Struts in Action

Struts in Action

Building web applications
with the leading Java framework

Ted Husted
Cedric Dumoulin
George Franciscus
David Winterfeldt

MANNING
Greenwich
(74° w. long.)

The following figures were adapted from other Manning books: figure 2.1 from *Swing* by
Matthew Robinson and Pavel Vorobiev (figure 1.3); figures 2.8, 10.6, 11.1, and 11.2 from
Web Development with JavaServer Pages Second Edition by Duane Fields and Mark Kolb (figures 10.1,
10.5, 6.2, and 10.4). Figure 2.9 by Jean-Michel Garnier is reproduced with permission from the
Apache Software Foundation.

 Manning Publications Co.   Copyeditor: Liz Welch
32 Lafayette Place   Typesetter: Tony Roberts
Greenwich, CT 06830   Cover designer: Leslie Haimes

ISBN 1-930110-50-2

Fourth, corrected, printing. April 2003.

Printed in the United States of America

6 7 8 9 10 – VHG – 05 04 03

brief contents

contents

13   **_Localizing content   409_**

foreword

You're holding in your hands the result of the hard labor of some of Struts' most important developers. Ted, Cedric, George, and David have done an outstanding job of explaining how Struts works *and* how it is used in practice. If you're a new developer, *Struts in Action* will make it much easier for you to learn the framework and quickly put it to work on your own projects. But even the most seasoned Struts developer is certain to learn something new by reading this book.

I became interested in web application development in the late 1990s. I was ready for a language that would let me address one of the most problematic aspects of advanced development—the need to free up dynamically allocated memory when I was through with it.

In the beginning, all I really hoped to accomplish was to make life a little easier for a few developers building web applications. The incredible popularity that Struts has achieved since then means that I wasn't the only one who struggled—Struts fills a very common need.

When the early public drafts of the JavaServer Pages specification (versions 0.91 and 0.92) became available, one of the intriguing concepts embedded in these documents was the idea of two basic design styles for JSP-based applications. A *Model 1* design is characterized by form submits that go back to the servlet or JSP page that created the form. This design encourages you to mix the *presentation* logic (used to create the form) with the *business* logic (used to validate the form input and process the requested transaction). Such a design is often used when developers of only one skill set (either page authors who know a little programming, or Java developers who know a little HTML) are available. It is also useful when time is of the essence ("The prototype needs to work by next Monday or we don't get our venture capital funding"). Experience has taught us that Model 1 designs can be difficult to maintain and enhance in the future.

In contrast, a *Model 2* design submits forms to a *controller* component. The controller component dispatches to an appropriate *business-logic* component to perform the requested transaction. The business-logic component interacts with the *database* and acquires the information it needs for the next user interaction. The controller component delegates the creation of the response page to a *presentation* component whose sole purpose is to create that response.

You're probably thinking that the Model 2 style sounds much more complicated—perhaps even like overkill for simple applications. Indeed, creating an application based on the Model 2 design does take *longer* than building the same application in a Model 1 style. But the primary benefits show up quickly. If you've created the proper architecture, major changes to one tier should have relatively little (if any) impact on the other tier, and you can reuse the logic in the unaffected tier immediately.

While all of this intellectual investigation of web application architectures was going on, my professional career was leading me in interesting directions as well. I was working for a company that provided information services to the long-haul trucking industry in the United States, and we wanted to expand this service into Europe. This created the need to deal with multiple languages and internationalization. I quickly whipped up a simple controller servlet that let me implement the basic MVC architecture, but it didn't address, say, the need to include a Select Language control.

Our first effort at internationalization started me down the path of creating "user interface components" using the new custom tags facilities of JSP 1.1—which led ultimately to things like the `<bean:message>` tag that is a part of Struts today.

Shortly after this, I joined Sun Microsystems to work with the Tomcat servlet and JSP container (I was the primary architect of the Catalina servlet container that is the basis of Tomcat 4). A large portion of this development took place in the open source community at Apache, as part of the Jakarta Project—initiated when Sun contributed the source code of what had been the servlet and JSP reference implementation to Apache in 1999. However, I was never happy with the state of Model 2-oriented application designs, so I resolved to do something about it.

Although I had a pretty good idea of how to solve the remaining problems, the actual code for Struts did not come into being until, much to the chagrin of my wife, I took my laptop along with me to the 2000 Memorial Day weekend with my family on the Oregon coast. The very first version of what became the ActionForm was born that weekend, and it turned out to solve a number of interesting design problems. In addition, the idea of defining logical names for the presentation and business logic components—and centralizing the definition of those names in a single configuration file—was clearly beneficial in solving the overlapping problems of coordination between the development of the two tiers and the goal of insulating tiers from changes in the other.

Through my work on Tomcat I had recognized the benefits of open source development so it was a natural choice to bring Struts to the world of open source as well. This choice—and the elegance of how Struts deals with some of the most basic problems of web application design—has resulted in acceptance that is truly astounding. Thousands of developers have downloaded Struts, gone through the learning curve, asked questions (and received answers) through the STRUTS-USER mailing list, and have successfully deployed applications based on Struts all over the world.

Of course, I was not able to accomplish all of this on my own. Ted, Cedric, David, and all the other past and present Committers for the Struts project, along with George and the community of Struts developers, have made the framework far more useful than I ever could have done alone. To them, I offer my heartfelt thanks. To you, the reader of this much-needed book, I hope that you find Struts a useful addition to your arsenal, well worth the investment of time to learn its techniques and APIs.

Enjoy!

Craig McClanahan
Portland, Oregon

preface

By 2000, Java had come of age. The dust from the early hype had settled and some very interesting development tools and libraries were cropping up. I had already been writing web applications for several years. Like many developers, I started with simple apps in JavaScript and Perl. A powerful combination, but a bear to maintain. Next came ColdFusion, which was much more powerful but at the time too expensive for my client's pocketbook. I even tried FileMaker Pro, which was fun, but very, very proprietary.

My major client for this succession of web applications was a public broadcasting station. The station's major fund-raiser was (and still is) an annual auction. Local vendors donate goods and services, and people buy them at auction to support the station. Of course, we were quick to post images of the high-end items on the web site: *objets d'art*, a car, vacation packages, autographed items, and so forth.

In 1998, we used an application written with JavaScript and Perl to accept "pre-bids" on the high-end items. The actual bidding on these items took place in live television bid-downs. All the application really did was set the starting bid price. In 1999, we accepted both online and phone bids right up to when the item sold. Each year, I used a different platform to put the auction online, because each year I found that the platform didn't meet all my needs.

Since we were already satisfied users of the Apache HTTPD server, I invested some time in wandering through the nascent Jakarta site, where I discovered Struts. At first, I wasn't even sure the project was still active. But the documentation seemed promising, so I subscribed to the list to see if anyone was home. An example application was already bundled with the documentation. I started working my way through the example, trying to figure out the framework as I went along. This journey turned into the "Walking Tour of the Struts Application," which describes how the example application works, screen by screen. I posted the tour to the list, where some of the subscribers gently corrected my understanding of the finer points.

I continued to follow the list, helping others when I could, and being helped by those who had traveled this road before me. Traffic on the list grew steadily. Toward the end of the year, Struts' architect and lead developer, Craig McClanahan, was looking for people to help with the documentation for the 1.0 release. I was elected a Struts Committer in December 2000, and we finally shipped Struts 1.0 in June 2001.

Along the way, I started my "More About Struts" page. At first, it was just a place where I could keep the links to the Struts material I was writing. Then I began adding links to the Struts "extensions" people had started to distribute, and then to the many Struts articles that had begun to appear. My Struts Resources page grew larger, and more popular, and so I moved it to the main Struts site. It is now a set of several pages with links to everything known about the Struts universe.

The Struts list remained a treasure trove of helpful information, especially since Craig himself was usually on hand to shed light on the implementation details and architectural philosophy. But finding the best bits in the list archive could be a challenge. So, I started a "threads page" within links to the best email nuggets, which grew into a fairly large FAQ. In June 2001, JGuru decided to open a Struts forum and FAQ, and we moved the main Struts FAQ to JGuru, where I continue to manage it.

Around the same time, publishers started to take notice of Struts, and offers began to arrive in my mailbox. After consulting with some of the other Struts Committers, we eventually decided to work with Manning Publications. Like Apache, Manning has a longstanding commitment to quality. While we wanted to get a Struts book out as soon as we could, we also wanted to be sure that it would be the best book possible.

The result is *Struts in Action*. It is very much a "team book." David Winterfeldt, the creator of the Struts Validator, was kind enough to draft our Validator chapter. Likewise, Cedric Dumoulin, the creator of Tiles, drafted the Tiles chapter. George Franciscus provided the critical chapter 1 of the book, which is designed to help bring newbies into the fold. We even dragged a foreword out of Craig (who would "rather be programming"). Of course, other Struts developers and Committers reviewed the manuscript at every stage, and we are thankful for the many helpful comments.

Oh, and the auction? We are going on our third year using Struts. Now instead of *rewriting* it every year, we *improve* it every year.

Ted Husted
Fairport, New York

acknowledgments

We recognize the support and understanding of the many people who helped make this book possible. We hope that the people we need to acknowledge most—the family and friends who stand by us while a project like this is under way—already know how much we appreciate their love and forbearance.

But a great many other people, who might otherwise have remained anonymous, have also contributed a great deal to this book.

First, there is the legion of volunteer developers responsible for the development of Struts. Literally hundreds of people have helped make Struts what is today. Most have contributed indirectly through thousands of invaluable, frank discussions on the Struts mailing lists. Others have contributed directly by donating code and documentation to the framework. As of the 1.02 release, these individuals include Arun M. Thomas, Chris Assenza, Chris Audley, Craig R. McClanahan, David Geary, dIon Gillard, Don Clasen, Ed Burns, Eric Wu, Florent Carpentier, Jeff Hutchison, Jimmy Larsson, John Rousseau, John Ueltzhoeffer, Larry McCay, Luis Arias, Marius Barduta, Martin Cooper, Matthias Kerkhoff, Mike Schachter, Niall Pemberton, Oleg V Alexeev, Paul Runyan, Ralph Schaer, Rob Leland, Robert Hayden, Sean Kelly, Stanley Santiago, and Wong Kok Kai.

Several Struts developers were also kind enough to review portions of the manuscript and provided many useful comments. Dan Malks' commentary contributed much to the final version of chapter 2. Richard Starr's thorough review of chapter 3 helped greatly in locking down our Hello World logon example. We are also grateful to many other developers who provided feedback on the manuscript, including Martin Cooper, Vincent Masool, John Yu, Jon Skeet, Max Loukianov, James Holmes, Bill Wallace, Nathan Anderson, Cody Burleson, Darryl Thompson, James F. McGovern, Steve Wilkinson, and Shawn Bayern. Our technical review editors, Steve Wilkinson and Stephen LeClair, deserve a special vote of thanks for picking every conceivable nit. We are also very grateful to our copyeditor, Liz Welch, who dotted our i's and crossed many a t.

This book also owes a great deal to our publisher, Marjan Bace, and the Manning editorial team. Manning didn't just want our work—they wanted our best work. That took more effort, and a lot more time, but when readers invest their own time and money into a book, they do deserve the very best we can give them.

about this book

The Struts framework joins together several related technologies so that web developers can create standards-based applications that are easier to build, extend, and maintain. Struts is already the framework of choice for both novice and experienced developers throughout the world

Struts in Action is a step-by-step introduction to the Struts framework. The text is complemented by several case study applications designed to demonstrate the best practices techniques introduced throughout the book. This book is intended for professional developers who want practical, battle-tested advice on how to get their own applications working the "Struts way."

Developers building web applications with Struts will typically use several related technologies as part of their project. A book that provided complete information on each of these would fill many volumes. To keep this work a single volume about Struts, we do not attempt to describe the HTML markup language, the syntax of JavaServer Pages, the conventions of JavaBean development, or the fine details of similar technologies. It is assumed that the reader is sufficiently familiar with these technologies to follow the examples presented. It is likewise assumed that the reader is familiar with URLs, document hierarchies, web application archives, and other concepts related to creating and publishing web applications.

We also do not include a primer on the Java programming language. As with HTML, JSP, JavaBeans, and related technologies, a wealth of information is already available. We assume that developers reading this book are familiar with Java syntax, the development cycle, and object-oriented design concepts. A basic understanding of relational database technology in general, and JDBC in particular, is recommended but not required.

Our focus here, then, is strictly on web applications and the Struts framework. The interaction between the technologies already mentioned—HTML, Java, databases, and others—is the focal point of this book and the subject that we cover in greatest depth.

However, for the benefit of readers not so well versed in some of the enabling technologies on which Struts depends, the text does include primers on the Hypertext Transfer Protocol (HTTP), Java servlets, JavaServer Pages, and custom JSP tags.

Roadmap

Chapter 1 introduces web application development in general and Struts in particular. We look at how Struts is written and distributed, the enabling technologies behind web applications, and the overall Struts architecture. To round out the chapter, we jump right in and develop our first Struts application.

Chapter 2 explores the Struts architecture. We start with a general overview of the Struts architecture followed by a close look at the how control flows through the framework. The chapter concludes with a frank discussion of Struts' strengths and weaknesses. The chapter is intended to give working developers a firm grounding in what working in Struts is really all about. It may also help product managers decide whether Struts is a good fit for their team.

Chapter 3 walks through the development of a simple application. Like the exercise in chapter 1, this is a very simple logon application, but it includes the same essentials as any web application. The goal here is to give a hands-on developer the "big picture" before we drill-down on the gory details in part 2. To add a touch of realism, we go back and upgrade the completed application from Struts 1.02 to the Struts 1.1 release.

Chapter 4 explores the backbone of the Struts framework—the configuration elements. We also describe configuring the web deployment descriptors and Ant build files to help you build and deploy your own application.

Chapter 5 covers the Struts ActionForm. This key object can be many things to the application: transfer object, firewall, API, data validator, and type transformer. We introduce several techniques to help you get the most out of the double-edged sword Struts likes to call form beans.

Chapter 6 covers the Struts ActionForward. The trickiest part of any Web application can be getting there from here. ActionForwards help you clearly define the entry points to your application, making it easier to see if you've covered all the bases.

Chapter 7 covers the Struts ActionMapping. The mappings are the foundation of the Struts controller. Actions classes can be designed for reuse and configured for different tasks with an ActionMapping. Here we explore how to use Action-Mappings to control the flow through your application, and get the most out of every Action class.

Chapter 8 covers the Struts Action object. These are the workhorses of a Struts application—and where the web developers spend most of their time. We take a close look at the Action classes bundled with Struts, and several goodies from the Scaffold package, along with the thorny problem of populating business classes from the incoming Struts ActionForms.

Chapter 9 covers the Struts ActionServlet. The controller servlet is the framework's "mouthpiece." It calls the shots but lets others do the dirty work. Here we look at the new ways to customize the ActionServlet to best suit the needs of your application or a specific application module.

Chapter 10 explores the Struts JSP tags and server pages generally. From the user's perspective, the web page *is* the application and represents everything the application is supposed to do. The key advantage of using Struts is that it helps you separate displaying content from acquiring content. In this chapter, we scrutinize the Struts JSP tags and briefly introduce using other presentation systems with Struts, such as XSLT and Velocity. Most Struts applications rely on JSP to create dynamic pages, but the framework can be used with any Java presentation technology.

Chapter 11 covers the Tiles page-assembly framework. Dynamic template systems, like Tiles, bring familiar programming patterns to the presentation layer of a web application. A tile encapsulates a block of markup, much like a method encapsulates a block of Java code. Building web pages with Tiles brings consistency and flexibility to the unruly, chaotic world of HTML.

Chapter 12 covers the important topic of validating user input. A popular extension to the Struts core is the Struts Validator. This is a very powerful component that provides both client-side and server-side validation from the same configuration. We show how to integrate validation into your Struts application, using both prewritten validators as well as any you write on your own.

Chapter 13 covers the Struts i18n features. Struts supports internationalization from the ground up. This chapter explores how and where i18n is built into Struts, and what you need to do to get it working properly. The underlying theme is what you must do to develop your application for one language today but be able to add others tomorrow.

Chapter 14 explores hooking up data services to Struts. This chapter shows how to use helper classes to connect a Struts Action with different types of enterprise data systems—including databases, search engines, and content-syndication services. Working examples are provided using JDBC, Lucene, and Rich Site Summary.

Chapter 15 is our feature application, Artimus. This enterprise-grade application pulls out all the stops and demonstrates the key Struts features and add-ons in one tidy, eminently reusable package. Authentication, customization, localization, Scaffold, Tiles, transactions, Validator, and more—it's an A-to-Z walkthrough of the best and brightest Struts has to offer.

Chapter 16 is our Struts 1.1 upgrade guide. Here we take the Artimus application from chapter 15 and retrofit it for the new 1.1 features, including DynaForms, plug-ins, and multiple modules. If you have a legacy Struts 1.0 application ready for upgrade, this is the chapter for you!

Chapter 17 shows how you can use Velocity templates with Struts. We revise our logon application (from chapter 3) to use with Velocity templates, and show you how the Velocity templates and JavaServer Pages compare, side by side.

Code

The source code for the example applications in this book has been donated to the Apache Software Foundation. The source code is now available as part of the Struts distribution and is also freely available from Manning's website, www.manning.com/husted.

Much of the source code shown in the earlier part of the book consists of fragments designed to illustrate the text. When a complete segment of code is given, it is shown as a numbered listing; code annotations accompany some listings. When we present source code, we sometimes use a **bold font** to draw attention to specific elements.

In the text, Courier typeface is used to denote code (JSP, Java, and HTML) as well as Java methods, JSP tag names, and other source code identifiers:

- A reference to a method in the text will generally not include the signature, because there may be more than one form of the method call.

- A reference to a JSP tag will include the braces and default prefix, but not the list of properties the tag accepts (`<bean:write>`).

- A reference to an XML element in the text will include the braces but not the properties or closing tag (`<action>`).

- When a Java class or tag library is first introduced in a section, the full package identifier is given in braces and set in a Courier font (`java.util.Map`); other references to the classname are set in normal body type.

- When JSP is interspersed with HTML in the code listings or code fragments, we have used UPPERCASE letters for the HTML elements and lowercase letters for JSP elements.

References

Bibliographic references are indicated in square brackets in the body of the text; for example, [ASF, Artimus]. Full publication details and/or URLs are provided in the "References" section on page 614 of this book.

Author Online

Purchase of *Struts in Action* includes free access to a private web forum run by Manning Publications where you can make comments about the book, ask technical questions, and receive help from other users and advice from the authors. To access the forum and subscribe to it, point your web browser to www.manning.com/husted. This page provides information on how to get on the forum once you are registered, what kind of help is available, and the rules of conduct on the forum.

Manning's commitment to our readers is to provide a venue where a meaningful dialog between individual readers and between readers and the author can take place. It is not a commitment to any specific amount of participation on the part of the author, whose contribution to the AO remains voluntary (and unpaid). We suggest you try asking the author some challenging questions lest his interest stray!

The Author Online forum and the archives of previous discussions will be accessible from the publisher's web site as long as the book is in print.

About the authors

Ted Husted is an acknowledged Struts authority, an active member of the Struts development team, and manager of the JGuru Struts Forum. As a consultant, Ted has worked with professional Struts development teams throughout the United States. Ted also helps manage the Apache Jakarta project, which hosts the Struts framework. Ted lives in Fairport, New York, with his wife, two children, four computers, and an aging cat.

Cedric Dumoulin is an active member of the Struts development team and author of the Tiles framework. Cedric is presently a researcher at the University of Lille. He has also worked in the R&D department of a leading international Internet banking company. He lives in Lille, France.

George Franciscus is a principal at Nexcel, providing technical and management consulting services in several industries, including telecommunications, banking, life insurance, and property and casualty insurance. George has expertise in Java, J2EE, Domino, relational databases, and mainframe technologies. He holds a BSc in Computer Science from the University of Toronto. George lives in Toronto, Ontario, with his wife and three children.

David Winterfeldt is a Struts Committer and author of the Commons Validator package. He works as a senior developer at a major company implementing J2EE technology. David currently lives in New York City.

Craig McClanahan, creator of the Struts framework, contributed the foreword to this book. Craig was the primary architect of Tomcat 4 and the implementation architect of the Java Web Services Developer Pack. He is now Sun's Specification Lead for JavaServer Faces (JSR-127) as well as the Web Layer Architect for the J2EE platform. Craig, as the primary developer of Struts, perhaps provided the most important part of this book—a framework for us to write about.

About the title

By combining introductions, overviews, and how-to examples, the *In Action* books are designed to help learning *and* remembering. According to research in cognitive science the things people remember are things they discover during self-motivated exploration.

Although no one at Manning is a cognitive scientist, we are convinced that for learning to become permanent it must pass through stages of exploration, play, and, interestingly, retelling of what is being learned. People understand and remember new things, which is to say they master them, only after actively exploring them. Humans learn *in action*. An essential part of an *In Action* book is that it is example-driven. It encourages the reader to try things out, to play with new code, and explore new ideas.

There is another, more mundane, reason for the title of this book: our readers are busy. They use books to do a job or solve a problem. They need books that allow them to jump in and jump out easily and learn just what they want just when they want it. They need books that aid them *in action*. The books in this series are designed for such readers.

About the cover

The figure on the cover of *Struts in Action* is a shepherd from the moors of Bordeaux, "Berger des Landes de Bordeaux." The region of Bordeaux in southwestern France has sunny hills that are ideal for viniculture, as well as many open and marshy fields dotted with small farms and flocks of grazing sheep. Perched on his stilts, the shepherd was better able to navigate the boggy fields and tend to his charges.

The illustration is taken from a French travel book, *Encyclopedie des Voyages* by J. G. St. Saveur, published in 1796. Travel for pleasure was a relatively new phenomenon at the time and travel guides such as this one were popular, introducing both the tourist as well as the armchair traveler to the inhabitants of other regions of France and abroad.

The diversity of the drawings in the *Encyclopedie des Voyages* speaks vividly of the uniqueness and individuality of the world's towns and provinces just 200 years ago. This was a time when the dress codes of two regions separated by a few dozen miles identified people uniquely as belonging to one or the other. The travel guide brings to life a sense of isolation and distance of that period and of every other historic period except our own hyperkinetic present.

Dress codes have changed since then and the diversity by region, so rich at the time, has faded away. It is now often hard to tell the inhabitant of one continent from another. Perhaps, trying to view it optimistically, we have traded a cultural and visual diversity for a more varied personal life. Or a more varied and interesting intellectual and technical life.

We at Manning celebrate the inventiveness, the initiative, and the fun of the computer business with book covers based on the rich diversity of regional life two centuries ago brought back to life by the pictures from this travel guide.

Part 1

Getting started with Struts

Part 1 is Struts distilled. We introduce Java web applications, examine the framework's architecture, build two simple applications, and walk through configuring the Struts components.

Introduction

Co-authored by George Franciscus and Ted Husted

This chapter covers

- Introducing application frameworks
- Understanding HTTP, CGI, servlets, and JSPs
- Using the Model 2 architecture
- Building a simple application

3

The only stupid question is the one you never ask.

—Anonymous

1.1   What is this book about?

Welcome to *Struts in Action*. We wrote this book to help web developers make the best possible use of the Struts web application framework.

Struts is open source software that helps developers build web applications quickly and easily. Struts relies on standard technologies—such as JavaBeans, Java servlets, and JavaServer Pages (JSP)—that most developers already know how to use. By taking a standards-based, "fill-in-the-blanks" approach to software development, Struts can alleviate much of the time-consuming grunt work that comes with every new project.

1.1.1   Who makes the Struts software?

Struts is hosted by the Apache Software Foundation (ASF) as part of its Jakarta project. Besides Struts, Jakarta hosts several successful open source products, including Tomcat, Ant, and Velocity.

The initial Struts codebase was developed between May 2000 and June 2001 when version 1.0 was released. More than 30 developers contributed to the Struts distribution, and thousands more follow the Struts mailing lists. The Struts codebase is managed by a team of volunteer "Committers." By 2002, the Struts team included nine active Committers.

The primary architect and developer of the Struts framework is Craig R. McClanahan. Craig is also the primary architect of Tomcat 4 and the implementation architect of the Java Web Services Developer Pack. He is now Sun's specification lead for JavaServer Faces (JSR-127) as well as the Web Layer Architect for the Java 2 Enterprise Edition (J2EE) platform.

Struts is available to the public at no charge under the Apache Software License [ASF, License]. There are no acquisition or other recurring costs for using the software. Unlike some other open source licenses, the Apache Software License is business-friendly. You can use Struts to create a commercial project and distribute the Struts binary without any red tape, fees, or other hassles. You can also integrate the Struts components into your own framework just as if they were written in-house. For complete details, see the Apache Software License at www.apache.org/LICENSE.

1.1.2 *Why is Struts open source?*

Most of the leading Java utilities and frameworks are now open source projects. Many of the developers working on these projects do so as part of their regular jobs with companies like IBM, Sun Microsystems, and Apple. Collaborating openly on this type of software benefits the entire marketplace. Today, many open source components are integrated into commercial products. Companies then sell professional documentation, guaranteed support levels, and other valuable aftermarket services to their clients.

When software is freely available, it becomes much easier for the marketplace to support. Struts is a prime example of this. Although still a youngster, it has already been featured in dozens of articles and seminars, not to mention books like this one.

Many development teams do not like to use software that was not "invented" in-house. Open source components provide all the benefits of writing the same software in-house but do not lock you into a proprietary solution that only your team understands.

Open source frameworks are a win-win for everyone.

1.1.3 *Why is it called Struts?*

The framework is called "Struts" to remind us of the invisible underpinnings that hold up our houses, buildings, bridges, and, indeed, ourselves when we are on stilts. This is an excellent description of the role Struts plays in developing web applications. When raising physical structures, construction engineers use struts to provide support for each floor of a building. Likewise, software engineers use Struts to support each layer of a business application.

1.2 *What are application frameworks?*

A framework is a reusable, semi-complete application that can be specialized to produce custom applications [Johnson]. Like people, software applications are more alike than they are different. They run on the same computers, expect input from the same devices, output to the same displays, and save data to the same hard disks. Developers working on conventional desktop applications are accustomed to toolkits and development environments that leverage the sameness between applications. Application frameworks build on this common ground to provide developers with a reusable structure that can serve as the foundation for their own products.

A framework provides developers with a set of backbone components that have the following characteristics:

- They are known to work well in other applications.
- They are ready to use with the next project.
- They can also be used by other teams in the organization.

Frameworks are the classic build-versus-buy proposition. If you build it, you will understand it when you are done—but how long will it be before you can roll your own? If you buy it, you will have to climb the learning curve—and how long is that going to take? There is no right answer here, but most observers would agree that frameworks such as Struts provide a significant return on investment compared to starting from scratch, especially for larger projects.

1.2.1 *Other types of frameworks*

The idea of a framework applies not only to applications but to application components as well. Throughout this book, we introduce other types of frameworks that you can use with Struts. These include the Lucene search engine, the Scaffold toolkit, the Struts validator, and the Tiles tag library. Like application frameworks, these tools provide semi-complete versions of a subsystem that can be specialized to provide a custom component.

Some frameworks have been linked to a proprietary development environment. This is not the case with Struts or any of the other frameworks shown in this book. You can use any development environment with Struts: Visual Age for Java, JBuilder, Eclipse, Emacs, and Textpad are all popular choices among Struts developers. If you can use it with Java, you can use it with Struts.

1.3 *Enabling technologies*

Applications developed with Struts are based on a number of enabling technologies. These components are not specific to Struts and underlie every Java web application. A reason that developers use frameworks like Struts is to hide the nasty details behind acronyms like HTTP, CGI, and JSP. As a Struts developer, you don't need to be an alphabet soup guru, but a working knowledge of these base technologies can help you devise creative solutions to tricky problems.

If you are already all-too-familiar with the fundamentals, feel free to skip ahead to section 1.4.

1.3.1 *Hypertext Transfer Protocol (HTTP)*

When mediating talks between nations, diplomats often follow a formal *protocol*. Diplomatic protocols are designed to avoid misunderstandings and to keep negotiations from breaking down. In a similar vein, when computers need to talk, they also follow a formal protocol. The protocol defines how data is transmitted and how to decode it once it arrives. Web applications use the Hypertext Transfer Protocol (HTTP) to move data between the browser running on your computer and the application running on the server.

Many server applications communicate using protocols other than HTTP. Some of these maintain an ongoing connection between the computers. The application server knows exactly who is connected at all times and can tell when a connection is dropped. Because they know the state of each connection and the identity of each person using it, these are known as *stateful* protocols.

By contrast, HTTP is known as a *stateless* protocol. An HTTP server will accept any request from any client and will always provide some type of response, even if the response is just to say *no*. Without the overhead of negotiating and retaining a connection, stateless protocols can handle a large volume of requests. This is one reason why the Internet has been able to scale to millions of computers.

Another reason HTTP has become the universal standard is its simplicity. An HTTP request looks like an ordinary text document. This has made it easy for applications to make HTTP requests. You can even send an HTTP request by hand using a standard utility such as Telnet. When the HTTP response comes back, it is also in plain text that developers can read.

The first line in the HTTP request contains the method, followed by the location of the requested resource and the version of HTTP. Zero or more HTTP request headers follow the initial line. The HTTP headers provide additional information to the server. This can include the browser type and version, acceptable document types, and the browser's cookies, just to name a few. Of the seven request methods, GET and POST are by far the most popular.

Once the server has received and serviced the request, it will issue an HTTP response. The first line in the response is called the status line and carries the HTTP protocol version, a numeric status, and a brief description of the status. Following the status line, the server will return a set of HTTP response headers that work in a way similar to the request headers.

As we mentioned, HTTP does not preserve state information between requests. The server logs the request, sends the response, and goes blissfully on to the next request. While simple and efficient, a stateless protocol is problematic for dynamic applications that need to keep track of their users. (Ignorance is not always bliss.)

Cookies and URL rewriting are two common ways to keep track of users between requests. A cookie is a special packet of information on the user's computer. URL rewriting stores a special reference in the page address that a Java server can use to track users. Neither approach is seamless, and using either means extra work when developing a web application. On its own, a standard HTTP web server does not traffic in *dynamic content*. It mainly uses the request to locate a file and then returns that file in the response. The file is typically formatted using Hypertext Markup Language (HTML) [W3C, HTML] that the web browser can format and display. The HTML page often includes hypertext links to other web pages and may display any number of other goodies, such as images and videos. The user clicks a link to make another request, and the process begins anew.

Standard web servers handle static content and images quite well but need a helping hand to provide users with a customized, dynamic response.

DEFINITION   *Static* content on the Web comes directly from text or data files, like HTML or JPEG files. These files might be changed from time to time, but they are not altered automatically when requested by a web browser. *Dynamic* content, on the other hand, is generated on the fly, typically in response to an individualized request from a browser.

1.3.2   *Common Gateway Interface (CGI)*

The first widely used standard for producing dynamic content was the Common Gateway Interface (CGI). CGI uses standard operating system features, such as environment variables and standard input and output, to create a bridge, or *gateway*, between the web server and other applications on the host machine. The other applications can look at the request sent to them by the web server and create a customized response.

When a web server receives a request that's intended for a CGI program, it runs that program and provides the program with information from the incoming request. The CGI program runs and sends its output back to the server. The web server then relays the response to the browser.

CGI defines a set of conventions regarding what information it will pass as environment variables and how it expects standard input and output to be used. Like HTTP, CGI is flexible and easy to implement, and a great number of CGI-aware programs have been written.

The main drawback to CGI is that it must run a new copy of the CGI-aware program for each request. This is a relatively expensive process that can bog down high-volume sites where thousands of requests are serviced per minute. Another drawback is that CGI programs tend to be platform dependent. A CGI program written for one operating system may not run on another.

1.3.3 *Java servlets*

Sun's Java Servlet platform directly addresses the two main drawbacks of CGI programs. First, servlets offer better performance and utilization of resources than conventional CGI programs. Second, the write-once, run-anywhere nature of Java means that servlets are portable between operating systems that have a Java Virtual Machine (JVM).

A servlet looks and feels like a miniature web server. It receives a request and renders a response. But, unlike conventional web servers, the servlet application programming interface (API) is specifically designed to help Java developers create dynamic applications.

The servlet itself is simply a Java class that has been compiled into byte code, like any other Java object. The servlet has access to a rich API of HTTP-specific services, but it is still just another Java object running in an application and can leverage all your other Java assets.

To give conventional web servers access to servlets, the servlets are plugged into *containers*. The servlet container is attached to the web server. Each servlet can declare what URL patterns it would like to handle. When a request matching a registered pattern arrives, the web server passes the request to the container, and the container invokes the servlet.

But unlike CGI programs, a new servlet is not created for each request. Once the container instantiates the servlet, it will just assign a new *thread* for each request. Java threads are much less expensive than the server processes used by CGI programs. Once the servlet has been created, using it for additional requests incurs very little overhead. Servlet developers can use the init() method to hold references to expensive resources, such as database connections or EJB Home Interfaces, so that they can be shared between requests. Acquiring resources like these can take several seconds—which is longer than many surfers are willing to wait.

The other edge of the sword is that, since servlets are multithreaded, servlet developers must take special care to be sure their servlets are thread-safe. To learn more about servlet programming, we recommend *Java Servlets by Example*, by Alan R. Williamson [Williamson]. The definitive source for Servlet information is the Java Servlet Specification [Sun, JST].

1.3.4 *JavaServer Pages*

While Java servlets are a big step up from CGI programs, they are not a panacea. To generate the response, developers are still stuck with using `println` statements to render the HTML. Code that looks like

```
out.println("<P>One line of HTML.</P>");
out.println("<P>Another line of HTML.</P>");
```

is all too common in servlets that generate the HTTP response. There are libraries that can help you generate HTML, but as applications grow more complex, Java developers end up being cast into the role of HTML page designers.

Meanwhile, given the choice, most project managers prefer to divide development teams into specialized groups. They like HTML designers to be working on the presentation while Java engineers sweat the business logic. Using servlets alone encourages mixing markup with business logic, making it difficult for team members to specialize.

To solve this problem, Sun turned to the idea of using server pages to combine scripting and templating technologies into a single component. To build Java-Server Pages, developers start by creating HTML pages in the same old way, using the same old HTML syntax. To bring dynamic content into the page, the developer can also place JSP scripting elements on the page. Scripting elements are tags that encapsulate logic that is recognized by the JSP. You can easily pick out scripting elements on JSP pages by looking for code that begins with `<%` and ends with `%>`. For instance, to display the last modified date on the page, the developer would place the following code in the page:

```
<B>This page was accessed at <%= new Date() %></B>
```

There are three different types of scripting elements: expressions, scriptlets, and declarations, as shown in table 1.1.

Table 1.1 JSP scripting elements

Element	Purpose
Expressions	Java code, bound by `<%=` and `%>`, used to evaluate Java language statements and insert the result into the servlet's output
Scriptlets	Java code, bound by `<%` and `%>`, often used to create dynamic content
Declarations	Java code, bound by `<%!` and `%>`, used to add code to the body of the servlet class

To be seen as a JSP page, the file just needs to be saved with an extension of .jsp. When a client requests the JSP page, the container translates the page into a source code file for a Java servlet and compiles the source into a Java class file— just as you would do if you were writing a servlet from scratch. At runtime, the container can also check the last modified date of the JSP file against the class file. If the JSP file has changed since it was last compiled, the container will retranslate and rebuild the page all over again.

Project managers can now assign the presentation layer to HTML developers, who then pass on their work to Java developers to complete the business-logic portion. The important thing to remember is that a JSP page is really just a servlet. Anything you can do with a servlet, you can do with a JSP.

1.3.5 *JSP tags*

Scripting elements are only one of the two ways to generate dynamic JSP content. Scriptlets are quick, easy, and powerful but require that developers mix Java code with HTML. Experience has taught us that embedding logic into JSP pages leads to non-maintainable applications with minimal opportunity for reuse. A popular alternative is to use JSP tags.

JSP tags are mixed in with the HTML markup and can be used as if they were ordinary HTML tags. A single JSP tag may represent dozens of Java statements, but all the developer needs to know is to how to insert the tag. The programming code is hidden away in a Java class file.

To use the same code on another page, the developer only has to insert the tag markup again. If the code for the tag changes, all the tags will automatically use the updated version. The JSP page using the tag does not need to be revised. JSP tags provide much better reuse than scriptlets and can be easier for page developers

---

JSPs vs. ASPs

Microsoft and Sun both offer their own brand of server pages. Sun offers JavaServer Pages and Microsoft offers Active Server Pages (ASP). Both JSPs and ASPs are designed so that developers can create dynamic web pages customized with back-office data. While similar on the surface, there are several differences between ASPs and JSPs:

- JSPs are platform independent—write once, run anywhere.

- Developers have input to the direction of JSPs through the Java Community Process (JCP).

- JSP developers can extend the JSP tag set with custom tags.

- JavaBeans and Enterprise JavaBeans (EJB) can be used with JSPs to increase reusability and reduce maintenance.

- JSPs can access many other Java libraries, including Java Database Connectivity (JDBC), Java Mail, Java Message Service (JMS), and Java Naming and Directory Interface (JNDI).

- JSPs are compiled into a binary class file and do not need to be interpreted for every request.

- JSPs find wide support with tool vendors, containers, and web servers.

to use, since they look like the familiar HTML tags.

A number of prebuilt JSP tags libraries are available that will perform useful functionality for developers. Among these is the new JSP Standard Tag Library (JSTL). This new standard provides a rich library of reusable JSP tags. For more on JSTL, we highly recommend *JSTL in Action*, by Shawn Bayern [Bayern]. Struts works well with JSTL and other publicly available tag libraries, as well as any you might write yourself.

For more on JSP and JSP pages, we highly recommend *Web Development with JavaServer Pages*, by Duane K. Fields, Mark A. Kolb, and Shawn Bayern [Fields]. The definitive source for JSP information is the JavaServer Pages Specification [Sun, JSP].

JSP pages are an integral part of the Struts developer's toolbox. Most Struts developers use JSP pages and custom tags to create all the dynamic content for their applications.

Rolling your own

Entire books have been written on developing your own JSP tags, but here's a quick overview of the process:

1 Create a class that implements `javax.servlet.jsp.tagext.TagSupport` or `javax.servlet.jsp.tagext.BodyTagSupport` by implementing the `doStart()` or `doEnd()` method. These methods obtain a JspWriter object to write out any valid HTML content you need.

2 Create a tag library descriptor (TLD) file to map the classes you just created to a JSP tag name.

3 Define your `<taglib>` elements in the web application descriptor file (web.xml). Tell the JSP page that you will be using your tags by placing a `@taglib` statement at the top of the page:

```
<%@taglib uri="/tags/app.tld
  prefix="app" %>
```

4 This statement imports the library for use on this page and assigns it a tag prefix. For more, see the JSP Tag Library technology page.

1.3.6 *JavaBeans*

JavaBeans are Java classes which conform to a set of design patterns that make them easier to use with development tools and other components.

DEFINITION   A *JavaBean* is a reusable software component written in Java. To qualify as a JavaBean, the class must be concrete and public, and have a no-argument constructor. JavaBeans expose internal fields as *properties* by providing public methods that follow a consistent design pattern. Knowing that the property names follow this pattern, other Java classes are able to use *introspection* to discover and manipulate JavaBean properties.

The JavaBean design patterns provide access to the bean's internal state through two flavors of methods: *accessors* are used to read a JavaBean's state; *mutators* are used to change a JavaBean's state.

Mutators are always prefixed with lowercase token *set* followed by the property name. The first character in the property name must be uppercase. The return value is always void—mutators only change property values; they do not retrieve them. The mutator for a simple property takes only one parameter in its signature, which can be of any type. Mutators are often nicknamed *setters* after their prefix.

The mutator method signature for a `weight` property of the type `Double` would be

```
public void setWeight(Double weight)
```

A similar design pattern is used to create the accessor method signature. Accessor methods are always prefixed with the lowercase token *get*, followed by the property name. The first character in the property name must be uppercase. The return value will match the method parameter in the corresponding mutator. Accessors for simple properties cannot accept parameters in their method signature. Not surprisingly, accessors are often called *getters*.

The accessor method signature for our `weight` property is

```
public Double getWeight()
```

If the accessor returns a logical value, there is a variant pattern. Instead of using the lowercase token get, a logical property can use the prefix *is*, followed by the property name. The first character in the property name must be uppercase. The return value will always be a logical value—either boolean or Boolean. Logical accessors cannot accept parameters in their method signature.

The boolean accessor method signature for an `on` property would be

```
public boolean isOn()
```

The canonical method signatures play an important role when working with Java-Beans. Other components are able to use the Java Reflection API to discover a JavaBean's properties by looking for methods prefixed by *set*, *is*, or *get*. If a component finds such a signature on a JavaBean, it knows that the method can be used to access or change the bean's properties.

Sun introduced JavaBeans to work with GUI components, but they are now used with every aspect of Java development, including web applications. When Sun engineers developed the JSP tag extension classes, they designed them to work with JavaBeans. The dynamic data for a page can be passed as a JavaBean, and the JSP tag can then use the bean's properties to customize the output.

For more on JavaBeans, we highly recommend *The Awesome Power of JavaBeans*, by Lawrence H. Rodrigues [Rodrigues]. The definitive source for JavaBean information is the JavaBean Specification [Sun, JBS].

1.3.7 Model 2

The 0.92 release of the Servlet/JSP Specification described Model 2 as an architecture that uses servlets and JSP pages together in the same application. The term *Model 2* disappeared from later releases, but it remains in popular use among Java web developers.

Under Model 2, servlets handle the data access and navigational flow, while JSP pages handle the presentation. Model 2 lets Java engineers and HTML developers each work on their own part of the application. A change in one part of a Model 2 application does not mandate a change to another part of the application. HTML developers can often change the look and feel of an application without changing how the back-office servlets work.

The Struts framework is based on the Model 2 architecture. It provides a controller servlet to handle the navigational flow and special classes to help with the data access. A substantial custom tag library is bundled with the framework to make Struts easy to use with JSP pages.

1.4 Struts from 30,000 feet

Hold on to your hats! Now that we've covered the basics, it's time for a whirlwind tour of Struts. Before we try to get into the nuts and bolts of the framework components, let's start with the *big* picture.

Struts uses a Model 2 architecture. The Struts *ActionServlet* controls the navigational flow. Another Struts class, the *Action*, is used to access the business classes. When the ActionServlet receives a request from the container, it uses the URI (or "path") to determine which Action it will use to handle the request. An Action can validate input and access the business layer to retrieve information from databases and other data services.

To validate input or use the input to update a database, the Action needs to know what values were submitted. Rather than force each Action to pull these values out of the request, the ActionServlet bundles the input into a JavaBean. The input beans are subclasses of the Struts *ActionForm* class. The ActionServlet can determine which ActionForm to use by looking at the path of the request, in the same way the Action was selected. An ActionForm extends `org.apache.struts.action.ActionForm`.

Each HTTP request must be answered with an HTTP response. Usually, a Struts Action does not render the response itself but forwards the request on to another resource, such as a JSP page. Struts provides an *ActionForward* class that can be used to store the path to a page under a logical name. When it has completed the business logic, the Action selects and returns an ActionForward to the servlet. The servlet then uses the path stored in the ActionForward object to call the page and complete the response.

Struts bundles these details together into an *ActionMapping* object. Each ActionMapping is related to a specific path. When that path is requested, the servlet retrieves the ActionMapping object. The mapping tells the servlet which Actions, ActionForms, and ActionForwards to use.

All of these details, the Actions, ActionForms, ActionForwards, ActionMappings, and some other things, are declared in the *struts-config.xml* file. The ActionServlet reads this file at startup and creates a database of configuration objects. At runtime, Struts refers to the objects created with the configuration file, not the file itself. Figure 1.1 illustrates how these components fit together.

Believe it or not, you already know enough about Struts to assemble a simple application. It won't do much, but it will illustrate how Struts actually works.

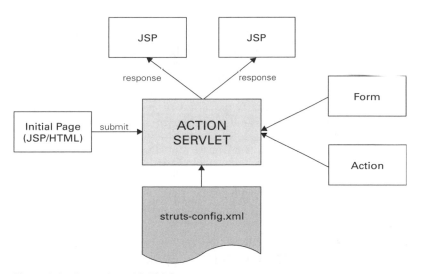

Figure 1.1　Struts from 30,000 feet

1.4.1 *Building a simple application*

Developers develop, and most of us learn best through example. Although we have spent barely a page describing how Struts works, let's just go ahead and build something so you can see how it's done. To close this chapter, we will put together a very simple but fully functional web application. The application will be used to register usernames and passwords. Once we are done you will have touched all the pieces you need to develop your own applications with Struts.

1.4.2 *Jump-starting development*

We have all felt frustration when we were eager to get started with a product but then hit a roadblock in just setting up the environment. To follow along with this chapter, all you need is the Java Development Kit (JDK), a modern web container (Tomcat 4, for example), and a simple text editor (such as Windows Notepad). If you do not already have Java and a web container set up, here's what you need to do:

- Download and install JDK 1.4.
- Download and install Tomcat (full version).
- Verify that Tomcat is working.
- Download and install the starter registration application.

To keep it simple, we will walk through the Windows installation for each of these steps.

A hyperlinked version of this section is available at the book's website [Husted], to make it easier for you to find the files you need to download.

NOTE The references to web addresses and other resources are given in the References section of this book. For your convenience in getting started, here are the URLs for the downloads you will need for this section:

- The Sun JDK [Sun, JDK], http://java.sun.com/j2se/
- Tomcat 4 [ASF, Tomcat], http://jakarta.apache.org/tomcat
- The book's website [Husted], http://www.manning.com/husted/

Installing the Java Development Kit

The Sun JDK 1.4 download [Sun, JDK] for Windows is now bundled with a Windows installation program. The setup wizard leads you through all the steps to install the JDK.

Installing Tomcat 4

Once JDK 1.4 is installed on your machine, you are ready to download and install Tomcat 4.0.4 (or later) [ASF, Tomcat]. A Windows setup wizard for Tomcat is available that will handle the installation details for you. To use the Windows setup program, choose the download with the .exe extension. Then, just double-click on the downloaded file to run the wizard.

The Tomcat defaults should work fine for most people, so installing Tomcat is mainly a matter of clicking Next. Let's step through the process so that you will know what to expect:

1 A small window will pop up indicating the location of the JDK.

2 Click OK and you will see the Acceptance Agreement. Review the agreement before clicking Next.

3 The next screen presents your installation options. You should be able to just accept the defaults and click Next.

4 You will be given the option to select a base directory. The default choice will usually be C:\PROGRAM FILES\APACHE TOMCAT 4.0. This should work fine for most people. If you need to put it on a different drive, we recommend just changing the drive letter and keeping the rest of the path as it is. This will make it easier to follow along later. This book and the Tomcat documentation will refer to this location as your Tomcat *base* directory.

5 Click Install, and the wizard will copy and expand files. A progress bar advises you how the installation is going.

6 When installation is complete, click the Close button.

Congratulations; you have installed Tomcat 4. Now it's time to fire it up and test it out. The Windows installer places a Tomcat Start item in your Start menu. Navigate your way through the Start menu until you find the Tomcat Start item. You stop Tomcat in the same way, except you select Tomcat Stop.

Tomcat provides several working servlets and JSP examples. Running these proves that your installation went according to plan. To test Tomcat (using the factory defaults), point your browser to http://localhost:8080. If all went well, a Welcome page with links to the examples will open. Try a few of the examples, just to be sure everything is hunky-dory. Then, install the Register application.

The easiest way to deploy a web application is with a Web Archive file (WAR). A WAR file is a compressed file containing all the application files a web application needs to function. To deploy a WAR file, you simply place it in the webapps directory under the Tomcat base directory (for example, C:\PROGRAM FILES\APACHE TOMCAT 4.0\webapps). The next time you restart Tomcat, you will see that the WAR file has been expanded. The entire application directory structure will have been re-created.

In the next section, you will be creating your first Struts application. To get you started quickly, we have provided a starter application for you to complete. Deployment will be a breeze because the starter application is a WAR file. You can download the starter application at the book's website [Husted]. The remainder of this chapter will have you add a few files to complete the application. The fully complete Register application is also available at the book's website in a separate WAR file. By default, the starter application will deploy under *register* and the completed version will deploy under *register-complete*.

Congratulations—if you have set up the JDK, Tomcat 4, and the Register application, you are ready to start development.

1.4.3 *Where the rubber meets the road*

Your first Struts application will be a simple user registration application. The user will be presented with a registration screen that will contain three fields—username, password, and confirmation password. A successful registration requires that the two passwords match. If the registration is successful, control flows to a page that says *successful!*. If the two passwords do not match, control flows to a page that says *failure*.

This simple exercise is designed to demonstrate the following:

- Creating HTML forms
- Capturing input from an HTML form
- Processing input (business logic)
- Changing the control flow based on dynamic input

To complete the starter application, you need to create:

- An ActionForm
- An Action
- The struts-config.xml file
- Three pages

That's it!

Creating the ActionForm

An ActionForm is a JavaBean that extends `org.apache.struts.action.ActionForm`. This object captures the input fields sent through the request. When a web browser submits a form, it creates a parameter in the request for each field on the form. The ActionForm has a corresponding property for each field on the HTML form. The ActionServlet matches the parameters in the request with the properties on the ActionForm. When they correspond, the ActionServlet calls the setter method for the property and passes it the value from the request.

In our exercise, the username field on the HTML form will need to have a `setUsername(String)` method. The password fields will need the `setPassword1(String)` and `setPassword2(String)` methods. These methods are responsible for populating the instance variables hidden within the RegisterForm JavaBean. The source code for our RegisterForm is shown in listing 1.1.

Create a file called RegisterForm.java that contains the code in listing 1.1. Save it under *<Base Directory>*/webapps/register/WEB-INF/classes/app. For the default Windows installation, the *<Base Directory>* would be C:/PROGRAM FILES/APACHE TOMCAT 4.0. For other containers, use the path to the classes directory for the deployed Register application.

Listing 1.1   RegisterForm.java

```java
package app;
import org.apache.struts.action.*;

public class RegisterForm extends ActionForm {
   protected String username;
   protected String password1;
   protected String password2;

   public String getUsername () {return username;}
   public String getPassword1() {return password1;}
   public String getPassword2() {return password2;}

   public void    setUsername (String username) {this.username = username;}
   public void    setPassword1(String password) {this.password1 = password;}
   public void    setPassword2(String password) {this.password2 = password;}
}
```

Creating the RegisterAction

An Action is a Java class that extends `org.apache.struts.Action`. The ActionServlet populates the ActionForm and then passes it to the Action. An Action is generally responsible for validating input, accessing business information, and determining which ActionForward to return to the servlet.

Now, create a file called RegisterAction.java that contains the code in listing 1.2. Save the file under *<Base Directory>*/webapps/register/WEB-INF/classes/app.

We also will focus only on the *Struts* source files you need to create. For example, the UserDirectory class is part of the application's business logic. The Struts framework interacts with this class, but the UserDirectory is **not** part of the Struts layer. (You would need this class whether you used Struts or not.) If you are interested, the source code for UserDirectory is provided in the WEB-INF/classes folder of the register application.

Listing 1.2   RegisterAction.java

```java
package app;
import org.apache.struts.action.*;
import javax.servlet.http.*;
import java.io.*;

public class RegisterAction extends Action {

public ActionForward perform (ActionMapping mapping,
                                ActionForm form,
                                HttpServletRequest req,
                                HttpServletResponse res) {

// ❶ Cast the form to the RegisterForm

RegisterForm rf = (RegisterForm) form;

String username  = rf.getUsername();
String password1 = rf.getPassword1();
String password2 = rf.getPassword2();

// ❷ Apply business logic

if (password1.equals(password2)) {

    try {

// ❸ Return ActionForward for success

UserDirectory.getInstance().setUser(username,password1);
        return mapping.findForward("success");
    } catch (UserDirectoryException e) {
        return mapping.findForward("failure");
    }
}

// ❹ Return ActionForward for failure

return mapping.findForward("failure");
}
}
```

While very simple, our RegisterAction does all the things Actions typically do. At ❶, the incoming ActionForm is cast to the RegisterForm. We can then extract the username, password1, and password2. If the two passwords match at ❷, we add the user to the *UserDirectory* at ❸ and return the ActionForward associated with *success*. The UserDirectory is a helper class that will record usernames and passwords into a standard properties file. Otherwise, the *failure* ActionForward is returned at ❹.

When we create our struts-config file in the next step, we will specify the ActionForward objects that represent the success and failure outcomes cited here.

NOTE   Struts 1.1 offers an alternative entry method, named execute. This method provides for better exception handling but is otherwise the same as the Struts 1.0 perform method. We will refer to the perform method in this chapter so the code will work with both versions.

To keep things simple, we won't try to compile this source file into a Java class. A precompiled class is provided with the Starter application that we can use to test the other components. In practice, you would have to build the Java classes as you went along. In this exercise, we focus on what source files you need to create and leave some of the technicalities for later.

Creating the Struts configuration file (struts-config.xml)

The struts-config.xml file contains details that the ActionServlet needs to handle the requests made to your application. For the purposes of this exercise, we have created a shell of the struts-config.xml file for you. All you need to do is fill in a few of the specifics. Let's look at the changes you need to make to *<Base Directory>*/webapps/register/WEB-INF/struts-config.xml.

First, add

```
/register
```

to the path attribute in the <action> element. The ActionServlet uses the URI forwarded to it by the web container to select the correct Action class. The URI is matched with the path attribute of an ActionMapping. In this case, the path given by the request must match /register after trimming any prefix or suffix.

The prefix or suffix is usually either */do/* or *.do*. For our exercise, it was set to .do. When the URI has a .do extension, the container knows to forward the request to our ActionServlet. Struts trims the extension automatically so we don't need to include it here.

The next step is to add

```
registerForm
```

to the `name` attribute in the `<action>` element. The `<action>` element uses the `name` attribute to indicate which ActionForm bean will be created by the Action-Servlet and populated with the submitted fields.

Next, add

```
app.RegisterAction
```

to the `type` attribute in the `<action>` element. The `type` attribute is used by the ActionServlet to identify the Action used to process the request.

At this point, in a `<forward>` element, add

```
success
```

to the `name` attribute and

```
/success.html
```

to the `path` attribute. Finally, add

```
failure
```

to the `name` attribute and

```
/failure.html
```

to the `path` attribute of the other `<forward>` tag. These elements will create the ActionForward objects that we use to alter the application's control flow. The `<forward>` elements define the association between the logical names used in the RegisterAction.

The source code for our struts-config.xml is shown in listing 1.3. Modify the file, found in *<Base Directory>*/webapps/register/WEB-INF/struts-config.xml, as shown in listing 1.3 and save it to the same place.

Listing 1.3   The struts-config.xml file

```
<?xml version="1.0" encoding="ISO-8859-1" ?>

<!DOCTYPE struts-config PUBLIC
"-//Apache Software Foundation//DTD Struts Configuration 1.0//EN"
"http://jakarta.apache.org/struts/dtds/struts-config_1_0.dtd">
<struts-config>
   <form-beans>
     <form-bean name="registerForm" type="app.RegisterForm"/>
   </form-beans>
<action-mappings>
```

```
<action        path="/register"
               type="app.RegisterAction"
               name="registerForm"
               input="/register.jsp">
   <forward name="success" path="/success.html"/>
   <forward name="failure" path="/failure.html"/>
  </action>
 </action-mappings>
</struts-config>
```

The framework uses the struts-config.xml file as a deployment descriptor. It lets us create and change the ActionMapping associated with a path without recompiling a Java class. We can also change how pages are linked together without changing the JSP templates.

Creating the pages

The final step is to create the success.html, failure.html, and register.jsp pages. Create the three pages as described in listings 1.4, 1.5, and 1.6. Save your work in *<Base Directory>*/webapps/register.

Listing 1.4   The success.html file

```
<HTML>
<HEAD>
   <TITLE>SUCCESS</TITLE>
</HEAD>
<BODY>
   Registration succeeded!
   <P><A href="register.jsp">try another?</A></P>
</BODY>
</HTML>
```

Listing 1.5   The failure.html file

```
<HTML>
<HEAD>
   <TITLE>FAILURE</TITLE>
</HEAD>
<BODY>
   Registration failed!
   <P><A href="register.jsp">try again?</A></P>
</BODY>
</HTML>
```

Listing 1.6   The register.jsp file

```
<%@ taglib uri="/WEB-INF/struts-html.tld" prefix="form" %>

<form:form action="/register">
   UserName:<form:text property="username"/><br>
   enter password:<form:password property="password1"/><br>
   re-enter password:<form:password property="password2"/><br>
<form:submit value="Register"/>
</form:form>
```

At this point, you have done everything you need to build a simple web application with Struts. Now let's try it out.

If Tomcat is not already running, you can start it by going to the Apache Tomcat menu on your Programs menu and selecting Tomcat Start.

With your web container running, point your browser to http://localhost:8080/register/register.jsp (see figure 1.2).

Figure 1.2   The Register application

1.4.4   *Looking back*

Let's take a step back to review what we did, how it worked, and what else you need to do to build your own Struts application.

What we did

To assemble the Register application we had to create the following:

- The RegisterForm ActionForm

- The RegisterAction Action
- Three pages (the register page, the success page, and the failure page)
- The struts-config.xml file (to tell Struts how to wire the pieces together)

How it works

When you point your browser to http://localhost:8080/register/register.jsp, Tomcat renders it as it would any JSP page. You enter a username and password, and click Register to submit the page. The browser posts the contents of the form as an HTTP request. The container sees that the request is being sent to a path registered to the Struts ActionServlet. The request is then forwarded to the ActionServlet and processed by the RegisterAction. The RegisterAction validates the user input before returning a success or failure ActionForward. The servlet forwards control to the page indicated by the ActionForward. Figure 1.3 shows the Register application architecture.

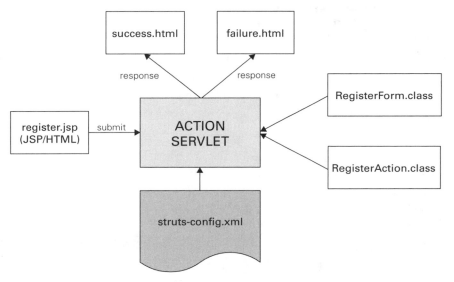

Figure 1.3   The Register application architecture

Looking back at register.jsp in listing 1.6, you will see that the form submits to the URI /register. But if you watch as the page is being submitted, you will see that it is actually sent to register.do. The Struts form tag adds the .do suffix for you. When we set up the application shell you downloaded, we asked that all request paths matching *.do be sent to our ActionServlet.

When it receives a request, the first thing the ActionServlet does is check the mappings for a matching path. The mappings are JavaBeans that Struts creates by reading the struts-config.xml file. We will show the XML for reference, but at runtime Struts refers to the objects, not the XML document.

You'll see from listing 1.3 that we created a mapping for the path /register using this element:

```
<action
  path="/register"
  type="app.RegisterAction"
  name="registerForm"
  input="/register.jsp">
```

Next, the ActionServlet checks to see if a `name` property is associated with the mapping:

```
<action
  path="/register"
  type="app.RegisterAction"
  name="registerForm"
  input="/register.jsp">
```

Our /register mapping specifies a form bean by the name of `registerForm`. The servlet uses this name to look up the corresponding ActionFormBean object. The type specified by the form bean is used to create the ActionForm object:

```
<form-beans>
  <form-bean
    name="registerForm"
    type="app.RegisterForm"/>
</form-beans>

<action-mappings>
  <action
    path="/register"
    type="app.RegisterAction"
    name="registerForm"
    input="/register.jsp">
    <forward
      name="success"
      path="/success.html"/>
    <forward
        name="failure"
      path="/failure.html"/>
  </action>
</action-mappings>
```

In this case, the servlet will use our RegisterForm class:

```
<form-beans>
  <form-bean
    name="registerForm"
    type="app.RegisterForm"/>
</form-beans>
```

Once RegisterForm is instantiated, the ActionServlet will try to call setter methods on RegisterForm for any input fields in the request. In our example, these are `setUsername`, `setPassword1`, and `setPassword2`. If a setter method doesn't exist for an input parameter, that parameter is ignored.

The `type` attribute of the ActionMapping object is the name of the class that the ActionServlet will use to instantiate an Action. In this case, it will use the RegisterAction object you created. The `perform` method of the RegisterAction object is invoked and passed a reference to the RegisterForm, which was created and populated in the previous step:

```
<action
  path="/register"
  type="app.RegisterAction"
  name="registerForm"
  input="/register.jsp">
  <forward
    name="success"
    path="/success.html"/>
  <forward
    name="failure"
    path="/failure.html"/>
</action>
```

Depending on the outcome of the `perform` method (see listing 1.2), one of the two ActionForwards is returned. The `findForward()` method uses its single `String` parameter to find a `forward` object that matches the `name` property. The `path` property is used by the ActionServlet to determine which of our pages should complete the response:

```
<forward
  name="success"
  path="/success.html"/>
<forward
  name="failure"
  path="/failure.html"/>
```

While very simple, our little exercise has shown you the essential components of any Struts application.

What we didn't do

To get you started as quickly as possible, our exercise cut a corner. Rather than have you compile the Java source files, we skipped that step and relied on the class files bundled with the starter application. We wanted to give you a chance to develop a Struts application without being distracted by routine technicalities, such as Ant build files.

In chapter 3, we develop another simple application to demonstrate other features of the framework. Here, we also get you started with Ant and an actual programmer's editor (jEdit). We also start to cover the Struts components in greater depth. Part 2 of the book covers the framework components in the greatest detail. In part 4, we put it all together and build a realistic production application called Artimus.

1.5 Summary

In this chapter, we introduced Struts as an application framework. We examined the technology behind HTTP, the Common Gateway Interface, Java servlets, JSPs, and JavaBeans. We also looked at the Model 2 application architecture to see how it is used to combine servlets and JSPs in the same application.

Toward the end of the chapter, we moved into the fast lane and assembled our first Struts application. Now that you have had a taste of what it is like to develop a web application with Struts, in chapter 2 we dig deeper into the theory and practice behind the Struts architecture.

Exploring the
Struts architecture

2

This chapter covers

- Introducing application frameworks, MVC, and Model 2
- Understanding how Struts works
- Using the Struts control flow
- Exploring the strengths and weaknesses of Struts

A common mistake that people make when trying to design something completely foolproof is to underestimate the ingenuity of complete fools.

—Douglas Adams, *Mostly Harmless*

2.1 Talking the talk

This chapter explores the Struts framework in depth and highlights the benefits Struts can bring to your development efforts. We believe that once you can "talk the talk" of web architecture and design, you will be better equipped to use Struts with your own applications.

With a sound overview of the Struts architecture in place, we outline the Struts control flow and the way it handles the request-response event cycle. A good understanding of this process makes it much easier to create applications that make the best use of the framework.

Choosing a web application framework should not be a casual decision. Many people will use this book, and especially this chapter, as part of evaluating Struts for their project. Accordingly, we conclude this chapter with a candid look at the strengths and weaknesses of the Struts framework and address concerns regarding overall performance. Struts is designed for professional developers. To make informed decisions, professionals need to be aware of both a tool's capabilities and its limitations.

2.2 Why we need Struts

Today's web applications are critical components of the corporate mission. As always, development teams need to build applications in record time, but they have to build them right and build them to last.

Java web developers already have utilities for building presentation pages, such as JavaServer Pages and Velocity templates. We also have mechanisms for handling databases—JDBC and Enterprise JavaBeans (EJBs), for example. But what do we use to put these components together? We have the plumbing and the drywall … what else do we need?

2.2.1 One step back, three steps forward

In the late 1970s, when graphical user interfaces (GUIs) were being invented, software architects saw applications as having three major parts: the part that manages data, the part that creates screens and reports, and the part that handles interactions between the user and the other subsystems [Ooram]. In the early 1980s, the ObjectWorks/Smalltalk programming environment introduced this triumvirate as a development framework. In Smalltalk 80 parlance, the data system is dubbed the *Model*, the presentation system is called the *View*, and the interaction system is the *Controller*. Many modern development environments, including Java's Swing, use this *Model/View/Controller (MVC)* architecture (see figure 2.1) as the foundation of their own frameworks.

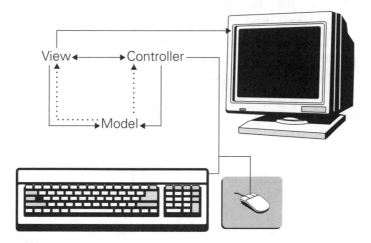

Figure 2.1   The Model/View/Controller architecture

Java web developers already have capable tools, such as JDBC and JSP, for consulting the Model and creating the View, but where's the Controller for our web applications?

2.2.2   *Enter Struts*

The centerpiece of Struts is an MVC-style Controller. The Struts Controller bridges the gap between Model and View. The framework also includes other missing pieces developers need to write scalable, leading-edge web applications. Struts is a collection of "invisible underpinnings" that help developers turn raw materials like databases and web pages into a coherent application.

2.2.3   *Struts controller components*

The Struts controller is a set of programmable components that allow developers to define exactly how their application interacts with the user. These components hide nasty, cumbersome implementation details behind logical names. Developers can program these details once, then go back to thinking in terms of *what* the program does rather than *how* it does it.

Users interact with a web application through hyperlinks and HTML forms. The hyperlinks lead to pages that display data and other elements, such as text and images. The forms generally submit data to the application via some type of custom action.

As shown in figure 2.2, Struts provides components that programmers can use to define the hyperlinks, forms, and custom actions that web applications use to interact with the user. We used these components to build a starter application in chapter 1. In chapter 3, we walk through using these components to build another simple application. Then, in chapter 4, we provide a detailed overview of configuring these components. Later chapters provide more detail about putting each component to use within your application. In part 4 we demonstrate using the components in the context of working applications. But, since this chapter is the architectural overview, let's go ahead and introduce the major Struts components now.

Figure 2.2   Major Struts components

NOTE   The Struts components are configured via XML. In practice, the configuration elements are an integral part of the Struts framework. To help you put it all together, we show a sample of each component's XML element as it is introduced.

Hyperlinks

To the application developer, a hyperlink is a path to some resource in the application. This may be a web page or a custom action. It may also include special parameters. In Struts, developers can define a hyperlink as an *ActionForward*. These objects have a logical name and a `path` property. This lets developers set the path and then refer to the ActionForward by name.

ActionForwards are usually defined in an XML configuration file that Struts reads when the web application loads. Struts uses the XML definitions to create the

Struts configuration, which includes a list of ActionForwards. The XML element that would create an ActionForward for a welcome hyperlink might look like this:

```
<forward
    name="welcome"
    path="/pages/index.jsp"/>
```

This element would create an ActionForward JavaBean with its name property set to welcome and its path property set to /pages/index.jsp.

JSP pages and other components can then refer to the welcome forward. The Struts framework will look up the welcome ActionForward bean and retrieve the path to complete the hyperlink. This allows developers to change the destination of a link without changing all the components that refer to that link. In most web applications, details like this are hardcoded into JSP and Java code, making changes difficult and prone to error. In a Struts application, these details can be changed throughout the application without touching a single page or Java class.

For more about ActionForwards, see chapter 6.

HTML forms

The web protocols, HTTP and HTML, provide a mechanism for submitting data from a form but leave receiving the data as an exercise for the developer. The Struts framework provides an *ActionForm* class, which is designed to handle input from an HTML form, validate the input, and redisplay the form to the user for correction (when needed), along with any corresponding prompts or messages.

ActionForms are just JavaBeans with a couple of standard methods to manage the validation and revision cycle. Struts automatically matches the JavaBean properties with the attributes of the HTML controls. The developer defines the Action-Form class. Struts does the rest.

This class will automatically populate the username field from a form with an HTML form element of the same name, as shown here:

```
public final class LogonForm extends ActionForm {
    private String username = null;
    public String getUsername() {
    return (this.username);
    }
    public void setUsername(String username) {
    this.username = username;
    }
}
```

Other properties would be added for each field of the form. This lets other components get what they need from a standard JavaBean, so everyone does not have to sift through an HTTP request.

The ActionForm classes are created using normal Java classes. The Struts configuration refers to the ActionForm classes through a set of descriptors: the `<form-beans>` and `<form-bean>` elements. The `<form-bean>` elements are descriptors that the framework uses to identify and instantiate the ActionForm objects, as shown here:

```
<form-bean
      name="articleForm"
      type="org.apache.artimus.struts.Form"/>
```

The Struts configuration lists the ActionForm beans it uses and gives the Action-Form classes a logical name to use within the application.

1.0 vs 1.1   In Struts 1.1 the ActionForm can also use a Map (`java.util.Map`) to store the attribute names rather than define individual properties. A new type of JavaBean, the *DynaBean*, can also be used with Struts 1.1 and later. You can specify the properties for a DynaActionForm by using an XML element. In effect, this does let you define ActionForms in the Struts configuration file.

For more about ActionForms, see chapter 5.

Custom actions

An HTML form uses an `action` parameter to tell the browser where to send the form's data. The Struts framework supplies a corresponding *Action* class to receive such data. The framework automatically creates, populates, validates, and finally passes the appropriate ActionForm to the Action object. The Action can then get the data it needs directly from the ActionForm bean. Here's an example:

```
public final class LogonAction extends Action {
  public ActionForward perform(ActionMapping mapping,
      ActionForm form,
      HttpServletRequest request,
      HttpServletResponse response)
      throws IOException, ServletException {
    MyForm myForm = (MyForm) form;
    // ...
    return mapping.findForward("continue");
  }
}
```

An Action concludes by returning an ActionForward object to the controller. This allows the Action to choose a definition using logical names, like *continue* or *cancel*, rather than system paths.

To ensure extensibility, the controller also passes the current request and response object. In practice, an Action can do anything a Java Servlet can do.

1.0 vs 1.1   In Struts 1.1 a new `execute` method is preferred over the `perform` method shown in our example. The `perform` method is deprecated but supported for backward compatibility. The `execute` method signature allows for better exception handling. The new ExceptionHandler is covered in chapter 9.

For more about Action objects, see chapter 8.

In addition to the ActionForward, ActionForm, and Action objects, the Struts controller layer provides several other specialized components, including *ActionMappings* and the *ActionServlet*. Struts also supports localizing your application from the controller layer.

ActionMappings

In a web application, every resource must be referred to through a Uniform Resource Identifier (URI). This includes HTML pages, JSP pages, and any custom actions. To give the custom Actions a URI, or path, the Struts framework provides an *ActionMapping* object. Like the ActionForwards and ActionForms, the mappings are usually defined in the XML configuration file:

```
<action-mappings>
    <action
    path="/logonSubmit"
    type="app.LogonAction"
    name="logonForm"
    scope="request"
    validate="true"
    input="/pages/logon.jsp"/>
</action-mappings>
```

This also allows the same Action object to be used by different mappings. For example, one mapping may require validation; another may not.

For more about ActionMappings, see chapter 7.

ActionServlet

The Struts *ActionServlet* works quietly behind the scenes, binding the other components together. Although it can be subclassed, most Struts 1.0 developers treat the ActionServlet as a blackbox: they configure it and leave it alone. For more about configuring Struts, see chapter 4.

In Struts 1.1, the ActionServlet is easier to extend. Chapter 9 covers the new extension points and configuration options for the Struts 1.1 ActionServlet.

Localization

Web applications also interact with users through prompts and messages. The Struts components have localization features built in so that applications can be written for an international audience. We refer to the localization features throughout the book. A general overview is provided in chapter 13.

2.2.4 Developing a web application with Struts

To build a web application with Struts, developers will define the hyperlinks they need as ActionForwards, the HTML forms they need as ActionForms, and whatever custom server-side actions they need as Action classes.

Developers who need to access EJBs or JDBC databases can do so by way of the Action object. This way, the presentation page does not need to interact with the Model layer.

The Struts Action object will collect whatever data a View may need and then forward it to the presentation page. Struts provides a JSP tag library for use with JSP pages that simplifies writing HTML forms and accessing other data that an Action may forward. Other presentation devices, such as Velocity templates, can also access the Struts framework to create dynamic web pages. This process is shown in figure 2.3.

Figure 2.3 Delivering data back to the view

For more about using various data systems with Struts, see chapter 14. See chapters 10 and 11 to learn more about creating presentation pages with Struts.

Before moving deeper into the Struts architecture, let's take a look at the issues faced by a web application framework that the architecture must address.

2.3 Why we need frameworks

In chapter 1, we introduced application frameworks and briefly discussed why frameworks are important. But to really understand a solution, you need to appreciate the problem. Developing for the web, while rewarding, brings its own set of challenges. Let's take a quick look at what makes web development so challenging.

2.3.1 The Web—a never-ending kluge

Web developers are hampered by a double web whammy. First, we are expected to use web browsers for clients. Second, we must use the web protocol to communicate.

Web browsers communicate via Hypertext Transmission Protocol (HTTP) and display pages created with Hypertext Markup Language (HTML). A web browser sends out the HTTP request and renders the HTML it receives in response. This is an excellent platform for serving prewritten pages that rarely change. But most of us are writing dynamic applications with pages that are customized for each user. While there are some handy "hooks" for dynamic features, web applications go against the HTTP/HTML grain.

As shown in table 2.1, restrictions imposed by the web protocol and the web clients predetermine how web applications can be written.

Table 2.1 Difficulties web applications face and web application frameworks must address

Restrictions imposed by...	Result in these difficulties...
The protocol	By default, HTTP will accept a connection from any client on the network. Changing this behavior varies from server to server.
	Primarily, HTTP transfers data using simple text fields. Transferring binary data requires use of a complicated extension to the protocol.
	HTTP is sessionless and requires extra effort to track people using the application.
	HTTP is trusting and expects that clients will provide accurate information.
The clients	Browsers are separate applications outside the application's direct control.
	All browsers are not equal and support different subsets of the official standards.
	Input from a browser may be incorrect or incomplete. Input may even be hostile and contrived to harm the application.

Table 2.1 **Difficulties web applications face and web application frameworks must address** (continued)

Restrictions imposed by...	Result in these difficulties...
	The standard web formatting language, HTML, cannot construct many of the interface elements found in desktop environments.
	Creating HTML controls with default data is an exercise left to the application.

Sadly, the situation is not going to change any time soon. Web developers must see these shortcomings as challenges to overcome. Since there are so many obstacles to writing robust web applications, using a framework is vital, lest your application become an endless series of workarounds and kluges.

The challenges we face when developing web applications are great. But so are the rewards. The duo of the HTTP protocol and the HTML client makes web applications accessible to people the world over. No other platform has ever been able to make that claim.

2.3.2 *The servlet solution*

As mentioned in chapter 1, the Java Servlet platform [Sun, JST] acts like a base framework to provide Java web applications with a number of important capabilities. The servlet class provides a base interface for handling HTTP requests and the ensuing response. It builds on HTTP to provide a "session" context to help track users in the application. It provides other contexts to help applications pass data to the browsers or to other servlets in the application. Java web applications also have uniform access to basic security features that would otherwise be managed differently by different HTTP servers.

To put this all together, the servlet specification describes a *container* to manage the servlets. The container may also provide other services, such as a handler for JSPs. A servlet container can include its own web server or simply act as an adjunct to an existing web server.

For database access, Java applications have another common framework at their disposal: JDBC. Developers can write to a standard SQL interface while an adapter takes care of the hoary details. This makes it easier to change database vendors without rewriting the source code.

For high-performance applications that access database systems on remote servers, web developers can use the Enterprise JavaBean platform. Most Java application frameworks, including Struts, can be used with EJBs when they are needed.

Overall, this makes web applications based on Java servlets very portable and relatively easy to write and maintain. Servlets and JSPs have made a real difference in the way we write applications. Java web application frameworks like Struts build on the servlet platform and try to provide developers with a seamless, kluge-free environment.

2.3.3 Servlet frameworks

Most, if not all, Java web frameworks use the Sun Servlet platform as a foundation. These frameworks bundle one or more prewritten servlets that you can plug into your application. A framework will also include a hierarchy of classes that you can implement or extend within your own application.

In general, the focus of a web application framework is to help get the data you need out of a browser and into a programming structure, where your application can use it—or out of a programming structure and into a browser, where your user can see it.

Some frameworks, such as Turbine [ASF, Turbine], also provide helper classes for working with JDBC databases. Other frameworks, like Struts, are model-neutral. They don't hinder database access but neither do they help. Even other frameworks, like dbForms [dbForms], specialize in database access and leave other tasks as an exercise for the developer (or to another framework, like Struts).

Common framework strategies

As shown in figure 2.4, Java web application frameworks use several common techniques to help make products easier to design, write, and maintain, including:

External configuration files.   Provide implementation details that developers do not want to embed in their source code.

A central controller.   Provides a way to funnel the HTTP requests into a more easily managed queue. This design is sometimes referred to as a *Front Controller* [Go3].

External presentation systems.   Let different people work on different parts of the application at the same time. For example, Java engineers can be working on classes related to the central controller, while page designers work with the JSPs. Aside from JSPs, other presentation systems, like Velocity Templates or XSLT, can be used with Struts.

Frameworks often have more components, but most share these hallmarks. These common strategies are rooted in the programming paradigms expounded in books like *Design Patterns* [Go4] and *Core J2EE Patterns* [Go3]. Many developers are

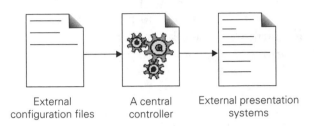

External   A central   External presentation
configuration files   controller   systems

Figure 2.4   Frameworks commonly use a configuration file, a controller, and a presentation system.

comfortable discussing and using these patterns but may not be up to the task of implementing them for the first time in a web environment.

They make it easy to do the Right Thing and build your application using proven design patterns, like Model-View-Controller (see section 2.2). The benefit of using patterns when developing desktop applications is well known, but deploying these same patterns in a web environment is still unfamiliar ground for most developers.

2.3.4 *The whitebox-blackbox continuum*

Frameworks are sometimes categorized into a continuum with poles labeled *whitebox* and *blackbox* [Fayad]. Whitebox frameworks rely heavily on object-oriented language features such as inheritance and dynamic binding. Blackbox frameworks tend to define interfaces for pluggable components and then provide base starter components based on those interfaces. The interface and base components will often provide *hotspot* methods that can be used as is or overridden to provide special behavior.

DEFINITION   Also called flexible points or extension points, *hotspots* are locations where code may be added to customize a framework. Hotspots (the hotspot subsystem) describe the different characteristics of each application that can be supported by the framework. In essence, they represent the problems that a framework solves. Many object-orientated frameworks consist of a kernel subsystem and a hotspot subsystem. [Braga, et al]

Like many real-life frameworks, Struts uses a mix of whitebox and blackbox techniques. But overall, the framework would be placed toward the blackbox end of the continuum.

Blackbox frameworks often rely strongly on design patterns. Struts is no exception. In fact, design patterns are often used to provide higher-level descriptions of frameworks [Johnson]. In keeping with this trend, let's introduce the design patterns and show how they are used within the Struts framework.

For more about Struts and design patterns, see appendix A.

2.4 Struts, Model 2, and MVC

One of the first things Struts says about itself is that the framework:

> *...encourages application architectures based on the Model 2*
> *approach, a variation of the classic Model-View-Controller (MVC)*
> *design paradigm.*

This statement reassures some web developers but befuddles others who have not been introduced to the mysteries of Model 2 or MVC. It can in fact be very difficult to understand much of the Struts literature without a thorough grounding in MVC and Sun's Model 2.

To be sure we are all on the same page, sections 2.4.1 and 2.4.2 are MVC and Model 2 primers. Then in section 2.4.3, we look at how Struts implements these classic patterns.

2.4.1 The evolution of MVC

As you will recall from section 2.1, originally, Model/View/Controller was a framework for building Smalltalk applications. The framework supported a triad of classes representing the application state, the screen presentation, and control flow—which it termed the Model, View, and Controller. See figure 2.5.

The Smalltalk MVC framework is used as a case study in a very popular book called *Design Patterns: Elements of Reusable Object-Oriented Software* [Go4]. The *Design Patterns* book has four primary authors, who have come to be known as the Gang of Four. For more about design patterns, see appendix A.

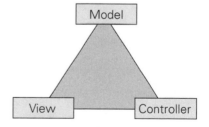

Figure 2.5   The Smalltalk MVC triad of classes

The MVC example in *Design Patterns* extols its use of the notify/subscribe protocol and the Observer pattern. The essentials of the example are that a system needs to display several different views of the same data, such as a bar chart, pie chart, and spreadsheet. This is an excellent justification for compartmentalizing applications, and the example has been often repeated.

In the example shown in figure 2.6, each of the views could be displayed to different users at the same time. The application must keep the views updated whenever the underlying data, or Model, changes. To update the Model, users submit a request to the Controller, which coordinates the change with the Model. The views of the data must then be updated to reflect the latest state of the Model.

The Smalltalk MVC solution is to use an Observer notification pattern. In this pattern, each View registers as an observer of the Model's data. The Model can then notify the Views of changes by sending a message to all its registered observers.

Others have since generalized the Smalltalk MVC framework into the Model-View-Controller architectural paradigm, which can be applied to the construction of applications on any platform.

2.4.2 *The rise of Model 2*

JavaServer Pages are intended to make dynamic web pages easier to write. JSPs were first introduced as an alternative to servlets, as well as to Microsoft's Active Server Pages. Developers were offered the power of servlets as easy-to-create server pages.

But with great power comes great responsibility. Many teams found that if they were not careful, a project could easily collapse under the weight of hopelessly intertwined pages. Advanced features required the use of complex scriptlets. But

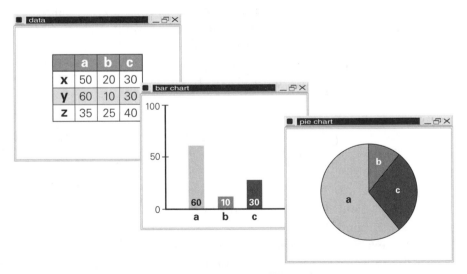

Figure 2.6   The Model data can be used in several different views.

scriptlets are difficult to reuse—unless you're pasting the code from page to page. Utility pages can be included, but they are difficult to keep organized and make for some very ugly "source" trees. Something was wrong with this picture.

Many developers soon realized that JSPs *and* servlets could be used together to deploy web applications. The servlets could cope with the control flow; the JSPs could focus on the nasty task of writing HTML. In due course, using JSPs and servlets together became known as Model 2 (using JSPs alone was referred to as Model 1).

Of course, there is nothing new under the Sun... and many have been quick to point out that JSP's Model 2 resembles the classic Model-View-Controller architecture. In some circles, it is now commonplace to use the terms Model 2 and MVC interchangeably, although some dispute whether an application can be MVC and not support the classic Observer notification pattern. Model-View-Controller without the notification pattern is sometimes called MVC2 or Web MVC.

2.4.3 *Application layers—decoupling the view*

One reason Model 2 is held to be distinct from MVC is that the Observer notification pattern doesn't work well in a web environment. HTTP is a "pull" protocol: the client requests and the server responds. No request, no response. The Observer pattern requires a push protocol for notification, so the server can push a message to the client when the model changes. While there are ways to simulate pushing data to a web client, they go against the grain and could be considered a kluge.

Figure 2.7 shows the Model-View-Controller paradigm as it is most commonly depicted: a triangle of three interconnected components. It can be difficult for a web application to maintain the "change notification" portion of this diagram. This sort of thing works well when all the resources are on the same server and the clients have an open connection with that server. It does not work so well when resources are distributed over several servers and clients do not maintain an open connection with the application.

Many architects of distributed systems, including web applications, wince at the idea of the view making a state query. Most often, remote applications are designed around the Layers pattern [POSA]. Essentially, the Layers pattern says that classes may interact with classes in their own layer or classes in an adjacent layer. In a complex application, this keeps dependencies from growing exponentially as components are added. Layering is a core pattern in the design of remote applications.

From an MVC context, introducing the Layers pattern puts the responsibility for both state changes and state queries onto the Controller along with any change notifications.

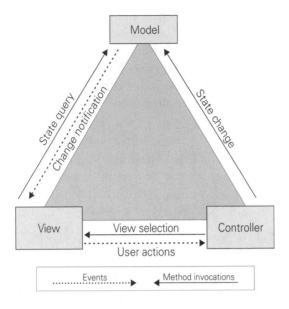

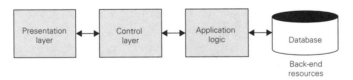

Figure 2.7
MVC is usually represented as
three interconnected components.

As shown in figure 2.8, layered web applications use a "flatter" design than conventional MVC. The controller is sandwiched between the presentation layer (View) and the application logic (Model).

Figure 2.8   Web application layers

The major responsibilities of each component are unchanged. The flow changes slightly in that any state query or change notification must pass through the Controller. Another difference is that when the View, or presentation layer, renders dynamic content, it uses data passed by the Controller rather than data returned directly by the Model. This change decouples the View from the Model, allowing the Controller to select both the data and View that displays the data.

2.4.4   How Struts implements Model 2, MVC, and layers

Struts implements Sun's Model 2 architecture by providing a controller servlet that can be used to manage the flow between JSP pages and other presentation layer devices. Struts implements the MVC/Layers pattern through the use of ActionForwards and ActionMappings to keep control-flow decisions out of the presentation layer. The JSPs can refer to logical destinations. The Controller components provide the actual URIs at runtime.

Table 2.2 maps the Struts core classes to the classic responsibilities of MVC components.

Table 2.2 Core Struts classes as they relate to MVC

Class	Description
ActionForward	A user gesture or view selection
ActionForm	The data for a state change
ActionMapping	The state change event
ActionServlet	The part of the Controller that receives user gestures and state changes and issues view selections
Action classes	The part of the Controller that interacts with the model to execute a state change or query and advises the ActionServlet of the next view to select

In addition to these core classes, Struts uses a number of configuration files and view helpers to bridge the gap between the Controller and the Model. Table 2.3 lists the Struts configuration files and describes their role in the architecture.

Table 2.3 Struts configuration files

File	Purpose
ApplicationResources.properties	Stores localized messages and labels so that your application can be internationalized
struts-config.xml	Stores the default configuration for the controller objects, which includes the user gestures, state changes, and state queries supported by your model

To expose the data in the Struts configuration to the view, the framework provides a number of helpers in the form of JSP tags, shown in table 2.4.

Table 2.4   Struts view helpers

Tag Library Descriptor	Purpose
struts-html.tld	JSP tag extension for HTML forms
struts-bean.tld	JSP tag extension for handling JavaBeans
struts-logic.tld	JSP tag extension for testing the values of properties

Putting this all together, table 2.5 indexes the Struts components by layer.

Table 2.5   Struts components indexed by layer

View layer	Controller layer	Model layer
JSP tag extensions	ActionForwards ActionForm classes ActionMappings ActionServlet Action classes ActionErrors MessageResources	GenericDataSource
JavaServer Pages, Velocity templates, and other presentation vehicles provided by the developer	Various utility classes, such as the Commons-Digester and Commons-BeanUtils	Other data services and APIs provided by the developer

Note that in accord with the Layers pattern (see section 2.4.3), the components should interact only with other components in their column or the adjacent column. To wit, the Model components should not interact directly with the View components.

In practice, the Controller and the View interact through the request, session, and application contexts provided by the servlet platform (see section 2.3.2). The Controller and Model interact through the file and memory system (in the case of loading XML documents or Properties files) or through other services, like TCP, to create a connection with a JDBC database.

2.5 Struts control flow

Since web applications are dynamic, it's difficult to represent the "One True Control Flow." Depending on the circumstances, a lot of different things can happen in different ways—especially in web applications. But there is still a general order to things that we can review here.

If you are new to Struts, or application frameworks, or even web applications, this process may seem hard to follow at first. The various problems it is trying to solve may not be evident. We'll be covering those in detail throughout the book. Here, we try to take a look at the forest before introducing the trees. As you read through the book, we recommend that you revisit this section occasionally to see how the pieces fit into the big picture.

2.5.1 *The big picture*

Figure 2.9 lays out the Struts request-response process in a visual sequence. Let's walk through a description of the request-response. The numbers in parentheses refer to figure 2.9 where appropriate:

- A client requests a path that matches the Action URI pattern (1).
- The container passes the request to the ActionServlet.
- If this is a modular application, the ActionServlet selects the appropriate module.
- The ActionServlet looks up the mapping for the path.
- If the mapping specifies a form bean, the ActionServlet sees if there is one already or creates one (1.1).
- If a form bean is in play, the ActionServlet resets and populates it from the HTTP request.
- If the mapping has the `validate` property set to true, it calls `validate` on the form bean (1.2).
- If it fails, the servlet forwards to the path specified by the `input` property and this control flow ends.
- If the mapping specifies an Action type, it is reused if it already exists or instantiated (1.3).
- The Action's `perform` or `execute` method is called and passed the instantiated form bean (or null).
- The Action may populate the form bean, call business objects, and do whatever else is needed (1.3.1-1.3.4).
- The Action returns an ActionForward to the ActionServlet (1.3.5).
- If the ActionForward is to another Action URI, we begin again; otherwise, it's off to a display page or some other resource. Most often, it is a JSP, in which case Jasper, or the equivalent (*not* Struts), renders the page (2, 3).

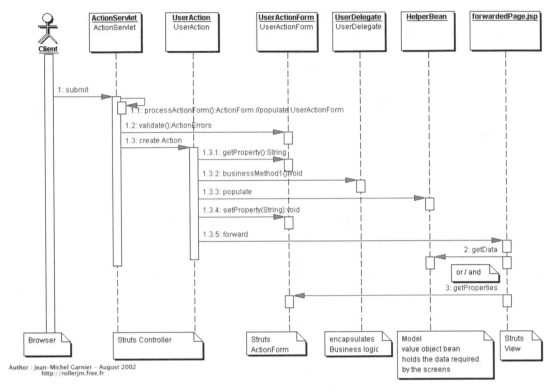

Figure 2.9 **The Struts Request-Response process. UML by Jean-Michel Garnier.**

- If the JSP uses Struts HTML tags, and they see the right ActionForm in the request (1.1), they populate their controls from the ActionForm. Otherwise, the `<html:form>` tag creates one. Since Struts 1.1, the form tag also calls reset on the ActionForm if it creates the object itself.

If you just need to create a blank form (1.1), you can use a standard ForwardAction (see chapter 8) to pass control through an Action and then out to the page.

2.5.2 *The finer details*

The devil, as they say, is in the details. The synopsis and diagram in the prior sections do a good job of outlining the big picture but omit important details. Let's drill down now and visit the finer points. Since this is HTTP, everything starts with an incoming request.

Request is received by our container

The backbone component of the Struts framework is the ActionServlet. Like all servlets, it lives in a container, such as Tomcat, Resin, or WebLogic. When the container boots, it reads a deployment descriptor (web.xml) that tells it which servlets to load.

One of the standard servlet settings is the *servlet mapping*. The container uses this setting to decide which requests are sent to which servlet:

```
<servlet-mapping>

    <servlet-name>action</servlet-name>

    <url-pattern>/do/*</url-pattern>

</servlet-mapping>
```

Here, we have asked the container to give our ActionServlet any request that matches the pattern /do/*. That would include /do/This or /do/That and /do/something/Whatever.

Many applications like to use suffix mapping instead:

```
<servlet-mapping>
    <servlet-name>action</servlet-name>
    <url-pattern>*.do</url-pattern>
</servlet-mapping>
```

This URL pattern would likewise match this.do or that.do or /something/whatever.do. Any valid extension or prefix can be used; .do is simply a popular choice. When a request comes in with a path component that matches our servlet context, the container forwards it to our ActionServlet. Requests that don't match our pattern are not sent to the ActionServlet. A request matching *.jsp, for example, would be forwarded to the container's JSP service, such as Jasper if you are using Tomcat or WebSphere. There may be other servlets in your applications that handle other patterns. Any pattern that doesn't match a servlet mapping is sent to the container's default web server.

Request is received by our ActionServlet

When our ActionServlet receives a request, it runs the request through a gauntlet that processes the locale, mapping, form bean, and finally the Action. Some of these steps apply only to Struts 1.1 applications:

Process MultipartRequest.   If this is a multipart request (a form with a Multipurpose Internet Mail Extension [MIME] attachment), the servlet wraps the request with a special handler, to avoid errors later in the process.

Process Path.   The ActionServlet checks to see if this path is for an application module. If so the configuration for the appropriate module is selected. [Struts 1.1]

Process Locale.   By default, the ActionServlet will check to see if there is a standard locale object in the user's session. If there is no locale object, the ActionServlet will put one there. This object can be used to provide a localized presentation for each user.

Process Content and NoCache.   The default MIME type and optional request headers are added to the response.

Process Mapping.   The ActionServlet checks the ActionMappings for a mapping keyed to a path that matches the one we are processing. If one is not found, the ActionServlet forwards to the default (or "unknown") Action, if one has been set, or generates a "bad request" error. If the mapping is found, it is placed into the request for future reference.

Process Roles.   The ActionServlet checks to see if the user is authorized to access this action. [Struts 1.1]

Process ActionForm.   The ActionServlet checks whether the mapping specifies an ActionForm. If it does, the servlet checks to see if one already exists in the specified scope. (The default is session.) If one does not exist, the ActionServlet creates one.

Process Populate.   The ActionForm's `reset` method is called, and then it is auto-populated via reflection. Parameters that match the ActionForm's properties are applied. Other parameters and properties are ignored.

Process Validate.   The ActionForm's `validate` method is called. If the method returns false, control is passed to the `input` property specified on the mapping, and the Action is not processed.

Process Forward or Include.   If the ActionMapping specifies the `forward` or `include` attribute, control is transferred to another resource. Otherwise, the ActionServlet delegates the request to an Action object.

Process Action.   If the mapping specifies an Action type, the servlet checks to see if one has already been instantiated. If it doesn't find one, the Action object is instantiated. There is only one Action object per class (the Singleton pattern), which handles all the requests for that Action through multithreading. The servlet calls the Action's `perform` or `execute` method, passing the request, response, mapping, and any form bean.

The Action executes whatever behavior is required, which may include:

- Accessing a data system, such as a JDBC database
- Creating objects in the request to be used by the view
- Creating objects in the user session, if required
- Updating session objects, such as the user's locale, as needed
- Performing any other business function required by the application
- Handling exceptions and other error conditions
- Sending a direct response or (most often) returning an ActionForward to the servlet

Some of this behavior, like accessing a database, is often handled by a business object that is invoked by the Action (the Business Delegate pattern). The Action is there to handle any web-specific tasks, but any code that can be placed in a business object should be placed in a business object. The Action is a Controller class and should not be used to handle your application's core business logic.

The Action returns an ActionForward

When the Action completes, it returns an ActionForward. If the ActionForward is null, the ActionServlet assumes the response has been generated and does nothing. Otherwise, the ActionServlet reads the ActionForward and either redirects or forwards the request as appropriate.

If the request is another Action URI, the container will return the request to the ActionServlet. Otherwise, the container sends the request to another servlet or service.

If the ActionForward is set for redirect, the request is sent back to the client with instructions to submit a new request to the specified location.

Jasper (or equivalent) renders a JavaServer Page

When the ActionServlet sends a request to a JSP, the request is handled by another service, such as Jasper. Typically, the Struts and other tag extensions are used to write the dynamic portions of the page. Sometimes a JSP template may be used so that the page is built up from other components.

Most often, the dynamic data is passed to the page in the request context in a JavaBean. This is known as the *View Helper* pattern [Go3]. The tag extensions simply call methods on the JavaBeans that return the formatted data. How data is positioned on a page is considered part of the presentation logic. The format of the data itself is usually part of the business logic, so it's delegated to the bean.

The Struts tags may also access view helpers provided by the framework. These include localized labels and prompts, error messages, and hyperlink paths. In addition, Struts tags can evaluate expressions, iterate through lists, and populate the controls in an HTML form.

Another servlet renders the response

After processing an Action, the request can be sent to any other servlet or service in the application. Other presentation systems, such as Velocity templates, can access framework resources through the servlet contexts.

2.5.3 Is Struts performant?

After a detailed description of the Struts process, you might wonder how long all this is going to take. In general, Struts should improve the performance of most properly designed web applications. In this section, we examine a few specific design points that contribute to the framework's efficiency.

DEFINITION   *Performant* is a French word meaning *efficient*. Software engineers often use the word *performant* to describe a process or device that performs well in practice.

Struts is not only thread-safe but thread-dependent.   A lightweight Action object, rather than an individual servlet, handles the response to a request. Struts instantiates each Action class once and allows other requests to be threaded through the original object. This core strategy conserves resources and provides the best possible throughput. A properly designed application will exploit this further by routing related operations through a single Action.

ActionForm beans minimize subclass code and shorten subclass hierarchies.   A key point in the Struts framework is automatically populating any ActionForm bean from any request. Without this component, custom code may have to be written and instantiated to populate each class of bean. The careful use of reflection saves resources, which are always finite, allowing them to be put to better use.

The Struts tag libraries provide general-purpose functionality.   The bean and logic taglibs bundled with Struts can meet most JSP tag needs. They reduce or even eliminate the need to write and instantiate additional tags. The JSP specification includes tag reuse within a JSP. Using the same general-purpose tag three times is more performant than using three different tags.

The Struts components are reusable by the application. Utilities bundled with the framework have uses throughout most applications. The `BeanUtil.populate` method is a good example. This method is used to populate form beans from an HTTP request but can also be used to populate any bean from any type of map. Reusing components reduces overhead and conserves resources.

The Struts localization strategies reduce the need for redundant JSPs. By allowing localized messages to be retrieved at runtime, internationalized applications can provide a single page where one page for each language would otherwise be needed. Meanwhile, the same messaging system is also used to handle error messages, providing dual use of the same objects.

Struts is designed with an open architecture. Struts components are designed so that they can be subclassed by an application to provide additional functionality. This allows developers to extend existing classes rather than add the overhead of creating and integrating new classes. Also, Struts shares its resources with the application. This allows developers to leverage existing components, so they do not have to write and instantiate their own.

Struts is lightweight. Similar frameworks may provide hundreds of classes or tags and dozens of packages. The entire Struts framework is made up of five tag libraries and five core packages.

Struts is standards compliant. Many containers are designed to perform best when using standard components—JSPs and JavaBeans, for example.

Struts is open source and well documented. This means developers can easily examine the code to identify and resolve any potential bottlenecks.

Struts is model neutral. Since Struts does not make any assumptions about the backend model, an application can implement the Model layer in the most efficient way possible. Struts Actions can call a set of helper classes to access needed data. Once the data is retrieved, Struts' reliance on JavaBeans makes it easy to retain value objects and reduce the number of calls to the Model layer.

2.6 *The strengths and weaknesses of Struts*

Like any complex system, Struts is a package deal. It has both its strengths and its weaknesses. Some of these points will be subjective but hopefully still instructive.

2.6.1 *The weak points*

As much as we love Struts, it's important that we see the framework for what it is, warts and all. Several similar weak points were cured by the Struts 1.1 release. Table 2.6 lists Struts 1.0 weaknesses that were addressed by Struts 1.1. If you had looked at Struts before, and any of these were showstoppers, Struts may now better meet your needs. Table 2.7 examines some of the framework's current weak points.

In the next section, you may notice that we shamelessly turn many of these points around and describe them as assets instead. "Goofus" or "Gallant," the choice is yours.

Table 2.6   Struts 1.0 weaknesses addressed by Struts 1.1

Weak point	Remarks
Logging	Struts uses the container's default logging system and does not provide a ready mechanism for applications to provide their own logging package. (Struts 1.1 implements the Commons-Logging interface package.)
Loads a single configuration file per application	Larger projects need to use multiple configuration files that do not need to be shared by the entire team. (Struts 1.1 supports multiple configuration files.)
Loads a single resource file per locale	Larger projects need to use multiple resource files that do not need to be shared by the entire team. (Struts 1.1 supports multiple resource files.)
No service manager	ActionServlets must be subclassed to be extended with additional services, such as a custom logger or authentication system. (Struts 1.1 offers several new extension points and components.)
ActionForm red tape	Struts 1.0 expects developers to create custom JavaBeans for use with HTML input forms. (Struts 1.1 supports Maps and DynaBeans in place of custom JavaBeans.)

Table 2.7   Struts 1.1 weaknesses

Weak point	Remarks
No event model	Struts is tightly coupled with the request-response model used by HTTP. This can be restricting to developers used to finely grained events.
Debugging	There is no support for automatic debugging. Developers have to resort to creating manual "breakpoints" by writing to standard out or the container's log.
No default data model or concrete recommendations	Access to a persistent data model is left entirely as an exercise for the developer.
Single ActionServlet	Only one ActionServlet can be used in a single application. This restriction can lead to configuration conflicts.

Table 2.7   Struts 1.1 weaknesses *(continued)*

Weak point	Remarks
Requires understanding of Struts components	To work in Struts, a developer needs to understand several special classes and how they interact.
Vendor does not offer priority support	The Apache Software Foundation is an all-volunteer organization without a paid staff that can provide a guaranteed response.
Mailing list is a embarrassment of riches	Struts has already outgrown its mailing list. It can be difficult to find the best advice among the many daily posts.
Formal releases are not rapid	The Struts formal releases have been relatively slow compared to some other projects. Developers must often use the "nightly build" to use the latest improvements. There is also no set schedule for releases.
i18n limitations	The Struts message resources are quite good at internationalizing labels and error messages but are not appropriate for managing larger blocks of text.
JSP mindset	While its use of a Model-View-Controller architecture can make its resources available to any presentation system, there is a longstanding Struts predisposition to JSP.
JSP exception localization	Many system-level messages, like the JSP exceptions, are not localized and always display in English.
Tag properties are verbose	The Struts tag extensions can require several parameters and can be clumsy to program.
The `perform` and `execute` signatures	The key to the Struts architecture is delegating a request to an Action class or dispatcher. The Action class is the only dispatcher supported by Struts and is invoked only through its `perform` method. This locks an application into working with the data passed by the `perform` signature. While there are ways to work around this restriction, the `perform` signature is still an architectural bottleneck. One common request is for the ActionServlet to populate more than one ActionForm. But since `perform` accepts a single ActionForm parameter, permitting this is not feasible without a significant architectural change. Struts 1.1 adds an alternate `execute` signature, which helps with the other major stumbling block with `perform`: the exceptions it returns. However, the other consequences remain.

Table 2.7   Struts 1.1 weaknesses *(continued)*

Weak point	Remarks
Fuzzy nomenclature	The Struts framework "grew in the telling." The names given to some of the application options and classes can be confusing. For example, the "validate" option in web.xml is not related to the Action `validate` method but to how the configuration file is parsed. Likewise, the mysterious "null" option refers to whether an error message is returned when a message key is not found.
	There is also a tendency toward compound names in the class hierarchy. Every class in the action package is prefixed "Action," which is redundant and confusing. Meanwhile, in the Struts configuration, the element name for ActionMapping definition is "Action" rather than "ActionMapping." If developers refer to "an action," it's hard to tell if they mean the Action class or the ActionMapping that configures the class.
	In the Struts config, a "name" field identifies ActionForwards and Action-Forms. A "path" field identifies ActionMappings. The "name" property in an action-mapping element refers to which ActionForm to use. The URI field for an ActionForward is also named "path" but may also include a query component along with the path. The "path" to an ActionMapping does not include the servlet pattern, like *.do, but the ActionForward path does include the *.do extension. The Application Resources are really the Message Resources. And so forth. While not showstoppers, these little inconsistencies do confuse new developers and make the framework harder to learn.

2.6.2 *Struts' strong points*

As mentioned, many of Struts' strong points outlined in table 2.8 are the flip side of the weaknesses found in tables 2.6 and 2.7. One developer's treasure...

Table 2.8   Struts' strengths

Strength	Remarks
HTTP-centric	Struts is designed around the standard HTTP request-response model, familiar to many web developers.
Standard logging	Struts can use the container's default logging system and does not require another package to be configured or understood.
Optional debug logging	Struts optionally logs a number of status messages during processing that can be helpful in debugging.
Model neutral	Struts is not predisposed to any particular persistence layer.
Collects implementation detail in a centralized configuration	The Struts configuration encapsulates the implementation detail for an application, or application module [Struts 1.1], so it can be reviewed and managed as a whole.

Table 2.8 Struts' strengths *(continued)*

Strength	Remarks
Permits a different message resources file for each locale	Different translators can work on their own copy of the message resource file. Adding support for a new locale is simply a matter of adding another message resource file.
Lightweight	Struts has relatively few core classes for developers to learn.
Open source	Full source code is provided under the liberal Apache Software License, leaving all your options open.
Strong developer community	There is a strong development community behind Struts. The mailing is very active. Many developer extensions are available.
Strong vendor community	Struts is incorporated by several other products, including Jcorporate's Expresso and IBM's WebSphere. Struts-specific tools are also available from several vendors.
Strong product support	Struts has its own professionally managed JGuru forum. The Struts mailing list is available through at least two other support portals. Struts has been covered in dozens of articles and several books, and has been addressed at professional seminars by several organizations.
Strong development team	Over 30 developers contributed to Struts 1.1. The Struts team is currently composed of nine active Committers, who share full responsibility for the source code.
Stable releases	The Struts formal releases follow a long testing period with no set deadline, so teams can be assured of a high-quality product.
i18n support	Support for localization is built into Struts from the ground up.
High compliance/mainstream mindset	Struts is dedicated to providing a product that is 100 percent compliant with public standards and that is in line with the development mainstream.
Full-service tag extensions	Struts includes a set of general-purpose tag extensions in addition to those that use framework-specific resources. Together, they can meet all of your JSP needs, without you having to resort to scriptlets.
Well-documented source code	The Struts JavaDocs are so detailed that you rarely, if ever, need to refer to the source. This is in addition to a high-level user guide to introduce developers to the framework.
Strongly founded in design patterns	The Struts framework implements several classic patterns in its architecture that are familiar to most developers.
Extensible	All default settings can be configured. The core Struts classes may be overridden and subclasses loaded in their place. The developer can customize key classes such as ActionForm and Action.

2.7 Summary

Today's developers need to build full-featured applications that can be maintained over time. Web application frameworks such as Struts solve common problems, so developers can focus on their application's unique functionality. Frameworks are especially important when building web applications since the way HTTP and HTML work makes creating dynamic applications difficult.

Struts makes the most of the standard Java servlet API and has even become an informal compliance test for servlet containers. Struts also builds on the common design patterns, especially the MVC architectural paradigm. The framework encourages a "layered" design for applications. This design helps make applications both robust and scalable.

A key part of the Struts architecture is the way it extends the flow of the base HTTP request-response cycle. The Struts controller manages the paths used by your application, helps to safely collect input from users, and can localize application messages—especially error messages.

Struts is a performant solution. It will not hold your application back and usually frees resources that can be better used elsewhere.

Of course, Struts has its flaws. Many of the classnames were hastily chosen during development and can be confusing; other areas could also be improved. Despite any drawback, Struts is easily the most popular web application framework available today.

In the next chapter, we put Struts back to work and build yet another web application with it.

Building a
simple application

3

This chapter covers
- Creating a simple application
- Extending an application
- Changing an application
- Using JavaServer Pages in an application

*A human being should be able to change a diaper, plan an invasion,
butcher a hog, conn a ship, design a building, write a sonnet, balance accounts, build a wall, set a bone, comfort the dying, take
orders, give orders, cooperate, act alone, solve equations, analyze a
new problem, pitch manure, program a computer, cook a tasty meal,
fight efficiently, die gallantly. Specialization is for insects.*

—Excerpt from the notebooks of Lazarus Long,
from Robert Heinlein's *Time Enough for Love*

3.1 *Strut by Strut*

Today, teams write many web applications. Using a layered architecture [POSA]
for your application, as described in chapters 1 and 2, can make it easier for team
members to specialize and work on different parts of an application. But it is still
useful for everyone to understand the entire process from beginning to end.
Before getting into the details of how Struts widgets are ratcheted, let's put
together a simple but useful program from square one. In this chapter, we say
hello to Struts by touring, dissecting, and then constructing an application for logging users in and out.

While not quite as trivial as the exercise in chapter 1, we will still keep it simple
for now. A practical application is presented in part 4.

In this chapter, we walk through a classic logon application from a user's perspective. The exercise in chapter 1 compared the passwords entered into a regis-
tration` form. Depending on whether the entries matched, control branched to
one page or another. This application lets you use the accounts created by the
chapter 1 exercise to actually log in. The control flow and page content change
depending on your status.

After introducing the application, we break it down and zoom in on each component. If you have Struts installed on your development machine, you are welcome to follow along if you like. But if you are leaning back in your armchair,
sipping cappuccino, that works too.

Then, with the groundwork laid, we step through constructing the application.
Each piece is presented as you might write it yourself, in the order you might write
it (less much of the tedious *re*writing). If you are working at your terminal, you
could enter the source as we go. If not, every detail is presented so you can follow
along from the book alone.

3.1.1 *Why a logon application?*

Our sample program allows a user to log in to the application. Once the user has logged in, the pages change to reflect that the user is now authorized. Typically this is the first step to a larger application that enables authorized users to do something interesting. But for our purposes, just logging in a user is enough to show you how a Struts application actually works.

As shown in table 3.1, we chose doing just a logon application since the process is well understood, simple, self-contained, and needed by most applications.

Table 3.1 Why we chose a logon application

Reason	Explanation
Well understood	Most of us have logged in to our share of applications, so the process is well understood.
Simple and self-contained	A sample application that accepts a user logon can be simple to write and can also be self-contained. It does not require a complicated model.
Needed by many applications	Most of us will eventually need to write an application that uses some type of logon workflow, so this is code we can use.

3.2 *Touring a logon application*

To begin our tour, we first discuss the scope of the logon application and how you can follow along. We then look at the screens used by the application and note how they change after you've logged in. After we conclude our nickel tour, we go back and take a peek under the hood.

3.2.1 *Start here*

The purpose of our logon application is to give you a look at the nuts and bolts of a Struts application. To help us stay on track, this application contains only the components needed to demonstrate the framework. It contains no real business logic, unit tests, or fancy dialog boxes. Such things are important elements of a shipping application, but we need to walk before we can run.

The logon application is also intentionally stark. It contains no HTML chrome designed to please the eye—just the raw functionality we need to accept a logon. Of course, *your* Struts applications can be as pretty as *you* please.

If you are interested in running the application on your own machine as we go, look for the logon application on the book site's download page [Husted]. This is packaged as a WAR ready to autodeploy. (See chapter 1 if you don't know how to autodeploy a web application.)

Having the application open is not required but can be interesting at some points. Everything you need to follow along is printed in the chapter.

First, let's tour the screens from the user's viewpoint. Then, we can go back and walk through the actual code.

3.2.2 Screens we'll see

As shown in table 3.2, our logon application has two screens: welcome and logon.

Table 3.2   Logon application screens

Screen	Purpose
Welcome	Greets visitor and offers links into the application
Logon	Allows input of username and password

If you are following along and have the application deployed on your local machine, you can reach the welcome page with your browser by opening:

```
http://localhost:8080/logon/
```

3.2.3 The welcome screen

The first time you visit the welcome screen, there will be only one link, which reads, "Sign in" (see figure 3.1). If you click this link, the logon screen will appear.

Figure 3.1
The welcome screen of our logon application

3.2.4 The logon screen

The logon screen submits the username and password, as you can see in figure 3.2. To see the logon form in action, try clicking Submit without entering anything. If you do, the logon screen returns but with a message, like the one shown in figure 3.3.

If you enter a username but forget the password and click Submit, the message changes to the one shown in figure 3.4.

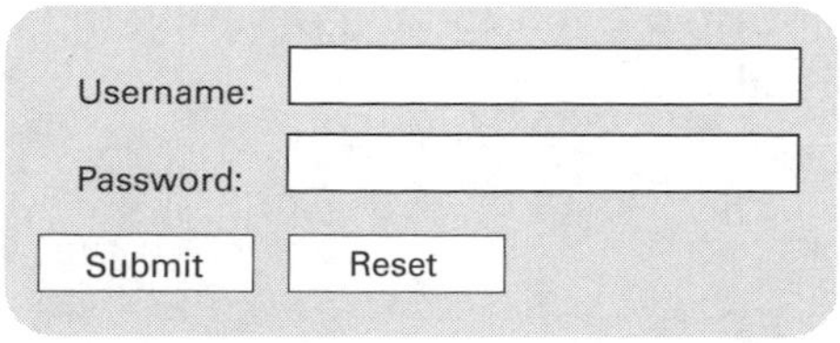

Username: [   ]

Password: [   ]

[Submit] [Reset]

Figure 3.2
The logon screen

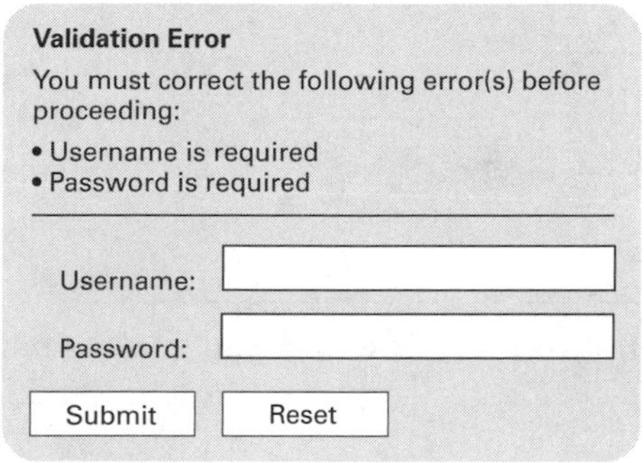

Validation Error

You must correct the following error(s) before proceeding:

• Username is required
• Password is required

Username: [   ]

Password: [   ]

[Submit] [Reset]

Figure 3.3
The logon screen tells you the
password and username are missing.

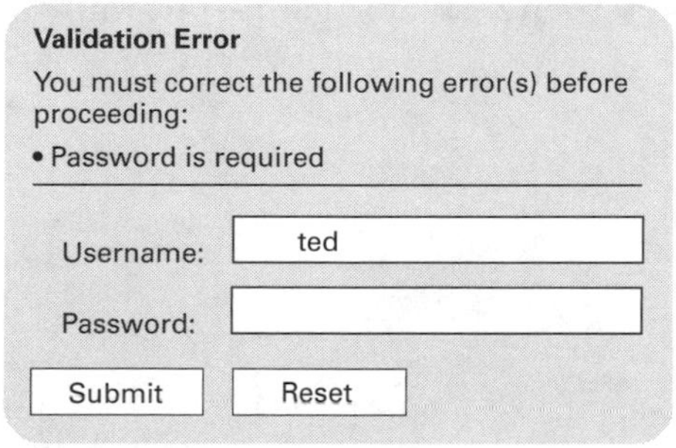

Validation Error

You must correct the following error(s) before proceeding:

• Password is required

Username: [ted   ]

Password: [   ]

[Submit] [Reset]

Figure 3.4
The logon screen reminds you that
you must enter the password.

Here are the important things to note about this workflow, from a user's viewpoint:

- It tells the user everything that is missing all at once.

- When the user submits one thing, it reminds the user only about the other thing.

- It redisplays on the screen what the user has entered so far, without asking the user to press the Back key.

- If the user manages to enter both a username and a password, the form is accepted and the next screen is displayed.

The logon application validates the logons against a Properties file, like the one used with the registration application from chapter 1. If you download the logon application from the book's web site [Husted], you can log on using the names of any of the book's authors, as shown in table 3.3.

Table 3.3   Default logons

Username (or userid)	Password
Ted	Husted
Cedric	Dumoulin
George	Franciscus
David	Winterfeldt
Craig	McClanahan

NOTE   The passwords are case sensitive, so be sure to use an initial capital letter.

3.2.5   *The welcome screen, again*

After a successful login, the welcome screen displays again—but with two differences, as you can see in figure 3.5.

Welcome Ted!
- Sign in
- Sign out

Powered by
Struts

**Figure 3.5
The welcome screen after
the user has logged on**

First, the screen has been tailored for the user. Instead of just saying "Welcome World!" it now greets the user by name.

In addition, you'll notice that another link has been added. Besides signing in (again), we can now sign out.

3.2.6   *The welcome screen, good-bye*

To close the loop, if we click the sign-out link, we are returned to the original welcome screen—the same screen shown in figure 3.1.

3.2.7 Feature roundup

Although simple, our application demonstrates several important techniques:

- Writing links
- Writing forms
- Validating input
- Displaying error messages
- Repopulating forms
- Displaying alternative content

While not as obvious, it also demonstrates:

- Referencing images from dynamic pages
- Rewriting hyperlinks

In the next section, we look at the source code for the application to show how the core features are implemented.

3.3 Dissecting the logon application

Now that we've said hello to our Struts logon application, let's wander back and take a closer look. We now present the code for each page, along with its related components, and explore what each piece does. After we introduce all the widgets, we show how you can assemble the application from scratch.

3.3.1 The browser source for the welcome screen

As you will recall, our application opens with the welcome screen. Let's have a peek at the browser source for the welcome page—just to see what's there (see listing 3.1). The part in bold is what prints on the screen.

Listing 3.1 The browser source for our welcome page

```
<HTML>
<HEAD>
<TITLE>Welcome World!!</TITLE>
<base href="http://localhost:8080/logon/pages/Welcome.jsp">
</HEAD>
<BODY>
<H3>Welcome World!</H3>
<UL>
<LI><a href="/logon/logon.do">Sign in</a></LI>
</UL>
```

```
<IMG src='struts-power.gif' alt='Powered by Struts'>
</BODY>
</HTML>
```

If you are new to web applications, an important thing to note is that there is nothing here but standard HTML. In fact, there can *never* be anything in a web page but the usual markup that browsers understand. All web applications are constrained to the limitations of HTML and cannot do anything that you can't do with HTML. Struts makes it easier to get Velocity templates, JSP, and other systems to write the HTML we want, but everything has to done with markup the browsers understand.

The jsessionid key

There may be one thing in the browser source that you might not recognize as standard HTML. The first time you visit this page, the sign-in link may actually look like this:

```
<LI><a href="/logon.do;jsessionid=aa6XkGuY8qc">Sign in</a></LI>
```

Most web applications need to keep track of the people using the application. HTTP has some rudimentary support for maintaining a user logon, but the approach is limited and not secure. The Java servlet framework does provide support for a robust user session but needs a mechanism to maintain the session across HTTP.

The *jsessionid* is a key maintained by the container to track the user session via HTTP. Including the session key in a hyperlink is called *URL rewriting*. The Servlet Specification [Sun, JST] encourages the use of cookies to maintain the session. When that is not possible, URL rewriting is used instead. The first time a browser makes a request to the container, the container does not know whether the browser will accept a cookie. The container can offer the browser a cookie, but can't tell if it was accepted until the next time a request is made. (HTTP has no "handshaking.") In the meantime, the response for the current request must be written. So, the first page written for a browser will *always* need to use URL rewriting. If on subsequent requests the container finds that its cookie was accepted, it can skip rewriting the URLs.

3.3.2 The JSP source for the welcome screen

Now let's peek at the JSP source that generated the page shown in figure 3.1. The JSP tags appear in bold in listing 3.2.

Listing 3.2 The JSP source for our welcome page (/pages/Welcome.jsp)

```
<%@ taglib uri="/tags/struts-bean" prefix="bean" %>
<%@ taglib uri="/tags/struts-html" prefix="html" %>
<%@ taglib uri="/tags/struts-logic" prefix="logic" %>
<HTML>
<HEAD>
<TITLE>Welcome World!!</TITLE>
<html:base/>
</HEAD>
<BODY>
<logic:present scope="session" name="user">
<H3>Welcome <bean:write name="user" property="username"/>!</H3>
</logic:present>
<logic:notPresent scope="session" name="user">
<H3>Welcome World!</H3>
</logic:notPresent>
<html:errors/>
<UL>
<LI><html:link forward="logon">Sign in</html:link></LI>
<logic:present scope="session" name="user">
<LI><html:link forward="logoff">Sign out</html:link></LI>
</logic:present>
</UL>
<IMG src='struts-power.gif' alt='Powered by Struts'>
</BODY>
</HTML>
```

Now let's take a look at what the lines in bold do:

```
<%@ taglib uri="/tags/struts-html" prefix="html" %>
<%@ taglib uri="/tags/struts-logic" prefix="logic" %>
```

These are the JSP equivalents to import statements and make the tag extensions available to the rest of the page. The code

```
<html:base/>
```

generates a standard HTML base tag, so that references to such things as images can be relative to the location of the original JSP page. You may have noticed that the logon application sometimes refers to .do pages. These aren't actual files on the server but references to Java classes, or Actions, written by the application developer. These Actions then forward to a JSP that creates the response.

JSPs often include references to HTML resources such as images and style sheets. The most convenient way to refer to these resources is through paths that are relative to the JSP template. But when the Action forwards control, it does so without alerting the browser. If the browser is given any relative references, it will resolve them according to the Action URI, not the location of the JSP template.

Depending on when you access the welcome page, its "location" is shown by the browser:

- http://localhost:8080/*logon/*
- http://localhost:8080/*logon/LogonSubmit.do*
- http://localhost:8080/*logon/Logoff.do*

This is a common problem for dynamic applications. The HTML specification [W3C, HTML] provides the base tag as a solution. Struts provides a companion html-base tag that inserts the location of the JSP. If you look at the HTML source for the logon page for each of its apparent locations, you will see that in every case the base tag renders as:

```
<base href="http://localhost:8080/logon/pages/Welcome.jsp">
```

This lets the browser find the "Powered by Struts" image, which is also stored in the pages folder.

Now let's take a look at this code:

```
<logic:present name="user">
<H3>Welcome <bean:write name="user" property="username"/>!</H3>
</logic:present>
```

You'll remember that the welcome page customizes itself depending on whether the user is logged in. This segment looks to see if we have stored a "user" bean in the client's session. If such a bean is present, then the user is welcomed by name.

The following code shows why maintaining the user's session is so important (see section 3.3.1). Happily, the Struts tags and servlet container cooperate to maintain the session automatically (regardless of whether the browser is set to use cookies). To the developer, it feels as if the session has been built into HTTP—which is what frameworks are all about. Frameworks extend the underlying environment so developers can focus on higher-level tasks:

```
<logic:notPresent scope="session" name="user">
<H3>Welcome!</H3>
</logic:notPresent>
```

Conversely, if the user bean is present, then we use a customized welcome. All of the Struts logic tags use "this" and "notThis" forms. Else tags are not provided. While this means that some tests need to be repeated, it simplifies the overall syntax and implementation of tags. Of course, other tag extensions can also be used;

you are not constrained to what is offered in the Struts distribution. Several contributor tag extensions are listed on the Struts resource page [ASF, Struts], even one with an if/then/else syntax, if you prefer to use that instead.

As mentioned in section 3.3.1, Struts automatically rewrites hyperlinks to maintain the user session. It also lets you give links a logical name and then store the actual links in a configuration file. This is like referring to a database record with a key. The name and address in the record can change as needed. Other tables will find the updated version using the key. In this case:

```
<LI><html:link forward="logon">Sign in</html:link></LI>
```

we are using `logon` as the key for a record that stores the hyperlink to use for logging on. If we need to change that link later, we can change it once in the configuration file and restart the application. The pages will start using the new link when they are next rendered.

This code combines the `<logic:present>` and the `<html:link>` tags to display the logoff link only when the user is already logged in:

```
<logic:present name="user">
<LI><html:link forward="logoff">Sign out</html:link></LI>
</logic:present>
```

3.3.3 *The configuration source for the welcome screen*

Struts uses a configuration file to define several things about your application, including the logical names for hyperlinks. This is an XML document that Struts reads at startup and uses to create a database of objects. Various Struts components refer to this database to provide the framework's services. The default name of the configuration file is struts-config.xml.

Since the configuration file is used by several different components, presenting the configuration all at once would be getting ahead of ourselves. For now, we'll provide the relevant portions as we go. Later, when we build the application from scratch, we'll present the configuration file in its entirety.

In the initial welcome screen, we refer to a `logon` forward. This is defined in the Struts configuration as such:

```
<forward
    name="logon"
    path="/Logon.do"/>
```

Here, `logon` is a key that is used to look up the actual path for the hyperlink. A Struts action is referenced here, but the path could just as easily refer to a JSP page, Velocity template, HTML page, or any resource with a URI [W3C, URI].

DEFINITION A *uniform resource identifier (URI)* is a short string that identifies a resource on the Internet or other computer network. A resource could be a document, image, downloadable file, or electronic mailbox, among other things. A URI may correspond to a path on a server's file system but is often an alias. Many URIs in a Struts application are aliases for Java classes or Actions.

Since the path is defined in the configuration file, you can change your mind at any time without touching the JSP source. If you update and reload the configuration, the change will be reflected when pages next render.

3.3.4 *The browser source for the logon screen*

If we follow the sign-in link on the welcome page, it brings us to the logon screen, shown earlier in figure 3.2. Listing 3.3 shows the browser source code for this screen. Again, the part in bold is what prints on the screen.

> **Listing 3.3   The browser source for our logon screen**

```
<HTML>
<HEAD>
<TITLE>Sign in, Please!</TITLE>
</HEAD>
<BODY>
<form name="logonForm" method="POST" action="/logon/LogonSubmit.do">
<TABLE border="0" width="100%">
<TR>
<TH align="right">Username:</TH>
<TD align="left"><input type="text" name="username" value=""></TD>
</TR>
<TR>
<TH align="right">Password:</TH>
<TD align="left"><input type="password" name="password" value=""></TD>
</TR>
<TR>
<TD align="right"><input type="submit" name="submit" value="Submit"></TD>
<TD align="left"><input type="reset" name="reset" value="Reset"></TD>
</TR>
</TABLE>
</form>
<script language="JavaScript" type="text/javascript">
  <!--
    document.forms["logonForm"].elements["username"].focus()
  // -->
</script>
</BODY>
</HTML>
```

Listing 3.4 shows the corresponding JSP source.

Listing 3.4 The JSP source for our logon screen (/pages/logon.jsp)

```
<%@ taglib uri="/tags/struts-html" prefix="html" %>
<HTML>
<HEAD>
<TITLE>Sign in, Please!</TITLE>
</HEAD>
<BODY>
<html:errors/>
<html:form action="/LogonSubmit" focus="username">
<TABLE border="0" width="100%">
<TR>
<TH align="right">Username:</TH>
<TD align="left"><html:text property="username"/></TD>
</TR>
<TR>
<TH align="right">Password:</TH>
<TD align="left"><html:password property="password"/></TD>
</TR>
<TR>
<TD align="right"><html:submit/></TD>
<TD align="left"><html:reset/></TD>
</TR>
</TABLE>
</html:form>
</BODY>
</HTML>
```

Let's step through each block here as we did with the welcome page. First, as before, this code makes the Struts html tag extension available to the rest of the page:

```
<%@ taglib uri="/tags/struts-html" prefix="html" %>
```

Like the Struts actions, the taglib URI is a logical reference. The location of the tag library descriptor (TLD) is given in web.xml.

You'll remember that if we tried to submit the form without entering a logon, an error message displayed. The following tag renders the error messages. When there are no messages, the tag outputs nothing and disappears from the output page:

```
<html:errors/>
```

The <html:form> tag produces an HTML form for data entry. It also generates a simple JavaScript to move the focus to the first field on the form. The action property is a reference to an ActionMapping in the Struts configuration. This tells the form which JavaBean helper to use to populate the HTML controls. The Java-Bean helpers are based on a Struts framework class, ActionForm:

```
<html:form action="/LogonSubmit" focus="username">
```

The `<html:text>` tag creates an HTML input control for a text field. It will also populate the field with the `username` property of the JavaBean helper for this form:

```
<TR><TH align="right">Username: </TH><TD align="left">
   <html:text property="username"/></TD>
```

So, if the form were being returned for validation, and the last username submitted was `Ted`, the tag would then output:

```
<input type="text" name="username" value="Ted">
```

Otherwise, the tag would use the initial default value for `username` as specified by the JavaBean helper class. Usually, this is `null`, but it could be any value.

Likewise, the `<html:password>` tag creates an HTML input control:

```
<TR><TH align="right">Password: </TH>
<TD align="left"><html:password property="password"/></TD>
```

The password control is like a text field but displays asterisks instead of the characters input. If the form is being returned for validation, by default the password tag will rewrite the prior value so that it doesn't need to be entered again. If you would prefer that the password be input each time, you can turn off redisplay.

If the initial logon attempt fails, this code keeps the password out of the browser's cache and require the password to be input again, even if it passed validation:

```
<html:password property="password" redisplay="false"/>
```

These tags create standard HTML Submit and Reset buttons:

```
<TD align="right"><html:submit/></TD>
<TD align="left"><html:reset/></TD>
```

When the form is submitted, two framework objects come into play: the Action-Form and the Action. Both of these objects must be created by the developer to include the details for their application. As shown in figure 3.6, the ActionServlet uses the Struts configuration to decide which ActionForm or Action subclass to use.

Let's look at the Struts configuration for the logon screen's ActionForm and Action. Then we can look at the source for these classes.

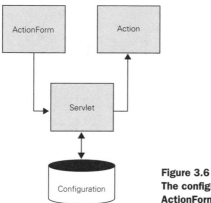

Figure 3.6
**The configuration determines which
ActionForm and Action to use.**

3.3.5 *The configuration source for the logon screen*

The logon screen itself refers to only one element in the Struts configuration file: the /LogonSubmit ActionMapping. This element in turn refers to two other objects, app.LogonForm and app.LogonAction. All three elements are shown in table 3.4. Let's explore each element in turn.

Table 3.4   The logon screen configuration elements

Element	Description
/LogonSubmit ActionMapping	Encapsulates several details needed when building and submitting an HTML form with the Struts framework
app.LogonForm	Describes properties used by the HTML form
app.LogonAction	Completes the processing of the submitted form

3.3.6 *The LogonSubmit source*

In the previous section, we mentioned that the <html:form> tag works closely with the Struts configuration to make HTML forms more useful:

```
<html:form action="/LogonSubmit" focus="username">
```

The action parameter tells the <html:form> tag which ActionMapping to use. In this case, the Struts configuration mapping would look like this:

```
<action
    path="/LogonSubmit"
    type="app.LogonAction"
    name="logonForm"
```

```
scope="request"
validate="true"
input="/pages/Logon.jsp"/>
```

Table 3.5 provides an index to what the settings on this mapping mean.

Table 3.5   ActionMapping settings

Property	Purpose
path	A unique identifier for this mapping. It is included in the web address, as in *http://local-host:8080/logon/*LogonSubmit.*do*.
type	The Action object to call when the path is requested.
name	The JavaBean helper (ActionForm) to use with an HTML form.
scope	A property that specifies whether to store the helper in the request or the session.
validate	A property that specifies whether to call the standard validate method on the form bean helper (specified by **name**) before calling the Action object (specified by type).
input	A property that specifies where to send control if the validate method returns false.

As we mentioned in chapter 2, many of the object and property names used by the Struts framework are vague. For example, the name property is *not* the name of the mapping; it's the name of the JavaBean helper, or ActionForm bean, to be used with this mapping.

The same form beans are also specified in the configuration:

```
<form-bean
    name="logonForm"
    type="app.LogonForm"/>
```

This element relates the logical name logonForm with a specific Java class, app.Logonform. This will be a subclass of a Struts ActionForm. The ActionForm class provides standard methods for the framework to use, including the validate method.

Let's take a look at the source for the LogonForm and then come back to the LogonAction.

3.3.7   *The LogonForm source*

While HTML forms give users a place to enter data, they do not give applications a place to put it. When the user clicks Submit, the browser collects the data in the form and sends it up to the server as a list of *name-values* pairs (or couplets). So, if a user enters a username and a password into the logon page and clicks Submit, this is what our application sees:

```
username=Ted
password=LetMeIn
```

The browser submits everything as a string of characters. You can put in JavaScript validations to force people to enter only numerals into a given field or to use a prescribed format for dates, but that's just smoke and mirrors. Everything is still going to be transferred to your application as a string—*not* as a binary object ready to pass to a Java method.

It's important to remember that this is the way the browsers and HTML work. Web applications cannot control this. Frameworks such as Struts exist to make the best of what we have to work with. The Struts solution to HTTP data-entry snarls is the ActionForm.

In an environment like Swing, data-entry controls have a built-in text buffer that can validate characters as they are entered. When the user leaves the control, the buffer can be converted to a binary type, ready for delivery to the business layer.

Unfortunately, the HTTP/HTML platform doesn't provide a component that can buffer, validate, and convert input. So, the Struts framework offers the Action-Form (`org.apache.struts.action.ActionForm`) to bridge the gap between web browser and business object. ActionForms provide the missing buffer/validate/convert mechanism we need to ensure that users enter what they are supposed to enter.

When an HTML form is submitted, the name-value couplets are caught by the Struts controller and applied to an ActionForm. The ActionForm is a JavaBean with properties that correspond to the controls on an HTML form. Struts compares the names of the ActionForm properties with the names of the incoming couplets. When they match, the controller sets the property to the value of the corresponding couplet. Extra properties are ignored. Missing properties retain their default value (usually null or false).

Here are the public properties from our LogonForm:

```
private String password = null;
public String getPassword() {
    return (this.password);
}
public void setPassword(String password) {
    this.password = password;
}

private String username = null;
public String getUsername() {
    return (this.username);
}
```

```
public void setUsername(String username) {
    this.username = username;
}
```

The properties of most Struts ActionForms look just like this. Thrifty developers can create them with a macro that simply prompts them for the property name. Others may use code skeletons and the search-and-replace feature of their code editors. Struts code generators are also available that create ActionForms by parsing HTML or JSPs.

NOTE   In Struts 1.1, creating ActionForms is even simpler if you use a Dyna-ActionForm or Map-backed ActionForm. See chapter 5 for details.

The base ActionForm also includes two standard methods—reset and validate. The reset method is helpful when you are using ActionForms as part of a wizard workflow. This method doesn't need to be implemented if the mapping is set to request scope.

When the mapping is set to validate=true, the validate method is called after the form is populated from the HTTP request. The validate method is most often used as a prima facie validation. It just checks that the data "looks" correct and that all required fields have been submitted. Again, this is something that a Swing control would do internally before passing the data along to the application. You can do these checks by hand, or use something like the *ValidatorForm* (see chapter 12), which can be programmed from a configuration file.

Here's the validate method from our LogonForm. It checks that both fields have something entered into them. If your application had any rules regarding the length of a username or password, you could enforce those rules here as well.

```
public ActionErrors validate(ActionMapping mapping,
    HttpServletRequest request) {

    ActionErrors errors = new ActionErrors();

    if ((username == null) || (username.length() < 1))
        errors.add ("username",
                new ActionError("error.username.required"));

    if ((password == null) || (password.length() < 1))
        errors.add("password",
                new ActionError("error.password.required"));

    return errors;

}
```

The ActionErrors object returned by `validate` is another framework class. If `validate` returns an ActionErrors collection which is neither null nor empty, then the controller will save the ActionErrors object in the request context under a known key. The `<html:errors>` tag knows the key and will render the error messages when they exist, or do nothing when they do not.

The tokens `error.username.required` and `error.password.required` are also keys. They are used to look up the actual messages from the Struts message resources file. Each locale can have its own resource file, which makes the messages easy to localize.

The Struts message resources file uses the common name-value format. The entries for our messages look like this:

```
error.username.required=<li>Username is required</li>
error.password.required=<li>Password is required</li>
```

NOTE   In Struts 1.1 there are ways to keep the markup out of the messages. A new `errors.prefix/error.suffix` feature can be used to specify that `<li>` and `</li>` should wrap each message. A new set of message tags is also available that can be used in place of the original `<html:errors>` tag. The message tags make it easy to keep the markup in the presentation page (where it belongs). See chapter 10 for more about the Struts JSP tags.

Even when localization is not being used, the Struts application resource file collects all the messages into a single place where they can be reviewed and revised, without touching the Java source code.

3.3.8 *The LogonAction source*

After collecting the data entry into an ActionForm and performing any initial validations, the controller passes the form along to the Action class given by the mapping.

The Struts architecture expects that you will use your own Java classes to do most of the request processing. A JSP page may *render* the result, but the Action *obtains* the result. As you saw in chapter 2, this is known as an MVC or Model 2 approach, where the Action serves as a request dispatcher.

When a request for an Action is sent to the Struts servlet, it invokes (or dispatches) the Action by calling its `perform` (or `execute`) method.

NOTE	There is an alternative entry method in Struts 1.1, named execute. This method provides for better exception handling but is otherwise the same as the Struts 1.0 perform method. We will refer to the perform method in this chapter so the code will work with both versions. Other applications in the book are based on Struts 1.1 and make good use of the new features.

Listing 3.5 contains the source in its entirety.

**Listing 3.5   The Java source for the LogonAction class
(/WEB-INF/src/java/app/LogonAction.java)**

```
package app;

import java.io.IOException;
import javax.servlet.ServletException;
import javax.servlet.http.HttpServletRequest;
import javax.servlet.http.HttpSession;
import javax.servlet.http.HttpServletResponse;
import org.apache.struts.action.Action;
import org.apache.struts.action.ActionError;
import org.apache.struts.action.ActionErrors;
import org.apache.struts.action.ActionForm;
import org.apache.struts.action.ActionForward;
import org.apache.struts.action.ActionMapping;
import org.apache.struts.action.ActionServlet;

public final class LogonAction extends Action {

// Validate credentials with business tier
public boolean isUserLogon (String username,
        String password) throws UserDirectoryException {

return (UserDirectory.getInstance().
isValidPassword(username,password));

} // end isUserLogon

public ActionForward perform(ActionMapping mapping,
        ActionForm form,
        HttpServletRequest request,
        HttpServletResponse response)
    throws IOException, ServletException {

// Obtain username and password from web tier
String username = ((LogonForm) form).getUsername();
String password = ((LogonForm) form).getPassword();

// Validate credentials
boolean validated = false;
try {
validated = isUserLogon(username,password);
```

```
    }
catch (UserDirectoryException ude) {
// couldn't connect to user directory
        ActionErrors errors = new ActionErrors();
        errors.add (ActionErrors.GLOBAL_ERROR,
        new ActionError("error.logon.connect"));
        saveErrors(request,errors);
        // return to input page
        return (new ActionForward (mapping.getInput()));
    }

if (!validated){
        // credentials don't match
        ActionErrors errors = new ActionErrors();
        errors.add(ActionErrors.GLOBAL_ERROR,
        new ActionError("error.logon.invalid"));
        saveErrors(request,errors);
        // return to input page
        return (new ActionForward(mapping.getInput()));
    }

// Save our logged-in user in the session,
// because we use it again later.
HttpSession session = request.getSession();
session.setAttribute(Constants.USER_KEY, form);

// Log this event, if appropriate
if (servlet.getDebug() >= Constants.DEBUG) {
    StringBuffer message =
        new StringBuffer("LogonAction: User '");
    message.append(username);
    message.append("' logged on in session ");
    message.append(session.getId());
    servlet.log(message.toString());
}

// Return success
return (mapping.findForward (Constants.SUCCESS));

} // end perform
} // end LogonAction
```

And now the blow by blow.

The Action is at the top of the Struts food chain and so imports several classes. We've specified each class used here, so that you can see where everything comes from:

```
package app;
import java.io.IOException;
import javax.servlet.ServletException;
import javax.servlet.http.HttpServletRequest;
```

```
import javax.servlet.http.HttpSession;
import javax.servlet.http.HttpServletResponse;
import org.apache.struts.action.Action;
import org.apache.struts.action.ActionError;
import org.apache.struts.action.ActionErrors;
import org.apache.struts.action.ActionForm;
import org.apache.struts.action.ActionForward;
import org.apache.struts.action.ActionMapping;
import org.apache.struts.action.ActionServlet;
```

If we were lazy, this block could also be expressed as:

```
package app;
import java.io.*;
import javax.servlet.*;
import javax.servlet.http.*;
import org.apache.struts.action.*;
```

But that would not be as instructive. Like most Apache products, the Struts source code follows best practices and doesn't cut corners. We follow suit in our own code. While we've omitted the JavaDoc here, both our code and the Struts code are fully documented.

Next, we use a helper method to call a business tier method. We could have put this same code into the Action's `perform` method, but it is always a good idea to strongly separate the generic business code from the Struts controller code. If you let even one line in, that soon turns into three, then five, and before long your Actions are a big ball of mud [Foote]. The best way to avoid "code creep" is to always encapsulate business tier code in a helper method before calling it from an Action:

```
// Validate credentials with business tier
public boolean isUserLogon (String username,
        String password) throws UserDirectoryException {

return (UserDirectory.getInstance().
isValidPassword(username,password));

} // end isUserLogon
```

As we've mentioned elsewhere, Struts 1.1 prefers the new `execute` method over the original `perform` method, but either one still works. We used `perform` in this application so the code will work with either version:

```
public ActionForward perform(ActionMapping mapping,
        ActionForm form,
        HttpServletRequest request,
        HttpServletResponse response)
    throws IOException, ServletException {
```

The purpose of an Action is to ferry input from the web tier to the business tier, where the rest of your application lives. Here, we extract the username and password from the ActionForm (JavaBean helper) and save them as plain `Strings`:

```
// Obtain username and password from web tier
String username = ((LogonForm) form).getUsername();
String password = ((LogonForm) form).getPassword();
```

We can then pass the `username` and `password` `Strings` to a business tier function to see if they validate. Here, we take care to encapsulate the call in a separate method and not bury the code in the Action's `perform` method. This call is to another method in this class, but it could just as easily be to any method in any Java class:

```
// Validate credentials
boolean validated = false;
try {
validated = isUserLogon(username,password);
}
catch (UserDirectoryException ude) {
// couldn't connect to user directory
        ActionErrors errors = new ActionErrors();
        errors.add (ActionErrors.GLOBAL_ERROR,
        new ActionError("error.logon.connect"));
        saveErrors(request,errors);
        // return to input page
        return (new ActionForward (mapping.getInput()));
}
```

The API for the `isUserLogon` method specifies that it return true if the credentials match, false if they don't, and throw an exception if it doesn't know (say, for instance, because it couldn't connect to the directory to find out). Should the exception occur, our Action catches it, converts the event into an ActionError, and forwards back to the `input` page.

If the business tier comes back and says the logon is no good, the Action posts the error message and routes control back to the input page. This is the same thing that happens when the `validate` method on the ActionForm fails (see section 3.3.7):

```
if (!validated) {
        // post the error
        ActionErrors errors = new ActionErrors();
        errors.add (ActionErrors.GLOBAL_ERROR,
            new ActionError("error.logon.invalid"));
        saveErrors(request,errors);
        // return to input page
        return (new ActionForward (mapping.getInput()));
}
```

Since the error does not pertain to a particular property, we log the error under the generic `ActionErrors.GLOBAL_ERROR` flag instead of a property name. To indicate that the logon itself is invalid, we also specify a different error message than `validate`. In the Struts application resources, this is shown as:

```
error.logon.invalid=<li>Username/password combination is invalid</li>
```

The presentation layer substitutes the `error.login.invalid` token for the proper message when it is displayed. If there is a separate message for a user's locale, then the user will receive the localized version of this message.

If the business tier says the logon is good, then we can tell the web tier to retain the user's credentials. The Java Servlet framework provides a user session for exactly this purpose. Here we store the user's `logonForm` in their session context. Each user has a context, maintained by the servlet container. Users who have a `logonForm` stored in their session context are logged in. Otherwise, the user is not logged in:

```
// Save our logged-in user in the session,
// because we use it again later.
HttpSession session = request.getSession();
session.setAttribute(Constants.USER_KEY, form);
```

This strategy is known as application-based security. Many Java web applications use this approach, since it is portable and easy to implement. Any approach to authentication can be used in your own applications.

The Struts framework relies on the container's default logging system. Here, we log an event only if the debug level for the servlet was set high enough in the web deployment descriptor (web.xml):

```
// Log this event, if appropriate
if (servlet.getDebug() >= Constants.DEBUG) {
    StringBuffer message =
        new StringBuffer("LogonAction: User '");
    message.append(username);
    message.append("' logged on in session ");
    message.append(session.getId());
    servlet.log(message.toString());
}
```

We set this with an `init-param`, like this:

```
<init-param>
    <param-name>debug</param-name>
    <param-value>2</param-value>
</init-param>
```

In a production application, you can set debug to 0, and entries like this one won't appear. To plug in another logging package, developers subclass the Struts ActionServlet class and override the log method.

NOTE   In Struts 1.1, using alternate logging packages is made even easier through support of the Jakarta Commons Logging Component [ASF Commons].

When all is said and done, the perform method returns an ActionForward to the controller (ActionServlet). Here, we send control to the success forward:

```
// return success
return mapping.findForward("success");
}
```

This is defined in the Struts configuration as:

```
<forward
    name="success"
    path="/pages/Welcome.jsp"/>
```

Now that we are logged in, the presentation of this page will vary slightly. A logoff link will be available.

3.3.9 *The LogoffAction source*

Look back to figure 3.5 to see how the welcome page changes once the user is logged in. In Welcome.jsp, the <logic:present> tag sees the user bean placed into the session context by the LogonAction

```
<logic:present name="user">
```

and exposes an <html:link> tag that references the logoff forward:

```
<html:link forward="logoff">Sign out</html:link>
```

In the Struts configuration, the logoff forward is defined as:

```
<forward
        name="logoff"
        path="/logoff.do"/>
```

The path here refers to a .do file. There should be a corresponding /logoff ActionMapping elsewhere in the Struts configuration:

```
<action
        path="/logoff"
        type="app.LogoffAction"/>
```

As you can see, /logoff is an extremely simple mapping; it simply passes control to the LogoffAction class, without any special parameters or settings. The job of the LogoffAction class is also very simple. It just removes the user's `logonForm` object from the session context. If there is no `logonForm` in the session context, then the user is considered to be logged out. Let's have a look at the LogoffAction source, which is the last class remaining in our walkthrough (see listing 3.6).

Listing 3.6 The Java source for LogoffAction class (/WEB-INF/src/java/app/LogoffAction.java)

```java
public ActionForward perform(ActionMapping mapping,
        ActionForm form,
        HttpServletRequest request,
        HttpServletResponse response)
            throws IOException, ServletException {

    // Extract attributes we will need
    HttpSession session = request.getSession();
    LogonForm user = (LogonForm)
      session.getAttribute(Constants.USER_KEY);

    // Log this user off
    if (user != null) {

        if (servlet.getDebug() >= Constants.DEBUG) {
            StringBuffer message =
                new StringBuffer("LogoffAction: User '");
            message.append(user.getUsername());
            message.append("' logged off in session ");
            message.append(session.getId());
            servlet.log(message.toString());
        }
    }

    else {

        if (servlet.getDebug() >= Constants.DEBUG) {
            StringBuffer message =
                new StringBuffer("LogoffAction: User '");
            message.append(session.getId());
            servlet.log(message.toString());
        }
    }

    // Remove user login
    session.removeAttribute(Constants.USER_KEY);

    // Return success
    return (mapping.findForward(Constants.SUCCESS));

    }
} // end LogoffAction
```

First, we obtain the user's logon object. The convention of this application is to store the user's logon object in the session context, under the key given by Constants.USER_KEY, so that's where we look:

```
// Extract attributes we will need
HttpSession session = request.getSession();
LogonForm user = (LogonForm) session.getAttribute(Constants.USER_KEY);

// Log this user off
if (user != null) {

  if (servlet.getDebug() >= Constants.DEBUG) {
      StringBuffer message =
          new StringBuffer("LogoffAction: User '");
      message.append(user.getUsername());
      message.append("' logged off in session ");
      message.append(session.getId());
      servlet.log(message.toString());
  }
}
```

As before, we log some detail if the debug level has been set high enough in the web deployment descriptor (web.xml).

This is the core operation in the class. We remove any object stored under the USER_KEY, and voila, the user is logged out:

```
// Remove user login
    session.removeAttribute(Constants.USER_KEY);
```

If we wanted to remove everything from the session that might be stored for the user, we could simply invalidate the session instead:

```
session.invalidate();
```

But this also destroys objects such as the user's locale, which is used to display localized messages.

As with logon, when the operation completes, we return to the welcome page:

```
// Return success
return (mapping.findForward(Constants.SUCCESS));
```

In the next section, we will step back and show how this application would be built from scratch. So far, we've been stepping through the guts of the pages and classes. Now we will take a wider look at the application by moving the focus to the Struts configuration file and the source code tree.

3.4 *Constructing an application*

We've taken the application for a drive, kicked the tires, and taken a good look under the hood. We know what it is supposed to do and how it does it, but where would you start building your own? In this section, we go back to square one and show how you can build an application like this from beginning to end.

Since we have a good grasp of what we need the application to do, we can start with a practical set of requirements. From this, we can create a whiteboard plan that includes the obvious objects and what we will call them. Then, we'll start coding the objects, refining and expanding on the plan as we go. This type of plan/code, refine-plan/refine-code approach to software development is often called a "spiral" methodology.

Of course, there are many other ways to approach software development. Any methodology should work fine with Struts. But the goal of this section is not to explore software methodologies. We're here to demonstrate what it is like to construct a simple Struts application. So, let's have at it…

3.4.1 *Defining the requirements*

> *Requirements are the effects that the computer is to exert in*
> *the problem domain, by virtue of the computer's programming*
> —*Practical Software Requirements*, by Benjamin L. Kovitz

Although we have a sound working understanding of what the application needs to do, it's always a good practice to start from a set of requirements. Following suit with the rest of this chapter, we'll just draw up the simplest possible set of useful requirements.

Our simple requirements document will have three main sections: goal, requirements, and specification, as shown in table 3.6.

Table 3.6 Headings in our requirements document

Heading	Purpose
Goal	What result we need to achieve within the problem domain
Domain requirements	What we need to accomplish to realize the goal
Program specifications	What we need to do to realize the requirements

Goal

- Allow privileged users to identify themselves to the application

Domain requirements

- Allow users to present their credentials (username and password)
- Verify that the credentials presented are valid
- Allow correction of invalid credentials
- Inform user when credentials are verified
- Allow validated users access to privileged features
- Allow user to invalidate access on demand

Program specifications

- Be accessible from a standard web browser, with or without JavaScript enabled
- Offer logon to new visitors from a welcome page
- Allow entry of credentials (username and password) on a logon page
- Require that each credential contain 1 to 20 characters, inclusive
- Require that both username and password be entered
- Submit credentials to business tier method for validation
- Return invalid credentials to user for correction
- Log on user if credentials are valid
- Customize welcome page with username when logged on
- Allow validated users to log off from welcome page

Of course, this is very simple specification for a very simple application. Many specifications consume reams of paper and are embellished with diagrams, data tables, screen definitions, and detailed descriptions of the problem domain. For more about writing specifications for your own applications, we recommend *Practical Software Requirements*, by Benjamin L. Kovitz [Kovitz].

3.4.2 Planning the application

With our requirements in hand, we can start to sketch the application and plan which objects we will need to realize the program specification. One way to approach this is to list the specifications and the components that would help realize them. Often, a team will do something like this on a large whiteboard as part of an initial design meeting.

NOTE	An important point to note in this process is that there is often not a 1:1 correlation between the specification items and the components that realize them. While both the specification and the program serve the same goal, they approach the goal from different perspectives. So, a list like this will not be "normalized." Some specifications will appear more than once, as will some components.

View

In practice, many applications start out as storyboards. JSPs define the visible parts of our application. Table 3.7 outlines our requirements for the presentation layer.

Table 3.7   Our "whiteboard" view plan

Specification	JavaServer Pages
Offers logon to new visitors from a welcome page	Welcome.jsp
Allows entry of credentials (username and password) on a logon page	Logon.jsp
Returns invalid credentials to user for correction	Logon.jsp
Customizes welcome page with username when logged on	Welcome.jsp
Allows validated users to log off from welcome page	Welcome.jsp
Is accessible from a standard web browser with or without JavaScript enabled	Logon.jsp; Welcome.jsp
Directs users to welcome activity	index.jsp

Note that we added a specification of our own at the end of this list. A good trick in a Struts application is to have the application's welcome page redirect to a Struts action. This puts the control flow into the framework as soon as possible and helps to minimize change as the application grows.

Controller

In a strongly layered application (see chapter 2), all requests for pages or data pass through the control layer. Table 3.8 outlines our requirements for the controller (or "Front Controller" [Go3]).

Table 3.8 Our "whiteboard" controller plan

Specification	ActionForms
Allows entry of credentials (username and password) on a logon page	LogonForm
	Actions
Validates credentials with business tier method	LogonAction
Returns invalid credentials to user for correction	LogonForm; LogonAction
Logs on user if credentials are valid	LogonAction
Allows validated users to log off from welcome page	LogoffAction
	ActionForwards
Offers logon to new visitors from a welcome page	welcome; logon
Allows validated users to log off from welcome page	logoff
	ActionMappings
Submits credentials to business tier method for validation	LogonSubmit
	Utility
Documents all internal constants	Constants

Note that we added another specification of our own, "Document all internal constants." This is especially important in a layered application, where some of the constants will be "loosely bound." The Java compiler can't validate tokens that we use in an XML configuration file, so it's important we carefully track whatever tokens we use.

Model

We have only one requirement for our data access layer, shown in table 3.9.

Table 3.9 Our "whiteboard" model plan

Specification	Method interface
Submits credentials to business tier method for validation	`boolean isUserLogon(String username, String password);`

3.4.3 *Planning the source tree*

With a baseline plan for the application in place, we can sketch a source tree for the application. Since our application is very simple, we can use a single subdirectory for the pages and a single package for Java classes. Our tree is shown in figure 3.7.

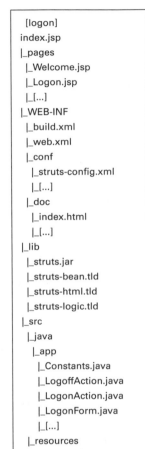

NOTE   Struts expects there to be an Application Resources bundle on your classpath. The logon application places its property file in its own "resources" package. Internationalized applications will have several property files. Giving them their own package helps keep things organized. Our build file copies these to the classes folder so that they will be on the classpath at runtime. Just be sure to rebuild the application after any change to a resource file.

If you are following along and building your own logon application, a good way to get a jumpstart on the tree and the Struts classes is to deploy the Blank application:

- Download the Blank application from the book site [Husted].

- Copy the blank.war file as logon.war.

- Put the WAR in your container's autodeployment folder (usually webapps).

This is why the Blank application is provided. It's meant as a generic template for other applications. We

Figure 3.7   The source tree for our logon application

present the base Blank infrastructure in sections 3.4.4 through 3.4.8. Then, we begin work on the source for our logon application.

To modify and rebuild the application, you may need to install some development tools.

3.4.4 *Setting up your development tools*

Aside from the Java Development Kit and a web container, you need two other pieces to be able to create and deploy web applications: a build tool and a programmer's editor. Like many development teams, the Struts Committers use Jakarta's Ant to build the Struts distribution and its sample applications. Other tools could be used, but Ant is quickly becoming the de facto standard build tool for Java applications.

The choice of a programming editor is a still a subjective decision. Any programming editor can be used with Struts (and probably is). If you do not have a preference, a likely starting point is the open source programmer's editor, jEdit.

Installing Ant

Deploying applications generally involves many steps. Automating those steps is your best chance that things will go as planned. Ant is an Apache XML scripting tool designed to ensure that deployments are quick and free from human error. Ant uses an XML build file to run a series of tasks. Ant predefines the most common tasks. If the predefined tasks don't meet your needs, you can also create your own.

To install Ant, you need to:

1 Download from Jakarta [ASF, Ant].

2 Unzip the download to the directory of your choice.

3 Set up three environment variables: `ANT_HOME`, `JAVA_HOME`, and `PATH`.

4 Set `ANT_HOME=<location of the unzipped download>`.

5 Set `JAVA_HOME=<location of the JDK>`.

6 Set `PATH=%PATH%;%ANT_HOME%\bin`.

As part of constructing our application, we provide a build.xml file to use with Ant.

Installing jEdit

If you do not already have a preferred programming editor, you can download and install jEdit to get started with Struts. The Java-based installer bundled with jEdit makes it as simple to install as the latest versions of the JDK and Tomcat (see chapter 1).

Let's step through the installation process:

1 Download jEdit from SourceForge [jEdit].

2 If the installer doesn't run automatically, you can start it from a DOS prompt using:

```
java -jar <downloaded jar file>
```

3 The first screen you will see is a welcome screen.

4 Clicking Next will present you with the GNU General Public License.

5 Clicking Next will provide you with the opportunity to select an installation directory.

6 Clicking Next will present you with a list of components to install. We recommend that you select them all.

7 Clicking Next again will initiate the install.

8 After the installation completes, you can launch jEdit by navigating through the Windows Start menu.

A number of jEdit plug-ins are available that allow you to edit over FTP, build Ant projects, edit XML files, and much more.

3.4.5 *Setting up the build.xml file*

Like many Java products these days, Struts expects that the Jakarta Ant tool [ASF, Ant] will be used as part of the build process. Ant also uses an XML configuration file, named build.xml. Typically, you can set up a stock build file for your application that does not change throughout. In chapter 4, we present the build file used by the logon application.

3.4.6 *Setting up the web.xml file*

The Java 2 Servlet framework uses a configuration file to help set up your application. The web deployment descriptor, or web.xml, identifies the servlets you'll need, and other settings for your application. The format is prescribed by the servlet specification [Sun, JST]. Most Struts applications need to deploy only a single servlet and the tag libraries, and tend to be relatively simple. We present the web.xml file used by the logon application in chapter 4.

3.4.7 *Setting up the struts-config.xml file*

Much like the web deployment descriptor, Struts also has an XML configuration file. This is where your application registers its ActionForms, ActionForwards, and ActionMappings. Each class has its own section in the file where you can define the default objects to be created at startup. Listing 3.7 shows our starter Struts configuration file.

Listing 3.7 The Struts configuration file (/WEB-INF/conf/struts-config.xml)

```xml
<?xml version="1.0" encoding="ISO-8859-1" ?>
<!DOCTYPE struts-config PUBLIC
"-//Apache Software Foundation//DTD Struts Configuration 1.0//EN"
"http://jakarta.apache.org/struts/dtds/struts-config_1_0.dtd">
<struts-config>
    <form-beans>
      <!-- ... -->
    </form-beans>
    <global-forwards>
      <forward
          name="welcome"
         path=" /Welcome.do"/>
      <!-- ... -->
    </global-forwards>
    <action-mappings>
    <action
          path="/Welcome"
          type="org.apache.struts.actions.ForwardAction"
          parameter="/pages/Welcome.jsp"/>

          <!-- ... -->
        </action-mappings>
</struts-config>
```

When you set up your application, you can start with a blank configuration file, like this one, and add the objects you need as you go along. We'll do just that through the balance of the chapter so you can see how the Struts configuration is used in practice. Chapter 4 covers the Struts configuration files in depth. You may have noticed that our starter configuration is not totally blank. A default `welcome` forward has been provided for your convenience.

The welcome action

Usually, it's helpful to route the page flow through the Struts controller as soon as possible. This keeps the big picture in the Struts configuration. You can adjust the control flow for the entire application from a single point. Unfortunately, the containers require a physical page for the welcome page. Listing a Struts action URI as a welcome page in the web deployment descriptor (web.xml) doesn't work.

The best all-around solution is to put in a stub index.jsp that redirects to your welcome action. The struts-blank provides one such stub. This is a very simple utility page, with just two lines:

```jsp
<%@ taglib uri="/tags/struts-logic" prefix="logic" %>
<logic:redirect forward="welcome"/>
```

The Blank application provides both the index.jsp forwarding page and a default welcome page. We will continue to use the index.jsp as is but will be making some changes to the welcome page. However, before we do anything else, let's test our deployment.

3.4.8 *Testing the deployment*

To be sure all is well before testing a new application, it's helpful to open a working application as a baseline. The Struts Blank application is a good choice for a baseline application. Its default welcome page includes some basic system checks to see that configuration files are loading properly, that the tag extensions can be found, and that the message resources are available.

The WAR file for the Struts Blank application can be found in the Struts distribution or on this book's website. Just place the blank.war file in your container's autodeploy folder and restart it if necessary. You can then open the application's welcome page using a URL such as

```
http://localhost:8080/blank
```

If all is well, a page like the one shown in figure 3.8 should display.

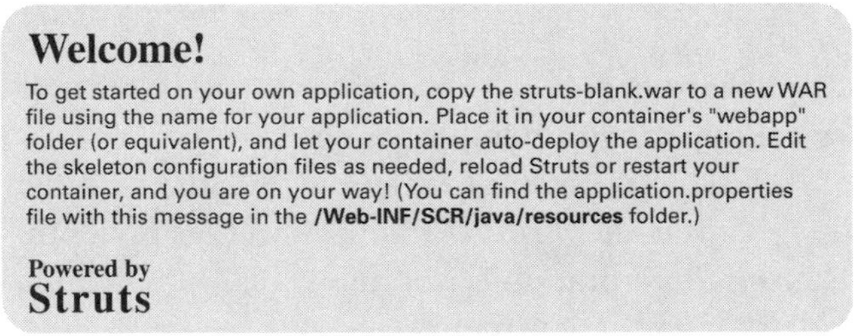

Welcome!

To get started on your own application, copy the struts-blank.war to a new WAR file using the name for your application. Place it in your container's "webapp" folder (or equivalent), and let your container auto-deploy the application. Edit the skeleton configuration files as needed, reload Struts or restart your container, and you are on your way! (You can find the application.properties file with this message in the **/Web-INF/SCR/java/resources** folder.)

Powered by
Struts

Figure 3.8   The welcome screen of the Blank application

The source for this page appears in listing 3.8.

Listing 3.8   The default welcome page for the Blank application

```
<%@ taglib uri="/tags/struts-bean" prefix="bean" %>
<%@ taglib uri="/tags/struts-html" prefix="html" %>
<%@ taglib uri="/tags/struts-logic" prefix="logic" %>
<html:html locale="true">
<head>
<title><bean:message key="welcome.title"/></title>
<html:base/>
</head
```

```
<body>
<logic:notPresent name="org.apache.struts.action.MESSAGE"
  scope="application">

<b>ERROR: Application resources not loaded -- check servlet container
  logs for error messages.</b>

</logic:notPresent>
<h3><bean:message key="welcome.heading"/></h3>
<p><bean:message key="welcome.message"/></p>
</body>
</html:html>
```

3.4.9 *Constructing our welcome page*

A basic tenet of most software methodologies is to get a working prototype up and running as soon as possible. If we follow that advice, then the first thing we should do is put up the welcome page called for by our specification. An early version of our welcome page, without the conditional logic, might look like the one shown in listing 3.9.

Listing 3.9   An early version of the welcome page

```
<%@ taglib uri="/tags/struts-html" prefix="html" %>
<html>
<head>
<title>Welcome World!!</title>
<html:base/>
</head>
<body>
</ul>
<li><html:link forward="logon">Sign in</html:link></li>
</ul>
<img src='struts-power.gif' alt='Powered by Struts'>
</body>
</html>
```

Since this refers to the logon ActionForward, we need to add that to our Struts configuration. We can also change the default welcome page from Index.jsp to Welcome.jsp:

```
<global-forwards>
  <forward
      name="logon"
      path /Logon.do"/>
  <forward
```

```
        name="welcome"
        path /Welcome.do"/>
    <!-- ... -->
</global-forwards>
```

At this point, we can restart the container to reload the Struts configuration. Some containers, like Tomcat, let you reload a single application.

1.0 vs 1.1 In Struts 1.0, there were number of administrative Actions available, including one to reload the Struts configuration. These were removed in Struts 1.1 because they conflicted with the support for multiple application modules.

Once the new configuration is loaded, we can try opening our new welcome page:

```
http://localhost:8080/logon/
```

You should see the screen shown in figure 3.9.

Figure 3.9
The welcome screen before logon

However, if you were to try and click on the link, you wouldn't get very far, as shown in figure 3.10.

404 Not Found
/logon/pages/Logon.jsp was not found on this server.

Figure 3.10
The file not found error

To fix this error, we need to move on to the next object and construct the logon page.

3.4.10 *Constructing the logon page*

Looking back at our whiteboard in section 3.4.2, we see that our logon page needs to collect the username and password, and submit them to a mapping named /LogonSubmit. This means that we need to create a Struts form that specifies the /LogonSubmit action, with input controls for a text field and a password field, as shown in listing 3.10.

Listing 3.10   The JSP source for our logon page (/pages/Logon.jsp)

```
<%@ taglib uri="/tags/struts-html" prefix="html" %>
<html><head><title>Sign in, Please!</title></head>
<body>
<html:errors/>
<html:form action="/LogonSubmit" focus="username">
<table border="0" width="100%">
<tr>
<th align="right">Username: </th>
<td align="left"><html:text property="username"/></td>
</tr>
<tr><th align="right">Password: </th>
<td align="left"><html:password property="password"/></td>
</tr>
<tr>
<td align="right"><html:submit property="submit" value="Submit"/></td>
<td align="left"><html:reset/></td>
</tr>
</table>
</html:form>
</body>
</html>
```

The `<html:form>` tag refers to an ActionMapping object, which in turns refers to other objects (`org.apache.struts.action.ActionMapping`). Let's write the ActionMapping first and then the objects that go with it:

```
<action-mappings>
    <action
      type="app.LogonAction"
      path="/LogonSubmit"
      name="logonForm"
      scope="request"
      validate="true"
      input="/pages/Logon.jsp"/>
    <!-- ... -->
</action-mappings>
```

The two related objects are the `logonForm` form bean and the LogonAction. We also need to register the ActionForm beans in the Struts configuration. The name we use becomes the default attribute name for the object when it is created in the request or session context:

```
<form-beans
    <form-bean
      name="logonForm"
      type="app.LogonForm"/>
    <!-- ... -->
</form-beans>
```

This brings us to adding the two specified Java classes, LogonForm and LogonAction.

3.4.11 *Constructing the Constants class*

While not strictly required, documenting the ActionForward names and other magic tokens is strongly recommended. This is simple to do and can make your codebase much easier to manage over time. When we present code, we usually omit the JavaDoc comments. But in this case we will leave them in. Why? Because the whole point of this class is to *document* the constants. So, in this case, the documentation *is* the code. Listing 3.11 contains the Java source for the Constants class.

Listing 3.11   Java source for Constants class (/WEB-INF/src/java/app/Constants.java)

```java
package app;
public final class Constants {

/**
 * The session scope attribute under which the LogonForm
 * for the currently logged in user is stored.
 */
public static final String USER_KEY = "user";

/**
 * The value to indicate debug logging.
 */
public static final int DEBUG = 1;

/**
 * The value to indicate normal logging.
 */
public static final int NORMAL = 0;
/**
 * The token that represents a nominal outcome
 * in an ActionForward.
 */
   public static final String SUCCESS= "success";

/**
 * The token that represents the logon activity
 * in an ActionForward.
 */
public static final String LOGON = "logon";

/**
 * The token that represents the welcome activity
 * in an ActionForward.
 */
public static final String WELCOME = "welcome";

}
```

3.4.12 *Constructing the other classes*

We presented the source for the LogonAction and LogonForm classes in sections 3.3.8 and 3.3.9. We also need to include the UserDirectory and UserDirectoryException classes introduced in chapter 1. We can add all of these to our new application unchanged. Our source tree from section 3.4 places them under /WEB-INF/src/java/app/, as shown in figure 3.11.

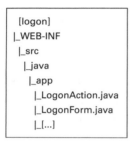

```
[logon]
|_WEB-INF
 |_src
  |_java
   |_app
    |_LogonAction.java
    |_LogonForm.java
    |_[...]
```

Figure 3.11
The location of LogonAction,
LogonForm, and other Java files

The LogonAction also refers to a Constants class. We need to add that before the source will compile.

3.4.13 *Creating the user directory*

In chapter 1, we introduced a simple registration application that stored a user ID and password. These logon accounts are stored in a standard Properties file named user.properties. This can be brought over from that application or re-created under WEB-INF/src/java/resources, as shown in figure 3.12.

```
[logon]
|_WEB-INF
 |_src
  |_java
   |_app
   |_resources
    |_application.properties
    |_user.properties
```

Figure 3.12
The location of user.properties
and other resource files

Properties files are simple text files. Here's an example that uses the first names of this book's authors as the user ID and their last names as a password:

```
TED=Husted
CEDRIC=Dumoulin
```

```
GEORGE=Franciscus
DAVID=Winterfeldt
CRAIG=McClanahan
```

If you like, you can just type these, or the logins of your choice, into a text file and save it under /WEB-INF/src/java/resources/user.properties. Just be sure to enter the user IDs in all uppercase letters, since this is required by the business logic.

Of course, your application can just as easily validate logins against a JNDI service or a database, or use the container's security realm. We cover using data services with Struts in chapter 14.

3.4.14 *Configuring the ActionErrors*

As you will remember, both the LogonForm and LogonAction may generate error messages. The ActionError system is integrated with the application messages. Before putting LogonForm and LogonAction to the test, we need to add these messages to the application.properties document:

```
errors.header=<H3><font color="red">Validation Error</font></H3>You must
    correct the following error(s) before proceeding:<UL>
errors.footer=</UL><HR>
error.username.required=<LI>Username is required</LI>
error.password.required=<LI>Password is required</LI>
error.logon.invalid=<LI>Username and password provided not found in user
    directory. Password must match exactly, including any lower or upper case
    characters.</LI>
```

1.0 vs 1.1   New tags in Struts 1.1 allow you to omit markup from the message. See chapter 10 for more about the Struts JSP tags.

As part of the build process, we copy the application resource documents from /WEB-INF/src/java/resource to a resources package under the classes folder where the ActionServlet can find them. Be sure to edit the copy under /WEB-INF/scr/java/resource and to launch the build process before running any tests.

3.4.15 *Compiling and testing the logon page*

In section 3.4.8, we created the JSP page for our logon form. But to make this work, we need to add the related configuration elements and Java classes, as shown in table 3.10.

Table 3.10 Logon page configuration elements

Configuration elements	Java classes
LogonSubmit action-mapping *logonForm* form-bean	*LogonAction,* subclass of Action *LogonForm,* subclass of ActionForm

Since these are now in place, we can compile the application and test the logon page. There is a stock build.xml in the WEB-INF directory that you can use with Ant. The default build target, `compile`, will build the Java classes from the Java source files and copy the application resources message file into the classes directory.

When the build is successful, you can enter the application and follow the link to the logon page. (Depending on how well your container reloads Java classes, you may need to restart the container after a build. When in doubt, restart.)

The logon application should now behave much as it did during our original tour (see sections 3.3.3 through 3.3.6). The difference is that the welcome page does not change after we have logged in, nor does it offer the opportunity to log out. We can fix that in the next section, and our initial application will be complete.

3.4.16 *Amending the welcome page*

Our original draft of the welcome page omitted the conditional logic regarding whether the user was logged in. Now that people can log in, we can add that back so it matches the version from section 3.3.2 (see listing 3.12). The lines we are adding appear in bold.

Listing 3.12 The revised source for the welcome page (/pages/Welcome.jsp)

```
<%@ taglib uri="/tags/struts-bean" prefix="bean" %>
<%@ taglib uri="/tags/struts-html" prefix="html" %>
<%@ taglib uri="/tags/struts-logic" prefix="logic" %>
<html>
<head>
<title>Welcome!</title>
<html:base/>
</head>
<body>
<logic:present scope="session" name="user">
```

```
<h3>Welcome <bean:write name="user" property="username"/>!</h3>
</logic:present>
<logic:notPresent scope="session" name="user"/>
<h3>Welcome World!</h3>
</logic:notPresent>
<html:errors/>
<ul>
<li><html:link forward="logon">Sign in</html:link></li>
<logic:present scope="session" name="user">
<li><html:link forward="logoff">Sign out</html:link></li>
</logic:present>
</ul>
<img src='struts-power.gif' alt='Powered by Struts'>
</body>
</html>
```

As shown in figure 3.13, this puts us back where we started. When guests arrive, they are invited to sign in. Once they log on, they are greeted by name and can then sign out. That's progress for you!

Figure 3.13   The welcome screen before and after logon

3.4.17   *The Struts ForwardAction Action*

If you've kept an eye on your browser's location bar, you may have noticed that we never reveal the location of our JSP pages. Many applications don't bother with this nicety, but if you would like to use a strict Model-View-Controller architecture (as described in chapter 2), you may not want to expose any implementation details regarding your View, including whether you are using JSP pages or where you happen to store them. Ideally, all navigation should pass through .do Actions that are managed by the controller.

Of course, many times there really isn't anything for the controller to, well, do. This was the case for our logon and welcome pages. They don't require any information from the model and can be displayed by linking directly to the JSP page. But this allows people to bookmark the location of the page. Later, you may need to perform some background action before displaying the logon page, or you may want to move or rename the JSP pages. If people have bookmarked the JSP page, they will try to go back to the old location and either bypass your logic or generate a file not found error. In practice, this usually leads to putting legacy checks into the server page and redirects into the web server—more ways for things to go wrong and more code to maintain.

The moral? We must "virtualize" as many navigation details as possible; otherwise, we will be forced to continually compensate for what the browser may (or may not) cache or store. Instead of linking directly to a "physical" JSP, we should always link to a "virtual" Struts Action, which can then provide the appropriate page.

Of course, writing a custom Action for every page, whether or not it needed one, would be a lot of busy work. A more efficient solution is to deploy a single utility Action that can be customized in the Struts configuration and reused whenever it is needed. Since Struts creates one multithreaded instance of each Action class, this is a very efficient way to ensure that control stays with the controller. All we need to do is pass the Action and the path to the page.

Happily, you can do this using the standard ForwardAction bundled in the struts.jar. You simply pass the target path as the `parameter` property of the ActionMapping:

```
<action
        path="/Welcome"
        type="org.apache.struts.actions.ForwardAction"
        parameter="/pages/Welcome.jsp"/>
```

The ForwardAction will then look up the target path from the mapping and use it to return an ActionForward to the servlet.

The practical upshot is that instead of

```
http://localhost:8080/logon/pages/Welcome.jsp
```

appearing on the browser's address bar, where it could be bookmarked for direct access, the Action URI appears instead:

```
http://localhost:8080/logon/Welcome.do
```

Users can still bookmark this address, but you have much more control now and can change the implementation of the logon activity without worrying about what some browser has bookmarked. Before, you would have had to consider what should happen if they try to go directly to the old server page.

In a Model-View-Controller architecture, the actions are your API. The server pages are an implementation detail. If the JSPs are exposed to the browser as part of the navigation system, then the Controller and View layers become mixed, and the benefits of MVC are diluted.

We can add other instances of the ForwardAction whenever we want to go directly to a page. Since only one ForwardAction will be instantiated for the application, all we are really adding is an ActionMapping object. If the usual MVC reasons for using ForwardAction weren't enough, the modular application feature introduced in Struts 1.1 *requires* that all JSP requests go through an Action. This is because each module has its own configuration context and control has to pass through the ActionServlet controller in order to select the configuration for the JSP page. This is not a requirement if you are using a single, default application. But if you follow this practice from the beginning, you can make your application a module without making any changes.

3.5 *Summary*

Regardless of what role you play on a development team—engineer, designer, architect, QA—it's helpful to have the big picture of how the application works as a whole. In this chapter, we took a comprehensive look at a small but useful application. By touring, dissecting, and then constructing a logon application, we were able to show you how the Struts framework actually works. As part of the construction phase, we created a design document to outline our goals, client requirements, and program specifications. Given a design to work from, we configured the application's web.xml, our Ant build.xml script, and the Struts config file. With the right infrastructure in place, we built each component in the order they were needed. Along the way, we pointed out some best practices and emphasized the importance of separating the model, view, and controller.

In chapter 4, we take a closer look at the Struts configuration file. As we have seen here, the configuration plays a strong role in Struts and makes applications easier to design and maintain.

Configuring
Struts components

Co-authored by Ted Husted and George Franciscus

This chapter covers

- The Web application deployment descriptor
- The Struts configuration file
- The application resources file
- The Ant build file

Change alone is unchanging.

—Heraclitus (c 535–c 475 B.C.)

4.1 Three XMLs and a Properties file

In addition to Java classes and JavaServer Pages, a developer must create, or change, several configuration files to get a Struts application up and running:

web.xml. The web application deployment descriptor required by the Java Servlet specification. The servlet/JSP container uses this file to load and configure your application.

struts-config.xml. The framework's deployment descriptor. It is used to load and configure various components used by the Struts framework.

build.xml. A file used by the Jakarta Ant build tool to compile and deploy your application. Using Ant is not a requirement, but it is a popular choice among Struts developers.

application.properties. This file provides the message resources for your Struts application. Like the build.xml file, it is not a strict requirement but is used by most Struts applications.

While working with these files might not seem like "Java development," using them correctly is an essential part of getting a web application out the door. In this chapter, we take a close look at how these files work and what they contribute to the development *and deployment* of your application.

4.1.1 The rest of the family

In addition to the configuration files that every Struts application needs, there are some others that many Struts applications will also want to use. Additional XML configuration files are needed to utilize optional components, such as the Tiles framework and the Struts Validator. If you elect to subdivide your application into multiple modules, each module may also have its own Struts configuration and message resource files.

In this chapter, we focus on the core configuration files first and then turn to configuring the standard options available in Struts 1.1.

1.0 vs 1.1   When this book was written, Struts 1.1 beta release 2 was in circulation. Some details may have changed between beta 2 and the final release. Be sure to check the book's site [Husted] for any errata.

4.2 *The web application deployment descriptor*

The core of the framework is the ActionServlet, which Struts uses as a controller. Although it can be subclassed, most developers treat the ActionServlet as a blackbox. They configure it from the web application deployment descriptor (web.xml) and leave it alone.

The ActionServlet can accept a number of initialization parameters. Most have reasonable default values and do not need to be set. Others must be set in order for your application to work correctly.

In this section, we examine a typical Struts web deployment descriptor and take a close look at the initialization parameters for the ActionServlet.

4.2.1 *The web.xml file*

The purpose and format of the web application deployment descriptor are covered by the Sun Servlet Specification [Sun, JST]. Basically, it is used to tell the servlet container how to configure the servlets and other high-level objects your application needs.

The Struts framework includes two components that need to be configured through your application's deployment descriptor: the ActionServlet and, optionally, the tag libraries. While most Struts applications do make use of the tag libraries, they are not strictly required. Applications using only XSLT or Velocity templates do not need to configure the tag libraries at all.

Listing 4.1 shows the web.xml file from our logon application (see chapter 3). The numbered comments correlate to annotations following the listing.

Listing 4.1   The logon application's web.xml file

```
<!-- ❶ -->
<?xml version="1.0" encoding="ISO-8859-1"?>
<!DOCTYPE web-app
   PUBLIC "-//Sun Microsystems, Inc.//DTD Web Application 2.2//EN"
   "http://java.sun.com/j2ee/dtds/web-app_2_2.dtd">

<web-app>
   <!-- ❷ -->
   <servlet>
     <servlet-name>action</servlet-name>
```

```
    <servlet-class>org.apache.struts.action.ActionServlet</servlet-class>
    <init-param>
      <param-name>application</param-name>
      <param-value>Application</param-value>
    </init-param>
    <init-param>
      <param-name>config</param-name>
      <param-value>/WEB-INF/conf/struts-config.xml</param-value>
    </init-param>
    <init-param>
      <param-name>debug</param-name>
      <param-value>2</param-value>
    </init-param>
    <init-param>
      <param-name>detail</param-name>
      <param-value>2</param-value>
    </init-param>
    <load-on-startup>2</load-on-startup>
  </servlet>

  <!-- ❸ -->
  <servlet-mapping>
    <servlet-name>action</servlet-name>
    <url-pattern>*.do</url-pattern>
  </servlet-mapping>

  <!-- ❹ -->
  <welcome-file-list>
    <welcome-file>index.jsp</welcome-file>
  </welcome-file-list>

  <!-- ❺ -->
  <taglib>
    <taglib-uri>/tags/struts-bean</taglib-uri>
    <taglib-location>/WEB-INF/lib/struts-bean.tld</taglib-location>
  </taglib>
  <taglib>
    <taglib-uri>/tags/struts-html</taglib-uri>
    <taglib-location>/WEB-INF/lib/struts-html.tld</taglib-location>
  </taglib>
  <taglib>
    <taglib-uri>/tags/struts-logic</taglib-uri>
    <taglib-location>/WEB-INF/lib/struts-logic.tld</taglib-location>
  </taglib>
</web-app>
```

❶ *Identify as web application deployment descriptor*—The first two lines identify the file as a web application deployment descriptor.

❷ *Configure the ActionServlet*—This block tells the container to load the ActionServlet under the name action. Four parameters are passed to the ActionServlet: `application`, `config`, `debug`, and `detail`. (There are several other parameters that the ActionServlet can accept; we cover those in the next sections.) The final setting in this block, `<load-on-startup>`, gives the action servlet a weighting with the container. Setting it to 2 allows other servlets to load first if needed. This would be important if you subclassed the ActionServlet so that it could make use of resources loaded by some other servlet.

Only one ActionServlet or ActionServlet subclass can be loaded for an application. The ActionServlet is designed to share resources with other components in the application. Loading more than one will cause contention; one ActionServlet will overwrite resources posted by another ActionServlet. Struts 1.1 supports modular applications but still only one ActionServlet.

❸ *Identify Struts requests*—This block tells the container to forward any file requests matching the pattern *.do to the action servlet. This is the ActionServlet that we configured in block (2). Requests for files not matching this pattern are *not* handled by Struts. Requests for *.html or *.jsp files are usually handed by services built into the container.

❹ *Create the welcome file*—Unfortunately, putting an index.do file here won't work. The container expects a welcome file to also be a physical file. In chapter 3, we showed you how to use the welcome file to forward to a Struts action.

❺ *Configure tag libraries*—Here we configure the tag libraries that our application uses. The three core Struts taglibs—bean, html, and logic—will be used by most applications. If your application uses other taglibs, they would be configured here too. The first element, `<taglib-uri>`, gives the library a logical name. This will usually look like a file path, but it's not. The JSPs can refer to this URI when they import the taglibs. The second element, `<taglib-location>`, provides the context-relative path to the taglibs descriptor (*.tld). The TLD specifies the actual type (Java class) for the library. When the library is needed, the container searches the classpath for the taglib's class file. In the case of the Struts taglibs, the container will find these packaged in the struts.jar file.

For more about the web application deployment descriptor, see the Java Servlet Specification [Sun, JST] and *Web Development with JavaServer Pages* [Fields].

4.2.2 *ActionServlet parameters*

The Struts ActionServlet accepts several parameters, which are summarized in table 4.1. Most of these were deprecated in Struts 1.1 in favor of components in the new config package, which provides support for modular applications.

Table 4.1 ActionServlet parameters

Parameter	Default	Description	Notes
config	/WEB-INF/struts-config.xml	The context-relative path to the XML resource containing our configuration information.	
config/${prefix}		The context-relative path to the XML resource containing the configuration information for the application module that will use the specified prefix (${prefix}). This can be repeated as many times as required for multiple application modules.	
convertNull	false	A parameter that forces simulation of the Struts 1.0 behavior when populating forms. If it's set to true, the numeric Java wrapper class types (such as java.lang.Integer) will default to null (rather than 0).	
debug	0	The debugging detail level that controls how much information is logged for this servlet. Accepts values 0 (off) and 1 (least serious) through 6 (most serious). Most Struts components use either level 0 or 2.	
detail	0	The debugging detail level for the Digester that we use to process the application configuration files. Accepts the values 0 (off) and 1 (least serious) through 6 (most serious).	
validating	true	Specifies whether we should we use a validating XML parser to process the configuration file (strongly recommended).	

Since Struts 1.1

Since Struts 1.1

Table 4.1 **ActionServlet parameters** *(continued)*

Parameter	Default	Description	Notes
`application`	No default value	The name of the application resource bundle, styled as a classname. To refer to a file named application.properties in a package named `resources`, use resources.application here. In this case, resources can be a subdirectory under classes (or a package in a JAR file).	Deprecated; configure this using the `parameter` attribute of the `<message-resources>` element.
`bufferSize`	4096	The size of the input buffer used when processing file uploads.	Deprecated; configure this using the `buffer-Size` attribute of the `<controller>` element.
`content`	text/html	The default content type and character encoding that is to be set on each response; may be overridden by a forwarded-to servlet or JSP.	Deprecated; configure this using the `contentType` attribute of the `<controller>` element.
`factory`	org.apache.struts .util.PropertyMessageResources-Factory	The Java classname of the MessageResourcesFactory used to create the application MessageResources object.	Deprecated; configure this using the `factory` attribute of the `<message-resources>` element.
`formBean`	org.apache.struts .action.Action-FormBean	The Java class name of the Action-FormBean implementation to use.	Deprecated; configure this using the `class-Name` attribute of each `<form-bean>` element.
`forward`	org.apache.struts .action.Action-Forward	The Java classname of the Action-Forward implementation to use.	Deprecated; configure this using the `className` attribute of each `<forward>` element.
`locale`	true	If set to true, and there is a user session, identifies and stores an appropriate `java.util.Locale` object (under the standard key identified by Action.LOCALE_KEY) in the user's session (if there is no Locale object already there).	Deprecated; configure this using the `locale` attribute of the `<controller>` element.

Table 4.1   ActionServlet parameters *(continued)*

Parameter	Default	Description	Notes
`mapping`	org.apache.struts .action.Action- Mapping	The Java class name of the Action-Mapping implementation to use.	Deprecated; configure this using the `className` attribute of each `<action>` element, or globally for an application module by using the `type` attribute of the `<action-mappings>` element.
`maxFileSize`	250M	The maximum size (in bytes) of a file that is to be accepted as a file upload. Can be expressed as a number followed by a "K", "M", or "G", interpreted to mean kilobytes, megabytes, or gigabytes, respectively.	Deprecated; configure this using the `maxFileSize` attribute of the `<con- troller>` element.
`multipartClass`	org.apache.struts .uploadDiskMulti- partRequest- Handler	The fully qualified name of the MultiPartRequestHandler implementation class that is to be used for processing file uploads. If set to none, disables Struts multipart request handling.	
`nocache`	false	If set to true, adds HTTP headers to every response. Intended to defeat browser caching of any response we generate or forward to.	Deprecated; configure this using the `nocache` attribute of the `<controller>` element.
`null`	True	If set to true, sets our application resources to return null if an unknown message key is used. Otherwise, an error message including the offending message key will be returned.	Deprecated; configure this using the `null` attribute of the `<mes- sage-resources>` element.
`tempDir`	The working direc- tory provided to this web applica- tion as a servlet context attribute	The temporary working directory to use when processing file uploads.	Deprecated, configure this using the `tempDir` attribute of the `<controller>` element.

4.3 *The Struts configuration*

The Struts configuration file (struts-config.xml) is used to load several critical framework components. Together, these objects make up the Struts configuration. The Struts configuration and Struts ActionServlet work together to create the control layer of your application. In this section, we explore why we need the Struts configuration. In the next section, we look at how Struts developers create and maintain the configuration.

> **NOTE**   Since Struts 1.1, an application can be subdivided into multiple modules. Each module has its own Struts configuration. Every Struts application has at least one default, or "root," module. If you are not using multiple modules, or are using Struts 1.0, then when we refer to a *module*, you can think *application*. We discuss configuring a Struts 1.1 application for modules at the end of this chapter.

4.3.1 *Details, details*

The Struts configuration is a living blueprint of your application. It knows what fields are on your forms. It knows where your JSPs can be found. It knows about every action your application performs and exactly what resources each of these actions need.

This may seem like a lot of information to collect in one place. And it is. But by keeping all these implementation details together, many developers find that their applications are much easier to create and maintain.

Every component in the Struts configuration is a Java object. The ActionForm objects know about the fields and forms. The ActionForward objects know where to find your JSPs. The ActionMapping objects know which forms and forwards are used with each command your application understands.

A very simple application could create all of these informational objects in an initialization method and then set each object to the default values needed. For example:

```
ActionForwards globals = new ActionForwards();
ActionForward logoff = new ActionForward();
logoff.setName("logoff");
logoff.setPath("/Logoff.do");
globals.addForward (logoff);
ActionForward logon = new ActionForward();
logoff.setName("logon");
logoff.setPath("/Logon.do");
globals.addForward (logon);
```

and so forth. But, in practice, initialization methods quickly become maintenance burdens and can cause as many problems as they solve.

Ironically, a class like this does not involve any real programming. It just instantiates objects from existing classes. Heck, it almost doesn't need to be in Java at all.

And, in fact, it doesn't. The Java language can create any given class by name. Java also supports features such as reflection that can determine which methods a class supports at runtime.

DEFINITION *Reflection* tells us what methods are provided by any Java class. *Introspection* helps us deduce which of those methods are properties that can be used to configure a JavaBean at runtime. Java tools and frameworks (like Struts) use reflection and introspection to automate loading and configuring JavaBean objects. This eliminates the mindless, error-prone task of writing and loading custom objects that simply load other objects.

Put these features together and you really don't need a Java class. You need a document that describes how to instantiate a Java class as a fully functioning object.

Of course, frameworks like Struts are not the only ones that have this problem. The servlet container needs to do the same thing for the same reason. Developers have to tell the container what servlets and other objects are needed by their applications. Rather than have you write a Java class and plug it into the container, the Sun engineers chose to use an XML document instead. The container reads the XML document and uses it to instantiate and configure whatever servlets an application needs.

The Struts configuration file is to Struts what the deployment descriptor is to your container. The Struts controller reads the configuration file and uses it to create and configure whatever objects the framework needs.

Every web developer who has written a deployment descriptor (web.xml) file has used an XML element to create a Java object. For example, here's how we might deploy a servlet in a web.xml:

```
<servlet>
    <servlet-name>action</servlet-name>
    <servlet-class>org.apache.struts.action.ActionServlet</servlet-class>
    <load-on-startup>2</load-on-startup>
</servlet>
```

Here's how we would deploy the forward objects from the previous Java code segment in a Struts configuration file:

```
<global-forwards>
        <forward
            name="logoff"
            path="/Logoff.do"/>
        <forward
            name="logon"
            path="/Logon.do"/>
</global-forwards>
```

Point in fact, the struts-config does not *configure* your application as much as it *deploys* it. But for most developers, it is very natural to think of these objects as the "configuration," and so that is the term we tend to use.

4.3.2 *Change management*

Deploying preconfigured Java objects this way is a very powerful feature. And with great power comes great responsibility. Because the Struts configuration file loads the framework objects, it also becomes *responsible* for the framework objects.

By describing how framework components interact, the Struts configuration file becomes a very effective tool for managing change within your application. In practice, the file transcends a simple object loader and is used as a dynamic design document.

It is not hard to imagine a tool that could read the Struts configuration file and use it to create a Universal Modeling Language (UML) diagram. Several Struts GUIs are now available that help you maintain the XML (see section 4.4). It may not be long before a visual tool can help you maintain the architectural design that is expressed by the Struts configuration file.

4.3.3 *The principle of Protected Variation*

The Struts configuration file helps your application react to change quickly with minimal effort. If an object needs to be initialized to another value, you do not have to edit, compile, and deploy a Java class. Many of the configuration details involve the presentation layer. The members of your team working on that layer may not be Java engineers. Using an XML document makes the configuration accessible to page designers and project administrators. A Java engineer is needed to create and modify the base objects for an application, but configuring these objects can be delegated to other personnel.

In practice, we are separating things that rarely change—the underlying Java classes—from things that often change—how the Java objects are deployed at runtime. This is known as the principle of *Protected Variation* [Larman].

DEFINITION   *Protected Variation* is a design principle that encourages the encapsulation of predicted points of variation by using a stable interface. Data-driven design, service lookup, interpreter-driven design, and reflective design are some of the mechanisms available to implement Protected Variation.

Protected Variation reminds us that a single point of change will yield a single point of maintenance. By separating implementation details (which often change) from the base objects (which rarely change), we reduce the effort it takes to maintain an application.

4.4 *The Struts configuration elements*

As discussed in section 4.3, the Struts configuration file is an XML document that is used to deploy Java objects. Each element in the configuration corresponds to a Java object. When you insert an element in the Struts configuration file, you are telling the Struts controller to create a Java object when the application initializes.

By starting from a blank configuration file with some commented examples, it's easy to cobble together a configuration file for your own application. But it's also easy to miss an important feature if all you do is follow some generic examples.

Most Java developers know to look for the JavaDocs if they want more information about a Java class, but where do you go for more information about an XML document?

Every well-formed XML document, including the Struts configuration file, includes a pointer to the document that describes the elements it can use. This is the document type definition (DTD). If you look at the top of the struts-config.xml, you will find this element:

```
<!DOCTYPE struts-config PUBLIC
  "-//Apache Software Foundation//DTD Struts Configuration 1.1//EN"
  "http://jakarta.apache.org/struts/dtds/struts-config_1_1.dtd">
```

This tells us that the official reference copy of this document's DTD can be found at the indicated URL. Internally, Struts uses the Digester, from the Jakarta Commons [ASF, Commons], to parse the Struts configuration file. The Digester uses the struts-config DTD to validate the format of the document and creates the Java objects the file describes. If the XML file contains undocumented elements or uses the elements in an undocumented way, the Digester will not process the file.

If for any reason XML validation causes a problem, you can turn it off using the `validating` servlet parameter described in section 4.3. But we don't recommend doing this.

Internally, Struts uses its own copy of the DTD to process the configuration. It does not fetch the reference copy from the Internet every time your application loads. (For some mysterious reason, however, a small number of developers have reported that setting `validating=false` seems to help some applications load when no Internet connection is available. In general, you should leave `validating=true` whether or not you are connected to the Internet.)

Table 4.2 summarizes the struts-config elements that can be used with Struts 1.1. We've indicated when elements have been added since Struts 1.1.

Table 4.2   The struts-config elements

Element	Description
`data-sources`	Contains a set of DataSource objects (JDBC 2.0 Standard Extension).
`data-source`	Specifies a DataSource object that is to be instantiated, configured, and made available as a servlet context attribute (or application-scope bean).
`set-property`	Specifies the method name and initial value of an additional JavaBean configuration property.
`global-exceptions`	Describes a set of exceptions that might be thrown by an Action object.
`exceptions`	Registers an ExceptionHandler for an exception type.
`form-beans`	Describes the set of form bean descriptors for this application module.
`form-bean`	Describes an ActionForm subclass that can be referenced by an `<action>` element.
`form-properties`	Describes a JavaBean property that can be used to configure an instance of a DynaActionForm or a subclass thereof.
`global-forwards`	Describes a set of ActionForward objects that are available to all Action objects as a return value.
`forward`	Describes an ActionForward that is to be made available to an Action as a return value.
`action-mappings`	Describes a set of ActionMappings that are available to process requests matching the `url-pattern` our ActionServlet registered with the container.
`action`	Describes an ActionMapping object that is to be used to process a request for a specific module-relative URI.
`controller`	Describes the ControllerConfig bean that encapsulates an application module's runtime configuration.

Table 4.2 **The struts-config elements** *(continued)*

Element	Description
message-resources	Describes a MessageResources object with message templates for this module.
plug-in	Specifies the fully qualified class name of a general-purpose application plug-in module that receives notification of application startup and shutdown events.

For your convenience, appendix B presents the struts-config DTD in a standard API format. In this section, we examine the elements and provide usage examples. For the nuts-and-bolts detail of each element and the attributes it accepts, we refer you to appendix B.

NOTE If you don't like editing XML by hand, or you are using Struts in an integrated development environment (IDE), visual tools are available to help you maintain the Struts configuration. Scioworks Camino [Camino] and Struts Console [Console] directly manage the Struts configuration file. Other products, such as Adalon by Synthis [Adalon] and ObjectAssembler by ObjectVenture [ObjectAssembler], help you design your application visually and then write the initial Struts configuration, Java classes, and JSPs for you. For a current listing of the latest Struts-related products, visit the Struts Resources page [ASF, Struts].

As mentioned, many programming components are configured with XML files these days, including the Java servlet container. For more about Java and XML, we recommend *J2EE and XML Development* [Gabrick].

4.4.1 *<global-exceptions>*

In a Struts application, the ActionServlet is at the top of the call tree, but the work is delegated to an Action object. This divide-and-conquer strategy works well in most circumstances, the exception being exception handling. Many applications like to handle exceptions in a consistent way, but that could mean replicating exception-handling code throughout several Actions.

To treat an exception in a consistent way throughout all your Action objects, you can register an ExceptionHandler for it with the Struts configuration file. The framework provides a default ExceptionHandler (org.apache.struts.action. ExceptionHandler) that stores the exception under a request-scope attribute, creates an ActionError for your exception message, and forwards control to the

JSP or other URI of your choice. The Struts `<html:errors>` tag will automatically print the localized version of your exception message. So, you can use the same page to display an exception error that you would use to display a validation error.

If you need to do something else as well, the ExceptionHandler can be sub-classed to add new behavior. Each exception can specify its own handler class, if need be.

You can register a global handler for an exception as well as a local handler for a specific ActionMapping. To register an exception, you need to provide the `Exception` type, the message resource key, and the response path, as shown here:

```
<exception
    type="org.apache.struts.webapp.example.ExpiredPasswordException"
    key="expired.password"
    path="/changePassword.jsp"/>
```

See chapter 9 for more about writing your own exception handlers.

4.4.2 *<form-beans>*

The Struts ActionForm (`org.apache.struts.action.ActionForm`) provides a handy place to store the input properties submitted with an HTTP request. But to store the input properties, the controller must first create an ActionForm and save it in the request or session context, where the rest of the framework components—such as JSP tags—can find it.

When there are several forms on an input page, each needs a different attribute name for its ActionForm object. So, we can't just use one standard name. Since the bean's attribute name is part of its public API, we should be able to provide developer-friendly names for the ActionForm—*logonForm*, for example.

Some flavors of ActionForms, such as DynaActionForms (`org.apache.struts.action.DynaActionForm`), need to be passed additional properties when they are created. So, we need a place to put these elements as well.

The ActionFormBean (`org.apache.struts.action.ActionFormBean`) resolves all of these issues by serving as a descriptor for an ActionForm object. Each ActionFormBean has properties that describe an ActionForm's attribute name and type. The ActionFormBean can also contain property attributes to use with DynaActionForms.

The Struts configuration file provides a `<form-bean>` element to catalog the ActionFormBeans used by a module. Each ActionFormBean is created by a corresponding `<form-bean>` element. At runtime, the controller calls up the appropriate ActionFormBean to find out which ActionForm object to create, where to store it, and what attribute name to use.

Here's an example of a `<form-bean>` element for a conventional ActionForm and another for a DynaActionForm:

```
<form-bean
  name="menuForm"
  type="org.apache.struts.scaffold.MenuForm"/>

<form-bean
  name="logonForm"
  type="org.apache.struts.action.DynaActionForm">
<form-property
  name="username"
  type="java.lang.String"/>
<form-property
  name="password"
  type="java.lang.String"/>
 </form-bean>
```

The menuForm `<form-bean>` represents a conventional ActionForm subclass; it requires that a corresponding Java class be maintained. The logonForm `<form-bean>` does not require use of a specialized subclass, but can use the DynaAction-Form as is. (DynamicActionForms were introduced in Struts 1.1.)

See chapter 5 for more about ActionForms, including DynaActionForms.

4.4.3 *<global-forwards>*

By centralizing detail, the Struts configuration minimizes change. When circumstances change, most of the implementation detail can be changed through the configuration without touching any of the Java or JSP code.

One of the thorniest details in a web application is the Uniform Resource Identifiers (URI) [W3C, URI]. Most URIs map directly to physical files in the application's directory tree. This makes life easy for conventional websites. To "put a page on the web," you just need to save the page to one of the website's directories. The directories are already mapped to the site's public URI, and there is nothing else to configure. Publishing a web page is just a matter of transferring a file.

This is great until you want to move the page or decide to use a different page instead. When that happens (and it always does), you have to update all your references to the page wherever they appear in your application.

If you miss any, and there's still a reference to the old page someplace, you've created what our database friends call an "update anomaly." Two facts that are supposed to be the same are now different.

The database solution to this problem is *normalization*. We put the fact in a table and have everyone look it up from the table. If the fact changes, then we just update the fact table, and everyone stays on the same page.

The Struts answer to a URI table is the *ActionForward*. An ActionForward associates a logical name with an URI. Other components can refer to the name without knowing anything about the URI. If the URI changes, we change its ActionForward. When other components ask for the ActionForward's path, they then get the updated URI. As usual, by encapsulating detail behind a logical name, we minimize change and reduce the potential for error.

The major consumers of ActionForwards are the Action objects. When an Action completes, it returns an ActionForward or null. If the Action does not return null, the ActionServlet forwards control to whatever path is returned by the ActionForward. Typically, the Action will look up the ActionForward by name and does not need to know anything about URIs. You can deploy global ActionForwards within the `<global-forwards>` element, like these:

```
<global-forwards>
        <forward
            name="logoff"
            path="/logoff.do"/>
        <forward
            name="logon"
            path="/logon.do"/>
        <forward
            name="welcome"
            path="/welcome.do"/>
</global-forwards>
```

These forwards are available to all the Actions in your application. You can also deploy local ActionForwards with the `<action>` element. These local forwards are available only to that ActionMapping.

See chapter 6 for more about ActionForwards.

4.4.4 *<action-mappings>*

ActionForms store data that the application needs to collect. ActionForwards catalog what URIs the application will use. *ActionMappings* describe what operations, or commands, the application can undertake.

The Action object handles the actual work of an operation. But a number of administrative details are associated with an operation. The ActionMapping is used to package those details.

One important detail is what URI [W3C, URI] will be used to call the Action object. The Action's URI is used as the logical identifier, or *path*, for the ActionMapping. When a web browser makes a request for an Action's URI, the ActionServlet first looks for a corresponding ActionMapping. The ActionMapping tells the ActionServlet which Action object to use for its URI.

Besides the URI path and Action type, an ActionMapping contains several other properties that can be used to control what happens when an Action is called. Changing these properties can change how the Action object behaves. This helps developers get more use out of the same Action object. Without an ActionMapping object, developers would need to create many more Action classes than they do now.

You can also use an ActionMapping to simply forward or redirect control to another path. But most often they are used in connection with an Action object.

The `<action-mappings>` element describes the set of ActionMapping objects (`org.apache.struts.action.ActionMapping`) that our application will use to process requests. For the request to reach our application and then our Action-Servlet, it must match the context and `url-pattern` we registered with the container. Since all the requests match this pattern, we do not need to use the context or `url-pattern` to identify an ActionMapping. So if the URL is for

```
http://localhost/myApp/myAction.do
```

we only need to refer to

```
/myAction
```

as the ActionMapping path. Each ActionMapping is created by a corresponding `<action>` element, nested within the `<action-mappings>` element, as shown here:

```
<action-mappings>
    <action
        path="/logoff"
        type="app.LogoffAction"/>
    <action
        path="/logonSubmit"
        type="app.LogonAction"
        name="logonForm"
        scope="request"
        validate="true"
        input="/pages/Logon.jsp"/>
    <action
        path="/logon"
        type="app.ContinueAction">
        <forward
            name="continue"
            path="/pages/Logon.jsp"/>
    </action>
    <action
        path="/welcome"
        type="app.ContinueAction">
        <forward
            name="continue"
```

```
                    path="/pages/Welcome.jsp"/>
    </action>
```

An ActionMapping can refer to over a dozen properties. Next to the Action objects, ActionMappings are probably the most important part of a Struts application. For more about ActionMappings, see chapter 7.

4.4.5 *<controller>*

Struts allows multiple application modules to share a single controller servlet. Each module has its own Struts configuration and can be developed independently of the other modules. The `<controller>` element allows each module to specify a different set of configuration parameters for the ActionServlet. Most of these were originally `<init-params>` set in the deployment descriptor.

The attributes set by the `<controller>` element are stored in a Controller-Config bean (`org.apache.struts.config.ControllerConfig`). A Controller-Config is created for every application module, including the default root module. If the module's struts-config provides a `<controller>` element, it is used to set the properties on the module's ControllerConfig bean.

Since the modules share the ActionServlet, you can also plug in a different RequestProcessor for each module. This lets each module process a request in its own way without subclassing the shared servlet.

Here's a `<controller>` element that sets the `nocache` and `null` configuration properties to true and loads a custom request processor:

```
<controller
   nocache="true"
   null="true"
   processorClass="com.myCompany.struts.RequestProcessor"/>
```

The RequestProcessor is the heart of the ActionServlet's processing cycle. In most cases, you should be able to write and load a RequestProcessor as an alternative to creating your own ActionServlet subclass. See chapter 9 for more about the ActionServlet and RequestProcessors.

4.4.6 *<message-resources>*

Each module should have a default message resource bundle. This is the bundle that Struts components, like the JSP tags, will use when no other is specified. You may also want to load additional bundles with specialized message templates. For example, many developers like to keep a separate bundle with image-related messages.

The `<message-resources>` element is used to deploy whatever bundles your application may need to use. Here's an example of a `<message-resources>` element that deploys the default bundle for this module, and another that deploys a bundle for image messages:

```
<message-resources
  parameter="resources.application"/>

<message-resources
  parameter="resources.image"/>
```

When needed, the framework will look for the default message bundle in a file named application.properties in a package named `resources`. The package, or file folder, can be anyplace on the container's classpath. Typically, the bundles are either in a JAR file or under the WEB-INF/classes folder.

If a JSP tag, or other component, specifies the resources.image bundle, the framework will look for a file named image.properties in the `resources` package.

See section 4.5 of this chapter for more about message resources and chapter 13 for more about localizing applications.

4.4.7 *<plug-in>*

 It's not unusual for an Action to need special resources to get its job done. It may need to use a connection pool that is not DataSource compliant. It may need to create application beans for its forms to use. It may need to read its own configuration file to create a series of objects, in the same way the struts-config does.

In a conventional web application, these tasks would usually be delegated to a special servlet. In a Struts application, we tend to delegate everything to Actions instead. When an Action needs to initialize and destroy its own resources, it can implement the `PlugIn` interface (`org.apache.struts.action.PlugIn`). This interface declares `init` and `destroy` methods that the controller can call at the appropriate times.

The PlugIn Action can then be registered with the Struts configuration via the `<plug-in>` element. Here's the standard plug-in for initializing the Struts Validator:

```
<plug-in className="org.apache.struts.validator.ValidatorPlugIn">
<set-property
  property="pathname"
  value="/WEB-INF/validator-rules.xml"/>
<set-property
  property="pathname"
  value="/WEB-INF/validation.xml"/>
</plug-in>
```

See chapter 9 for more about the ActionServlet and PlugIn Actions.

4.4.8 <data-sources>

While the Struts framework is model-neutral (see chapter 2), it may still need to interact with the business and even the data-access layers. It is not unusual for a component to expect the caller to pass it a live SQL Connection (java.sql. Connection). This then makes the caller (for example, Struts) responsible for managing the connection's life cycle.

To provide applications more flexibility in the way they connect to data-access components, the JDBC 2.0 Standard Extension package offers a factory-based approach to acquiring connections. The preferred way for an application to connect to a database, or other data service, is to go through an object that implements the DataSource interface (javax.sql.DataSource).

In a web application, a DataSource object usually represents a pool of connections that can be shared by all users of the application. Acquiring a database connection can be expensive, in terms of both time and other resources. Typically, a web application logs on to the database under a single account and then manages the security concerns for individual users on its own.

To help developers work with connections, Struts provides a DataSource management component. You can use this component to instantiate and configure any object that implements DataSource and that can be configured entirely from JavaBean properties.

If your database management system does not provide its own component that meets these two requirements, you can use the Jakarta Commons DataBase Connection Pool BasicDataSource class (org.apache.commons.dbcp.BasicData-Source). In Struts 1.1, the Struts GenericDataSource (org.apache.struts. util.GenericDataSource) is a wrapper around the BasicDataSource class. (The Struts class is now deprecated and provided only for backward compatibility.)

If your database management system provides its own DataSource that can be used with Struts, you should consider using that implementation instead. Using the BasicDataSource or GenericDataSource with Struts is no more efficient than using any other class. Choose the implementation that will work best in your environment.

You can also configure more than one DataSource and then select them by name. This feature can be used to provide better security or scalability, or to compare one DataSource implementation with another.

Here's a DataSource configuration that uses the Struts default with a MySQL database:

```
<data-sources>
   <data-source>
     <set-property property="maxCount"
                        value="4"/>
     <set-property property="minCount"
                        value="2"/>
     <set-property property="description"
                        value="Artimus:MySQL Data Source Configuration"/>
     <set-property property="driverClass"
                        value="org.gjt.mm.mysql.Driver"/>
     <set-property property="url"
                        value="jdbc:mysql://localhost:3306/artimus"/>
     <set-property property="autoCommit"
                        value="true"/>
     <set-property property="user"
                        value="root"/>
     <set-property property="password"
                        value=""/>
   </data-source>
</data-sources>
```

Unlike the other struts-config elements, the `<data-source>` element relies heavily on the `<set-property>` element. Since developers will often need to configure their own DataSource subclass, fewer attributes were built into the `<data-source>` element. The DataSource objects are a bridge between Struts and the data-access layer. The other components in the configuration make up the Struts control layer.

4.4.9 *Rolling your own*

If you subclass any of the struts-config objects, you can use the `<set-property>` element to pass your own properties to your subclass. This lets you extend the framework classes without changing how the configuration file is parsed. Here's an example of passing an XSL stylesheet reference to a (hypothetical) custom implementation of the ActionForward object:

```
<global-forwards type="app.struts.XslForward">
  <forward name="logon">
    <set-property property="styleName"
      value="default"/>
    <set-property property="stylePath"
      value="/logon.xsl"/>
  </forward>
</global-forwards>
```

When the XslForward object for the `logon` element is instantiated, the Digester will also call the equivalent of

```
logon.setStyleName("default");
logon.setStylePath("/logon.xls");
```

You can use this approach with any of the Struts configuration elements, making all the objects fully pluggable.

4.4.10 *A skeleton Struts config*

Listing 4.2 is a skeleton Struts configuration file showing the most commonly used elements and attributes. This file is much like the one that ships with the Struts Blank application.

Listing 4.2   A skeleton struts-config

```xml
<?xml version="1.0" encoding="ISO-8859-1" ?>
<!DOCTYPE struts-config PUBLIC
"-//Apache Software Foundation//DTD Struts Configuration 1.1//EN"
"http://jakarta.apache.org/struts/dtds/struts-config_1_1.dtd">
<struts-config>

  <data-sources>
    <data-source>
 <set-property
        name="${}"
        value="${}"/>
    </data-source>
  </data-sources>

  <form-beans>
    <form-bean
        name="${}"
        type="${}">
    <form-property
        name="${}"
        type="${}"/>
    </form-bean>
  </form-beans>

  <global-exceptions>
    <exception
        type="${}"
        key="${}"
        path="${}"/>
  </global-exceptions>

  <global-forwards>
    <forward
        name="${}"
        path="${}"/>
  </global-forwards>

  <action-mappings>
```

```
<action
    path="${}"
    type="${}"
    name="${}"
    scope="${}"
    validate="${}"
    input="${}">
    <forward
        name="${}"
        path="${}"/>
    <exception
        type="${}"
        key="${}"
        path="${}"/>
    </action>
</action-mappings>

<controller processorClass="${}"  />

<message-resources
  parameter="${}"/>

<plug-in
  className="${}">
  <set-property
      property="${}"
      value="${}"/>
</plug-in>
</struts-config>
```

For the complete listing of Struts configuration elements and attributes, see the struts-config API in appendix B.

4.5 *The application resources file*

The Struts framework provides a capable and flexible messaging system. We touched on this system in chapter 3, and chapter 13 covers it more extensively. In this section, we discuss the configuration files needed to get the system up and running. In section 4.4.6, we looked at how you tell Struts *where* to find your resource bundle. In this section, we look at *how* you create the resource bundle. The text for the messages is stored in a standard Java Propertics file (`java.util.Properties`). In the Java and JSP code, a key for the message is given; the text of the message is retrieved from the Properties file at runtime. The framework documentation refers to the message Properties file as the *application resources* or *message resource bundle*.

If you want to localize your application, you can include additional application resources files for the locales you would like to support. This creates a *resource bun-*

dle (`java.util.ResourceBundle`). The framework maintains a standard Locale object for each user (`java.util.Locale`). The best message for the user's locale will be automatically selected from the resource bundle. For more about localizing Struts applications, see chapter 13.

DEFINITIONS A *Locale* object is an identifier for a particular combination of language and region.

ResourceBundle objects contain locale-specific objects. When you need a locale-specific object, you fetch it from a ResourceBundle, which returns the object that matches the end user's locale. The Struts framework uses a String-based bundle for text messages.

The Properties file itself is a plain-text file with a key-value pair on each line. You can create one with any plain-text editor, including Windows Notepad.

The default name for the application resources file is determined by passing an initialization parameter to the Struts ActionServlet in your web.xml. As you can see in this code snippet, the parameter's name is `application`:

```
<init-param>
    <param-name>application</param-name>
    <param-value>application</param-value>
</init-param>
```

There is no default value for this parameter. It must be specified before you can use a Struts application resources bundle in your application.

The application resources file must be on your application's CLASSPATH for Struts to find it. The best thing is to place it with your application's class files. This would either be under WEB-INF/classes or in a JAR file under WEB-INF/lib if you are deploying your binaries files that way.

The `param-value` should be the fully qualified name of your file in package format. This means that if you're putting your application resources file directly under classes, you can just state the filename, as shown in the previous code snippet.

If you are putting the file under a subdirectory, then that directory equates to a Java package. If the application resources bundle is in a subdirectory named resources, you would specify it like this:

```
<init-param>
    <param-name>application</param-name>
    <param-value>resources.application</param-value>
</init-param>
```

The system path to the physical file would then be

```
WEB-INF/classes/resources/application.properties
```

If you moved the classes to a JAR, nothing would need to be changed. Struts would find it in the JAR instead, along with your other classes.

To localize your application, add resource files for each supported local by appending the locale identifier to the base name, as shown here:

```
WEB-INF/classes/resources/
        application.properties
        application_es.properties
        application_fr_CA.properties
```

The `application` name is only a convention. There is no framework default. You can change the name to whatever works best for you. Another common default is to use `ApplicationResources` as the base name, since that was used in some early Struts examples.

For more about Properties files and resource bundles, see the Sun Java Tutorial, Internationalization Trail [Sun, i18n] along with chapter 13 of this book.

The Ant build file presented later in this chapter helps you manage application resources bundles by automatically copying them from your source tree to the binary class folder when the application is built. This keeps the original files with the rest of the source code.

4.6 *The Ant build file*

While not strictly a necessary part of using or configuring Struts, many developers now rely on Ant and its build file to assemble, deploy, and even test their applications. The build.xml file from our logon application (see chapter 2) is based on the pragmatic skeleton file provided with our blank Struts application.

This build file is set up to use a project tree that stores the source code in a subdirectory under WEB-INF. This puts the entire application, source and binaries, together in the same subdirectory system. This can be the application's working directory on your development server. If your container is good about reloading class files, you can rebuild your application and try the latest changes without restarting.

See section 3.4.3 for a schematic of the source tree this build.xml expects. Listing 4.3 shows our simple build.xml file in its entirety.

Listing 4.3   The logon application's build.xml file

```xml
<!-- ❶ -->
<project name="logon" basedir="." default="dist">
<property name="project.title" value="Logon"/>
<property name="project.version" value="1.2"/>
<property name="dist.name" value="logon"/>

    <!-- ❷ -->
    <path id="project.class.path">
        <pathelement path="lib/struts.jar"/>
        <pathelement path="./classes/"/>
        <pathelement path="${classpath}"/>
    </path>

    <!-- ❸ -->
    <target name="prepare">
        <tstamp/>
    </target>

  <!-- ❹ -->
  <target name="resources">
      <copy todir="classes" includeEmptyDirs="no">
          <fileset dir="src/resources">
          <patternset>
              <include name="**/*.properties"/>
          </patternset>
          </fileset>
      </copy>
  </target>

    <!-- ❺ -->
    <target name="compile" depends="prepare,resources">
        <!-- property name="build.compiler" value="jikes"/ -->
        <javac srcdir="src" destdir="classes">
            <classpath refid="project.class.path"/>
        </javac>
    </target>

    <!-- ❻ -->
    <target name="clean" description="Prepare for clean build">
      <delete dir="classes"/>
      <mkdir  dir="classes"/>
    </target>

    <!-- ❼ -->
    <target name="javadoc" description="Generate JavaDoc API docs">
        <delete dir="./doc/api"/>
        <mkdir dir="./doc/api"/>
        <javadoc sourcepath="./src/java"
            destdir="./doc/api"
            classpath="lib/struts.jar:"
            packagenames="app.*"
```

```
                author="true"
                private="true"
                version="true"
                windowtitle=" API Documentation"
                doctitle="&lt;h1&gt;${project.title} Documentation (Version
    ${project.version})&lt;/h1&gt;"
                bottom="Copyright &#169; 2002"/>
      </target>

      <!-- ❽ -->
      <target name="dist" description="Create binary distribution">
        <delete dir="./dist"/>
        <mkdir dir="./dist"/>
        <war warfile="./dist/${dist.name}.war"
                webxml="../WEB-INF/web.xml"
                manifest="../META-INF/MANIFEST.MF"
                basedir="../"
                excludes="WEB-INF/dist,WEB-INF/web.xml,META-INF/MANIFEST.MF"/>
      </target>

      <!-- ❾ -->
      <target name="project" depends="clean,prepare,compile,javadoc,dist"/>
    </project>
```

❶ The *project* block gives the overall build file a name, and specifies the base directory and the default target. When Ant loads the file, the target is the first block it
calls. To use a different target, change the default and save the file or override the
target on the command line. The default base directory is set to be the build.xml's
current directory. Other parts of the script assume that this is the WEB-INF folder,
and will look for the source code in a subdirectory under the base directory. Several other properties are set in this block that are used later. To use this file for
another application, you can just change these properties and leave the rest of the
build file be.

❷ The *path* block builds the classpath Ant will use when building our application. It
is executed each time regardless of what target is selected. Generally, this would
be a list of whatever JARs are in the WEB-INF/lib folder.

❸ The *prepare* target helps minimize the classes Ant compiles by comparing the
timestamp of the class file against the source file.

❹ The *resources* target copies any Properties files (`java.util.Properties`) from
the source tree to the classes tree. This way, you can keep the original Properties
files with the rest of your source code.

❺ The *compile* target first calls the *prepare* and *resources* targets and then builds your
source files. Either Jikes [Jikes] or the standard javac compiler can be used.

❻ The *clean* target ensures that everything will be rebuilt from scratch by dropping and restoring the classes folder.

❼ The *javadoc* target builds the JavaDocs for the application. Generally, you will need to specify the same JARs on the JavaDoc classpath as we specified for the project's path. Note that this is a *colon*-separated list. The JavaDoc compiler will complain if it cannot find a class but should still generate documentation for the classes it does find.

❽ The *dist* target creates a Web Archive (WAR) file for your application. This can be used to deploy your application on your production server.

❾ The *project* target builds everything from scratch and prepares a binary distribution.

For more about Ant, we highly recommend you read *Java Development with Ant* [Hatcher].

4.7 Configuring the Struts core

So far, we've covered the four files that you need to create or customize to get your Struts application up and running:

- The deployment descriptor (web.xml)
- The Struts configuration file (struts-config.xml)
- The application resources bundle (application.properties)
- The Ant build file (build.xml)

Now, let's put it all together as a Struts configuration checklist.

4.7.1 Installing Java and a Java servlet container

The first step is to set up a servlet container, like Tomcat. We walked through this in chapter 1, but here's a quick checklist for Windows that starts you from scratch:

- Download and install Java 1.4 (or later) from the JavaSoft website [Sun, Java].
- Download and install Tomcat 4 LE (or later) from Jakarta [ASF, Tomcat].

Of course, Struts works with other web containers and other Java Virtual Machines. These are only suggestions. The documentation in the Struts distribution includes the technical specifications and notes on configuring various servlet containers.

4.7.2 *Installing a development environment*

We touched on setting up a development environment in chapter 3. Struts works well in most Java environments. If you don't already have one, a good place to start is with jEdit and Ant:

- Download and install Ant 1.4 (or later) [ASF, Ant].

- Download and install jEdit [jEdit].

- Install the Ant add-in for jEdit.

But again, these are only suggestions. If you are already using something else, it should work just as well.

4.7.3 *Installing the Struts core files*

All the stock files that you need to run Struts are provided in the Struts library distribution (jakarta-struts-1.1-lib.zip). These include several JARs, the tag library descriptors, DTDs, and standard XML configuration files. This set of stock files, combined with the four files you provide, create a complete core Struts configuration.

Here's the checklist:

- Download and unzip the Struts library distribution [ASF, Struts].

- Copy all the *.jar files to your application's /WEB-INF/lib folder.

- Copy all the *.tld files to your /WEB-INF folder.

- Copy all the *.xml and *.dtd files to your /WEB-INF folder.

- Create your deployment descriptor (see 4.2).

- Create your Struts configuration file (see 4.4).

- Create your message resources bundle (see 4.5).

- Create your Ant build file (see 4.6).

4.8 *Configuring the Tiles framework*

Tiles, an optional component of the Struts framework, is a powerful page assembly tool and really a framework in its own right. We cover using Tiles in chapter 11. You do not need to use or configure Tiles to use the rest of the Struts framework. But if you would like to use Tiles, here's the drill.

NOTE This Tiles setup example is based on Struts 1.1 beta release 2. The procedure changed between beta 1 and beta 2 and could change again by Struts 1.1 final. Please check the book's website [Husted] for any errata.

All of the files you will need to use Tiles are provided with the Struts library distribution (see section 4.7). If you based your application on the Struts Blank application (see section 4.10) or have otherwise already installed everything from the Struts library distribution folder to your application's /WEB-INF or /WEB-INF/lib folder, then the essential files should already be present.

Here's the Tiles checklist:

1 Copy the struts-tiles.tld and tiles-config.dtd files (if missing) from the Struts lib folder to your /WEB-INF folder.

2 Insert the following block (if missing) in your /WEB-INF/web.xml file, next to any other `<taglib>` elements:

```
<taglib>
        <taglib-uri>/tags/tiles</taglib-uri>
        <taglib-location>/WEB-INF/tiles.tld</taglib-location>
</taglib>
```

3 Create a blank tiles-defs.xml (if missing) in your /WEB-INF folder, like this one:

```
<!DOCTYPE tiles-definitions PUBLIC
        "-//Apache Software Foundation//DTD Tiles Configuration//EN"
        "http://jakarta.apache.org/struts/dtds/tiles-config.dtd">

<tiles-definitions>
    <!-- skeleton definition
    <definition
name="${name}"
path="${path}">
      <put
name="${name}"
value="${value}"/>
   </definition>
    end blank definition -->
</tiles-definitions>
```

4 Insert this `<plug-in>` element into your struts-config.xml, just before the closing `</struts-config>` element:

```
<plug-in className="org.apache.struts.tiles.TilesPlugin" >
    <set-property
        property="definitions-config"
    value="/WEB-INF/tiles-defs.xml" />
</plug-in>
```

For examples of working Tiles applications, see the Tiles example application that is bundled with the Struts distribution as well as our Artimus 1.1 example application from chapter 16. The Struts Blank application (see section 4.10) also ships with Tiles enabled.

For an example of a working Tiles application for Struts 1.0, see our Artimus 1.0 example application in chapter 15.

4.9 *Configuring the Struts Validator*

Like Tiles, the Struts Validator is an optional component of the Struts framework. We cover using the Struts Validator in chapter 12. You do not need to use or configure the Validator to use the rest of the Struts framework. But if you would like to use the Validator, here's the drill.

> **NOTE** This Validator setup example is based on Struts 1.1 beta release 2. The procedure changed between beta 1 and beta 2 and could change again by Struts 1.1 final. Please check the book's website [Husted] for any errata.

All of the files you will need to use the Validator are provided with the Struts library distribution (see section 4.7). If you based your application on the Struts Blank application (see section 4.10) or have otherwise already installed everything from the Struts library distribution folder to your application's /WEB-INF or /WEB-INF/lib folder, then the essential files should already be present.

Here's the Validator checklist:

1 Copy the struts-validator.tld and validator-rules.xml files (if missing) from the Struts library distribution to your /WEB-INF folder.

2 Insert the following block (if missing) in your /WEB-INF/web.xml file, next to any other `<taglib>` elements:

```
<taglib>
        <taglib-uri>/tags/validator</taglib-uri>
        <taglib-location>/WEB-INF/struts-validator.tld</taglib-location>
</taglib>
```

3 Create a blank validations.xml (if missing) in your /WEB-INF folder, like this one:

```
<form-validation>
    <formset>
        <!-- skeleton form -->
    <form name="${}">
```

```
            <field
                property="${}"
                depends="${}">
                    <arg0 key="${}"/>
            </field>
        </form>
        end skeleton form -->
    </formset>
</form-validation>
```

4 Insert this `<plug-in>` element at the end of your /WEB-INF/struts-config.xml immediately before `</struts-config>`:

```
<plug-in className="org.apache.struts.validator.ValidatorPlugIn">
    <set-property
      property="pathnames"
      value="/WEB-INF/validator-rules.xml,/WEB-INF/validation.xml"/>
</plug-in>
```

For examples of working Validator applications, see the Validator example application that is bundled with the Struts binary distribution as well as our Artimus 1.1 example application from chapter 16. The Struts Blank application (see section 4.10) also ships with Validator enabled.

For an example of a working Validator application for Struts 1.0, see our Artimus 1.0 example application in chapter 15.

4.10 Getting started with the Struts Blank application

The *Struts Blank* application in the Struts binary distribution provides a skeleton configuration that new applications can adopt and adapt. It contains all the base files from the distribution and starter versions of the four configuration files that developers provide (see section 4.7), along with skeleton configurations for Tiles and the Validator.

Struts Blank is distributed as a WAR file. To get started all you need to do is

1 Copy the struts-blank.war file from the webapps folder in the Struts binary distribution to the WAR deployment directory for your container (usually webapps).

2 Rename struts-blank.war to the name you want to use for your application.

3 Start or restart your servlet container.

The Struts Blank application will deploy under the name for your new application. If you access the default page

```
http://localhost/myApp
```

your new blank application will display a simple welcome page.

The Blank application does not ship with any Java source files—that's your job—but it does include the files and pages that we've summarized in table 4.3.

Table 4.3   The Struts Blank starter files

Filename	Purpose
/index.jsp	A stock welcome page that forwards to a Struts Welcome action.
/pages/Welcome.jsp	A Welcome JSP reached through the Welcome action.
/classes/resources/application.properties	The deployed ApplicationResource files. This is a working copy; the original is kept with the other source code files.
/WEB-INF/struts-config.xml	A starter Struts configuration file with commented examples of common elements.
/WEB-INF/tiles-def.xml	A starter Tiles configuration file with commented examples of some definitions.
/WEB-INF/validator-rules.xml	The standard Validator configuration file that sets up the basic validators.
/WEB-INF/validations.xml	A starter Validations configuration file where you would describe your own forms.
/WEB-INF/*.tld	The tag library descriptor files for the Struts taglibs.
/WEB-INF/lib/*.jar	The JARs upon which the framework classes depend.
/WEB-INF/src/build.xml	A working Ant build file.
/WEB-INF/src/java/	A starter directory for your Java source files.
/WEB-INF/src/resources/application.properties	The original application.properties file. Edit this one and then rebuild.

The Struts Blank application is designed to make it easy for you to get started on a Struts project. If you deploy it on a local copy of a servlet container, like Tomcat or Resin, you can start working on it right away. The build file is designed so that you can work on the application "in place" and just restart the container, or reload the application as you go.

If you are working on a team, you may need to use a different layout since you may need to check files in and out. But the simple things can still be simple, and the Struts Blank application makes getting started with Struts very simple indeed!

The one thing to note is that the build.xml file refers to some paths on your local system that may or may not exist:

```
<property name=" jdbc20ext.jar"
value="/javasoft/lib/jdbc2_0-stdext.jar"/>
<property name="servlet.jar"
value="/javasoft/lib/servlet.jar"/>
<property name="distpath.project"
value="/projects/lib"/>
```

The jdbc2_0-stdext.jar and servlet.jar are needed to generate the JavaDocs. The Blank build.xml will look for these under a /javasoft/lib folder on your default drive. If necessary, you can change the path setting in build.xml to point to wherever you keep these JARs:

- Your container should include a servlet.jar for the servlet API it supports (for example, 2.2 or 2.3). Tomcat 4 keeps its servlet.jar in the $TOMCAT/ common/lib folder.

- The jdbc2_0-stdext.jar is included with the Struts library distribution. It is not bundled with the Struts web applications. Many containers, like Tomcat, will share a copy of this JAR. Putting another in the WEB-INF/lib folder could possibly cause conflicts.

The other directory is a location to hold a distribution WAR for your application. This can be used to deploy your application on a production server when development is complete or when you are ready for testing. Again, you can change the path or create the directory. The Blank build.xml factory setting is /projects/lib on your default drive.

4.11 *Configuring modular applications*

A key benefit of the Struts architecture is that you can guarantee that all requests flow through a single point of control. Developers can centralize functionality that should be applied to every request and avoid repeating code throughout the application. Since Java is a multithreaded platform, Struts' use of a single controller servlet also provides the best possible performance. Developers write less code and the machine runs faster on fewer resources. Pretty good deal all around.

In Struts 1.0, the singleton mindset ran all the way down to the Struts configuration files. They came one to a customer. If several developers were working on an application, they needed to find a way to manage updates to the Struts configuration.

In practice, developers working on teams tend to divide their work up into logical units, much the same way we divvy up Java code into packages. It's not unusual for team members to have their own "namespace" within the application. In an online auction application, one team might be working on the registration module; another team may be working on the bidding module. The first team might have a /reg folder for their JSP pages and an app.reg package for their Java code. Likewise, team 2 might have a /bid folder for their JSP pages and an app.bid package for their Java code. In the message resource file, each team might also prefix their message keys with reg. or bid.

Of course, you don't need to be on a large team to want to organize a large project in this way. Many solo developers do the same thing. Limiting the number of files in a folder or classes in a package is considered good project management. Many developers will organize an application into logical modules whether or not they need to share files.

4.11.1 *Divide and conquer*

In Struts 1.1, the idea of dividing an application into modules became more than a convention—it's now built into the framework. Let's step back and take a look at how Struts organizes an application into modules.

The web application container lets us share use of the server by creating a context for each application. This context maps to a subdirectory in the server's webapp directory. In the same way, Struts 1.1 lets you share use of an application by creating a prefix for each application. Multiple modules can run within the same application space, each under its own prefix, in much the same way that multiple applications can run in the same server space—each under its own context.

When we write web applications, we often refer to a context-relative URI. This is a path that does not include the name, or context, of our application. Likewise, when we write Struts applications, we often refer to a module-relative URI. Not surprisingly, this is a path that does not include the module-name, or prefix, of our module. Table 4.4 shows the absolute, context-relative, and module-relative portions of the same URI.

Table 4.4   Absolute, context-relative, and module-relative portions of the same URI

Portion	URI
absolute URL	http://localhost/myApp/myModule/myAction.do
domain-relative	/myApp/myModule/myAction.do
context-relative	/myModule/myAction.do
module-relative	/myAction.do

Just as you can write a web application and configure it to run under any context, you can write a Struts application module and configure it to run under any prefix. Writing a module is not much different than writing a stand-alone application. All the real configuration takes place in the deployment descriptor. If you move a module from the prefix to the root, or from the root to the prefix, or to another prefix, none of the JSPs, Java code, or XML code in the module needs to change.

To set up an application to use separate reg and bid modules, we could configure our servlet descriptor like this:

```
<servlet>
  <servlet-name>action</servlet-name>
   <servlet-class>org.apache.struts.action.ActionServlet</servlet-class>
    <!-- The default  (or "root") module  -->
     <init-param>
       <param-name>config</param-name>
       <param-value>/WEB-INF/struts-config.xml</param-value>
     </init-param>

     <!-- The register module -->
     <init-param>
       <param-name>config/reg</param-name> <-- Includes prefix! -->
       <param-value>/WEB-INF/struts-config-reg.xml</param-value>
     </init-param>

     <!-- The bidding module -->
     <init-param>
       <param-name>config/bid</param-name> <-- Includes prefix! -->
       <param-value>/WEB-INF/struts-config-bid.xml</param-value>
     </init-param>

     <!--  ... other servlet elements  ...  -- >
   </servlet>
```

In this example, the reg team can now work with the struts-config-reg.xml and the bid team can now work with the struts-config-bid.xml. Each can work on their module just as if they were working alone on a single-module application. The framework makes all the adjustments for the module prefix, just as the container can make adjustments for the application context.

Well, almost all the adjustments...

4.11.2 *Prefixing pages*

When the framework adjusts the URIs for a module prefix, it adjusts *all* the URIs, whether they are to an ActionMapping or some other resource in the module's namespace, such as a JSP. Inside the struts-config-bid.xml, we might have a module-relative URI, like /index.do. The context-relative version of this becomes /bid/index.do. Likewise, we might have a reference to /pages/Index.jsp, and the context-relative rendition of this will be /bid/pages/Index.jsp.

Moving the ActionMappings around is easy enough; they're virtual anyway. But many of the URIs reference JSPs, which correlate to physical files. Other URIs may also refer to HTML pages, image files, and so forth.

This means that while the bid team can omit the module prefix from the URIs in the Struts configuration, they still need to know which prefix they are using, so they know where to store their pages. And if the prefix changes, they need to rename that directory. They will not need to change any of the JSP, Java, or XML coding, however, although they will have to synchronize the name of their pages directory with the module name.

This really isn't any different than what we have to do with applications. If we are uploading files to an application, we need to know what context-directory it is under. And if we are uploading files to a module, we need to know what module-directory it is under.

4.11.3 *Retrofitting a configuration*

If you already have a Struts 1.0 application set up like a modular application, the only real trick is to take the module-prefix out of the module's configuration file. If the pages are already under a subdirectory keyed to the module name, they can stay where they are, and you're done. If not, you *should* be able to move them under the module-directory without making any other changes (unless of course, some nasty hardcoded links snuck in where <html:link> tags *should* have been).

4.12 *Sharing the Struts JAR*

The Struts JAR can be shared by all the applications in your web container, if your container supports this functionality. (Most do or soon will.) Consult your container's documentation to learn how to install shared JARs. In most cases, you simply place the Struts JAR in a shared lib folder and then remove it from all the /WEB-INF/lib folders.

For Tomcat 4, the shared library folder is at

```
$TOMCAT/common/lib
```

For a default Windows installation, that would map to \Program Files\Apache Tomcat 4\common\lib.

Of course, this means that all Struts applications sharing this JAR must be using the same version.

4.13 *Summary*

No application is an island. To get all the components of an application working together, you have to create and maintain several configuration files. To get a Struts application up and running, most developers need to provide a Struts configuration file, an application resources file, the web application deployment descriptor file, and an Ant build file. This chapter stepped through the nuts and bolts of creating these files.

A key benefit of the Struts configuration is that it embraces change. Since the implementation details are centralized, a Struts application can be completely rewired from the Struts configuration, without making any changes to Action classes or the presentation pages.

The components initialized by the Struts configuration—ActionForms, ActionForwards, and ActionMappings—form the core of the Struts controller. Taken together, these objects represent the external and internal API of the application—the rest is implementation detail. These core components map out the input to accept, the places to go, and the things to do in your application.

So what's next?

In part 2 of this book, we drill down on each of the core components to help you get the most out of them. In part 3, we focus on the visible portions of your application: the pages. Part 4 puts it all back together again by presenting several case studies using techniques introduced in parts 1 through 3.

But if you are itching to get started, at this point you should have enough knowledge at your fingertips to get started on your own application. Then, if you like, as the rest of the book unfolds, you can refactor, improve, and extend your application as new techniques are introduced.

Part 2

Raising your framework

Part 2 zooms in on each of the core framework components. Our goal is to brief you on how each component works and show you how the component is used by working developers. In most cases, we present several alternative ways to use the components, since we know that different developers and different applications have their own needs.

Coping with ActionForms

Co-authored by Ted Husted and George Franciscus

This chapter covers
- Understanding the ActionForm life cycle
- Examining the responsibilities of an ActionForm
- Discussing ActionForm design characteristics
- Using ActionForm best practices
- Populating and debriefing ActionForms
- Introducing the Scaffold BaseForm

> *The sweat of hard work is not to be displayed. It is much*
> *more graceful to appear favored by the gods.*
>
> —Maxine Hong Kingston,
> *The Woman Warrior: Memoirs of a Girlhood among Ghosts*

5.1 Garbage in, treasure out

People who use web applications often spend a lot of time submitting data through HTML forms. Sometimes it's new data being submitted through a blank form. Other times, it's data that's being updated and submitted again.

HTML forms provide the web developer with two challenges: capturing the data when it submitted and prepopulating a form with any data the user may have to revise. If the user selects an address record that has to be updated, we need to copy the data from that record into an HTML form. This means we must be able to change the page for each request by passing the form *dynamic values*.

HTML does not have a built-in facility for prepopulating a control with dynamic values. A page that needs customization is written to the response at runtime by a component that mixes the static and dynamic HTML together in its own proprietary way.

There are several ways to write dynamic HTML in a Java web application, the most common being JavaServer Pages. The Struts distribution includes a set of JSP tags that you can use to write dynamic HTML controls. Like many taglibs, the Struts tags are designed to work with JavaBeans. As we saw in chapter 1, JavaBeans are simple but powerful objects that follow a set of design guidelines.

Unlike the HTML elements, the Struts tags provide a standard way to populate a control. Each HTML tag corresponds to a standard HTML element. Each JSP tag has a `property` attribute that provides the name of a property on the bean. The return value of the JavaBean property is used as the `value` attribute of the control.

So, if there is an element like this:

```
<input name="address"/>
```

it can be substituted for a Struts JSP tag like this:

```
<html:input property="address"/>
```

The tag retrieves the `address` property from the JavaBean and inserts it as the HTML element's `value`. When the browser gets the markup, it looks something like this:

```
<input name="address" value="6 Lost Feather Drive"/>
```

where calling the `ActionForm`'s `getAddress()` method returns the `String` "6 Lost Feather Drive".

NOTE   In some programming contexts, the word "property" is synonymous with an attribute, field, or variable. In these cases, a property represents a storage location. JavaBean properties will most often use a field to store a value, but the JavaBean "properties" are actually the *methods* that are used to retrieve the value. When we talk about public properties, we are not talking about fields on the JavaBean object. We are talking about the methods that are used to retrieve or set a value. Sometimes these values are stored in a field. Other times, they may be calculated from several fields or retrieved from other objects. The power of JavaBeans is that the object can control how the value is stored but still make it publicly accessible through the mutator and accessor methods.

To complete the process, when the form is submitted to the Struts controller, it converts the HTTP parameters back into a JavaBean. Most of the input from an HTML form will have to be validated before it can be passed to the business tier. If a field is supposed to contain a number, it's our job to make sure it is indeed a number. When validation checks fail, we can pass the JavaBean back to the page. The JSP tags populate the HTML elements from the JavaBean properties, and the user can correct the input and try again.

Any JavaBean can be used with the Struts JSP tags to populate a control. But to provide automatic validation of the input, Struts uses its own JavaBean subclass, called the ActionForm.

Once the input from an HTML form is transformed into an ActionForm bean and the properties are validated, the form's input is delivered to the Action as a nice, tidy JavaBean. The Struts Action object uses the form bean while it conducts the business operation, handles any errors, and selects the response page. Chapter 8 covers the Action object in depth.

5.1.1 ActionForm requirements

Creating an ActionForm subclass is not difficult, but your class must meet some simple requirements:

- An ActionForm must extend from `org.apache.struts.action.ActionForm`. The base ActionForm class cannot be instantiated.

- An ActionForm must define a public property for each HTML control it should harvest from the request. (Struts 1.0 requires both a mutator and accessor for each property. Struts 1.1 is not so strict.)

The ActionForm may also meet the following optional requirements:

- If you want the ActionForm to validate the input before passing it to the Action, you can implement the `validate` method.

- If you want to initialize properties before they are populated, you can implement the `reset` method, which is called before the ActionForm is populated.

Listing 5.1 shows a simple ActionForm class.

Listing 5.1   MyForm.java

```java
import org.apache.struts.action.*;
public class MyForm extends ActionForm {
    protected String name;
    protected String address;

    public String getName()
      {return this.name;};
    public String getAddress()
      {return this.address;};

    public void setName(String name)
      {this.name = name;};
    public void setAddress(String address)
      {this.address = address;};

};
```

In Struts 1.1, you can also use the DynaActionForm class and declare your properties in the Struts configuration file. Listing 5.2 shows the same simple ActionForm as a DynaActionForm.

Listing 5.2   myForm form bean

```
<form-bean
        name="myForm"
        type="org.apache.struts.action.DynaActionForm">
        <form-property
            name="name"
        type="java.lang.String"/>
        <form-property
            name="address"
            type="java.lang.String"/>
</form-bean>
```

For more about the Struts configuration file, see chapter 4.

While the requirements for ActionForms start out simply, they play a surprisingly strong role in the development of many applications. ActionForms may be the most misunderstood aspect of the Struts framework. These hardworking Java-Beans play the role of field harvester, firewall, data buffer, data validator, type transformer, and transfer object.

Sometimes they seem redundant, sometimes they seem invaluable, but at every turn, ActionForms are a focal part of the framework—a key part of what makes Struts Struts.

In this chapter, we explore the ins and outs of the ActionForm so that your application can get the most from this Struts cornerstone class.

5.2   The many faces of an ActionForm

ActionForms are versatile objects. As we explained earlier, they can play the role of field harvester, data buffer, type transformer, and transfer object—all within the span of a single request. Let's step through some of the responsibilities an ActionForm may have in your application.

5.2.1   The ActionForm as a field harvester

Most applications need data from their users. Many applications need *a lot* of data. In a web environment, collecting data presents its own set of challenges. HTML defines a barely adequate set of data-entry controls. HTTP defines a barely adequate protocol for data transfer. Struts uses ActionForms to help compensate for the shortcomings of HTML and HTTP.

HTTP is a surprisingly simple protocol that transfers everything in the most basic way possible. As protocols go, it's easy to implement and even efficient in its own way. But when used for applications, HTTP leaves many implementation details as an exercise for the developer.

Submitting fields via HTTP

When an HTML form is submitted via HTTP, everything is reduced to text. The form elements a web server receives come in as name-value pairs. These are text-only strings, not binary data.

Figure 5.1 shows a simple form, with two fields, Name and Amount. Figure 5.2 shows the URI that a browser would submit for this form.

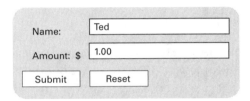

Figure 5.1   A simple form with two fields

```
http://localhost/app/submit.do?name=ted&amount=1.00
```

Figure 5.2   A GET request from a form

The POST method, shown in Figure 5.3, can be used to hide what is submitted, but the result is the same: whatever is typed into the form is submitted as pairs of URL-encoded name-value strings.

```
POST /app/submit.do HTTP/1.0
Content-Type: application/x-www-form-URL-encoded
Content-Length: 22

name=ted
&amount=1.00
```

Figure 5.3   A POST request from a form (simplified)

DEFINITION   The HTTP specification allows form data to be submitted as part of the URI, but not every character can be used in a URI. If other characters are needed by the form data, they must be encoded. *URL encoding* of a character consists of a % symbol, followed by the two-digit hexadecimal representation (not case-sensitive) of the ISO-Latin code point for the character. For more, see RFCs 1738 and 2396 [W3C URL; W3C URI] and the HTML 4.01 specification at 17.13.4 [W3C HTML4].

Submitting files via HTTP

Some forms allow you to attach a file that users can upload. In that case, the attachment is specially encoded so that only text characters are submitted. This workaround lets us transmit binary files via HTTP, but only because the files have been converted to a stream of text characters and then converted back again.

Submitting blank fields via HTTP

If a text field is blank, most browsers will submit a blank parameter. But if a checkbox is blank, the browser may not submit anything at all. The application must deduce that since the checkbox is absent, it must be false or null. In practice, this applies only to checkboxes, but the specification allows a browser to omit any empty field.

Receiving it all via HTTP

Parsing the HTTP text stream looking for name-value pairs is not a pleasant task. The Servlet API provides several useful methods to help you discover what was submitted and pull out just what you need. But a lot of tedious coding can still be involved.

The ActionForm solution

The Struts solution to HTTP parameter handling is to transform the input fields into JavaBean properties. When a property on the ActionForm matches a parameter in the request, the framework automatically sets the property to the value of the parameter. A Struts developer can work with a trusty JavaBean and leave the HTTP rigmarole to the framework.

To harvest request parameters, all the Struts developer needs to do is provide an ActionForm with JavaBean properties that match the names of the HTTP parameters. The rest is automatic.

5.2.2 The ActionForm as a data buffer

In a conventional (non-web) user interface, controls have an internal buffer that captures the user's input so it can be validated. If validation fails, the user can't leave the control. If validation succeeds, the data is transferred to another field of the appropriate type. The developer does not usually "see" the internal buffer, but it's there.

HTML controls do not have a built-in buffer or any *reliable* way to ensure a field is validated before it is submitted. There are things you can do with JavaScript, but JavaScript can be disabled.

The ActionForm serves as the missing buffer for HTML controls. It preserves the input until it can be validated and transferred to another field of the appropriate type. If the user enters letters in an `Integer` field, the original input should be returned, including the invalid characters. A user can see what went wrong, correct the data, and try again. This also means that the ActionForm properties should be `Strings` so that *any* input can be captured, valid or not.

ActionForm fields are not the *destination* of the input, but a *buffer* to be validated before the input is committed.

5.2.3 *The ActionForm as a data validator*

While existing projects will often already have JavaBeans that perform validation, few if any of these beans will be able to buffer invalid input so it can be corrected. The ActionForm's `validate` method is an extension point where you can insert calls to business-tier methods (that know how to validate the data). When validation fails, the ActionForm can ferry the whole shebang back to the web page, where the user can try again.

But ActionForms are not about validation as much as they are about correction. Many fields must be the correct type before they can be processed by the business logic. Data on its way to an `Integer` field must not contain alphabetic characters. If it does, you can have the user correct the data before moving forward.

Usually, this is just a prima facie validation. Knowing that a field is an `Integer` doesn't tell us that it is the *right* `Integer`. Many applications perform validation in two phases. First, they use the ActionForm `validate` method to determine whether the input is the right type and whether it can even be used with the business process. Once that phase is completed, the Action may perform additional validation to determine whether the input matches other requirements of the business tier. If the business validation fails, you can return control to the input page just as if it had failed the ActionForm `validate` method.

The Struts framework gives you the flexibility of handling data validations in the ActionForm, in the Action, or in both, as your needs dictate.

In chapter 12, we explore the Struts Validator, which extends the use of the ActionForm `validate` method.

5.2.4 *The ActionForm as a type transformer*

A sticky point of ActionForms is that they should use only `String` and `boolean` properties. In practice, this means that properties must be converted from one type to another. Most applications also require that some properties, such as telephone numbers or amounts, be formatted in specific ways. The core Java packages provide tools for doing this sort of thing, but cleanly integrating these features into a web application is still a challenge.

Struts developers often include helper methods on ActionForms to help with type conversions and transformations. The helper methods are implemented in various ways, which we cover in section 5.6.

5.2.5 *The ActionForm as a transfer object*

An ActionForm is a carrier for data to be used by another bean or process—which is to say, an ActionForm is a *transfer* object. Like other transfer objects, the data it carries often maps to more than one entity in the persistent store (for example, a database table). But unlike with conventional transfer objects, the individual properties of an ActionForm must be mutable. HTTP will represent each property as a separate name-value pair. It is much simpler if each property can be set independently. By contrast, other transfer objects are often set only when instantiated and cannot be changed afterward.

DEFINITIONS *Transfer objects* (also known as *value objects* [Go3]) are designed to efficiently commute fine-grained data by sending a coarse-grained view of the data. Often used in remote applications, a transfer object can group several related properties so that they can be serialized and sent to the remote server in a single operation.

Mutable means "capable of or subject to change or alteration." Computer programs may contain both mutable and immutable elements. Some objects are designed so that they cannot be changed and are referred to as *immutable*. Most objects are designed so that they can be changed and are referred to as *mutable*.

STRUTS TIP Use coarse-grained ActionForms to reduce class maintenance. In practice, the forms in your application will often share properties. It is often easier to create a base ActionForm with all the properties needed by your forms. If necessary, you can subclass the coarse-grained properties bean and provide specialized `validate` and `reset` methods.

5.2.6 *The ActionForm as a firewall*

When a request is submitted, the ActionServlet uses an autopopulation mechanism to set the request's ActionForm properties from the request parameters. This lets you control which request parameters are accepted by controlling which ActionForm properties are exposed. It also means that you can *lose* control of which parameters are accepted if your ActionForm design is careless. An Action-Form must not include methods that look like JavaBean properties but are not meant to be set from an HTTP request.

You should keep in mind the *automatic* aspect of the population mechanism when you're designing ActionForms. The autopopulation mechanism will happily set from the request whatever public properties are on an ActionForm, whether or not they came from one of the HTML forms. So if you were to reuse a bean as an ActionForm, any public property on that bean—and its super classes—can be set from an HTTP request. Since the references can be nested and chained, any bean that is a member property is also exposed, along with any of its super classes and any of their member properties. If any of these beans can make some immediate change in the system state, then a spoofer could affect that state change—even though it was not an intended use of the program.

If you are creating ActionForms from scratch for their intended purpose, you should have nothing to fear from autopopulation. But some developers like to place business objects on ActionForms so they can pass through values from the request. If you do this, any method that looks like a JavaBean property, and accepts a `String` value, can be invoked from an HTTP request.

An example is the upload buffer size in the ActionServlet. In Struts 1.0, the ActionServlet was exposed as a member property on the ActionForm. This means in Struts 1.0, you could call `ActionServlet.setBufferSize` from any HTTP request to a Struts application. Fortunately, doing that had no effect, since the ActionServlet uses the value only on initialization. However, if the servlet did refer to it at runtime, a spoofer could have set the buffer size to 0, creating a denial-of-service exploit.

Using a bean that can affect the system state as an ActionForm, or part of an ActionForm, is like passing input fields straight through to a shell script. There is no telling what hijinks clever but misguided people may come up with. The ActionForm is like a demilitarized zone (DMZ) in a firewall system: it lets you examine the input being offered before that data is allowed through to the rest of the application.

5.3 *ActionForm design consequences*

The design of ActionForms yields several consequences. An ActionForm may:

- Share property names with business logic beans
- Minimize custom code
- Encapsulate helper methods
- Contain other JavaBeans

5.3.1 *ActionForms may share names*

Since they interact with business logic beans, ActionForms may often use the same set of property names found on a corresponding business logic bean. Usually there is no correlation between the properties, so this is generally a good practice to follow. While the form and logic beans may ultimately represent the same data, they represent the data at different points of its life cycle. The logic beans represent the state of the model. The form beans represent a proposed change to that state. ActionForm beans collect and validate input ("in the wild"). The business logic beans then process the captured data ("back in the office") and incorporate the new data into the model.

So while the beans may share property names and create a common protocol, they really do not share data. Data that *has been* accepted into the model is one thing; data that *may be* accepted into the model is another.

DEFINITION   A *message protocol* (or message interface) is a technique based on reflection that allows objects to share information by observing a common naming convention in lieu of sharing a common hierarchy. Two Java-Beans share the same message protocol if they have properties of the same name that return comparable values. Whether the JavaBeans are of the same class or super class doesn't matter. A message protocol operates by reflection and cares only about the property (or "message") names. Different JavaBeans can use the same Struts JSP as long as the beans follow the same protocol. If the beans have properties of the same name, the Struts tags can find the right methods to call. Many Struts applications will return a bean directly from the business tier and pass it to an HTML form. When that page is submitted, an ActionForm bean sharing the same protocol is used to catch and validate the parameters. If validation fails, control may be returned to the same page. The tags will now use the properties from the ActionForm bean. Each bean was of a different class, but since the JSP tags are based on reflection, the tags do not care as long as the beans use the same message protocol (or set of method names). [Johnson]

5.3.2 *ActionForms may minimize custom code*

In a typical deployment, the code used in an ActionForm is directly related to the presentation layer and often specific to an HTML presentation layer. Custom helper methods, with business-specific outputs, are usually found in the business logic beans, where they can be reused in another environment. Both ActionForms and Action classes are designed to be adaptors, to encourage keeping the business code on the business tier and the presentation code on the presentation tier. See chapter 1 for more about the importance of layers and tiers.

5.3.3 *ActionForms may encapsulate helpers*

In practice, developers find it helpful for an ActionForm to format or validate data according to specific business rules used by their application. Since the ActionForm is a JavaBean, it can pass the input to a business helper method to perform that actual formatting and validating, and then pass the result back to the presentation tier.

Static methods are useful here since the operation is usually a simple filtering process:

```
public String getTelephoneText() {
    return ContactBean.formatTelephone(
        this.telephoneText,getLocale());
}
```

Here, the ActionForm imported a `ContactBean` from the business layer. Most developers agree that the control layer can import from the business layer (but not the other way around!).

5.3.4 *ActionForms may nest other beans*

Both the Struts tag extensions and the autopopulation mechanism support a dotted syntax to access beans with the ActionForm beans. This can be a convenient way to populate an existing bean via an ActionForm. In a JSP page, you can refer to a nested bean like this:

```
<html:text
  property="values.telephoneText"
  size="14"
  maxlength="14"/>
```

This the calls the equivalent of

```
aForm.getValues().getTelephoneText()
```

The browser will then submit the parameter via HTTP as

```
values.telephoneText=555-1234
```

and the autopopulate mechanism will then call the equivalent of

```
aForm.getValues().setTelephoneText((String)request.getParameter("val-
    ues.telephoneText"));
```

Protecting yourself from the Nesting Exploit

When nesting beans, do remember that your ActionForm must be prepared to handle any type of HTTP request, not just the ones submitted from the forms you control. HTTP requests are very easy to spoof. If your nested bean has any methods that accept a `String` parameter and look like a JavaBean property, that method can be passed a value from an HTTP request.

In Struts 1.0, the base ActionForm exposed a servlet property linked to the application's ActionServlet. Access to the servlet was needed to process a multi-part Multipurpose Internet Mail Extension (MIME) request. A side effect was that this query string could be sent to any Struts 1.0 Action to change the `TempDir` property on the ActionServlet at runtime:

```
?servlet.setTempDir=/whatever
```

which calls the equivalent of

```
ActionForm.getServlet().setTempDir("/whatever")
```

In practice, this usually has no effect, since the property is used only at instantiation. In Struts 1.0.1 and later, a wrapper class is used to protect the ActionServlet object:

```
public class ActionServletWrapper {
        protected transient ActionServlet servlet = null;

        public void log (String message, int level) {
                servlet.log(message,level);
        }

        public void log(String message) {
                servlet.log(message);
        }

        public String getMultipartClass() {
                return servlet.multipartClass;
        }
```

```
public void setServletFor(MultipartRequestHandler object) {
        object.setServlet(this.servlet);
}

public ActionServletWrapper (ActionServlet servlet) {
        super();
        this.servlet = servlet;
}
}
```

The wrapper discloses only the properties the framework needs. Other properties of the ActionServlet are protected from tampering.

The Nesting Exploit stresses the fundamental design principle that an object should expose only what it expects to be changed. This is a good principle for designing not only ActionForms but any JavaBean.

Nesting beans is a powerful technique but must be used with care.

5.4 *ActionForm flavors*

In Struts 1.1, two standard alternatives are available to the base ActionForm: map-backed ActionForms and DynaActionForms.

5.4.1 *Map-backed ActionForms*

 Many large web applications need to use hundreds of properties. Developers of these applications chaff at creating and maintaining ActionForm beans that do little more than declare a field, a getter, and a setter. These applications often hook up with a mature business-tier component that is being used with other platforms and is now being adapted to a web application. Since the bean protocol is already well defined, all these applications really want to do is store whatever fields are submitted with a minimum of fuss.

Of course, at the same time, not every property on the form is a simple property—maybe just eight out of ten.

In Struts 1.1, ActionForms can support mapped properties. Among other things, this makes it possible to mix using a Map with conventional JavaBean properties on the same ActionForm. The Map can be used to trap whatever parameters are submitted without defining any of the properties in advance. Each field is just another entry on the Map.

From the ActionForm, you can define these methods to access the entries of your Map:

```
public void setValue(String key, Object value)
public Object getValue(String key)
```

Then you can use this notation in the JSP:

```
<html:text property="value(key)"/>
```

and

```
<bean:write name="formBean" property="value(key)"/>
```

This lets you use a Map for simple properties that do not need to be helped along in any way. The Map still has an accessor, so if a property needs special handling, you can watch for it and interject a helper method. In this code:

```
public Object getValue(String key) throws Exception {
        // telephone number needs to be reformatted.
        if ("telephone".equals(key)) {
            return (Object) getTelephone();
        }
        return getMap().get(key);
    }
```

you need to define an accessor for the telephone property, but everything else can just pass through and be stored in the Map. Transparently calling the telephone property takes a bit more work. But a lot more work is saved by not having to define whatever other properties the ActionForm uses. Since ActionForms may have dozens of simple properties, the savings can be significant.

The trade-off is that the page reference for a mapped value is different than the reference to a standard property. If the pages were already using the standard JavaBean property notation, the JSP code needs to be revised to use the mapped notation instead.

Whereas an HTML tag referred to

```
<html:text property="telephone"/>
```

you would now refer to

```
<html:text property="value(telephone)"/>
```

instead.

The fields stored in the Map are also not exposed as normal JavaBean properties. Some Java development tools let you work directly with JavaBeans. These tools would not see these fields as distinct properties, and you may not get full use of the tools' capabilities.

If seeing each field as a JavaBean property is important, and you also need to minimize property maintenance, then the next thing to consider is the DynaActionForm class.

5.4.2 *DynaActionForms*

 Declaring simple properties in the usual way can add up to a lot of work in a larger application. To create a conventional JavaBean property, you need to code a field, a getter, and a setter—a lot of infrastructure just to say *get this and set that*. It would be much faster and safer if we could just declare the JavaBean properties instead of having to code each one.

The DynaActionForm (`org.apache.struts.action.DynaActionForm`) is designed so that you can specify simple JavaBean properties through the Struts configuration file, as we saw back in listing 5.2. The DynaActionForm is based on the DynaBean component of the Jakarta Commons [ASF, Commons]. This is a clever object that stores the fields in an internal map but exposes them as standard JavaBean properties.

You can use a DynaActionForm anywhere an ActionForm can be used. You can also substitute a DynaActionForm for a conventional ActionForm without changing any of the existing Java or JSP code.

But watch that reset

There's one caveat: By default, the `reset` method of a DynaActionForm will set all of the fields to their initial value. With a conventional ActionForm, the developer determined which fields were affected by reset. Many developers reset them all anyway, so in most cases the behavior will be consistent if you change from an ActionForm to a DynaActionForm.

5.5 *Why isn't an ActionForm...*

In the open source community, few designs go unchallenged. Here are some popular questions that developers raise regarding the design of the Struts ActionForm class.

5.5.1 Why isn't an ActionForm just a Map?

There are several design justifications for using a JavaBean rather than a Map, as you can see in table 5.1.

Table 5.1   Design justifications for JavaBeans versus Maps

Justification	Explanation
Encapsulation	Most often, a property will return a simple value, but sometimes values do need to be generated instead.
Extensibility	A Map can't be extended to provide related methods, like the `validate` and `reset` methods.
Introspection	A bean with clearly defined properties can be adopted into a GUI interface and other tools.

Struts 1.1 provides the best of both worlds. You can define your own Map to store your fields or just use a DynaActionForm to declare the properties automagically (see section 5.4.2).

5.5.2 Why isn't an ActionForm a plain JavaBean?

While any JavaBean can be used with the Struts JSP tags to populate an HTML form, a class with known methods is needed to manage the input after it is submitted. When accepting input over HTTP, validation is critical. Any data coming up from the web tier must be carefully examined before use and rejected if inappropriate. The ActionForm has a `validate` method that is called by the ActionServlet to help ensure data is entered correctly. Other validations may occur later, but having the initial validation part of the ActionForm makes for a robust design.

Another issue is checkboxes. If a checkbox is not checked, then the browser does not send anything. Present is true; absent is false. The workaround is to reset a checkbox to false before populating it. This way, the present checkboxes turn the property true. Otherwise, it stays false. To help with issues like this, the Action-Form has a built-in `reset` method. Since these methods are needed to properly handle the incoming data, any old JavaBean won't do. The form bean has to provide these two methods for the framework's use.

5.5.3 Why isn't an ActionForm an interface?

Good question. After all, using a base class rather than an interface means we have to extend the class rather than reuse a preexisting class. An ActionForm will most often expose properties from a business object. If it were an interface, we might be able to use our business objects directly and avoid passing everything through a separate ActionForm object.

This sounds good, but in practice, there are several showstoppers. Table 5.2 summarizes some of the issues.

Table 5.2   Why an ActionForm is not an interface

Reason	Explanation
Extensibility	Adding a new method to an ActionForm interface (in some future version of Struts) will break an application's form bean if it relied solely on the prior version's interface. As a base class, we can add a new method with a default behavior. Existing subclasses will simply inherit the default behavior.
Correct use	If an ActionForm were an interface, developers would be tempted to use existing data beans as ActionForms. The ActionForm should be considered part of the control layer, and the provided APIs should encourage using it as such. The core API contract for an ActionForm is that it must faithfully represent the input that a user submits, whether or not that input is semantically valid. This allows the user to correct the input and try again. Most value objects are not designed to buffer *incorrect* data, and many are immutable.
Performance	Some data beans, especially Enterprise JavaBeans, may be designed to start transactions and lock resources in the underlying database when used. Applications will scale better if database transactions are delayed until semantically valid input is available.
Security	The Struts autopopulation mechanism works by setting the property first and validating it second. An existing object may be designed to change the system state when a new value is passed to one of its properties. In this case, a hostile user could pass a property to your Action from a browser and make unauthorized state changes, even if you never intended for that property to be set from a browser. The ActionServlet doesn't know whether a property is used in an HTML form; it only knows that it was found in the request.

Here's another good question: "Why isn't your business bean an interface?" The ActionForm can implement your business interface and, once validated, be passed up to the business tier.

Transferring data from ActionForms to the business tier is an important step that we explore in the next section.

5.6 *Debriefing ActionForms*

The Struts tag extensions help you populate HTML controls from an ActionForm. The ActionServlet handles populating the ActionForm from an HTTP request. But, as shown in figure 5.4, we still need to traverse "the last mile." For our data to

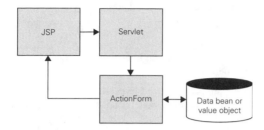

Figure 5.4   The cycle of data: Data beans populate ActionForms; ActionForms populate JSPs; the ActionServlet populates ActionForms; ActionForms populate data beans.

complete its life cycle, we have to transfer values between the ActionForms and business objects.

Struts developers use several strategies to transfer values between tiers. In this section, we examine the most popular strategies. The requirements of your business layer will often determine which approach is best for your project. Many web developers are required to use a preexisting layer of business methods, which can limit their options. Sometimes the entire application is being created at once, and developers have the luxury of choosing their favorite solution

In our discussion, we use the term *transfer object* to describe a JavaBean whose main purpose is to carry data from one place to another. This approach is often used in Enterprise JavaBean environments to reduce the number of calls an application needs to make on a remote database. The idea is that several properties are bundled together into a single JavaBean. The properties on the bean may relate to more than one table, but that is handled on the remote side.

Your own application may not use transfer objects per se, but some type of "data bean" that might be used to access a local data system. The approach works the same in either case. The strategies we'll cover are summarized in table 5.3.

Table 5.3   Strategies for populating and debriefing ActionForms

Strategy	Description
Implementing a business layer interface	The ActionForm implements a business-layer interface so it can be used directly.
Nesting a mutable value object	A value object with individual properties is a member property of the ActionForm.
Setting an immutable value object	A bulk constructor or setter is called by the Action.
Setting a mutable value object	One or more setters are called by the Action.
Using a factory method	A helper method encapsulates, instantiates, and populates a business tier bean.

Table 5.3 Strategies for populating and debriefing ActionForms *(continued)*

Strategy	Description
Passing a Map	A Map of the data is passed by the Action to a business layer entity.
Transferring values by reflection	Data is transferred from one bean to the other by matching the property names.
Using an adaptor class	A specialized class copies properties from one Action-Form to several business layer entities.

To help in your selection process, we've included a "Consequences" and a "Converting data types" section for each strategy.

5.6.1 Implementing a business-layer interface

Business layers often define interfaces for their beans (and those that don't should consider doing so). When a business-layer interface is available, you can have your ActionForm implement that interface so it can be passed directly to business methods:

```
public class ArticleForm extends ActionForm
        implements ArticleBean {

    // ...
}
```

Then, in your Action, you could pass the validated ActionForm directly to any method expecting the business-layer type:

```
articleModel.save((ArticleBean) form);
```

Converting data types

At some point, much of the String-based input submitted by a web client must be converted to native types needed by the business tier. Unfortunately, the JavaBean specification does not allow property getters and setters to be overloaded. If you attempt such a thing on an ActionForm, the ActionServlet's autopopulation mechanism will throw an exception.

One useful technique is to use a helper method with a predictable name to convert the property on demand:

```
private String keyDisplay = null;
public String getKeyDisplay {
  return keyDisplay;
}
```

```
public Integer getKey() {
  return new Integer( getKeyDisplay() );
}
```

The tag extensions would refer to the `keyDisplay` version:

```
<html:text property="keyDisplay"/>
```

But the Action or a business-tier method can simply refer to the original method:

```
ArticleBean articleBean = (ArticleBean) form;
articleModel.update(articleBean.getKey(),articleBean);
```

Consequences

- ActionForms become a seamless part of the business API.
- Care must be taken that input is validated before being used in business methods.
- Non-`String` properties will be converted on the fly.

5.6.2 Nesting a mutable value object

If you are fortunate enough to be using a value object with only `String` and `boolean` properties, then you can make your value object a property on the Action-Form. The properties on the value object can then be referred to using a dotted syntax, like this:

```
values.telephone
```

This calls the equivalent of

```
getValues().getTelephone();
```

and

```
getValues().setTelephone(values.telephone);
```

Converting data types

Not applicable. This strategy requires `String` and `boolean` values that do not need conversion.

Consequences

- This strategy is quick and easy to implement.
- This strategy does not apply to nontext types, such as `Integer` or `Date`.
- This strategy may not work well if the value object rejects badly formatted data.

- This strategy binds the presentation layer to specific value objects. If values are moved between objects, the presentation code would need to reflect that change.

NOTE   The first two strategies, implementing a business-tier interface and nesting a mutable value object, transfer data automatically. The other strategies require the assistance of the Action to trigger the transfer. The code snippets in the remaining strategies would be found in an Action class.

5.6.3 *Setting an immutable value object*

If you're provided with an immutable value object that uses a bulk constructor, then populating it boils down to this:

```
ArticleForm aForm = (ArticleForm) form;
ArticleBean aBean  = new ArticleBean(
        aForm.getArticleKey(),
        aForm.getContributor(),
        aForm.getCreator(),
        aForm.getTitle(),
        aForm.getContent()
);
```

A bulk setter would look the same, except the bean would be created and then the setter called. If a good number of parameters are involved, it can help to break them into groups and define a setter for each group (if that's an option). Classic divide and conquer:

```
ArticleForm aForm = (ArticleForm) form;
ArticleBean aBean  = new ArticleBean();
aBean.setRecordHeader(
        aForm.getArticleKey(),
        aForm.getEditor());
aBean.setPeople(
        aForm.getContributor(),
        aForm.getCreator());
aBean.setText(
        aForm.getTitle(),
        aForm.getContent());
```

Of course, for this to be worthwhile, each block would take several more parameters, but you get the idea. Sometimes, multiple setters can correlate to partial updates, where, say, the text fields are being updated but the people fields are not touched. If the data is being sent over a remote connection, sending only the data you mean to change can be important.

Converting data types

If the property types need to be converted, you can do that as data is being trans-ferred or put a helper method in your ActionForm. Since the fields would have already been validated and prequalified for conversion, the ActionForm helpers can be optimistic and assume that the conversion will succeed. For example:

```
Integer getArticleKeyInteger() {
        return new Integer(this.getArticle())
}
ArticleBean  aBean  = new ArticleBean(
        aForm.getArticleKeyInteger(),
        aForm.getContributor(),
        aForm.getCreator(),
        aForm.getTitle(),
        aForm.getContent()
)
```

Of course, you can also use `try … catch` with this segment and throw an exception if something unexpected happens:

```
try {
        ArticleBean aBean = new ArticleBean(
            aForm.getArticleKeyInteger(),
            aForm.getContributor(),
            aForm.getCreator(),
            aForm.getTitle(),
            aForm.getContent())
}
catch (Throwable t) {
        errors.add(ActionErrors.GLOBAL_ERROR,
            new ActionError("error.conversion"));
}
```

Consequences

- This strategy can provide type checking.
- This strategy works with any value object.
- This strategy involves high maintenance if properties are changing.
- This strategy strongly couples an Action class with a particular ActionForm.
- Value objects with dozens of properties are difficult to manage this way.

5.6.4 *Setting a mutable value object*

If your value objects don't have bulk setters and new methods can't be added for some reason, then it gets messy:

```
ArticleBean aBean = new ArticleBean();
aBean.setArticleKey(aForm.getArticleKeyInteger());
aBean.setContributor(aForm.getContributor());
aBean.setCreator(aForm.getCreator());
aBean.setTitle(aForm.getTitle());
aBean.setContent(aForm.getContent());
```

Consequences and data-type conversion considerations are the same as for immutable value objects.

5.6.5 *Using a factory method*

If ActionForm values are being transferred to another value object, you can encapsulate the transfer in the ActionForm rather than expose the process to the Action class.

   If the value object has to be created anyway, a good approach is to use a factory method that instantiates, populates, and returns the value object. Here's a sample method that would be found on an ActionForm:

```
public ArticleBean getArticleBean() {

    ArticleBean aBean  = new ArticleBean(
        this.getArticleKey(),
        this.getContributor(),
        this.getCreator(),
        this.getTitle(),
        this.getContent()
    );

    return aBean;
}
```

Alternatively, you can pass an existing value object:

```
public void setArticleBean(ArticleBean aBean) {

    aBean.set (
        this.getArticleKey(),
        this.getContributor(),
        this.getCreator(),
        this.getTitle(),
        this.getContent()
    );
}
```

Converting data types

The same considerations apply to this strategy as for the setting a mutable object and setting an immutable object strategies. This strategy simply moves the code from the Action to the ActionForm.

Consequences

- This strategy binds the ActionForm to the business-tier type.

- This strategy simplifies the ActionForm.

- This strategy allows more than one Action to transfer data without replicating code.

5.6.6 Passing a Map

It is not uncommon for value objects to pass properties through a Map (java.util.Map). If the ActionForm properties and the value object properties match, then transferring the data can be very easy.

If you have a value object that accepts Maps, there are two approaches for using Maps with ActionForms, depending on whether you are using Struts 1.0 or Struts 1.1 and later.

Struts 1.0

The BeanUtils class includes a describe method that returns a Map of a Java-Bean's public properties. It also offers a corresponding populate method that will set the public properties of a JavaBean from a Map. In the following example, let's assume that our hypothetical value object has setMap and getMap properties that represent its values.

Here we're going from the form to the value object

```
Map map = BeanUtils.describe(form);
bean.setMap(map);
```

and from the value object to the form:

```
Map map = bean.getMap();
BeanUtils.populate(form,map);
```

(For clarity, we showed the Map as an intermediate variable. In your own code, you can combine the statements.)

If the property names do not match for some reason, the ActionForm can be given alias properties

```
public String getKey() {
        return getArticle();
}
public String getAuthor() {
        return getCreator();
}
```

or the ActionForm can be given a custom method to return the appropriate Map:

```
public class ArticleForm extends ActionForm {
// ...
       public Map describe() {
              map = new HashMap();
           map.add("key",this.getArticle());
           map.add("author",this.getCreator());
           // ...
           return map;
       }
}
```

In the latter case, you would call the ActionForm's describe method instead of
BeanUtil's:

```
bean.setMap(form.describe());
```

Struts 1.1

If your model accepts incoming data in a Map (java.util.Map), then most likely it
can also return data as a Map. Since Struts 1.1, you can combine the enhanced
capabilities of the Commons BeanUtils [ASF, Commons] class with the Struts dotted syntax. This makes it easy to use a Map to store your ActionForm properties.

The technique is quite simple. First, add a property to your ActionForm to
access the Map:

```
private Map map = null;
public void setMap(Map map) {
    this.map = map;
}
public Map getMap() {
    return this.map;
}
```

Then add a property to access an element of the Map:

```
public void setValue(String key, Object value) throws Exception {
    getMap().put(key,value);
}

public Object getValue(String key) throws Exception {
    return getMap().get(key);
}
```

In the Struts 1.1 JSP tags (see chapter 10), you can access the elements of the Map
like this:

```
<html:text property="value(key)"/>
```

and

```
<bean:write name="formBean" property="value (key)"/>
```

where `key` is the name of the property.

If your business-tier value objects are already using Maps, you can just transfer the data by using the respective `getMap` and `setMap` methods (or equivalent):

```
form.setMap(bean.getMap());
```

```
bean.setMap(form.getMap());
```

For more on using Maps with Struts 1.1 ActionForms, see section 5.7.

Converting data types

If the business tier expects a Map of native types rather than `Strings`, an Action-Form helper method may be required to convert the `Strings` to native types and return a modified Map:

```
public Map getTypedMap() {
    Map map = this.getMap();
    String keyString = (String) map.get("key");
    Integer keyInteger = new Integer(keyString);
    map.put("key",keyInteger);
    return map;
}
```

Consequences

- This strategy results in good integration with the business tier when Maps are already used for data transfer.

- Since a Map will return null if the entry is not present, some extra validation code may be needed to watch for missing parameters.

5.6.7 *Transferring values by reflection*

If you are using a modern JVM, an excellent way to get ActionForm data into another JavaBean is to use reflection. Initially, reflection carried a performance penalty, but each JVM release reduced that penalty. In Sun's Java 1.3 and later, the difference is moot.

You can add some simple methods to an ActionForm base class to make it easy to transfer data to and from any other bean using reflection, like those methods shown in listing 5.3. The methods are just wrappers around the BeanUtils class methods used elsewhere in the framework. The ActionServlet uses BeanUtils to populate the ActionForm from the HTTP request.

Listing 5.3 Data-transfer methods

```
public Map describe() throws Exception {
        try {
                return BeanUtils.describe(this);
        } catch (Throwable t) {
                throw new PopulateException(t);
        }
}

public void set(Object o) throws Exception {
        try {
                BeanUtils.populate(this,BeanUtils.describe(o));
        } catch (Throwable t) {
                throw new PopulateException(t);
        }
}

public void populate(Object o) throws Exception {
        try {
                BeanUtils.populate(o,this.describe());
        } catch (Throwable t) {
                throw new PopulateException(t);
        }
}
```

1.0 vs 1.1 The Commons `BeanUtil` package used by Struts 1.1 provides much better type conversion than the original Struts 1.0 version. If you are using reflection to transfer your own data, we recommend importing the Commons `BeanUtil` package, regardless of what version of Struts you are using. The best all-around data transfer method is `BeanUtils.copyProperties`. Here's how to use `copyProperties` to populate your bean from any other bean:

```
BeanUtils.copyProperties(this,source);
```

The `copyProperties` method will automatically apply any `String` to native type conversions in either direction. The new `copyProperties` makes it very easy to "round-trip" your ActionForms and business beans:

```
BeanUtils.copyProperties(myBusinessBean,myActionForm);
  myBusinessOperation(myBusinessbean);
  BeanUtils.copyProperties(myActionForm,myBusinessBean);
```

The code in this snippet transfers the `String` properties in myAction-Form to native types in myBusinessBeans, allows the business operation to update the values, and then transfers the native types back to the all-String myActionForm. *Sweet*!

You can also register custom converters with BeanUtils to handle your own types. See the Commons site for details [JSF, Commons].

Converting data types

The BeanUtils methods can convert data between Strings and native types, so you do not need to write as many "bridge" methods as you might when implementing another interface (though non-native types become more of a problem).

When using the BeanUtils methods to transfer data, everything has to pass through a native type. This is not an issue on the ActionForm side since it uses only Strings or booleans. It *is* a problem on the business bean side since trying to transfer data between

```
String setCurrent();
```

and

```
Date getCurrent() ;
```

or any other non-native type is not supported by the Struts 1.0 BeanUtils class.

One solution is to provide transformation methods on the business side that can move the Date into a String and back again.

Here's a set of business methods for converting a String into a Timestamp and back. These methods should be members of the business-layer bean—*not* the ActionForm. By putting them on the business tier, we make them available to any other component that may also need to deal in Strings:

```
public String getTicklerDisplay() {
        Timestamp tickler = getTickler();
        if (ConvertUtils.isNull(tickler)) return null;
        return tickler.toString();
}
public void setTicklerDisplay(String ticklerDisplay) {
        if (ticklerDisplay==null)
                setTickler(null);
        else try {
                setTickler(Timestamp.valueOf(ticklerDisplay));
        } catch (Throwable t) {
                setTickler(null);
        }
}
```

Elsewhere on the business-layer bean are a getter and setter for the actual `Time-stamp` that is stored in a database:

```
private Timestamp tickler = null;
public Timestamp getTickler() {
        return (this.tickler);
}
public void setTickler(Timestamp tickler) {
        this.tickler = tickler;
}
```

On the ActionForm side, we can just use simple `String` properties but named with the `Display` suffix:

```
private string ticklerDisplay = null;
public String getTicklerDisplay() {
    return this.ticklerDisplay;
    };
public void setTicklerDisplay(String ticklerDisplay)
    this.ticklerDisplay = ticklerDisplay;
    };
```

When set or populated with reflection, the mechanism calls the equivalent of

```
bean.setTicklerDisplay(form.getTicklerDisplay());
```

or

```
form.setTicklerDisplay(bean.getTicklerDisplay());
```

depending on which direction we are going. The business method handles the conversion between `String` and `Timestamp`, so that the ActionForm can just use `String` properties as usual.

STRUTS TIP   Use display helpers on your business beans to automatically convert complex types. By letting the business bean handle the conversions to and from a `String`, you ensure that the business requirements stay on the business tier and can also be reused on other platforms.

In practice, your application would probably need these methods anyway, since we can rarely display data in its native form. Even without the conversion issue, something like the `getDateDisplay` method shown in listing 5.4 is usually needed to render the value in a localized or user-friendly format.

Listing 5.4   A method for displaying a date

```
public String getDateDisplay() {

  if (this.dateDisplay==null) return null;

  DateFormat dateFormatter = DateFormat.getDateInstance(
      DateFormat.DEFAULT,
      this.getLocale()
  );

  return dateFormatter.parse(this.dateDisplay);
}
```

For something like a timestamp, you might need to decompose a single value into several fields so that each component can be selected from a drop-down box on an HTML form.

The setTicklerDisplay in listing 5.5 extracts components from a Timestamp string so they can be used in different controls.

Listing 5.5   A method for decomposing a timestamp

```
public void setTicklerDisplay(String ticklerDisplay) {

      this.ticklerDisplay = ticklerDisplay;

      boolean longEnough = ((this.ticklerDisplay!=null) &&
        (this.ticklerDisplay.length()>11+2));

      if (longEnough) {

          // Snag components: YYYY-MM-DD HH:MM
          setTicklerYear(this.ticklerDisplay.substring(0,0+4));
          setTicklerMonth(this.ticklerDisplay.substring(5,5+2));
          setTicklerDay(this.ticklerDisplay.substring(8,8+2));
          setTicklerHour(this.ticklerDisplay.substring(11,11+2));

          // Parse AM/PM/EV
          Integer hour = null;
          try {
              hour = Integer.valueOf(getTicklerHour());
          }
          catch (Throwable t)  {
              hour = null;
          }
          int tod = 0;
          if (hour!=null) tod = hour.intValue();
          setTicklerTod(AM);
          if (tod>12) setTicklerTod(PM); // after 1pm
          if (tod>16) setTicklerTod(EV); // after 5pm
      }

  }
```

In many cases, the `Display` methods will just be doing double duty. They format the value as `Strings` to transfer it to the ActionForm. The ActionForm methods can then display the value in whatever format may be required.

Consequences

- The size of the codebase is reduced.
- Overall maintenance is reduced.
- Coupling between the Action class and other components is reduced.
- This strategy may require creating some bridge methods or classes.
- Some developers relying on dated information may hesitate to use reflection.

5.6.8 Using an adaptor class

Often the ActionForm beans and model beans are very much alike. Other times, they may have little in common. The fields in a single ActionForm may need to be transferred to several different model beans. Or the property names of the ActionForms may need to differ from the property names used on the business object. In this case, an adaptor class may be helpful to map the business object methods to the ActionForm properties.

An adaptor and an ActionForm will share one or more methods with the same signature. The adaptor class is designed as a wrapper around one or more of the business objects. The getters and setters on the adaptor call the corresponding methods on the business object. The adaptor can then be used in place of the business bean (as a proxy or delegate):

```
// Get data into ActionForm
DataBean dBean = new DataBean();
dBean.execute(something);
AdaptorBean aBean = new AdaptorBean(dBean);
aBean.populate(form);

// Fetch data from ActionForm
AdaptorBean adaptor = new AdaptorBean(new DataBean());
BaseForm actionForm = (BaseForm) form;
adaptor.set(actionForm);
DataBean model = (DataBean) adaptor.getBean();
model.execute();
```

Any of the data-transfer techniques we've already discussed can be used within an adaptor class. The main point of the adaptor is that it encapsulates differences between the ActionForm and business classes. This can be especially useful when the business model is complex, since the adaptor can cleanly decouple the Action from the business implementation.

Converting data types

An adaptor can encapsulate any existing data conversion methods or implement new conversions as needed.

Workarounds

If you need your value objects to be immutable elsewhere, you may be able to have the same object implement both mutable and immutable interfaces. The business and data layers would use the object via the read-only interface. The Action could use the mutable interface, but both would share the same underlying data field.

Consequences

- Classes are often application specific, with little reuse.

- This strategy increases the number of objects in the application.

- This strategy is sensitive to changes in both the business and presentation layers.

- This strategy can shield each layer from changes in the other (helps to decouple layers).

5.7 *BaseForm*

The Scaffold package provides a base ActionForm that implements several techniques discussed in this book (`org.apache.struts.scaffold.BaseForm`). This class includes methods for handling locales, dispatching control, and managing auto-population. Table 5.4 shows the BaseForm methods.

STRUTS TIP If your application uses several ActionForm classes, define a base object to include any properties or utilities that may be common to the forms in your application. Once you start to look, you may be surprised at how many you find.

Table 5.4 BaseForm methods

Category	Methods

SessionLocale	`public void setSessionLocale(Locale locale);`
	`public Locale getSessionLocale();`
	`protected void resetSessionLocale (HttpServletRequest request);`

Dispatch	`public void setDispatch(String dispatch);` `public String getDispatch();`
Mutable	`public void setMutable(boolean mutable);` `public boolean isMutable();`

Autopopulation	`public Map describe() throws Exception;`
	`public void set(Object o) throws Exception;`
	`public void populate(Object o) throws Exception;`
	`public Map merge(Object profile) throws Exception;`

5.7.1 SessionLocale

By default, the ActionServlet will automatically create a Locale object for users in their session context. These methods are designed to help you manage that Locale object:

```
public void setSessionLocale(Locale locale);
public Locale getSessionLocale();
protected void resetSessionLocale(HttpServletRequest request);
```

The `resetLocale` method is called by the BaseForm's `reset` method. It retrieves the Locale object from the session so that it is available to your ActionForm. If you provide an HTML control to change the locale, you can make the change in the `validate` method. Since the Locale object here refers to the session object, any changes will persist through the user's session.

For more about the Struts localization features, see chapter 13.

5.7.2 Dispatch

Struts developers often have the same Action handle related operations. One popular technique to select the operation is to use a hidden property on an HTML form. The `dispatch` property on BaseForm can be used for this purpose:

```
public void setDispatch(String dispatch);
    public String getDispatch();
```

For other ways of dispatching operations within an Action, see chapter 8.

5.7.3 *Autopopulation*

The ActionServlet handles the default autopopulation of an ActionForm. This set of utility methods is designed to help Action objects perform other data-transfer tasks. The describe method returns a Map of the ActionForm bean. The set method populates this ActionForm from another JavaBean. The populate method sets another JavaBean's properties to match this bean:

```
public Map describe() throws Exception;
public void set(Object o) throws Exception {
public void populate(Object o) throws Exception {
protected Map merge(Object profile) throws Exception {
```

The merge method is a trifle more complicated. The underlying idea is that your application may have a profile bean in session scope that overrides the application defaults with user-specific settings. The merge method lets you combine the user-specific settings with the standard settings in an ActionForm into a unified Map. So, if the ActionForm had a sessionLocale property and the profile bean also had a sessionLocale property, the profile bean's setting would be returned in the Map. If the profile bean did not have a sessionProfile property, or the property was null, then the property from this ActionForm would be returned in the Map instead.

5.7.4 *BaseMapForm*

With Struts 1.1 and later, we can use Maps as ActionForm properties. A value from a Map is referenced differently than a regular JavaBean property:

```
// form.getValue(key);
<html:text property="value(key)"/>
```

But this is often a fair trade-off for the flexibility that Maps can bring to your ActionForms.

The BaseMapForm in Scaffold (org.apache.struts.scaffold.BaseMapForm) provides a standard method for storing and retrieving fields using a Map property. It extends BaseForm and so also offers all the functionality of that class. Table 5.5 shows the BaseMapForm methods.

Table 5.5   BaseMapForm methods

Category	Methods

Value Map	```public void setValue(String key, Object value);```
	```public Object getValue(String key);```
	```public void setValues(Map values);```
	```public Map getValues();```

Value Map

To initialize the ActionForm with a prepopulated Map, use the setValues method. To return the Map representing the current BaseMapForm values, call the getValues method. To add or change a specific value, use the setValue and getValue methods as shown in table 5.5.

5.8 Summary

Traditionally, ActionForms have been a source of aggravation for many Struts developers. This may begin to change in Struts 1.1, where Maps and DynaBeans can reduce ActionForm maintenance.

In this chapter, we explored the design principles behind ActionForms to help crystallize their role in the framework. We also explored various ways to transfer data between ActionForms and your business objects.

The Scaffold BaseForm class supports many of the data-transfer strategies covered by this chapter and can be an excellent choice as the base for your own ActionForms.

ActionForms describe *what* people can enter into your application. In the next chapter, we look at ActionForwards, which describe *where* people can go in your application.

Wiring with
ActionForwards

6

This chapter covers

- Understanding ActionForward best practices
- Using runtime parameters
- Using dynamic forwards

> *Inanimate objects are classified scientifically into three major*
> *categories—those that don't work, those that break down*
> *and those that get lost.*
>
> —Russell Baker

6.1   *What ActionForwards do*

Throughout an application, many components, such as Action objects, will ask questions like "OK, the operation succeeded, now what?" The Struts configuration will respond with an ActionForward linked to "success" for that operation. The ActionForward is passed back to the ActionServlet. The ActionServlet uses the path inside to send control to one place or another. None of the other components know anything about the path; they only know that the ActionForward says this is where we go next.

NOTE   Technically, the *path* is only one part of the URI that the ActionForward stores. The URI can also contain a query component with any parameters that your application might use. But here when we say *path*, we mean the complete URI.

If every hyperlink goes through a forward, the ActionForwards document an application's workflow. Ideally, ActionForwards should be used at every entry point to an application—any place where one page links to another.

1.0 vs 1.1   In Struts 1.1, ActionForward subclasses ForwardConfig (`org.apache.struts.config.ForwardConfig`) and adds API methods required for backward compatibility. ActionForward is not deprecated, and how the hierarchy will be handled in future releases has not been determined. For now, we will refer to the ActionForward class, but you should note that, in Struts 1.1, all of the forward properties are actually defined by the ForwardConfig super class. ActionForward otherwise works the same way in both versions.

ActionForwards represent a URI [W3C, URI] to the application. Although the property is called a *path*, the ActionForwards can contain any complete URI and can also include a query component. This means you can also use strings like

```
path="/do/item?dispatch=edit"
```

in your ActionForward paths. If /do/item is an Action class, and its ActionForm has a property named `dispatch`, this URI will have Struts set the `dispatch` property to `edit`. Of course, more complex query strings work just as well. The URI

```
path="/do/item?dispatch=edit&amp;key=17"
```

would have Struts set the `dispatch` property to edit and a key property to 17.

> **NOTE**   Since the path is a URI, we encoded the ampersand as &. Ampersands are a restricted character in the query component of a URI. See "Uniform Resource Identifiers (URI): Generic Syntax" [W3C, URI] for more about the syntax expected here.

6.2 How ActionForwards work

The ActionForward is a simple but effective wrapper. The base class is just storage space for four properties: `name`, `path`, `redirect`, and `className`, which are summarized in table 6.1.

Table 6.1   The ActionForward properties

Property	Description
name	Specifies a logical name for this ActionForward. Other components refer to the ActionForward by name so that the other properties can be easily changed.
path	Specifies the URI for this ActionForward. URIs are an important way that web applications communicate.
redirect	If true, control is redirected instead. The default is false and is almost always the better choice. We take a closer look at a forward versus a redirect in the next section.
className	Optionally specifies a subclass of org.apache.struts.action.ActionForward when instantiating this forward [Struts 1.1].

6.2.1 Forward versus redirect

Very little stands still on the web. The HTTP protocol even has a built-in "redirect" command that a server can use to send control from one page to another. Java web developers have a similar command at their disposal, called a forward. Both are useful in their own way.

- *Forward*   Retains everything in the HTTP request and request context. Can be used only within the same application.

■ *Redirect* Instructs the web client to make a new HTTP request. The resource may be in the same application or elsewhere.

Forwarding requests

Java Servlet containers have an internal mechanism that enables a request to be passed along to another component, or *forwarded*. This allows a request to be handled by several different components before the response is generated. Along the way, components can add and update objects in the request context and even amend the request parameters.

When an Action object returns an ActionForward, the servlet creates a Request-Dispatcher for the ActionForward's path. If the path includes a query string component, the query string parameters become part of the forwarded request. You can then retrieve the parameters using a method on the request object:

```
Object parameter = request.getParameter("parameterName");
```

If it is a new parameter, it is also passed to any subsequent forwards. If the parameter already exists, the new value overrides the original for the duration of the forward. After that, the old parameter surfaces again. For more about how servlets handle requests, see "Dispatching Requests" in the Servlet Specification [Sun, JST].

Parameters should not be confused with request attributes. The parameters are part of the HTTP request. The attributes are stored in the request context, which is something Java provides. The elements of the HTTP request are made available from the Java request context, so they sometimes seem like the same thing.

The parameters of the HTTP request are used to populate the ActionForm (see chapter 5). Typically, the ActionForm will contain all the input an application expects. Struts developers do not need to work directly with request parameters. Struts developers do most of their work through request attributes. A request attribute will be available throughout a forwarded request but disappears if the request is redirected.

Redirecting requests

When an ActionForward's `redirect` property is set to true, the ActionServlet sends the browser an HTTP response that tells the browser to submit a new request to this path. The original request parameters are not retained; the original request context disappears. The new HTTP request contains only the parameters contained in the ActionForward's `path` property, if any. The URI is encoded before it is sent to the client, and the user's session context is maintained if the path is within the same application. But a redirect always clears the request context.

6.3 Global and local forwards

The Struts configuration provides two levels of nesting for ActionForwards:

- *Global* ActionForwards are available to any Action object throughout the application.
- *Local* ActionForwards are defined within the ActionMapping element. These are only available to the Action object when it is called from that ActionMapping.

From within an Action object, a forward is usually chosen like this:

```
ActionForward forward = mapping.findForward("continue");
```

An Action's mapping object is passed to it when the ActionServlet invokes the Action. The mapping object includes a list of its local forwards and a link to the global forwards. The mapping's findForward method will check its local forwards first. A failure to find a local forward will trigger a search through the global forwards. If a forward is not found in either scope, the findForward method will return null. Should that happen accidentally, because the Action class and Struts configuration disagree, the Action object could return a null ActionForward, leaving the browser to report the error.

Ideally, whatever globals you use should be defined as String constants to avoid any misunderstandings or typographical errors. This also makes them available to the JSPs (but, sadly, not to the XML configuration file). The Jakarta Commons Scaffold [ASF, Scaffold] package defines several constants for commonly used globals in its Tokens class:

```
public static final String CANCEL = "cancel";
public static final String CONTINUE = "continue";
public static final String DONE = "done";
public static final String EMPTY = "empty";
public static final String ERROR = "error";
public static final String EXIT = "exit";
public static final String FORWARD = "forward";
public static final String LOGON = "logon";
public static final String LOGOFF = "logoff";
public static final String MENU = "menu";
public static final String NEXT = "next";
public static final String PREVIOUS = "previous";
public static final String TOKEN = "token";
public static final String WELCOME = "welcome";
```

6.4 *Runtime parameters*

Of course, the driving force behind a web application is that it is supposed to be dynamic and allow changes to be made at runtime. There are two points at which ActionForwards can be adjusted at runtime to add or amend its query component: in the page and in the Action class.

6.4.1 *Adding parameters in the page*

If you use ActionForwards with the `<html:link>` tag (`org.apache.struts.taglib.html`), you can also add runtime parameters to the query component:

```
<html:link
  forward="article"
  paramId="key"
  paramProperty="key"
  name="articleForm">
  <bean:write name="articleForm" property="name">
</html:link>
```

Given an `articleForm` bean with the method `getKey`, the tag will retrieve the `key` property and append its value to the URI. Given an ActionForward like this:

```
<forward
  name="article"
  path="/do/article?dispatch=view"/>
```

an `<html:link>` tag like this:

```
<html:link forward="article" paramName="articleForm"
paramProperty="articleKey" paramId="key">
News from the edge
</html:link>
```

would generate an HTML tag like this:

```
<a href="http://localhost/artimus/do/article?dispatch=view&key=17">News from
  the edge</a>
```

Note that the tag is smart enough to append additional parameters if there is an existing query string.

For more information about tag extensions, see chapter 10.

6.4.2 *Adding parameters in the Action class*

You can also add parameters to an ActionForward within an Action class, using a fragment like this:

```
ActionForward forward = mapping.findForward("article");
```

```
StringBuffer path = new StringBuffer(forward.getPath());
boolean isQuery = (path.indexOf("?")>=0);
if (isQuery)
    path.append("&amp;dispatch=view");
else
    path.append("?dispatch=view");
return new ActionForward(path.toString());
```

The Scaffold ConvertUtils class (`org.apache.scaffold.text.ConvertUtils`) provides a method to help automate this—the addParam method, as shown here:

```
    // Base path and one parameter
aForward.setPath(
    ConvertUtils.addParam("/do/article","dispatch","view"));
    // Current path and an additional parameter
aForward.setPath(
    ConvertUtils.addParam(aForward.getPath(),"key","17"));
```

This resolves to

```
/do/article?dispatch=view&key=17
```

Unless the ActionForward is set to redirect, the parameters are merged with any parameters in the current request. If any of the new parameters use the same name as an existing parameter, the new one is used for the duration of the new forward.

6.5 *Dynamic forwards*

While it may be better to document your ActionForwards by defining them in the Struts configuration, if necessary you can even create an ActionForward from scratch, setting its path and any parameters:

```
ActionForward forward = new ActionForward("/do/itemEdit?action=edit");
```

Once you've created the ActionForward, you can use the runtime parameter techniques from the previous section to help build your ActionForward path.

If you're interested in learning more about setting runtime parameters and dynamic forwards, see chapter 8 (section 8.4).

NOTE   If you find yourself continually creating dynamic forwards and chaining Actions, it may be a warning sign that too much business logic is being expressed within an Action class. Ideally, you should be able to reuse business objects between Action classes, so that you do not need to "pass the baton" this way. For more about keeping business logic out of Action classes, see chapter 8.

6.6 *Why doesn't the address bar change?*

Something that confuses new developers is why an Action URI, such as /do/article/View, remains on the browser's address bar, even though a presentation page, such as /pages/article/View.jsp, is displayed in the window.

The address bar displays the last URL the browser was given. After the URL is submitted, your application may forward the request several times before one of the components returns a response to the browser. All this happens server-side without the browser knowing that it happens. When an HTTP response is returned, it does not include a value for the address bar. The browser displays only the address it used for the initial request.

NOTE   Of course, usually this is what you want anyway. The name or location of the page being presented is immaterial. Often, it is not even useful. The presentation of a dynamic page typically relies on data provided by the Action object. If the page is accessed directly, data may be missing.

The only way to change what is displayed on the address bar is to use a redirect rather than a forward (see section 6.2.1). This sends a standard response to the browser instructing it to submit a new request. Accordingly, the browser will update its address bar to reflect the new URL. Unfortunately, this also means that data cannot be passed to a page through the request context. It must be passed in the URI.

6.7 *Rolling your own ActionForward*

Developers may also provide their own ActionForward subclass with additional properties or methods. In Struts 1.0, you configure this in the deployment descriptor (web.xml) for the ActionServlet, as shown here:

```
<init-param>
<param-name>forward</param-name>
<param-value>app.MyActionForward</param-value>
</init-param>
```

In Struts 1.1, you configure this in the Struts configuration file as an attribute to the `<global-forwards>` element:

```
<global-forwards type="app.MyActionMapping">
```

Individual forwards may also be set to use another type through the `className` attribute:

```
<forward className="app.MyActionMapping">
```

For more about configuring Struts, see chapter 4.

The framework provides two base ActionForward classes, shown in table 6.2. These can be selected as the default or used as a base for your own subclasses.

Table 6.2   The default ActionForward classes

Object name	Description
`org.apache.struts.action.ForwardingActionForward`	Defaults the `redirect` property to false
`org.apache.struts.action.RedirectingActionForward`	Defaults the `redirect` property to true

The framework default is ForwardingActionForward (`redirect=false`).

Subclasses that provide new properties may set them in the Struts configuration file using a standard mechanism:

```
<set-property property="myProperty" value="myValue" />
```

This trick avoids subclassing the ActionServlet just to recognize the new properties when it digests the file.

6.8   *Summary*

Although very simple objects, ActionForwards play a vital role in the design of a Struts application. Used correctly, they can make it much easier to see the forest *and* the trees. A web application is a morass of arcane URIs that ActionForwards can reduce to neat, logical boxes—like the flowchart on your wall.

In the next chapter, we get closer to the bone of the application with our look at ActionMappings. ActionForms describe what people can enter. ActionForwards describe where people can go. ActionMappings tell us what the application can actually do.

7

Designing with
ActionMappings

This chapter covers
- Understanding ActionMappings
- Defining ActionMapping properties
- Using local and global ActionForwards

> *Decide what you want, decide what you are willing to exchange for it.*
> *Establish your priorities and go to work.*
>
> —H. L. Hunt

7.1   *Enter ActionMappings*

The Model 2 architecture (see chapter 1) encourages us to use servlets and Java-Server Pages in the same application. Under Model 2, we start by calling a servlet. The servlet handles the business logic and directs control to the appropriate page to complete the response.

The web application deployment descriptor (web.xml) lets us map a URL pattern to a servlet. This can be a general pattern, like *.do, or a specific path, like saveRecord.do.

Some applications implement Model 2 by mapping a servlet to each business operation. This approach works, but many applications involve dozens or hundreds of business operations. Since servlets are *multithreaded,* instantiating so many servlets is not the best use of server resources. Servlets are designed to handle any number of parallel requests. There is no performance benefit in simply creating more and more servlets.

The servlet's primary job is to interact with the container and HTTP. Handling a business operation is something that a servlet could delegate to another component. Struts does this by having the ActionServlet delegate the business operation to an object. Using a servlet to receive a request and route it to a handler is known as the *Front Controller* pattern [Go3].

Of course, simply delegating the business operation to another component does not solve the problem of mapping URIs [W3C, URI] to business operations. Our only way of communicating with a web browser is through HTTP requests and URIs. Arranging for a URI to trigger a business operation is an essential part of developing a web application.

Meanwhile, in practice many business operations are handled in similar ways. Since Java is multithreaded, we could get better use of our server resources if we could use the same Action object to handle similar operations. But for this to work, we might need to pass the object a set of configuration parameters to use with each operation.

So what's the bottom line? To implement Model 2 in an efficient and flexible way, we need to:

- Route requests for our business operations to a single servlet
- Determine which business operation is related to the request
- Load a multithreaded helper object to handle the business operation
- Pass the helper object the specifics of each request along with any configuration detail used by this operation

This is where ActionMappings come in.

7.1.1 *The ActionMapping bean*

An ActionMapping (`org.apache.struts.action.ActionMapping`) describes how the framework handles each discrete business operation (or *action*). In Struts, each ActionMapping is associated with a specific URI through its `path` property. When a request comes in, the ActionServlet uses the `path` property to select the corresponding ActionMapping. The set of ActionMapping objects is kept in an *ActionMappings* collection (`org.apache.struts.action.ActionMappings`).

Originally, the ActionMapping object was used to extend the Action *object* rather than the Action *class*. When used with an Action, a mapping gives a specific Action object additional responsibilities and new functionality. So, it was essentially an Action *decorator* [Go4]. Along the way, the ActionMapping evolved into an object in its own right and can be used with or without an Action.

DEFINITION   The intent of the *decorator pattern* is to attach additional responsibilities to an object dynamically. Decorators provide a flexible alternative to subclassing for extending functionality [Go4].

The ActionMappings are usually created through the Struts configuration file. For more about this file, see chapter 4.

7.1.2 *The ActionMappings catalog*

The ActionMappings catalog the business logic available to a Struts application. When a request comes in, the servlet finds its entry in the ActionMappings catalog and pulls the corresponding bean.

The ActionServlet uses the ActionMapping bean to decide what to do next. It may need to forward control off to another resource. Or it may need to populate and validate an ActionForm bean. At some point, it may have to pass control to an Action object, and when the Action returns, it may have to look up an Action-Forward associated with this mapping.

The ActionMapping works like a routing slip for the servlet. Depending on how the mapping is filled out, the request could go just about anywhere.

The ActionMappings represent the core design of a Struts application. If you want to figure out how a Struts application works, start with the ActionMappings. If you want to figure out how to write a new Struts application, start with the Action-Mappings. The mappings are at the absolute center of every Struts application.

In this chapter, we take a close look at the ActionMapping properties and explore how they help you design the flow of a Struts application.

1.0 vs 1.1   In Struts 1.1, ActionMapping subclasses ActionConfig (`org.apache.struts.config.ActionConfig`) and adds API methods required for backward compatibility. ActionMapping is not deprecated, and how the hierarchy will be handled in future releases has not been determined. For now, we refer to the ActionMapping class, but you should note that in Struts 1.1 all of the action properties are actually defined by the Ac-tionConfig super class. The ActionMapping class otherwise works the same way in both versions.

7.2 *ActionMapping properties*

Table 7.1 describes the base ActionMapping properties. As with other configuration components, developers may extend ActionMapping to provide additional properties.

Table 7.1   The base ActionMapping properties

Property	Description
path	The URI path from the request used to select this mapping. (API command)
forward	The context-relative path of the resource that should serve this request via a forward. Exactly one of the `forward`, `include`, or `type` properties must be specified.
or	
include	The context-relative path of the resource that should serve this request via an include. Exactly one of the `forward`, `include`, or `type` properties must be specified.
or	
type	The fully qualified name of the Action class used by this mapping.
className	Optionally specifies a subclass of `org.apache.struts.action.ActionMapping` that should be used when instantiating this mapping.

Since Struts 1.1

Table 7.1   The base ActionMapping properties *(continued)*

Property	Description
name	The name of the form bean, if any, associated with this action. This is not the class name. It is the logical name used in the form bean configuration.
roles	The list of security roles that may access this mapping.
scope	The identifier of the scope (request or session) within which the form bean, if any, associated with this mapping will be created.
validate	Set to true if the validate method of the form bean (if any) associated with this mapping should be called.
input	Context-relative path of the input form to which control should be returned if a validation error is encountered. This can be any URI: HTML, JSP, VM, or another ActionMapping.
parameter	General-purpose configuration parameter that can be used to pass extra information to the Action selected by this ActionMapping.
attribute	Name of the request-scope or session-scope attribute under which our form bean is accessed, if it is other than the bean's specified name.
prefix	Prefix used to match request parameter names to form bean property names, if any.
suffix	Suffix used to match request parameter names when populating the properties of our ActionForm bean, if any.
unknown	Can be set to true if this mapping should be configured as the default for this application (to handle all requests not handled by another mapping). Only one mapping can be defined as the default unknown mapping within an application.
forwards(s)	Block of ActionForwards for this mapping to use, if any.
exception(s)	Block of ExceptionHandlers for this mapping to use, if any.

In the sections that follow, we take a look at each of these properties.

7.2.1 *The path property*

The ActionMapping URI, or path, will look to the user like just another file on the web server. But it does not represent a file. It is a *virtual* reference to our ActionMapping.

Because it is exposed to other systems, the path is not really a logical name, like those we use with ActionForward. The path can include slashes and an extension—as if it referred to a file system—but they are all just part of a single name. The ActionMappings themselves are a "flat" namespace with no type of internal hierarchy whatsoever. They just happen to use the same characters that we are used to seeing in hierarchical file systems.

Of course, it can still be useful to treat your ActionMappings as if they were part of a hierarchy and group related commands under the same "folder." The only restriction is that the names must match whatever pattern is used in the application's deployment description (web.xml) for the ActionServlet. This is usually either /do/* or *.do, but any similar pattern can be used.

If you are working in a team environment, different team members can be given different ActionMapping namespaces to use. Some people may be working with the /customer ActionMappings, others may be working with the /vendor ActionMappings. This may also relate to the Java package hierarchy the team is using. Since the ActionMapping URIs are logical constructs, they can be organized in any way that suits your project.

With Struts 1.1, these types of namespaces can be promoted to application modules. Each team can work independently on its own module, with its own set of configuration files and presentation pages. Configuring your application to use multiple modules is covered in chapter 4.

DEFINITION   The web runs on URIs, and most URIs map to physical files. If you want to change the resource, you change the corresponding file. Some URIs, like Struts actions, are *virtual* references. They do not have a corresponding file but are handled by a programming component. To change the resource, we change how the component is programmed. But since the path is a URI and interacts with other systems outside our control, the path is not a true *logical* reference—the name of an ActionForward, for instance. We can change the name of an ActionForward without consulting other systems. It's an internal, logical reference. If we change the path to an ActionMapping, we might need to update other systems that refer to the ActionMapping through its public URI.

7.2.2 *The forward property*

When the forward property is specified, the servlet will not pass the request to an Action class but will make a call to RequestDispatcher.forward. Since the operation does not use an Action class, it can be used to integrate Struts with other resources and to prototype systems. The forward, include, and type properties are mutually exclusive. (See chapter 6 for more information.)

7.2.3 *The include property*

When the include property is specified, the servlet will not pass the request to an Action class but will make a call to RequestDispatcher.include. The operation does not use an Action class and can be used to integrate Struts with other components. The `forward`, `include`, and `type` properties are mutually exclusive. (See chapter 6 for more information.)

7.2.4 *The type property*

Most mappings will specify an Action class type rather than a forward or include. An Action class may be used by more than one mapping. The mappings may specify form beans, parameters, forwards, or exceptions. The `forward`, `include`, and `type` properties are mutually exclusive.

7.2.5 *The className property*

When specified, `className` is the fully qualified Java classname of the ActionMapping subclass that should be used for this object. This allows you to use your own ActionMapping subclass with specialized methods and properties. See also section 7.4.

7.2.6 *The name property*

This property specifies the logical name for the form bean, as given in the form-bean segment of the Struts configuration file. By default, this is also the name to be used when placing the form bean in the request or session context. Use the `attribute` property of this class to specify a different attribute key.

7.2.7 *The roles property*

This property is a comma-delimited list of the security role names that are allowed access to this ActionMapping object. By default, the same system that is used with standard container-based security is applied to the list of roles given here. This means you can use action-based security in lieu of specifying URL patterns in the deployment descriptor, or you can use both together.

The security check is handled by the `processRoles` method of the Request-Processor (`org.apache.struts.action.RequestProcessor`). By subclassing RequestProcessor, you can also use the `roles` property with application-based security. See chapter 9 for more about subclassing RequestProcessor.

7.2.8 *The scope property*

The ActionForm bean can be stored in the current request or in the session scope (where it will be available to additional requests). While most developers use request scope for the ActionForm, the framework default is session scope. To make request the default, see section 7.4.

7.2.9 *The validate property*

An important step in the lifecycle of an ActionForm is to validate its data before offering it to the business layer. When the `validate` property for a mapping is true, the ActionServlet will call the ActionForm's `validate` method. If `validate` returns false, the request is forwarded to the resource given by the `input` property.

Often, developers will create a pair of mappings for each data entry form. One mapping will have `validate` set to false, so you can create an empty form. The other has `validate` set to true and is used to submit the completed form.

NOTE   Whether or not the ActionForm `validate` method is called does *not* relate to the ActionServlet's `validating` property. That switch controls how the Struts configuration file is processed.

7.2.10 *The input property*

When `validate` is set to true, it is important that a valid path for input be provided. This is where control will pass should the ActionForm `validate` method return false. Often, this is the address for a presentation page. Sometimes it will be another Action path (with `validate` set to false) that is required to generate data objects needed by the page.

NOTE   The input path often leads back to the page that submitted the request. While it seems natural for the framework to return the request to where it originated, this is not a simple task in a web application. A request is often passed from component to component before a response is sent back to the browser. The browser only knows the path it used to retrieve the input page, which may or may not also be the correct path to use for the input property. While it may be possible to try and generate a default input page based on the HTTP `referrer` attribute, the Struts designers deemed that approach unreliable.

---

inputForward

In Struts 1.0, the ActionMapping `input` property is always a literal URI. In Struts 1.1, it may optionally be the name of an ActionForward instead. The ActionForward is retrieved and its `path` property is used as the `input` property. This can be a global or local ActionForward.

To use ActionForwards here instead of literal paths, set the `inputForward` attribute on the `<controller>` element for this module to true:

```
<controller inputForward="true">
```

For more about configuring Struts, see chapter 4. For more about ActionForwards, see chapter 6.

7.2.11 *The parameter property*

The generic `parameter` property allows Actions to be configured at runtime. Several of the standard Struts Actions make use of this property, and the standard Scaffold Actions often use it, too. The `parameter` property may contain a URI, the name of a method, the name of a class, or any other bit of information an Action may need at runtime. This flexibility allows some Actions to do double and triple duty, slashing the number of distinct Action classes an application needs on hand.

Within an Action class, the `parameter` property is retrieved from the mapping passed to `perform`:

```
parameter = mapping.getParameter();
```

Multiple parameters

While multiple parameters are not supported by the standard ActionMappings class, there are some easy ways to implement this, including using `HttpUtils`, a `StringTokenizer`, or a Properties file (`java.util.Properties`).

HttpUtils.   Although deprecated as of the Servlet API 2.3 specification, the `HttpUtils` package (`javax.servlet.http.HttpUtils`) provides a static method that parses any string as if it were a query string and returns a `Hashtable` (`java.util.Hashtable`):

```
Hashtable parameters = parseQueryString(parameter);
```

The `parameter` property for your mapping then becomes just another query string, because you might use it elsewhere in the Struts configuration.

stringTokenizer.   Another simple approach is to delimit the parameters using the token of your choice—such as a comma, colon, or semicolon—and use the `StringTokenizer` to read them back:

```
StringTokenizer incoming =
    new StringTokenizer(mapping.getParameter(),";");
int i = 0;
String[] parameters = new String[incoming.countTokens()];
while (incoming.hasMoreTokens()) {
    parameters[i++] = incoming.nextToken().trim();
}
```

Properties file.   While slightly more complicated than the others, another popular approach to providing multiple parameters to an ActionMapping is with a standard Properties files (`java.util.Properties`). Depending on your needs, the Properties file could be stored in an absolute location in your file system or anywhere on your application's `CLASSPATH`.

The Commons Scaffold package [ASF, Commons] provides a `ResourceUtils` package (`org.apache.commons.scaffold.util.ResourceUtils`) with methods for loading a Properties file from an absolute location or from your application's `CLASSPATH`.

7.2.12 *The attribute property*

From time to time, you may need to store two copies of the same ActionForm in the same context at the same time. This most often happens when ActionForms are being stored in the session context as part of a workflow. To keep their names from conflicting, you can use the `attribute` property to give one ActionForm bean a different name.

An alternative approach is to define another ActionForm bean in the configuration, using the same type but under a different name.

7.2.13 *The prefix and suffix properties*

Like `attribute`, the `prefix` and `suffix` properties can be used to help avoid naming conflicts in your application. When specified, these switches enable a prefix or suffix for the property name, forming an alias when it is populated from the request.

If the prefix `this` was specified, then

```
thisName=McClanahan
```

becomes equivalent to

```
name=McClanahan
```

for the purpose of populating the ActionForm. Either or both parameters would call

```
getName("McClanahan");
```

This does not affect how the properties are written by the tag extensions. It affects how the autopopulation mechanism perceives them in the request.

7.2.14 *The unknown ActionMapping*

While surfing the Web, most of us have encountered the dreaded *404— page not found* message. Most web servers provide some special features for processing requests for unknown pages, so webmasters can steer users in the right direction.

Struts offers a similar service for ActionMapping 404s—*the unknown ActionMapping*. In the Struts configuration file, you can specify one ActionMapping to receive any requests for an ActionMapping that would not otherwise be matched:

```
<action
    name="/debug"
    unknown="true"
    forward="/pages/debug.jsp"/>
```

When this option is not set, a request for an ActionMapping that cannot be matched throws

```
400 Invalid path /notHere was requested
```

Note that by a *request for an ActionMapping*, we mean a URI that matches the prefix or suffix specified for the servlet (usually /do/* or *.do). Requests for other URI patterns, good or bad, will be handled by other servlets or by the container:

```
/do/notHere (goes to the unknown ActionMapping)
/notHere.txt (goes to the container)
```

7.3 *Nested components*

The ActionMapping properties are helpful when it comes to getting an Action to run a business operation. But they tell only part of the story. There is still much to do when the Action returns.

An Action may have more than one outcome. We may need to register several ActionForwards so that the Action can take its pick.

7.3.1 *Local forwards*

In the normal course, an ActionMapping is used to select an Action object to handle the request. The Action returns an ActionForward that indicates which page should complete the response.

The reason we use ActionForwards is that, in practice, presentation pages are either often reused or often changed, or both. In either case, it is good practice to encapsulate the page's location behind a logical name, like "success" or "failure." The ActionForward object lets us assign a logical name to any given URI.

Of course, logical concepts like success or failure are often relative. What represents success to one Action may represent failure to another. Each ActionMapping can have its own set of local ActionForwards. When the Action asks for a forward (by name), the local set is checked before trying the global forwards. See chapter 6 for more about ActionForwards.

Local forwards are usually specified in the Struts configuration file. See chapter 4 for details.

7.3.2 *Local exceptions*

Most often, an application's exception handlers (`org.apache.struts.action.ExceptionHandler`) can be declared globally. However, if a given ActionMapping needs to handle an exception differently, it can have its own set of local exception handlers that are checked before the global set.

Local exceptions are usually specified in the Struts configuration file. See chapter 4 for details.

7.4 *Rolling your own ActionMapping*

While ActionMapping provides an impressive array of properties, developers may also provide their own subclass with additional properties or methods. In Struts 1.0, this is configured in the deployment descriptor (web.xml) for the ActionServlet:

```
<init-param>
    <param-name>mapping</param-name>
    <param-value>app.MyActionMapping</param-value>
</init-param>
```

In Struts 1.1, this is configured in the Struts configuration file as an attribute to the `<action-mappings>` element:

```
<action-mappings type="app.MyActionMapping">
```

Individual mappings may also be set to use another type through the `className` attribute:

```
<action className="app.MyActionMapping">
```

For more about configuring Struts, see chapter 4.

The framework provides two base ActionMapping classes, shown in table 7.2. They can be selected as the default or used as a base for your own subclasses.

Table 7.2   The default ActionMapping classes

ActionMapping	Description
org.apache.struts.action.SessionActionMapping	Defaults the scope property to session
org.apache.struts.action.RequestActionMapping	Defaults the scope property to request

The framework default is SessionActionMapping, so scope defaults to session.

Subclasses that provide new properties may set them in the Struts configuration using a standard mechanism:

```
<set-property property="myProperty" value="myValue" />
```

Using this standard mechanism helps developers avoid subclassing the Action-Servlet just to recognize the new properties when it digests the configuration file. This is actually a feature of the Digester that Struts simply inherits.

7.5   *Summary*

Sun's Model 2 architecture teaches that servlets and JavaServer Pages should be used together in the same application. The servlets can handle flow control and data acquisition, and the JavaServer Pages can handle the HTML.

Struts takes this one step further and delegates much of the flow control and data acquisition to Action objects. The application then needs only a single servlet to act as a traffic cop. All the real work is parceled out to the Actions and the Struts configuration objects.

Like servlets, Actions are efficient, multithreaded singletons. A single Action object can be handling any number of requests at the same time, optimizing your server's resources.

To get the most use out of your Actions, the ActionMapping object is used as a decorator for the Action object. It gives the Action a URI, or several URIs, and a way to pass different configuration settings to an Action depending on which URI is called.

In this chapter, we took a close look at the ActionMapping properties and explained each property's role in the scheme of things. We also looked at extending the standard ActionMapping object with custom properties—just in case your scheme needs even more things.

In chapter 8, the real fun begins. The configuration objects covered so far are mainly a support system. They help the controller match an incoming request with a server-side operation. Now that we have the supporting players, let's meet the Struts diva: the Action object.

Working with
Action objects

> *I will work harder!*
>
> —Boxer (*Animal Farm,* by George Orwell)

8.1 *Ready, set, action!*

If the Struts configuration is an application's brain, the Action classes are its brawn. These are the workhorses of a Struts application and where the web developers spend most of their time.

Actions are the most flexible classes in the Struts framework. These chimeras can be used to create whatever functionality you need whenever you need it.

The core responsibilities of a Struts Action are to:

- Access the business layer
- Prepare data objects for the presentation layer
- Deal with any errors that spring up in between

But this list does not begin to touch on everything that an Action can do. When the ActionServlet dispatches the request to the Action, it also "deputizes" the object so that it can do whatever a servlet might usually do. For example, an Action can:

- Create its own response to the request
- Access or create other objects in any servlet scope
- Include or forward to another servlet via a RequestDispatcher

While many Actions are customized to a particular task, others can be well-factored utilities, configured by their mapping, and reused throughout your application.

In this chapter we take a close look at the standard Action classes bundled with Struts, the standard Action classes in the Scaffold package, and reusable coding techniques for Actions.

8.2 *Getting it done with Action objects*

Most of the other components in a Struts application simply provide infrastructure so that an Action object can *do* whatever the application *does.*

If the application needs to save a record to a database:

- The ActionForward provides a link to the input page.
- The ActionForm captures the input.

- The ActionMapping configures the Action.
- The Action sends the input up to the database.

NOTE In practice, most developers will send the data to a business delegate (see chapter 14) rather than the actual database. But that's up to you, not Struts. The framework delegates the business operation to the Action and lets the Action do the job in its own way.

In this section, we describe the basics of this vital class: what Actions are, when they are called, what they do, and what they look like.

8.2.1 *What are Actions?*

Compared to a conventional web application, the Struts Action classes work like mini-servlets. In most Java applications, such tasks as accessing the business layer and error handling are handled by a servlet. In a Struts application, the servlet acts as a dispatcher. It's the Action objects that do the actual work. Like servlets, Action objects are multithreaded. Only one instance of an Action class is used per application.

Although they do the work of a servlet, Action objects are not themselves servlets. The Action is a simple, lightweight Java class to which the ActionServlet delegates the handling of the request and its response. The Action class is connected to the ActionServlet and can call any of its public properties but without the overhead of instantiating another servlet.

The servlet refers to the list of ActionMappings (see chapter 7) to select an Action to handle a request. The servlet then calls an entry method on the Action and passes in several useful objects. When the Action's entry method completes, it returns an ActionForward. The ActionServlet uses the ActionForward to determine where control should next pass to complete the request.

Typically, the ActionForward directs control to a presentation component, such as a JSP or Velocity template. The ActionForward could also refer to another Action, an HTML page, or any resource with a URI [W3C, URI]. To signal that it has already generated the response and completed the request, the Action can just return a null value.

From the outside, an Action looks like a mini-servlet that returns an ActionForward. In the rest of this chapter, we explore what Actions look like from the inside.

Thread safety

Actions are multithreaded; there is a single instance of any given Action subclass per application. This means that Actions must be written to be thread-safe. When you're writing an Action subclass, the most important thing to remember is that class properties cannot be used to share values between member methods. If member methods are used, then all values must be passed through the method's signature. This passes the values through the stack, which is thread-safe.

DEFINITION   The term *thread-safe* means that a given library function is implemented in such a manner that it can be executed by multiple concurrent threads of execution. For more about thread safety and multithreading, see chapter 7 of *The Java Language Environment* [Gosling, JLE].

Member methods are an important design element and will often be found in well-written Action subclasses (including several Actions we present later in this chapter). Just be sure to pass all shared values through the method signatures as you would if the methods were on separate objects.

8.2.2   When are Actions called?

When an Action is needed, it is called by the ActionServlet through the Action's `perform` or `execute` method.

STRUTS 1.1   The `execute` method was added in Struts 1.1 to improve exception handling. It is otherwise used in the same way as the original `perform` method. The `perform` method is deprecated in Struts 1.1 but still supported to provide backward compatibility with Struts 1.0.

The `perform` or `execute` method is the only entry point to the Action. The methods accept four parameters, as shown in table 8.1.

Table 8.1   Parameters passed to the Action perform or execute method

Parameter	Description
mapping	The ActionMapping used to invoke this Action
form	The ActionForm specified by the mapping, if any
request	The request context
response	The response we are creating

The `mapping` and `form` parameters are passed as a matter of convenience. At this point, they have already been placed in the request and could be retrieved from there:

```
ActionMapping mapping =
    (ActionMapping) request.getAttribute(MAPPING_KEY);
ActionForm form =
    (ActionForm) request.getAttribute(mapping.getName());
```

But since nearly every Action class will need to use these objects, it's simpler for the servlet to pass them along in the signature. By contrast, the servlet does not pass the session object since most Action classes do not need to use the session context. When the session is needed, it can be retrieved from the request:

```
HttpSession session = request.getSession();
```

It is important to remember that the ActionForm passed to an Action class may differ between requests. The ActionMapping determines which ActionForm subclass is passed to the Action. The ActionServlet will use whatever ActionForm type is in the request. This lets you create flexible Action classes that can be used with a variety of ActionForms.

However, in practice, many Action classes are designed to use a particular ActionForm type and will cast it to access the properties it expects:

```
MyActionForm myForm = (MyActionForm) form;
```

If the form passed were not a MyActionForm or subclass, a runtime exception would be thrown. But as long as the proper type is specified in the ActionMapping, this technique works well.

8.2.3 *What do Actions do?*

The general responsibilities of a typical Action are to:

1 Validate preconditions or assertions.
2 Call any needed business logic methods.
3 Detect any other processing errors.
4 Route control to the appropriate view.

This list is not meant to restrict what an Action *can* do. An Action can do nearly anything a full-fledged servlet can do. If it wants to write a response back to the client, the Action can. If it wants to forward to another servlet, the Action can. But, in practice, most developers write Actions that do these four things and then let the controller forward the request on to another component to render the view.

Actions validate assertions

The primary role of an Action is to serve as an adaptor between the web and business tiers. The Action takes what we can get from the web tier and passes it off to the business operation. But business operations can be finicky and web operations can be vague. Given the loosely coupled nature of the web, most Actions need to validate the data as to form and check other assertions before conducting the requested business operation.

Many times data validation can be delegated to the ActionForm. So, all the Action needs to do is confirm that the ActionForm is of the expected type. Usually this is done with a casual cast of the incoming ActionForm into the expected class (as shown in the prior section):

```
MyActionForm myform = (MyActionForm) form;
```

Other assertions may include whether the user is logged in and has the appropriate clearance. In Struts 1.1, this can be handled automatically using the `roles` property of the ActionMapping (see chapter 7). In some cases, there may be other assertions, such as whether the user has performed another step in the workflow.

If any of the preconditions fail, the Action can generate a list of localized messages and route control to an error page. We'll come back to error handling shortly.

The Action's first responsibility is to confirm any preconditions. Job two is to call the business logic.

Actions call business logic

> *Business logic, in a very broad sense, is the set of guidelines to manage a specific business function. Taking the object-oriented approach enables the developer to decompose a business function into a set of components or elements called business objects.... The business-specific rules that help us identify the structure and behavior of the business objects, along with the pre- and post-conditions that must be met when an object exposes its behavior to other objects in the system, is known as business logic.*
>
> — Taken from the J2EE Blueprints at 5.1 [Sun, Blueprints]

An Action class is an adaptor between HTTP and the rest of your application. It is important to avoid placing any business logic in the Action class itself. The Action class should simply gather whatever data the business methods need and pass it along. If you are writing the business classes and the Action classes at the same time, it is tempting to put them together. You should avoid this and put the business methods in a separate class that the Action can call. The Java Virtual Machine

(JVM) is optimized for calling methods; the performance penalty is slim to nonexistent. Meanwhile, you gain several design advantages, described in table 8.2.

Table 8.2   Why we decouple business logic from Actions

Reason	Explanation
A more robust design	If your business methods are in another class, you don't have to worry about breaking them while you are writing the Action class.
A simpler design	It is easier to see how your Action class works if the business methods are encapsulated behind a method call rather than buried in another paragraph of code.
A broader design	Today they just want a Struts web application. Tomorrow, they refactor the requirements and want something else. If the business logic is not embedded in your Action classes, then it can be reused in another environment.
A more flexible design	Eventually, you may find yourself wanting to use the same business logic in another Action class. Some developers then start forwarding requests between Actions. If the business methods are in a separate class, you have the flexibility of calling them from more than one Action.

Actions detect errors

Struts has a well-developed error-handling system that allows you to:

- Catch several errors at once
- Pass the error packet in the request
- Display a localized message

The process involves two objects (ActionErrors and ActionError) and a utility method (`saveErrors`) to register errors. Two other objects (MessageResources and a custom tag) display the message on the other end. We cover the objects and servlet method here. For more about displaying the error messages using JSP tags, see chapter 10.

Registering errors

The overall process boils down to:

- Creating an empty ActionErrors instance
- Adding keys for error messages as they occur
- Checking to see if any messages have been added
- Saving the `ActionErrors` collection to the request

- Forwarding control to an error page to display the messages
- Otherwise, continuing normally

Or, for example:

```
ActionErrors errors = new ActionErrors();
try {
    // * call a business object *
}
catch (ModelException e) {
    errors.add(ActionErrors.GLOBAL_ERROR,
    new ActionError("error.detail",e.getMessage()));
}
if (!errors.empty()) {
    saveErrors(request, errors);
    return (mapping.findForward("error"));
}
// * continue normally *
```

Of course, `error.detail` is not what the user sees. This is a key to the message resources. The message associated with the key will be merged with any replacement parameters and the result displayed to the user. There can be different message resources for different locales. The messages will differ, but each resource will usually have the same set of keys.

The example just sends the message from the exception to the error page. In the resource file, the key `error.detail` is just one big replacement parameter:

```
error.detail={0}
```

Typically, you may want to use a user-friendlier message like this:

```
error.database=An error occurred while accessing the database
```

You can send both the friendly error and the actual exception message with

```
errors.add(ActionErrors.GLOBAL_ERROR,
    new ActionError("error.database"));
errors.add(ActionErrors.GLOBAL_ERROR,
    new ActionError("error.detail",e.getMessage()));
```

Struts messages can accept up to four replacement parameters. You can use these to customize the message with record numbers or other specifics. For more about the message resources and internationalizing your application, see chapter 13.

In the JSP, you can print the errors using the trusty Struts 1.0 tag:

```
<html:errors/>
```

or the more flexible message tags in Struts 1.1:

```
<logic:messagesPresent>
<UL>
   <html:messages id="error">
      <LI><bean:write name="error"/></LI>
   </html:messages>
   </UL>
</logic:messagesPresent>
```

Queuing messages with Struts 1.0

In Struts 1.0, you can use the same queue for confirmation messages. Whether or not a message is an error is typically a matter of context. It's not difficult for users to tell the difference between

```
"The Amount field is required"
```

and

```
"Record #1412 deleted"
```

Queuing messages with Struts 1.1

In Struts 1.1, you can register both messages and errors to separate queues. On the presentation page, you can then print each queue separately, perhaps using different styles. The process for registering a message is the same general process as registering an error:

- Create an empty ActionMessages instance.
- Add keys for the messages as needed.
- Call saveMessages(HttpServletRequest, ActionMessages).

On the JSP, you can check for messages, as opposed to errors, by specifying message=true in any of the message tags:

```
<logic:messagesPresent message="true">
<UL>
   <html:messages id="message" message="true">
      <LI><bean:write name="message"/></LI>
   </html:messages>
   </UL>
</logic:messagesPresent>
```

To check for errors, as opposed to messages, omit the message attribute (which defaults to false).

Exception handling in Struts 1.0

In a Struts 1.0 application, the Action object sits at the top of the call tree. Any exception that is not caught here does not get caught. It ends up as either a "white screen" or as filler for your JSP error page.

The `perform` method is documented to throw IOExceptions and ServletExceptions. If these exceptions do occur, letting them go to a default error page may be the best thing, since something nasty has happened.

The exceptions you *must* watch for are those thrown by your business logic. The recommended approach is for business objects to throw their own class of exception. This makes it easier to watch for the right ones. It can also give your business layer the chance to frame the exception in a business context.

Exception handling in Struts 1.1

In Struts 1.1, the preferred entry point to an Action is the `execute` method. This method is designed to be used with the Struts ExceptionHandler object (`org.apache.struts.action.ExceptionHandler`). You can register both global and local exception handlers with the Struts configuration. If you like, you can delegate all responsibility for exceptions to the Struts handler. Or you can still handle recoverable exceptions from the Action and allow others to pass up to the handler. The choice is yours.

For more about configuring a Struts exception handler, see chapter 4. For more about writing your own ExceptionHandlers, see chapter 9.

Actions route control

The Struts ActionForwards may *define* the "places to go," but it's the Action object that selects the runtime itinerary. The ActionForward defines where; the Action object decides when.

mapping.findForward.   The ActionServlet invokes an Action object through its `perform` or `execute` method and exits by returning an ActionForward or null. The most common way for an Action class to select a forward is through the `findForward` method of the ActionMapping:

```
return mapping.findForward("continue");
```

The mapping will first search for a local forward before checking the global forwards. If the named forward is not found, then `findForward` returns null.

Usually, an Action returns null to indicate a response has already been sent. If you receive a message from a browser indicating that there was no response, most often it's because `findForward` returned null. This means that either a forward is missing or the Action class has the name wrong.

STRUTS TIP One way to avoid errors like this is to define `String` tokens for the ActionForwards. Unfortunately, you can't use them in the XML configuration file and they are clumsy to use in a JSP. But they do at least document what the forwards are *supposed* to be called and prevent typing errors in the Action classes.

Dynamic selection. While passing a `String` constant is the most common way to select an ActionForward, it is not the only way. The `mapping.findForward` method is resolved at runtime, and so the forward name can be determined at runtime too. For example, a base Action could provide a `getForward` method that could be subclassed to provide specialized behavior. The main `execute` block calls your method to return the result:

```
return mapping.findForward( this.getForward() );
```

Your subclass can override the `getForward` method to return a different outcome without changing the main `execute` method. An Action class might also select a forward based on the outcome of an operation. For example, a special page might be used if a search result came back empty.

```
Collection result = businessClass.getResult();
if (0==result.size()) {
return mapping.findForward(Tokens.EMPTY);
}
request.setAttribute(Tokens.RESULT,result);
return mapping.findForward(Tokens.SUCCESS);
```

Although not a common practice, an Action could also transparently select one forward or another based on the user's locale, browser, security role, or other criteria.

Dynamic construction. The ActionForward itself can also be constructed at runtime. This is a handy way to add parameters to an ActionForward before sending it along to another Action. For more about constructing ActionForwards, see chapter 6.

8.2.4 *What does an Action look like?*

Here's a skeleton `execute` method that synthesizes some of the fragments presented earlier (for Struts 1.0, you can use the same code within a `perform` method):

```
public ActionForward execute(ActionMapping mapping,
  ActionForm form,
  HttpServletRequest request,
  HttpServletResponse response)
    throws Exception {

ActionErrors errors = new ActionErrors();
```

// If all exceptions are registered with handlers
// the try .. catch clause can be omitted
```
try {

        // * business logic here *

}
```

// * Catch your business exceptions here *

```
catch (ChainedException e) {
```
  // Log and print to error console
```
        servlet.log("Exception: ", e );
        e.printStackTrace();
```
  // General error message
```
        errors.add(ActionErrors.GLOBAL_ERROR,
            new ActionError("error.general"));
```
  // Generate error message from exceptions
```
        errors.add(ActionErrors.GLOBAL_ERROR,
            new ActionError("error.detail",e.getMessage()));
        if (e.isCause()) {
                errors.add(ActionErrors.GLOBAL_ERROR,
                        new
ActionError("error.detail",e.getCauseMessage()));
        }
}
```

  // Report any errors
```
if (!errors.empty()) {
        saveErrors(request, errors);
        if (mapping.getInput()!=null)
                return (new ActionForward(mapping.getInput()));
```
        // If no input page, use error forwarding
```
                return (mapping.findForward(Tokens.ERROR));
        }
```

  // * If your business logic created any *
  // * helper objects, save them before returning *
  // * request.setAttribute("yourKey",yourBusinessObject); *

  // * Return the ActionForward you use for success *
```
return findForward("continue");
}
```

Of course, there are several other clever things your Action could do, but this is the basic skeleton that most Actions will follow.

The Scaffold package provides a refactored version of this skeleton that can be used as a base Action in your applications (`org.apache.struts.scaffold.Base-Action`). It replaces each block of code shown previously with a public or protected method that your subclasses can override as needed.

8.3 *The standard Actions*

Many Struts Action classes are written to do a particular job in a particular application. Other Actions are written to be used by any application. Some Actions are written so they can do several jobs. Other Actions may only provide flow control to an application without doing anything themselves. Still others are written to provide a common base for other Actions.

The Struts distribution provides several "standard" Actions that do different things. There are *bridge* Actions that help Struts work with other servlets in your application, and several *base* Actions designed to be extended with new functionality. Table 8.3 describes these Actions.

Table 8.3   The Struts standard Actions (org.apache.struts.actions)

Action	Purpose	Example
Bridge Actions	Integrate Struts with other servlets	ForwardAction IncludeAction
Base Actions	Extend your functionality	DispatchAction LookupDispatchAction [Struts 1.1] SwitchAction [Struts 1.1] BaseAction [ASF, Scaffold]

8.3.1 *Standard bridge Action classes*

Struts likes to play well with others and even provides standard classes to help integrate Struts with other servlets in your application. These work by calling the standard servlet RequestDispatcher class (`javax.servlet.RequestDispatcher`), using either its forward or include method, as shown in table 8.4.

Table 8.4   The standard bridge Actions

Action	Purpose
ForwardAction	Issues a RequestDispatcher forward
IncludeAction	Issues a RequestDispatcher include

ForwardAction

True to its name, the ForwardAction simply forwards control to another resource. This can be another Action, a JSP, another servlet, or any other application resource with a URI [W3C, URI].

The ForwardAction creates a request dispatcher and forwards control to a context-relative URI supplied by the ActionMapping. The context-relative path is given as the ActionMapping's `parameter` property:

```
<action
        path="/saveSubscription"
        type="org.apache.struts.actions.ForwardAction"
        name="subscriptionForm"
        scope="request"
        input="/subscription.jsp"
        parameter="/path/to/application/resource"/>
```

The ActionServlet will run through its normal routine of instantiating any form bean and validating it, if appropriate, before forwarding the request along.

The most common use of the ForwardAction is to serve as a placeholder Action. Many Struts developers avoid linking from one page to another and try to always pass control through an Action or ActionForward. This keeps the workflow under the control of the Struts configuration where it can be centrally managed.

However, many pages do not require any special preprocessing (at least not yet). If an ActionMapping is created for these pages, you can start by using the ForwardAction to just route control. Later, if requirements change and preprocessing is required, you can change the mapping to refer to an Action for that page. Since the links refer to the mapping, not the Action class, you can change the Action class without changing the links.

1.0 vs 1.1 Support for modular application, was introduced in Struts 1.1. Use of this feature requires that control passes through the ActionServlet before processing a JSP page using the Struts taglibs. Even if you are not using a modular design now, you can make your application easier to refactor by linking only to Actions and never to JSPs. If your page does not require an Action, use the ForwardAction instead.

The ForwardAction can also be used to integrate Struts with any other components in an application that expects to be handed a URI. Many servlets, such as Cocoon [ASF, Cocoon], are designed to be accessed through a URI. The URI for these servlets can be encapsulated using a ForwardAction. This makes it easier to leverage the Struts control flow and form bean capabilities without giving up the special services the other servlet offers.

The other servlet would also have access to the form bean in the request, if that were needed. The mapping would also be available under the key given by `Action.MAPPING_KEY`, along with the original HTTP request parameters. Any of these objects can be used to provide information to the other servlet (if it is able to import the Struts classes):

```
ActionMapping mapping = (ActionMapping)
        request.getAttribute(Action.MAPPING_KEY);

EditForm editForm = (EditForm)
        request.getAttribute(mapping.getName());
```

If you need to put objects in the request that are expected by the other component, then simply create your own Action subclass and return an ActionForward to the component's URI. This forward could be created dynamically or read from the Struts configuration in the usual way.

IncludeAction

Similar to the ForwardAction, the IncludeAction helps you integrate other application components into the Struts framework. Rather than forward to the path specified as the `parameter` property, it issues an `include` directive.

With an include, you can start responding to a client and still issue the include. When the other servlet completes, control returns. By contrast, a forward cannot be issued once a response begins, and control does not return to the issuing servlet, as shown in table 8.5.

Table 8.5   Forward versus include

Action	Response	Control
Forward	Cannot be issued once response begins	Control does not return
Include	Can be issued during the response	Controls does return

Includes are most often used as part of the presentation and are the basis for most JSP template systems, like the Tiles library covered in chapter 11. For more about how servlets dispatch requests, see the servlet specification [Sun, JTS].

The place where an IncludeAction can come into play is when an Action object begins a response and then wants some other servlet to finish it. Somewhat esoteric ... but there it is. In practice, the source code from an IncludeAction may be a helpful guide in developing your own Action classes that need to include output from other servlets.

8.3.2 Standard base Actions

The standard base Actions include the following:

- BaseAction (Scaffold)
- DispatchAction
- LookupDispatchAction
- SwitchAction

BaseAction (Scaffold)

Earlier in this chapter, we outlined the things Actions usually do:

- Detect errors and queue messages
- Call business methods
- Catch exceptions
- Log messages
- Route control

If you put all these tasks together into a well-factored Action, you end up with something like this:

```
public ActionForward execute(ActionMapping mapping,
    ActionForm form,
    HttpServletRequest request,
    HttpServletResponse response)
throws Exception {
        // Check for precondition errors; fail if found
        preProcess(mapping,form,request,response);
        if (isErrors(request)) {
            return findFailure(mapping,form,request,response);
        }
        // Try the logic; Call catchException() if needed
        try {
            executeLogic(mapping,form,request,response);
        }
        catch (Exception e) {
                // Store Exception; call extension point
            setException(request,e);
            catchException(mapping,form,request,response);
        }
        finally {
            postProcess(mapping,form,request,response);
```

```
        }
            // If errors queued, fail
        if (isErrors(request)) {
            return findFailure(mapping,form,request,response);
        }
            // Otherwise, check for messages and succeed (only I_0)
        if ((isStruts_1_0()) && (isMessages(request))) {
            saveErrors(request,getMessages(request,false));
        }
        return findSuccess(mapping,form,request,response);
    }
```

This is the execute method from the Struts BaseAction (org.apache.scaffold. http.BaseAction) in the optional Scaffold package. This Action provides hotspot methods for the major events in an Action's workflow. A subclass can override just the hotspot methods it needs to change.

STRUTS TIP   Always create a base class for the custom Actions in your application. The Actions are instantiated only once, so there is little penalty for creating a deep Action hierarchy. If you watch for places where you can abstract common needs into utility methods, there can be a lot of code to share between your Actions.

In practice, you would usually override the executeLogic method and sometimes postProcess, but the other methods have default behaviors that will work well in most circumstances. If not, you can override any of these hotspot methods to provide special behavior for special circumstances, as shown in table 8.6.

Table 8.6   Base Action hotspots

Action	Description
preProcess	Optional extension point to handle any preconditions for this Action.
findFailure	Returns the appropriate ActionForward for an error condition. The default method returns a forward to the input path, when there is one, or the error forward when not.
executeLogic	Executes the business logic for this Action. Overrides to provide functionality.
catchException	Processes the exception handling for this Action.
postProcess	Optional extension point to handle any post conditions for this Action.
findSuccess	Returns the appropriate ActionForward for the nominal, nonerror state. The default returns mapping.findForward("success").

You can use BaseAction as the ancestor class for your own Actions, or adopt and adapt the techniques to any base Action that you may already use.

1.0 vs 1.1   The BaseAction Scaffold 1.0 release is written to be forward-compatible with Struts 1.1. It includes a stub `process` method that calls the now-preferred `execute` method. This lets you base your code on `execute` regardless of whether it is now used with Struts 1.0 or Struts 1.1. In Struts 1.1, the `execute` method will be called directly and the old `perform` method ignored. Under Struts 1.0, calling the `perform` method in turn invokes the newer `execute` method. Other hooks are included to accommodate other changes, like the new message queue.

For more about moving from Struts 1.0 to Struts 1.1, see chapter 16.

DispatchAction

A common strategy among Struts developers is to use the same Action class to handle several related tasks. A good example is performing the basic CRUD (Create Read Update Delete) operations on a data record. Since these operations have much in common, it can be simplest to maintain them from the same class.

Without the DispatchAction, the usual approach is to use a hidden field in the ActionForm to select the appropriate Action. With the DispatchAction (`org.apache.struts.actions.DispatchAction`), developers can group multiple methods within a single Action. The DispatchAction can automatically select the correct method by keying on the hidden field; it uses reflection to replace the fragile if/then logic most developers would use instead.

Each of the dispatch methods must use the same signature as the usual Action `perform` or `execute` method. (Read as `perform` for Struts 1.0 and `execute` for Struts 1.1.) The name of the hidden field is passed to the Action in the generic `parameter` property of the ActionMapping. The DispatchAction then grabs the value of the field from the request and uses reflection to call the appropriate method.

STRUTS TIP   Use DispatchAction to organize related operations into a unified Action. Keeping related operations together simplifies maintenance and flow control.

For example, your DispatchAction subclass might contain "dispatch" methods like these:

```
public ActionForward create(
        ActionMapping mapping, ActionForm form,
        HttpServletRequest request, HttpServletResponse response)
        throws IOException,ServletException;

public ActionForward read(
        ActionMapping mapping, ActionForm form,
        HttpServletRequest request, HttpServletResponse response)
        throws IOException, ServletException;

public ActionForward update(
        ActionMapping mapping, ActionForm form,
        HttpServletRequest request, HttpServletResponse response)
        throws IOException, ServletException;

public ActionForward delete(
        ActionMapping mapping, ActionForm form,
        HttpServletRequest request, HttpServletResponse response)
        throws IOException, ServletException;
```

And your Struts configuration could create an entry like this:

```
<action
        path="/dataRecord"
        type="app.recordDispatchAction"
        name="dataForm"
        scope="request"
        input="/data.jsp"
        parameter="method"/>
```

To select the delete method, you could call

```
http://localhost/app/dataRecord?method=delete
```

and include whatever other property is needed to select the record.

In practice, the value of the method field is usually the name of one of the buttons or a hidden property in the form (set with a JavaScript).

The dispatch mechanism itself is transparent and efficient. The developer need only subclass DispatchAction and supply the appropriate methods. The perform or execute method should not be overridden, since it is used to select one of the other methods. Whatever functionality would usually be placed in a perform or execute method would be placed into the dispatch methods.

LookupDispatchAction

A convenient way to select a dispatch method is by linking it with a button. This can be problematic in a localized application, since the label of the button may change according to the user's locale. For one user, the button may read *Delete*; for another, it may read *Borre*.

STRUTS TIP Use DispatchLookupAction instead of DispatchAction when it is important to both localize your controls and avoid reliance on JavaScript to select the dispatch operation.

The DispatchLookupAction (`org.apache.struts.actions.DispatchLookup-Action`) solves this problem by mapping the labels back to their original message key. The key can then be mapped to the appropriate dispatch method. Since the message key may not be an appropriate name for a Java method, the developer provides a hash table that maps the message keys to the dispatch method names:

```
protected Map getKeyMethodMap(ActionMapping mapping,
            ActionForm form,HttpServletRequest request) {
    Map map = new HashMap();
    map.put("button.add", "create");
    map.put("button.view", "read");
    map.put("button.update", "update");
    map.put("button.delete", "delete");
    return map;
}
```

In a JSP, the buttons could be created like this:

```
<html:form action="/dataRecord">
  <html:submit property="method">
    <bean:message key="button.add">
  </html:submit>
  <html:submit property="method">
    <bean:message key="button.view">
  </html:submit>
  <html:submit property="method">
    <bean:message key="button.update">
  </html:submit>
  <html:submit property="method">
    <bean:message key="button.delete">
  </html:submit>
</html:form>
```

The labels for the buttons may vary by user locale, but the same method will be selected regardless.

To sum up, the difference between the DispatchAction and DispatchLookupAction is that the latter does a reverse lookup to match the localized value submitted for the button back to the message key. The message key is then mapped to the name of the dispatch method.

Factoring dispatch methods

Often, the dispatch methods will need to do similar things while undertaking their individual operations: watch for exceptions, check for errors, log messages, and so forth—all the things an Action would usually do.

While Action classes need to be thread-safe, you can still provide utilities for the dispatch methods to share. The important thing is to pass whatever variables are needed by the utility through its signature. This places the variables on the stack, which is thread-safe.

For example, if each dispatch method needs to check the locale of the user, they can all call the same utility to look this up, as long as each instance passes their copy of the request:

```
Locale locale = getLocale(request);
```

The same principle applies to any other data structure. A multithreaded class, like an Action, cannot share data between methods using class variables, but methods may pass instance variables to each other through their signatures. The Base-Action class covered earlier in this section relies on this technique.

If you like routing related operations to the same Action but sometimes need to handle one of them through its own Action, you can always have the dispatch method return a forward so that the other Action can finish the job.

SwitchAction

All Struts applications have at least one module. Some applications may be configured to use multiple modules. Each module has its own set of configuration files and presentation pages and can be developed as if it were the only module in the application.

Of course, at some point the modules need to interact if they are going to work as a single application. SwitchAction (`org.apache.struts.actions.SwitchAction`) is a standard Action that can switch to another module and then forward control to a path within that module.

SwitchAction expects two request parameters to be passed:

- `page`: A module-relative URI (beginning with /) to which control should be forwarded after switching.

- `prefix`: The module prefix (beginning with /) of the application module to which control should be switched. Use a zero-length string for the default module. The appropriate ApplicationConfig object will be stored as a request attribute, so any subsequent logic will assume the new application module.

8.4 Chaining Actions

As an application grows, its Actions tend to evolve into an internal API. Developers find themselves wanting to join Action classes in a chain, creating a workflow or macro process. Generally, this is a sign that the business logic is too strongly coupled with the Action or that the Action hierarchy is too shallow. If there is functionality that should be shared between Actions, it should be factored into separate business classes or provided as helper methods in an Action super class. However, there are techniques you can use to chain Actions together if need be.

The ActionForward returned by an Action's `perform` method can be any URI, including another Action. Developers often use this technique to create workflows where each Action plays its own part in processing the request.

If you forward from one Action to another in this way, the ActionServlet treats the forwarded request just as if it had come directly from the client. The Action-Form bean is reset, repopulated, and revalidated, and, if all goes well, passed to the second Action. This often upsets developers, since they usually want to set a property on the form bean and pass that value along to the next Action in the chain.

The best solution here is to add a switch to your bean to make its properties immutable:

```
private boolean mutable = true;
public void setMutable(boolean mutable) {
        this.mutable = mutable;
}
// ...
public setProperty(String property) {
        if (isMutable()) this.property = property;
}
```

After modifying properties in the first action, call `setMutable(false)`. Then go on to the second Action.

If your `reset` method calls the public setters, then `reset` will be effectively disabled as well. If `reset` sets the properties directly, then it will need to be modified to check the immutable state. If validation might be a problem, then have `validate` return true whenever `mutable` is false. However, the data you want to pass between Actions is likely to be valid and shouldn't fail in the normal course.

A variation on this technique is to create a new form bean for the second Action, populate it, and add it to the request. If both Actions use the same bean type, and you need them both, you can add an `attribute` property to one of the Action's mappings so that it is stored under a different attribute name:

```
<action
        path="/item/Edit"
        type="org.apache.gavel.http.ModelHelper"
        name="itemForm"
        attribute="itemFormAdd"
        scope="request"
        validate="false"
        parameter="org.apache.gavel.item.Select">
        <forward
                name="continue"
                path="/pages/item/Form.jsp"/>
</action>
```

8.4.1 *Starting fresh*

On the other hand, if you would like to clear the request context so that the chained Action starts with a clean slate, make it a redirect instead:

```
ActionForward startOver = mapping.findForward("start");
startOver.setRedirect(true);
return startOver;
```

NOTE Speaking as a software architect, chaining Actions in any way is not something that I like to do. Ideally, you should be able to call the business objects from any Action where they are needed. Wanting to forward control to another Action implies that the business objects may be too tightly coupled. Or it may imply that the Actions should descend from a common super class with hotspots that subclasses could override. Be sure to study the design of the Scaffold BaseAction before you kluge two Actions together. There are occasions when chaining Actions makes sense—for example, if the other Action is being used to render the response in lieu of a presentation page. But valid use cases are rare. The best general practice is to stay with a one-request, one-Action regimen.

8.5 *Scaffold Actions*

The Scaffold package includes several standard Action classes that are designed to be used multiple times in multiple applications. These fall into two general categories, as shown in table 8.7.

Table 8.7 Scaffold Actions

Forward-only Actions	Helper Actions
SuccessAction	BaseHelperAction
RelayAction	ProcessAction
ParameterAction	AttributeExistsAction
FindForwardAction	RemoveAttributeAction

All of the Scaffold standard Actions subclass BaseAction. The Struts 1.0 version of BaseAction provides a forward-compatible `execute` signature. In this section, when we refer to `execute` we are referring to the same method for both versions.

8.5.1 *Forward-only Actions*

This is a very simple but powerful technique. Here the Action class is used as a simple dispatcher. It looks for a given ActionForward and relays control. The Scaffold package provides four variations on this theme, as shown in table 8.8.

Table 8.8 Scaffold's forward-only Actions

Action	Purpose
SuccessAction	Just forwards to success
RelayAction	Looks up a forward based on a known runtime parameter
ParameterAction	Adds a runtime parameter before relaying
FindForwardAction	Dynamically finds a forward based on the runtime parameters

SuccessAction

Similar to the standard ForwardAction, the SuccessAction (`org.apache.struts.scaffold.SuccessAction`) routes control to another resource, usually a JSP. But instead of getting the URI from the `parameter` property, it looks for a local or global forward.

The `execute` method for a SuccessAction can be implemented as one line:

```
return mapping.findForward("success");
```

An ActionMapping element might look like this:

```
<action
        path="/myPackage/myForm"
        type="org.apache.scaffold.http.SuccessAction"
        name="myFormBean"
        scope="request"
        validate="false">
```

```
<forward
        name="success"
        path="/pages/myPackage/myForm.jsp"/>
</action>
```

The SuccessAction has the same effect as the ForwardAction but lets you specify the resource using a forward rather than the mapping's `parameter` property. Of course, since the SuccessAction is very simple, if you wish to use a token other than `success`, creating your own version for a given project is trivial.

RelayAction

The RelayAction (`org.apache.struts.scaffold.RelayAction`) looks for a given parameter and uses its value to look up the forward. This can be useful when there is more than one Submit button on a page and a different ActionMapping should be called for each.

NOTE   This is an alternative approach to DispatchAction and LookupDispatchAction, which expect related operations to be submitted to the same ActionMapping. Other designs may need to route different operations through different ActionMappings.

A simple JavaScript is used to set a hidden property on the form. Like the SuccessAction, the implementation of the Action `execute` method is a single line:

```
return mapping.findForward(request.getParameter(Tokens.DISPATCH));
```

But here, we look up a parameter from the request and pass its value to `findForward()`. In contrast, the SuccessAction always passes the same value to `findForward ("success")`.

If passed a URL like

```
http://whatever.com/artimus/do/prospect/Submit?dispatch=update
```

the RelayAction would check the mappings for an ActionForward named `update` and return that. Here's an example of a RelayAction mapping:

```
<action
        path="/prospect/Submit"
        type="org.apache.scaffold.http.RelayAction"
        name="prospectForm"
        scope="request"
        validate="false">
        <forward
                name="update"
```

```
                    path="/do/prospect/Store"/>
        <forward
                name="cancel"
                path="/do/prospect/Current"/>
        <forward
                name="create"
                path="/do/prospect/CreateDonor"/>
        <forward
                name="donor"
                path="/do/donor/Detail"/>
</action>
```

Depending on the value of the dispatch parameter, this mapping can relay control to four other ActionMappings: Store, Current, CreateDonor, or Detail.

In a JSP, the forward parameter can be set using a smidgen of JavaScript, like this:

```
<html:form>
// ...
<html:hidden property="dispatch" value="error"/>
<html:submit onclick="set('update');">UPDATE PROSPECT</html:submit>
<html:cancel onclick="set('cancel');">CANCEL</html:cancel>
<html:submit onclick="set('create');">CREATE DONOR</html:submit>
<html:submit onclick="set('donor');">UPDATE DONOR</html:submit>
</html:form>
<script>
function set(target) {document.forms[0].dispatch.value=target;};
</script>
```

NOTE The hidden dispatch property defaults to error. If JavaScript were disabled, then the user would be forwarded to an error page, where the requirement could be explained. This assumes that dispatch is a property on the ActionForm (recommended). If dispatch is not an ActionForm property, then

```
<input type="hidden" name="dispatch" value="error">
```

could be used instead.

Another technique that does not require JavaScript is the FindForwardAction covered in this chapter.

STRUTS TIP Use the RelayAction to select and dispatch Actions from the Struts configuration. This helps keep the control-flow code in the "open" rather than buried in an Action.

ParameterAction

Many menu pages offer lists of business operations. Often, these menu items require a parameter in order to operate correctly. For example, a search operation may need a String parameter to narrow the search. Typically, we start out with a URI like

```
/do/find/Content
```

and want to customize it to be something like

```
/do/find/Content?content=glockenspiel
```

where glockenspiel is provided by the user at runtime.

The ParameterAction (org.apache.struts.scaffold.ParameterAction) starts out like a RelayAction. It looks for a request parameter named dispatch and uses the dispatch value to look up a forward. But then it goes on to look up a second request parameter. The value of this parameter is appended to the end of the URI. The request parameter the Action should look up is specified by the parameter property of the ActionMapping.

Here's a sample ActionMapping:

```
<action
        path="/menu/Find"
        type="org.apache.struts.scaffold.ParameterAction"
        name="menuForm"
        validate="false"
        parameter="keyValue">
        <forward
            name="title"
            path="/do/find/Title?title="/>
        <forward
            name="author"
            path="/do/find/Author?creator="/>
        <forward
            name="content"
            path="/do/find/Content?content="/>
</action>
```

and a JSP code fragment that uses it:

```
<html:form action="/menu/Find">
<TR>
<TD>Find articles by: </TD>
<TD>
<html:select property="dispatch">
        <html:option value="title">Title</html:option>
        <html:option value="author">Author</html:option>
        <html:option value="content">Content</html:option>
```

```
</html:select>
<html:text property="keyValue"/>
</TD>
<TD><html:submit>GO</html:submit></TD>
</TR>
</html:form>
```

If the user selects Content and enters `glockenspiel` in the text field, the browser will submit

```
dispatch=content
keyValue=glockenspiel
```

The ParameterAction will then look up the forward for `content` and append the keyValue to the end of its URI, yielding

```
/do/find/Content?content=glockenspiel
```

For more about creating menu pages, see section 8.8.

FindForwardAction

Using multiple Submit buttons on a page can get complicated—especially when some might be localized or use an image. The browser submits the button's name and its label when a standard HTML button is used. But when an image button is used, the browser submits the x/y coordinates instead (by appending `.x` and `.y` to the button name). The original name is not passed at all.

In either case, the value submitted is usually of no value. The label may be localized or changed on a designer's whim. Even the x and y coordinates are subject to change.

The one reliable piece of information here is the button's name, which can be used as a key to determine which task is required. An Action object could loop through the set of possible button keys, but changing the set of buttons could mean changing the Action's source code.

A better approach is to map the buttons to their corresponding ActionMapping from within the Struts configuration. FindForwardAction (`org.apache.struts.actions.FindForwardAction`) makes this easy to do. Since the technique is indirect, let's start with a concrete example of a JSP and work from there.

This example displays two buttons. One is a standard Submit button named *add* with a localized label. The other is an image button named *delete*.

```
<html:form action="/addDelete">
<!-- BUTTON --!>
<html:submit property="button_add">
      <bean:message key="button.add"/>
</html:submit>
```

```
<!-- IMAGE --!>
        <html:image page="/images/delete.gif" property="image_delete" />
</html:form>
```

When submitted, the request will contain either a parameter named `button_add` or a set of parameters named `image_delete.x` and `image_delete.y`.

Here is a sample ActionMapping for handling this form. Note that it specifies a local forward for each button. In the case of the `image_delete` button, the `image_delete.x` name was used since it is an image button (`image_delete.y` would work as well):

```
<action path="/addDelete"
        type="org.apache.scaffold.http.FindForwardAction"
        name="addDeleteForm"
        scope="request"
        input="/pages/addDelete.jsp">
        <forward name="button_add" path="/do/Add"/>
        <forward name="image_delete.x" path="/do/Delete"/>
</action>
```

Or , if you need to include a parameter:

```
<action path="/addDelete"
        type="org.apache.scaffold.http.FindForwardAction"
        name="addDeleteForm"
        scope="request"
        input="/pages/addDelete.jsp">
        <forward name="button_add" path="/do/crud?dispatch=add"/>
        <forward name="image_delete.x" path="/do/crud?dispatch=delete"/>
</action>
```

While the other forward-only Action classes looked for a forward by a given name, FindForwardAction is more dynamic. It obtains the list of available ActionForward names and checks to see if any of them match the name of a request parameter. If one does, it is selected as the ActionForward. So, if the method finds `button_add`, the local forward for `button_add` fires. If the method finds `image_delete.x`, the local forward for `image_delete.x` fires instead.

The FindForwardAction `perform` method is a whopping five lines:

```
String forwards[] = mapping.findForwards();
for (int i=0; i<forwards.length; i++) {
        if (request.getParameter(forwards[i])!=null) {
                return mapping.findForward(forwards[i]);
        }
}
return null;
```

This decouples button names from the Action classes they call. If the page changes the buttons it uses, or how it uses them, any corresponding changes would take place only in the Struts configuration.

8.5.2 *Helper Actions*

Scaffold provides several Action classes that provide services above and beyond what is usually expected of an Action. In addition to being dispatchers, these classes manage special helper objects that are used to complete the task at hand, as shown in table 8.9.

Table 8.9   Helper Actions

Action	Purpose
BaseHelperAction	Creates arbitrary helper objects
ProcessAction	Instantiates and executes helper beans and processes the result
ExistsAttributeAction	Checks whether an attribute exists in a given scope
RemoveAttributeAction	Deletes an object from session context

BaseHelperAction

Nearly all the object types used by the Struts framework can be specified in the Struts configuration—ActionForwards, ActionForms, ActionMappings, and the Action objects—everything but the business objects. The business objects are usually encapsulated (or "buried") in the Action class.

STRUTS TIP   Specifying a helper object in the ActionMapping puts everything under the control of the Struts configuration, making the application architecture easier to design, review, and modify.

If you are using lightweight business objects, then the BaseHelperAction can allow you to bring the business objects out into the open. The business object type to be associated with a mapping can be specified as its `parameter` property:

```
<action
     path="/search/Content"
     type="org.apache.struts.scaffold.BaseActionHelper"
     name="articleForm"
     validate="false"
     parameter="org.apache.artimus.article.SearchContent">
     <forward
```

```
                  name="continue"
                  path="/pages/article/Result.jsp"/>
   </action>
```

The BaseHelperAction (`org.apache.struts.scaffold.BaseHelperAction`) sub-classes BaseAction. The BaseAction supplies the default control flow for an Action so that subclasses, such as BaseHelperAction, can override one hotspot and inherit the rest of the process. Since these helpers are intended as business objects, BaseHelperAction overrides the `executeLogic` method to instantiate the helpers. It then calls a new hotspot of its own, with an array of all the helpers:

```
executeLogic(mapping,form,request,response,helpers);
```

Subclasses should override this new `executeLogic` signature to make use of the helpers passed by the BaseHelperAction class. The default version provides some test code that just prints the `String` representation of each helper as the response:

```
protected void executeLogic(
            ActionMapping mapping,
            ActionForm form,
            HttpServletRequest request,
            HttpServletResponse response,
            Object[] helpers)
        throws Exception {
        // override to provide new functionality
        response.setContentType(Tokens.TEXT_PLAIN);
        for (int i = 0; i < helpers.length; i++)
            response.getWriter().print(helpers[i].toString());
    }
```

ProcessAction

The Scaffold ProcessAction (`org.apache.struts.scaffold.ProcessAction`) class is a BaseHelperAction subclass that uses the helper business objects and builds on the control flow provided by the BaseAction.

ProcessAction expects the underlying helpers to be subclasses of another Scaffold class, ProcessBean (`org.apache.commons.scaffold.util.ProcessBean`). This is a lightweight class designed to encapsulate business operations. Like a Struts Action, a ProcessBean is accessed through an `execute` method.

When used with ProcessAction, the ProcessBean `execute` method is expected to return a ProcessResult (`org.apache.commons.scaffold.ProcessResult`). This is a transfer object designed to encapsulate the result of an arbitrary business operation that may return any combination of data, messages, or both.

The ProcessAction analyzes the ProcessResult. If the result returns messages, the action calls `saveMessage` to expose the messages to Struts. If the result returns data, it saves the data to a servlet context where a presentation page can find it.

ProcessAction is designed as a "graybox" component, like the Struts ActionServlet. You can use it as is or start overriding the extension points to modify or extend the default behavior. The real programming takes place in the ProcessBeans.

For a working example of implementing ProcessBeans and using them with ProcessAction, see the Artimus application in chapter 15.

ExistsAttributeAction

Some workflows may expect that an attribute has already been created. This may be a value object that is being used to collect fields as part of a wizard. It may be an object that provides the options for an HTML control. It may be a user profile record that is used as part of a security scheme, or several other things.

The chaotic nature of web applications can make it difficult for us to ensure that such attributes are available. There are many ways that users can skip around an application and end up at step 2 without going through step 1. There are also objects that we may not want to bother creating until they are needed, but once we create them we do not need them again.

The ExistsAttributeAction is one solution for these types of problems. It checks to see if a given attribute exists in a given scope, or in any scope. If so, it goes on to the `success` forward. If not, it goes on to the `failure` forward:

```
<action
        path="/Menu"
        name="menuForm"
        type="org.apache.struts.scaffold.ExistsAttributeAction"
        parameter="*;HOURS">
        <forward
            name="success"
            path="/pages/article/Menu.jsp "/>
        <forward
            name="failure"
            path="/do/MenuCreate"/>
</action>
```

The scope and attribute are specified as the `parameter` property. The first token is the scope (application, session, request). To indicate any scope, use an asterisk. The second token is the attribute. Remember that Java is case sensitive, so `HOURS` and `hours` are not the same attribute.

RemoveAttributeAction

This Action class can be used with any workflow that needs to remove an attribute from the session context. It simply removes the attribute specified as the Action-Mapping's parameter and forwards to success:

```
<action
        path="/account/Logoff"
        type="org.apache.gavel.http.RemoveAttributeAction"
        validate="false"
        parameter="userProfile">
        <forward
                name="success"
                path="/pages/account/Logon.jsp"/>
</action>
```

This can be used as part of logging out a user or at the end of a wizard workflow.

8.6 Base View Actions

For the most part, the Struts framework is designed to provide the Controller component of a Model/View/Controller architecture (see chapter 1).

But that doesn't mean an Action can't create the response and render the View. The framework directly supports the idea that the Action may create the response. All an Action has to do is return null and the framework considers the request/response fulfilled. If your application has special requirements for the View, an Action can do whatever you need it to do. You might want to create your own View Action for rendering dynamic images, creating PDFs, or merging XML with a XSL stylesheet.

One approach is to simply chain your View Action and have the usual Controller Action forward to another that renders the View. This way, your Controller Actions can continue to prepare the data and forward it on for someone else to display. Instead of a JSP or Velocity template, the "someone else" is an Action.

Another approach is to create a base View Action and then extend that to create whatever Controller Actions you may need. The base Action can implement a method like this:

```
public ActionForward render(
    ActionMapping mapping, ActionForm form,
    HttpServletRequest request, HttpServletResponse response)
    throws IOException, ServletException;
```

Taking this approach has several consequences:

- Since this method passes the runtime variables in its signature, it is thread safe.

- The code can be easy to maintain. One team can work on the ancestor class while others focus on the classes that extend it.

- Since `render` uses the `perform` signature, the method's interface is as stable as the rest of the Action.

- Since the request does not need to be forwarded, everything can be completed then and there.

- The ActionServlet will not process the request again or overwrite the original ActionForm and ActionMapping.

- If you have more than one special rendering technique, there could be more than one base class. If the interfaces were compatible, you could just change which one it extends.

- If the base class extends DispatchAction (`org.apache.struts.actions.DispatchAction`), then you could also call the render method directly and forego the subclass.

- Properly factored, the request-rendered code can be portable. The Action can pass the request, the response, and any other needed data to a method in another class. The second class can write the actual response, just as it might call a business layer method to access the actual database.

8.7 *Helper Action techniques*

In the preceding section, we looked at some standard Action classes that were designed for reuse. These Action classes implement several techniques that you can include in your classes to make them more flexible. To save you prowling through the source code to scavenge for the best bits, we present several reusable techniques here (see table 8.10 for a summary).

Table 8.10   Helper Action techniques

Action	Purpose
Optional forwarding	Engages logic if a certain forward is present
Calling ahead	Invokes base method intended to be overridden
Catching chained exceptions	Displays a message for each exception in a chain
Smart error forwarding	Optionally forwards to input or standard error page
Confirming success	Queues messages to report status
Alternate views	Selects view helper based on business logic event

Table 8.10 Helper Action techniques *(continued)*

Action	Purpose
Reflecting methods	Invokes a method of an Action by name
Reflecting classes	Invokes a helper object with an Action by name

8.7.1 *Optional forwarding*

This technique is used several times in the helpers to provide optional behavior depending on how an Action object is configured. This permits the same Action class to be used in different ways. In the Struts framework, an Action object is configured by an ActionMapping. The ActionMapping defines several properties and also provides a list of local ActionForwards.

STRUTS TIP   Use optional forwarding to make your base Actions more flexible and easier to reuse.

The optional forwarding technique first checks to see whether a particular ActionForward has been defined. If not, the optional behavior is skipped. If so, the optional behavior may occur if circumstances warrant.

A good example is checking for a *cancel* state. Canceling the submission of an HTML form is built into the Struts framework. Of course, not every form can be canceled, and when it can, where the control should flow may vary from mapping to mapping.

Here's an ActionMapping that includes a forward for routing a cancel event:

```
<action
        path="/item/Store"
        type="org.apache.gavel.http.ModelHelper"
        name="itemForm"
        scope="request"
        validate="true"
        input="/pages/item/Form.jsp"
        parameter="org.apache.gavel.item.Store">
        <forward
                name="cancel"
                path="/do/item/Detail"/>
        <forward
                name="token"
                path="/pages/item/tokenError.jsp"/>
        <forward
                name="continue"
```

```
                    path="/do/item/Detail"/>
    </action>
```

Here's how the BaseAction uses our optional forwarding technique to check for a cancel command. This is the first statement of the BaseAction's execute method:

```
ActionForward forward = mapping.findForward(Tokens.CANCEL);
if ((forward!=null) && (isCancelled(request))) {
        return (forward);
}
```

First, it checks to see if a cancel ActionForward has been defined. If an appropriate ActionForward has been defined (!=null) *and* the request was in fact canceled, the cancel ActionForward is returned, ending the method.

Another built-in feature is *synchronizer tokens* (see also chapter 10). These ensure that a form is not submitted more than once. Again, if an ActionForward for token has been defined, and the token is actually invalid, then the token ActionForward is returned. The balance of the method is not processed.

```
forward = mapping.findForward(Tokens.TOKEN);
if ((forward!=null) && (!isTokenValid(request))) {
        return (forward);
}
```

Is it is important to note that the names of any optional forward (like cancel or token) should be used only in a local context. If there are also global forwards using these names, looping and other problems can occur. The findForward method will always search the local forwards first, but if the forward is not found, it will also search the global forwards before returning null.

8.7.2 Calling ahead

As a general pattern, it is often useful to have an ancestor method call an abstract or base method that is expected to be subclassed. Many Struts developers do this with the Action execute method in order to ensure that some standard operation happens first. (In Struts 1.0, the perform method would be called instead of execute.) A common use case is authenticating users with application-based security. The base ancestor Action object first checks that the user is logged in (often by checking for an object in the HTTP session). If so, the ancestor execute calls another method that has been subclassed to provide the actual functionality. If not, the user is routed to a login page.

Often the other method is given a similar but different name (for example, doExecute). Developers can then extend the application's base Action class, and override doExecute instead of execute.

Another approach is to call

```
super.execute(mapping,form,request,response)
```

from the subclassed `execute` and return any non-null result.

The BaseHelperAction uses a third variation. It calls another method named `perform` that uses a different signature. After the method has instantiated the business object, it closes with

```
return execute(mapping,form,request,response,helpers);
```

This invokes the "other" `execute` method and passes it an array of helper objects. When the subclass method returns, that is the result that passes up the stack to the ActionServlet.

8.7.3 *Catching chained exceptions*

Many Java mavens recommend that business objects throw their own exceptions. Internally, a component may catch a SQL or IO exception, but what we really need is to tell the user that a data access error occurred. Of course, at the same time, we do not want to sacrifice any detail from the original exception. Retaining detail from the exception can be especially important in a layered, multitiered, or multiplatform application. The business component may not have direct access to the log, and the exception is its only way of telling us what went wrong.

In short, we need a way to keep the detail of the original message but at the same time also add a user-friendly business exception. The former may complain that it could not process a SQL query. The latter may simply report that a data-access error occurred and suggest that you contact the database administration. We would also want to be sure to log both exceptions, to ensure that all the detail is maintained.

As the exception class was originally designed, doing something like this is a problem. The Java exception mechanism allows you to throw only one exception, not two or three. It's easy to wrap exceptions, using one to initialize the next, but the result is a loss of detail over multiple layers. What we really need to do is *stack*, or *chain*, the exceptions, so that each layer can add its own viewpoint to the incident. Then, at the end, we can display them all, with the originating exception at the bottom of the list.

This approach works surprisingly well in a layered architecture. The topmost layer is closest to the user, and so throws the most user-friendly exceptions. The lowest layer throws the "geek-friendly" errors that we need to solve the problem. When we chain exceptions by linking them together, the user-friendly message comes first, followed by the more detailed messages. The user is told what he or she needs to know first, and can leave the rest to the system administrators.

The best part is that chaining exceptions is very easy to implement in Struts!

Java 1.4 provides new functionality for chaining exceptions, but it is not difficult to write your own ChainedException class to use with another JVM. The Commons Scaffold toolkit [ASF, Scaffold] includes a ChainedException class that works with older JVMs.

Here's a `try`/`catch` block from a base Action that uses the Scaffold Chained-Exception class. It calls a member method to perform the business operation and then analyzes the result:

```
// ❶
ActionErrors errors = new ActionErrors();
try {
    executeLogic(mapping,form,request,response);
}
catch (Exception exception) {
    // ❷
  servlet.log("*** ACTION EXCEPTION: ", exception);
 exception.printStackTrace();
    // ❸
    errors.add(ActionErrors.GLOBAL_ERROR,
      new ActionError("error.general"));
    // ❹
    StringBuffer sb = new StringBuffer();
    if (exception instanceof ChainedException) {
      ChainedException e = (ChainedException) exception;
      e.getMessage(sb);
    }
    else {
      sb.append(exception.getMessage());
    }
}
// ❺
errors.add(ActionErrors.GLOBAL_ERROR,
    new ActionError("error.detail",sb.toString()));
// ❻
```

❶ We set up an empty ActionErrors collection for later use, call the business operation, and catch any and all exceptions it might throw.

❷ If an exception is thrown, we start by logging the message and including a marker so that it is easier to find later. We also print the stack trace, to ensure that it is recorded for future reference.

❸ We start by adding our own general error message to the errors collection. This just says something like "The process did not complete. Details should follow."

❹ If the business operation passes back a subclass of ChainedException, we trundle through the chain and collect all the messages.

❺ To make the messages easy to display a presentation page, we wrap them in a generic message template. The message template is a single substitution code:

```
error.detail={0}
```

so that it just prints everything verbatim.

This results in an error messages like

1 The process did not complete. Details should follow.

2 A required resource is not available.

3 Cannot connect to MySQL server on localhost:3307. Is there a MySQL server running on the machine port you are trying to connect to? (`java.net.ConnectException`)

being (using the same reference numbers):

1 The general error message

2 The business object message

3 The original message from the JDBC driver

❻ We branch to an error page if the error collection is not empty.

The key advantage to this approach is that it provides a high-level message for the user ("A required resource is not available") and a low-level message for technical support ("Cannot connect to MySQL server..."). So, everybody's happy! The user gets a reasonable message. Support gets the detail needed to solve the problem.

8.7.4 *Smart error forwarding*

The Struts ActionErrors class is designed so that you can add any number of messages and then send them through the request to be displayed by a page component. This class is also used for validation errors. If a validation error occurs, the ActionServlet automatically forwards to the mapping's input property. So, when an input property exists, it would be a reasonable target for other error messages.

This block of code checks to see whether any error messages have been collected. If so, it checks to see whether there is an input property for the current mapping, or lacking an input property, looks for a standard error mapping instead:

```
if (!errors.empty()) {
        saveErrors(request, errors);
        if (mapping.getInput()!=null)
                return (new ActionForward(mapping.getInput()));
        return (mapping.findForward(Tokens.ERROR));
}
```

8.7.5 *Confirming success*

The Scaffold ProcessResult class (org.apache.commons.scaffold.util.Process-Result) provides its own collection of messages. These are intended to provide confirmation of a successful operation, or alerts, rather than to report an error condition. This message collection is not coupled with the ActionErrors class. The BaseAction provides a utility method so they can collaborate. The utility method, mergeAlerts, works as an adapter between a list of message tokens and a Struts ActionErrors class. Here's the signature for the utility message:

```
protected void mergeAlerts(
        HttpServletRequest request,
        ActionErrors alerts,
        List list) {
```

The mergeAlerts method assumes that the messages are replacement parameters for a Struts-style messages. The first element on the list is taken as the template. Any other items are taken to be parameters. mergeAlerts calls the appropriate errors.add method for up to a maximum of four parameters.

The BaseAction provides other support methods that create the message queue, as needed, and place it in the request context. If the queue is already in the request, mergeAlerts appends to it. An application would usually just call the saveMessages(HttpServletRequest,List) method.

Struts 1.1 also has a saveMessages(HttpServletRequest,ActionMessages) method. The BaseAction version is designed to be compatible with the stock Struts 1.1 method and also works with the Struts 1.1 messages tags.

In a Struts 1.0 application, the BaseAction automatically saves the message queue as the error queue so that the Struts 1.0 tags can find it.

8.7.6 *Alternate views*

The final task that most Actions perform is to forward control on to the next player. An Action may also return null it if responds to the request itself—but that is rare. Actions will typically branch to an error page along the way or look for a success or continue forward at the end. Sometimes, there may be more than one successful outcome. For example, search operations often return an empty set. A page, like the one shown earlier, might contain presentation logic to deal with this gracefully. Alternatively, control might be sent to an empty set page instead.

NOTE Whether an MVC page should contain presentation logic is open to debate. One argument is that a View should not cope with business logic events such as an empty result set or whether a user is logged in. Another argument is that without presentation logic, the number of Views in some applications would increase exponentially. Such a mass of Views can become a support burden and defeat the purpose of the MVC architecture. Our suggestion is that you make the decision based on the needs of your application.

Here's an example of forking to an alternate forward. Inverting the optional forward technique, this block looks for a trigger first (an empty result set) and then checks for a valid ActionForward. This block would come at the end of an Action.execute method:

```
ActionForward forward = null;

if (resultList.getSize()==0)
        forward = mapping.findForward(Tokens.EMPTY);
if (forward!=null)        return forward;
return mapping.findForward(Tokens.SUCCESS);
```

Here, if the ActionMapping included an empty forward, we would branch to that page when the result set has no entries. Otherwise, we branch to the usual success page, the presumption being that the version of the success page (for this mapping) can handle an empty result set. If another mapping provided an empty forward, the Action would use that forward for an empty result set and the usual success page when one or more entries were returned.

8.7.7 *Reflecting methods*

Many Struts developers like to gather related tasks into a single Action class. This can simplify application design and reduce the cost of maintenance. One way to select which task to perform is to invoke it via reflection. The Struts DispatchAction (`org.apache.struts.actions.DispatchAction`) uses this technique.

The basic strategy is to first identify the name of the method. DispatchAction uses the mapping's `parameter` property to do this. Once the method name is determined, you can look up the method by its signature. Here's a streamlined version of looking up the method as is done by DispatchAction:

```
protected Class clazz == this.getClass();
protected Class types[] = {
        ActionMapping.class, ActionForm.class,
        HttpServletRequest.class, HttpServletResponse.class }
protected Method getMethod(String name)
                throws NoSuchMethodException {
{
        return clazz.getMethod(name, types);
}
```

DispatchAction also caches the methods to improve performance, but we removed that portion of the code to simplify the example. You can find the full source in the Struts source distribution [ASF, Struts].

8.7.8 *Reflecting classes*

A similar strategy is to pass to the Action class the names of one or more business classes to invoke. The Scaffold BaseHelper class does this—again using the mapping's `parameter` property to obtain the class names. Given Java's reflection techniques, creating an object from its classname is simple:

```
Object helper = null;
try {
        helper  = Class.forName(className).newInstance();
} catch (Throwable t) {
        // error handling
}
```

If the helper uses a known ancestor class or interface, it can be cast and the operative method called. Here's an example of invoking a ProcessBean, using an ActionForm as input:

```
ProcessBean processBean = (ProcessBean) helper;
ProcessResult processResult = processBean.execute(
beanUtils.describe(form));
```

8.8 *Using smart forwarding*

One thing that has made the World Wide Web so popular is ease of navigation. Any swatch of text on a page can be turned into a hyperlink. Users just have to point and click, and off they go to the target page. Behind the swatch of text is a path to the page, which may be long and cumbersome, but the users don't need to know that. They just click on the description, and the system does the rest.

Besides the ubiquitous hyperlink, HTML also provides us with an assortment of user interface widgets, like radio buttons, checkboxes, and select lists. Like hyperlinks, they allow us to display a plain language description to the user but return a technical descriptor to the server. Most often, these controls are used to make it easier to fill out a form, but they can also be used to create menu systems. Users choose a location from the select list, and the system whisks them off to the relevant page.

The simplest way to build a menu system would be to just embed the page locations, or URLs, into the control. And many, many web applications have been written using that approach, especially those using CGI systems like Perl. But embedding systems paths is not the way we build applications with Struts. We want to design pages using logical identifiers, and let Struts do the matching between identifiers with system paths. This way we can move things around without the pages being any the wiser.

The fundamental way Struts matches identifiers with system paths is through the Struts configuration (struts-config.xml). Struts applications continually use the configuration to match IDs like success and failure to various locations with the application. Now how can we do the same thing to support menu systems?

Earlier in this chapter, we introduced a standard RelayAction that can be used to select between multiple Submit buttons. Now let's look at how we can use the RelayAction and some other standard Actions to select between multiple options on a select list.

This is a multidisciplinary technique that uses standard Actions, ActionForm beans, JSP tags, and the Struts configuration. To bring it all together, we will introduce code for each of these components.

The simplest instance would be selecting between various locations in an application. Here's an example with two options:

```
<html:select property="dispatch" >
<html:option value="reload">Reload Config</html:option>
<html:option value="create">Create Resources</html:option>
</html:select>
```

This control can be used just like the multiple Submit buttons technique. The form's `dispatch` property is set to whatever is selected. The form is submitted to a RelayAction with a local forward for each option. The RelayAction then forwards the request along to whatever path is indicated by the forward:

```
<action
  path="/menu/Manager"
  type="org.apache.struts.scaffold.RelayAction"
  name="menuForm"
  validate="false">
    <forward
      name="reload"
      path="/do/admin/Reload"/>
    <forward
      name="createResources"
      path="/do/admin/CreateResources"/>
</action>
```

This is great for simple requests, but what if we need to include a parameter?

If the control is being used to select parameters for the same ActionMapping, or mappings that use the same parameter name, you can just give the option the parameter name. Here's a radio button control that displays identifiers like *Day* and *Week* but passes the corresponding number of hours to the mapping:

```
<html:form action="/find/Hours">
<P>List articles posted in the last:</P>
<P>
<INPUT type="radio" name="hours" value="24">Day <INPUT type="radio"
name="hours" value="168">Week <INPUT type="radio" name="hours"
value="720">Month
</P>
<P>
<html:submit property="submit" value="GO"/>
</p>
</html:form>
```

When users submit the form, the browser generates a URI like

```
/find/Hours?hours=24
```

or

```
/find/Hours?hours=168
```

or

```
/find/Hours?hours=720
```

depending on which radio button is selected.

In practice, we might want to write this control from a collection, using code like this:

```
<html:form action="/find/Hours">
<P>List articles posted in the last:</P>
<P>
<html:options collection="FIND" property="value" labelProperty="label"/>
</P>
<P>
<html:submit property="submit" value="GO"/>
</p>
</html:form>
```

But that would not be an instructive example. So, we show our options hardcoded instead, even if that is not what we would do in practice.

Hardcoding a parameter, or passing it down with a collection, works fine when all our options go to the same option or goto actions that use the same parameter name. But what if the parameter names are different? We may have a number of actions for looking up a record based on this field or that field, and may need to provide the field as the parameter name, like this:

```
/do/find/Title?title=Struts
/do/find/Author?creator=husted
/do/find/Content?content=menus
/do/article/View?article=12
```

There are many times when we would like to provide locations like these as a single combo control, which lets us select the search type (Title, Author, Content, ID), and then provide a user-supplied parameter, like those shown.

In each case, all we really need to do is paste the parameter to the end of the URI. The form would still need to submit the parameter under the same name, but if we could take something like this:

```
/do/menu/Find?dispatch=title&value=Struts
```

and turn it into this:

```
/do/find/Title?title=Struts
```

we'd be in business.

Happily, this is exactly what the standard ParameterAction does. Here's the action-mapping element that sets it up:

```
<action
  path="/menu/Find"
  type="org.apache.scaffold.struts.ParameterAction"
  name="menuForm"
```

```
      validate="false"
      parameter="keyValue">
    <forward
      name="title"
      path="/do/find/Title?title="/>
    <forward
      name="author"
      path="/do/find/Author?creator="/>
    <forward
      name="content"
      path="/do/find/Content?content="/>
    <forward
      name="article"
      path="/do/article/View?article="/>
    </action>
```

You may note that the action uses a form bean called `menuForm`. This is a simple bean with properties common to many menu items. Here's the source:

```java
private String keyName = null;
public String getKeyName() {
    return this.keyName;
}
public void setKeyName(String keyName) {
    this.keyName = keyName;
}

private String keyValue = null;
public String getKeyValue() {
    return this.keyValue;
}
public void setKeyValue(String keyValue) {
    this.keyValue = keyValue;
}

private String dispatch = null;
public String getDispatch() {
    return this.dispatch;
}
public void setDispatch(String dispatch) {
    this.dispatch = dispatch;
}
```

The version in the Scaffold package (`org.apache.struts.scaffold.MenuForm`) includes some other convenience properties, but these three are the important ones.

Of course, your form can still use all the properties it needs. They all go into the request and stay there for the duration. When one of the standard actions forwards the request, all the original parameters go with it. You can populate as many ActionForms as you like from the same request. When the request arrives at the mapping for the target action, whatever form bean it uses is populated normally.

So far, we've looked at using the RelayAction to select between different Submit buttons or menu selections, and the ParameterAction to append a value to a query string. There is one more action like this in our repertoire: the FindForwardAction (`org.apache.struts.scaffold.FindForwardAction`).

The RelayAction relies on there being a parameter with a known name in a request—for example, [dispatch=save]. It looks for the parameter named `dispatch`, then looks for a forward named `save`. The FindForwardAction is even more dynamic. It runs through all the parameter names and checks to see if any are also the name of a forward. If so, it returns the matching ActionForward.

This can be a good way to match multiple Submit buttons without using JavaScript to set the `dispatch` property. If you have buttons named Save, Create, and Delete, and forwards also named `save`, `create`, and `delete`, the FindFowardAction will automatically match one with the other.

Here is an example of JSP code that creates multiple Submit buttons:

```
<html:submit name="save">SAVE</html:submit>
<html:submit name="create">SAVE AS NEW</html:submitl>
<html:submit name="delete">DELETE</html:submit>
```

Then, in the Struts configuration file, we enter forwards for each of the buttons:

```
<action
    name="articleForm"
    path="/do/article/Submit"
    type="org.apache.scaffold.FindForwardAction">
    <forward
        name="create"
        path="/do/article/Create"/>
    <forward
        name="save"
        path="/do/article/Store"/>
    <forward
        name="delete"
        path="/do/article/Recycle"/>
</action>
```

The only caveat here is that you have to manage your forward and control names more carefully. The FindForwardAction will check all the parameters on the form against all the available forwards, and the first one it finds wins. So if any of your control names match any of your forward names, it might come up with an unexpected match.

This can be useful when you cannot add a `dispatch` property to a form, or cannot use JavaScript to set the `dispatch` property. But the RelayAction should be preferred when possible, since it is more deterministic.

Using these techniques together can fill a surprising number of your menu needs and keeps all the flow control within the Struts configuration.

8.9 *Summary*

This chapter explored the ins and outs of the workhorses of a Struts application: the Action classes. Reload and the other admin Actions can update the Struts configuration at runtime, a very handy development feature. Other standard Actions, such as ForwardAction and IncludeAction, help integrate Struts with other servlets in the application. The handy DispatchAction and the new LookupDispatchAction can be used to select a method within an Action object at runtime and help reduce the number of individual Action classes. The reusable Actions in the Scaffold package can be used throughout your application and can help slash the number of custom Actions you need to write and maintain.

Extending ActionServlet

This chapter covers

- Understanding the ActionServlet's role in your application
- Using ActionServlet extension components
- Using ActionServlet extension points

255

> *If the only tool you have is a hammer, you tend to see*
> *every problem as a nail.*
>
> —Abraham Maslow

9.1 Where's the beef?

First, let it be said that, for the most part, the Struts ActionServlet components can be used as they are. They do not need to be subclassed (but can be), and the default classes get the job done with a minimum of fuss. From an architectural perspective, the Struts ActionServlet is a blackbox component [Johnson].

Throughout this book, we have often referred to the Struts controller servlet and described how it fits in with the various components that make up the Struts framework. This jibes well with actual practice, since to work with Struts on a day-to-day basis, most developers only *need* to know how the ActionServlet interacts with the other components they use. Struts developers, rarely, if ever, work with the ActionServlet directly.

1.0 vs 1.1   The implementation of the ActionServlet changed quite a bit between Struts 1.0 and Struts 1.1—so much so, that we will cover only the Struts 1.1 ActionServlet here. Most developers did not subclass the Struts 1.0 ActionServlet, or did so in very minor ways. Moreover, the ActionServlet is designed as a singleton. At most, applications will subclass ActionServlet exactly once. Since Struts developers do not work with the ActionServlet on a day-to-day basis, we will not contrast the differences between the releases, as we have done elsewhere. By simply describing the ActionServlet as it now stands, if necessary, Struts 1.0 developers will be able to adapt any changes they might have made.

There are two key reasons why Struts developers are so detached from the ActionServlet. First, it is a true *singleton*. There is exactly one ActionServlet present in any Struts application. We do not create new ActionServlets the way we create new Actions or ActionForms. In Struts, there is simply not much development work left to do with a servlet.

Second, the ActionServlet spends most of its time invoking other objects. Rather than code to the servlet, we code to the objects the servlet calls. Many frameworks use this approach. In fact, it is considered a formal design pattern, Inversion of Control [Johnson]. The ActionServlet coordinates the application's activities, but the methods defined by the user to tailor the framework are only called *by* the servlet. They are not declared *within* the servlet.

DEFINITION *Inversion of Control* (a.k.a. the "Hollywood Principle," or "Don't call us, we'll call you") is a design pattern where objects register with a framework as a handler for an event. When the event occurs, the framework invokes a hook method on the registered object. The object then performs whatever application-specific processing is required for the event. This allows frameworks to manage the event life cycle while allowing developers to plug in customized handlers for the framework events. [Earles]

Many of the other classes in the Struts framework, like ActionForms and Actions, are designed to be subclassed and tailored for each application. These are the framework's whitebox components [Johnson]. On the other end of the spectrum is the framework's chief blackbox component, the ActionServlet. Figure 9.1 depicts the ActionServlet at the center of the application, calling other objects into service.

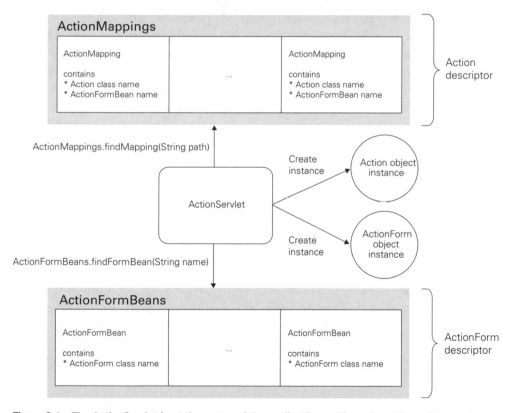

Figure 9.1   The ActionServlet is at the center of the application, calling other objects into service.

While still very much a blackbox, the Struts 1.1 ActionServlet is designed to be more extensible. A number of new extension points are available that make it easier to design a subclass that cleanly changes a specific behavior.

Most of the extension points are provided through objects that can be plugged into the controller. Using pluggable components allows you to change key behaviors without actually creating a new ActionServlet subclass. One reason for these new components is to allow different application modules to use different behaviors. (Configuring Struts for modular applications is covered in chapter 4.)

9.1.1 *The servlet's Gang of Three*

Of all the pluggable components, the *RequestProcessor* (org.apache.struts.action.RequestProcessor) is the most powerful. The RequestProcessor is the meat of the ActionServlet; it handles the top-level request routing the way that an Action handles a request for a specific URI.

One of the top-level issues that the RequestProcessor handles is exception handling. Exception classes can be registered for a handler. If one of the registered Exceptions is thrown, the RequestProcessor hands the Exception off to its *ExceptionHandler* (org.apache.struts.action.ExceptionHandler). You can use the default class or provide your own subclass for each Exception type.

Many applications need access to their own specialized resources. To make it easy to initialize custom resources with Struts, you can register a PlugIn Action with the controller. The controller then calls the Action's init method on startup and its destroy method on shutdown. The Action has access to the calling servlet and can be used to do whatever a conventional servlet can do.

This extensible triad—the RequestProcessor, ExceptionHandler, and PlugIn Action—doesn't leave much else for the ActionServlet to do. In fact, all the ActionServlet class does at runtime is select the RequestProcessor for the appropriate application module. The rest of the class "simply" manages the Struts configuration life cycle. It uses the Digester to create the objects called for by the configuration files, and then destroys them when the application is shut down.

The rest of this chapter will be about using this "Gang of Three" to extend ActionServlet, without ever subclassing the servlet itself. Each of these classes, or its subclass, can be plugged into the controller through the Struts configuration file, covered in chapter 4.

9.2 The RequestProcessor

When a request comes in, the servlet selects the application module and hands it off to the RequestProcessor. Each module can load its own RequestProcessor subclass, or just use the default RequestProcessor that ships with the framework.

The RequestProcessor is a "graybox" component. You can use it as is, like a blackbox component, or extend it to provide some special behavior, like a whitebox component. Wearing its white hat, the RequestProcessor provides several extension methods that you can override to cleanly change any of its behaviors. Wearing its black hat, the RequestProcessor provides default behaviors for all of these methods that are suitable for most applications. The extension methods are summarized in table 9.1.

Table 9.1   The RequestProcessor extension methods

Extension method	Remark
processMultipart	Wraps multipart requests with a special wrapper
processPath	Identifies the path component we will use to select a mapping
processLocale	Selects a locale for the current user if requested
processContent	Sets the content type in the request
processNoCache	Sets the no-caching headers in the request, if enabled for this module
processPreprocess	Serves as a general-purpose preprocessing hook
processMapping	Identifies the mapping for this request
processRoles	Checks for any role required to perform this action
processActionForm	Creates or acquires the ActionForm bean for this mapping
processPopulate	Populates the ActionForm from the request
processValidate	Processes any ActionForm bean related to this request
processForward	Processes a forward specified by this mapping
processInclude	Processes an include specified by this mapping
processActionCreate	Creates or acquires the Action instance to process this request
processActionPerform	Calls the Action instance processing this request, returning an ActionForward
processActionForward	Processes the returned ActionForward instance

A RequestProcessor subclass is registered with the controller through the Struts configuration file, using an element like this:

```
<controller
        processorClass="myApp.MyRequestProcessor"/>
```

For more about registering objects through the Struts configuration file, see chapter 4.

9.2.1 *The process method*

The extension methods are all called in turn from the process method. The process method has responsibility for processing an HttpServletRequest and creating the corresponding HttpServletResponse. The default RequestProcessor does this by calling the extension methods listed in table 9.1.

To create the response, the processActionForward method will typically send the request off to a JSP page or other resource. But when process returns, the API contract states that the response should have been completed.

Overriding any of the extension methods, if needed, is usually a straightforward process, especially since you have the full source at your disposal. Generally, you would probably want to execute your custom behavior and then call the super class method for the default behavior.

9.2.2 *processRoles*

The RequestProcessor extension most likely to be completely overridden may be processRoles. The assigned task of processRoles is to check whether the user is permitted access to an action. The default behavior uses the standard Java security API [Sun, JAAS], but many applications have their own schemes. By overriding processRoles, you can call your own API instead.

The default behavior is to run the list of roles specified by the ActionMapping against the standard isUserInRole method exposed by the request parameter. If the user is in any of the specified roles, access is granted.

The standard container-based system has you specify a url-pattern and the roles that may access resources matching that pattern. The Struts action-based security system lets you specify which roles may access a particular ActionMapping. When the standard API is being used, these systems do not conflict and may be used together. Listing 9.1 shows the implementation of the processRoles method.

Listing 9.1   The RequestProcessor processRoles method

```
protected boolean processRoles(
            HttpServletRequest request,
            HttpServletResponse response,
            ActionMapping mapping)
                throws IOException, ServletException {

    // Is this action protected by role requirements?
    String roles[] = mapping.getRoleNames();
    if ((roles == null) || (roles.length < 1)) {
        return (true);
    }

    // Check the current user against the list of required roles
    for (int i = 0; i < roles.length; i++) {
        if (request.isUserInRole(roles[i])) {
            if (log.isDebugEnabled()) {
                log.debug(" User '" + request.getRemoteUser() +
                    "' has role '" + roles[i] + "', granting access");
            }
            return (true);
        }
    }

    // The current user is not authorized for this action
    if (log.isDebugEnabled()) {
        log.debug(" User '" + request.getRemoteUser() +
                "' does not have any required role, denying access");
    }
    response.sendError(HttpServletResponse.SC_BAD_REQUEST,
                    getInternal().getMessage("notAuthorized",
                                            mapping.getPath()));
    return (false);
}
```

By overriding `processRoles`, you can easily adapt this feature to a proprietary application-based security scheme. Instead of calling `request.isUserInRole`, your subclass method could call the equivalent method in your own API. Of course, the roles do not have to be roles per se, but could contain whatever tokens your system uses to quantify access.

Depending on your security profile, you could also require that each Action-Mapping have a role property, even if it is just a token, like *, that represents anonymous access. You don't even *need* to use the `roles` property at all. The method is called regardless and could be used to implement any variety of access scheme. The `request` and `mapping` objects are passed in the signature, which means you have access to whatever you might need to check a user's credentials.

The implementation of `processRoles` is typical of the RequestProcessor extension methods. Any of these can be overridden in the same general way to provide whatever specialized behavior you may need.

9.3 *The ExceptionHandler*

The Action object is the ActionServlet's delegate in most matters, which can include exception handling. Alternatively, you can let Actions pass all or some of the checked Exceptions back up to the ActionServlet, which catches all Exceptions. If the servlet does catch an Exception, it checks to see if you have registered a handler for that Exception type or its super types. Any local exception handlers for the ActionMapping are checked first, and then the global Exceptions.

If the servlet finds a handler, it invokes that handler with the details of the Exception. If not, the servlet rethrows the Exception, and it will probably end up on an infamous "white screen."

The ExceptionHandler can be registered through an element in the Struts configuration file (see chapter 4), like this one:

```
<exception
    type="org.apache.struts.webapp.example.ExpiredPasswordException"
    key="expired.password"
    path="/changePassword.jsp"/>
```

If the ExpiredPasswordException is thrown, the default handler will create an ActionError using the specified key and an ActionForward for the specified path. Control will then be forwarded to the /changePassword.jsp in this module. Presumably, the JSP will look up and display the message for the key `expired.password` from the module's default message resource bundle and give the user the chance to try again. If we had omitted the `path` attribute, the default handler would have used the ActionMapping's `input` property instead.

The `<exception>` element can accept several other attributes, all of which are listed in the struts-config API reference in appendix B. The attributes include `handler` and `className`, which can be used to specify a custom ExceptionHandler and (if needed) a custom configuration bean for that handler.

Your ExceptionHandler must be a subclass of the default handler (`org.apache.struts.action.ExceptionHandler`). The entry method is `execute`, which provides a well-heeled set of parameters:

```
public ActionForward execute(
    Exception ex,
    ExceptionConfig ae,
    ActionMapping mapping,
```

```
ActionForm formInstance,
HttpServletRequest request,
HttpServletResponse response)
    throws ServletException
```

Just as with writing an Action execute method, you have carte blanche as long as you return an ActionForward when you are done. If for some reason your handler completed the response, you can even return a null ActionForward.

The ExceptionConfig bean (org.apache.struts.config.ExceptionConfig) represents the original <exception> element from the Struts configuration file. If you need any special properties set, you can create your own subclass of ExceptionConfig and use the <set-property> element to initialize them from the module's configuration file.

For more about configuring Struts, see chapter 4.

9.4 *PlugIn*

Many applications need access to specialized resources. These may be data access components, Properties files, or any number of business-tier components. Many of the developer extensions to Struts, such as menu systems, alternate validators, data transformers, XSL converters, and so forth, need to parse their own configuration files and create their own controller objects.

In a conventional Java web application, these objects would usually be initialized as part of the servlet's init method and released as part of its destroy method. We could subclass the ActionServlet and do the same thing, but that can lead to contention when a developer wants to use more than one third-party Struts extension.

Since Actions are already the servlet's delegate in most matters, the framework offers a PlugIn interface (org.apache.stuts.action.PlugIn) that allows an Action to implement init and destroy methods, like those on a servlet. Since the Action has access to the servlet as a member variable, any resource that could be initialized or released by a servlet can be handled through a PlugIn Action.

The PlugIn is registered with the controller through the Struts configuration using an element like this:

```
<plug-in className="myApp.MyAction>
    <set-property
      property="key"
      value="MY_APP_KEY"/>
    </plug-in>
```

The Action specified by the `className` attribute must implement the PlugIn interface and provide an `init` and a `destroy` method. If the Action has any member variables that need to be initialized, the standard `<set-property>` elements can be used to pass a value to any arbitrary property.

On startup, the controller initializes the PlugIn Actions, sets any properties, and calls the `init` method. On shutdown, the controller calls the `destroy` method on each PlugIn Action before releasing it.

9.5 *Summary*

To extend the controller servlet, most applications will not need to subclass the Struts 1.1 ActionServlet at all. Most often, you can create the desired behavior by subclassing one of the controller extension components or plugging in a prewritten component, such as the Tiles RequestProcessor or the Validator PlugIn. By plugging in one of the standard components, or your own subclass, you should be able to cleanly modify the controller to produce any reasonable behavior.

In part 3 of this book, we move past the Struts control layer and take a closer look at how Struts works with the presentation layer, so you can write the *rest* of the application.

Part 3

Building your pages

Part 3 moves the focus to building the visible portion of your application—the pages. Discussing pages later in the book reflects a key tenet of the Struts/Model-View-Controller architecture: most of the real work is done before a page is ever displayed.

10

Displaying dynamic content

This chapter covers

- Understanding why we use JSP tags
- Installing tag extensions
- Using the Struts JSP tags
- Glimpsing the future of JSP tags

Nothing is particularly hard if you divide it into small jobs.

—Henry Ford

10.1 Tag—you're it

In part 1 of this book, we covered processing business data and rules. In this chapter, we can concentrate on what happens *after* the data has been acquired, the top-level logic has been applied, and the nanosecond has come for the controller to send the request out to the presentation layer—equipped with all the materials needed to finish the job.

The Struts distribution includes a powerful set of prewritten JSP tags that integrate the framework with JSP pages. A new standard taglib, the JavaServer Tag Library [Sun, JSTL], is also on the horizon.

In this chapter, we introduce using the Struts tag extensions in your application. You can use JSP tags to prepopulate text fields or select lists and to manage arrays of checkboxes and radio buttons. Struts works well with JavaScript, so you can create the other clever widgets that page designers adore but that HTML barely supports.

10.1.1 JSP tags—what are they good for?

We've referred to JSPs throughout the book, but we haven't really talked about what they are or why we use them. Let's step back and quickly review *why* we would want to use JSP tags to build web pages. If you're already a custom tag devotee and easily bored, feel free to skip ahead to section 10.3.

Most web applications rely on standard browsers to display information. In turn, standard browsers rely on standard HTML as a formatting language. Often, the information an application needs to display is not a static, prewritten page, but dynamic content intended for a particular user. At first, this doesn't sound too difficult. After all, Java servlets make it easy to write HTML on the fly—we can write HTML the same way we would send plain text to the display or printer: just `out.println("whatever")`. Figure 10.1 shows how you'd write a web page using a standard Java servlet.

As the HTML code is being created, a couple of dynamic variables, `dog` and `cat`, are being merged into the page. The web browser will receive and display a page sent this way just as it would a static, prewritten page. If the `ChaseBean` was set to something like `fox` or `hound`, the user would get a different story. Figure 10.2 shows the markup that the browser would receive and how it might be displayed.

```
ChaseBean chase = new Chase("dog","cat");
// ...
out.println("<HTML>");
out.println("<HEAD><TITLE>The Chase<TITLE><HEAD>");
out.println("<BODY>");
out.println("<H1>Welcome to the Chase</H1>");
out.println("<H2>Our story so far:</H2>");
out.println("<FONT SIZE=\"+1\" FACE=\"Times\" COLOR=\"#FFFFFF">);
out.print("The big ");
out.print(chase.getChaser());
out.print(" &amp; ");
out.print("the little )"
out.print(chase.getChasee());
out.println(" chased each other. ");
out.println("</FONT>");
out.println("</BODY>");
out.println("</HTML>");
```

Figure 10.1   Rendering HTML the old-fashioned way

What the browser sees:

```
<HTML>
<HEAD><TITLE>The
Chase<TITLE><HEAD>
<BODY>
<H1>Welcome to the Chase</H1>
<H2>Our story so far:</H2>
<FONT SIZE=\"+1\" FACE=\"Times\"
COLOR=\"#FFFFFF">The big dog &amp;
the little cat chased each other.
</FONT>
</BODY>
</HTML>
```

What the browser displays:

Welcome to the Chase

Our story so far:

The big dog & the little cat chased each other.

Figure 10.2   What the browser sees and displays

But complex pages output this way are maddening to create and burdensome to maintain. The next step up from println is to use special Java classes and methods to generate the HTML. Figure 10.3 shows another approach to rendering HTML, generating the markup using nested classes.

At least the approach in figure 10.3 takes working with raw HTML out of the equation. But even the best HTML generators make it hard to see the forest for the trees. Few developers can imagine what the page is going to look like. To see the latest version, the developer has to recompile the class and possibly redeploy it.

```
ChaseBean chase = new Chase("dog","cat");
// ...
Html html = new Html()
.addElement(new Head()
.addElement(new Title("The Chase")))
.addElement(new Body()
.addElement(new H1("Welcome to the Chase"))
.addElement(new H2("Our story so far:"))
.addElement(new Font().setSize("+1")
.setColor(HtmlColor.WHITE)
.setFace("Times")
.addElement(chase.getChaser());
.addElement(" &amp; ");
.addElement("the little )"
.addElement(chase.getChasee());
.addElement(" chased each other. ");
output(out);
```

Figure 10.3   A step up from `println`, packages like the Element Construction Set
[ASF, ECS] generate HTML using deeply nested classes.

Server pages

One popular solution to the problem of authoring dynamic screens is the *server page*. There are many flavors of server pages: ActiveServer Pages, ColdFusion pages, PHP pages, server-side includes, Velocity templates, and of course JSPs. But they all use the same basic approach:

- You create an HTML-like page that uses a server page markup to indicate dynamic features.
- When a request for the page is received, the server page is used to construct a dynamic response.
- The response is returned as standard HTML.

Here are the key advantages:

- The server page is not a program file that is compiled into the core application.
- The syntax of the server page resembles a standard web page.

These advantages make server pages much easier to create and maintain, especially by nonprogrammers. Scrver pages can even be maintained using graphical editors, such as Macromedia's Dreamweaver [Macromedia].

JavaServer Pages

JSPs offer two distinct approaches to server page markup. Developers can place Java code directly into the page using *scriptlets*. Scriptlets are quick, relatively easy, and quite powerful. Figure 10.4 shows the JSP scriptlet approach.

```
<jsp:useBean id="chase" scope="page" class="app.ChaseBean"/>
<HTML>
<HEAD><TITLE>The Chase</TITLE></HEAD>
<BODY>
<H1>Welcome to the Chase</H1>
<H2>Our story so far:</H2>
<FONT SIZE="+1" FACE="Times" COLOR="#FFFFFF">
The big "<%= chase.getChaser() %>" &amp; the little "<%= chase.getChasee()
%>"> chased each other.
</FONT>
</BODY>
</HTML>
```

Figure 10.4   Scriptlets allow Java code and expressions to be mixed with HTML.

The second approach to JSP markup is to use tag extensions. JSP tags resemble HTML tags, and use a similar format and syntax. They require more effort to write, but once written, JSP tags are easier to use and much easier to maintain over the long run. Figure 10.5 shows the JSP tag approach.

```
<%@ taglib uri="/tags/struts-bean" prefix="bean" %
<HTML>
<HEAD><TITLE>The Chase</TITLE></HEAD>
<BODY>
<H1>Welcome to the Chase</H1>
<H2>Our story so far:</H2>
<FONT SIZE="+1" FACE="Times" COLOR="#FFFFFF">
The big <bean:write name="chase" property="chaser"/> &amp; the little
<bean:write name="chase" property="chasee"/> chased each other.
</FONT>
</BODY>
</HTML>
```

Figure 10.5   A JSP page looks and feels like HTML.

10.1.2 Struts and JSTL

While the Struts tags are quite capable and easy to use, they are not the only game in town. Sun's new JavaServer Pages Standard Tag Library (JSTL) implementation sports a useful set of tags, many of which overlap with the Struts taglibs. JSTL requires a container that supports Servlets 2.3 and JSP 1.2, such as Tomcat 4 or

Resin 2. In short order, we can expect containers to be optimized for JSTL, making it the base taglib of choice for most applications.

Of course, JSTL does not eliminate the need for custom tag extensions. There will be many instances when a developer will find it convenient to write a tag that does exactly this in exactly this way. But, like the original Struts taglibs, JSTL eliminates the need to write tags that perform the common operations most applications undertake.

Should you use JSTL tags instead of Struts tags whenever you can? Sure, if your container supports Servlets 2.3 and JSP 1.2, and that's what *you* want to do. Most of the Struts tags were provided to fill a void and are not strongly coupled with the framework. If JSTL already existed, most of the Struts tags would never have been written.

Of course, at this time, the Struts tags are an integral part of a great many applications and will be part of the Struts distribution for some time to come. But you can rest assured that the Struts team will not be competing with JSTL. You can expect any new Struts tags to either be based on JSTL or work as adjuncts to it.

NOTE   As this book went to press, a JSTL version of the Struts taglibs was being added to the development build. This library should be part of the final release of Struts 1.1. See the book's website [Husted] for any Struts 1.1 errata or addenda.

The JSTL expression language

JSTL includes an expression language (EL) that provides a clear alternative to scriptlets. An expression language is especially useful to the many custom tag users who want to pass several dynamic parameters to their JSP tags.

Right now, there is a blind spot in the syntax for custom tags. One property can be passed in the body of the tag, which could include the output of another custom tag. All other properties must be passed in the tag itself, and nesting other tags is not permitted here.

So this

```
<some:tag attribute="<bean:message key='...'/>">
```

will not compile, since the JSP syntax expects you to do something like this

```
<some:tag><bean:message key="..." /></some:tag>
```

instead. This generally works, but sometimes more than one attribute needs to be dynamic. The Struts tags get around this by having you specify the names of beans rather than the data. The tag then gets the properties from the bean. But for other tags, you may need to use a runtime expression, like

```
<some:tag attribute='<%=myDynamicString + "txt" %>'/>
```

When using runtime expressions with JSP tag attributes, it is important to use a complete expression for the attribute value, as we have done here, or the expression won't compile.

The JSTL expression language can provide another alternative:

```
<c:set var="msg"><bean:message key="..." /></c:set>
<tag attribute="$msg"/>
```

Here we first trapped the output of the `<bean:message>` tag as a page-scoped attribute, and then we used the JSTL expression language to write that attribute with the other (non-JSTL) tag.

Of course, there is much more to JSTL than is shown by this simple example. Generally, you should be able to use JSTL instead of the generic Struts bean and logic tags (if that's what you want). But you will probably need to continue using the Struts html tags for the time being, since those tags are more specialized.

JSTL and the Struts framework work well together because they share some common goals. Both try to avoid the use of scriptlets, and both encourage using JavaServer Pages as the View in a Model-View-Controller architecture.

10.1.3   *Struts tags and MVC*

The Struts JSP tags provide all the functionality most applications need to create an MVC-style presentation page. (For more about the Model-View-Controller architecture, see chapter 2.) This is important since many developers want to make a clean break with the bad old days of page-centric, Model 1 web applications. In a proper Model 2–MVC application, a request does not go directly to the presentation page. The request goes first to the Controller. As shown in figure 10.6, only after the business data has been acquired and the business rules applied does the Controller hand off to the presentation page.

Since everything else has already been done, the page's only responsibility is writing the result—which is where the JSP tags come in. JSP tags can access value objects stored in the servlet contexts and use data from these objects to create dynamic content.

If you haven't guessed by now, the heading for section 10.1 has a dual meaning. In an MVC environment, the Controller hands off to the page, saying, in essence, "Tag—you're it." And, compared to the elder alternatives, tags are *it*.

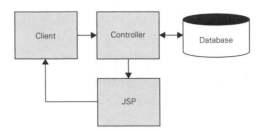

Figure 10.6   Program flow in a Model 2–MVC application

Moving forward, in section 10.2 we briefly cover the fundamentals of working with tag extensions, including how to write and install them, and what you can't do with them. In section 10.3, we introduce the Struts taglibs, with a focus on the overall design of the libraries. Then, in section 10.4, the rubber hits the road, and we put the Struts taglibs to work. Here we explore the specifics of using the tags, including the fundamentals, important techniques, and common applications.

The goal of this chapter is to shorten your learning curve so that you can quickly integrate the Struts tags into your own projects. The Struts Taglib Developer Guides and technical documentation [ASF, Struts] are quite good and are still recommended reading. But to help you get started with those, this chapter provides a gentle introduction to tag extensions and the Struts tags, with an emphasis on how they work and how you can put them to use in your own applications.

10.2   Working with tag extensions

In section 10.1, we took a brisk walk down memory lane to show how Java web applications have progressed from rendering output using a command-line format to using templates and server pages that can be managed with an external graphical editor. In this section, we look at how tag extensions are written and what tag extensions are not, and then we introduce the Struts tags. With this foundation, the balance of the chapter shows how to put the Struts tags to work.

10.2.1   How are tag extensions written?

JSP tags are written in Java using the tag extension API. The classes are designed to parse a tag in XML format and use the tag's properties as parameters to the class's methods. In practice, tag extensions let you call Java functions using an XML syntax that resembles standard HTML. For example, the standard HTML base tag looks like this:

```
<base href="http://mydomain.com/myapp/index.jsp">
```

and the Struts base tag looks like this:

```
<html:base/>
```

When rendered by the JSP page, the Struts `<html:base>` tag will be converted into a standard HTML base tag, with the appropriate path (or URI) automatically included.

Under the hood, there is a BaseTag class corresponding to the base JSP tag. BaseTag extends an API class, TagSupport (see listing 10.1), and overrides the *hotspot* method, `doStartTag`. This is a run-of-the-mill Java method that constructs the HTML markup, much as you would if you were using a plain servlet to generate the response (see section 10.1.1).

Listing 10.1   A sample BaseTag class

```java
public class BaseTag extends TagSupport {
// ...
public int doStartTag() throws JspException {
  HttpServletRequest request = (HttpServletRequest)pageContext.getRequest();
   StringBuffer buf = new StringBuffer("<base href=\"");
   buf.append(request.getScheme());
   buf.append("://");
   buf.append(request.getServerName());
   buf.append(request.getRequestURI());
   buf.append("\"");
   if (target != null) {
       buf.append(" target=\"");
       buf.append(target);
       buf.append("\"");
   }
   buf.append(">");
   JspWriter out = pageContext.getOut();
   try {
       out.write(buf.toString());
   }
   catch (IOException e) {
       pageContext.setAttribute(Action.EXCEPTION_KEY, e,
       PageContext.REQUEST_SCOPE);
       throw new JspException(messages.getMessage(
           "common.io", e.toString()));
   }
   return EVAL_BODY_INCLUDE;
}
}
```

This code may remind you of what we presented in figures 10.1 and 10.3. The major difference is that a specialized class, designed for reuse, encapsulates the markup here. Applications can share custom tag libraries, and the tag markup integrates well with ordinary JSP/HTML markup.

In practice, most developers do not need to write their own tags. Many general-purpose libraries are available, including the new JSTL. But it's nice to have the option should the need arise. Typically, a developer will simply import an existing taglib into a page (can you say *reuse?*) and go to work on the markup, which looks and feels like an extension to HTML.

Developers use a number of related terms when discussing tag extensions. A quick glossary may help you keep everything straight. Table 10.1 defines some of the vocabulary used to discuss JSP tag extension.

Table 10.1   JSP taglibs glossary

Term	Definition
Tag extension	The mechanism (or API) by which tag libraries are made available to a JSP.
Tag library	A collection of actions (or tags) that encapsulate some functionality to be used within a JSP.
Taglib	Common abbreviation for tab library. Often pronounced *tag-libe*.
Custom tag or JSP tag	The individual actions (or tags) that make up a tag library.

10.2.2   How are tag extensions installed?

Installing a tag extension and using it in your page is a three-step process:

1 Install the JAR and TLD files.

2 Update the application's web.xml file.

3 Import the new taglib to your page.

1. Install the JAR and TLD files

Tag extensions are typically distributed in a binary Java Archive (JAR) file. You can place the taglib JARs under the WEB-INF/lib folder, like any other jar'd component. There is a second part to a taglib distribution: the Tag Library Descriptor (TLD) file. The TLDs are often placed directly under WEB-INF. The JSP service uses the TLD to check the syntax of the tags when compiling your JSP:

```
\WEB-INF\lib\struts.jar
\WEB-INF\struts-bean.tld
\WEB-INF\struts-html.tld
\WEB-INF\struts-logic.tld
```

2. Update the application's web.xml file

To provide the best flexibility, your JSP will use a logical reference to refer to the taglib. This lets you move or even change the taglib without affecting any of your pages (as long as the libraries are binary compatible). The logical references are mapped to the actual taglibs in your application's deployment descriptor file (web.xml).

Here's a block of taglib elements for the Struts tags we cover in this chapter:

```
<web-app>
<!-- ... other web-app elements ... -->
<taglib>
<taglib-uri>/tags/struts-bean</taglib-uri>
<taglib-location>/WEB-INF/struts-bean.tld</taglib-location>
</taglib>

<taglib>
<taglib-uri>/tags/struts-html</taglib-uri>
<taglib-location>/WEB-INF/struts-html.tld</taglib-location>
</taglib>

<taglib>
<taglib-uri>/tags/struts-logic</taglib-uri>
<taglib-location>/WEB-INF/struts-logic.tld</taglib-location>
</taglib>

</web-app>
```

Some developers will use the same string for both the uri and the location, but that practice defeats the purpose of this feature and leads to confusion if the location of the TLDs changes.

NOTE   Since taglibs are often distributed in JARs, some developers place the TLDs under \WEB-INF\lib with the JAR files. This keeps everything together. Another common convention is to create a separate folder for the TLDs. Since the location of the TLD is specified in the web.xml, any of these places work as well.

---

3. Import the new taglib to your page

Which tags are available to which page is a decision left to the developer. The specification provides developers with good flexibility. You can both import a taglib and give it an identifying prefix for the current page. Note that when we import the taglib, we are referring to the uri from the web.xml—not the location:

```
<%@ taglib uri="/tags/struts-bean" prefix="bean" %>
<%@ taglib uri="/tags/struts-html" prefix="html" %>
```

```
<%@ taglib uri="/tags/struts-logic" prefix="logic" %>
```

The individual tags can then be referenced by the prefix defined for the page:

```
<bean:write name="userForm" property="firstName"/>
```

This approach neatly resolves taglib name conflicts and makes it easy to switch among compatible libraries.

Most often, developers will use the same prefix through the application, but this is not required. If there were a conflict, you could use different prefixes in different pages. You can also change the taglib imported to a page and use the old prefix (as long as the DTDs are compatible).

NOTE If you find that a JSP tag on a page is acting strangely, or perhaps not working, check to see that its taglib has been imported. Both the JSP compiler and web browser will ignore tags they don't understand. So if you use a taglib on a page but don't import it, nothing happens!

10.2.3 *What tag extensions are not*

Tag extensions both useful *and* promising—but, at this writing, a technology still under development. Here are some points to remember:

- Tag extensions are not supported by all HTML visual editors.
- Tag extensions are not a drop-in replacement for scriptlets.
- Tag extensions are not JavaServer Faces.

Tag extensions are not supported by all HTML visual editors

There is some plug-in support available for Macromedia's UltraDev 4 [ASF, CTLX], but it is currently incomplete. UltraDev 4 only supports JSP 1.0, which predates the introduction of custom tags. Another Macromedia product, HomeBase, also supports custom tags, but that product is designed for the handcoders among us. Of course, GUI support for JSP tags is likely to grow as custom tags become more widely used.

Tag extensions are not a drop-in replacement for scriptlets

Almost everything you'd want to do with an MVC-style JSP can be done with the Struts taglibs or JSTL. But that's still just *almost*. Developers still find themselves resorting to scriptlets to do some things. Most often, the continued use of scriptlets is to overcome design flaws in a tag, or to avoid writing or extending a new tag. A real honest-to-goodness *need* for a scriptlet is rare.

The scripting features of JSTL are designed to overcome any need to revert to scriptlets. But at this writing, the JSTL is brand new and requires a container supporting the relatively new Servlet 2.3 and JSP 1.2 APIs. The JSTL expression language features will make replacing scriptlets even easier.

Tag extensions are not JavaServer Faces

An initiative is under way to define a standard set of JSP tags and Java classes that will simplify building JavaServer application GUIs, called JavaServer Faces (JSF) [Sun, JSF]. While JSF will apparently build on the tag extension API, it will be a component framework of its own. The JSF components will overlap with some of the Struts tags, but the Struts team is sure to provide a clear migration path when the time comes.

NOTE   As this book went to press, the Struts team announced the development of a struts-faces taglib that will be released to coincide with JavaServer Faces 1.0. The struts-faces taglib is designed so that developers can migrate from the Struts tags to JavaServer Faces a page at a time. For the latest details, see the book's website [Husted].

For more about tag extensions, we recommend *JSP Tag Libraries* [Shachor], another Manning Publications book.

10.3 *The Struts taglibs*

First, your application is not constrained to using only the Struts tags. Tag extensions are a standard Java technology. Other standard libraries are available, including Sun's JSP Standard Tag Library [Sun, JSTL], the Jakarta Taglibs [ASF, Taglibs], and Struts-Layout tags by Improve [Improve], to name a few. All of these, and more, can be used in your application alongside the Struts taglibs. If you have needs that are not met by a prewritten extension, or would like to streamline a tag's processing, you can also write your own custom tags. Your own tags can then be mixed and matched with those from other sources.

The Struts distribution includes four key tag libraries: *bean, html, logic,* and *nested,* as listed in table 10.2. Most of the tags in the html library (`org.apache.struts.taglibs.html`) depend on the framework. Most of the tags in the other libraries do *not* rely on the framework and could be used in other applications. In this section, we look at common features shared by the Struts taglib, and then introduce each of the libraries. This material is not meant to replace the Struts

Table 10.2   The four key Struts tag libraries

Library	Description
bean	Tags useful in accessing JavaBeans and their properties, as well as defining new beans
html	Tags used to create HTML input forms that can interact with the Struts framework, and related HTML tags
logic	Tags for managing the conditional generation of output, looping over object collections for repetitive generation of output, and application flow management
nested	Tags that provide enhanced nesting capabilities to the other Struts tags

Developer Guides and technical documentation. For detailed specifics regarding each tag, we refer you to the technical documentation. This section is designed to build a foundation for section 10.4, where we explore putting the Struts tag to work.

10.3.1   *Features common to Struts tags*

The JSP tags in the Struts taglibs offer a number of common features that help to make the tags convenient to use, including automatic scoping, common property names, extended syntax, runtime expressions, and a common error attribute.

Automatic scoping

Java servlets can store objects in a number of shared areas called *contexts*. Contexts are like public bulletin boards. Any servlet in an application can post whatever it wants, and any other servlet in that application can see whatever is posted.

When searching for an object, the Struts tags can automatically check all the standard contexts—page, request, session, and application—and use the first instance found. You can also specify a context (or *scope*) to be sure the tag locks on to the right object.

Common property names

An important thing to realize about the Struts tags is that they are designed to expose JavaBeans passed to the page. The properties common to the tags—id, name, property, and scope—revolve around working with some helper bean, presumably passed by the controller. Table 10.3 itemizes these four most common properties.

Table 10.3   Struts taglibs use a consistent set of property names.

Property	Description
id	Names any scripting variable to be created by a custom tag.
name	Indicates the key value under which an existing bean will be found. If a scope is given, only that context is searched. Otherwise, the contexts are searched in the standard order (page, request, session, application).
property	Indicates a property on the bean from which to retrieve a value. If not specified, the value of the object itself is used.
scope	Identifies the context (page, request, session, or application) in which the bean is to be found. If not specified, the scopes are searched in the standard order. Any scripting variable (see id) is created in the same scope.

Here's an example of a Struts tag using all four of the common properties:

```
<logic:iterate scope="request" name="result"
     property="collection" id="row"> <%-- markup --%> </logic:iterate>
```

This particular example says to look in the standard request context for a bean named result. Then, retrieve a property on that bean, called collection (for example, getCollection). Iterate over that collection, expose each element in turn as a scripting variable named row, and process the markup up to the closing </logic:iterate> tag.

Other Struts tags will use these properties in similar ways, which helps to flatten the learning curve.

Extended syntax

Struts tags support both the standard *simple references* found in JSP actions as well as *nested references*. Using nested references, you can express a property in a Struts tag as

```
property="foo.bar.baz"
```

which tells Struts to call the equivalent of

```
getFoo().getBar().getBaz();
```

or, as a setter,

```
getFoo().getBar().setBaz(value);
```

Since Struts 1.1, you can also include *indexed references*:

```
property="foo[2]"
```

which calls the equivalent of

```
getFoo(2);
```

or, as a setter,

```
setFoo(2, value);
```

Note that the references are zero-relative, as is typical for a Java expression.

Runtime expressions

Although the Struts tags are designed so that you can avoid using scriptlets in your JSPs, all of the Struts tag properties can be provided by a runtime expression (scriptlet), in case there is no alternative. When using a scriptlet to generate a property, be sure to use a complete expression:

  Incorrect

```
<html:link href='<%= "/" + name %>/index.jsp>'>
```

  Correct

```
<html:link href='<%= "/" + name + "/index.jsp" %>'>
```

As shown in the snippet, the expression must provide the entire property, quote to quote. For more examples of mixing scriptlets with JSP tags, see the Struts Bean Taglib Developers Guide [ASF, Struts]. Do note that the Struts team, and many other developers, now consider using scriptlets a last resort.

Common error handling

The JavaServer Pages specification [Sun, JSP] allows you to define a default error page. If an exception occurs when processing the page, the container will direct control to the error page rather than throw up the standard "white page." If a Struts tag throws an exception, it is passed to the error page under a request attribute using the key

```
org.apache.struts.action.EXCEPTION
```

This gives your JSP error page the opportunity to process the actual exception that caused the problem.

10.3.2 The bean tags

There is a strong relationship between custom tags and JavaBeans. One of the original design justifications for custom tags was to provide an interface between JSPs and JavaBeans. Toward that end, Struts provides a small but extremely useful library of tags devoted to manipulating JavaBeans and related objects. The 11 bean tags are summarized in table 10.4. These tags can be used to do the following:

- Create a JSP scripting variable from an HTTP header, request parameter, cookie, or any existing object in any scope.
- Create a new bean from the response to another request (include), from an application resource, or from a Struts configuration object.
- Determine the number of elements in a collection or a map.
- Automatically write a localized message for the current user from an application resource.
- Write the value of a given property on any available bean.

Of these, only two, the `message` and `struts` tags, are bound to the framework in any way. The other nine will work just as well in any application.

Table 10.4 The Struts bean tags

Tag name	Description
cookie	Defines a scripting variable based on the value(s) of the specified request cookie
define	Defines a scripting variable based on the value(s) of the specified bean property
header	Defines a scripting variable based on the value(s) of the specified request header
include	Loads the response from a dynamic application request and makes it available as a bean
message	Renders an internationalized message string
page	Exposes a specified item from the page context as a bean
parameter	Defines a scripting variable based on the value(s) of the specified request parameter
resource	Loads a web application resource and makes it available as a bean
size	Defines a bean containing the number of elements in a Collection or Map
struts	Exposes a Struts internal configuration object as a bean
write	Renders the value of the specified bean property

Used together, these tags provide a great deal of functionality that JSP designers can usually access only through scriptlets. These include the usual CGI tricks, like writing HTTP headers:

```
<bean:header id="browser" name="User-Agent"/>
<P>You are viewing this page with: <bean:write name="browser"/></P>
```

along with more useful things, like creating a new bean based on a cookie:

```
<bean:cookie id="username" name="username" scope="session"
    value="New User" />
<P>Welcome <bean:write name="username" property="value"/!</P>
```

If the username had already been stored as a cookie, then it would be displayed instead of *New User.*

Bean tag best practices

The Struts bean taglib provides many advanced capabilities that can be useful when developers are migrating from JSP Model 1 to Model 2 applications (see chapter 1). Many of the tags, like `<bean:cookie>` and `<bean:header>`, provide services that can also be handled by the Struts Action. Many Struts developers prefer to reduce JavaServer Pages to a mail-merge task. Anything that smacks of business logic, like managing cookies, might best be handled in a Struts Action and then passed to the page.

In general practice, the most often used bean tags are `<bean:write>` and `<bean:message>`.

The bean write and message tags

The `<bean:write>` tag is the read-only complement to the Struts html tags discussed in the next section. It is a flexible and efficient tag that uses reflection to print the value of any given property:

```
<bean:write name="shoppingCart" property="itemSum"/>
```

If the property is not a Java primitive, the standard `toString()` method for the object is called.

The `<bean:message>` tag helps localize your application. Java defines a standard object for storing a user's region and language, called the *locale* (`java.util.locale`). By default, the Struts controller creates a locale object for each user and stores it in the session context under a known key.

All the developer need do is provide the key for the message. The pertinent Struts components, like the `<bean:message>` tag, look up the message related to that key. The framework automatically provides the related message from the resource for the user's locale.

Given a tag like this:

```
<bean:message key="inquiry"/>
```

the bean message tag could render

```
"Comment allez-vous?"
```

for a user set to the French/Canada locale, but render

```
"How are you?"
```

for a user in the English/United States locale. For more about localizing applications, see chapter 13.

10.3.3 *The html tags*

The HTML format [W3C, HTML] provides a small but useful set of controls that browsers must support. These include buttons, checkboxes, radio buttons, menus, text fields, and hidden controls. All of these are designed so that they can be pre-populated with dynamic data. Actually getting the data into the control is left up to the application.

Dynamic applications written with scripting languages, including JSP scriptlets, often populate HTML tags by writing a mix of HTML and script. For example, to populate an HTML text form tag using a standard JavaBean and JSP scriptlet, most developers would write something like this:

```
<input type="text" name="firstName"
    value="<%= formBean.getFirstName() %>"/>
```

NOTE Incidentally, there is nothing to prevent you from writing HTML tags using scriptlets. The Struts tags have no special preference. When the form is submitted to the Struts controller, all the controller sees is a standard HTTP request. Regardless of how the request was initiated, the controller will dutifully run through the gauntlet: populate any associated Action-Form bean, call the ActionForm bean's `validate` method, and pass the ActionForm along to the Action `perform` method or forward the request back for additional input. How the HTML form underlying the request was rendered isn't important. What *is* important (at least to the Struts team) is that JSP developers have a complete set of tags they can use to write HTML controls without resorting to scriptlets.

Here's how we would populate that same control using a Struts html tag:

```
<html:text property="firstName"/>
```

Note some differences between the two:

- Although not shown, the scriptlet version requires that the formBean be declared on the page as a scripting variable before use. The Struts tags will find the bean without any red tape.
- By default, the Struts tags will use the same bean as the rest of the form, so the bean does not have to be specified for each control.

Corresponding HTML elements

The Struts html taglib provides a set of more than 20 tags to help you prepopulate HTML controls and related elements. As shown in table 10.5, most of these correspond to standard HTML elements.

Table 10.5   How Struts html tags correspond to HTML elements

Struts html tag	Corresponding HTML element	Struts html tag	Corresponding HTML element
base	`<base>`	messages	None—displays a set of accumulated error message [Struts 1.1]
button	`<input type="button">`	option, options	`<option>`
checkbox, multibox	`<input type="checkbox">`	password	`<input type="password">`
errors	None—displays a set of accumulated error messages	radio	`<input type="radio">`
file	`<input type="file">`	reset	`<input type="reset">`
form	`<form>`	rewrite	None—outputs a URL-encoded path
hidden	`<input type="hidden">`	select	`<select>`
html	`<html>`	submit	`<input type="submit">`
image	`<input type="image">`	text	`<input type="text">`
img	`<img>`	textarea	`<textarea>`
link	`<a>`		

This one-to-one correspondence makes converting existing HTML or JSP pages to Struts a very straightforward process. For example, wherever an HTML element like

```
<input type="text" name="username">
```

is found, it can be replaced with the corresponding Struts html tag:

```
<html:text property="username"/>
```

There are already converters available that read existing HTML pages and automatically create the corresponding Struts version [Objectwave], [Ramaiah]. Tools like this can give you a good head start on your project.

Common properties

Like the Struts tags overall, the Struts html tags share a number of common properties, as shown in table 10.6.

Table 10.6   Struts html taglibs use a consistent set of property names.

Property	Purpose
name	The name of the ActionForm, or other JavaBean, that provides the data for this control. If not specified, the ActionForm bean associated with the enclosing form tag is used.
on*	Each of the html tags includes the appropriate JavaScript event handlers [Netscape], including onblur, onchange, onclick, ondblclick, onfocus, onkeydown, onkeypress, onkeyup, onmousedown, onmousemove, onmouseout, onmouseover, onmouseup, onreset, and onsubmit. These are all rendered in lowercase for compatibility with XML.
accesskey	Accessibility key character (ignored by some browsers). Pressing an access key assigned to an element gives focus to the element.
tabindex	An attribute that specifies the position of the current element in the tabbing order for the current document. The tabbing order defines the order in which elements will receive focus when navigated by the user via the keyboard.
style	CSS styles [W3C, CSS] to be applied to this HTML element.
StyleClass	CSS style sheet class [W3C, CSS] to be applied to this HTML element.

10.3.4   The logic tags

As shown in table 10.7, Struts offers three flavors of logic tags: evaluation tags, control-flow tags, and a repeat tag.

Table 10.7   The three kinds of Struts logic tags

Tag	Purpose
Evaluation tags	For testing if values are equal, less than, greater than, empty (blank or null), or even present
Control-flow tags	For redirecting or forwarding the request
Repeat tag	For iterating over any type of collection

Evaluation tags

The Struts logic tags are often used to provide alternative versions of the same presentation page. Depending on the existence or value of an object or property, a given block of markup is selected and presented to the user:

```
<logic:notPresent name="logonForm">
    <html:link forward="logon">Sign in here</html:link>
</logic:notPresent>
<logic:present name="logonForm">
    <html:link forward="logoff">Sign out</html:link>
</logic:present>
```

Many pages will differ slightly depending on certain circumstances, such as whether a user is logged in. Logged-in users may see a dialog box offering them the chance to log out. Logged-out users may see a dialog box offering them the chance to log in. When users are logged in, they may also have access to administrative controls. In addition, users may have access to different controls based on their security role. Often, most of the page remains the same, the only difference being a line or two of markup.

While the MVC architecture allows us to process the application's business logic in the Model and Controller layers, being able to apply some logical constructs in the View is still useful. In practice, creating separate pages for every possible circumstance creates a maintenance burden. If similar pages are created and then need to be updated, every variation of the page will have to be updated separately. This does not meet the MVC's prime directive to help us create robust, easy-to-maintain applications. So, as a practical matter many developers place a smidgen of presentation logic into a page, just to reduce the total number of pages to maintain.

NOTE   The Tiles library discussed in chapter 11 provides another solution to this problem. Various page definitions can be created for each circumstance without creating redundant markup files. Using Tiles in this way can reduce or eliminate presentation logic from an application.

Since it is expected that the majority of logic will be processed in the Action, the Struts logic tags are rudimentary. You may have noticed that the lack of an if...then...else structure in the foregoing code fragment. One tag, present, was used to test to see whether the logonForm exists, and another, notPresent, was used to test whether the ActionForm did not exist. This same pattern follows for all the Struts evaluation tags. There is no kind of if...then...else structure available in the logic tag library. These structures are difficult to formulate as custom tags, and given the restricted amount of logic that is processed on a Struts page, deemed not worth the trouble by the development team.

Evaluation tags—common properties

As mentioned, Struts provides a full complement of evaluation tags: `empty` [Struts 1.1], `notEmpty` [Struts 1.1], `equal`, `notEqual`, `greaterEqual`, `lessEqual`, `greaterThan`, `lessThan`, `match`, `notMatch`, `present`, and `notPresent`. All of these tags require a `value` property upon which to base the evaluation. Of course, the value property can be determined by runtime expression if needed:

```
<bean:define id="value2" name="bean2" property="value"/>
<logic:equal value="<%=(String) value2 %>" name="bean1" property="value">
<%-- markup for when bean1.value equals bean2.value --%>
HIT!
</logic:equal>
```

As shown in table 10.8, the evaluation tags can compare the value with a cookie, HTTP header, request parameter, bean, or property on a bean.

Table 10.8   Comparison attributes for evaluation tags

Attribute	Purpose
cookie	The value is compared with a cookie's property.
header	The value is compared with the HTTP header.
parameter	The value is compared with a request parameter.
name	The value is compared with the object by this name.
property	The value is compared with this property of the named object.

The `match` and `notMatch` tags also take an optional `location` property. This can be used to indicate whether the `start` or `end` of the string is to be matched. Otherwise, the match runs across the entire string.

For details regarding what attributes each of the Struts tags accepts, see the technical documentation provided with the Struts distribution.

Control-flow tags

Again, while it is better to provide the control flow in the controller, the Struts `redirect` and `forward` tags can also handle task this from a JSP. Typically, flow will be forwarded or redirected based on the outcome of an evaluation tag.

A very good use of the `redirect` or `forward` tag is to send control from a default welcome page to an Action. Virtual URIs, like the Struts Action, cannot be used as the welcome page for an application. (The container looks for a physical page.) Alternatively, you can provide an index.jsp page that forwards control to an element controlled by the Struts configuration:

```
<%@ taglib uri="/tags/struts-logic" prefix="logic" %>
<logic:forward name="welcome"/>
```

The repeat tag

The Struts `<logic:iterate>` tag is quite flexible. It provides all the looping functionality most MVC presentation pages require. A collection is passed as a bean, or as a property of a bean. The tag then repeats over each element, exposing it as a scripting variable. The `bean` and `html` tags can then be used to write out the element as it iterates:

```
<UL>
<logic:iterate id="item" name="list">
    <LI><bean:write name="item"/></LI>
</logic:iterate>
</UL>
```

We will return to `iterate` in the next section, which covers putting the tags to work.

The complete API for the Struts tag libraries is included with the Struts distribution [ASF, Struts]. As you start to use the tags in your own application, it is recommended that you review the Struts Taglib Developer Guides, which include additional usage information and several handy examples. The exercise-taglib application in the Struts distribution also includes several interesting test cases for various tags. Many of these can be used as a starting point for your own widgets.

To complement what is distributed with Struts, appendix C provides a Struts taglibs quick reference with descriptions of the tags in each library, along with a list of properties each tag accepts.

10.4 Using Struts JSP tags

In part 1 of this book, we stressed the importance of using a layered architecture. With this approach, all the data processing takes place through an Action class. The presentation layer can then focus on displaying data rather than acquiring it. In this section, we cut to the chase and show you how to use the Struts custom tags to display dynamic data.

One last note before we get started. It's important to remember that, in the end, *it all comes down to HTML*. By the time the page reaches the browser, it is no longer "in JSP" or "in Struts." What the browser sees is regular HTML, rendered in the usual way. This must be the case, since JSP and Struts are designed to work with any existing browser, as is, without adaptation. There are technologies, such as Java applets, that can plug into a browser and provide special capabilities. But JSP and Struts are designed to work with stock web browsers. They can do only whatever HTML can do. Conversely, you can do *anything* with Struts that you can do with JSP and HTML. That by itself opens a world of possibilities.

10.4.1 *The Struts tag team*

In practice, tags from the various Struts libraries are often used together. Some properties on a form may be read-only and rendered with a `<bean:write>` rather than an `<html:text>` tag. A logic tag may be used to provide or exclude a control on a form based on evaluating a value at runtime. The `<html:link>` tag is often used with `<logic:iterate>` to render a list of hyperlinks. And so forth.

In this section, we focus on how the Struts tags are used together to provide a desired effect. Creating web pages from dynamic data is an interesting topic and could easily fill an entire book on its own. Many of the more interesting effects rely on client-side JavaScript rather than server-side dynamic data. Accordingly, we focus here on how to get the dynamic, server-side data into your page, where other assets, such as JavaScripts, can then make use of it.

First, in the "Fundamentals" section, we look at the basics of populating controls and setting defaults. Then, in the "Techniques" section, we examine several key features of the Struts tags that provide a broad range of solutions to common problems. These include using arrays to capture duplicate elements and using `rewrite` to render paths to other assets.

10.4.2 *Fundamentals*

The material in this section is designed to help you get started with your own application. First, we cover the base essentials, such as declaring a form and populating a control. Then we touch upon some of the finer points that new Struts developers tend to overlook or struggle with, including how to do the following:

- Select a radio button
- Filter (or not filter) HTML
- Clear passwords
- Use transactional tokens
- Use collections with the `options` tag
- Use `multibox` to handle checkbox arrays
- Localize buttons and labels

Chapter 13 covers localization in depth. In this section, we cover localization issues specific to using the Struts tags only.

Declaring a form

The Struts html tags are designed to populate their corresponding element from a JavaBean. The JavaBean represents the overall form. The properties of the Java-Bean represent the form's elements. While any JavaBean will work with the tags, the architecture encourages developers to use ActionForms (see chapter 5). ActionForms are specially designed to ferry data from HTML forms to the rest of your application.

STRUTS TIP   The best way to get started with the Struts JSP tags is to begin replacing the HTML elements in your pages with the corresponding tag from the html taglib.

Like its HTML counterpart, Struts begins a form with an <html:form> tag, followed by whatever control elements are needed, and concludes with a closing </html:form> tag, as shown in listing 10.2.

Listing 10.2   A simple login form page

```
<%@ taglib uri="/tags/struts-html" prefix="html" %>
<html:html>
<HEAD><TITLE>Sign in, Please!</title></head>
<BODY>
<html:errors/>
<html:form action="/logonSubmit"
    name="logonForm" type="app.LogonForm" scope="request">
<TABLE border="0" width="100%">
<TR><TH>Username: </TH>
<TD><html:text property="username"/></TD>
</TR>
<TR>
<TH>Password: </TH>
<TD><html:password property="password"/></TD>
</TR>
<TR>
<TD><html:submit/></TD>
<TD><html:reset/></TD>
</TR>
</TABLE>
</html:form>
</BODY>
</html:html>
```

In listing 10.2, we specified the name, type, and scope for the default JavaBean to be used by the form. In practice, these properties are usually omitted, and the <html:form> tag looks them up from the ActionMapping (chapter 7). If the Java-Bean does not exist, the <html:form> tag will create it, making the bean's default values available to other elements on the page.

Populating an html control element

By default, the text and password tags in listing 10.2 will populate themselves from the logonForm bean. If the bean was placed in the request before forwarding to the page, any preexisting values will be used. This lets you set the bean properties in a Struts Action class and then forward to the page, where the properties can be displayed.

So

```
<html:text property="username"/>
```

as a scriptlet would equate to something like

```
<input type="text" value="<%= logonForm.getUsername() %>"">
```

where logonForm had been already exposed as scripting variable.

Every element on the form does not have to be populated from the same bean. The bean used by the <html:form> tag is simply the default. The snippet

```
<html:text property="username" name="accountBean"/>
```

will populate the element from a bean named accountBean. Since the scope was not specified, the usual order is followed: page, request, session, application. The first bean found by that name is used.

NOTE   When the form is submitted, the browser will send this element as user-name= . . . . The Struts controller will populate only the ActionForm associated with the form's action. If additional beans are used, it is the developer's responsibility to capture the additional parameters. Whenever possible, it is best to have all the properties used by the form represented on the same ActionForm bean.

Selecting a radio button

Each radio button element requires an assigned value that distinguishes it from the other radio buttons. When creating a *static* array of radio buttons, you need to indicate which one of these, if any, is checked. This does *not* need to be done when the radio buttons are being populated from dynamic data. The control can compare itself to the form bean's property and then check itself when appropriate.

Given a set of `<html:radio>` controls like this:

```
<html:radio property="expectedVia" value="UPS"/>UPS
<html:radio property="expectedVia" value="FEDX"/>Federal Express
<html:radio property="expectedVia" value="AIRB"/>Airborne
```

and that the `expectedVia` property on the form bean was already set to UPS, then the HTML radio elements would be rendered like this:

```
<input type="radio" name="expectedVia" value="UPS" checked="checked">UPS
<input type="radio" name="expectedVia" value="FEDX">Federal Express
<input type="radio" name="expectedVia" value="AIRB" >Airborne
```

Filtering HTML

There are several characters that HTML treats specially, including the braces around markup tags, the ampersand, and some others. If these characters are rendered as part of a text field, as is, they can ruin the HTML and produce other nasty side effects. By default, these characters are filtered by the Struts `<bean:write>` tag and replaced with their HTML equivalents. This lets you store the actual characters in your data file but safely and automatically render them on a web page.

Occasionally, you may need to use a field to capture actual HTML (entered by trusted and knowledgeable people) and display that as part of the page. When this happens, you can switch the filtering off:

```
<bean:write name="scriptForm" property="article" filter="false"/>
```

But this should only be done when you really, really know what you are doing. Rendering raw input to a page is a security risk and should avoided whenever possible.

Clearing passwords

By default, the `<html:password>` field will repopulate itself, like any other html tag. If there is a validation error on the page, the `password` property will be read back from the form bean and placed into the `password` tag. The actual password will be masked by the browser and hidden from casual onlookers, but will still be visible in the HTML source. If this behavior is considered a security risk, then the `password` tag can set to bypass autopopulation:

```
<html:password property="password" redisplay="false"/>
```

This means that the `password` field will always start out blank. If the form fails validation when submitted, the password will have to be entered again, even if the original input was valid. Setting `redisplay` to false on logon forms is a good practice for production applications.

Using transactional tokens

Duplicate submissions can often be a problem for web applications. Struts supports a strategy to prevent duplication submissions using a *synchronizing token*. Using synchronizing tokens is automatic for the Struts `<html:form>` tag. If it sees that tokens are being used, it automatically includes the appropriate hidden field.

On the Action side, you can enable transactional tokens by calling

```
saveToken(request);
```

anywhere in the Action's perform or execute method. On the return trip, to have an Action check if a token is still good, call

```
boolean valid = isTokenValid(request);
```

If this method returns false, branch to an error page. If it returns true, call

```
resetToken(request);
```

While participating in a transaction most often occurs with forms, there are also applications for hyperlinks and other assets. Accordingly, the Struts `<html:link>` and `<html:rewrite>` tags provide optional support for transactions. To include the appropriate token in the link, set the `transaction` property to true. A tag like this:

```
<html:link forward="addItem" paramName="row" paramProperty="itemId"
   paramId="id" transaction="true"/>
```

will then generate a hyperlink like this:

```
<a href="/gavel/do/addItem?
    id=3017&amp;org.apache.struts.taglib.html.TOKEN=72da1d3fdede66c">
```

Using collections for options

The `options` tag is used to write the options for a menu selection from one or more collections. You can use one collection for both the `labels` option and `values` option, or you can use a separate collection for each. Alternatively, you can use one collection with elements that have accessors for the `label` and `value` properties. With a little help from `<bean:define>`, you can also pass the collections as part of the form bean.

The syntax for the `options` tag is complex. The best thing might be to provide examples of the popular use cases:

- One collection, stored as a property on the ActionForm

- One collection, stored as a separate bean
- One collection, with `labelName` and `labelProperty` accessors, stored as a separate bean
- One collection with `CodeName` and `LabelProperty` accessors

One collection, stored as a property on the ActionForm.   The same string will be used for the value and the property. The collection is being returned by a method with the signature `Collection getImageOptions()`:

```
<TR>
<TD>Item Image Source:</TD>
<TD><html:select property="hasImage">
<html:options property="imageOptions" />
</html:select>
</TD>
</TR>
```

One collection, stored as a separate bean.   Here the collection has been put directly in the request, session, or application scope under the name `imageOptions`:

```
<TR>
<TD>Item Image Source:</TD>
<TD><html:select property="hasImage">
<html:options collection="imageOptions"/>
</html:select>
</TD>
</TR>
```

One collection, with `labelName` *and* `labelProperty` *accessors, stored as a separate bean.* This will call the `getValue()` and `getLabel()` properties for each element in the collection:

```
<TR>
<TD>Item Image Source:</TD>
<TD><html:select property="hasImage">
<html:options collection="imageOptions" property="value"
    labelProperty="label"/>
</html:select>
</TD>
</TR>
```

One collection, with `labelName` *and* `labelProperty` *accessors.*   This will call the `getValue()` and `getLabel()` methods for each element in the collection. Here we need to use `<bean:define>` to expose the collection so that it can be used like the prior example:

```
<TR>
<TD>Item Image Source:</TD>
<TD><html:select property="hasImage">
<bean:define id="imageOptions" name="itemForm">
    property="imageOptions" type="java.util.Collection"/>
<html:options collection="imageOptions" property="value"
  labelProperty="label"/>
</html:select>
</TD>
</TR>
```

Since Struts 1.1, a LabelValueBean class is provided with the Struts distribution (org.apache.struts.util.LabelValueBean), but any compatible class can be used. For more about localizing LabelValue classes, see chapter 13.

Using arrays for checkboxes

Many applications need to use a large number of checkboxes to track options or selected items. To help with this, Struts provides the multibox control. It's quite handy but a little tricky to understand at first.

The multibox leverages the way HTML handles checkboxes. If the box is not checked, the browser does not submit a value for the control. If the box is checked, then the name of the control and its value are submitted. This behavior is the reason there is a reset method on the ActionForm. Since the browser will never signal that a box has been *un*-checked, the only solution is to reset all the boxes, and then check the ones that are now present in the request.

STRUTS TIP Use the <html:multibox> tag to manage a set of checkboxes as an array.

The multibox control is designed to use an array of Strings. Each element in the array represents a checked box. To select a box, add a String to the array with the box's value. To deselect a box, remove the element from the array. (Sound familiar?)

When passed a value, the multibox control scans the elements of its array to see if there is a match. If so, the box is checked. If not, the box is left unchecked. If the user checks the box and submits the form, the box's value will be included in the request. The controller will then add that box to the checked array. If a box is unchecked, nothing is submitted, and nothing is added to the array. If the ActionForm bean is kept in the session context, in between requests, the reset method needs to reduce the array to zero length (but not null).

In this example

```
<logic:iterate id="item" property="items">
    <html:multibox property="selectedItems">
        <bean:write name="item"/>
    </html:multibox>
        <bean:write name="item"/>
</logic:iterate>
```

the labels for the individual checkboxes are in the items property. The list of selected items is in an array named selectedItems. Items that are not selected are not present in the selectedItems array. The multibox checks the selectedItems array for the current item. If it is present, it writes a checked checkbox. If not, it writes an unchecked checkbox.

Given an ActionForm setup like this

```
private String[] selectedItems = {};
private String[] items = {"UPS","FedEx","Airborne"};
public String[] getSelectedItems() {
    return this.selectedItems;
}
public void setSelectedItems(String[] selectedItems) {
    this.selectedItems = selectedItems;
}
```

the markup in the example would generate three checkboxes, labeled UPS, FedEx, and Airborne:

```
<input type="checkbox" name="selectedItems" value="UPS">UPS
<input type="checkbox" name="selectedItems" value="FedEx">FedEx
<input type="checkbox" name="selectedItems" value="Airborne">Airborne
```

Initially, the selectedItems array would be empty. If UPS were checked and submitted, it would become the equivalent of

```
private String[] selectedItems = {"UPS"};
```

If UPS and Airborne were both checked, it would become the equivalent of

```
private String[] selectedItems = {"UPS","Airborne"};
```

And when the checkboxes are rendered, the appropriate elements are automatically checked by the multibox tag:

```
<input type="checkbox" name="selectedItems"
    value="UPS" checked="checked">UPS
<input type="checkbox" name="selectedItems"
    value="FedEx">FedEx
<input type="checkbox" name="selectedItems"
    value="Airborne" checked="checked">Airborne
```

To provide different sets of labels and values, the standard LabelValueBean class (org.apache.struts.util.LabelValueBean) (since Struts 1.1) can be used with the multibox control:

```
<logic:iterate id="item" property="items"
    <html:multibox property="selectedItems">
        <bean:write name="item" property="value"/>
    </html:multibox>
        <bean:write name="item" property="label"/>
</logic:iterate>
```

Localizing labels

You can use <bean:message> to create localized labels for the html tags, as in

```
<TH><bean:message  key="username"/></TH>
<TD><html:text property="username"/></TD>
```

where username is a key in the application's message resources.

A message resource may be provided for each supported locale. The message for the current user's locale will be rendered automatically. For more about localization, see chapter 13.

In the case of button tags, the <bean:message> may be given as the button's content:

```
<html:submit><bean:message key="submit"/></html:submit>
```

Since the button's label is also its value, the localized message is what the browser will submit.

Localizing options

The <html:options> tags allow you to provide a collection for the option labels and another for the optional values. This allows you to forward a label collection for a given user's locale. There are no changes to the markup in this case, since the tag simply outputs what it is given. The actual collection is best generated in the Action class. See chapter 13 for more about generating localized content.

If you are hardcoding the options in your page, then you can also localize options using <bean:message>:

```
<html:option value="status"><bean:message key="status"/></html:option>
```

Localizing collections

For more about preparing localized collections, including collections based on LabelValueBean, turn to chapter 13. When a localized collection is passed to a page, no changes to the markup are needed, since the page simply renders whatever is provided in the collection.

10.4.3 *Techniques*

Now that we're past the fundamentals, let's look at several advanced techniques Struts developers find useful, including:

- Using an ImageButtonBean to represent an ImageButton
- Using bean tags to create custom controls
- Using an array to catch duplicate parameters
- Using `<bean:size>` to test the size of a collection
- Iterating over part of a collection
- Exposing the iteration index if needed

- Using nested `<present>` and `<notEmpty>` tags to test bean properties
- Using application scope objects for stable option lists
- Using `rewrite` to render URLs for style sheets, JavaScripts, and other assets
- Using Struts JSP tags to render JavaScript
- Using `<bean:write>` to render JavaScript from a bean
- Renaming the Submit button to avoid JavaScript conflicts
- Using formless buttons
- Using an Action as the input property to re-create dependent objects
- Using dynamic form actions
- Using alternative message tags

Using an ImageButtonBean to represent an ImageButton

An endless source of aggravation is the HTML input `image` element. The specification says that browsers should treat this control like an image map. Unlike other buttons, it does not submit a string representing the button's label; it submits the x and y coordinates. If you look at the HTTP post for an image button, you'll see it looks something like this:

```
myImageButton.x=200
myImageButton.y=300
```

For most other controls, a Struts developer can create a simple `String` property to represent the element. This clearly won't work with an image button, because it submits two "dotted" properties instead of a simple name-value entry like other elements.

Happily, Struts does allow an ActionForm to contain, or nest, other JavaBeans, and will automatically populate the beans using the same syntax as the image element. (What a co-inky-dink!)

To represent an image input element in your ActionForm, say what you mean, and use an ImageButtonBean to capture the x and y parameters, like that shown in listing 10.3.

Listing 10.3   An ImageButtonBean class

```
public final class ImageButtonBean extends Object {
    private String x = null;
    private String y = null;
    public String getX() {
        return (this.x);
    }
    public void setX(String x) {
        this.x = x;
    }
    public String getY() {
    return (this.y);
    }
    public void setY(String y) {
        this.y = y;
    }
    public boolean isSelected() {
            return ((x!=null) || (y!=null));
    }
} // End ImageButtonBean
```

Note that we've included a helper method on this bean, isSelected. This method just returns true if either the x or y property is not null. If both are still null, then isSelected returns false.

Here's how you could declare two ImageButtonBeans on an ActionForm:

```
// ..
    private ImageButtonBean logonButton = new ImageButtonBean();
    public void setLogonButton(ImageButtonBean button) {
        this.logonButton = button;
    }
    public ImageButtonBean getLogonButton() {
        return this.logonButton;
    }
    private ImageButtonBean cancelButton = new ImageButtonBean();
```

```
    public void setCancelButton(ImageButtonBean button) {
        this.cancelButton = button;
    }
    public ImageButtonBean getCancelButton() {
        return this.cancelButton;
    }
// ...
```

The next question will be "OK, which button did they click?" so let's define another helper method on the ActionForm to tell us:

```
public String getSelected() {
    if (getLogonButton().isSelected()) {
      return Constants.LOGON;
  }

    if (getCancelButton().isSelected()) {
      return Constants.CANCEL;
  }

      return null; // nobody home
  }
```

In an Action, determining which button is clicked is then a simple matter of asking the form what was selected:

```
String selected = ((MyForm) form).getSelected();
if (Constants.CANCEL.equals(selected)) ...
```

Of course, since `getSelected` would be called within the Action, the method doesn't need to return a `String`. It could be an `int`, a custom type to represent your API functions, or even the name of another method for use with a DispatchAction (`org.apache.struts.actions.DispatchAction`).

Using bean tags to create custom controls

As good as the html tags are, they cannot cover every circumstance. When you need to write an HTML form element in a way not supported by the stock tags, you can cobble your own with `<bean:write>`. Here are some popular use cases:

Adding `wrap="soft"` to the `textarea` control:

```
<textarea name="description" rows="5" cols="60" wrap="soft">
<bean:write name="scriptForm" property="description"/></textarea>
```

Renaming a property:

```
<input type='hidden' name='prospect'
    value='<bean:write name="donorForm" property="donor"/>'>
```

Setting a control to a parameter from the request:

```
<bean:parameter id="item" name="item"/>
<input type='text' name='item' value='<bean:write name="item"/>'>
```

Setting a control to the value of a cookie:

```
<bean:cookie id="username" name="username"/>
<input type='text' name="username" value='<bean:write name="username"
property="value"/>'>
```

Of course, these three cases are only the most popular examples. There are many other use cases that follow the same pattern shown here.

Using an array to catch duplicate parameters

HTML and HTTP allow for parameters with the same name to be added to the same request. You can capture duplicate parameters by making the properties on your ActionForm a String array:

```
private String items = {""};
public String[] getItems() {
    return this.item;
}
public void setItem(String item[]) {
    this.item = item;
}
```

Note that you must code your arrays so that they are never null; otherwise an Exception will be thrown when iterate tries to loop through the entries.

In the form, you can then write out the array out using the iterate tag:

```
<logic:iterate name="logonForm" property="items" id="item">
    <TR>
    <TD>Item:</TD>
    <TD>
    <input type='text' name="item"
        value='<bean:write name="item"/>'>
    </TD>
    </TR>
</logic:iterate>
```

STRUTS TIP   The properties on your ActionForm can include collections and arrays as well as simple properties. If you submit parameters with duplicate names, they can be captured in an array property.

Using <bean:size> to test the size of a collection

Some of the standard Java collections, like ArrayList, do not use JavaBean conventions for their properties. To work around this problem, the <bean:size> tag returns the size of any given collection. One good use of this tag is to print a special message if the collection is empty, rather than iterate over zero elements:

```
<bean:size id="listSize" name="list"/>
<logic:equal name="listSize" value="0">
    <P>No records were selected.</P>
</logic:equal>
<logic:notEqual name="listSize" value="0">
<logic:iterate id="row" name="list" >
    <%-- markup for each row --%>
</logic:iterate>
</logic:notEqual>
```

However, if an application often returns a set of search results, it can be worthwhile to define a convenience class to wrap the collection and associated properties. See the ResultList class in the Scaffold package for an example (org.apache. commons.scaffold.util.ResultList).

Iterating over part of a collection

The <logic:iterate> tag can take an offset and count, in the event only part of the collection should be exposed. For example, use this to start from the fifth element and display the next five elements:

```
<logic:iterate id="element" name="list" offset="5" length="5">
```

Exposing the iteration index if needed

 It can be useful to have access to the index for each iterator in order to generate unique form names or other elements:

```
<OL>
<logic:iterate id="element" name="list" indexId="index">
<LI><EM><bean:write name="element"/></EM>
  [<bean:write name="index"/>]</LI>
</logic:iterate>
</OL>
```

index is actually a scripting variable, and so this could also be written as

```
<OL>
<logic:iterate id="element" name="list" indexId="index">
<LI><EM><bean:write name="element"/></EM>
    [<% index %>"/>]</LI>
</logic:iterate>
</OL>
```

Using nested <present> and <notEmpty> tags to test bean properties

If you need to test whether a property on a bean is present or empty, and the bean itself may not exist, you can nest the evaluations:

```
<logic:present name="bean"><logic:notEmpty name="bean" property="value">
   <bean:write name="bean" property="value"/>
</logic:notEmpty></logic:present>
```

NOTES   The `<logic:empty>` tag was added in Struts 1.1.

In Struts 1.0, `<notPresent>` can be used to test for null values. In Struts 1.1, `<empty>` can be used to test for both null values and empty `Strings`.

Using application scope objects for stable option lists

Many applications need to use static, or semi-static, sets of option lists that may be used on several different pages. Often, these lists are drawn from a database table or other resource. This makes them good candidates for collections. If the collections are the same for every user, that makes them good candidates for application scope objects. Here's an example:

```
<TR>
<TD>Item Image Source:</TD>
<TD><html:select property="hasImage">
<html:options collection="imageOptions" scope="application"
    property="value" labelProperty="label"/>
</html:select>
</TD>
</TR>
```

If the list needs to be filtered or localized for a user, a proxy object can be placed in the session, which uses the application object as a data source.

Using rewrite to render URLs for style sheets, JavaScripts, and other assets

The Struts `<html:rewrite>` tag can convert a context-relative URI into a base URI that can be used to access style sheets, JavaScripts, images, and other HTML assets. For example:

```
<LINK rel="stylesheet" type="text/css"
    href="<html:rewrite page='/assets/styles/base.css'/>">
```

If you want to hedge your bets about where the style sheets will be located, an ActionForward may also be used:

```
<LINK rel="stylesheet" type="text/css"
    href="<html:rewrite forward='baseStyleSheet'/>">
```

Likewise, references to JavaScripts, as well as URIs to be processed by JavaScripts, can be rendered this way:

```
<SCRIPT language='javascript'
    src='<html:rewrite page="/assets/scripts/remote.js"/>'></SCRIPT>
<SCRIPT>
<!--
function doPreview (aRecord) {
    aBase = '<html:rewrite forward="preview"/>';
    doOpenRemote(aBase + '?record=' + aRecord);
}
// --
</SCRIPT>
```

In the latter example, we first included a set of JavaScripts from another page (including the doOpenRemote script). Before calling the script, we look up the base URI for the JavaScript function from an ActionForward. Finally, as we call the JavaScript, we append the script number to the function. This type of function would usually be called from a hyperlink like this

```
<a href='javascript:doScript(10011)'>10011</a>
```

that was generated using JSP code like this:

```
<a href='javascript:doPreview(<bean:write name="row" property="script"/>)'>
    <bean:write name="row" property="script"/>
</a>
```

STRUTS TIP   Use <html:rewrite> to reference HTML assets.

Since we are calling a JavaScript function, we did not bother with an <html:link> tag to provide URL encoding. The hyperlink will be handled client-side, so maintaining the session is not an issue. The URI generated by the rewrite tag, and subsequently used *by* the JavaScript, will be URL encoded, so that the session will be maintained if cookies are not present.

Using Struts JSP tags to render JavaScript

The Struts framework ensures that we can perform data validation without the benefit of JavaScript. But that doesn't mean we can't use JavaScript in our Struts applications. Most web developers rely on JavaScript to provide core features on the presentation layer, and Struts developers are no exception.

Most JavaScripts can be used on a Struts JSP like any other page. After all, in the end, it all comes down to HTML.

Because it all comes down to HTML, you can mix JSP tags in with references to your JavaScript. The JSP code renders first, so by the time the browser sees it, any dynamic references have been resolved and it just looks just like a static reference. Let's look at a script to open a remote window to preview a record from a database.

First, here's a basic remote window script, just like you would use on a static page:

```
// Open window
function openWin(newURL, newName, newFeatures, orgName) {
  var newWin = open(newURL, newName, newFeatures);
  if (newWin.opener == null)
    newWin.opener = window;
  newWin.opener.name = orgName;
  return newWin;
}
```

```
// Open centered remote
function doOpenRemote(aURL, newName, aHEIGHT, aWIDTH, aFeatures, orgName){
  if (aHEIGHT == "*"){ aHEIGHT = (screen.availHeight - 80) };
  if (aWIDTH == "*"){ aWIDTH = (screen.availWidth - 30) };
  var newFeatures = "height=" + aHEIGHT + ",innerHeight=" + aHEIGHT;
  newFeatures += ",width=" + aWIDTH + ",innerWidth=" + aWIDTH;
  if (window.screen){
    var ah = (screen.availHeight - 30);
    var aw = (screen.availWidth - 10);
    var xc = (( aw - aWIDTH ) / 2);
    var yc = (( ah - aHEIGHT ) / 2);
    newFeatures += ",left=" + xc + ",screenX=" + xc;
    newFeatures += ",top=" + yc + ",screenY=" + yc;
    newFeatures += "," + aFeatures;
  }
  var newWin = openWin(aURL, newName, newFeatures, orgName);
  newWin.focus();
  return newWin;
}
```

We'll take this script as a given and not step through how it works. The sample script is not the point of the exercise. Let's move on to how it is called from the JSP.

We want to use this script to open different database records at different times. To do this, we need to feed it a different URI to indicate which database record to open this time. In many applications, the URI would look something like this:

```
/do/item/View?item=117
```

The /do/item/View part is relatively static. It just needs to be rewritten to maintain the session. We can store it as an ActionForward and use the <html:rewrite> tag to render it at runtime, and ensure it is URL-encoded if necessary. For example, in the Struts configuration file, we can place

```
<forward
    name="item"
    path="/do/item/View"/>
```

and then use this tag in the JSP:

```
<html:rewrite forward="item"/>
```

The dicey part is the `?item=117`. This is the truly dynamic portion of the URI, and the part that we actively need to pass to the script. That being so, let's make it a parameter to our JavaScript function. Here's the result:

```
<script>
<!--
function doItem(aItem) {
  aBase = '<html:rewrite forward="item"/>';
  doOpenRemote(aBase + '?item=' +
                 aItem,'preview','*','600','scrollbars','form');
}
// -->
</script>
```

Note that we only need to pass the item number (for example, `117`) to this function. The function then takes the base part of the URI and concatenates it with the query string and our parameter.

All that's left now is passing the parameter to the script. The item number would be passed to the page within a JavaBean, so we can use `<bean:write>` for that:

```
<a href='javascript:doItem(<bean:write name="itemForm"
property="item"/>)'>Item Number</a>
```

At runtime, this would resolve to

```
<a href='javascript:doItem(117)'>Item Number</a>
```

Since the JavaScript is rewriting the URI, we don't have to worry about that part of it here and can use a conventional hyperlink tag.

Using `<bean:write>` to render JavaScript from a bean

Another way to go is to just write the entire script into the page from scratch:

```
<SCRIPT>
<!--
<bean:write name="fancyForm" property="javaScript" filter="off"/>
// -->
</SCRIPT>
```

This will write out whatever is returned by the String `fancyForm.getJavaScript()` method. This lets you create the JavaScript by any means necessary. The Struts

Validator uses this approach to create a complex series of scripts that are rendered into the page from a single JSP tag.

Of course, the same technique applies to any HTML text asset, including Cascading Style Sheets (CSS).

Renaming the Submit button to avoid JavaScript conflicts

Some JavaScripts may try to call the submit operation for a form. By default, the <html:submit> button is also named (surprise) Submit. To avoid conflicts, give the Submit button another name:

```
<html:submit property="submitButton"/>
```

Using formless buttons

It is often useful to use a button to represent a hyperlink or JavaScript action. Problem is, the <html:form> tag expects each form to have a corresponding ActionForm bean. The solution is to give the tag what it wants and define a simple form with no properties:

```
public class BlankForm extends ValidatorForm {
    // blank form
};
```

This form can then be cited in the Struts configuration whenever a "formless" form is needed. For example, to provide a JavaScript back button:

Struts configuration file:

```
<action
    path="/Back"
    type="org.apache.struts.ForwardAction"
    name="blankForm"
    scope="request"
    validate="false"
    parameter="/do/Menu"/>
```

JSP page:

```
<html:form action="/Back">
    <html:button property="page"
        onclick="history.go(-1)">DONE</html:button>
</html:form>
```

Using an Action as the input property to re-create dependent objects

If a page displays options or other controls from objects placed in the request, these objects must be re-created if validation fails. So *instead* of an input property like

```
<action
  path="/item/RecvStore"
  // ...
  validate="true"
 input="/pages/item/RecvForm.jsp"/>
```

you should use something like

```
<action path="/item/RecvStore"
 // ...
 validate="true"
 input="/do/item/RecvForm"/>
```

where the RecvForm action will re-create any objects the page expects to find in the request.

If the dependent objects are properties on the ActionForm, you can also preserve them out as hidden properties on the form. The dependent objects can then be reconstructed from the request along with the user-supplied values.

Using dynamic form actions

A form collects properties and submits them to an Action object. In practice, different Actions may expect the same set of properties but carry out different operations on those properties. The classic example is inserting versus updating a record. To a database, these are distinct operations. To an application, they may look like the same form.

Problem is, the <html:form> tag assumes that a particular form always use the same value for the action property. The framework does not provide an automatic way to pass the action property to a form.

When they want to reuse the same form with different ActionMappings, developers typically hardcode the action property into the tag:

```
<html:form action="/saveRecord'>
  <%-- ... --%>
</html:form>
```

and then use smoke and mirrors to change the ultimate target of the submit. Chapter 6 shows ways to handle this with ActionForwards. Chapter 8 offers other solutions using the standard Dispatch Actions and the Scaffold FindForward Action. The Tiles framework covered in chapter 11 can also help out by putting the content of the form in a separate tile. Yet another workaround is to use a *(ugh!)* runtime expression.

Like all Struts tag properties, the value of the action property can be provided as an expression at runtime. You can have your Action object pass the value for the form's `action` property through the request. The page can place it into the `<html:form>` tag when the page is rendered:

```
<bean:define name="dispatch" id="dispatch" type="java.lang.String">
<html:form action ="<%=dispatch %>">
  <%-- ... -->%
</html:form>
```

If the `dispatch` `String` is being passed through the request, as shown here, you must be sure that the request always passes through the page's Action first. Otherwise, the `dispatch` `String` will not be in the request, and the `<html:form>` tag will throw an exception.

NOTE The same principle applies to any dependent properties. See "Using an Action as the input property to re-create dependent objects" earlier in this section.

A way to avoid this routing issue is to make `dispatch` a property on the Action-Form bean:

```
<bean:define name="recordForm" property="dispatch"
    id="dispatch" type="java.lang.String">
<html:form action ="<%=dispatch %>">
<html:hidden property="dispatch"/>
```

By also including the `dispatch` property as a hidden field, you ensure that it will be automatically populated during the validation step along with the other ActionForm properties. If validation fails, the `dispatch` property will be written back into the `<html:form>`, like any other ActionForm value.

If you use this technique, a good practice is to put the `dispatch` property in a base ActionForm object that your other ActionForms can extend. The Base-Form class (see chapter 5) in the Scaffold package (`org.apache.scaffold.http.BaseForm`) provides a `dispatch` property, among others.

Using alternative message tags

Many Struts applications can get by with a simple

```
<html:error/>
```

tag at the top of a page. If any error messages are present, it's this tag's job to print them all out. To help prettify the output, `<html:error>` checks for `errors.header` and `errors.footer` messages in the application resources. If found, the tag prints these before and after the block of messages. A common setup is:

```
errors.header=<UL>
errors.footer=</UL>
```

Struts 1.0 developers can then include `<LI>` and `</LI>` tags with the text of each message to be used this way. In Struts 1.1, the situation improves with the addition of the `errors.prefix` and `errors.suffix` messages. Just as the header and footer print before and after the block of messages, the prefix and suffix print before the individual messages. So to print a simple list of any message that might arise, you can just include

```
errors.header=<UL>
errors.footer</UL>
errors.prefix=<LI>
errors.suffix=</LI>
```

in your application resources, and the `<html:error>` tag will take care of the rest.

However, purists would complain that HTML markup has no place in a message resources file. And they would be right. Even with the Struts 1.1 prefix and suffix feature, you may still need to use different markup on different pages.

For Struts 1.0 applications, the Struts Validation extension (see chapter 12) offers a useful alternative to the standard `<html:error/>` tag. You can use these tags whether you are using the rest of the Validator package or not. Instead of providing one omnibus tag, the Validator approach is to use an iterator to expose each message, and then leave it up to the page to provide whatever other formatting is necessary. Here's an example:

```
<validator:errorsExist>
  <UL>
  <validator:errors id="error">
    <LI><bean:write name="error"/></LI>
  </validator:errors>
  </UL>
</validator:errorsExist>
```

In Struts 1.1, these tags were adopted into the core taglibs. Here's the same example using the Struts 1.1 rendition:

```
<logic:messagesPresent>
  <UL>
  <html:messages id="error">
    <LI><bean:write name="error"/></LI>
  </html:messages>
  </UL>
</logic:messagesPresent>
```

This is all great if you just want to print your messages as a batch. But many messages are related to data-entry validation and involve a specific field. Many page designs expect a message concerning a field to print next to a field.

Not a problem. When the error message is queued, you can specify a "property" to go with it. If you don't specify a property (using any of the tags we described), then all the messages print. If you do specify a property, then only the messages queued for that property print.

The default code for queuing an error message is:

```
errors.add(ActionErrors.GLOBAL_ERROR,
    new ActionError("error.username.required"));
```

To specify that this message is for the `username` property, we would use this code instead:

```
errors.add("username", new ActionError("error.username.required"));
```

If we specify a property, we can use the `<html:errors/>` tag (or any of the alternatives) like this:

```
<P>Username: <html:text property="username"/><html:errors
    property="username"/></P>
<P>Password: <html:password property="property"/><html:errors
    property="password"/></P>
```

The `username` errors print next to the username field, and any `password` errors print next to the password field.

But what if you need to print both specific and general errors?

Again, no problem. You can also specify the generic property just like you did in the Java code. First, at the top of your JSP, import the Action and ActionErrors package, so you can reference the appropriate constants:

```
<%@ page import="org.apache.struts.action.Action" %>
<%@ page import="org.apache.struts.action.ActionErrors" %>
```

Then, in the tags, use a runtime expression to specify the constants:

```
<logic:present name="<%=Action.ERROR_KEY%>">
<P><html:errors property="<%=ActionErrors.GLOBAL_ERROR%>"/>/P>
</logic:present>
```

Viola! Specific messages print out in specific places, and any general errors can still print out in a place of their own.

Of course, you don't have to settle for *any* of these standard tags. If these variations still don't meet your specific needs, take a peek at the source code and cobble up your own. The framework provides the queue, but how it prints is up to you.

10.4.4 *Successful controls*

Many of the dynamic pages we write involve submitting HTML forms. When you're working with HTML forms, it's important to keep in mind how empty, or "unsuccessful," controls are handled. If a control is not successful, then the browser may not include it in the request. In this case, you will not get back an empty string or anything representing null. The parameter for the control will simply not be there.

Here are some notes from the HTML 4.01 specification [W3C, HTML] regarding successful controls:

- Controls that are disabled cannot be successful.

- Hidden controls and controls that are not rendered because of style sheet settings may still be successful.

- If a control doesn't have a current value when the form is submitted, user agents (for example, web browsers) are not required to treat it as a successful control.

- If a form contains more than one Submit button, only the activated Submit button is successful.

- All on checkboxes may be successful.

- For radio buttons that share the same value of the name attribute, only the on radio button may be successful.

- For menus, the control name is provided by a SELECT element and values are provided by OPTION elements. Only selected options may be successful. When no options are selected, the control is not successful and neither the name nor any values are submitted to the server when the form is submitted.

Because of the way HTML treats unsuccessful controls, the Struts ActionForms have a reset method. The reset method can be used to set a control to its default value in case it is unsuccessful and not submitted by the browser. The problematic case is when a form using checkboxes is resubmitted and the ActionForm is being maintained in the user's session. If the user deselects a checkbox, the control becomes unsuccessful and is not resubmitted. As a result, the ActionForm value in the session object does not become unchecked. The workaround is to use reset to turn off all the checkboxes and let the request turn on the successful ones.

10.5 *Alternate views*

Struts isn't just for JSP any more. Several new extensions are available that connect other presentation systems to the framework, making XSLT (Extensible Stylesheet Language Transformations) and Velocity first-class citizens in a Struts application.

10.5.1 *Struts and JSPs*

In chapter 2, we explored the Model-View-Controller architectural pattern and the framework's role as a web-aware Controller. Of course, no Controller is an island. To be useful, an application also needs Model and View components. JSPs are the standard means for creating dynamic views in a Java web application. To help JSP developers integrate controller elements with the rest of their application, the Struts distribution includes a comprehensive JSP taglib that we covered earlier in this chapter.

Of course, Struts does not itself render the JSPs. That's the container's job. Internally, the .jsp extension is mapped to a service running within the container. When anyone, including Struts, wants a JSP, the container's service takes over the request and delivers the response. The JSP may include tags from our Struts-supplied taglib, but it's the JSP service that invokes the code behind the tags.

A benefit of this arrangement is that it enforces layering between Struts and the JSPs. Since Struts does not actually render the JSPs and has no special privileges within the container, Struts communicates with JSPs in the same way any servlet would—through the servlet contexts [Sun, JST].

10.5.2 *Servlet contexts*

Sun's Java web architecture encourages developers to create applications as a collection of cooperating servlets. Each servlet can be assigned to handle a particular type of request and then either return the response or forward it to another servlet. In practice, a servlet often needs to include additional information with the HTTP request. Information could be added to a raw HTTP request as it was forwarded, but the HTTP request is String-based and encoded in arcane ways, making that a clumsy option at best.

To provide servlets with both the HTTP request and runtime information about the request, the container wraps the HTTP request in a Java object, called, well, the *HttpServletRequest*. Among other things, the HttpServletRequest provides a clipboard-like component that servlets can use to exchange information, called a *context*.

DEFINITION	Java servlets can store objects in a number of shared areas called *contexts*. Each variable in a context has a name and an associated object. Any servlet in the same application can retrieve any object from a context by name. The servlets in an application often need to share information that outlasts a single HTTP request. To help manage the life cycle of shared variables, three standard contexts are provided: *application, session,* and *request*. A *page* scope is also available to a JSP. Objects in page scope cannot be shared with other JSPs or servlets.

Application frameworks such as Struts rely on the standard servlet contexts to allow their components to communicate and collaborate. The servlet framework provides various scopes, so that different types of objects can have their own life cycle. If the Struts controller posts a Locale object under the name `org.apache.struts.action.LOCALE`, any other servlet in the application can access that object by referring to the same name. Table 10.9 shows the standard contexts.

Table 10.9   The standard contexts

Context	Purpose
application	Objects are available to all servlets in the application.
session	Objects are available to all servlets that have access to the user's HttpSession object. This is usually found by calling a method on the HttpRequest. The session context may be invalidated by a servlet or by the container.
request	Objects are available to each servlet processing the HttpRequest. The request may be forwarded from one servlet to another. Objects in the request may also be shared when one servlet includes another. (See chapter 8.)
page	Objects are available to the current JSP for the lifetime of the request. Page scope is available to JSPs but not to standard servlets.

The Struts controller makes extensive use of the standard contexts. All of its resources are exposed in one context or another. The contexts are how JSPs, *and any other object in the application,* can be integrated with the Struts controller.

This allows Struts to be used by any view or model technology with access to the standard contexts. The contexts are available to every servlet in the application. So, if you can do it with a servlet, you can do it with Struts.

> **NOTE** Although we've introduced the idea of servlet requests and contexts from a web perspective, the HTTP versions of these classes extend interfaces that are also available to conventional applications. So, it's not just a web thing.

10.5.3 *Beyond JSPs*

While the vast majority of Struts applications are written solely with JSPs, many developers are using other presentation servlets in their applications. Extensions for using Struts with XSLT and Velocity are already available. More are sure to follow. Struts developers can now mix and match their presentation technologies, using XSLT where it makes sense and JSP or Velocity templates where they make sense—or just one or the other, as best meets the requirements of a specific application.

In chapter 17, we look at moving from JSP tags to Velocity templates.

10.6 *Summary*

JSP tags are part of a development continuum that started with writing raw HTML to the HTTP response and is progressing toward creating server pages using GUI editors. The ultimate design goal of JSP tags is simply to expose the properties of JavaBeans that software engineers can define and page designers can use. Recent initiatives like the JavaServer Page Standard Tag Library and JavaServer Faces are moving us closer to that goal, but there is still work to be done.

The Struts JSP tags provide Java developers with the functionality they need today. The tags in the HTML library correspond closely to the standard HTML elements and often can be swapped one for one. Other Struts tags are designed to wean developers from scriptlets and help them refactor Model 1 applications for Model 2. Overall, combining JSP tags with a Model 2–MVC architecture provides a more robust design today and opens the door to future possibilities.

Of course, any journey starts with the first step. The fundamental how-tos in this chapter get developers started on the right foot as they build their pages around the Struts tags. To lay the foundation for more complex pages, we explored several advanced techniques Struts developers commonly use to build real pages for real applications.

That's great, but now how do I...

At this point, the answer to most "How do I?" questions is going to be "However you would usually do it." Custom tags are not a new environment but simply a way to get dynamic data into the tried-and-true HTML environment. By leveraging the fundamentals and techniques described here, you should be able to take any existing HTML or JSP form and adapt it to Struts.

In the next chapter, we explore taking JSPs to the next level with the Tiles framework. Tiles helps you build your pages from specialized components so that pages become easier to design and maintain.

11 Developing applications with Tiles

Co-authored by Cedric Dumoulin and Ted Husted

This chapter covers
- Designing applications with dynamic includes
- Using the Struts and Tiles frameworks together
- Understanding Tiles Definitions and attributes
- Migrating applications to Tiles

319

> *A foolish consistency is the hobgoblin of little minds, adored by little*
> *statesmen and philosophers and divines.*
>
> —Ralph Waldo Emerson

11.1 Leveraging layouts

Usability is a prime concern in the design of today's applications—and consistency is a prime ingredient of usability. Users want to stay focused on the task at hand and are easily annoyed by any small inconsistency in an application's interface or screen layout.

Consistency is no small challenge for a dynamic web application; it is commonplace for each page to be coded by hand. Layout tools for static pages are available to most designers today, but few of these are available to applications based on JavaServer Pages.

Worse, the look and feel of an application is usually the last detail to be finalized, and then it will often change between versions—or even arbitrarily as part of a greater website "relaunch." This can create a nightmarish round of last-minute coding and testing—even if only to alter the background color or add a new link to the menu bar.

Of course, consistency is more than a hobgoblin; it's a hallmark of good design. Like any other component, web pages contain many common elements, headers, footers, menus, and so forth. Often, these are cut-and-pasted from one page to the next. But like any component, bugs are found and features are enhanced, leading to another round of cut-and-paste "reuse."

In a web application, page markup is a programming component like any other and should be held to the same standard of reuse.

11.1.1 Layering with dynamic templates

In the first part of this book, we stressed the importance of layering an application to isolate the effects of change. By compartmentalizing an application, we can change one piece without disrupting the other pieces. The same concept can be applied within the presentation layer to separate the look and feel from the actual content.

One approach to separating layout from content is the use of dynamic JSP includes. The JSP specification provides for both static and dynamic includes. The standard JSP action for a dynamic include is `<jsp:include>`.

We make use of dynamic includes by breaking the server page into several fragments, each with its own job to do. A background template can set the default format and layout, and page fragments can be included at runtime to provide the content. A dynamic include folds the output of the included page into the original page. It acts like a switch that moves processing over to a page fragment and then back to the caller. As shown in figure 11.1, the included template is processed normally, just as if it had been called on its own.

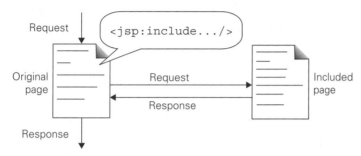

Figure 11.1   The effect of the `<jsp:include>` action on the processing of a request

The Tiles framework, which we explore in this chapter, uses a more advanced form of the JSP include action. In a Tiles application, the background, or layout, template usually defines the position of a header, menu body, content, and footer. Other pages are then included to fill each of these positions. If the header changes, then only that template file need be changed. The change is automatically reflected in all pages that include that template. The effects of changes are minimized—and the hobgoblins appeased.

Standard HTML components, like Cascading Style Sheets (CSSs), also work well with dynamic templates. A style sheet can help keep the templates internally consistent and further minimizes the effects of change.

11.1.2 *Template consequences*

Every technology comes bundled with compromises. Here are some consequences—pro, con, and mixed—that come with using dynamic templates in your application:

- The JSP include technology is well established and reliable, and tends to scale well in larger applications. The underlying technology for including dynamic templates is part of the core Java Servlet API.

- Most containers are optimized for JSPs and standard features like servlet include.

- The included pages typically output HTML fragments and are not synoptically complete. This can prevent you from maintaining templates with standard HTML editors, which expect markup to be part of a complete, stand-alone page.

- Most sites recompile JSP pages when the source changes. Templates create more pages to be monitored for such changes.

- Templates actually reuse code that would otherwise be duplicated from page to page. This can result in a significantly smaller footprint and conserve server resources.

11.1.3 Using templates

We take a close look at using dynamic templates in this chapter, especially as the Tiles framework implements them. Tiles is a mature product and integrates well with the Struts framework. Tiles templates can even be deployed from a Struts ActionForward, eliminating a good many "red tape" files other template systems require.

Struts and Tiles are a powerful combination. Using dynamic templates to generate presentation pages jibes well with the other programming practices involved in writing a web application. In this chapter, we show how to best combine Tiles with Struts and other assets, like CSS. After introducing Tiles, we provide a refactoring guide to help you migrate an existing product to Tiles.

If you find that Tiles is a good match for your application, be sure to study the example application in chapter 15. See table 11.1 for a glossary of some of the special terms we use in this chapter.

Table 11.1   A glossary of dynamic template terms

Term	Definition
Dynamic element	A portion of a JSP that is recognized by the JSP translator, including an action, directive, expression, JSP tag, or scriptlet.
Template data	A portion of a JSP that is not recognized by the JSP translator and is passed to the response verbatim. Usually markup and visible text.
Template page	A JSP that includes, or is included by, another page.
Template file	A static file or JSP that is included by a template page.
Tile	A synonym for template page.
Layout	A description of where template files, or tiles, should be positioned on a page.

Table 11.1   A glossary of dynamic template terms *(continued)*

Term	Definition
Tiles	A framework that makes templates and layouts easier and more powerful.
Definition	A Tiles feature that allows a layout to be specified as a template page or as a JavaBean. Definitions can also be described by an XML document.

11.1.4 Combining templates, Tiles, and Struts

When HTML tables were first invented, page designers immediately adopted them as a layout mechanism. A borderless table can be used to contain other tables and content and create layouts that were otherwise impossible.

The same idea is often used with dynamic templates. As shown in figure 11.2, a master template is used to provide the layout for the page and position the elements; page fragments are then included to fill in the elements. The page fragments can be included in any type of layout: those that use borderless tables, those that use <div> tags, and even very simple layouts that just stack one component over the other.

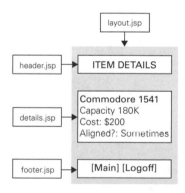

**Figure 11.2
A master template provides
the layout for a page.**

Tiles is a framework that makes using template layouts much easier through use of a simple but effective tag library. It can be used as a drop-in replacement for the Template taglib distributed with Struts 1.0 but provides more functionality. The Tiles package can be used with any JSP application.

1.0 vs 1.1 Tiles is bundled with Struts 1.1. Configuring Tiles for Struts 1.1 is covered in chapter 4. Tiles is also available for Struts 1.0. See the Extensions category on the Struts Resources page for details [ASF, Struts].

Most often, a JSP template system will use one template for the layout and another for the fill-in components. Tiles calls these layout files *Definitions*. Most template systems require that an extra file be used just to specify the layout. To avoid this overhead, Tiles allows the layout Definitions to be stored as a JavaBean. What's more, there is an extension to Struts that allows Definitions to be the target of an ActionForward. This is an exciting feature, which we discuss in section 11.3.3. In section 11.5, we return to Definitions again when we walk through refactoring an existing product into a Tiles-based application using Definitions and Struts.

But, for now, let's start at the beginning and create a new layout from scratch.

11.2 *Building a layout template*

The first step in building any layout is to identify the component parts. For a classic web page, the parts would be a header, menu, body, and footer. Often a simple sketch can help to bring the layout into focus.

To provide a quick example, we will build a layout for a classic web page with a header, a menu, a body, and footer. Our layout sketch is provided in figure 11.3.

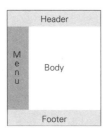

Figure 11.3
The classic master template layout includes a header, body, menu, and footer.

Creating the template page for a layout like the one in figure 11.3 is as easy as it looks:

1 Open a new JSP page.
2 Import the Tiles taglib.
3 Create an HTML table with cells that match the sketch.
4 Use a Tiles JSP tag (`<tiles:insert>`) to name each part of the layout.

As you can see in listing 11.1, wherever we create a cell to include one of our layout components, we place a JSP tag like `<tiles:insert attribute="aName"/>`. This tag says to insert the tile (or template file) identified by the value of the specified attribute. When it is time to use this layout in an application, we pass to it the paths to use for each of these tiles. This allows us to use the same layout over and over again, simply by passing a different path for one or more of the tiles.

Listing 11.1 Markup fragment for our layout page

```
<%@ taglib uri="/tags/tiles" prefix="tiles" %>
<TABLE border="0" width="100%" cellspacing="5">
<TR>
  <TD colspan="2"><tiles:insert attribute="header"/></TD>
</TR>
<TR>
  <TD width="140" valign="top">
    <tiles:insert attribute="menu"/>
  </TD>
  <TD valign="top"  align="left">
    <tiles:insert attribute="body"/>
  </TD>
</TR>
<TR>
  <TD colspan="2">
    <tiles:insert attribute="footer" />
  </TD>
</TR>
</TABLE>
```

In most cases, the body tile will change for each page, but all pages in the same area could share the same header and menu tiles. Meanwhile, all pages on the same site might share a single footer tile. When a new year rolls around and it is time to update the copyright notice to display the new current year on every page, only the one footer tile need be edited.

Our classic layout can be made into a complete, stand-alone template page just by adding the rest of the HTML markup.

In listing 11.2, you'll note that we slipped in a new Tiles tag, `<tiles:getAsString name="title"/>`. This tag says to return an attribute value as a literal string rather than as a pathname or other command. To do this, Tiles calls the object's standard `toString()` method. The result is inserted directly into the page at runtime.

Listing 11.2   Classic layout as a complete template page: myLayout.jsp

```
<%@ taglib uri="/tags/tiles" prefix="tiles" %>
<HTML>
  <HEAD>
    <TITLE><tiles:getAsString name="title"/></TITLE>
  </HEAD>
<BODY>
<TABLE border="0" width="100%" cellspacing="5">
<TR>
  <TD colspan="2"><tiles:insert attribute="header" /></TD>
</TR>
<TR>
  <TD width="140" valign="top">
    <tiles:insert attribute='menu'/>
  </TD>
<TD valign="top" align="left">
    <tiles:insert attribute='body' />
  </TD>
</TR>
<TR>
  <TD colspan="2">
    <tiles:insert attribute="footer" />
  </TD>
</TR>
</TABLE>
</BODY>
</HTML>
```

11.2.1 *But what is a tile?*

The template features offered by the Tiles framework far surpass what the standard Servlet and JSP includes offer. The framework refers to its templates as *tiles*. This is to help indicate that tiles are more powerful than simple JSP templates. Tiles are building blocks for your presentation layer.

Technically, a tile is a rectangular area in a JSP, sometimes referred to as a *region*. A tile may be assembled from other tiles. Tiles can be built recursively and represented as a tree, as shown in figure 11.4. Each node on the tree is a region. The root node is usually the page. Final nodes, or leaves, contain the page content. Intermediate nodes are usually layouts. The layout nodes are utility tiles that either position a tile within the page or provide background markup for the content tiles.

The tile objects support several important features, including parameters and Definitions.

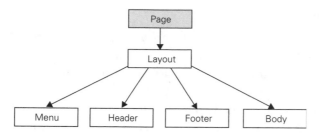

Figure 11.4 Tiles can be represented as a tree: the page is the root, and the layout tile is a branch (intermediate node), which then includes its own leaves (final nodes).

Parameters

A tile can accept variable information at runtime in the form of parameters or attributes. This means that tiles are parameterizable. They can accept variable information and act upon themselves accordingly. The tiles parameters are usually called *attributes* to avoid confusion with request parameters.

Tile attributes are defined when inserting the tile and are visible within the tile only. They aren't visible in subtiles or to a page enclosing the tile. This avoids name conflicts when the same tile is used several times in the same page. Developers can stay focused on making the best use of Tiles without worrying about name contention.

Tile attributes can be strings and other types. See section 11.4 for more about tile attributes.

Definitions

Taken together, the various attributes passed to a tile create a description of the screen. In practice, many of these descriptions are related and tend to build on one another.

Definitions store a set of attributes so that a screen description becomes a discrete object with its own identity. Declare a base screen Definition and then create other Definitions derived from that base. If the particulars of a base screen change, then all the Definitions extended from that base are also changed. This brings the object-oriented principles of inheritance and encapsulation to your dynamic pages. We cover the Tiles Definition in section 11.4.

Definitions are optional. You can also deploy a tile at any time using a simple JSP tag.

11.2.2 *Deploying a Tiles template*

The layout template we built in 11.2.1 defined *where* to position its tiles but not *what* tiles to use. Those details—and any other particulars—are passed to the layout when it is deployed. The simplest way to do this is to call the layout from another JSP.

Listing 11.3 shows a JavaServer Page being used to pass to a layout what tiles it should use. When hello.jsp is rendered, it will return myLayout.jsp with the content of the specified tiles.

Listing 11.3 Deploying an instance of the classic layout: /pages/hello.jsp

```
<%@ taglib uri="/tags/tiles" prefix="tiles" %>
<tiles:insert page="/layouts/myLayout.jsp" flush="true">
  <tiles:put name="title"  value="Hello World" />
  <tiles:put name="header" value="/tiles/header.jsp" />
  <tiles:put name="footer" value="/tiles/footer.jsp" />
  <tiles:put name="menu"   value="/tiles/menu.jsp" />
  <tiles:put name="body"   value="/tiles/helloBody.jsp" />
</tiles:insert>
```

To use the same layout with a different body, we simply substitute the tags

```
<tiles:put name="title"  value="Hello World" />
<tiles:put name="body"   value="/tiles/helloBody.jsp" />
```

with new particulars, like

```
<tiles:put name="title"  value="Hello Again" />
<tiles:put name="body"   value="/tiles/pageTwo.jsp" />
```

This new page would look much like the original hello.jsp, except with a different title (Hello Again) and a different body tile (the contents of pageTwo.jsp).

You can continue to reuse a layout this way, substituting different attribute values as needed. This passing of parameters makes it possible to use a single base template to lay out every page on a site. If the website layout has to be altered, then only the one base template need be changed.

However, to get the full value of this approach, you have to create at least two JSP files for each new page deployed: one file for the new content and then a second file to insert the template and include the new content in the first file. Later in the chapter, we show you how to use Tiles Definitions with Struts to avoid the overhead of a second file. The body-wrap deployment approach covered in the next section is another way to avoid the second file.

Body-wrap deployments

Any tile can be used any number of times in an application. In practice, though, most of the tiles in your application will be *content* tiles that provide the distinct portion of any given page.

Typically, a page's content tile is used only once in the application. The header, footer, and menu tiles may be used over and over again from page to page. But the multiuse tiles are usually window dressing for each page's singular content tile.

When this is the case, you can simply wrap the content tile with the rest of the screen definition. The trick is to just provide the markup as the value of the put tag. As shown in listing 11.4, be sure to specify type="string" so that Tiles does not mistake it for the path to a page.

Listing 11.4   Deploying a layout using the body-wrap technique

```
<%@ taglib uri="/tags/tiles" prefix="tiles" %>
<tiles:insert page="/layouts/myLayout.jsp" flush="true">
  <tiles:put name="title" value="Hello World" />
  <tiles:put name="header" value="/tiles/header.jsp" />
  <tiles:put name="body" type="string">

  <%-- Place the content from /tiles/pageTwo.jsp here --%>

  </tiles:put>
  <tiles:put name="footer" value="/tiles/footer.jsp" />
  <tiles:put name="menu"   value="/tiles/menu.jsp" />
</tiles:insert>
```

This avoids creating an extra tile. A side effect is that it prevents a body tile from being reused on another page. When the body markup does need to be used in more than one place, you would have to refactor the page so that the content is a separate tile again. But for nearly all your pages, the content tile will be used only once.

The body wrap is a very effective approach. The only downside is that the screen definitions are dispersed throughout the site, which can make some global changes more difficult. The Tiles Definitions, described in section 11.3, provide a more centralized approach that works very well with the Struts architecture. But the body-wrap deployment pattern can still be a good choice for smaller applications.

11.2.3 Adding a style sheet

Since tiles are JSP pages, all the usual accouterments are available, including CSSs [W3C, CSS]. Using a style sheet with your tiles is not required but can be helpful.

While full support of CSSs eludes today's browsers, they are still a useful way to define color schemes and some other key attributes. Style sheets help ensure that these niceties remain consistent from tile to tile.

To specify a style sheet, simply insert the usual tag. The `<html:base>` tag can help resolve relative paths to the style sheets and other assets. Better yet, use the `<html:rewrite>` tag to render the path for you, and URL-encode it in the bargain. Listing 11.5 shows how to use both tags.

Listing 11.5 Using <html:base> and <html:rewrite>

```
<%@ taglib uri="/tags/struts-html" prefix="html" %>
<HTML>
  <HEAD>
    <TITLE><tiles:getAsString name="title"/></TITLE>
    <html:base/>
    <LINK rel="stylesheet" type="text/css"
    ref="<html:rewrite page='/assets/styles/global.css'/>">
  </HEAD>
<BODY>
```

11.2.4 *Templates and MVC*

Dynamic templates work especially well within a Model-View-Controller architecture. (See chapter 2 for more about MVC.) Used correctly, dynamic templates cleanly separate markup from content. In practice, the portion of a page with the actual content is often tucked away in the center, surrounded by areas devoted to markup and navigation. Content, markup, and navigation map easily to the roles of Model, View, and Controller.

Often, an MVC template system can be created from an existing application just by using standard refactoring techniques. The base markup for the page can be extracted into a master template. The site header and footer are extracted into their own files; the center square with the actual content goes into its own template file as well. The base template includes them back again. Related technologies, like CSS, can be used to define formatting in the base template and have it apply seamlessly to the others that form the final page.

DEFINITION *Refactoring* is the process of improving software by restructuring its source code for clarity and flexibility and by eliminating redundant or unused code.

The Tiles package takes this one step further with its Definition feature. Using Definitions, we can streamline the number of physical templates an application needs and move the implementation details into a central JavaServer Page or, better yet, an XML document.

11.3 *Tiles Definitions*

In listing 11.3, we saw that even the simplest layout can require a good number of parameters. We also saw that in most cases only one or two of those parameters change from page to page.

What's needed is a way to define all these attributes and properties in a single reusable bundle that could just be overloaded with the parameters that change—which, as it happens, it just what the Tiles Definitions do.

11.3.1 *Declaring Definitions*

Since they serve similar purposes, writing a Tiles Definition is much like writing a `<tiles:insert>` tag, as we did in 11.2.2. A Definition requires the following information:

- A path to the base template file
- A list of zero or more attributes (name-value couplets) to pass to the template
- An identifier (or name) for the Definition

As you can see, the real difference between a Definition and a `<tiles:insert>` tag is that a Definition can be named. But just by adding *identity* to the feature list, several doors are opened:

- A Definition can be overloaded by passing additional or replacement attributes when it is deployed.
- A Definition can be extended by using one Definition as the base for another.
- A Definition can be reused by storing it in a JSP or loading it from an XML document.
- A Definition can be the target of a Struts ActionForward.

Let's look at the two ways of specifying a Tiles Definition: with a JSP or via an XML document.

11.3.2 *JSP declarations*

A quick and easy way to get started with Definitions is to declare them with a JSP. This does not reduce the number of template files your application needs but does allow for reuse through overloading. You can declare a base Definition, and then in other Definitions specify how the new Definition differs from its predecessor. This requires the use of a stub file to deploy the Definition at runtime.

In section 11.3.3, we will look at placing these same Definitions in an XML document and deploying them directly from a Struts ActionForward. Since the underlying process is the same, let's discuss the now-familiar JSP-type declaration first.

The process for using Tiles Definitions with JavaServer Pages includes:

- Declaring a Definition with a JSP
- Deploying a JSP-declared Definition
- Overloading a Definition
- Reusing Definitions with JSPs

Let's discuss each in turn.

Declaring a Definition with a JSP

Listing 11.6 specifies the same particulars as listing 11.4 but uses a Definition.

Listing 11.6   A simple Definition

```
<%@ taglib uri="/tags/tiles" prefix="tiles" %>
<tiles:definition id="definitionName" page="/layouts/myLayout.jsp">
  <tiles:put name="title"  value="Hello World" />
  <tiles:put name="header" value="/tiles/header.jsp" />
  <tiles:put name="footer" value="/tiles/footer.jsp" />
  <tiles:put name="menu"   value="/tiles/menu.jsp" />
  <tiles:put name="body"   value="/tiles/helloBody.jsp" />
</tiles:definition>
```

The Definition in listing 11.6 would be saved as a bean in the JSP context scope, using `id` as the attribute key. Like many Struts tags, the `<tiles:definition>` tag supports a `scope` property for specifying a certain context (application, session, request, page). The default is page context. This Definition would be available to the rest of this JSP only.

Deploying a JSP-declared Definition

To put a Definition to use, you can use the `<tiles:insert>` tag, specifying the bean name (Definition ID) and also the scope if needed, as shown in listing 11.7.

Listing 11.7   Deploying a Definition

```
<%@ taglib uri="/tags/tiles" prefix="tiles" %>
<tiles:definition id="definitionName" page="/layouts/myLayout.jsp">
  <tiles:put name="title"  value="Hello World" />
  <tiles:put name="header" value="/tiles/header.jsp" />
  <tiles:put name="footer" value="/tiles/footer.jsp" />
  <tiles:put name="menu"   value="/tiles/menu.jsp" />
  <tiles:put name="body"   value="/tiles/helloBody.jsp" />
</tiles:definition>
<tiles:insert beanName="definitionName" flush="true"/>
```

At startup, Tiles uses the XML element to create a Definition object (or bean) with the id definitionName. At runtime, the `<tiles:insert>` tag refers to the Definition id through its beanName property.

Overloading a Definition

Once we have declared a Definition, we can refer to it by name and overload some or all of its attributes. To overload an attribute, just specify it again with a new value. To create a new attribute, include a new attribute name and its value. This allows you to create a base Definition and then just specify the changes needed to create a new page, as shown in listing 11.8.

Listing 11.8   Overloading a Definition

```
<%@ taglib uri="/tags/tiles" prefix="tiles" %>
<tiles:definition id="definitionName" page="/layouts/myLayout.jsp">
  <tiles:put name="title"  value="Hello World" />
  <tiles:put name="header" value="/tiles/header.jsp" />
  <tiles:put name="footer" value="/tiles/footer.jsp" />
  <tiles:put name="menu"   value="/tiles/menu.jsp" />
  <tiles:put name="body"   value="/tiles/helloBody.jsp" />
</tiles:definition>

<tiles:insert beanName="definitionName" flush="true" >
  <tiles:put name="title"  value="New PageTitle" />
  <tiles:put name="body"   value="/tiles/anotherBody.jsp" />
  <tiles:put name="extra"  value="/extra.jsp" />
</tiles:insert>
```

Here, after declaring the Definition, our `<insert>` tag specifies a new page `title` and a different `body`, and throws in an `extra` attribute that was not used in the original Definition. This implies that the layout can manage without this tile but can also display it when provided. A layout can indicate an optional tile using the `ignore` property. When `ignore` is set to true, an error will not be reported if the attribute is not present.

This is how the myLayout.jsp from the original Definition would specify the extra tile:

```
<tiles:insert attribute="extra" ignore="true" />
```

Reusing Definitions with JSPs

In the preceding example, we had to repeat the Definition before we could overload any of the attributes. Of course, this is not a very practical approach to reuse. A slightly better approach, shown in listing 11.9, is to declare and reuse Definitions by using a utility page and including that page wherever any of the Definitions are needed.

Listing 11.9   Including a Definition

```
<%@ taglib uri="/tags/tiles" prefix="tiles" %>
<%@ include file="definitionsConfig.jsp" %>
<tiles:insert beanName="definitionName" beanScope="request" />
  <tiles:put name="title"  value="Another Page" />
  <tiles:put name="body"   value="/tiles/anotherBody.jsp" />
</tiles:insert>
```

The key here is the standard JSP `include` directive that brings in the file containing our Definitions. The Definitions are created normally; you can use any of the Definitions in the usual way. The example also overloads the `title` and `body` attributes to customize the page.

This approach to reuse is fine if you have a small number of Definitions, but it doesn't scale well. Each time the file is included, by default all the Definition objects are re-created, draining performance. This can still be a useful approach during development, since any change to the Definitions will be reflected in the next page load.

In production, one workaround would be to create the Definitions in application scope and protect the block with the Struts `<logic:notPresent>` tag (or equivalent), as shown in listing 11.10.

Listing 11.10   Including a Definition using <logic:notPresent>

```
<%@ taglib uri="/tags/struts-logic" prefix="logic" %>
<%@ taglib uri="/tags/tiles" prefix="tiles" %>
<logic:notPresent name="definitionName" scope="application">
<tiles:definition id="definitionName" page="/layouts/myLayout.jsp">
  <tiles:put name="title"   value="Hello World" />
  <tiles:put name="header"  value="/tiles/header.jsp" />
  <tiles:put name="footer"  value="/tiles/footer.jsp" />
  <tiles:put name="menu"    value="/tiles/menu.jsp" />
  <tiles:put name="body"    value="/tiles/helloBody.jsp" />
</tiles:definition>
<%-- … other definitions … --%>
</logic:notPresent>
```

If the Definitions have already been created and stored in application scope, they will not be created again. Each page still has to include the Definitions, and each page will be looking to see if they exist, but at least they won't be continually re-created.

Tiles offers a better approach to loading and reusing Definitions. The Definitions can be declared and loaded once from an XML document. Internally, Tiles renders the Definitions directly from ActionForwards. This is a truly excellent way to manage Tiles Definitions, which we explore in the next section.

1.0 vs 1.1   Tiles for Struts 1.0 subclasses the ActionServlet to render the Definitions. In Struts 1.1, Tiles subclasses the RequestProcessor to do the same thing.

11.3.3 *Configuration file declarations*

By declaring your Definitions in an XML configuration file, you can make your application load the file at startup and create a "Definition factory" containing your Definitions. Each Definition is identified by the name property that should be unique to all your Definitions. Other components, like ActionForwards, can then refer to the Definition by name.

Declaring Tiles Definitions from a configuration file requires some additional setup to enable support for reading the configuration file when the application initializes. See chapter 4 for more about installing Tiles with Struts 1.1.

The XML configuration file is read when the application is initialized and parsed into a Definition factory that contains an instance of each declared Definition. Each Definition should have a unique name so that it can be referenced by

JSP tags or the Struts ActionForwards. The Definition name is an internal reference only. It is not a URI and can't be referenced directly by a client.

The process of using Definitions declared from an XML document is no different than using includes from a JSP file. The main difference is how they are created, how they can be extended, and how the Definitions can be used as Struts ActionForwards.

Creating the configuration

The overall format of the XML configuration is similar to the Struts configuration (since they are both proper XML documents). Unsurprisingly, the syntax used within the XML configuration file is similar to the Tiles `<definition>` tag, as shown in listing 11.11.

Listing 11.11   The Tiles XML configuration file

```
<!DOCTYPE tiles-definitions PUBLIC
        "-//Apache Software Foundation//DTD Tiles Configuration 1.1//EN"
        "http://jakarta.apache.org/struts/dtds/tiles-config_1_1.dtd">
<tiles-definitions>
<definition name="definitionName" page="/layouts/myLayout.jsp">
  <put name="title"   value="Hello World" />
  <put name="header" value="/tiles/header.jsp" />
  <put name="footer" value="/tiles/footer.jsp" />
  <put name="menu"    value="/tiles/menu.jsp" />
  <put name="body"    value="/tiles/helloBody.jsp" />
  </definition>
  <!-- ... more definitions ... -->
</tiles-definitions>
```

An empty Tiles Definitions file is provided with the Blank application on the book's website [Husted].

NOTE   The name and location of the Tiles Definitions file can be specified in the web application deployment descriptor (web.xml). We recommend creating a conf folder under WEB-INF to store the growing number of configuration files that a Struts application can use.

Extending Definitions

A Definition can be declared as a subclass of another Definition. In this case, the new Definition inherits all the attributes and properties of the parent Definition. The property `extends` is used to indicate the parent Definition:

```
<definition name="portal.page" extends="portal.masterPage">
    <put name="title"  value="Tiles 1.1 Portal" />
    <put name="body"   value="portal.body" />
</definition>
```

In this code segment, we specify a new Definition named `portal.page` that extends the Definition `portal.masterPage`. The new Definition inherits all the attributes and properties of its parent. In the preceding fragment, the attributes `title` and `body` are overloaded. This inheritance capability allows us to have root Definitions—declaring default attributes—and extended Definitions with specialized attributes (like `title` and `body`). If all your Definitions extend one root Definition, changing a value in the root Definition will change that value for all Definitions extended from that root

Extending is similar to overloading but adds persistence. Overloading describes the process where we specify a Definition and pass it new parameters (or attributes), rather like making a call to a method and passing it parameters. But a `<tiles:insert>` tag cannot call another `<tiles:insert>` tag, so the overloaded Definition cannot be referenced and reused. By using the `extend` property, you are creating a new Definition. This new Definition can then be inserted and overloaded and even extended by another Definition. It is still linked back to its ancestor Definitions through the usual type of inheritance tree, as shown in figure 11.5.

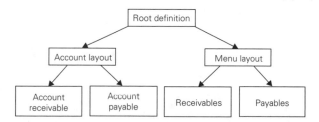

Figure 11.5   Definitions can be extended to create new Definitions.

Extending and overloading Definitions can dramatically reduce the amount of redundant information in your page declarations. Each markup, navigation, and content component in your website schema need be declared only once. The component can then be reused wherever it is needed.

While this is all quite cool, we would still need an extra page to host the Definition. This means to add a new page of content, we need to add the content page and then another page to insert the Definition that specifies the new content. A conventional application will have 60 pages for 60 pages of content. A templated application will use at least 120 pages to cover the same ground. Each of the

template pages are smaller and simpler than their conventional counterparts, but
file management can be an issue.

A good solution to the page boom is to host the Definitions as Struts Action-
Forwards.

11.3.4 *Using Definitions as ActionForwards*

In a Struts application, most pages are not referenced directly but encapsulated
by an ActionForward object. The ActionForward is given a unique logical name
along with a URI that usually refers to a presentation page. A Struts Action selects
and returns an ActionForward to the controller servlet. The ActionServlet then
forwards control to the URI specified by the ActionForward's `path` property. (For
more about ActionForwards, see part 1 of this book.)

The Tiles package includes an ActionServlet subclass that also checks the `path`
property against your Definitions. If the Definition `id` and ActionForward `path`
properties match, then the Definition bean is placed in the request scope, control
forwarded to the layout, and your assembled templates are displayed.

Accordingly, you can define ActionForwards that use Definition names instead
of URIs:

```
<action
  path="/tutorial/testAction2"
  type="org.apache.struts.example.tiles.tutorial.ForwardExampleAction">
  <forward
    name="failure"
    path=".forward.example.failure.page"/>
   <forward
    name="success"
    path=".forward.example.success.page"/>
</action>
```

Of course, you could also name your Definitions using the traditional slash
instead of a dot:

```
<action
  path="/tutorial/testAction2"
  type="org.apache.struts.example.tiles.tutorial.ForwardExampleAction">
  <forward
    name="failure"
    path="/forward/example/failure.page"/>
  <forward
    name="success"
    path="/forward/example/success.page"/>
</action>
```

However, the second naming scheme could be confused with other identifiers related to Actions and page URIs. A good practice is to use dot separators (the first scheme) for the Tile Definitions and the slash separators for ActionForwards. This ensures that the names do not intersect.

The code in your Action is exactly the same as before. If you are switching from presentation page URIs in an ActionForward to a Tiles Definition, most Action classes would *not* need to be rebuilt. Typically, Action classes ignore the ActionForward path and just deal with the ActionForward by its name.

You can mix and match conventional ActionForwards and Tiles-Definition-ActionForwards in an application. The Tiles ActionServlet deals with each request on its own terms.

When ActionForwards are used this way, the number of template pages in an application drops dramatically. To host 60 pages of content, we just need 60 content pages, plus a small number of utility tiles to provide the standard navigation and layout features. But creating page 61 can mean creating only one more content-only JSP and one more XML Definition, with the latter often being a single line.

Deploying Tiles Definitions as ActionForwards gives you all the power and flexibility of dynamic templates without the usual red tape.

11.4 *Tile attributes*

Being able to extend Definitions and overload attributes is a very powerful feature. But so far, we've only shown examples where the attributes are static values hardcoded into the pages. What if you would like to specify an attribute at runtime? Shouldn't an Action be able to pass the value of an attribute to a tile?

Yes, it can. The secret is that Tiles stores the attributes in its own context. Just as JSP stores attributes in a page context, Tiles stores its attributes in a Tiles context associated with the user's request.

There is nothing mysterious about the Tiles context. It is simply a collection that Tiles creates in the request for the use of its components. Specialized contexts are a popular technique for managing the various objects components create and then share with others, especially when control may pass from one application layer to another. Several of the Tiles tags are designed to be used with the Tiles context, including `useAttribute`.

11.4.1 *useAttribute*

The `<tiles:useAttribute>` tag makes one of the Tiles context attributes available through the page context. This makes the attribute available to other tags that read the page context, like the Struts `<bean:write>` tag.

The same attribute name can be used in either context

```
<tiles:useAttribute name="myAttribute" />
```

or another name can be specified:

```
<tiles:useAttribute attributeName="anAttribute" name="myAttribute" />
```

Once Tiles has put the attribute into page scope, the Struts bean tag can refer to the message in the usual way:

```
<bean:write name="myAttribute" />
```

The `<useAttribute>` tag can also be used to declare a scripting variable for use in a JSP scriptlet:

```
<tiles:useAttribute id="list" name="myAttribute"
                    classname="java.util.List" />
```

In general, the `<useAttribute>` tag corresponds to the `<useBean>` action and the Struts `<bean:define>` tag but allows access to the attributes in the Tiles context.

Note that each tile is an individual JSP and therefore has its own page context. To export an attribute so that it is available to other tiles that may make up the completed response page, specify another scope. For example,

```
<tiles:useAttribute name="myAttribute" scope="request"/>
```

puts the attribute in request scope where a tag in another tile would be able to find it.

Since each tile is technically a different "page," each is in its own page scope. If you want to avoid conflicts with attributes on another tile, you can use page scope. If you want an attribute to be shared with another tile, you can use request scope instead.

The `<useAttribute>` operations are rendered sequentially. A tile rendering further down the page would be able to use the attribute, but one rendering earlier would not be able to find it (since it doesn't exist yet).

11.4.2 *importAttribute*

By default, the `<tiles:importAttribute>` tag imports all of the Tiles context attributes into the page context:

```
<tiles:importAttribute/>
```

Any and all attributes stored in the current Tiles context would now be available through the standard page context.

Optionally, a single attribute or another context may be specified:

```
<tiles:importAttribute name="myAttribute" scope="request"/>
```

But, unlike `<useAttribute>`, `<importAttribute>` does not support renaming attributes or exposing them as scripting variables.

11.4.3 *put*

The `<tiles:put>` tag is used to associate a value to an attribute. The `name` property will usually be specified as a simple string, but the value may be specified in a variety of ways: as a tag property, as a tag body, and as a JavaBean.

put as tag property

When used in a JSP, this is the most common form of the `put` command. The value is usually set using a simple string but can also be a runtime value:

```
<tiles:put name="title"  value="My first page" />
```

or

```
<tiles:put name="title"  value="<%=myObject%>" />
```

put as tag body

As is the case with many JSP tags, the value property can also be set as the tag's body:

```
<tiles:put name="title">My first page</tiles:put>
```

This approach can also be used to nest the output of other JSP tags:

```
<tiles:put name="title"><bean:write message="first.pageTitle"/></tiles:put>
```

put as a bean defined in some scope

Like many of the Struts tags, the attribute can be passed via a bean:

```
<tiles:put name="title" beanName="myBean" />
```

The object identified by `beanName` is retrieved, and its value used as the attribute value. If `myBean` is not a `String`, the Struts or Tiles JSP tags will automatically call the object's default `toString()` method so that the result of `myBean.toString()` will be used to set the `value` property.

By default, the scopes will be searched in the usual order, until the first instance of `myBean` is found. You may also specify a particular scope:

```
<tiles:put name="title" beanName="myBean" beanScope="session"/>
```

This would ignore any instance of myBean in the page or request scope and check the session instead. Tiles adds a context of its own, called tiles, that is checked after the standard scopes. The values accepted by beanScope are page, request, application, and tiles.

put as a property of a bean defined in some scope

Again like many of the Struts tags, you can also specify a certain property on a JavaBean. The <put> tag will then call that method to set the attribute value:

```
<tiles:put name="title" beanName="myBean" beanProperty="myProperty"/>
```

This would call the equivalent of myBean.getMyProperty() to set the value of the title attribute.

Specifying the attribute type

The <put> tag is used to set an attribute that will be used by another tag, usually either <tiles:insert> or <tiles:get>. The corresponding tag may use the value passed in various ways. It may represent a direct string, a page URL, or another Definition to insert. The type of data the attribute is meant to represent can be specified in the put tag with the optional type property. This can help the corresponding tag insert the value as intended:

```
<tiles:put name="footer" value="/tiles/footer.jsp" type="page"/>
```

The type, when specified, can be any one of the tokens: string, page, or definition. Table 11.2 provides a description of each of the tokens.

Table 11.2   Valid tokens for the type property of the put tag

Token	Description
string	The value property denotes a String.
page	The value property denotes a URL.
definition	The value property denotes a Definition name.

Specifying the security role

When container-based authentication is being used, you can also specify the role for a tile. If the user is not in the specified role, then the attribute value is not set. This allows you to specify a tile for each security role and let the framework select the appropriate one for the current user:

```
<tiles:put name="title"  value="myValue" role="myManager"/>
<tiles:put name="title"  value="myValue" role="myStaff"/>
```

If `<put>` is being used in a `<tiles:insert>` tag, the role is checked immediately. If `<put>` is being used within a `<tiles:definition>` tag, the role is checked when the Tiles context is initialized.

11.4.4 *putList and add*

In addition to accepting single objects, Tiles attributes can be of type `java.util.List`. You can specify a series of objects for an attribute and pass them as a single attribute. The `<tiles:add>` tag is nested within `<tiles:putList>` to specify the items to be placed on the list:

```
<tiles:insert page="menu.jsp" >
  <tiles:putList name="items">
    <tiles:add value="home" />
    <tiles:add value="documentation"/>
  </tiles:putList>
</tiles:insert>
```

The `<putList>` tag is often used with the `<useAttribute>` or `<importAttribute>` tag to make the list accessible to other tags on the page:

```
<tiles:importAttribute/>
<TABLE>
<logic:iterate id="item" name="items" >
<TR>
  <TD>
    <bean:write name="item">
  </TD>
</TR>
</logic:iterate>
</TABLE>
```

11.5 *Migrating an application to Tiles*

At the beginning of this chapter we portrayed Tiles as a means of making your applications more consistent and easier to use. We also mentioned that consistency is a hallmark of good design. This is because consistency implies reuse. Reuse leads to applications that are hard to break and easy to maintain.

Often, you will have an existing application that you would like to adapt for Tiles. You may want it to improve the look so it is more consistent, or you may want to improve its functional design—or both. Improving the design of existing software is called *refactoring* [Fowler].

If you are familiar with conventional refactoring techniques, migrating an application to Tiles resembles the *Extract Method*. The tiles equate to methods that are called to render the page. When we are done, pages are reduced to a layout and a punch list of tiles to call. This works much like the central method in a class that just calls one member method after another.

Once we have extracted our tiles and reduced the page to a punch list, we can take the process a step further and replace the page with an XML element. Struts can use this element to render the tiles directly without bothering with a punch list page. But like all good refactorings, ours begins with the smallest step.

11.5.1 *Setting up the Tiles framework*

First, make an extra backup of everything, regardless of how many backups are made in the normal course. Migrating to Tiles can be tricky at first, and, realistically, you may need to make more than one pass before everything clicks into place. So be ready to roll back and try again. An extra backup on your desktop may be enough to lure you away from a three-hour debugging session spurred by some incidental typo.

Struts 1.0

If you haven't done so, the first step is to install the Tiles 1.0 package and load the Tiles servlet through your application's deployment descriptor. (See the package for details.) The 1.0 version of Artimus (see chapter 16) is based on Tiles and can be used for a working example. Then, test your application to be sure all is well by clicking through a few pages.

Also, be sure to set up a skeleton Tiles Definitions XML document so you can start filling it out as the refactoring proceeds.

Struts 1.1

Tiles is integrated with Struts 1.1. We cover the steps for enabling Tiles in Struts 1.1 in section 4.8 of this book.

11.5.2 *Testing the default configuration*

Set the `debug` and `detail` parameters in the deployment descriptor (web.xml) to level 2, and restart the application. Check the log entries carefully for any new error messages. Run any unit tests and click through the application to confirm that operation is still nominal.

11.5.3 *Reviewing the pages*

With Tiles up and running, the next thing is to take a good hard look at your pages and determine the overall layout types and the regions within each layout. It's also time to start thinking about a naming scheme. Each component will need its own identifier.

Identifying the layouts

When you look through an application, you will find varieties of menu or dialog pages—list pages, view pages, and edit pages—among others. Here the focus should not be on what the pages contain but how the parts of the page fit together. Does it have a header or a footer? Does it have a menu? Is the menu along the side or at the top? At this point, the relative position of elements like the navigation bar is more important than the actual links on the bar.

From this group, try to identify some common layouts. Again, the focus is on the visual layouts used throughout your application, not on the page content.

Identifying the tiles

Next take a closer look at each of the common layouts and identify the individual tiles. Determine how the parts of the page fit together. Then take a look at the page itself and identify the individual tiles. The presentation code for each tile will be saved as a separate file. We can use it in multiple layouts or edit it without touching the other tiles.

As mentioned, this process is similar to applying the Extract Method to a large Java class. One clue is to look for any existing comments in the presentation code, like `<!-- menu starts here -- >`. A block of markup prefaced with a comment is often a tile waiting to happen, like the block shown in listing 11.12.

Listing 11.12   A good candidate for a tile

```
<%-- messages --%>
<TR class="message">
<TD colspan="3">
<logic:messagesPresent>
   <bean:message key="errors.header"/>
   <html:messages id="error">
      <LI><bean:write name="error"/></LI>
   </html:messages>
   <bean:message key="errors.footer"/>
</logic:messagesPresent>
</TD>
</TR>
```

Style changes in a page are also a good indicator of a potential tile. If the designer put in a style to set off a portion of the page, that portion of the page may make for a good tile.

The best candidate is a block of self-contained code with a single, coherent purpose—again, not unlike a Java method.

If the presentation code does not have comments like these, it can be helpful to add them to some representative pages before making a pass to extract the tiles. If a page segment looks like a tile, except that each page prints something different on the tile, don't despair. Tiles can also pass string constants to a tile so that the rest of the markup can be reused. For now, just put in a marker, like ${subtitle}, where the replacement string would go.

Naming the candidates

It can help to start working on a naming scheme early in the process. What we call a component can crystallize its purpose. We will need names for the individual regions, the general layouts, and each page in the system.

Table 11.3 shows the Tiles nomenclature for these entities: tile, layout, and definition.

Table 11.3 Tiles nomenclature

Entity	Description
Tile	A reusable page fragment with HTML markup and JSP code.
Layout	A JSP that describes where to position the tiles on a page.
Definition	A JavaBean that represents a particular page. The Definition combines a layout with a set of tiles and other runtime options to generate a distinct page. The Definition may be expressed as a JSP or contained in an XML configuration file.

The *tiles* are coherent fragments of text and markup that you will extract from your existing pages. Tiles can host static content or markup, or a mix of both. Most tiles represent navigational controls and other common assets and will be reused between pages. Common assets might include a table that positions a logo somewhere on a page or a set of buttons, like Save and Cancel, that are used on several forms. If a style is already associated with the asset, consider naming the tile after the style.

DEFINITION   *Markup* is the collection of commands placed in a file to provide formatting instructions rather than visible text or content. HTML uses a tag-based markup system.

Other tiles will contain content that is used on a single page. These tiles are often found at the center of the page surrounded by other tiles that provide the menu bars and other HTML chrome.

DEFINITION   The *chrome* is that part of the application window that lies outside a window's content area. Toolbars, menu bars, progress bars, and window title bars are all examples of elements that are typically part of the chrome. HTML chrome is created by markup and lies within the application window but serves the same purpose.

You can use the same conventions to name the tiles that you would use for any HTML or JSP. It can be useful to separate the shared tiles from those designed for a particular page. An easy way to do this is to open a tiles folder next to the folder you would usually use for your pages:

```
/pages
   ./article/Form.jsp
   ./channel/Channels.jsp
/tiles
   ./header.jsp
   ./message.jsp
```

If a file resides in the *tiles* folder, it means that the file is meant to be used in more than one Definition. If a file resides in the *pages* folder, it means that the file contains unique content and is not expected to be shared.

The *layouts* are the containers for the tiles that describe where each component appears on the page. The layouts can be reused between Definitions. To keep everything together, you can create a layouts subdirectory beneath the tiles folder:

```
/tiles
   ./header.jsp
   ./message.jsp
   ./layouts
      ./Base.jsp
      ./Remote.jsp
```

The *Definitions* are stored as elements in an XML document. Each Definition element needs its own name. In practice, the Definitions share namespace with the

ActionForwards. The scheme should ensure that the ActionForward and Definition names do not collide. It can be helpful to group Definitions together in a directory/subdirectory type structure, so a name separator is also needed. One convention is to use a dot (.) for a separator in Definition names where many people might use a slash (/) in an ActionForward. To be sure there is no conflict with file system names, a leading dot can also be used where a leading slash would usually go:

```
<definition name=".account.logon"> . . . </definition>
```

Of course, any convention will do. You could use @ signs instead of dots, or preface each Definition with TILES: and then use slashes. Since these are logical references, any valid URI will do.

Once you have a general idea of what tiles, layouts, and Definitions you will need, and what you will call them, the next step is to extract the tiles and refactor a page.

11.5.4 *Refactoring a page with <tiles:insert>*

As with any refactoring, it's best to start slow, making one small change after another, until the first iteration is complete. As the process continues, you can take larger and larger steps, building on the prior work (and learning from your mistakes).

In most cases, the goal will be to reduce the pages to a Definition that can be declared in the Tiles configuration file and called from within an ActionForward (see section 11.3 for details). This approach saves creating an extra punch list page to insert the tiles. But to get started, it's simplest to build a page using the <tiles:insert> tags.

To get off on the right foot, remember to:

- Select a good starter page.
- Thoughtfully extract the tiles from that page.
- Develop a set of good (and bad) practices along the way.

Selecting a good starter page

It's best to start with a simple page, extract the common components, and insert them one at a time back into the original page. Your application's welcome or logon page can be a good candidate. These tend to be relatively simple pages with a nice mix of reusable and custom content. An interior page can also be a good choice, if it does not contain too much chrome. Listing 11.13 shows an interior page from the Artimus example application [ASF, Artimus] before it was migrated to Tiles.

Listing 11.13   Our starter page: /pages/View.jsp

```
<%@ taglib uri="/tags/struts-html" prefix="html" %>
<%@ taglib uri="/tags/struts-bean" prefix="bean" %>
<%@ taglib uri="/tags/struts-logic" prefix="logic" %>
<%@ taglib uri="/tags/request" prefix="req" %>
<!-- HEADER -->
<HTML>
<HEAD>
<html:base/>
<LINK rel="stylesheet" type="text/css" href="<html:rewrite
   forward='baseStyle'/>">
<TITLE>Artimus - Article</TITLE>
</HEAD>
<BODY>
<TABLE class="outer">
<TR>
<TD>
<TABLE class="inner">
<!-- MESSAGE -->
<TR>
<TD class="message" colspan="3" width="100%"><html:errors/></TD>
</TR>
<TR>
<TD class="heading" colspan="3">
<H2><bean:write name="articleForm" property="title"/></H2></TD>
</TR>
<TR>
<TD class="author" colspan="3">by <bean:write name="articleForm"
   property="creator"/>
</TD>
</TR>
<TR>
<TD class="article" colspan="3">
<bean:write name="articleForm" property="content" filter="false"/></TD>
</TR>
<%-- CONTRIBUTOR PANEL --%>
<req:isUserInRole role="contributor">
<TR>
<TD colspan="3"><HR /></TD>
</TR>
<TR>
<%-- DELETE --%>
<logic:equal name="articleForm" property="marked" value="0">
<html:form action="/admin/article/Delete">
<TD class="input"><html:submit >DELETE</html:submit></TD>
<html:hidden property="article"/>
</html:form>
</logic:equal>
<%-- RESTORE --%>
<logic:equal name="articleForm" property="marked" value="1">
```

```
<html:form action="/admin/article/Restore">
<TD class="input">
<html:submit>RESTORE</html:submit>
</TD>
<html:hidden property="article"/>
</html:form>
</logic:equal>
<html:form action="/admin/article/Edit">
<TD class="button" colspan="2">
<html:hidden property="article"/>
<html:submit>EDIT</html:submit>
<html:cancel>CANCEL</html:cancel>
</TD>
</html:form>
</TR>
</req:isUserInRole>
<!-- NAVBAR -->
</TABLE>
</TD>
</TR>
<TR>
<TD class="navbar">
<html:link forward="done">DONE</html:link>
</TD>
</TR>
</TABLE>
</BODY>
</HTML>
```

Once you've selected your starter page, go through it and extract each logical block into its own tile and insert it back again. After each extraction, test the page to be sure it still renders. Listing 11.14 shows a fragment extracted into its own tile.

Listing 11.14 An extracted tile: /tiles/header.jsp

```
<%@ taglib uri="/tags/struts-html" prefix="html" %>
<HTML>
<HEAD>
<html:base/>
<LINK rel="stylesheet" type="text/css" href="<html:rewrite
    forward='baseStyle'/>">
<TITLE>Artimus - View Article</TITLE>
</HEAD>
<BODY onload="document.forms[0].elements[0].focus();">
<!-- OUTER TABLE -->
<TABLE class="outer">
<TR>
<TD align="center">
```

```
<!-- INNER TABLE -->
<TABLE class="inner">
<TR>
<TD class="navbar" colspan="3">View Article</TD>
</TR>
```

Listing 11.15 shows how the View.jsp can include the Header tile again after it has been extracted.

Listing 11.15 Inserting an extracted tile: /pages/article/View.jsp

```
<%@ taglib uri="/tags/struts-html" prefix="html" %>
<%@ taglib uri="/tags/struts-bean" prefix="bean" %>
<%@ taglib uri="/tags/struts-logic" prefix="logic" %>
<%@ taglib uri="/tags/tiles" prefix="tiles" %>
<%@ taglib uri="/tags/request" prefix="req" %>
<!-- HEAD -->
<tiles:insert page="/tiles/header.jsp"/>
<!-- MESSAGE -->
<TR>
<TD class="message" colspan="3" width="100%"><html:errors/></TD>
</TR>

<!-- ... -->

</HTML>
```

As soon as your first tile is extracted and inserted back, be sure to test opening the page before moving on to the next tile.

When this process is complete, the page will consist of a series of insert tiles, as shown in listing 11.16.

Listing 11.16 A refactored page: /pages/View.jsp (completed)

```
<%@ taglib uri="/tags/tiles" prefix="tiles" %>
<tiles:insert page="/tiles/header.jsp"/>
<tiles:insert page="/tiles/message.jsp"/>
<tiles:insert page="/tiles/view.jsp"/>
<tiles:insert page="/tiles/navbar.jsp"/>
```

If the text in some of the tiles has to be customized, say with the page title, you can use the <tiles:put> tag to send a custom value along to the tile. The <tiles:getAsString> tag can then write it out when the page renders. Listing 11.17 shows how to send the text to the tile; listing 11.18 shows how to write the dynamic text out again.

Listing 11.17   Inserting dynamic content: /pages/View.jsp (revised)

```
<%@ taglib uri="/tags/tiles" prefix="tiles" %>
<tiles:insert page="/tiles/header.jsp">
<tiles:put name="title" value ="Artimus - View Article"/>
<tiles:put name="subtitle" value ="View Article"/>
</tiles:insert>
<tiles:insert page="/tiles/message.jsp"/>
<tiles:insert page="/tiles/view.jsp"/>
<tiles:insert page="/tiles/navbar.jsp"/>
```

Listing 11.18   Writing dynamic content with getAsString

```
<%@ taglib uri="/tags/struts-html" prefix="html" %>
<%@ taglib uri="/tags/tiles" prefix="tiles" %>
<HTML>
<HEAD>
<html:base/>
<LINK rel="stylesheet" type="text/css" href="<html:rewrite
   forward='baseStyle'/>">
<TITLE><tiles:getAsString name="title"/></TITLE>
</HEAD>
<BODY onload="document.forms[0].elements[0].focus();">
<!-- OUTER TABLE -->
<TABLE class="outer">
<TR>
<TD align="center">
<!-- INNER TABLE -->
<TABLE class="inner">
<TR>
<TD class="navbar" colspan="3"><tiles:getAsString name="subtitle"/></TD>
</TR>
```

If you prefer, the Struts `<bean:write>` or `<bean:message>` tag can also be substituted for `<tiles:getAsString>`. The attributes are being saved to the standard contexts, so any standard tag will work as well.

Extracting tiles

The main work of the refactoring is to determine which part of the page is part of which tile, moving that fragment into its own file and then inserting it back again. Here's a step-by-step checklist:

1   Select and cut the block.

2   Open a new file.

3   Paste in the block.

4   Save and name the file as a JSP (or HTML file if you can).

5   Insert any taglib import statements the tile requires.

6   Close the new tile.

7   Place a `<tile:insert page="/path/to/new/page"/>` tag where the segment used to be.

NOTE   The Tiles Definitions represent the set of pages that were in use before the refactoring began. The pages are being composed differently, but the content and appearance should remain the same. Most often, the Definition includes a body or content tile as part of the Definition. Some distinct pages may not have a unique *tile* but are represented by a unique *list* of shared tiles. You may have a form that uses different buttons under different circumstances. One page may include the set of buttons for creating a new record. Another page may include the set of buttons for updating a record. But other pages may share the sets of buttons and other tiles in the Definition. Distinct pages may also be created from the same Definition by passing a title string and the dynamic content retrieved from a data service. You might have several different ways of searching for records but display them all using the same Definition.

Extraction practices

Here are some caveats and practice notes regarding the extraction process. Since this will become a routine, it is important to have clear practices and to learn from past mistakes:

- All custom tags used by the tile must be imported into the tile.
- All custom tag elements must begin and end in the same tile.
- Avoid carrying HTML elements over to another tile.
- Mark up by contract.
- Consider trade-offs.
- Leverage technology.

All custom tags used by the tile must be imported into the tile.   The tile will inherit HTML assets, like style sheets. It will not inherit references to JSP assets, like tag libraries. The web browser applies the style sheet when the page renders, but since each tile is in fact a stand-alone JSP servlet, it needs its own references to JSP resources.

All custom tag elements must begin and end in the same tile.   If you use the `<html:html>` tag in your file, place the elements for this tag at the top and bottom of your layout (which is a single tile). This restriction does not apply to HTML elements. You can, for example, open the `<BODY>` element in a header tile and close the `</BODY>` element in a footer tile, but custom tags are validated when the tile is compiled. JSP tag elements must begin and end within the same tile.

Avoid carrying HTML elements over to another tile.   In practice, you may decide that one tile should open an element, like a table; a second should provide the content, like the rows in a table; and a third should close the element. When this pattern is useful, you should use it but still try to begin and end as many elements as possible in the same tile. This makes finding markup errors much easier. Even if the middle tile only provides the rows for a table, it can do so as complete `<TR>`...`</TR>` rows.

Mark up by contract.   When you decide to use something like Tiles, you are also deciding to treat markup like code. Accordingly, all the usual paradigms apply, like assertions and program by contract. When you design your tiles, think about the preconditions and postconditions for each tile, just as you would for a method in a class. Don't hesitate to document the conditions for each tile, just as you would for a method. A good approach is to just use standard JavaDoc conventions in a JSP comment, which avoids creating a new wheel:

```
<%--
/**
 * Global page header, without automatic form select.
 * See headerForm.jsp for version with form select.
 * Imports global style sheet.
 * Opens HEAD, BODY, and TABLE. Another tile must close these.
 * @author Ted Husted
 * @license ASF 1.0
 */
--%>
```

For HTML tiles, just use HTML comment braces instead. Unlike JSP comments, HTML comments will be visible in the source of the page. You may wish to be brief and discreet when using HTML comments.

Consider trade-offs.   Dissembling a page into tiles is much like normalizing a database. You can strip out absolutely all the redundant information, but if you do, some of the parts become so small that maintenance and performances issues can appear. In practice, you may have two or three varieties of header or footer files that may replicate markup. But if the markup changes, it is still easier to conform 3 files than 30 or 300. As with any programming task, the usual trade-offs apply.

Leverage technology. If you are also introducing style sheets and other markup changes at the same time, don't hesitate to create skeleton files and use editing macros with search-and-replace to automate some of the work. It's easy to forget how much time you can save with these old friends.

11.5.5 *Extracting the <tiles:insert> tags into a Definition*

After you have applied the process in section 11.5.3 to your starter page and have confirmed that it still works, you can finish the job by extracting the <tiles:insert> tags into an XML Definition. This is a four-step process:

1 Move the page to the layouts folder.
2 Rename the body tile.
3 Convert the insert tag to a layout and Definition.
4 Update the ActionForward.

Move the page to the layouts folder

Move the refactored page to the location you've chosen for layout tiles, under /tiles/layouts, for example. At this point, the refactored page should be a punch list of <tile:insert> tags, and the original content of the page should have been reduced to a set of tiles.

Rename the body tile

One of the extracted tiles probably represents the body, or "guts," of the original page. If so, consider renaming it as the original page you just moved. The implication is that the core content of the original page will still be where the original page stood. This helps to minimize change. If you need to edit the page's content, the content will still be where it always was. If you do this, update the <tiles:insert> tag after moving or renaming the file. Working from listing 11.16, we would change

```
<tiles:insert page="/tiles/view.jsp"/>
```

to

```
<tiles:insert page="/pages/view.jsp"/>
```

Convert the insert tag to a layout and Definition

Add a `name` property to each of the insert tags. This will often match the name of the JSP. The exception might be the tile representing the original body of your page. This will usually have a more generic name, like *content*.

Copy the `<tiles:insert>` statements from your refactored page into the starter tiles.xml configuration file that we set up at the beginning of this section and place them inside a `<definition>` element. If you used any `<tiles:put>` elements, you can promote those to top-level elements now:

```
<definition>
     <tiles:insert put="title"     value ="Artimus - View Article"/>
     <tiles:insert put="subtitle" value ="View Article"/>
     <tiles:insert name="header"   page="/tiles/header.jsp"/>
     <tiles:insert name="message"  page="/tiles/message.jsp"/>
     <tiles:insert name="content"  page="/pages/view.jsp"/>
     <tiles:insert name="navbar"   page="/tiles/navbar.jsp"/>
   </definition>
```

Then, rename the `<tiles:insert>` tags as `<tiles:put>` elements and the `page` attribute as a `value` attribute. To the `<definition>` element, add `name` and `path` properties. The `path` property should be to your layout page (see step 1). The `name` property can correspond to the name of your original page, but substitute dots for the slashes. Listing 11.19 shows our complete tiles.xml file.

Listing 11.19   A Tiles configuration file: /WEB-INF/conf/tiles.xml

```
<!DOCTYPE tiles-definitions PUBLIC
       "-//Apache Software Foundation//DTD Tiles Configuration//EN"
       "http://jakarta.apache.org/struts/dtds/tiles-config.dtd">

<tiles-definitions>
    <definition name=".article.view" path="/pages/tiles/layouts/Base.jsp>
      <tiles:put name="title"     value ="Artimus - View Article"/>
      <tiles:put name="subtitle" value="View Article"/>
      <tiles:put name="header"   value="/tiles/header.jsp"/>
      <tiles:put name="message"  value="/tiles/message.jsp"/>
      <tiles:put name="content"  value="/pages/view.jsp"/>
      <tiles:put name="navbar"   value="/tiles/navbar.jsp"/>
    </definition>
</tiles-definitions>
```

Now, in the layout page, change the `<tiles:insert>` tags to `<tiles:get>` tags and delete the `page` attribute (since that is now part of the Definition)

Any `<tiles:put>` tags can be changed to `<tiles:useAttribute>` tags. Keep the name attribute, but delete the value attribute (since the value is part of the Definition now).

Listing 11.20 shows a complete layout JSP.

Listing 11.20 A Tiles layout page: /tiles/layouts/Base.jsp

```
<%@ taglib uri="/tags/tiles" prefix="tiles" %>
<tiles:useAttribute name="title"/>
<tiles:useAttribute name="subtitle"/>
<tiles:get name="header">
<tiles:get name="message"/>
<tiles:get name="content"/>
<tiles:get name="navbar"/>
```

Update the ActionForward

Finally, replace the ActionForward that referred to the original JSP with a reference to the Tiles Definition:

```
<action
        path="/article/View"
        type="org.apache.scaffold.struts.ProcessAction"
        parameter="org.apache.artimus.article.FindByArticle"
        name="articleForm"
        scope="request"
        validate="false">
    <forward
        name="success"
        path=".article.View"/>
</action>
```

As shown in figure 11.6, the Tiles ActionServlet will intercept the reference and apply the Definition to the layout page.

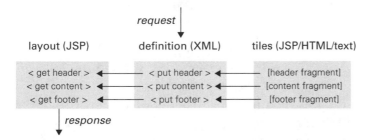

Figure 11.6 The Tiles ActionServlet uses the definition to help create the response.

If you were forwarding directly to the JSP before, you can use the standard Scaffold SuccessAction to route control through the controller so the Definition can be used to select and render the layout. You can use the Definition anywhere you were using a system path to the JSP. If there are enough references, you can even use the search-and-replace feature of your editor to change them all automatically.

At runtime, the Tiles ActionServlet will intercept the ActionForward and check its path against the Definitions in the Tiles configuration. If it finds a match, it includes each tile of the Definition in the response. The container then processes each included tile normally. The HTML tiles are rendered by the container's HTML service, and the JSP tiles are rendered by the container's JSP service.

If the ActionForward path is not the name of a Definition, the ActionServlet handles it as a normal URI, same as always.

NOTES If your refactored page does not display the same as the original, first make sure that you have imported any needed tag libraries in the tiles. If the taglib is not included, the tag will not be rendered and will be ignored by the browser (and you will see it in the HTML page source). If that is not the problem, create a new page and start reassembling the page by hand to uncover the error. Most often, you will find that a tile broke its "API contract" by opening or closing an element improperly. Another API contract to check is the path for the input property of the ActionMapping. This should also point to the Definition name rather than the physical JSP page.

If you expose the *Path must be absolute* error after switching over to Tiles, it means that you've tried to use a Definition as the path for a forward but it was not found in the Tiles configuration. After checking for a Definition, Tiles passes the path up to the super class method, and Struts treats it like a system path. Our leading dot is being interpreted as a relative reference to a directory, hence the *Path must be absolute* advice. The bottom line is there is usually a typo in either the Struts or Tiles configuration file.

To test your changes, be sure to reload the application so that the current Struts and Tiles configurations are loaded into memory. If you've been following along, you can try this now.

Once you have gone through the process of refactoring a page with `<tiles:insert>` and then converting it to a Definition, you may wish to convert other pages directly to a Definition. To do this, you:

- Copy an existing Definition using the same layout and give it a new name.
- Clip out and save the content segment of the page you are refactoring.
- Change the new Definition to refer to the segment you just saved and converted.
- Test and repeat.

NOTE When you first switch a block of pages over to Tiles, it may take a little extra time for the pages to render at first. This is because the JSPs for the new tiles are being created *in addition to* the usual one you need for the content. Once the JSP for each tile is created, it will not be re-created until it is changed, and everything goes back to normal. In the future, if you edit the content tile, only that one JSP will be recompiled.

11.5.6 *Normalizing your base layout*

Back in listing 11.20, we showed the layout file as a series of `<tiles:insert>` tags. If you like, you can also use regular HTML and JSP code on your layout page. This is a good place to put the topmost tags, like `<HTML>` or `<html:html>`, so that these do not need to be put inside other tiles, which might really be intended to do other things.

Listing 11.21 shows a revised base layout page that extracts the topmost elements from the header and navbar tiles and puts them on the base layout. We've also renamed it from Base.jsp to Article.jsp to indicate its role as the Article layout tile. Other pages in the application may need to use a different layout.

Listing 11.21 Revised layout tile (/tiles/layouts/Article.jsp)

```
<%@ taglib uri="/tags/tiles" prefix="tiles" %>
<%@ taglib uri="/tags/struts-html" prefix="html" %>
<html:html>
<HEAD>
<html:base/>
<LINK rel="stylesheet" type="text/css" href="<html:rewrite
   forward='baseStyle'/>">
<TITLE>Artimus - <bean:write name="title"/></TITLE>
</HEAD>
<tiles:useAttribute name="title"/>
<tiles:get name="header"/>
<tiles:get name="message"/>
<tiles:get name="content"/>
<tiles:get name="navbar"/>
</BODY>
</html:html>
```

11.5.7 *Refining your Definitions into base and extended classes*

As you commute your pages to layouts and Definitions, it's easy to end up with sets like this:

```
<definition name=".article.View" path="/tiles/layouts/Article.jsp">
  <put name="title"       value="View Article" />
  <put name="header"      value="/tiles/header.jsp" />
  <put name="messages"    value="/tiles/messages.jsp" />
  <put name="content"     value="/pages/articles/view.jsp" />
  <put name="navbar"      value="/tiles/navbar.jsp" />
</definition>

<definition name=".article.Result" path="/tiles/layouts/Article.jsp">
  <put name="title"       value="Search Result" />
  <put name="header"      value="/tiles/header.jsp" />
  <put name="messages"    value="/tiles/messages.jsp" />
  <put name="content"     value="/pages/articles/result.jsp" />
  <put name="navbar"      value="/tiles/navbar.jsp" />
</definition>
```

If you look closely, you'll see that the first and third items differ but the others are the same. A better way to write them, and any like them, is to create a base Definition. The Tiles Definition supports an `extends` property, which lets a Definition inherit attributes and overload only what needs to be changed. Here, we extend `.article.Base` and overload `title` and `content`:

```
<definition name=".article.Base" path="/tiles/layouts/Article.jsp">
    <put name="title"      value="${title}"/>
    <put name="header"     value="/tiles/header.jsp"/>
    <put name="message"    value="/tiles/message.jsp"/>
    <put name="content"    value="${content}"/>
    <put name="navbar"     value="/tiles/navbar.jsp"/>
</definition>
<definition name=".article.View" extends=".article.Base">
    <put name="title"      value="View Article"/>
    <put name="content"    value="/pages/article/view.jsp"/>
</definition>
<definition name=".article.Result" extends=".article.Base">
  <put name="title"       value ="Article Search Result"/>
  <put name="content"     value="/pages/article/result.jsp"/>
</definition>
```

With the base Definition in place, we now have to supply only two lines for each of our subDefinitions. The other settings fall through and do not need to be specified. If there are attributes that will be used throughout your site, you can put those in a base Definition and extend everything else from that. Then, if any of the base attributes change, you need to make the change in only one place.

As a convention, we put markers in for the values of the first and third items (title and content) to indicate that these are extension points that subDefinitions need to override. If the base Definition were used directly, then these markers would just print out as literals. The ${} markers have no special meaning to Tiles.

Another convention shown here is to use an initial capital letter for the layout JSP but an initial lowercase letter for the tile JSPs. This is to indicate that the layout page can be called directly, because it is a fully formed JSP class. The tile pages are like methods invoked by the layout JSP, and so use the same naming convention as a method. But this is only a convention; any other consistent naming scheme would work just as well.

11.5.8 *Developing a routine*

After the first few pages, you should be able to develop a routine that goes something like this:

1. Create a new Definition (in tag.xml), often by copying a similar one.
2. Update the Definition with the path to the existing page, page title, and any other custom information.
3. Open the existing page.
4. Delete the top and bottom, leaving the core content and tag import statements.
5. Review and revise the core content to ensure that the markup keeps its API contract with the tiles before and after it in the Definition. One tile may need to open an element, like a <TABLE>, and another tile may need to close it. Remove any unneeded tag import statements. Optionally, add a comment block.
6. Update the paths in the Struts configuration (struts-config.xml) to reference the new Definition, including any input properties.
7. Reload the tag configuration and the Struts configuration.
8. Review the page.
9. Rinse and repeat.

At first, you will probably start with pages as they appear in your application's flow. Once you have the procedure down, it is not difficult to step through the page tree and refactor each page in turn. This will ensure that you don't miss any. It may also uncover some obsolete pages left over from prior development efforts.

DEFINITIONS A popular way to view a method's signature is as a *contract* between the method and its caller. The caller agrees to provide certain parameters and the method agrees to provide a certain result based on those parameters. Since an API is a collection of method signatures, the paradigm of seeing interactions between components as a binding agreement is generally referred to an *API contract*.

API is an acronym for application programming interface, any set of routines generally available for use by programmers. The operating system, for example, has APIs for a variety of disk/file-handling tasks. APIs are written to provide portable code. The programmer only has to worry about the call and its parameters and not the details of implementation, which may vary from system to system. [CKNOW]

11.5.9 *Managing the migration*

Moving an application over to Tiles is not difficult but neither is it trivial. Be sure to schedule enough time for the project. The first few pages may take several hours, but once the pattern is established, additional pages may take only a few minutes each.

If you also need to apply a new look to the site, it may be best to first convert it to Tiles and then apply the new design so that you are not doing two new things at once. Once the layout is migrated to Tiles, bringing up the new design will go more quickly.

A good time to schedule a migration is when you know a visual redesign is coming but don't have the new design in hand yet. If you can have the application migrated to Tiles while the redesign is being finalized, applying the changes will be a smoother process. Doing both at once is not recommended—especially for your first migration.

So what's the bottom line of a migration? Your mileage will vary, but a small application with 25 presentation pages consuming about 140,000 kbytes of markup code was migrated to 55 tiles of about 120,000 kbytes—the 15% difference being redundant markup that was removed.

Moving forward, new pages for the application can now be created much more quickly and will be more consistent with existing pages. To change the overall layout, you can edit the layout or a few individual tiles instead of every page on the site.

11.6 *Summary*

Dynamic template systems, like the Tiles framework, can bring familiar programming patterns to the presentation layer of a web application. They let us slice and dice the HTML markup and JSP commands into manageable pieces. We can then assemble a page by calling the individual pieces, or tiles, the way we would call Java methods to perform a larger process. A tile encapsulates a block of markup, much like a method encapsulates a block of Java code.

The pages of a web application are built around a common look and feel, or layout, that helps users navigate the site. When we assemble pages using Tiles, we start with a base layout that defines where the tiles are placed and gives each position a logical name. The paths to the tiles a particular page uses can then be passed at runtime. A typical page may use five or six tiles, with only one or two of those changing from page to page.

In Tiles, a complete page, including the layout and the paths to its tiles, can be represented as an object called a Definition. To assemble a particular page, we can simply refer to its Tiles Definition. Like the Struts framework components, the Definitions can be configured using an XML document and loaded at startup.

The Struts framework uses ActionForwards to encapsulate paths to system resources, including presentation pages and Action classes. The framework's controller, the ActionServlet, uses ActionForwards to route control. The other components refer to the ActionForward by name and rely on the controller to invoke the resource indicated by the forward's path.

A standard extension to the controller allows Definitions to be used as the ActionForward path. When a Definition is the target of an ActionForward, the controller includes the fragments in a combined response. The standard service for each fragment then finishes the job.

When an application is migrated to Struts, one consequence is that system paths become encapsulated in the Struts configuration. The presentation pages can then refer to other resources using a logical name rather than an actual path or URI. This lets us focus on what the page wants to do rather than the particulars of how it is done.

In the same fashion, when an application is migrated to Tiles, the configuration encapsulates the system paths. Struts can then refer to the page Definition by name and leave the particulars of assembling the page to the Tiles framework.

Tiles can be of most use to larger systems with dozens or hundreds of pages. Like decomposing a process into constituent methods, refactoring an application to use Tiles creates more component parts, but each individual part is simpler to understand and maintain. More important, the individual tiles can be reused, avoiding the need to make the same change in multiple places. As applications grow, the need to eliminate redundancy becomes increasingly important.

The focus of this chapter has been to provide you with enough information to put Tiles to work in your application. But it by no means covers everything that is possible with the Tiles framework. The Artimus example application (see chapter 15) is based on Tiles and demonstrates several of the best practices described in this chapter.

In the next chapter, we explore another "optional" component, the Struts Validator.

Validating user input

12

Co-authored by David Winterfeldt and Ted Husted

This chapter covers

- Understanding the need to validate data
- Configuring and using the Commons Validator
- Using multipage and localized validations
- Writing your own validators

> **Us:** *Programming today is a race between software engineers
> striving to build bigger and better idiot-proof programs, and the
> Universe trying to produce bigger and better idiots. So far, the
> Universe is winning.*
>
> —Rich Cook
>
> **Them:** *I never know how much of what I say is true.*
>
> —Bette Midler

12.1 I know it when I see it

Most web applications need to collect data from their users. The input may come via freeform text fields or GUI elements such as menu lists, radio buttons, and checkboxes. In practice, what the user enters does not always make sense. Some menu options may be mutually exclusive. A phone number may be lacking a digit. Letters might be entered into a numeric field. Numbers may be entered where letters are expected. This may be because the data-entry form isn't clear or because the users are not paying attention. But in any event it happens—and with great regularity.

Nothing is more frustrating for a user than getting garbage out of an application, even if it was the user who put the garbage in. A prudent application scrutinizes all input, guards against all foreseeable errors, and protects users from themselves. After all, if they mess up, we still have to fix it.

12.1.1 Input we can't refuse

In a conventional application, data-entry controls can simply refuse to accept bad values, but they have luxury of being modal.

DEFINITION   A user interface element is *modal* when it claims all the user input for an application. Other elements of the application cannot be accessed until the element is dismissed. To proceed, the user must either complete the modal dialog box or close the application. Most user interface elements are nonmodal.

Web applications, being inherently nonmodal, have fewer options. By default, the HTML elements displayed by the browser will accept anything typed into them. A given element has no clue what was entered elsewhere on the form. We can play tricks with JavaScript, but there is no guarantee that the user has enabled JavaScript.

Of course, we can validate the data when it reaches the business tier. (For more about application tiers and business objects, see chapter 2.) Many business logic objects do have some validation built in, but most business objects do not vet data before accepting it. Business-tier methods tend to be trusting creatures. They expect friendly objects will be offering reasonable data and just do as they are told. Even when business objects are more pessimistic, usually all they can do is throw an exception. It is not the responsibility of business objects to enter into a patient dialogue with the user to correct the erroneous input.

Of course, it *is* the responsibility of a business object to validate data *in context*—to see, for example, if a username and password correspond. But there are many objective validation rules that can be applied before data is ever commuted to the business tier. In a distributed application, the business object may reside on a remote machine. Creating roundtrips to resolve simple data-entry errors may be costly.

12.1.2 *Web-tier validations*

In real life, it often falls to the web application framework to provide objective validation routines and narrow the gap between model and view. In a nonmodal, distributed environment, we need validation routines that can do the following:

- Require that certain fields have values
- Confirm that a given value is in an expected pattern or range
- Check the entire form at once and return a list of messages
- Compare values between fields
- Return the original input for correction
- Display localized messages when required
- Perform server-side validations if JavaScript is disabled

Two other important hallmarks of a validation system are loose coupling and optional client-side validations.

Loose coupling

As a practical matter, input needs to be validated by the controller, but business validations are tied to the business tier. This implies that the validation rules should be stored separately from markup or Java code so that they can be reviewed and modified without changing any other source code. Keeping the validation rules loosely coupled makes it much easier to keep validations synchronized with business requirements.

DEFINITION   The degree of *coupling* refers to the strength of a connection between two components. Coupling is a complement to cohesion. Cohesion describes how strongly the internal contents of a component are related to each other. The goal is to create components with internal integrity (strong cohesion) and small, direct, visible, and flexible relations to other components (loose coupling). [McConnell]

Some validation rules may also need to be localized. When support for a new locale is added, we should be able to update the validation rules as easily we update the resource bundle.

While the validation rules may be provided as a convenience to the presentation layer, it is important to recognize they actually "belong" to the business tier. Validation rules should not be commingled with presentation source code.

Client-side validations

Client-side validations are inherently insecure. It is easy to spoof submitting a web page and bypass any scripting on the original page. While we cannot rely on client-side JavaScript validations, they are still useful. Immediate user feedback avoids another trip to the server, saving time and bandwidth for everyone. So, another ideal feature would be to generate JavaScript and server-side validations from the same set of rules. When JavaScript is enabled, the input can be validated client-side before it is submitted. If not, the input is still validated server-side to ensure nothing is amiss.

12.1.3 Validator consequences

Using the Jakarta Commons Validator [ASF, Validator] brings several consequences:

- The Validator is a framework component that meets these requirements— and more.
- The Validator is configured from an XML file that generates validation rules for the fields in your form.
- Rules are defined by a Validator that is also configured through XML.
- Validators for basic types, like dates and integers, are provided. If needed, you can create your own.
- Regular expressions can be used for pattern-based validations such as postal codes and phone numbers.

- Multipage and localized validations are supported, so you can write wizards in any language.

DEFINITION   A *regular expression* is a formula for matching strings that follow some pattern. Regular expressions are used by many Unix command-line and programming utilities. For more about regular expressions, see the "Using Regular Expressions" web page by Stephen Ramsay. [Ramsay]

Using the Jakarta Commons Validator in your application yields several benefits:

- Optimal use of resources: JavaScript validations are provided when enabled, and server-side validations are guaranteed.

- A single point of maintenance: Both client-side and server-side validations are generated from the same configuration.

- Extendibility: Custom validations can be defined as regular expressions or in Java code.

- Maintainability: It is loosely coupled to the application and can be maintained without changing markup or code.

- Localization: Localized validations can be defined only when and where they are needed.

- Integration with Struts: By default, validations share the Struts message bundle. Localized text can be centralized and reused.

- Easy deployment of server-side validation: To make use of the server-side validations, your Struts ActionForm can simply extend the ValidatorForm or ValidatorActionForm class. The rest is automatic.

- Easy deployment of client-side validation: To make use of the client-side validations, you just add a single JSP tag to generate the validation script and use that script to submit the form.

- Easy configuration: The Validator uses an XML file for configuration, just like the web application deployment descriptor and the Struts configuration.

But, of course, there are also drawbacks:

- Nonmodal client-side validations: The generated JavaScript is nonmodal; it does not engage until the form is submitted.

- Dependencies: The validations are detached from the fields and from the ActionForm properties. The page markup, the ActionForm, and the Validator and Struts configuration files must all be synchronized.

- Lack of data conversions and transformations: The package does not offer data conversions or transformations. When needed, conversions and transformations must be programmed separately.

Keep in mind that using the Jakarta Commons Validator in your application is not a panacea. Some validations may only be performed server-side. If these fail, the error messages are displayed differently than the JavaScript messages. Interface discontinuities confuse users.

DEFINITION   *Data conversion* is moving data from one type to another, as from a `String` to an `Integer`. *Data transformation* is changing the internal format of data, such as adding punctuation to a `String` before it is displayed or removing unwanted punctuation from a `String` before it is stored. Localization can require transforming data into a display format.

In this chapter, we show you how to make the best use of the Commons Validator framework in your application. We cover the overall design of the Validator, and present a simple example. We then look at each component of the Validator in depth along with often-needed techniques, such as overriding default messages, canceling validations, using multipage workflows, validating collections, and more.

It is important to emphasize that objective, data-entry validations are not an omnibus solution. There are many types of errors that cannot be found without accessing the model. We can look to see if a username and password meet the business requirements for length and composition. But to see if the username and password combination is valid, we need to go up to the business tier and talk to a data service. However, by checking to see whether data could possibly be valid before we even ask, we can eliminate expensive data-access transactions, which benefits everyone.

NOTE   You might be wondering, "So would I be using the Struts framework to build my application or the Struts Validator framework?" Both, actually. Most applications are built using several sets of framework components, including some that development teams create in-house. Struts builds on

Sun's Java J2SE framework. Likewise, the Struts Validator builds on the Struts framework. So, just as your application may use several classes in several packages, it may also use several frameworks. For more about working with framework architectures, see chapter 2.

Chapter 4 covers setting up the Validator with Struts 1.1. This chapter is a developer's guide to putting the Validator to work in your application.

12.2 *Overview of the Struts Validator*

Let's look at how the Struts Validator interacts with other components to provide both server-side and client-side validations from the same set of validation rules. You may be surprised at how easy it can be to validate your data once the Validator puts all the pieces together. Table 12.1 lists the various pieces that make up the Struts Validator.

Table 12.1   Major Struts Validator components

Component	Description
Validators	Handle native and other common types. The basic validators include `required`, `mask` (matches regular expression), `minLength`, `maxLength`, `range`, native types, `date`, `email`, and `creditCard`. Custom (or plug-in) validators may also be defined.
Resource bundle	Provides (localized) labels and messages. Shares Struts messages by default.
XML configuration file	Defines form set and validations for fields as needed. The validators can be defined in a separate file.
JSP tag	Generates JavaScript validations for a given form name or action path.
ValidatorForm	Automatically validates properties based on the form bean's name (passed to the `validate` method through the ActionMapping parameter at runtime). Must be extended to provide the properties expected on the form.
ValidatorActionForm	Automatically validates properties based on the action path (passed to the `validate` method through the ActionMapping parameter at runtime). Must be extended to provide the properties expected on the form.

Originally, the Commons Validator was created as an extension to the Struts framework. But since it could also be used outside the framework, the developers contributed it to another Jakarta subproject, the Commons.

The Struts distribution includes a Validator package with several classes that integrate the Commons Validator with Struts. This package, along with the Commons Validator package it extends, constitutes the Struts Validator. In the balance of this chapter, we refer to the Struts Validator as a superset of the Commons Validator. The Validator package is actually a collection of several Validator objects, written in Java. Each Validator object enforces a rule regarding a property on another object. In the Struts Validator, these objects are ActionForms. The validators have standard entry methods, like a Struts Action, that are used to call the Validator when needed. The Validator configuration file lets you associate one or more validators with each property in a form.

In practice, most applications need to perform a number of common validations. Some fields may require data to be entered. A postal code abbreviation may always be of a known length. Other common field types include numbers, dates, and credit card numbers.

The Validator comes equipped with several basic validators to handle these common needs, among others. If your Validator needs can't be met by one of the basic validators or a regular expression, you can roll your own Validator and plug it into the package. The basic validators are really just bundled plug-ins themselves. Your custom validators can do anything the basic validators do, and more.

The validators your application needs to use, basic or custom, can be specified in an XML configuration file, usually named validation.xml. To make maintenance easier, you can specify the rules that associate a Validator with your Action-Form properties in a separate file, usually named validator-rules.xml.

1.0 vs 1.1 The version of the Validator for Struts 1.0 uses a single validation.xml file that contains both the Validator definitions and the form validations. Struts 1.1 lets you split these components into separate files. In this chapter, we will refer to the separate files used by Struts 1.1. If you are using Struts 1.0, all configuration elements are kept in the single validation.xml file.

The validation-xml file has a `<form>` element that usually corresponds to the `<form-bean>` element in your Struts application. The `<form>` element in turn has `<field>` subelements. Each `<field>` can specify that it must pass one or more validators to succeed. If a validator fails, it can pass back a key to a message template in the application resources, along with any replacement parameters. Struts uses the key and parameters to generate a localized error message. If client-side validations are being used, the same message can be displayed in a JavaScript window, as shown in figure 12.1.

The validation file is where you plug in whatever basic or custom validations are needed by the validator rules. Here you specify which Validator classes to use, along with the optional client-side JavaScript validations. When used, the Java-Script validations must pass before the form is submitted back to the application.

Besides the JavaScript element in the validator configuration file, the other piece of client-side validations is the `<validator:javascript>` tag (Struts 1.0) or `<html:javascript>` tag (Struts 1.1). If you place this anywhere on your JSP, it will combine the JavaScript for all the validators into a single script that can be called from a standard entry method. You can then call the entry method using the `onsubmit` attribute to the `<html:form>` tag. If the JavaScript validations pass, the form is submitted. If not, a window pops up with the localized error messages.

To enable the server-side validations, you can simply extend your Action-Forms from one of the base classes in the Struts Validator package. The ValidatorForm (`org.apache.struts.validator.ValidatorForm`) class corresponds to the standard ActionForm. The DynaValidatorForm class (`org.apache.struts.validator.DynaValidatorForm`) corresponds to the DynaActionForm.

By default, the Validator `<form>` elements are matched to the ActionForms using the attribute or form bean name. Alternatively, you can use ValidatorActionForm

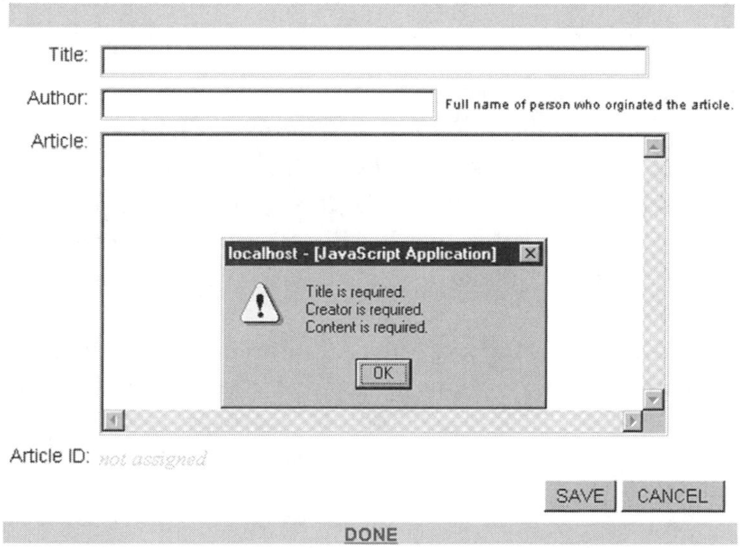

Figure 12.1   A JavaScript message window generated by the Struts Validator

(org.apache.struts.validator.ValidatorActionForm) or DynaValidatorAction-
Form (org.apache.struts.validator.DynaValidatorActionForm) to match up
the <form> elements using the ActionMapping path.

In the next section, we show you how to put it all together by using the logon
application as the backdrop for both client-side and server-side validation.

1.0 vs 1.1   In the 1.1 release, the Struts Validator was bundled into the Struts JAR
and made an optional component of the formal distribution. The im-
ports and some minor implementation details changed, but the package
is essentially unchanged. Where there are implementation differences,
we show separate listings for each release.

12.2.1 Logon example

Adapting the logon application from chapter 3 for the Struts Validator will help
illustrate how these components fit together. Then, in section 12.3, we explore
each component in depth.

After you set up the package (see chapter 4), your next step is to be sure the
validators you need are on hand. These can be kept in a separate file, named
validator-rules.xml by default. Our example only uses the required validator,
though most applications will use several others as well.

In the following sections, we will look at what we need in order to validate a
username and password using the Struts Validator.

validator-rules.xml

The Struts Validator distribution includes validators for native types and other
common needs, like e-mail and credit card validations. In practice, it's likely that
the basic validators will cover all your needs. If not, you can write your own and
define them in the validator-rules.xml file along with the basic validators. (As
noted, in Struts 1.0, both the validators and the form validations are defined in
the single validation.xml file.)

Listings 12.1 and 12.2 show the Java and XML source code for the required validator under Struts 1.1. For more about writing your own pluggable validators, see
section 12.9.

Listing 12.1   The XML source for the required validator (Struts 1.1)

```
<validator name="required"
<!-- ❶ -->
    classname="org.apache.struts.util.StrutsValidator"
    method="validateRequired"
      <!-- ❷ -->
    methodParams="java.lang.Object,
        org.apache.commons.validator.ValidatorAction,
        org.apache.commons.validator.Field,
        org.apache.struts.action.ActionErrors,
        javax.servlet.http.HttpServletRequest"
    msg="errors.required">
    <!-- ❸ -->
    <javascript><![CDATA[
        function validateRequired(form) {
        var bValid = true;
        var focusField = null;
        var i = 0;
        var fields = new Array();
        oRequired = new required();
        for (x in oRequired) {
            if ((form[oRequired[x][0]].type == 'text' ||
                form[oRequired[x][0]].type == 'textarea' ||
                form[oRequired[x][0]].type == 'select-one' ||
                form[oRequired[x][0]].type == 'radio' ||
                form[oRequired[x][0]].type == 'password') &&
                form[oRequired[x][0]].value == '') {
                if (i == 0)
                    focusField = form[oRequired[x][0]];
                fields[i++] = oRequired[x][1];
                bValid = false;
            }
        }
        if (fields.length==0) {
            focusField.focus();
            alert(fields.join('\n'));
        }
        return bValid;
        }
    ]]>
    </javascript>
</validator>
```

❶ This section contains the reference to the server-side validator (see listing 12.2).

❷ methodParams are used in Struts 1.1 only.

❸ The client-side JavaScript is included with the XML element.

As shown, the Validator elements are defined in two parts:

- A Java class and method for the server-side validation
- JavaScript for the client-side validation

The Java method the `required` validator invokes is shown in listing 12.2.

Listing 12.2   The Java source for the validateRequired method (Struts 1.1)

```
public static boolean validateRequired(Object bean,
        ValidatorAction va, Field field,
        ActionErrors errors,
        HttpServletRequest request) {
    String value = null;
    if (isString(bean)) {
        value = (String) bean;
    } else {
        value = ValidatorUtil.getValueAsString(bean, field.getProperty());
    }
    if (GenericValidator.isBlankOrNull(value)) {
        errors.add(field.getKey(),
                StrutsValidatorUtil.getActionError(request, va, field));
        return false;
    } else {
        return true;
    }
}
```

application.properties

If a validator fails, it passes back a message key and replacement parameters, which can be used with a standard resource bundle. By default, the Struts Validator shares the resource bundle used by the rest of your application. This is usually named ApplicationResources.properties, or just application.properties. When another message is not specified, the Struts Validator will automatically look for a message in the default resource bundle. Concatenating errors with a dot and the validator name usually creates the key for the message. Here is what the entry for our `required` validator looks like:

```
errors.required={0} is required.
```

When we configure a field to use the `required` validator, we also pass the field's label as a replaceable parameter. The validator can then reuse the same message for all the required fields. Alternatively, you can define your own messages to selectively override the defaults. (See section 12.4.3.)

The resource bundle will contain whatever other messages are needed by your application, along with specific labels and messages needed by the Struts Validator. Here is the block we will need for our `username` and `login` validations:

```
# -- logon --
logon.username.maskmsg=Username must be letters and numbers, no spaces.
logon.password.maskmsg=Password must be five characters long and contain a
    special character or numeral.
```

We also need labels for the `username` and `password` fields. However, these would already be provided if the application were localized:

```
logon.username.displayname=Username
logon.password.displayname=Password
```

Note that we prefix the labels and messages with `logon`. By giving each form its own namespace, we can avoid collisions as the application grows.

validator.xml

The validators and message keys are used when defining our `formset` element in the validator.xml file, as shown in listing 12.3.

Listing 12.3   A formset element

```
<!-- ❶ -->
<formset>
<!-- ❷ -->
<form name="logonForm">
<!-- ❸,❹ -->
<field
    property-"username"
    depends="required,mask">
<!-- ❺ -->
    <msg
        name="mask"
        key="logon.username.maskmsg"/>
<!-- ❻ -->
    <arg0
        key="logon.username.displayname"/>
<!-- ❼,❽ -->
    <var>
        <var-name>mask</var-name>
        <var-value>^[a-zA-Z0-9]*$</var-value>
    </var>
</field>
<!-- ❾ -->
<field
    property="password"
    depends="required,minlength">
```

```
<arg0
    key="logon.password.displayname"/>
<var>
    <var-name>minlength</var-name>
    <var-value>5</var-value>
</var>
</field>
</form>
<!-- ... -->
</formset>
```

❶ A `formset` is a wrapper for one or more forms.

❷ Each form element is given its own `name`. This should correspond to either the form bean name or the action path from your Struts configuration.

❸ Each `form` element is composed of a number of `field` elements.

❹ The `field` elements designate which validator(s) to use with the `depends` attribute.

❺ The optional `msg` element lets you specify a custom message key for a validator and the message key to use for any replacement parameters.

❻ The `arg0` element specifies the first replacement parameter to use with any messages that need them.

❼ The `var` element is used to pass variable properties to the validator.

❽ Here we pass a regular expression to the `mask` validator. The expression says usernames can contain only the alphabet characters and numerals.

❾ Here we say that a password is required and must be at least five characters long. The password length is a business requirement to help make the accounts more secure. The password validation message uses the default `minlength` or `required` messages, defined in validation-rules.xml (`errors.minlength` and `errors.required`).

JSP tag / logon.jsp

JavaScript validations are optional but easy to implement if you would like to use them in your application. Listing 12.4 shows the logon.jsp modified to display JavaScript validations.

Listing 12.4   logon.jsp prepared for JavaScript validations

```
<%@ taglib uri="/tags/struts-html" prefix="html" %>
<!-- ❶ -->
<%@ taglib uri="/tags/struts-validator" prefix="validator" %>
<HTML><HEAD><TITLE>Sign in, Please!</TITLE></HEAD>
<BODY>
```

```
<!-- ❷ -->
<html:form action="/logonSubmit" focus="username"
    onsubmit="return validateLogonForm(this)">
<TABLE border="0" width="100%">
<TR><TH align="right">Username:</TH>
<TD align="left"><html:text property="username"/></TD>
</TR>
<TR><th align="right">Password:</TH>
<TD align="left"><html:password property="password"/></TD>
</TR>
<TR>
<TD align="right"><html:submit property="submit" value="Submit"/></TD>
<TD align="left"><html:reset/></TD>
</TR>
</TABLE
</html:form>
<!-- ❸ -->
<validator:javascript formName="logonForm"/>
</BODY>
</HTML>
```

❶ Here we import the validator taglib.

❷ This section calls the validation script. Then, the form is submitted.

❸ Here, we add the tag to output the JavaScript anywhere on the page.

The validate method

To enable the server-side validations, all that needs to be done is to have the form bean extend ValidatorForm instead of ActionForm

```
public final class LogonForm extends
    org.apache.struts.validator.action.ValidatorForm {
```

and remove the old `validate` method. When the controller calls the `validate` method, the ValidatorForm method will kick in and follow the rules we defined in the validation.xml file.

12.3 *Basic validators*

As shown in table 12.2, the Struts Validator ships with 14 basic validators. These should cover the needs of most applications. If the need arises, as we will see in section 12.9, you can add custom, or plug-in, validators.

Table 12.2   Basic validators

Validator	Purpose
`required`	Succeeds if the field contains any characters other than whitespace.
`mask`	Succeeds if the value matches the regular expression given by the `mask` attribute.
`range`	Succeeds if the value is within the values given by the `min` and `max` attributes (`(value >= min) & (value <= max)`).
`maxLength`	Succeeds if the field's length is less than or equal to the `max` attribute.
`minLength`	Succeeds if the field's length is greater than or equal to the `min` attribute.
`byte, short, integer, long, float, double`	Succeeds if the value can be converted to the corresponding primitive.
`date`	Succeeds if the value represents a valid date. A date pattern may be provided.
`creditCard`	Succeeds if the value could be a valid credit card number.
`email`	Succeeds if the value could be a valid e-mail address.

12.3.1 *The required validator*

The `required` validator is both the simplest and the most commonly used of the validators:

```
<field
    property="customerId"
    depends="required"/>
```

If nothing or only whitespace is entered into a field, then the validation fails, and an error is passed back to the framework. Otherwise, the validation succeeds. To determine whether the field contains only whitespace, the standard `String.trim()` method is called (`value.trim().length() == 0`).

Since browsers do not submit empty fields, any field that isn't required will skip all validations if the field is null or has a length of zero.

12.3.2 *The mask validator*

The `mask` validator checks the value against a regular expression and succeeds if the pattern matches:

```
<field property="postalCode" depends="mask">
    <arg0 key="registrationForm.postalCode.displayname"/>
    <var>
        <var-name>mask</var-name>
```

```
        <var-value>^\d{5}\d*$</var-value>
    </var>
</field>
```

The Jakarta RegExp package [ASF, Regexp] is used to parse the expression. If an expression needs to be used by more than one field, it can also be defined as a constant in the validation.xml file—for example:

```
<constant>
    <constant-name>zip</constant-name>
    <constant-value>^\d{5}\d*$</constant-value>
</constant>
```

Like most of the other standard validators, the mask validator is declared to be dependent on the required validator. Therefore, if a field depends on both required and mask, then the required validator must complete successfully before the mask validator is applied.

12.3.3 *The range validator*

The range validator checks that the value falls within a specified minimum and maximum:

```
<field property="priority"
    depends="required,integer,range">
    <arg0 key="responseForm.priority.displayname"/>
    <var>
        <var-name>min</var-name>
        <var-value>1</var-value>
    </var>
    <var>
        <var-name>max</var-name>
        <var-value>4</var-value>
    </var>
</field
```

This validator would succeed if the digit 1, 2, 3, or 4 were entered into the field. In practice, the error message should display the minimum and maximum of the range, to help the user get it right. You can use the arg elements to include the min and max variables in the message by reference:

```
<field property="priority"
    depends="required,integer,range">
    <arg0 key="responseForm.priority.displayname"/>
    <arg1 name="range" key="${var:min}" resource="false"/>
    <arg2 name="range" key="${var:max}" resource="false"/>
    <var>
        <var-name>min</var-name>
        <var-value>1</var-value>
```

```
    </var>
    <var>
        <var-name>max</var-name>
        <var-value>4</var-value>
    </var>
</field
```

This implies that the template for the range messages looks something like this:

```
errors.range=Please enter a value between {1} and {2}.
```

If the range validator fails for the priority field, the validation message would read:

```
Please enter a value between 1 and 4.
```

By default, the validator assumes that the key of an arg element matches a key in the resource bundle and will substitute the value of the resource entry for the value of the key attribute. The resource=false switch tells the validator to use the value as is. If the values are being rendered by a select element, you may wish to map the messages to the first and last items on the select list:

```
<arg1 name="range" key="priority.range.first"/>
<arg2 name="range" key="priority.range.last"/>
```

This implies that there are also entries like these

```
priority.range.first=do-it-now
priority.range.last=forget-about-it
```

in the resource bundle. If validation failed, the message for priority would read:

```
Please enter a value between do-it-now and forget-about it.
```

12.3.4 *The maxLength validator*

The maxLength validator checks the high end of the range; it succeeds if the field's length is less than or equal to the max attribute:

```
<field property="remarks"
    depends="maxLength">
    <arg0 key="responseForm.remarks.displayname"/>
    <arg1 name="maxLength" key="${var:maxLength}" resource="false"/>
    <var>
        <var-name>maxLength</var-name>
        <var-value>1000</var-value>
    </var>
</field>
```

This field element makes sure that the length of the remarks (probably a text area field) does not exceed 1000 characters. Note that we pass the length as an argument to the validation message, as we did with the range validator.

12.3.5 *The minLength validator*

The `minLength` validator checks the low end of the range; it succeeds if the field's length is greater than or equal to the `min` attribute:

```
<field property="password"
    depends="required,minlength">
    <arg0 key="logon.password.displayname"/>
    <arg1 name="minlength" key="${var:minlength}" resource="false"/>
    <var>
        <var-name>minlength</var-name>
        <var-value>5</var-value>
    </var>
</field
```

The `field` element stipulates that the password must be entered and must have a length of at least five characters.

12.3.6 *The byte, short, integer, long, float, and double validators*

These validators all apply the standard `type.parseType` methods to the value. If an Exception is caught, the validator returns false. Otherwise, it succeeds:

```
<field property="amount"
    depends="required,double">
<arg0 key="typeForm.amount.displayname"/>
</field>
```

12.3.7 *The date validator*

The `date` validator checks to see if the value represents a valid date:

```
<field property="date"
    depends="required,date">
    <arg0 key="typeForm.date.displayname"/>
</field>
```

The validator passes the standard Locale object (`java.util.Locale`) maintained by the framework to the date utilities, so the result is automatically localized. The `datePattern` attribute will pass a standard date pattern to a `java.text.Simple-DateFormat` object:

```
<var>
    <var-name>datePattern</var-name>
    <var-value>MM/dd/yyyy</var-value>
</var>
```

Internally, the `datePattern` attribute is used in the SimpleDateFormat constructor and then used to parse the value:

```
SimpleDateFormat formatter = new SimpleDateFormat(datePattern);
Date date = formatter.parse(value);
```

If the parse succeeds, the validator succeeds.

If the `datePatternStrict` attribute is set instead, the length is also checked to ensure a leading zero is included when appropriate:

```
<var>
    <var-name>datePatternStrict</var-name>
    <var-value>MM/dd/yyyy</var-value>
</var>
```

When no pattern is specified, the `DateFormat.SHORT` format for the user's Locale is used. If the Struts Locale object is not available, the server's default Locale is used. The `setLenient` method is set to false for all date transformations.

12.3.8 *The creditCard validator*

The `creditCard` validator analyzes the value to see if it could be a credit card number:

```
<field property="creditCard"
    depends="required,creditCard">
    <arg0 key="typeForm.creditCard.displayname"/>
</field>
```

Credit card numbers include a parity-check digit. The validation checks for this digit and other business rules, such as whether the card's prefix matches one of the credit card vendors (American Express, Discover, MasterCard, VISA) and whether the length of the number is correct for the indicated vendor.

12.3.9 *The email validator*

The `email` validator employs an *extensive* check of the format of a prospective e-mail address to be sure it is in accordance with the published specification:

```
<field property="email"
    depends="required,email">
    <arg0 key="typeForm.email.displayname"/>
</field>
```

12.4 *Resource bundles*

The underlying purpose of validation is to get the user to fix the input and try again. Since that process involves displaying field labels and messages, the Struts Validator makes good use of the Java localization features and the framework's support for those features. (The Java localization features are covered in chapter 13.)

Of course, the framework also needs to provide localized labels for the fields. Since the Struts resource bundle is offered as an application-level resource, the Validator is able to share the same bundle with the framework, so you can keep all your labels and messages together. You simply need to add default messages for the validators you are using and any custom messages needed while validating a particular field.

12.4.1 *The default bundle*

The Struts bundle is configured through the deployment descriptor (see chapter 4). It is usually named ApplicationResources.properties or just application.properties. In our example applications, the bundles are stored in a package under /WEB-INF/src/java/resources. Our default Properties files (`java.util.Properties`) are named application.properties. Files for supported locales are then named application_*en*.properties, application_*es*.properties, application_*fr*.properties, and so forth. (Again, see chapter 13 for more about localization.)

You do not need to do anything special to start using the Struts resource bundle with the Validator. Just add whatever messages or labels you may need and then refer to the resource key in the Validator's configuration file. If the application is being localized, keys for the field labels should already be present, and you can share them with the rest of the framework, as shown here:

```
<field property="lastName"
    depends="required">
    <arg0 key="registrationForm.lastName.displayname"/>
</field>
```

12.4.2 *Default validator messages*

If a custom message is not provided by a field element, the default message for the validator is used when the validation fails. The key for a validator's default message is specified when it is defined. The convention is to add an `errors.` prefix to the validator's name. The default message for the `required` validator then becomes `errors.required`.

This convention dovetails with the Struts `<html:error>` tag, which looks for *errors.header* and *errors.footer* entries. Listing 12.5 shows the keys and templates you could add to an English resource bundle for the basic validators.

Listing 12.5   Default messages for the basic validators

```
# Struts Validator Basic Error Messages
errors.required={0} is required.
errors.minlength={0} cannot be less than {1} characters.
errors.maxlength={0} cannot be greater than {1} characters.
errors.invalid={0} is invalid.
errors.byte={0} must be a byte.
errors.short={0} must be a short.
errors.integer={0} must be an integer.
errors.long={0} must be a long.
errors.float={0} must be a float.
errors.double={0} must be a double.
errors.date={0} is not a date.
errors.range={0} is not in the range {1} through {2}.
errors.creditcard={0} is not a valid credit card number.
errors.email={0} is not a valid e-mail address.
```

You may note that there is no entry for errors.mask. For historical reasons, the definition for the mask validator specifies errors.invalid instead of errors.mask.

Each of the validator messages can take up to four replacement parameters, which are specified as arg elements within the field definition. The first parameter, arg0 or {0}, is usually the key for the field label. The validator will then look up the display text for the label from the resource bundle and merge the localized text into the message template.

12.4.3 *Custom validator messages*

A field can also specify a custom validation message to use instead of the default. This often happens when the mask validator is being used, so you can explain what pattern the regular expression expects. The key for the message is given in a msg element. Since more than one validator may be used by a field, the name of the validator is included as the msg element's name attribute:

```
<field
    property="username"
    depends="required,mask">
    <msg
        name="mask"
        key="logon.username.maskmsg"/>
    <arg0
        key="logon.username.displayname"/>
    <var>
        <var-name>mask</var-name>
        <var-value>^[a-zA-Z0-9]*$</var-value>
    </var>
</field>
```

In the Properties file, we could then place a key/template entry like this:

```
logon.username.maskmsg={0} must be letters and numbers, no spaces.
```

12.5 *Configuration files*

The strength of the Struts Validator is that the validations are declared outside the application source code using an XML configuration file. The configuration specifies which fields on a form need validation, the validators a field uses, and any special settings to be used with a field. Alternate formsets can be configured for different locales and override any locale-sensitive validations.

All of the validators used by the framework are configured through XML, including the basic validators that ship with the package. You can omit validators that your application doesn't need and plug in your own custom validators to use alongside those that ship with the framework.

This makes for a very flexible package, but combining all these configurations into a single file can result in a verbose document. As shown in table 12.3, the Struts Validator can actually use two XML files: one to set up the validators and another with the settings for your applications. (As noted, Struts 1.0 uses a single configuration file.)

Table 12.3   Struts Validator configuration files

Filename	Description
validator-rules.xml	Configuration files for the validators
validation.xml	The validations for your application

This makes for a very convenient arrangement. This way, it's easy to copy a standard set of validation rules between applications and then customize the validation.xml file. Or, if you prefer, you can still combine all the elements in a single validation.xml.

In Struts 1.1, the paths to the Validator configuration files are declared in the struts-config.xml file, as shown here:

```
<plug-in className="org.apache.struts.validator.ValidatorPlugIn">
    <set-property
      property="pathnames"
      value="/WEB-INF/validator-rules.xml,/WEB-INF/validation.xml"/>
</plug-in>
```

See chapter 4 for more about installing the Struts Validator 1.1 components into your application.

12.6 *Validator JSP tags*

The Struts Validator framework combines the (optional) JavaScripts needed to validate a form into a single script. You insert the script into your JavaServer Page via a custom tag. The script can then be called when the form is submitted. If the validation fails, the script displays an error message window, like the one back in figure 12.1, and the submit fails.

Otherwise, the submit succeeds and control passes to the validate method on the Struts ActionForm. This ensures that the validations are triggered even when JavaScript is not available.

In listing 12.4, we introduced the <javascript> tag. For simplicity, this listing retained the original <html:errors> tag. The original <errors> tag is quite easy to use on the page but requires that you mix markup in with the message. Otherwise, if the messages are presented as a block, they all run together into a single paragraph.

Under the Struts Validator framework, error messages are shared with the Java-Script validations. In practice, using the same markup in both cases is problematic. A much better way to go would be to use plain messages all around.

The Struts Validator taglib provides additional tags that help with this very problem. The <errorsPresent> or <messagesPresent> tag reports whether any messages are pending. The <messages> tag works like an iterator, so your page can loop through the queue, providing any markup entries needed along the way.

Listing 12.6 shows the code from listing 12.4 again, this time outfitted with the messages tags. Listing 12.7 shows the Struts 1.1 version.

Listing 12.6 Logon page with validations and additional JSP tags (1.0)

```
<%@ taglib uri="/tags/struts-bean" prefix="bean" %>
<%@ taglib uri="/tags/struts-validator" prefix="validator" %>
<%@ taglib uri="/tags/struts-html" prefix="html" %>
<!-- ❶ -->
<%@ taglib uri="/tags/struts-validator" prefix="validator" %>
<HTML><HEAD><TITLE>Sign in, Please!</TITLE></HEAD>
<BODY>
<!-- ❷ -->
<validator:errorsExist>
<UL>
<!-- ❸ -->
<validator:errors id="error">
<LI><bean:write name="error"/></LI>
```

```
</validator:errors>
</UL>
</validator:errorsExist>
<!-- ❹ -->
<html:form action="/logonSubmit" focus="username"
    onsubmit="return validateLogonForm(this)">
<TABLE border="0" width="100%">
<TR><TH align="right">Username:</th>
<TD align="left"><html:text property="username"/></TD>
</TR>
<TR><th align="right">Password:</TH>
<TD align="left"><html:password property="password"/></TD>
</TR>
<TR>
<TD align="right"><html:submit property="submit" value="Submit"/></TD>
<TD align="left"><html:reset/></TD>
<!-- ❺ -->
<TD align="left"><html:cancel onclick="bCancel=true"/></TD>
</TR>
</TABLE>
</html:form>
<!-- ❻ -->
<validator:javascript formName="logonForm"/>
</BODY>
</HTML>
```

Listing 12.7 Logon page with validations and additional JSP tags (1.1)

```
<%@ taglib uri="/tags/struts-html" prefix="html" %>
<!-- ❶ -->
<%@ taglib uri="/tags/struts-validator" prefix="validator" %>
<%@ taglib uri="/tags/struts-logic" prefix="logic" %>
<HTML><HEAD><TITLE>Sign in, Please!</TITLE></HEAD>
<BODY>
<!-- ❷ -->
<logic:messagesPresent>
<UL>
<!-- ❸ -->
<logic:messages id="error"
<LI><bean:write name="error"/></LI>
</logic:messages>
</UL>
</logic:messagesPresent>
<!-- ❹ -->
<html:form action="/logonSubmit" focus="username"
    onsubmit="return validateLogonForm(this)">
<TABLE border="0" width="100%">
<TR><TH align="right">Username:</th>
<TD align="left"><html:text property="username"/></TD>
</TR>
<TR><th align="right">Password:</TH>
```

```
<TD align="left"><html:password property="password"/></TD>
</TR>
<TR>
<TD align="right"><html:submit property="submit" value="Submit"/></TD>
<TD align="left"><html:reset/></TD>
<!-- 5 -->
<TD align="left"><html:cancel onclick="bCancel=true"/></TD>
</TR>
</TABLE
</html:form>
<!-- 6 -->
<validator:javascript formName="logonForm"/>
</BODY>
</HTML>
```

Here are some remarks that apply to both listings 12.6 and 12.7:

❶ Since we will be using the Struts Validator tags, we need to import the taglib. In Struts 1.1, we should also import the logic taglib, since it now includes tags we can use here.

❷ The Struts 1.0 error tags, or Struts 1.1 message tags, let us keep the HTML in the page and out of the error messages. If there are no messages, this entire block is skipped.

❸ The `<errors>` or `<messages>` tag works like an iterator. The tag will expose each message under the id errors so that the bean tag can write them out in turn.

❹ A JavaScript onsubmit event has been added to the `<html:form>` tag. This will call our validator JavaScript when any Submit button is pushed or a JavaScript submit event is triggered.

❺ To allow the user to cancel the submit and bypass the validations, a JavaScript flag can be set. If the Submit button sets bCancel to true, then the Struts Validator will pass control through to the Action.

❻ Last, but not least, is the actual `<javascript>` tag. At runtime, this will be replaced with a script combining the JavaScript validators for this form. The script, like the ActionForm, is named after the action-mapping attribute name, which in this case is logonForm.

The basic validators provided with the framework all include JavaScript validations. If a pluggable validator (section 12.9) provides a JavaScript validation, it will be included here as well. For the script to succeed, all the validations must succeed.

The generated JavaScript observes the page property of the ValidatorForm and will only generate validators for fields with a page number equal to or less than the form's page number. The default page number for both is 0. This is useful for multipage wizard forms. (See section 12.10.1.)

12.7 *ValidatorForm and ValidatorActionForm*

To enable the Struts Validator for Struts 1.1, just follow the initial setup instructions in chapter 4 and extend your ActionForm from ValidatorForm and ValidatorActionForm. The ValidatorForm will match the `formset` name with the `form-bean` name. The ValidatorActionForm will match the `formset` name with the `action-mapping` path.

In most cases, the Struts Validator can completely replace the need to write a custom `validate` method for an ActionForm. However, should you still need a `validate` method, it can easily work alongside the validation framework. In most cases, you would want to call the validator framework first, and then run your own validations if these pass. Listing 12.8 shows how this is done.

Listing 12.8 Logon page with validations

```
public ActionErrors validate(
        ActionMapping mapping,
        HttpServletRequest request) {
    // ❶
    ActionErrors errors = super.validate(mapping, request);
    // ❷
    if (errors==null) errors = new ActionErrors();
    if (errors.empty()) {
        // ❸
      if (notGood(mapping,request)) errors.add(ActionErrors.GLOBAL_ERROR,new
            ActionError("errors.notGood","goodProperty"));
    }
    if (errors.empty()) return null;
    return errors;
}
```

---

❶ First, we call the ancestor `validate` method. In this case, we're calling the Validator framework.

❷ Since the ancestor method could return null, we need to check for null first. Since we want to run our own validations, which may need to post errors, we create a new `ActionErrors` object if one wasn't returned. This implementation does not run our validations if the ancestor returns errors, though you could just as easily run your own if that was appropriate.

❸ Our sample validation calls a helper method called `notGood`, which returns the result of our custom validation. We pass the parameters from the `validate` method to be sure `notGood` knows everything `validate` knows.

12.8 Localized validations

The Validator configuration files include a `formset` element. The formset is a wrapper for a collection of forms that share a common locale setting. While some fields in some forms do need to be localized, usually the majority do not. The Struts Validator allows you to localize selected fields and use the default validations for the rest. The default formset omits the language, country, and variant properties. The localization is properly scoped; you can define a format to override just the language, or just the country, or both if need be. For more about internationalizing your applications, see chapter 13.

12.9 Pluggable validators

Each field element can specify a list of validators on which it depends. Some applications will use very few validators; others will use several. To allow developers to load only the validators their application needs and to make it easy to load custom objects, the validators are declared from a configuration file, essentially making them all pluggable.

DEFINITION *Pluggable* refers to an object-oriented design strategy that allows objects to be developed independently of an application and then incorporated without changing the base code. Pluggable components are often created by a third party.

12.9.1 Creating pluggable validators

Creating your own validator and plugging it in is a two-step process:

1 Create a method in a Java class to handle the server-side validations.

2 Update the validator-rules.xml file with an element for your validator. If your validator will have a client-side JavaScript component, you can make this part of the `validator` element.

Creating a validation method

Any class can be used to store your `validate` method. For Struts 1.0, the method must follow a specific signature:

```
public static boolean validateMyValidator(
        Object bean,
        ValidatorAction va,
        Field field,
        ActionErrors errors,
        HttpServletRequest request);
```

Table 12.4 provides a key to the parameters passed to your `validate` method.

Table 12.4   Validator method properties

Property	Description
`Object bean`	The bean on which validation is being performed.
`ValidatorAction va`	This is a JavaBean that represents the `validator` element for this validator from the validator-rules.xml. The bean is declared in the `org.apache.commons.validator` package.
`Field field`	This JavaBean represents the element for the field we are to validate. The bean is declared in the `org.apache.commons.validator` package.
`ActionErrors errors`	An ActionErrors object that will receive any validation errors that may occur.
`HttpServletRequest request`	The current request object underlying this operation.

In Struts 1.1, you may specify the signature for your method as part of the configuration.

For coding hints on how to get your pluggable validator to do what you need, see the `org.apache.struts.util.StrutsValidator` class. This class contains the methods for the basic validators that ship with the distribution. Your validations should work in exactly the same way as the basic ones, which themselves are essentially all plug-ins.

STRUTS TIP   When developing pluggable validators, keep an eye on the log file. Many programming errors will only be logged and will not be exposed in the application. A good example is getting the package name wrong in the validator-rules.xml. A `ClassNotFound` exception will be logged, but the application will act as if the validation succeeded!

Declaring a validator element

Listings 12.1 and 12.2 show the configuration element, which is the same one you would use for your own plug-in. The `required` portion is simply:

```
<validator
    name="required"
    classname="org.apache.struts.validator.util.StrutsValidator"
    method="validateRequired"
    msg="errors.required"/>
```

This element tells the Struts Validator which method to call on what class, and the message key to use when the validation fails. (Hey, it has to fail some time; otherwise, what's the point?)

In Struts 1.1, you can also specify the parameters your `validate` method will use:

```
<validator name="required"
    classname="org.apache.struts.util.StrutsValidator"
    method="validateRequired"
    methodParams="java.lang.Object,
        org.apache.commons.validator.ValidatorAction,
        org.apache.commons.validator.Field,
        org.apache.struts.action.ActionErrors,
        javax.servlet.http.HttpServletRequest"
    msg="errors.required"/>
```

In addition to declaring the server-side validation, you can specify a client-side JavaScript to use with your validator. The various JavaScript elements in the stock validator-rules.xml provide several working examples of how to write a compatible script.

12.10 *Techniques*

In addition to the everyday uses we've covered so far, there are several special techniques you can use with the Struts Validator. These include:

- Multipage validations
- Cancel buttons
- Custom messages
- Interrelated fields
- The combining of validators with the `validate` method

12.10.1 *Multipage validations*

Many developers like to use wizard forms. A wizard gathers the information needed for an operation through several different forms. Then, it combines the results at the end. Since not so much information is provided at once, it can be easier for a user to complete a large form. Some developers use a different form for each page. Others like to use one big form and expose only part of it at a time.

If you are using the one-big-form wizard approach, the Struts Validator includes a `page` property on the field element and provides a corresponding `page` property on the ValidatorForm. Before performing the validation on a field, the framework checks to see if the field page is less than or equal to the ValidatorForm page. This means that as part of validating page 3, we also double-check the validations for pages 1 and 2. This is to help to keep people from skipping pages.

If your one-big-form wizard has a `reset` method, you can also use the `page` property to reset values only for the current page:

```
if (page==1) {
    // reset page I properties
}
if (page==2) {
    // reset page 2 properties
}
```

12.10.2 *Cancel buttons*

Most forms give the user the opportunity to cancel the operation altogether, usually with a Cancel button. The problem here is that the Cancel button submits the form—so the JavaScript tries to validate it. The server-side pieces can be made to acknowledge the Cancel button, but the JavaScript is client-side and unaware of the framework. So, to cancel a form, a user must first appease the JavaScript validations. Not good.

To resolve this dilemma, the Struts Validator provides a `bCancel` JavaScript variable. If `bCancel` is set to true, the JavaScript validations will also return true, allowing the cancel request to pass through to the container. The server-side validations know about the Struts `<cancel>` button and will not fire if they see it in the request. The rest is up to the Action, which should check its own `isCancelled` method before committing any operation that a user might relay:

```
<html:cancel onclick="bCancel=true;">
<bean:message key="button.cancel"/>
</html:cancel>
```

12.10.3 *Custom messages*

Each validator can define a default error message to use when the validation fails. For example,

```
errors.integer={0} must be an integer.
```

would automatically display

```
Quantity must be an integer.
```

when someone tried to enter a letter into a field labeled Quantity.

For most validators, this works just fine, and the default message is all you need. The exception is the mask validator, which is used with regular expressions. Here, the default message is

```
errors.invalid={0} is invalid.
```

If used with a mask on a form for entering a new password that needed to be at least five characters long, the default message would be

```
Password is invalid.
```

which doesn't tell users what they need to do to fix it. A better message would be

```
Password must be five or more characters long.
```

Of course, that message would not work as well for some other field that used the mask validator with a different regular expression.

In most cases, whenever you use a mask validator, you should also specify a custom error message that explains what the regular expression expects:

```
<field property="password" depends="required,mask">
    <msg name="mask" key="accountForm.password.mask"/>
    <arg0 key="nameForm.password.displayname"/>
    <var>
        <var-name>mask</var-name>
        <var-value>^{5}*$</var-value>
    </var>
</field>
```

And in the application resources:

```
accountForm.password.mask ={0} must be five or more characters long.
```

While the message attribute is most often used with the mask validator, you can override the message for any validator on a field-by-field basis.

12.10.4 *Interrelated fields*

If users change their password, it's commonplace for a program to have users input the new password twice, to help ensure they have typed it correctly. Many other fields in a form may also be interrelated in some way. You can compare fields in any way you like by defining your own plug-in validator.

Used together in the same application, the components shown in listings 12.9, 12.10, and 12.11 create a plug-in validator that compares two fields to be sure they are identical.

Listing 12.9   validator-rules.xml

```xml
<validator name="identical"
    classname="com.mysite.StrutsValidator"
    method="validateIdentical"
    depends="required"
    msg="errors.identical"/>
```

Listing 12.10   validate.xml

```xml
<field property="password"
    depends="required,identical">
    <arg0 key="accountForm.password.displayname"/>
    <var>
        <var-name>secondProperty</var-name>
        <var-value>password2</var-value>
    </var>
</field
```

Listing 12.11   apps.ValidateUtils

```java
public static boolean validateIdentical(
        Object bean,
        ValidatorAction va,
        Field field,
        ActionErrors errors,
        HttpServletRequest request) {

    String value = ValidatorUtil.getValueAsString(bean,
        field.getProperty());
    String sProperty2 = field.getVarValue("secondProperty");
    String value2 = ValidatorUtil.getValueAsString(bean, sProperty2);

    if (!GenericValidator.isBlankOrNull(value)) {
        try {
            if (!value.equals(value2)) {
                errors.add(field.getKey(),
                ValidatorUtil.getActionError(application, request, va, field));
                return false;
```

```
            }
        }
            catch (Exception e) {
            errors.add(field.getKey(), ValidatorUtil.getActionError(
                application, request, va, field));
            return false;
        }
    }
    return true;
}
```

12.10.5 *Combining validators with the validate method*

Plug-in validators, like the one shown in section 12.10.4, can be used to ensure more complex relationships between fields are maintained. For example, if something may be picked up or shipped, and users choose Ship, you could plug in a validator to be sure a shipping option had been chosen.

The best candidates for plug-in validators are ones that you can reuse on several forms. If the validation would not be reusable, you can also override the validate method and use it in the normal way. Just be sure to also call the ancestor validate method, to ensure that any framework validations are triggered. Listing 12.12 shows how to combine a custom validate method with the Struts Validator.

Listing 12.12   Combining validate with validators

```
public ActionErrors validate(ActionMapping mapping,
        HttpServletRequest request) {
    ActionErrors errors = super.validate(mapping, request);

    if (errors==null) errors = new ActionErrors();
    // If selects shipping
    if ("S".equals(deliveryType)) {
        // Vendor required
        if ("".equals(getShipVendor().trim())) {
            errors.add(ActionErrors.GLOBAL_ERROR,
            new ActionError("item.shipVendor.maskmsg"));
    }

    if (errors.empty()) return null;
    return errors;
}
```

12.11   *Migrating an application to the Struts Validator*

While many Struts applications are written to use the Struts Validator from the get-go, most start out using their own routines before moving to the Validator. In this section, we walk through migrating a simple ActionForm `validate` method to its Struts Validator counterpart. The point of the exercise is not the example `validate` method, which is trivial, but the process of moving the method to the Struts Validator.

In chapter 11, we followed a similar process by migrating some example pages to Tiles.

12.11.1   *Setting up the Validator framework*

Setting up the validator varies slightly between Struts 1.0 and 1.1, but works just as well with either version.

NOTE   Before you begin, make an extra backup of everything, regardless of how many backups are made in the normal course. Migrating to the Validator can be tricky at first, and, realistically, you may need to make more than one pass before everything clicks into place. So, be ready to roll back and try again. 'Nuff said.

Struts 1.0

If you haven't done so, the first step is to install the Validator package and load the Validator servlet through your application's deployment descriptor. (The Validator servlet is just a resource loader and so does not conflict with the Tiles servlet.) Then, test your application to be sure all is well by clicking through a few pages.

The Blank application for Struts 1.0 on the book's website [Husted] includes an empty Validator configuration file and sample setup.

Struts 1.1

The Validator is integrated with Struts 1.1. The steps for enabling the Validator in Struts 1.1 are covered in section 4.9 of this book.

12.11.2   *Testing the default configuration*

Set the `debug` and `detail` parameters in the deployment descriptor (web.xml) to level 2, and restart the application. Check the log entries carefully for any new error messages. Run any unit tests and click through the application to confirm that operation is still nominal.

12.11.3 *Reviewing your validations*

With the Validator up and running, the next step is to take a good hard look at your `validate` methods. Identify which will correspond to a standard Struts Validator validation and which will have to be handled on a custom basis. The Validator is not an either/or proposition. You can continue to use the ActionForm `validate` method to handle some things, and the Validator to handle the rest.

Listing 12.13 shows a code skeleton that calls the Struts Validator and then tries any custom validations.

Listing 12.13   Calling the Validator and your own custom routines

```
public ActionErrors validate(
        ActionMapping mapping,
      HttpServletRequest request) {

      // ❶
    ActionErrors errors = super.validate(mapping, request);

      // ❷
    if (null==errors) errors = new ActionErrors();

    /* ❸
        if (!(dateCheck()))
        errors.add(ActionErrors.GLOBAL_ERROR,
            new ActionError("errors.invalid","Expiration Date"));
    */

      // ❹

    // ❺
    if (errors.empty()) return null;
    return errors;

} // end validate
```

---

❶ This method is meant to be used with a ValidatorForm subclass. By calling and capturing the super class `validate` method, we run any of the Struts Validator validations but leave room for calling our own.

❷ If the super class validations all pass, `validate` will return null. We might still find some errors of our own, so we create an ActionErrors collection to hold them. If the ValidatorForm super class returns some errors, we continue to use the same collection. This will provide a unified set of error messages to the user, regardless of which `validate` method ran the validation.

❸ This is an example of a commented-out validation that has been replaced by the Struts Validator. Once the method is fully tested, this would be removed.

4 Other validation routines that have not been moved to the Struts Validator can run here.

5 If there were no errors, this code returns null; otherwise, it returns the combined list of errors—the Struts Validator's and any of our own.

The moral of this method? If a standard validation won't be able to handle some of your validation routines, plan to leave them in for now. You might want to replace these routines with a custom validator later, but pick the low-hanging fruit first, and get the standard versions working.

12.11.4 *Extending ValidatorForm or the Scaffold BaseForm*

Before making any code changes to your ActionForm, ensure that it extends either the ValidatorForm or the Scaffold BaseForm:

```
import com.wintecinc.struts.action.ValidatorForm; // Struts 1.0.x
// import org.apache.struts.validator.ValidatorForm; // Struts 1.1

public class ActionForm extends ValidatorForm {
    // . . .
}
```

or

```
import org.apache.scaffold.struts.BaseForm;

public class ActionForm extends BaseForm {
    // . . .
}
```

In either case, you should be able to rebuild and test the application without error. Neither class changes the default ActionForm functionality. If you do expose any errors at this point, be sure to resolve them before continuing.

12.11.5 *Selecting a validation to migrate*

Let's look at a simple example validation from an early version of the Artimus example application [ASF, Artimus]. It tests to be sure that some required fields were present before storing an article. Listing 12.14 shows the complete class.

Listing 12.14   A simple validate method
(org.apache.artimus.articles.struts.ActionForm)

```
package org.apache.artimus.article.struts;
import javax.servlet.http.HttpServletRequest;
import org.apache.struts.action.ActionError;
import org.apache.struts.action.ActionErrors;
import org.apache.struts.action.ActionMapping;
import org.apache.artimus.struts.Form;

public class ArticleForm extends Form {

        // ❶
    private boolean isNotPresent(String field) {
        return ((null==field) || ("".equals(field)));
    }

    public ActionErrors validate(
        ActionMapping mapping,
        HttpServletRequest request) {

        // ❷
            ActionErrors errors = new ActionErrors();

        // ❸
            String title = getTitle();
        if (isNotPresent(title)) {
            errors.add(ActionErrors.GLOBAL_ERROR,
                new ActionError("errors.required","Title"));
        }
        String content = getContent();
        if (isNotPresent(content)) {
            errors.add(ActionErrors.GLOBAL_ERROR,
                new ActionError("errors.required","Article text"));
        }
        String creator = getCreator();
        if (isNotPresent(creator)) {
            errors.add(ActionErrors.GLOBAL_ERROR,
                new ActionError("errors.required","Author"));
        }

            if (errors.empty()) return null;
            return errors;

    } // end validate
//   end ArticleForm
```

❶ isNotPresent is a simple utility method to test whether a field is null or empty.

❷ This code creates an ActionErrors collection, so that it's there if we need it.

❸ This code runs our three simple validations. If any fail, it creates an ActionError. The `errors.required` template is used to create the ActionError, and the field is merged into the message.

As validation routines go, this is no biggie, but it's better to start with something simple and work your way up. Let's see how the title validation routine would be migrated to the Struts Validator.

12.11.6 *Adding the formset, form, and field elements*

First, add a default `<formset>` to the Validator configuration file (validation.xml), and add to that an element for the form and a `field` element for the property. Listing 12.15 shows the initial `<formset>` for our `articleForm` example.

Listing 12.15   An initial <formset> for the Struts Validator

```
<formset>
   <form name="articleForm">
      <field
         property="title"
         depends="required">
            <arg0 key="Title" resource="false"/>
      </field>
   </form>
</formset>
```

The title validation routine in listing 12.14 is just a test that it is required. Of course, the Struts Validator has a standard validator for that. In listing 12.15, we specify that in the form `articleForm`, the field `title` depends on the `required` validator. Our error message includes the field's name as the `{0}` replacement parameter, so we can pass that to the field as the `<arg0>` element.

12.11.7 *Adding new entries to the ApplicationResources*

The `<field>` element in listing 12.15 uses the `resource="false"` attribute to pass a literal `String`. At this point, it's better to get on the right track and extract the language elements into the ApplicationResources bundle. When you are writing your own validation methods, it's easy to embed these language elements into the Java code. But when you are using the Struts Validator, it's just as easy to put them in the ApplicationResources bundle (where they belong). Listing 12.16 shows our initial `<formset>` with a reference to the ApplicationResources bundle.

Listing 12.16   An initial <formset>for the Struts Validator

```
<formset>
   <form name="articleForm">
      <field
         property="title"
         depends="required">
            <arg0 key="article.title.displayname"/>
      </field>
   </form>
</formset>
```

We then need to add the appropriate entry to our ApplicationResources file (/WEB-INF/src/java/resources/application.properties):

```
# /**
#  * Messages for Artimus application
#  */

# ...

# -- article Form fields --
article.title.displayname=Title
article.creator.displayname=Creator
article.content.displayname=Content

# ...
```

12.11.8 *Calling the Struts Validator*

In the Java source for the ArticleForm class, we can now call the ValidatorForm super class to validate our `title` field. Initially, we can just comment out the original validation and leave everything else intact. Listing 12.17 shows the revised `validate` method for our `articleForm` example. This is the code skeleton from listing 12.13 applied to listing 12.16.

Listing 12.17   A revised validate method

```java
public ActionErrors validate(
        ActionMapping mapping,
        HttpServletRequest request) {
    ActionErrors errors = super.validate(mapping, request);
    if (null==errors) errors = new ActionErrors();
/*
    String title = getTitle();
    if (isNotPresent(title)) {
        errors.add(ActionErrors.GLOBAL_ERROR,
            new ActionError("errors.required","Title"));
    }
*/
    String content = getContent();
    if (isNotPresent(content)) {
        errors.add(ActionErrors.GLOBAL_ERROR,
            new ActionError("errors.required","Article text"));
    }
    String creator = getCreator();
    if ((isNotPresent(creator)) {
        errors.add(ActionErrors.GLOBAL_ERROR,
            new ActionError("errors.required","Author"));
    }
    if (errors.empty()) return null;
    return (errors);
    } // end validate
// end ArticleForm
```

12.11.9   *Test and repeat*

Rebuild and reload the application to be sure the latest versions of *everything* are in place. Try to defeat the validation. When operation is deemed nominal, continue to the next validation routine. In our example, we ended up with this:

```xml
<formset>
    <form name="articleForm">
      <field
         property="title"
         depends="required">
            <arg0 key="article.title.displayname"/>
      </field>
      <field
         property="creator"
         depends="required">
            <arg0 key="article.creator.displayname"/>
      </field>
      <field
```

```
                property="contentDisplayHtml"
                depends="required">
                    <arg0 key="article.content.displayname"/>
            </field>
        </form>
    </formset>
```

12.11.10 *Removing the ActionForm subclass*

Our sample ActionForm subclassed a coarse-grained ActionForm (see chapter 5). The ArticleForm class itself provided nothing but a `validate` method that acted on the inherited properties. All of the bean's properties are defined in a base class.

In this case, once all the validations are transferred to the Struts Validator, we can just remove the class and update the `<form-bean>` element to use the base class instead.

What was:

```
    <form-beans>
  <form-bean
      name="baseForm"
      type="org.apache.artimus.struts.Form"/>
   <form-bean
      name="articleForm"
      type="org.apache.artimus.article.struts.ActicleForm"/>
          <!-- ... -->
      </form-beans>
```

can now be:

```
    <form-beans>
  <form-bean
      name="baseForm"
      type="org.apache.artimus.struts.Form"/>
   <form-bean
      name="articleForm"
      type="org.apache.artimus.struts.Form"/>
          <!-- ... -->
      </form-beans>
```

The same ActionForm class can be used by any number of form beans, just as an Action class can be used by any number of action mappings. Each instance is just given a different attribute name, and the Struts Validator matches the `<form>` elements by the attribute name. With a coarse-grained ActionForm in place to define our properties, the Struts Validator `<form>` element does the work of a subclass.

In Struts 1.1, you can use the DynaValidatorForm class to avoid declaring any new ActionForm class whatsoever. You can declare whatever simple properties your form needs as part of the `<form-bean>` element.

Here's the `<form-bean>` configuration for the Artimus 1.1 ArticleForm:

```
<form-bean
  name="articleForm"
    type="org.apache.struts.validator.DynaValidatorForm">
    <form-property
      name="keyName"
      type="java.lang.String"/>
    <form-property
      name="keyValue"
      type="java.lang.String"/>
    <form-property
      name="marked"
      type="java.lang.String"
      initialValue="0"/>
    <form-property
      name="hours"
      type="java.lang.String"/>
    <form-property
      name="articles"
      type="java.lang.String"/>
    <form-property
      name="article"
      type="java.lang.String"/>
    <form-property
      name="contributor"
      type="java.lang.String"/>
    <form-property
      name="contributedDisplay"
      type="java.lang.String"/>
    <form-property
      name="creator"
      type="java.lang.String"/>
    <form-property
      name="title"
      type="java.lang.String"/>
    <form-property
      name="contentDisplayHtml"
      type="java.lang.String"/>
</form-bean>
```

The validator `<form>` for this DynaBean is shown in section 12.11.9.

These two XML constructs replace writing a conventional ActionForm class and its `Validate` method.

12.12 Summary

The Struts Validator is a powerful addition to the framework. It allows validations to be managed in a separate configuration file, where they can be reviewed and modified without changing Java or JavaServer Page code. This is important since, like localization, validations are tied to the business tier and should not be mixed with presentation code.

The framework ships with several basic validators that will meet most of your routine needs. You can easily add custom validators for special requirements. If required, the original Struts `validate` method can be used in tandem with the Struts Validator to be sure all your needs are met.

Like the main Struts framework, the Struts Validator is built for localization from the ground up. It can even share the standard message resource file with the main framework, providing a seamless solution for your translators.

Validating input is an essential service that a web application framework must provide, and the Struts Validator is a flexible solution that can scale to meet the needs of even the most complex applications.

Localizing content

409

Life is a foreign language; all men mispronounce it.

—Christopher Morley (1890–1957)

13.1 *By any other name*

A key feature of the Struts framework is the way it collects input from users, validates the input, and (if necessary) redisplays the input for correction. To help redisplay the input, Struts provides custom tags that can create HTML input controls and populate them from a JavaBean [Sun, JBS]. In order to alert users as to what data needs to be corrected, the framework also provides a system for posting messages.

While it would be easy to have these components use hardcoded strings, that would make the text difficult to change. To rephrase a label or message, both presentation code and Java code may need to be updated, perhaps by different teams. It would also mean that the same application could not be reused for different languages without recompiling the source code.

To avoid these sorts of problems, the Struts framework lets developers define labels and messages in a separate file, called a *resource bundle* (`java.util.Resource-Bundle`). When a message or label needs to be written, it can refer to the message by its key. The framework then retrieves the appropriate text for the label at runtime. The source path for an image or image button and its text alternative can also be read from a resource bundle. Resource bundles are part of Java's internationalization features. Like Java, Struts was internationalized from the ground up. This is one reason the framework is popular the world over.

DEFINITION   *Internationalization* is the process of designing an application so that it can be adapted to various languages and regions without engineering changes. Sometimes the term *internationalization* is abbreviated as *i18n* because there are 18 letters between the first *i* and the last *n*.

Struts builds directly on the standard features provided by the Java platform. Developers can then continue to use the same techniques to localize their own components without becoming directly dependent on the Struts framework.

DEFINITION   *Localization* is the process of adapting software for a specific region or language by adding locale-specific components and translating text. The term *localization* is often abbreviated as *l10n*, because there are 10 letters between the *l* and the *n*. Usually, the most time-consuming portion of the localization phase is the translation of text. Other types of data, such as sounds and images, may require localization if they are culturally sensitive. Localizers also verify that the formatting of dates, numbers, and currencies conforms to local requirements.

In this chapter, we first look at why so many developers localize their applications and how Java internationalization works. We discuss the Struts i18n components and how they can localize your application. Popular Struts add-ins, like the Struts Validator and Tiles, can also be localized, along with collections you may pass to HTML control elements. We close the chapter with a look at how localization for these components is handled.

13.1.1 *Why localize?*

A great deal of effort goes into creating today's web applications. Every organization wants to get the most mileage out of its investment. Given the worldwide span of the Internet, every web application is available to an international audience. If an application can be localized, it can be instantly accessible to a much wider audience. This is especially true in multilingual countries, such as Belgium, Canada, Switzerland, and even the United States.

Unfortunately, many applications are not internationalized, and making them so can be a tremendous effort. Since Struts has internationalization features built in, most applications based on Struts can be localized without much trouble. If a Struts application is built to use internationalization features from the start, localization may just be a matter of translating a single message file.

Even without localizing, making good use of the techniques described here can help you build a more robust application that will be easier to maintain. Localization helps to group common resources together, where they can be reviewed and updated together. Applications that are hard to localize may have other bad habits. Many of the internationalization techniques are based on general best practices, such as encapsulation, modularity, and separation of concerns.

While language is often the most important part of localization, it is not the only consideration. Dates, currency, and images also need to be localized. The

Java platform has built-in features to help you handle dates and currency; Struts conveniently adds support for selecting images by locale.

13.1.2 *How Java internationalization works*

To be internationalized, an application should be able to:

- Distinguish between different localities
- Display appropriate messages and labels for different localities using the same executable
- Provide support for new localities without compiling a new executable
- Automatically format elements sensitive to locality, such as dates and currencies, as appropriate to a given region and language

Java helps applications meet the requirements of internationalization through the use of three key classes: Locale, ResourceBundle, and MessageFormat, shown in table 13.1.

Table 13.1   Key classes for Java internationalization

Internationalization requirement	Java class
Distinguish between different localities	`java.util.`**`Locale`**
Display appropriate messages and labels for different localities using the same executable and provide support for new localities without compiling a new executable	`java.util.`**`ResourceBundle`**
Automatically format elements sensitive to locality, such as dates and currencies, as appropriate to the locality's region and language	`java.text.`**`MessageFormat`**

Let's discuss each of these in turn.

Locale

The absolute core of Java's support for internationalization is the Locale object (`java.util.Locale`). This deceptively simple object lets you combine a language, a country, and an optional variant into a single Locale entity. The languages and countries are defined by ISO standards [IS0-3166, ISO-639]. Some sample language and country codes are shown in table 13.2.

Table 13.2   Sample language and country codes

Language code	Description	Country code	Description
de	German	CN	China
es	Spanish	CA	Canada
en	English	DE	Germany
fr	French	FR	France
ja	Japanese	IN	India
jw	Javanese	US	United States
ko	Korean	zh	Chinese

The optional variant is often used to represent a dialect but can be any code useful to an application (perhaps to represent which browser is being used). The Struts framework does not make use of the variant field. But since the standard libraries are used, the variant field is available to applications if needed.

To create a Locale object, pass the language and country code in the constructor. The locale for French-speaking Canadians can be created like this:

```
locale = new Locale("fr", "CA");
```

Most often, the Locale object is passed to a utility method that formats output based on the Locale object's settings. Components that can alter their behavior by locality are called *locale-sensitive*. The locale is simply an identifier provided for informational purposes only. It's up to the locale-sensitive method to do the actual work of localization.

Several methods in the JVM are locale-sensitive and can render numbers, currencies, and dates using the conventions of a given locality:

```
NumberFormat.getInstance(myLocale)
NumberFormat.getCurrencyInstance(myLocale)
NumberFormat.getPercentInstance(myLocale)
```

A number of Struts components are also locale-sensitive and make use of a Locale object that the framework manages for each user. For more about the Struts i18n components, see section 13.2.

The Locale object can render user-friendly descriptions of its settings. This is helpful when you're displaying the current Locale setting to the user or when generating a list of supported Locales. Several methods are available for rendering the description that nicely fulfill the Locale object's role as an identifier. Most of these are overloaded so that you can also display the description in another Locale object. Table 13.3 shows two examples.

Table 13.3   Two overloaded methods for rendering the Locale object's description

Method	Purpose
getDisplayName()	Returns a name for the locale that is appropriate for display to the user
getDisplayName(Locale)	Returns a name for the locale that is appropriate for display to the user

The Locale object is immutable. If you need to change locales, a new Locale object must be created and used to replace the original. There are several ready-made Locale objects in the JVM for the commonly used locales. See the Java API for details (`java.util.Locale`).

ResourceBundle

When designing an internationalized application, you place your initial focus on the user interface. The various menus and dialog boxes used by an application are often called program *resources*. Many programming environments have been designed so that the user interface can be loaded from a separate file, or, in Java terminology, a *resource bundle*.

The Java *ResourceBundle* class (`java.util.ResourceBundle`) is not designed for reading in the application's entire user interface, but it is quite handy for storing the text and messages used with interface elements. Your application can request the bundle for a user's locale and retrieve the appropriate element. The same key is used for the element regardless of locale, but the `String` or `Object` it returns may be very different. To support another locale, just add a source file for that locale to your bundle.

DEFINITION   A *resource bundle* (`java.util.ResourceBundle`) is a collection of Properties objects (`java.util.Properties`). Each Properties object is keyed to a locality. Localities are identified by region and language using a Locale object (`java.util.Locale`). When a key is requested, a locale can also be specified. If a Properties object for the locale is not found in the bundle, the value from the closest matching locale is returned. In practice, ResourceBundles use the principle of inheritance. If the entry is not found for the closest locale, the next closest is checked, and so on. The bundle can include a default Properties object to be used when a better match is not found.

ResourceBundle is an abstract class with two stock implementations, ListResource-Bundle and PropertyResourceBundle.

The PropertyResourceBundle class (java.util.PropertyResourceBundle) is used to manage a set of text messages, and it is the one most commonly used with Struts applications. The messages can be loaded from a Properties file (java.util.Properties), usually with a call to a static method, like this:

```
message = ResourceBundle.getBundle("application",userLocale);
```

A Properties file is a simple text file that can be created with any plain text editor. The locale for each text file can be indicated using a simple naming convention. The language and country code is appended to the end of the filename, before the extension. The first argument in the preceding sample code, application, refers to a family of Properties files, like these:

```
application_es_ES.properties
application_fr_FR.properties
application.properties
```

A Properties file contains key-value pairs, called *entries*. The *key* is a token your application will use to retrieve a certain message. The *value* is the text to use as the message. The file for each locale can contain messages translated for the given language and country.

A Properties file for the es_ES locale (Spanish/Spain) might look like this:

```
greetings =  Hola
farewell =  Adios
inquiry =  Como estas?
```

Translated, the same set of properties for the fr_FR (French/France) locale would look like this:

```
greetings = Bonjour.
farewell = Au revoir.
inquiry = Comment allez-vous?
```

The default bundle is always used when the requested locale cannot be found. This means that you do not need to provide a separate bundle for your server's default locale. If your server's default locale is en_US, you can just provide an application.properties file and forego a duplicate application_en_US.properties file. You could just use this as the default application.properties file instead:

```
greetings = Hello
farewell = Goodbye
inquiry = How are you?
```

The Struts framework will automatically use the default ResourceBundle with its locale-sensitive components. See section 13.3 for the particulars of loading the default bundle.

The *ListResourceBundle* class (`java.util.ListResourceBundle`) can be used to load arbitrary non-`String` objects. The use of a ListResourceBundle is outside the scope of this chapter, but if it were used, the object could make use of the Locale object already managed by the framework. The same holds true for any standard Java, locale-sensitive object.

NOTE   For historical reasons, Struts 1.0 and Struts 1.1 do not use the actual ResourceBundle classes from the `java.util` package. However, the Struts versions are designed to work in the same way. For the purpose of developing your own applications, you can consider the classes interchangeable.

MessageFormat

To be useful, many messages must include runtime information or data particular to the instant user. These may be record numbers, or the current date, or an amount. In a non-internationalized application, we often concatenate `Strings` with runtime variables to create such messages, applying formatting along the way.

For an internationalized application, simple concatenation is not an option. The language elements being concatenated will vary from user to user and can't be hardcoded. Instead, message templates are loaded from a resource file and merged with other data. The *MessageFormat* class (`java.text.MessageFormat`) is designed to help you merge the message template with replaceable parameters at runtime.

A runtime message like this:

```
The disk named MyDisk contains 300 files.
```

can be based on a template like this:

```
The disk named {0} contains {1} files.
```

At runtime, the application can pass an array of objects to a formatter that merges the two together:

```
diskParameters[0] = (Object) diskName;
diskParameters[1] = (Object) fileCount;
formatter.applyPattern(messages.getString("disk.inventory"));
String output = formatter.format(diskParameters);
```

The first object in the array is merged with the {0} marker, the second with the {1} marker, and so forth.

As we will see in section 13.2, the Struts framework provides components that help you do the following:

- Manage a Locale object for each user.
- Automatically load a message bundle for your supported locales.
- Merge runtime parameters with message templates.

13.2 Struts' internationalized components

Before creating Struts, Craig McClanahan spent a couple of years telecommuting to Belgium to manage a software development project there. Many of the basic ideas for Struts originated with this web application, including its fundamental support for internationalization. Struts' worldwide popularity shows in its development team, which has members from Australia, France, Russia, Scotland, and even the United States. It is also interesting to note that, coincidentally, the illustration on the book depicts a character from the Bordeaux region, not so far from Brussels, Struts' ancestral home.

As shown in table 13.4, Struts provides several internationalized components that work together to help you localize your application.

Table 13.4   Struts' i18n components

Standard Locale object for each user	Session Locale attribute
Framework class for handling a message resource	MessageResources
Automatic loading of application-wide message templates	Default resource bundle
Special classes for queuing errors and other messages	ActionErrors and ActionMessages
Locale-sensitive view components	JSP tags

Let's take a look at how all these components fit together.

13.2.1 Session Locale attribute

As we saw in section 13.1.2, all of the standard Java localization tools rely on the Locale object. So the trick to localization then becomes maintaining a Locale object for each user.

The Java servlet framework provides a facility for temporarily storing an object for each user called the *session context*. By default, Struts will store a Locale attribute for each user in their session context under a known key. Initially, this attribute is set to the server's default locale. If your application replaces this object with one for the user's locale, the locale-sensitive objects in the framework will select messages written for the user's locale instead of the default locale.

NOTE But what about `ServletRequest.getLocale()`? This returns the locale set by the user's browser (passed via the HTTP Accept-Language header). Unfortunately, this setting is outside the application's direct control, and there is no guarantee that it has been set properly. For an alternative, Struts provides a locale in the session context that your application *can* control.

Of course, localization is not magic. The application must provide a set of messages for each locale it supports and provide a mechanism for selecting and updating the user's locale.

13.2.2 *MessageResources*

To streamline retrieving messages, Struts provides a *MessageResources* class (`org.apache.struts.util.MessageResources`). Struts developers rarely call this object directly, but work through other classes that use MessageResources behind the scenes to return the appropriate message.

MessageResources describes an API for retrieving locale-sensitive messages. The API can also use the MessageFormat class to merge parameters and customize messages at runtime (`java.text.MessageFormat`). The MessageResources interface does not specify how or where the messages are stored, only how they are retrieved. The default implementation uses a standard PropertyResourceBundle, but, with some effort, any storage mechanism, such as an XML file or SQL database, could be used instead.

Typically, the messages will be retrieved by JSP tags or another presentation system. The Action can also prepare a localized message by calling Message-Resources. Here's an example of retrieving the user's locale from the session context, passing it to MessageResources to obtain the appropriate message for that locale, and storing it in a bean for later use:

```
Locale locale = (Locale) session.getAttribute(Action.LOCALE_KEY);
MessageResources messages = servlet.getResources();
String message = messages.getMessage(locale,"important.message");
((messageForm) form).setMessage(message);
```

The getMessages signature is overloaded so that it can take up to five replacement parameters ({0}...{4}):

```
String message = getMessage(locale,"important.message",new Date());
```

The parameters are often Strings but can be any Java object. When other objects are used, the MessageFormat class can help format the object. See section 13.3 for more.

There are also getMessage signatures that omit the Locale object. In this case, the default locale for the server is used.

13.2.3 *The default resource bundle*

The framework uses an instance of MessageResources to provide access to a default resource bundle, loaded by the controller servlet. Each resource in the bundle is loaded from disk the first time it is needed and then retained in memory for the life of the application. The other Struts i18n components will retrieve message templates from this bundle unless another is specified.

Since by default Struts uses standard Properties files and a standard Property-ResourceBundle, all the usual features apply for formatting your message strings, like those shown in table 13.5.

Table 13.5 Formatting features for resource property files

Feature	Template	Example
Literal character	\	WEB-INF\\lib
Single quote	''	Struts'' ancestral home
Special formatting	{#,type,style}	{2,real,currency}

Message formatting

Since the standard Java libraries are used, the conventional techniques for formatting numbers, dates, and currencies can be used with your Struts messages. For example, if a message involved a date, the Properties file for the resource bundle might read:

```
detected.ufo = At {2,time,short} on {2,date,long}, we detected
{1,number,integer} spaceships on the planet {0}.
```

A single date property could be passed to the message template as the second parameter. It would then be used to display the time and the date at separate points in the message.

If the user's locale were en_US:

```
At 1:15 PM on April 13, 1998, we detected 7 spaceships on the planet Mars.
```

If the user's locale were de_DE:

```
Um 13.15 Uhr am 13. April 1998 haben wir 7 Raumschiffe auf dem Planeten Mars
    entdeckt.
```

In the Action class, the Date object can be passed to ActionError or ActionMessage:

```
Date today = new Date(System.currentTimeMillis());
messages.addActionMessages.GLOBAL_MESSAGE,
    new ActionMessage("detected.ufo",ufoPlanet,ufoCount,today));
saveMessages(requestmessages);
```

Displaying special characters

The Java platform is fully Unicode-based and capable of rendering characters from any language. However, the Java compiler and other Java tools can process only files that contain Latin-1 [ISO 8859-1] or Unicode-encoded characters. A Unicode-encoded character is expressed using a /u escape sequence followed by the character's number in the Unicode set—for example, /u0084.

DEFINITION   *Unicode* provides a unique number for every character, no matter what the platform, no matter what the program, no matter what the language. It is supported in many operating systems, all modern browsers, and many other products. The emergence of the Unicode Standard, and the availability of tools supporting it, are among the most significant recent global software technology trends. [Sun, i18n]

To help convert files using characters outside the Latin-1 group, the JDK provides a utility called *native2ascii*. This converts a file with native-encoded characters (non-Latin 1 and non-Unicode) to one with Unicode-encoded characters. While a Unicode-encoded file would not make much sense to a human being, the Java components won't give it a second thought.

You can also use the Message Tool in the Java Internationalization and Localization Toolkit 2.0 [Sun, JILKIT] to do the same thing. The toolkit has a number of other utilities that you might find useful if you are translating files on a larger scale. It's definitely worth the download if you are managing several large resource files.

13.2.4 *ActionErrors*

As mentioned in the introduction to this chapter, the Struts workflow (submit/validate/correct/submit) is an essential part of the framework. When validation is performed, the method needs a way to pass error messages back to the input form, where they can be displayed to the user. The *ActionErrors* (`org.apache.struts.Action.ActionErrors`) object is used to carry these messages.

Since more than one error may be detected during validation, ActionErrors is a collection. Any number of error messages can be queued and displayed to the user at once. Each message can be optionally associated with a particular property on the form. This gives developers the chance to display the error message next to its property.

Not surprisingly, ActionErrors is a collection of ActionError objects (`org.apache.struts.Action.ActionError`). Each error object holds the message key and an optional property name. The key is used to look up the message from a resource bundle (see section 13.1.2). To add an error message to the queue, a call like

```
errors.add(ActionErrors.GLOBAL_ERROR,
    new ActionError("prospect.statusDate"));
```

is used, where `prospect.statusDate` is a key in the resource bundle. Parameters can also be passed and merged into the message string:

```
errors.add(ActionErrors.GLOBAL_ERROR,
    new ActionError("record.updated",recordId));
```

When you have added all the errors you need, the collection can be saved to the request under a known key. The Action's `saveErrors` method can be used to do this:

```
saveErrors(request,errors);
```

Since it uses keys and resource bundles, localization support for ActionErrors is built in and will automatically display the correct message for each user's locale.

13.2.5 *ActionMessages*

ActionMessages (`org.apache.struts.Action.ActionMessages`) were introduced in Struts 1.1 along with a corresponding JSP tag. ActionMessages are intended to supplant the original ActionErrors, but, for backward compatibility, the original ActionError classes were left in place.

So, what's wrong with the ActionError classes? The design of the `<html:errors>` tag encouraged developers to place HTML markup in the messages file. But this can cause problems when the messages are reused in a different context, say in a

JavaScript. It also confuses language translators who may also be working with the file.

The ActionMessages tag (`org.apache.struts.taglib.html.MessagesTag`) provides additional functionality so that developers do not need to mix markup with messages. (See chapter 10 for more about the Struts JSP tags.)

Since they are meant as an enhanced version of the ActionErrors set, by default the message tags will use the ActionErrors queue. This makes it very easy to drop in ActionMessages where ActionErrors were previously used.

If you would like to pass both messages and errors, there is also a separate ActionMessages queue. To access the alternate queue, just call `saveMessages` instead of `saveErrors`

```
saveMessages(request,messages);
```

and then specify `messages=true` in the JSP tag:

```
<html:messages id="message" messages="true">
<bean:write name="message"/><BR>
</html:messages>
```

The `messages` queue can be used to send confirmation notices to the page, like *Record inserted* or *Message sent*. This leaves the `errors` queue open for actual *Houston, we have a problem* alerts. The same page could use the messages markup (see the previous code snippet) and also use the following markup to also display errors elsewhere on the page:

```
<html:messages id="error" messages="false">
<bean:write name="error"/><BR>
</html:messages>
```

In these examples, it is important to note that while the `<bean:write>` tag is being used to output localized data, it is not the locale-sensitive component. The `<html:messages>` tag pulls localized data from the ActionMessages or ActionErrors object, which in turn retrieves it from the default MessageResource object (a ResourceBundle).

In section 13.3, we look at other ways standard components can be used to output localized data. Several of the Struts tags do have locale-sensitive features, which we discuss in section 13.2.6.

13.2.6 *Locale-sensitive JSP tags*

We cover the fundamentals of using the Struts JSP tags in chapter 10. If you're just getting started with the Struts tags, you should read that chapter first. Here we focus on the localization features of the Strut tags.

As shown in table 13.6, the Struts tag libraries include several locale-sensitive tags. These tags can retrieve text messages from a resource bundle and customize the presentation for the instant user.

Table 13.6 Locale-sensitive tags

bean:message	html:file
bean:write	html:hidden
html:errors	html:multibox
html:html	html:password
html:image	html:radio
html:img	html:select
html:messages	html:submit
html:option	html:text
html:button	html:textarea
html:cancel	html:form
html:checkbox	html:link

Most of these tags simply offer keys for retrieving the alternative text and advisory title for an element. The image-related tags accept additional key properties to allow both the sources of the image and its alternate text to be localized. Table 13.7 summarizes the common property names in the locale-sensitive tags. The tags that use the property are listed as part of the description.

Table 13.7 Common property names in locale-sensitive tags

Property	Description and tags
arg0 ... arg4	Parametric replacement values, if any. [message write]
bundle	The name of the application scope bean under which the MessageResources object containing our messages is stored. If not specified, the default is used. [message write image img option errors messages]
key	The message key of the requested message that must have a corresponding value in the message resources. If not specified, the key is obtained from the name and property attributes. [message write image img option]
locale	The name of the session scope bean under which our currently selected Locale object is stored. If not specified, the default is used. [message write image img errors messages]
altKey, titleKey	The message resources key of the alternate text and advisory title for this element. [button cancel file hidden image img multibox password radio reset select submit text textarea]
titleKey	The message resources key for the advisory title. (No alternative text.) [form link]

Table 13.7 Common property names in locale-sensitive tags *(continued)*

Property	Description and tags
pageKey, srcKey	The key of the message resources string specifying the image for this input tag, either as an application-relative path or as a source URL. [image img]
formatKey	Specifies a key for a format string to retrieve from the application resources. [write]

Let's take a closer look at the more interesting tags: <bean:message>, <bean:write>, <html: errors>, <html:messages>, <html:html>, <html:image>, <html:img>, and <html:option>.

<bean:message>

<bean:message> is the primary JSP tag for rendering localized messages and labels. Although other tags can render error and confirmation messages, <bean:message> is most often used in HTML forms:

```
<html:cancel><bean:message key="button.cancel"/></html:cancel>
```

<bean:write>

In the Struts 1.1 release, <bean:write> gained the format property. This provides a way to apply a standard formatting template against the value being written:

```
<bean:write name="inputForm" property="amount" format="$#.##"/>
```

A formatKey property is provided that reads the template from the resource bundle:

```
<bean:write name="inputForm" property="amount" formatKey="pattern.currency"/>
```

A locale property is also provided if another Locale object is to be used instead of the framework's default. The locale property indicates the name of a session-scope attribute:

```
<bean:write name="inputForm" property="amount" formatKey="pattern.currency"
  locale="myLocale"/>
```

STRUTS TIP Don't use custom tags to format data. Instead, localize data inside an Action-Form or (even better) on the business tier. You can easily pass the Struts Locale object to the ActionForm (or your business bean) and apply the localization in the getter. To store the user's Locale object in your Action-Form, add a locale property and put this code in the reset method:

```
HttpSession session = request.getSession();
  if (session!=null) {
    setLocale((Locale)
```

```
                    session.getAttribute(Action.LOCALE_KEY));
  }
  else {
      setLocale(Locale.getDefault());
  }
```

You can then use the `locale` property with the standard MessageFormat objects. For more about using display properties to transform output, see chapter 5.

<html:errors> and <html:messages>

Both `<html:errors>` and `<html:messages>` will automatically print pending error messages from the resource for the user's locale. No additional effort is needed to localize these messages; it's already been done. For more about using the `<html:errors>` and `<html:messages>` tags in your application, see chapter 10.

<html:html>

Many browsers (or user agents) also support localization. Things that an internationalized user agent might localize include:

- Glyph variants for high-quality typography
- Quotation marks
- Decisions about hyphenation, ligatures, and spacing

To indicate to a user agent which language is being used on a page, you can provide a `lang` element within the standard `<HTML>` tag that encloses the rest of the markup. The corresponding `<html:html>` JSP tag creates this element automatically when Struts localization is enabled.

This could result in

```
<html:html> -> <html lang="en">
```

or

```
<html:html> -> <html lang="fr">
```

depending on the user's locale.

As a practical matter, your pages should localize fine without this element, but including it is a nice touch and may save you some trouble later.

<html:image> and <html:img>

Images in a web application often contain language elements. Images may also relate to a particular region or culture. The `<html:image>` and `<html:img>` tags provide properties that help you localize the images and image buttons in an application.

Consider these three factors when localizing an image or image button:

- The *source* of the binary image file
- The *alternative text* associated with the image
- The *advisory title* associated with the element

NOTE   The roles of the `alt` and `title` properties overlap when applied to an image. Refer to the HTML specification [W3C, HTML] for guidance on how these properties are to be used.

Each of these elements is represented by a property to the `<image>` and `<img>` tags, as shown in table 13.8. The `page` property allows the image URL to be given in application-relative terms.

Table 13.8   The `alt`, `title`, `src`, and `page` properties

Property	Description
`alt`	The alternate text of this element
`title`	The advisory title for this element
`src`	The URL of this image
`page`	The application-relative URI of the image

To support localization, a set of corresponding properties can be used instead that read the text or path from the resource file using a key. Table 13.9 describes these properties.

Table 13.9   The `altKey`, `titleKey`, `srcKey`, and `pageKey` properties

Property	Description
`altKey`	The message resources key of the alternate text of this element
`titleKey`	The message resources key of the advisory title for this element
`srcKey`	The message resources key of the URL of this image
`pageKey`	The message resources key of the application-relative URI of the image

These properties can be specified just like the corresponding properties:

```
<html:image pageKey="images.sign" altKey="images.sign.alt"
titleKey="images.sign.title">
```

This tag will insert the values assigned to the given keys from the resource file for the instant user's locale. This allows you to specify image files appropriate to each locale, along with translated `alt` and `title` elements.

<html:option>

The `<html:option>` tag usually accepts a `text` and a `value` property. The `text` property is displayed to the user. If the option is selected, the `value` is submitted with the request. To localize the `<option>` tag, you can specify a key in place of the text. This key will look in the resource file for the instant user and insert the value assigned to the given key.

Other properties

Each of these tags—`message`, `write`, `errors`, `messages`, `image`, `img`, and `option`— accept two other properties (shown in table 13.10) that you can use to fine-tune your localization effort.

Table 13.10   The `bundle` and `locale` properties

Property	Description
bundle	The name of an application-scoped attribute for an alternate MessageResources object
locale	The name of a session-scoped attribute for an alternate Locale object

These properties are provided because developers sometimes use separate bundles for certain elements, like images. An alternative locale is also sometimes useful in this case. In addition, these properties can be helpful when developers are migrating to Struts from another localized application.

13.3   *Localizing a Struts application*

Let's put it all together and step through the process of localizing a Struts application.

13.3.1 *Enabling localization*

There are just three points on the Struts localization checklist:

- Is the `locale` servlet parameter set correctly?
- Is the default `application` resource bundle parameter set correctly?
- Are localized JSP pages using the `<html:html>` tag?

Setting the locale servlet parameter

By default, the Struts framework will provide a Locale object in each user's session that any locale-sensitive component can use. Whether or not this object is automatically created is controlled by the `locale` parameter to the ActionServlet, which you set in the web application deployment descriptor (see chapter 4):

```
<init-param>
<param-name>
locale
</param-name>
<param-value>
true
</param-value>
</init-param>
```

The default is true, which enables localization.

Setting the application resources servlet parameter

The Struts locale-sensitive components rely on the MessageResources class, which in turn relies on the framework Locale object and the default application resource bundle. The location of the application resource file is also specified as a parameter to the Struts ActionServlet. The default is an empty string, so it is important that you specify a name for this file:

```
<init-param>
<param-name>
application
</param-name>
<param-value>
application
</param-value>
</init-param>
```

This tells the ActionServlet to look for a file named application.properties along the CLASSPATH. If a specific locale is requested, the ActionServlet will look for a file named application_*xx_XX*.properties, where _*xx_XX* is a given locale, like _fr_CA or _es_US (see also section 13.2).

You can also specify the default resource bundle as being part of a package:

```
<init-param>
<param-name>
application
</param-name>
<param-value>
resources.application
</param-value>
</init-param>
```

This example implies that your resources files can be found under

```
<app-context>/WEB-INF/classes/resources/application.properties
<app-context>/WEB-INF/classes/resources/application_fr_CA.properties
<app-context>/WEB-INF/classes/resources/application_es_US.properties
```

or packaged as a JAR in the WEB-INF/lib folder.

Generally, you would want to keep the properties with your other source files, and so you should make copying these into the classes directory part of the Ant build process. If your source files were under /WEB-INF/src/java, such an Ant task would look like this:

```
<target name="resources">
<copy todir="classes" includeEmptyDirs="no">
<fileset dir="src/java">
<patternset>
<include name="**/*.properties"/>
</patternset>
</fileset>
</copy>
</target>
```

This copies any *.properties files found in any of your source packages to the classes file tree.

Whenever the Properties files are stored in a directory outside /WEB-INF/, be sure to build the application after any change to the resource Properties files. The updated file must be deployed under classes where the application can find it. Whether or not an updated resource bundle is automatically reloaded depends on your container.

STRUTS TIP   Use Ant to build *and deploy* your application for you. Along with compiling your Java classes, Ant can also copy source, configuration, and JSP files from your source tree to your deployment tree. See the Artimus application in chapter 15 for a working example.

See chapter 4 for more about the ActionServlet parameters and Ant build files.

13.3.2 *Using the framework Locale object*

With localization enabled, the Struts ActionServlet places a Locale object in the user's session. The object is placed there for the benefit of the entire application. As we explained in section 13.2, the Struts i18n components will automatically make use of this object when it is present, and your components can do the same.

Checking the user's locale

You can retrieve the framework Locale object in an Action, like this:

```
Locale locale = request.getSession().getAttribute(Action.LOCALE_KEY);
```

If you base your Actions on the BaseAction class in the Scaffold package, you can use this instead:

```
Locale locale = getLocale(request); // BaseForm version
```

You can then pass this object to any locale-sensitive method, including those in the standard `java.text` package. This makes it easy to create localized data in the Action and pass it along to the presentation layer, ready to display.

Changing the user's locale

When the user's session is first created, the ActionServlet will simply create a default Locale object for the user. If the user is not in the default Locale for the application server, your application will need to replace the Locale object. Since Locale objects are not mutable, you *do* have to replace it with a new object. Of course, the best place to do this is in an Action, using code like this:

```
Locale locale = new Locale(myForm.getLanguage(),myForm.getCountry());
HttpSession session = request.getSession(true);
session.setAttribute(Action.LOCALE_KEY,locale);
```

If your Action is based on the Scaffold package's BaseAction, you can do this instead:

```
Locale locale = new
    Locale(myForm.getLanguage(),myForm.getCountry());
setLocale(request,locale);
```

If your application only localizes by language, an empty string can be used for the country.

Using the Struts locale-sensitive components

With Struts localization enabled, and the user's framework Locale object property set, the Struts locale-sensitive components will automatically localize data. See section 13.2 for more about using these components in your application.

13.3.3 Placing labels and messages in Properties files

By default, Struts uses a standard Properties file for the labels and messages used in your application. This is a simple text file that you can create with any text editor. The file itself is just a list of key-value pairs. The key is what your application passes in its request. The value is the label or message to be returned. See section 13.2.3 for more default properties files.

13.3.4 Creating language-specified Properties files

Your application will have a Properties file for every locale you will support. If properly named, these files will be loaded automatically. You just need to get the values translated and the new file stored where the application can find it (see section 13.3.1). If the application cannot find a key in the resource for a user's locale, it will use the resource for the default locale instead.

13.3.5 Specifying an appropriate key in localization-aware components

As outlined in section 13.2, the Struts locale-sensitive components will accept a key into the resource bundle and output the appropriate label or message for the current user. For more about each of these components, see section 13.2.

13.3.6 Using <bean:message> with other components

For components that do not have localization built in, you can usually use <bean:message> to provide the localized message. For example, to create a localized Cancel button, have <bean:message> provide the value:

```
<html:cancel><bean:message key="buttons.cancel"></html:cancel>
```

For a user in a German locale, this might render a button labeled *Abbrechen*. In a Norwegian locale, it might render *Kanseller.*

13.4 *Localizing other components*

To complete your internationalization task, you must also localize other parts of your application. These include any Struts add-ins, such as the Struts Validator and Tiles, as well as the collections your Action may pass to HTML elements.

13.4.1 *Localizing the Struts Validator*

The Struts Validator, covered in chapter 12, uses an XML configuration file to validate user input. This configuration can be used to generate JavaScript using a JSP tag. The same configuration can also be used by the Struts ActionForm `validate` method.

The Validator's configuration file is composed of one or more `FormSet` elements, which correspond to the `form-bean` elements in the Struts configuration. Each `FormSet` is composed of a collection of `Field` elements. Each `Field` element can have its own validation settings. The settings include labels and messages to display when the `Field` element's validation fails.

All the labels and messages used by the Validator are linked to the Struts message resource and will be automatically localized. If additional localization is needed, say to verify the format of a postal code or telephone number, you can also define a locale-specific `FormSet` element. A locale-specific `FormSet` element acts like a subclass of the default `FormSet`—you can just define the fields that change.

Given a default `FormSet` like this:

```
<form name="registrationForm">
<field property="name" depends="required">
<arg0 key="registrationForm.name.displayname"/>
</field>
<field property="address" depends="required">
<arg0 key="registrationForm.address.displayname"/>
</field>
<field property="postOffice" depends="required">
<arg0 key="registrationForm.postOffice.displayname"/>
<var>
<field property="postalCode" depends="required,mask">
<arg0 key="registrationForm.postalCode.displayname"/>
<var>
<var-name>mask</var-name>
<var-value>^\d{5}\d*$</var-value>
</var>
</field>
</form>
```

an application can provide an alternate validator for the `postalCode` field like this:

```
<form name="registrationForm" locale="fr" country="CA">
<field property="postalCode"
depends="required,mask">
<arg0 key="registrationForm.postalCode.displayname"/>
<var>
<var-name>mask</var-name>
<var-value>^[a-zA-Z]*$</var-value>
</var>
</field>
</form>
```

For more about the Struts Validator, see chapter 12.

13.4.2 Localizing Tiles

We covered the Tiles framework in chapter 11. As you saw, the powerful Tiles Definition feature allows you to create a high-level description of your application pages that builds the view up from smaller fragments. You can store the Definitions in an XML configuration file, much like the configuration files for Struts and the Struts Validator.

Just as you can create a Properties file for specific locales, you can also create a Tiles configuration file for each locale. You follow the same conventions. If you needed a Tiles configuration file for the French Canadian locale, it would be named

```
tiles_fr_CA.xml
```

and stored next to the default tiles.xml file.

In the locale-specific file, you need to replace only the Definitions that change. If an application does not find a Definition in a configuration for the user's locale, it uses the Definition in the default configuration instead.

This makes it very easy to create entire sub-sites that are locale specific. Just create a Tiles Definition file for each locale and change the paths in the Definitions to point to the localized version of each Tile. That way, you can reuse the layout tiles so that the site has a consistent look and feel, but change all the content tiles so that the site reads well in each locale.

13.4.3 Localizing collections

Some of the Struts JSP tags display select lists to the user based on a collection. Since these collections are often passed to the page from the Action, the Action has the opportunity to localize the collection before it is passed along.

<html:options>

The `<html:options>` tag supports two parallel lists: one for the values (what will be returned to the server for this field) and one for the labels (what the user sees in the combo box). The challenge is to select the labels in a locale-sensitive way without modifying the values.

In the Action, create an array or ArrayList (`java.util.ArrayList`) under a request attribute named `values` for the values component. Build a corresponding ArrayList or array under `labels` that does the MessageResource lookups based on the user's locale.

The MessageResource can be obtained from the servlet:

```
org.apache.struts.utils.MessageResources resources = servlet.getResources();
```

The locale can be obtained from the request:

```
Locale locale = request.getSession().getAttribute(Action.LOCALE_KEY);
```

And together they are used to look up the localized messages for each value:

```
String[] messages = new String[keys.length];
for (int i=0; i<keys.length; i++) {
  messages[i] = resources.getMessage(locale,keys[i]);
}
```

To save you the trouble of coding this, the Scaffold package provides a `getMessages` method in the MessageUtils class (`org.apache.scaffold.text.MessageUtils`) that does the same thing:

```
String[] messages = MessageUtils.getMessages(resources,locale,keys);
```

A similar method can also return a collection of LabelValueBeans if you prefer to use those instead:

```
ArrayList labelValueBeans =
  MessageUtils.getLabelValueBeans(resources,locale,keys);
```

For more about the `<options>` tag and LabelValueBeans, see chapter 10.

<html:multibox>

The `<html:multibox>` tag uses a collection of values to generate a set of checkbox elements. If the values and labels match, you can generate a set of checkboxes like this:

```
<logic:iterate id="item" property="items">
  <html:multibox property="selectedItems">
    <bean:write name="item"/>
  </html:multibox>
```

```
        <bean:write name="item"/>
    </logic:iterate>
```

If you need localized labels for your checkboxes, you can use `MessageUtils`. `getLabelValueBean()` to create localized labels, and use those instead:

```
<logic:iterate id="item" property="labelValueBeans">
    <html:multibox property="selectedItems">
        <bean:write name="item" property="value"/>
    </html:multibox>
        <bean:write name="item" property="label"/>
</logic:iterate>
```

13.5 *Summary*

In this chapter, you learned why so many developers localize their applications and how Java internationalization works. Since Struts builds directly on Java's internationalization, localizing Struts components takes very little effort. The popular Struts add-ins, Jakarta Tiles and the Struts Validator, are also easy to localize. The same techniques used to localize other Struts components can be applied to other objects, such as Collections.

This chapter covered only the highlights of the Java internationalization features. For more extensive coverage, see the Sun Java Tutorial, Internationalization Trail [Sun, i18n].

14

Using data services
with Struts

This chapter covers

- Understanding why and how applications use databases and other data services
- Integrating your application with a data service
- Using layers when connecting with a data service
- Defining the business layer of an application
- Connecting data access components with the business layer
- Connecting other data services, such as search engines and content syndication, with the business layer

There is a tendency to mistake data for wisdom.
—Norman Cousins (1912–1990), American editor, author

14.1 Stepping out

In addition to storing and retrieving their own data, today's applications need to access a variety of data maintained by others. Each system might have its own method, or protocol, for transmittal and storage. These include authentication services using the Lightweight Directory Access Protocol (LDAP) and publishing systems using XML.

Today's applications may also need to offer different "perspectives" on the same data. In addition to standard database retrievals, an application might require full-text search capabilities so that people can find the straws lost in our abundant haystacks. An application might also want to share its hard-earned content with others, using services like Rich Site Summary (RSS).

This chapter shows how your application can attach to various data services like these without compromising its design. We explore specific examples of using a database, a search engine, and content syndication in an application, but the techniques shown should be applicable to any data service. The strategies follow the classic Layers pattern [POSA] that is used throughout the Struts framework.

Let's look at how a familiar duo—a JDBC driver and its database—fit into the Layers pattern.

14.1.1 JDBC from a patterns perspective

From a patterns perspective, the JDBC driver used by a conventional database is part of the integration layer, while the actual database lives in the resource layer.

To the developer, the exchange between the driver and the database is transparent. It appears as if the application is talking directly to the database, but in fact Java is providing a thin layer between the two components. This arrangement is illustrated in figure 14.1. The benefit of this approach is that a developer can change databases without changing how the databases talk to the driver. All JDBC drivers accept SQL statements in the same way, even if the underlying databases do not.

Uncovering the business layer

The *driver:device*, or *facade*, pattern used by the JDBC driver is a strategy you can use when integrating any data service. In general, all your applications want to say is, "I have this piece of data; take care of it for me" or "What is the rest of the

Figure 14.1   The application talks to the driver, and the driver talks to the database.

record for this identifier?" The design goal is to provide an interface (or driver) that the application can use without it having to know anything about the data service behind that interface.

The part of an application that says, "This is what I have and this is what I want" is commonly called the business layer, or Model (the *M* in MVC). It's what makes your application different from all other applications.

Just as a Java application connects to a JDBC driver (which connects to a database), most pundits [Go3] advise that you have your application connect to a business layer, which then connects to an integration layer. The integration layer accesses the database and returns the result to the business layer, as shown in figure 14.2.

Figure 14.2   The application that Jack built [Jack]. The application connects to the business layer, which connects to the integration layer, which connects to the resource layer (JDBC), which connects to the database.

The hallmark of the Layers pattern is that a class within a given layer may only interact with other classes in that layer or with classes in an adjacent layer. By layering your code, coupling within the application is reduced, and your application becomes easier to maintain and enhance [Ambler]. We put this principle into practice throughout this chapter as we attach different data services to a single application.

Of course, like a lot of good advice, creating separate business and integration layers is a step often ignored in practice. Many applications connect directly to the resource layer (and have developers who live to regret it). The business and integration layers are still there, but they are buried in SQL commands, which makes it hard to see the forest for the trees.

14.1.2 *Introducing our data services*

For the purposes of this chapter, let's follow the best practice and hook Struts up to different data services using the recommended layers [Go3]. We start with a working example of a business layer and then hook that up to different implementations of the integration and resource layers.

First, we connect to a JDBC database service using the StatementUtils and ResultSetUtils classes from the Scaffold package. This is a simple, baseline strategy that uses reflection and metadata to transfer a SQL ResultSet into a collection of JavaBeans. You have to define the JavaBeans and SQL statements yourself, but the system is easy to understand and use.

Then, we step out of the "database box" and hook up with Lucene, a popular full-text search engine. Lucene is another open source product hosted at Jakarta. Adding Lucene to our resource layer is an important proof of concept. Here we show that a good layered design lets you integrate new services into your application without disruption.

Finally, we demonstrate how easy it can be to continue adding services, like Rich Site Summary (RSS), to your application. RSS is a great way for your application to selectively share information with others and is already a web services standard.

Our focus throughout the chapter is mainly on the *techniques* used to attach these products to your business layer, rather than the products themselves. The Struts framework is model-neutral and can be used with any general-purpose data access tool. You can deploy these examples as is or use them as a guide to attaching your own data-access solution.

14.2 *Exploring the business layer*

In the introduction to this book, we discussed the Model-View-Controller (MVC) pattern. Using this terminology, the business layer is part of the Model along with the aforementioned resource and integration layers. Development projects start by designing some type of business layer (even if they don't realize it) and then attach the resource and integration layers (even if they are all jumbled together). Accordingly, we first explore the ins and outs of the business layer and then attach our database system.

14.2.1 *Struts—bringing your own Model*

I like to say that Struts is a BYOM (Bring Your Own Model) framework. It brings data up from the HTTP layer and stops. Getting data to the Model and back again is an exercise that the framework leaves to the developer. The Struts User Guide

[ASF, Struts] recommends that we fill this void with *business logic beans,* also known as *business objects.* But just what are business objects, anyway? Not surprisingly, they are the movers and shakers of the business layer.

14.2.2 *Defining business objects*

We've already touched on business objects in chapter 8, as part of our discussion of Action objects. In general terms, the business objects can be the hardest part of an application to describe because they *are* the application. They represent the logic that makes your application different from every other application: your API.

To define the business objects, you must first isolate your application's core business logic. If your application relies on a JDBC database, then most of your API may be represented by your SQL queries. If so, your business object will look like a punch list of the queries your application uses (or will use). If you are using prepared statements, there will also be a close relationship between the replaceable parameters and the parameters to your bean's methods.

Here's a sample query from a poll application. It's used to tell whether someone from a given IP (host) has already voted in an online poll:

```
public static final String RESP_VOTED =
    "SELECT COUNT(*),poll,host FROM polls_resp " +
    "WHERE poll=? AND marked=0 AND host=? GROUP by poll;";
```

From a business logic perspective, however, we don't really care what the SQL command looks like. We just want to ask if a given voter is eligible to vote in a given poll. The signature for an eligibility method could look like this:

```
boolean isEligible(String poll, String host);
```

The method takes just two `String`s, one to identify the poll and another to identify the voter. There's no mention of SQL or HTTP, just the bottom line of who and what.

From a web application's perspective, the *who* is usually an IP address (or the RemoteHost). The *what* is something that would be passed in from a data-entry form (as represented by a Struts ActionForm). Here's how a Struts application might call the `isEligible()` business method. Remember that the method is only looking for `String`s; it doesn't care where they come from:

```
boolean voted = Access.isEligible(
    pollForm.getPoll(), request.getRemoteHost()
);
```

This call could be used in a Struts Action class. The Action just takes data from the ActionForm and request, both denizens of the web tier, and passes it along to the business object. The Action has no clear idea what the business object does with the data or what it means to be "eligible." It just knows that it needs to pass these `Strings`, catch this `boolean`, and watch for an exception. If the method comes back false, the Action can do one thing. If it comes back true, the Action can do something else. But that's all the Action needs to know.

This same pattern would hold true for any client that used this business object. The client acquires the data and interprets the result, but determining the result is delegated to another object.

So, is this a Business Delegate pattern? Yes, this strategy is an example of the Business Delegate pattern described in *Core J2EE Patterns* [Go3].

Does this work with Enterprise JavaBeans? Yes. You could change the implementation of a business method to use EJBs, and the rest of the application would not know the difference. The data requirements of a business method are the same regardless of the technology used to access the persistent store.

14.2.3 *Designing business objects*

To be an effective middleman, a business object should avoid dependencies on other classes and be as self-contained as possible (for example, it should be weakly coupled). Ideally, *business methods* should accept and return properties using ordinary Java types and throw their own set of exceptions.

So, business logic beans should:

- Represent the core logic of your program—its API
- Accept and return native Java types and classes as parameters when possible
- Define their own class of exceptions
- Expose minimal dependencies to other classes

Why a bean? A business object doesn't really have to follow the JavaBean specification. The other components of its design are much more important than the object's calling conventions. But if you are creating a new class these days, it's just as easy to follow the JavaBean design patterns, which cost little and gain much. For more about designing JavaBeans, see Sun's JavaBean Tutorial Trail [Sun, Trails] and the JavaBean Specification [Sun, JBS].

Why throw our own exceptions? First, to provide encapsulation. If we throw a SQL exception, we reveal a dependency on SQL, even if we decide to use something else later. Second, to provide control. By throwing its own version, a business object can interpret an exception and provide a more meaningful response. By using chained exceptions (see chapter 8), a business object can throw its own exception along with any underlying exception from another package. For more about writing Exception classes, see the online article "Exceptional Practices" [Goetz].

For more about business logic and the business object pattern, see section 14.1 of the J2EE Blueprints [Sun, Blueprints].

14.2.4 *Design consequences*

Table 14.1 describes some general consequences of using a business layer and business objects in your applications.

Table 14.1 **Design consequences of separating the business layer**

Consequence	Explanation
Reduces coupling, improves manageability	A business object reduces coupling between the client and the implementation details. This makes it easier to manage changes to an implementation, since the details are encapsulated within the business object.
Introduces an additional layer	Some people might feel that the integration layer is unnecessary and want to connect to the resources directly.
Provides a simple, uniform interface	A business object's signature shows exactly what inputs are required, and what output is desired, without the complication of implementation details.
May hide inefficiencies	Since the implementation is hidden, a developer may not realize that a remote resource is being accessed or that several queries are being executed and be careless with how often a business method is invoked.

14.2.5 *Mixing business with Actions (not)*

If a business layer is *not* used, there are number of Struts-specific consequences to consider:

- When people write their first Struts application, they often access a database directly from an Action class. This does work, but applications designed in this way can grow to become difficult to expand and maintain. The problems are similar to those discovered with Model 1 JSP applications.

- Any logic implemented in an Action cannot be used outside of the Struts framework or properly tested with tools like JUnit [JUnit].

- Data access, error handling, and other resource-layer code may be duplicated among Actions, and reused only through cut and paste.

- Critical elements, like SQL commands, can become buried and difficult to review.

- Actions become the application interface, encouraging developers to forward requests between Actions.

- When Actions become the API, new mechanisms are needed, either to create intermediate query strings or to have an Action check for semaphore objects in the request.

- Actions become complex and bloated as they try to handle business logic requests from both clients and other Actions.

- As Actions become interdependent and cohesive, the application can devolve into a morass of spaghetti code, as we have often seen happen with Model 1 JSP applications.

As discussed earlier, a better approach is to continue with the classic MVC pattern and cleanly separate what happens on the web and application tiers (the View and the Controller) from what happens on the business tier (the Model). For more about MVC, see the introduction to this book and the Struts User Guide [ASF, Struts].

14.2.6 *A simple example*

Let's take a look at the business API for the Artimus sample application. The balance of the chapter will then describe attaching a database to this API and then explain how to add the Lucene search engine to the mix.

Artimus is an application for posting news articles. The articles can be searched in various ways and also syndicated. It's a simple but useful application. Let's look at the initial business requirements.

Artimus—initial business requirements

Simply put, the initial business requirements for Artimus are:

- Store the title, author, and content of an article.
- List recent articles by descending entry order (newest to oldest).
- Filter and list articles by title, author, content, and other properties.

We'll be adding more requirements to this list later, but first let's take a look at a business API that realizes this set.

Artimus—starter API

A starter API for Artimus is shown in table 14.2.

Table 14.2   Sample API for Artimus application

Requirement	Method
Store the article	`int` **`insert`** `(Integer article, String title, String creator, String content)`
List recent articles	`Collection` **`searchLast`** `(int count)`
Filter articles	`Collection` **`searchTitle`**`(String value)`

For the balance of this chapter, we implement the Artimus business requirements using APIs like this one. We also add requirements regarding full-text searches and content syndication and then implement the requirements without changing the business API.

14.3 Using ProcessBeans and JDBC with Struts

There are several products that offer object-to-relational (O/R) mapping between a hierarchy of JavaBeans and a relational database. Products like these let you concentrate on the design of your object hierarchy and then automatically generate the SQL code needed to map your hierarchy to a relational database. Scott Ambler has written two classic white papers on O/R modeling and designing a persistence layer, both of which we highly recommend [Ambler].

The ProcessBean class uses the techniques broadly described in the Struts User Guide [ASF, Struts] in its discussion of business logic beans. These techniques include:

- Encapsulating the functional logic of an application
- Representing the state of a pending transaction, such as a shopping cart
- Avoiding use of classes from the web tier (for example, the http packages)
- Avoiding any code that presumes interaction with a web application
- Providing an `execute` (or equivalent) trigger method, to engage a specific behavior

In addition, a ProcessBean

- Uses a bulk setter to populate itself from another JavaBean
- Uses a bulk "populator" to copy values to another JavaBean

The ProcessBeans class is *not* an implementation of O/R mapping. Rather than encapsulate or hide the SQL, the ProcessBeans package provides a structured place where you can insert your query and get a collection of JavaBeans in return.

It also autopopulates your model beans from other beans (for example, Action-Forms) and moves data from a SQL ResultSet into a collection of your JavaBeans as quickly as possible. This final step may resemble O/R mapping, but the overall strategy is far too simple to earn the O/R stripe.

14.3.1 *Introducing ProcessBeans*

To get started, it's useful to think of the ProcessBeans as typed versions of the Struts ActionForm beans. The ActionForm beans need to use only `String` and `boolean` properties, mostly to remain compatible with HTTP. The ProcessBeans don't have that restriction and can use whatever types best represent your data.

So where you might have an ActionForm like this:

```
private String account = null;
public String getArticle() {
    return (this.account);
}
public void setArticle(String account) {
    this.account = account;
}
private String amount = null;
public String get Amount() {
    return (this.amount);
}
public void set Amount(String amount) {
    this.amount = amount;
}
```

you could have a ProcessBean like this:

```
private Integer account = null;
public Integer getArticle() {
    return (this.account);
}
public void setArticle(Integer account) {
    this.account = account;
}
private Double amount = null;
public Double getAmount() {
    return (this.amount);
}
public void set Amount(Double amount) {
    this.amount = amount;
}
```

Like ActionForm beans, ProcessBeans do *not* need to be direct representations of the tables in some database. They represent the business model as realized by the business API. Of course, the database will also represent the business model, and so the properties of these components will often intersect. Sometimes, the set of properties may even be identical. But that is a coincidence and not a design goal.

In relation to the database, the properties of a ProcessBean will intersect with the values needed by a SQL query and the columns returned in a result set. This is a necessity since the results of the queries are used to populate the ProcessBeans (and vice versa). Sometimes these properties happen to be all the columns from a single table. More often, the properties are a set of columns joined from several tables, or a *logical view.*

This is an important distinction. The purpose of the layers is to let the business objects be business objects and let the database be a database. Coupling these components too closely leads to brittle applications that are difficult to maintain. Over time, the way a database stores values may change. Columns that were in one table may be moved to another. Or the database may be replaced by some other component, such as a search engine. For these reasons, and many others, it is important for the resource and business layers to be loosely coupled and not allowed to become a monolithic lump.

So, again, ProcessBeans do not represent tables in a database; they represent logical views of the database. What properties belong in these logical views is determined by the business API.

Is the logical view the presentation View described by the MVC pattern? The MVC pattern would consider these separate objects. But, essentially, yes, we are talking about the same set of properties. We were careful to use the phrase *logical view* here, since the term has its own meaning in reference to databases. The same set of values is simply transferred from one object to another along the way.

14.3.2 *ProcessBeans as transfer objects*

Since they are intended to carry data from one layer to another, ProcessBeans can be seen as transfer objects, the flipside of ActionForm. Within the actual model, each property of a process bean may be available separately. But to avoid having to send each property individually, we collect them together into a single object that can be transferred with as a single operation.

Depending on the circumstances, some transfer objects may be read-only, or *immutable.* Here, the values are set when the object is constructed and not allowed to be changed later. (No public setters, or *mutators,* are provided.) Most often, this occurs in Enterprise JavaBean environments where the database is remote and updates are expensive. Immutable beans can specialize in displaying data as needed while another bean is used for judicious inserts and updates.

Since ProcessBeans are usually designed for use with local resources, they are also usually read-write, or *mutable*. Like many transfer object implementations, a ProcessBean uses a bulk mutator to set all its values at once. But unlike most transfer objects, a ProcessBean will usually make good use of reflection in its bulk setter.

14.3.3 *Populating ProcessBeans*

The Struts ActionServlet autopopulates ActionForm beans from an incoming HTTP request. The utilities Struts uses to do this can also be used separately and can populate any bean from another.

ProcessBean is actually an interface that defines two main signatures:

```
public Object execute() throws Exception;
public Object execute(Object parameters) throws Exception;
```

The ProcessBeanBase class provides an implementation of the execute(Object) method that uses reflection to populate any properties provided by a subclass. To work this wizardry, ProcessBeanBase uses methods from BeanUtils.

1.0 vs 1.1 In Struts 1.0, the BeanUtil class is provided in the Struts util package. Post 1.0, it was moved to the Jakarta Commons and is provided as a standalone package (jakarta.commons.BeanUtils). [ASF, Commons]

If you subclass your own ProcessBeans from ProcessBeanBase, the default implementation of execute(Object) can be used as is and doesn't need to be overridden. The magic of reflection will find whatever public properties you add.

Is reflection performant? Yes. Each release of the JVM has made improvements in the efficiency of reflection, and release 1.4 is a significant advance. The use of reflection eliminates scads of custom code that simply calls getters and setters. Instead, a single utility routine can be used throughout the application to do the same thing. In practice, this utility code will tend to stay in the JVM's execution cache and be optimized by a Java HotSpot compiler and may be more performant than any alternative.

14.3.4 *Executing ProcessBeans*

The other ProcessBean execute method has the ProcessBean do whatever it was designed to do. This could be inserting data, returning a result, or whatever operation is required.

The usual strategy is to create a base bean with the properties required by your business model. This base object is then extended for each business process required by your model. To populate the bean, you can pass a Map (`java.util.Map`) of the required properties to `execute(Object)`. The default implementation will populate any match properties and trigger the `execute` method to finish the job.

The `execute` methods return an object. Usually, this will be a ProcessResult object. The ProcessResult is designed to convey the result of a business operation to another layer (making it another transfer object). The ProcessResult may contain messages, data, or both, and it includes methods that can be used to automate processing the result.

If the business operation returns data, the data is usually contained in a ResultList object (`org.apache.commons.scaffold.util.ResultList`). This is a Collection (`java.util.Collection`) with some helper methods to make it easy to use with presentation pages. The ResultList is designed to take the place of a ResultSet (`java.sql.ResultSet`) so that you can work with disconnected Java-Beans instead.

If you subclass your own model beans from ProcessBeanBase, you need to:

- Add your properties. The use of the object wrappers, such as `Integer`, is recommended.

- Override `execute()` to perform the appropriate operation.

Since the interface signature accepts and returns `Object`, be sure to document the actual return type and the expected parameters.

14.3.5 *Accessing data services*

The ProcessBeans used by Artimus use a static class, named Access (`org.apache.artimus.article.Access`), to connect the business layer to the resource layer. This is not a requirement but simply a useful convention. The Access class represents the actual business API. The ProcessBeans represent the client objects using the API.

Under the hood, the Access class puts SQL commands together with SQL statements and prepared statements and plays the role of data access object. If you need to use more than one implementation, Access could be based on an interface, with the ProcessBeans connecting to a singleton rather than a static class.

The implementations of an Access class tend to be very simple. Scaffold provides some handy utilities for using SQL statements and prepared statements. The Access class puts these together with the appropriate SQL command and the runtime data passed by the bean. Listing 14.1 shows the `findByArticle` access method (`org.apache.artimus.article.Access.findByArticle`).

Listing 14.1   The findByArticle access method

```
public static final void findByArticle(
        Object target,
        Integer key) throws ResourceException {

    findElement(target,key,ARTICLE_SELECT_KEY);

} // end findByArticle
```

The static findElement method is provided by a base Access class. It in turn calls one of the Scaffold SQL utilities (org.apache.scaffold.StatementUtils). The implementation is shown in listing 14.2.

Listing 14.2   The findElement access method

```
public static final void findElement(
        Object target,
        Object key,
        String command) throws ResourceException {
    try {

        StatementUtils.getElement(null,target,
            getCommand(command),key);
    }
    catch (SQLException e) {
        throw new ResourceException(e);
    }
} // end findElement
```

The getElement method populates the target JavaBean in exchange for the parameters shown in table 14.3.

Table 14.3   StatementUtils.getElement parameters

Parameter	Purpose	Value of the parameter in listing 14.2
resource	The name of a data resource; null indicates the default.	null
target	The bean that the program should populate with the matching columns from the first row in the result set.	target
command	The SQL statement that the program should execute. The result set the statement generates will be used to populate the target JavaBean.	getCommand(ARTICLE _SELECT_KEY)

Most of the other basic data access methods in Scaffold are based on a similar utility, `getCollection` (`org.apache.commons.scaffold.sql.StatementUtils.getCollection`). In this method, instead of populating the target bean, the target is used as a factory to instantiate a bean for every row in the result set.

The Scaffold StatementUtils package provides several convenience signatures for passing common replacement parameters, like a `String` or an `Integer`. Under the hood, these methods all lead to the same `executeUpdate` or `executeQuery` method. These methods extract the replacement parameters from an array and match them up with the parameters in the SQL queries. The convenience signatures simply take care of creating the array for you.

The `getCommand` method in listing 14.2 returns an ordinary SQL statement from a standard Properties file. This keeps the SQL queries out of the Java code and puts them where a database administrator can work with them. In the sql_article. properties file, our query is just listed as

```
article.select.key = SELECT
article,marked,contributed,contributor,creator,cost,title,content FROM
artimus_article WHERE article=?;
```

along with the other `article` queries.

14.3.6 *Following a typical flow*

The high points of a typical workflow using a ProcessBean are:

- The Struts ActionServlet passes a populated ActionForm to the `perform` or `execute` method of an Action.

- The Action creates, populates, and executes the appropriate ProcessBean.

- If errors occur, the Action catches the exceptions and routes control to an error or input page.

- If the operation is successful, the Action usually refreshes the ActionForm from the bean and posts the ResultList object to the request context.

We'll return to this topic later in the chapter in our discussion of helper actions. For now, let's look at a working example from Artimus.

14.3.7 *Coding a business activity*

Let's look at the code needed to provide the view-article-by-ID activity in Artimus.

The Struts ActionServlet passes a populated ActionForm to the `perform` or `execute` method of an Action. The ActionForm and Action are specified in the Struts configuration, using settings like these:

```
<!-- Article Form bean -->
<form-bean
    name="articleForm"
    type="org.apache.artimus.article.struts.Form"/>
<!-- View Article action mapping -->
    <action
        path="/article/View"
        type="org.apache.struts.scaffold.ProcessAction"
        parameter="org.apache.artimus.article.FindByArticle"
        name="articleForm"
        scope="request"
        validate="false">
    <forward
        name="success"
        path="/article/pages/View.jsp"/>
    </action>
```

NOTE   The current implementation of Artimus uses Tiles. For clarity, the code
presented here is for a pre-Tiles version of the application.

Table 14.4 describes the configuration settings.

Table 14.4   Struts configuration elements

Element or property	Purpose	Value of parameter in the example listing
`form-bean` element	Creates an ActionForm object.	
`name` property	Associates a logical name with the ActionForm.	ArticleForm
`type` property	Specifies the class to use for the Action-Form object.	org.apache.artimus.artimus.http. Form
`action` element	Creates an ActionMapping object.	
`path` property	Relates a URI with this mapping.	/search/Article
`name` property	The name of the ActionForm to populate from the request (if any).	ArticleForm
`type` property	The class of the Action object to associate with this mapping.	org.apache.commons.scaffold.util. ProcessBean
`parameter` property	A general-purpose property. In this case, it is used to specify the business object for the ProcessAction to instantiate. This usage is an extension to the core Struts framework.	org.apache.artimus.article. FindByArticle

Following the same pattern as the Struts ActionServlet, the Scaffold ProcessAction uses reflection to create and populate a helper object. The helper is specified as the parameter property to the ActionMapping. The process is automatic, and the populated helper's execute method is invoked by the ProcessAction without developer intervention. Listing 14.3 shows a ProcessBean for a FindByArticle operation.

Listing 14.3   A FindByArticle ProcessBean

```
package org.apache.artimus.article;

import org.apache.commons.scaffold.lang.ParameterException;
import org.apache.commons.scaffold.util.ProcessResult;
import org.apache.commons.scaffold.util.ProcessResultBase;

public class FindByArticle extends Bean {

public Object execute() throws Exception {
        // ❶
        if (null==getArticle()) {
            throw new ParameterException();
        }

        // ❷
        Access.findByArticle(this,getArticle());

        // ❸
        ProcessResult result = new ProcessResultBase(this);
        result.setSingleForm(true);
        return result;

    } // end execute

} // end FindByArticle
```

Our FindByArticle bean, shown in listing 14.3, extends an article bean class (org.apache.artimus.article.Bean). The Bean class (which extends org.apache. commons.scaffold.util.ProcessBeanBase) provides all the properties common to ProcessBeans. Its execute(Object) method automatically populates these properties from a Map passed as the method's parameter and then calls the execute() method, which is the only method defined in the FindByArticle class. At ❶, we look for our base article property and do a "last chance" validation. If our article parameter is missing, a ParameterException is thrown.

At ❷, our ProcessBean calls Access.findByArticle using itself as the target type and passing the title to match. The findByArticle data-access method will return the records matching the title as a FindByArticle bean. If we wanted to use another bean type instead, we could pass an instance of that type instead of this.

The API contract for the Artimus ProcessBeans is that they return a Process-Result object. So, at ❸, we wrap the `FindByArticle` bean in a ProcessResult before returning.

As you can see, the ProcessBean code is mainly handling the administrative details and making sure the API contracts are fulfilled. The actual data access is left to the `Access.findByArticle` method, as shown back in listing 14.1.

In listing 14.1, we see that the `findByArticle` method is just a wrapper around the `Access.findElement` method. Several ProcessBeans use this particular method, and so it makes sense to provide it as a utility. In other cases, the access method may be provided in the ProcessBean itself. The utilities provided by the Scaffold Access and StatementUtils classes make this easy to do.

This is the end of the stack. The row is now returned to the ProcessBean class, wrapped in a ProcessResult object. The ProcessBean, in turn, hands the Process-Result back to the ProcessAction.

The ProcessAction class provides a reusable infrastructure to handle exceptions and route control within an application. Exception handling and control flow are an important part of using Struts with business classes and data systems. We return to the Scaffold helper actions later in the chapter.

STRUTS TIP   *What if the names of the SQL columns don't match the bean property conventions?* SQL allows you to rename columns on the fly. So if you're stuck with column names like FIRST_NAME and LAST_NAME, you can alias them in the SQL statement like this:

```
Select FIRST_NAME firstName, LAST_NAME lastName
        From CUSTOMER_TABLE Where ...
```

When the statement returns, `setFirstName` and `setLastName` will now correspond to the FIRST_NAME and LAST_NAME columns.

14.3.8 *ProcessBeans as a persistence layer*

Taken together, the ProcessBeans and other Scaffold objects described here form a simple persistence layer. Table 14.5 shows how the Scaffold/Artimus classes map to the persistence layer classes described by Scott Ambler [Ambler].

Table 14.5 Comparing Scaffold classes to Ambler's persistence layer

Scaffold/Artimus class	Ambler class	Description
ProcessBean	PersistenceObject	Provides behavior needed by the business domain
Access	PersistenceCriteria	Provides behavior needed to retrieve, update, or delete collections of objects
StatementUtils, Statements	PersistenceMechanism	Provides access to the data services (database, search engine, and so forth)
`getCommand()`, commands	SqlStatement	Provides SQL statements
ConnectionAdaptor	PersistenceBroker	Provides connections to the persistence mechanisms (StatementUtils)

The classes in the Ambler design do provide more functionality than those presented here. For a large-scale project, you should consider a comprehensive data persistence package like Osage [Osage] or ObjectRelationalBridge [ASF, OJB].

14.3.9 *Using other persistence layers*

Of course, ProcessBeans are *not* the only persistence layer you can use with Struts. Since Struts is model-neutral, you should be able to use the persistence layer of your choice. The patterns we have shown here should be adaptable to any persistence product, from Simper [Simper] to EJBs [Sun, J2EE].

If you do not already have a persistence layer, one likely candidate is Jakarta ObjectRelationalBridge (OJB) [ASF, OJB]. ObjectRelationalBridge is a relatively new product but is quickly attracting a substantial user base. Other open source products to consider include Castor [Castor], Simpler [Simper], and Osage [Osage].

14.4 *Using result objects*

Once the data is retrieved, you still need to commute it to the presentation layer. While you can use standard classes, such as Vectors and ArrayLists, it is often more convenient to create a specialized wrapper. Internally, the wrapper can use a standard collection as its data store, but externally it can expose methods to simplify rendering a view of your data.

14.4.1 *ResultList methods*

A good example of such a wrapper is the ResultList class (`org.apache.commons.scaffold.util.ResultList`). The ResultList class provides several methods that are helpful when creating a page listing the result of a search, including those shown in table 14.6.

Table 14.6   Some ResultList methods for creating a page listing

Method	Description
int getSize()	Returns the number of elements on the result list
String getLegend()	Returns a description of the result list
Iterator getIterator()	Returns an iterator for the result list

Since these methods follow the standard JavaBean naming conventions, they are easy to use with the Struts tags. Here's some JSP code for writing a simple HTML table from a result list. You can find the full source at pages/article/Result.jsp in the Artimus example application:

```
<TABLE><TR><TD align="center" colspan="3">
<bean:write name="RESULT" property="size"/>
matches for
<bean:write name="RESULT" property="legend"/>
</TD></TR>
<logic:notEqual name="RESULT" property="size" value="0" >
<TR bgcolor="FFFFEE">
<TH>id</TH><TH>article</TH><TH>contributed</TH>
</TR>
<TR>
<logic:iterate name="RESULT" property="iterator" id="row">
<TD><bean:write name="row" property="article"/></TD>
<TD>
<html:link forward="article" paramName="row" paramProperty="key"
  paramId="key">
<bean:write name="row" property="title"/>
</html:link>
</TD>
<TD><bean:write name="row" property="contributed"/></TD>
</TR>
</logic:iterate>
</TR>
</logic:notEqual>
</TABLE>
```

This page can be used for a number of different searches: by key, by author, or by title, for example. Each of these terms sets a different description, or legend, for the search, so that you can customize the page for each search type.

Like ProcessBean, ResultList is based on an interface that is implemented in a base class (`org.apache.commons.scaffold.util.ResultList`) that you can use in your own applications.

ResultList extends Collection and can be used anywhere a Collection is used. Table 14.7 contains a list of methods that ResultList implements aside from the Collection members.

Table 14.7   The ResultList interface (sans Collection methods)

Method	Description
Iterator **getIterator**()	Returns an iterator for the result list
int **getSize**()	Returns the number of elements on the result list
String **getLegend**()	Returns a description of the result list
public void **setLegend**(String description)	Sets the description for the result list
public void **setLegend**(String value, String property)	Uses the value and property to set the description as ${property} = ${value}
boolean **addMessage**(String message)	Adds a confirmation message to the internal list
public boolean **populate**(Object o, int index) throws Exception	Populates the given object from the element at index—the value of o may change
Map get**DisplayName**	Returns the displayName map (a HashMap)
set**DisplayName**(Map displayName);	Assigns a new displayName list

14.5 *Using helper Actions*

A common strategy among Struts developers is to use a single Action for several related operations. This helps to reuse code and streamline flow, and reduces the number of classes in an application. The helper Actions in the Scaffold package take this idea to its logical conclusion and implement a set of framework Actions that can be reused for nearly all operations in an application.

The strategy used by the helper Actions is to associate a set of business objects with an ActionMapping. The business objects are instantiated, populated, and invoked. The Action concentrates on exception handling and flow control. The polymorphic business objects are called in due course without the Action actually knowing what they do. This allows you to "wire" the better part of a web application from the Struts configuration, just by specifying which business object classes are used by which ActionMappings.

We've been saying *helper Actions* since ProcessAction builds on a base class, BaseHelperAction. ProcessAction is specialized to work with ProcessBeans, while the BaseHelperAction can be used with any type of business object. If you like helpers but don't want to use ProcessBeans, you could use BaseHelperAction as the basis of your own hierarchy. Table 14.8 shows the package references for our Action hierarchy.

Table 14.8   The helper Actions

Classname	Full package name
BaseAction	`org.apache.struts.scaffold.BaseAction`
BaseHelperAction	`org.apache.struts.scaffold.BaseHelperAction`
ProcessAction	`org.apache.struts.scaffold.ProcessAction`

Even if you do not use the helper Action strategy, the various techniques used by these Actions may be useful in your own classes. See chapter 8 for more about reusable Action techniques.

14.6 *Using Lucene*

Databases are indispensable, but they do have limitations—especially when it comes to searching a text field. Table 14.9 contains database behaviors and their consequences.

Table 14.9   Database behaviors and consequences

Behavior	Consequence
ANSI SQL text searches are case-sensitive.	`Text` does not match `TEXT`.
A SQL wildcard query considers the parameter to be a single string.	`Wildcards` does not match `Wildcard`.
SQL queries can only be ordered by the content of a field.	The most likely (or relevant) matches are not listed first.
Most database systems are not indexed for text searches.	A search on a text field may not be performant.
Many database systems are not optimized for complex boolean queries.	Text searches using boolean operations can be a bottleneck.
Database systems can only search data stored within their own tables.	Information external to a database table cannot be searched.

A good search engine package, such as Jakarta's Lucene [ASF, Lucene], solves all of these problems and more by providing:

- Word-based full-text searches
- Efficient term-based boolean searches
- Date range searches
- Matches in order of relevance

Given a good layered design, attaching Lucene to your application is really very simple. Let's see how Artimus does it.

14.6.1 *searchProperties redux*

Earlier, in listing 14.1, we looked at a `findByArticle` method from Artimus. The production version of Artimus actually uses Lucene to search for properties:

```
public static final Collection findByProperty(
        Object target,
        String property,
        String value) throws ParameterException, PopulateException,
        ResourceException {

    return SearchUtils.getCollection(target,
        Engine.getHits(
            Engine.getQuery(value,property)));

} // end findByProperty
```

In response to a search query, Lucene returns a hit list of matching articles, much like a SQL query returns a ResultSet of matching rows. The Scaffold package includes a `getCollection` method (`org.apache.scaffold.search.Lucene-Utils`) that transfers a Lucene hit list to a list of any type of JavaBean. This is the same functionality provided by the SQL version of `getCollection` (`org.apache.scaffold.sql.ResultSetUtils`), making it very easy to drop in a Lucene search to replace a SQL query.

NOTE The only changes we've made are within the data access method. The Collection returned will now be taken from the Lucene index rather than a SQL query, but the rest of the application is none the wiser. If you peruse the data access class for Artimus (`org.apache.artimus.articles.Access`), you'll see that methods access either the Artimus database or the Artimus search index, as best suits the intent of the method.

Lucene is a well-designed toolkit and surprisingly easy to use. A comprehensive treatment of Lucene is outside the scope of this chapter, but we can provide an overview to help you get started. Like Struts, Lucene is an open source project hosted at Jakarta [ASF, Lucene].

Introducing Lucene

Lucene is both a search engine and a toolkit for building search engines. It does not store data but simply indexes it. The data can be a record in a database or a page on a website. The only requirement is that your application will be able to retrieve it again later using some identifier. This could be a primary key, a URL, or anything else that your application might use.

Key objects.   Lucene works its magic using five key objects: Document, Field, Index, Query, and Hits, as shown in table 14.10.

Table 14.10   Key Lucene classes

Object	Description
Document	A logical construct that may be a record from a database, a page from a website, or any other piece of information that can retrieved again later. A Lucene Document is maintained as a set of fields, one of which contains the location of the original data source.
Field	A Field is a section of a Lucene Document. Each Lucene Field has two parts: a name and a value. The value may be indexed so that it can be queried and used to retrieve the original data source. A Field may be stored with the Lucene Document, in which case it is returned when a Query matches the Document. A Document will typically contain at least one stored Field to uniquely identify it.
Index	When Lucene analyzes the Fields in a Document, it creates an Index so that you can apply a Query to the Fields and retrieve the Document. Your application can then use one of the stored Fields in the Document to retrieve the original data. Documents are returned in a Hits list in response to a Query. The Index is created and maintained using an *IndexWriter.*
Query	Lucene supports several different Query types to make searches more effective. The flexible Query object can simply take a search string and create a full-text Query object, as is often done by directories and portals on the World Wide Web.
Hits	A ranked collection containing the Documents matched by a Query.

Typical workflow.   Starting from scratch, an application using Lucene would:

- Create Documents by adding Fields
- Create an IndexWriter and add documents to it with `addDocument`

- Call QueryParser.parse to build a Query from a string
- Create an IndexSearcher and pass the Query to its search method
- Render the Hits returned as a list displayed to the user

How Artimus works with Lucene

To bootstrap the SQL tables and Lucene index, Artimus provides a CreateResources ProcessBean (`org.apache.artimus.CreateResources`). After calling an Access method to initialize the index, CreateResources indexes any existing records. Once the index is created, Artimus continues to maintain it as records are added, updated, and deleted. As we have already seen, a Lucene search query can be swapped for a database management system (DBMS) whenever we like.

Creating the index. Like most things in Lucene, the overall indexing process is very simple:

1 Create an Index using an IndexWriter.

2 Create a Document object.

3 Retrieve your data source.

4 Add one or more Fields to the Document object, based on your data source.

5 Add the Document to the Index.

6 Repeat step 2 for each data source.

7 Optimize and close the Index.

The trickiest part is creating the Field objects for Lucene Documents. Lucene offers three switches for Fields that can be mixed and matched as needed, as shown in table 14.11.

Table 14.11 The Lucene Field switches

Switch	Specifies...
store	Whether to keep a copy of the field in the Document object
index	Whether to analyze the field so that it can be searched by a Query
tokenize	Whether to break the field down into tokens (or *words*)

You need to *store* fields that you want on the hit list displayed to the user and some others that might need to be searched verbatim. This would include things like keywords and dates. But most of the fields, especially the big ones, can be indexed but not stored.

You need to *index* fields that can be part of search query and used to find the document again later.

You need to *tokenize* fields that contain more than one word, and each of the words should be indexed as a separate entity.

Trying to visualize which switch you need for a given use case can make your head swim. In practice, four common field types emerge that cover most people's needs: Keyword, Text, Unindexed, and Stored. As a convenience, Lucene provides static factory methods to make it easy to generate just the object you need.

Table 14.12 correlates the static fields to the boolean properties.

Table 14.12   The field factory methods

Factory method	store	index	tokenize	Description
static Field **UnIndexed**(String name, String value)	***			Constructs a `String`-valued Field that is not tokenized or indexed but is stored for return with hits.
static Field **UnStored**(String name, String value)		***	***	Constructs a `String`-valued Field that is tokenized and indexed but that is not stored in the index.
static Field **Keyword**(String name, String value)	***	***		Constructs a `String`-valued Field that is not tokenized but is indexed and stored.
static Field **Text**(String name, String value) static Field **Text**(String name, Reader value)	***		***	Constructs a `String`-valued Field that is tokenized and indexed and is stored for return with hits.

This is a common pattern in Lucene. Common usages are provided in a high-level API or base class, but the full power of the package is still available to those who may need it.

Artimus encapsulates the Lucene indexing in separate methods that are kept in the Access class (`org.apache.artimus.Access`). Note how the `Field.factory` methods are used to indicate how the field should be stored and indexed:

```
public static final void index (
    String article, String contributor, String creator,
    String title, String content,IndexWriter index
) throws Exception {
```

```
    try {
        Document document = new Document();
        document.add(Field.Keyword("article",article));
        document.add(Field.Text("title",title));
        document.add(Field.UnStored("contributor",contributor));
        document.add(Field.UnStored("creator",creator));
        document.add(Field.UnStored("content",content));
        index.addDocument(document);
    }
    catch (IOException e) {
        throw new ResourceException(e);
    }
}
```

Lucene does not play well with null. When you are adding fields, it is your responsibility to ensure that the value passed is not null. An easy way to do this is to wrap the fields in a simple utility that returns a blank String if the property is null:

```
document.add(Field.Keyword("article",Engine.blankNull(article)));
```

This makes implementing the CreateIndex Action a very simple task. All it does is select the Article records from the database and then pass each one to the Access.index method:

```
ArrayList list = null;
Form article = null;
try {
    IndexWriter index =
        Engine.getIndexWriter(true);
    list = (ArrayList)
    Access.select(new Form());
    for (int i=0; i<list.size(); i++) {
        article = (Form) list.get(i);
        Access.index(
            article.getArticle(),
            article.getContributor(),
            article.getCreator(),
            article.getTitle(),
            article.getContent(),
            index);
    }
index.optimize();
index.close();
}
catch (Exception e) {
    e.printStackTrace();
}
```

As shown earlier, in section 14.6.1, once the index is created, retrieving a hit list is just a method call away.

While on the surface Lucene seems like a very different way to access data, our application architecture makes it surprisingly easy to plug in.

14.7 Using content syndication

Syndicating content has become a popular way for applications to provide more data to more people. The strategy is surprisingly simple, as well as standard, secure, and scalable.

Here's how it works:

- Available content is summarized in an XML file.
- The XML file is made available via HTTP, the same as any web page.

Other sites can then:

- Retrieve and cache that file.
- Render the summary to their own visitors.

If users see something they like, they can click through and retrieve the detail from your site.

With the help of the Struts Digester, creating and retrieving syndicated content couldn't be simpler. As you might have guessed, the Artimus application can act both as a content provider and syndication client.

Let's see how this is done.

14.7.1 Digesting RSS

Struts uses the Digester to create objects from the Struts configuration file (struts-config.xml). This is a general-purpose utility that can be used to both create Java-Beans from an XML description as well as write XML to represent a JavaBean.

The Digester ships with a special RSS version designed to read and write Rich Summary Site files. This is a popular format for content syndication. To use another format, you can create a new set of rules for the Digester.

1.0 vs 1.1   In Struts 1.0, the Digester was packaged in the Struts JAR file. It has now been moved to the Jakarta Commons and made a product in its own right. Later releases of Struts use the Commons version. For more about using the Digester in your own application, see the Jakarta Commons distribution. [ASF, Commons]

A Rich Site Summary file is a collection of *items* called a *channel*. Each item has several properties, including a link to the item itself, which would usually be someplace on your own site. The channel typically puts related items together, usually those that have just been released.

The Digester package provides classes that represent an RSS item and its channel. Since these are just JavaBeans, using them from a Java program is very straightforward.

14.7.2 *Retrieve and render*

To create an RSS channel object from an existing XML file, you simply need to create a Channel object and hand it a path, and the RSSDigester does the rest:

```
RSSDigester digester = new RSSDigester();
channel = (Channel) digester.parse(path);
request.setAttribute("CHANNEL",channel);
```

Channel has a getItems method that you can use to iterate through the items, either in your Action or in the presentation:

```
<logic:iterate name="CHANNEL" property="items" id="ITEM">
<TABLE cellspacing="2" cellpadding="4" border="1"
    width="90%" align="center">
<TR>
<TD>DESCRIPTION</TD>
<TD><bean:write name="ITEM" property="description"/></TD>
</TR>
<TR>
<TD>LINK</TD>
<TD><bean:write name="ITEM" property="link"/></TD>
</TR>
<TD>TITLE</TD>
<TD><bean:write name="ITEM" property="title"/></TD>
</TR>
</TABLE>
</logic:iterate>
```

Creating your own RSS file is just as easy. Simply create a new Channel object, add your items, and use a Writer to render the result:

```
Channel channel = new Channel();
Iterator rows = modelResult.getIterator();
while (rows.hasNext()) {
    ArticleForm article = (ArticleForm) rows.next();
    Item item = new Item();
    item.setTitle(article.getTitle());
    item.setLink(article.getLink());
channel.addItem(item);
```

```
response.setContentType("text/plain");
channel.render(response.getWriter());
eturn(null);
```

We return null at the end so that the controller knows the response is complete.

14.7.3 *Syndicating RSS*

Once the RSSDigester converts the XML into a JavaBean, we can render it like any other bean. But how do we close the loop and offer our own content as an RSS channel?

The Artimus application already offers a list of the latest stories that it sends to a JSP. If it were rendered as XML rather than HTML, this list would make for a very nice channel. Happily, the Digester is designed as a bidirectional filter. If we can transform our list into a ChannelBean, the `RSSDigester.render` method will gladly output the XML.

In a typical Struts request/response cycle, the Action class will create a Java-Bean and pass it to the view via the request context. This may be an ActionForm or some other JavaBean, but when it leaves the Action class it is simply an ordinary Java object. Typically, the Action class forwards the request on to a presentation component, such as a JSP, which renders the response as HTML using the objects in the request.

Rather than send the list object out to a JSP to render, we can just as easily send it to an RSS Action to render. The Action is passed the response and can render the response directly when appropriate. It's just usually easier to send things off to a presentation component.

Listing 14.4 shows the Artimus RenderRss Action (`org.apache.artimus.struts.RenderRss`) that takes an incoming ArticleHelper and uses it to create a Channel object. The Channel object renders the XML directly back to the client, and so the method returns null at the end.

> **Listing 14.4   org.apache.artimus.struts.RenderRss**

```
package org.apache.artimus.struts;

import java.io.IOException;
import java.io.PrintWriter;
import java.sql.SQLException;
import java.util.Iterator;
import javax.servlet.ServletException;
import javax.servlet.http.HttpServletRequest;
import javax.servlet.http.HttpServletResponse;
import org.apache.commons.digester.rss.Channel;
import org.apache.commons.digester.rss.Item;
```

```
import org.apache.scaffold.sql.AccessBean;
import org.apache.artimus.http.ArticleForm;
import org.apache.struts.action.Action;
import org.apache.struts.action.ActionError;
import org.apache.struts.action.ActionErrors;
import org.apache.struts.action.ActionForm;
import org.apache.struts.action.ActionForward;
import org.apache.struts.action.ActionMapping;
import org.apache.struts.action.ActionServlet;

public final class RenderRss extends Action {

public ActionForward perform(ActionMapping mapping,
                             ActionForm form,
                             HttpServletRequest request,
                             HttpServletResponse response)
        throws IOException, ServletException {

 ActionErrors errors = new ActionErrors();
Channel channel = new Channel();
ArticleHelper helper = (ArticleHelper)
    request.getAttribute(AccessBean.HELPER_KEY);
if (helper==null) {
    errors.add(ActionErrors.GLOBAL_ERROR,
    new ActionError("access.missing.parameter"));
}

if (errors.empty()) {
    try {
        channel.setTitle("Articles");
        channel.setDescription(DESCRIPTION_TEXT);
        channel.setLink(CHANNEL_LINK);
        Iterator rows = helper.getRows();
        while (rows.hasNext()) {
            ArticleForm article = (ArticleForm) rows.next();
            Item item = new Item();
            item.setTitle(article.getTitle());
            item.setLink(ARTICLE_BASE +
                article.getArticle());
            channel.addItem(item);
        }
    }
    catch (Exception e) {
        errors.add(ActionErrors.GLOBAL_ERROR,
        new ActionError("rss.access.error"));
        servlet.log(e.toString());
    }
}

if (!errors.empty()) {
    saveErrors(request, errors);
    return (mapping.findForward("error"));
}
```

```
response.setContentType("text/plain");
channel.render(response.getWriter());
return(null);

    } // ---- End perform ----

} // ---- End RenderRss ----
```

Here's how the Struts configuration is set up for the RenderRss Action:

```
<!-- Find recent articles -->
    <action
        path="/channel/Recent"
        type="org.apache.struts.scaffold.ProcessAction"
        name="articleForm"
        scope="request"
        validate="false"
        parameter="org.apache.artimus.article.FindByLast">
      <forward
          name="success"
          path="/do/channel/Render"/>
    </action>

    <!-- Render result as RSS channel -->
    <action
        path="/channel/Render"
        type="org.apache.artimus.struts.RenderRss"/>
```

This demonstrates two important ideas:

- When the view is decoupled from the data retrieval (or model), the same data can be processed differently to provide a different result. The original process was designed for a JSP, but we were able to extend it for RSS without making any change to the original process. Using the same technique, we can offer by RSS any information now being sent to a JSP. Likewise, we could offer it using any presentation device that can use a standard Java object in a standard servlet context.

- An Action can process the response if it chooses.

14.8 Using EJBs with Struts

Enterprise JavaBeans (EJBs) are designed to represent the model layer of an application. Developers often choose EJBs when building applications that will be distributed over several servers. Many developers also like to use EJBs because of the transparent way they handle transactions. Used properly, EJBs can be a good fit with Struts.

Whether or not to use EJBs for a given application is a complex question. EJBs can provide an application with a plethora of services that developers might otherwise have to write themselves. But there is no free lunch. Most developers will agree that EJBs are a good choice for distributed, enterprise-scale applications. But most applications do not fit in that category. Be sure to think carefully before deciding to use EJBs with your application. However, if your application is well designed, you should be able to switch to EJBs, or to any model layer, without affecting the rest of your application.

The most flexible approach is to use the *Facade* pattern to create a buffer zone between the Struts Actions and your EJBs. To Struts, the facade looks and acts like the actual model. In practice, the facade is talking to other components that do the actual work.

DEFINITION   A *facade* substitutes the interfaces of a set of classes with the interface of a single class. The facade hides implementation classes behind one interface. [Go4]

The Scaffold ProcessBeans (see section 14.3.1) are an example of the Facade pattern. To switch an application from plain-vanilla JDBC to something else, like EJBs, you can implement the business logic within a ProcessBean. The Action can continue to call the ProcessBean without knowing anything about EJBs, JDBC, or whatever else. (Of course, there is nothing special about ProcessBeans. Any similar object of your own creation will work as well.)

Using a facade to encapsulate calls to your business model is called the Business Delegate pattern.

DEFINITION   The *Business Delegate* hides the underlying implementation details of the business service, such as lookup and access details of the EJB architecture. [Go3]

The Business Delegate pattern is often used with an EJB pattern called *Session Facade*.

14.8.1 *Session Facade*

The classic Facade pattern is also the basis of the popular *Session Facade* pattern [Go3]. Here, an EJB component called a *session bean* is used to implement the facade. If your application is wedded to EJBs, you might choose to have the Actions call your Session Facade directly. This will bind your Action to EJB Session

Beans, but eliminates the need to build a generic facade between the Struts Action and your Session Facade. Like many implementation decisions, the best choice will depend on the circumstances.

14.8.2   *Data transfer objects*

To display the result of an operation, it is technically possible to pass an EJB to the presentation layer. The Struts Tags or Velocity View tools can display the properties of an EJB, the same as any JavaBean. However, there is some overhead to every call to an EJB. Consequently, most developers use another object to carry data between layers. Such carriers are called *data transfer objects* (DTOs). The Scaffold ResultList class is an example of a data transfer object.

The Struts ActionForm is also a type of DTO. When displaying data on the presentation layer, you have the option of populating an ActionForm from an EJB DTO or using the DTO directly. The deciding point is often how much control you have over the DTO. If you can control the DTO properties, then for displaying read-only data you might as well pass the DTO back. The Struts tags and Velocity View tools work by reflection. As long as the property names match, any object type can be used.

Of course, for input you should use a Struts ActionForm. Once validated, the ActionForm can be used to populate the EJB DTO. The DTO is then passed through the facade to the EJBs.

A popular tool for working with EJBs is XDoclet [XDoclet]. This component starts out as an enhancement to the standard JavaDoc tool and ends up as a very clever code generator. You can use it to create and maintain much of the bullwork code needed by most EJB applications, including DTOs.

Another EJB tool to pursue is the Struts-Expresso [Expresso] framework. Expresso supports creating applications with or without EJBs, making it easier to hedge your bets.

14.8.3   *Implementation patterns*

For the best scalability, many Struts/EJB developers follow this pattern:

- Re-create the reference to the remote interface as required.
- Use stateless session EJBs in preference to stateful EJBs.
- Avoid retaining a handle to the stateless EJBs.
- Avoid interacting directly with entities.
- Use a stateless facade that returns a data transfer object to the Action.

A discussion of the technologies behind EJBs (stateless versus stateful and so forth) is beyond the scope of this book. For more about the Enterprise JavaBean technology, we recommend *Mastering Enterprise JavaBeans* [Roman]. A good online article is "Enterprise Bean Best Practices" [Dragan].

14.9 Summary

We've covered a lot of ground in this chapter, but we hope at a pace that made it easy to understand. While the focus has been on techniques, you can see the complete strategies in action by exploring the Artimus example application at your leisure.

The major topics we discussed were:

- Layering data access
- Defining the business layer
- Attaching resources to the business layer
- Transferring data between layers
- Communicating user gestures between layers

Of these, the most important thing is that we saw how a layered design lets us attach different services, and different service implementations, to the same business layer without changing the rest of the application.

Along the way, we also peeked at the nuts and bolts of using some popular tools and frameworks with Struts, including:

- ProcessBeans
- Lucene
- The Digester (for content syndication)

We used the Artimus example application as our case study. Its business API easily supports using the different services we implemented:

- Storing data in a SQL table
- Indexing data with a search engine
- Providing syndicated content through XML

To conclude the chapter, we covered some best practices to follow when using Enterprise JavaBeans with Struts.

In part 4 of this book, "Struts by Example," we put into practice many of the techniques we have discussed.

Struts by example

P art 4 returns to the hands-on lab work we started in part 1. We walk through three case study applications. Together, these examples demonstrate using Struts with data services, implementing applications with Tiles and the Validator, upgrading from Struts 1.0 to 1.1, and using Velocity templates in your application.

Artimus: pulling out the stops

Artimus: pulling out the stops

This chapter covers

- Introducing the Artimus example application
- Using Tiles, the Validator, and Scaffold in the same application
- Understanding recommended practices for production applications

Just do it.

—Nike

15.1 *The framework's framework*

The Artimus example application demonstrates deploying an enterprise-grade, best-practices application using the Struts core together with all the optional components: Scaffold, Tiles, and the Validator.

Since many of the production applications written for Struts 1.0 will now be migrating to Struts 1.1, we will present the 1.0 version of Artimus in this chapter, and then show how to upgrade the codebase for Struts 1.1 in the next chapter.

> **WARNING**   Artimus is designed to show techniques that you would use in a real-life production application. The material in this case study may be more advanced than what is often presented in a programming book. (So, you might want to top off that cappuccino before getting started.)

Other chapters in this book are devoted to Tiles and the Validator, and we have also introduced several Scaffold classes along the way. But before getting started with our tour of Artimus, it might help to provide some additional background on the Scaffold toolkit.

> **NOTE**   Throughout this chapter we refer to the Struts *ActionMapping* objects as well as the Struts *Action* objects. In the Struts configuration file, the element for creating an ActionMapping is termed an *action*. When we refer to an *action* (lowercase), we are talking about the ActionMapping element. When we refer to an *Action* (initial cap), we are talking about the Action object. (The `<action>` element might have been better styled a `<mapping>` element, but that's not the case for Struts 1.0 or 1.1.)

15.2 *Scaffold—birth of a toolset*

Although originally designed to be an integrator of existing technologies, Struts is fast becoming a proving ground for new technologies.

The initial version of Struts gave rise to several utility packages. The Jakarta Commons BeanUtils, Collections, Digester, and Validator packages were all conceived within the Struts framework. Each of these packages had uses outside the framework; so, being good citizens, the Struts developers repackaged these utilities for the Jakarta Commons. Now other frameworks and applications can easily import these components and avoid reinventing yet another wheel.

Like Tiles and the Validator, Scaffold is a utility package born out of creating web applications with Struts. Over the course of developing several Struts applications, a number of common solutions to common needs were identified and assembled into a set of reusable classes under the name *Scaffold*. The core Scaffold packages are available through the Jakarta Commons [ASF, Commons]. An optional Struts-specific Scaffold package is available at the Struts website [ASF, Struts].

While Struts provides the invisible underpinnings for a web application, Scaffold provides a set of higher-level objects that help you assemble an application from component parts. Like Struts, Scaffold encourages a layered design and helps you keep business-tier code separated from web-tier code. We've introduced several Scaffold classes throughout the book. Here, we put these classes into context and show how they are used to create the Artimus example application.

Many Scaffold classes are designed to ease the transition from Struts 1.0 to Struts 1.1. They allow you to start using many of the Struts 1.1 techniques now and complete your migration later. When forward compatibility is not transparent, changing over is usually a matter of changing some import and extends clauses. This will simplify our migration from Struts 1.0 to Struts 1.1 in the next chapter.

1.0 vs 1.1   When this book went to press, the Struts 1.1 beta 2 was in circulation. It is likely that some details will change in the Struts 1.1 final release. Check the book's website [Husted] for any errata.

15.3 *About Artimus*

Artimus is a web-based news poster. Authorized users can add, edit, or delete articles. Any visitor to the site can view the articles online using various search features, including full text and by author, title, or time span.

Artimus can also publish its articles as a Rich Site Summary (RSS) channel. This hooks Artimus up with enterprise portals, such as Jakarta Jetspeed [ASF, Jetspeed].

Meanwhile, from a developer's viewpoint, Artimus is a full-blown example of a ready-to-ship Struts application. Here are some of the techno-bullets:

- Application settings can be configured through the deployment descriptor (web.xml) or an external Properties file.

- In the Struts 1.0 version, a helper servlet is used to load custom resources so ActionServlet does not need to be subclassed. In the Struts 1.1 version, a PlugIn Action is used instead.

- A connection pool adaptor allows use of the Struts connection pool, and many others, from the business tier. Connection pools can be changed from the deployment descriptor (or PlugIn configuration).

- SQL commands are also stored in external Properties files and can be changed without recompiling.

- The business tier is represented by a set of ProcessBeans, dispatched using the classic Command pattern. Business code is not embedded in any Struts or HTTP-bound class.

- A standard Action is used to dispatch the ProcessBeans, drastically reducing the number of custom Actions in the application.

- The application can be easily localized.

- The Jakarta Tiles framework is used to lay out and organize display pages.

- The Jakarta Struts Validator is used to validate input, both client- and server-side.

- The Jakarta Lucene search engine is used to provide full-text searches when appropriate.

The Struts 1.0 version of Artimus defines exactly three classes that extend Struts: two ActionForms and an adapter Action for the RSS channel. The rest of Artimus is pure business tier or standard classes imported from the Scaffold package. The architecture allows you to add any number of new business operations without requiring any additional Struts or Scaffold classes. You can just add more business beans. Everything else is designed for reuse.

The Struts 1.1 version of Artimus (see chapter 16) does not create any new Struts-based classes at all. Everything is used straight out of the Struts or Scaffold JARs.

The full source code and binary Web Archive (WAR) file for the versions of Artimus and Scaffold used by this chapter are available at the book's website [Husted]. Since both Artimus and Scaffold are actively maintained, new releases may also be available through the Jakarta Struts website [ASF, Struts].

15.3.1 *Building Artimus*

All of the configuration and source code files used by Artimus are kept under a centralized directory. The Ant build file is used to both compile the Java source files into classes and place other updated source files in their statutory locations.

In the Artimus WAR, the centralized directory for all the source code files, including JSPs and configuration files, is /WEB-INF/src. The build file at /WEB-INF/src/build.xml includes Ant targets that copy (or deploy) the appropriate files from under /WEB-INF/src to locations under the application root or WEB-INF folder.

Table 15.1 shows the location of the Artimus source files and where they end up when deployed.

Table 15.1   How Artimus source files are deployed

Source code location	Deployed to
/WEB-INF/src/**conf**	/WEB-INF
/WEB-INF/src/java/****/*.java**	/WEB-INF/classes/****/*.class**
/WEB-INF/src/**pages/**/*.jsp**	**/**/*.jsp**
/WEB-INF/src/**resources**	/WEB-INF/classes/**resources**

There are several advantages to this approach:

- It is compatible with code repositories, like CVS. The files under WEB-INF/src can be checked in and maintained under CVS. Other files in the system, such as the JARs under WEB-INF/lib, do not need to be checked in.

- It keeps all the source files used by your application together where they are easy to find and edit. In the web application folder, some of these files may be several directory layers removed from each other.

- Some files, like the message resources, have no default location and just need to be placed somewhere on the CLASSPATH. These can be kept in their own folder in your source tree and then copied under the /WEB-INF/classes folder when deployed.

- WEB-INF is the default location for a growing number of configuration files. If you are deploying these from your own source folders, you have the opportunity to organize them any way you like without creating nonstandard folders under WEB-INF.

- An omnibus source tree gives you a place to store alternate configurations and other information about the various files that make up a web application. Such files can be maintained with the source files, where they won't get lost, but not deployed, where they might confuse matters.

On the other hand, while many developers use this approach, it is by no means commonplace, and so needs to be explained (as we have done here). There is also the potential for error in that you might edit the wrong copy of the file. Ant itself mitigates this danger, though, since it will not overwrite a newer file with an older one on its own. You also need to rebuild after changing any source file, just as you would when changing a Java source file.

When we present the source files in this chapter, we will refer to the file's *deployment location*. If you base any of your own development on Artimus, just be aware that the original source for these files is maintained elsewhere within the directory tree. When the application is compiled, any modified source files are deployed to their proper place in the web application tree.

15.4 *The deployment descriptor (web.xml)*

The deployment descriptors for most Struts applications tend to be cut and dried. Usually, it's just a matter of specifying the one Struts ActionServlet, and maybe the standard Validator or Tiles servlets if you are using Struts 1.0. We cover the general format of the deployment descriptor in chapter 4.

The web.xml for Artimus 1.0 is a tad more interesting. Aside from the Struts standards, it includes configurations for its own ArtimusServlet and a Declarative Security setting. The ArtimusServlet is not a runtime servlet for processing requests, but a resource loader to initialize our business-tier classes. The Declarative Security setting protects the editing commands from unauthorized users.

1.0 vs 1.1   In the Struts 1.1 version of Artimus, we use a PlugIn Action instead of a separate servlet.

In this section, we present the configuration blocks for these two special items: the ArtimusServlet and Declarative Security. See chapter 4 for more about configuring the standard Struts components.

Listing 15.1 shows the initialization blocks for the ArtimusServlet and our Declarative Security. Each block of code is discussed in its own section following the listing. The numbers in the code comments refer to the appropriate section numbers.

Listing 15.1   /WEB-INF/web.xml (ArtimusServlet and Declarative Security)

```xml
<?xml version="1.0" encoding="ISO-8859-1"?>
<!DOCTYPE web-app
  PUBLIC "-//Sun Microsystems, Inc.//DTD Web Application 2.2//EN"
  "http://java.sun.com/j2ee/dtds/web-app_2_2.dtd">
<web-app>
  <!-- [15.4.1] Configuring Artimus -->
  <servlet>
    <servlet-name>artimus</servlet-name>
    <servlet-class>org.apache.artimus.http.ArtimusServlet</servlet-class>
<!-- [15.4.2] Our application properties -->
    <init-param>
<param-name>default</param-name>
      <param-value>resources/artimus.properties</param-value>
    </init-param>
<!-- [15.4.3] Our connection adaptor -->
    <init-param>
      <param-name>adaptor</param-name>
      <param-value>org.apache.commons.scaffold.sql.ServletAdaptor</param-
  value>
    </init-param>
    <init-param>
      <param-name>adaptor.key</param-name>
      <param-value>org.apache.struts.action.DATA_SOURCE</param-value>
    </init-param>
<!-- [15.4.4] Our startup priority -->
    <load-on-startup>1</load-on-startup>
  </servlet>

<!-- [15.4.5] other configuration blocks ... -->

<!-- [15.4.6] Our security settings-->
  <security-constraint>
    <web-resource-collection>
      <web-resource-name>Administrative</web-resource-name>
        <!-- [15.4.7] The URLs we protect -->
        <url-pattern>/do/admin/*</url-pattern>
      </web-resource-collection>
      <!-- [15.4.8] The authorized users -->
      <auth-constraint>
        <role-name>manager</role-name>
        <role-name>editor</role-name>
        <role-name>contributor</role-name>
      </auth-constraint>
  </security-constraint>
<!-- [15.4.9] Our authentication strategy -->
    <login-config>
    <auth-method>BASIC</auth-method>
    <realm-name>EBasic Authentication Area</realm-name>
  </login-config>
</web-app>
```

15.4.1 Configuring Artimus

Following the statutory XML red tape at the top of listing 15.1, we start by giving our Artimus servlet a reference name and specifying the class for the container to load. Note that this is *not* the Struts ActionServlet, which is configured elsewhere in the descriptor.

15.4.2 Our application properties

The Artimus servlet is designed to load a default Properties file, much the same way Struts loads a default message resource bundle. In listing 15.1, the `<default>` parameter indicates the path to our file. A Properties file is a standard Java component [Sun, Properties]. Ours is a text-based Properties file that uses the same format as a resource bundle (see chapter 13). We use it to store system paths and other settings that don't vary by locale.

Most system settings in a Java web application can be adjusted automatically using services provided by the container. Hyperlinks, for example, can be made relative or rewritten to include the correct path. Other system settings cannot be determined this way. Many intranet applications will hardcode settings like these, requiring that the application be recompiled if they change.

Artimus avoids hardcoding system settings by obtaining them from an external Properties file. For example, some packages, like Lucene, need to store files somewhere on your server. A setting in the Properties file lets us specify the path to use and then change it without recompiling the source code.

The Properties file can be modified with any text editor. Your application could even provide a simple Swing application to read and edit the custom properties for your application.

15.4.3 Our connection adaptor

To reach the widest audience, the Artimus example application presented here uses JDBC as the default storage system. For more about using Struts with various data services, see chapter 14.

In listing 15.1, we use the `<adaptor>` and `<adaptor.key>` elements to configure our connection adaptor to use the Struts generic connection pool. Struts stores a reference to its connection pool in the application context. Since this is a common approach, Scaffold provides a standard ServletAdaptor. This adaptor lets business-tier components use the pool without being bound directly to a web application.

The attribute key used to store the reference in the application context may vary. Here we specify use the default key used by Struts. We could also specify this key in the Properties file described in section 15.4.2. A database administrator could change the attribute key in the Properties file without touching the more complicated deployment descriptor.

Scaffold provides other standard connection adaptors for Poolman and JNDI-based pools, like Resin. You can also create your own custom adaptors by subclassing the base adaptor and overriding a method or two. See the Scaffold JavaDoc and source code for details.

15.4.4 *Our startup priority*

Since the Artimus servlet loads resources that might be used by other servlets, we use the `<load-on-startup>` element in listing 15.1 to give it a lower load-on-startup value. This means that the container will load it before servlets with a higher startup value.

15.4.5 *Other configuration settings*

See chapter 4 for more about configuring the standard Struts and taglibs components. Artimus does nothing unusual in this regard.

15.4.6 *Our security settings*

Artimus uses the standard Declarative Security scheme. The container manages this type of security, so in listing 15.1, we provide the necessary details to the `<security-constraint>` element.

15.4.7 *The URLs we protect*

The first step in defining Declarative Security is to identify the URL pattern(s) to secure. In listing 15.1, our `<url-pattern>` says to limit access to any location under /do/admin in our application. If a URI like /do/admin/article/Edit is requested, the container checks to see if the user has logged in to this application. If not, the container will bring up a challenge dialog box to require that the user log in to the application. If the user's credentials pass, the container will grant access to the resource.

An application can define any number of resources, each with its own URL pattern and set of constraints.

1.0 vs 1.1 In the Struts 1.1 version of Artimus (see chapter 16), we use the new security features built into the Struts ActionMappings. The same security roles are used in either case. The foundation we are laying here is forward-compatible with Struts 1.1.

15.4.8 *The authorized users*

Once a user logs in, the `<auth-constraint>` in listing 15.1 says to grant access to users in the roles of manager, editor, and contributor. A user can belong to more than one role, so a manager can also be a contributor. Separate resources could have been set up for each role. As we will see later, Artimus fine-tunes the security on its own by providing different menus to users based on their role.

15.4.9 *Our authentication strategy*

The `<auth-method>` element in listing 15.1 tells the container to use the Basic authentication strategy. There are other schemes that are more secure, but they are not supported by all browsers. Since Artimus does not need to be a *highly* secure application, the simplest, most compatible scheme is chosen.

This completes the roundup of our deployment descriptor. Next, let's take a closer look at the ArtimusServlet loaded through the descriptor and the resources it provides to our application.

15.5 *ArtimusServlet*

The ArtimusServlet is used to initialize several custom resources used by our application. This could be done by subclassing ActionServlet directly, but it is often better to use another servlet to load your resources. The advantages of using your own resource loader are that it:

- Can draw on standard subclasses to do most of the work
- Limits the amount of custom coding you bind to Struts
- Protects you from any changes that may later occur in the ActionServlet or PlugIn interface

All told, Artimus needs to load three properties files and initialize two internal services:

- The Artimus system Properties file
- Two SQL Properties files
- The Connection Adaptor
- The Lucene search engine

Our resource loaders extend standard base classes in the Scaffold package and do all this using very little custom code. The Scaffold package also has similar base classes for PlugIns, which we will use later in this chapter to migrate ArtimusServlet to a PlugIn.

Listing 15.2 shows the full source code for the ArtimusServlet.

Listing 15.2   ArtimusServlet

```
package org.apache.artimus.http;

import java.io.IOException;
import java.util.Properties;
import javax.servlet.ServletException;
import org.apache.commons.scaffold.lucene.Engine;
import org.apache.commons.scaffold.sql.ConnectionAdaptor;
import org.apache.commons.scaffold.http.ConnectionServlet;

<!-- [15.5.1] Our subclass -->
public class ArtimusServlet extends ConnectionServlet {

<!-- [15.5.2] Our String tokens -->
private static String KEYS_PARAMETER = "sql_keys";
private static String KEYS_PATH =
      "resources/sql_keys.properties";
private static String ARTICLE_PARAMETER = "sql_article";
private static String ARTICLE_PATH =
      "resources/sql_article.properties";
private static String INDEX_PARAMETER = "index.path";
private static String INDEX_PATH = "/var/lucene/artimus";

<!-- [15.5.3] Our extension point -->
  protected void initCustom()
throws IOException, ServletException {
            <!-- Fetch the SQL commands -->
Properties keysCommands =
            loadProperties(KEYS_PARAMETER,KEYS_PATH,null);
            org.apache.artimus.keys.Access.init(keysCommands);
            Properties articleCommands =
            loadProperties(ARTICLE_PARAMETER,ARTICLE_PATH,null);
            org.apache.artimus.article.Access.init(articleCommands);
            <!-- Initialize the Lucene index path -->
String indexPath =
getProperties().getProperty(INDEX_PARAMETER);
          if (null==indexPath) {
            indexPath = getInitString(INDEX_PARAMETER,INDEX_PATH);
        }
          Engine.init(indexPath);
} // end initCustom
} // end ArtimusServlet
```

15.5.1 *Our subclass*

The ArtimusServlet in listing 15.2 extends ConnectionServlet, a standard Scaffold class. The ConnectionServlet automatically initializes the connection adaptor (section 15.4.3), so we do not need to provide any code to handle that.

The ConnectionServlet in turn extends the Scaffold ResourceServlet. Likewise, this class automatically loads the default Properties file (section 15.4.2), so that's one less thing to worry about.

The ResourceServlet also provides a utility method for loading other Properties files. We will use this utility to load our application's SQL commands.

15.5.2 *Our String tokens*

The block of static Strings in listing 15.2 could have been provided inline. But as a matter of coding style, both Artimus and the Scaffold package provide static constants for all String literals. This provides the opportunity to document the literals and can avoid some hard-to-trace bugs. We do not show the JavaDocs here, but in the source, each static includes a description that documents the default value.

15.5.3 *Our extension point*

The ResourceServlet super class (section 15.5.1) provides an initCustom method as an extension point where subclasses (like ours) can add their own initialization code. In listing 15.2, the ArtimusServlet overrides initCustom to load our SQL commands and sets the path for the Lucene index file.

Fetching the SQL commands

Each of the SQL properties files are loaded using the loadProperties method provided by the ResourceServlet super class. This method checks the deployment descriptor (web.xml) for a custom setting or uses the provided default if a setting is not found in the descriptor.

To use loadProperties, we pass it:

- The name of the initialization parameter (the <param-name> element for the web.xml)
- The default setting to use, if one is not given in the web.xml
- Optionally, an attribute name for the application context

If an attribute name is passed, loadProperties will save a reference to the Properties file in the application context. The Artimus Properties files don't need to do this, so they pass null instead.

The ResourceServlet super class does use this feature to store a reference to the default application properties. Other classes in the Scaffold package look for this reference to obtain system properties. The core Struts framework uses this same strategy to expose the ApplicationResources to other components in the application.

After the SQL Properties objects are loaded from the external files, each object is passed to the data-access component that uses it (`Access.init(Properties commands)`). The components save the reference and provide it to the data-access routines at runtime.

Initializing the Lucene index path

The Lucene search engine creates a set of index files that must be stored within your server's file system. Scaffold provides a number of convenient utility methods for Lucene that need to know where to store the index file. Artimus lets you specify the index location in the default Properties file or the deployment descriptor. If neither is found, a default location is used instead.

In listing 15.2, this is done with two lines of code that call utility methods in the ResourceServlet super class. The `getProperties` method checks the default Properties file (automatically created by the super class). The `getInitString` method checks the deployment descriptor for a parameter, returning a default value if it is not found. The result is then passed to the Lucene utility class for use at runtime.

15.6 *The application and SQL Properties files*

As mentioned, the Artimus Properties file uses the same standard name-value format as used by the ResourceBundles. (Actually, it's the other way around. Resource files are an extension of the Properties file, but who's counting?) Although these files are very simple, let's have a peek anyway.

The working copies of these files are found under /artimus/WEB-INF/classes/ resource. The Artimus Properties file is shown in listing 15.3.

Listing 15.3 /WEB-INF/classes/resources/artimus.properties

```
index.path = /var/lucene/artimus
rss.link.base=http://localhost/artimus/
rss.link.view=http://localhost/artimus/article/View.do?article=
```

The first entry in listing 15.3 is the index path for the Lucene search utilities (section 15.5.3). The others are used to configure the default RSS channel. We put these out in the Properties files so that a system administrator could change them. An XML file could have been used, but that would be something that many mere mortals could easily mess up. One of the Properties files Artimus uses to store SQL commands is shown in listing 15.4.

Listing 15.4 /WEB/-INF/classes/resources/sql_keys.properties

```
keys.next = SELECT next FROM artimus_keys WHERE name=?;
keys.inc = UPDATE artimus_keys SET next=next+1 WHERE name=?;
```

Likewise, the SQL command file in listing 15.4 is something that any database administrator could easily review and edit. The two commands shown here are used to generate serial numbers. The `keys.next` command selects the current key, and the `keys.inc` command increments it for the next caller.

There are actually a few more commands in this file, including one to create the table, but they seemed rather long to present here. There is also a second SQL command file, sql_articles.properties, but that is just more of the same. (Two lines of SQL are the most many Java developers can stand anyway.)

At runtime, the data-access object retrieves the command it needs from the Properties file and uses it to retrieve or update database records. Accessing JDBC and other data services with Artimus is covered in chapter 14.

Keep in mind that these files are loaded once at startup. To activate any changes, you must reload the application.

15.7 *index.jsp*

Now that our resources are initialized, let's move past the web.xml and look at how Artimus unfolds at runtime. One of the standard appurtenances in our deployment descriptor is a reference to a standard welcome page, index.jsp. When a visitor does not request a specific page, the container looks for a welcome page to return instead.

Unfortunately, this request does not pass through the usual servlet gauntlet, and we cannot use something like index.do for our welcome page. It needs to be a physical file on the system, like an HTML page or JSP.

Meanwhile, many dynamic applications, like Artimus, are designed to avoid using direct references to a physical page. Control is expected to pass through a servlet and then out to a page.

As a compromise, Artimus uses a stock index.jsp page that forwards to a Struts Action. This is a page that can be used in any Struts application as is. The entire JSP is shown in listing 15.5; it's just two lines.

Listing 15.5   /index.jsp

```
<%@ taglib uri="/tags/struts-logic" prefix="logic" %>
              <logic:redirect forward="welcome"/>
```

The index.jsp uses a Struts logic tag to redirect control to `welcome`, which is defined as a global forward in the Struts configuration. We'll be presenting the struts-config.xml over several sections, starting with the global forwards in the next section.

15.8 *Global forwards*

A Struts configuration file has several sections. First, there's the statutory XML header followed by sections for the data sources, form beans, global forwards, and action mappings.

1.0 vs 1.1   In Struts 1.1, the configuration file may also include global exception, controller, message resource, and plug-in elements. See chapter 4 and chapter 16 for more about configuring Struts 1.1.

At 400+ lines, the struts-config.xml is actually the longest source file in the Artimus application. Accordingly, we'll present it piece by piece. Each piece will be a logical segment of the file, but to get the struts-config.xml big picture, see chapter 4, where it is covered in depth.

Listing 15.6 shows the `<global-forwards>` portion of our Struts configuration file.

Listing 15.6   /WEB-INF/struts-config.xml (global forwards)

```
<global-forwards>
    <!-- default forwards -->
     <forward
        name="welcome"
        path="/do/find/Recent"/>
     <forward
        name="cancel"
        path="/do/Menu"
```

```
          redirect="true"/>
      <forward
        name="done"
        path="/do/Menu"/>
      <forward
        name="exit"
        redirect="true"
        path="http://jakarta.apache.org/"/>
      <forward
        name="failure"
        path="/do/Menu"/>
      <forward
        name="baseStyle"
        path="/assets/styles/base.css"/>
     <!-- MENU forwards -->
      <forward
        name="logon"
        path="/do/admin/Menu"/>
     <!-- ARTICLE forwards -->
      <forward
        name="article"
        path="/do/article/View"/>
   </global-forwards>
```

We've already seen the first global forward, `welcome`, in action. The index.jsp in section 15.7 uses it to redirect control from the welcome page to the Struts portion of our application. The `welcome` forward in listing 15.6 sends control to the context-relative URI /do/find/Recent. If we wanted to change the welcome page later, we'd only need to change the path reference in the ActionForward.

In the web.xml setup for the Struts ActionServlet, we asked the container to forward all URLs beginning with /do/* to the servlet, instead of trying to find a file with that name. These are the Struts actions that we will route through the Action-Mappings object defined in the Struts configuration. We'll look at the /find/Recent action in the next section.

The global `cancel`, `done`, and `failure` ActionForwards are standard stock for many applications. If a particular ActionMapping doesn't provide its own forward for these common events, the global versions come into play. The `cancel` forward has `redirect` set to true. This forces a clean request to be sent back by the browser, helping to ensure that the request is indeed canceled. If an individual action wants to handle `cancel` differently, it can define its own local forward. The Artimus menu page is designed to display any pending errors or messages, making it a convenient place to route the unhandled `done`, `failure`, and `success` events. But if that changes, the paths can be changed here and these default events would be routed elsewhere. The exit forward just gives the menu some-place to go if users are done with the application. Here, we exit to one of our favorite sites, the Jakarta Project.

NOTE   You might note that there is no global success forward in listing 15.6. In most cases, each action will have its own place to go for success—usual-ly a display page. Since unhandled success seems like an exception rather than a rule, Artimus does not define one.

The logon and article forwards are more specialized than the others. If this were a modular Struts 1.1 application, they might be put into their own Struts configuration files with other menu and article elements.

The logon forward points to a URI under admin. This will trigger our security constraints (section 15.4.6). Once the user is logged in, the menu page will dis-play a set of menus appropriate for each role assigned to the user.

The article forward is used for creating links. At runtime, the Struts <html:link> tag is used to merge this path with a reference to an article. The JSP source looks like this:

```
<html:link forward="article" paramProperty="article" paramId="article">
```

But after the JSP tag renders, a proper hypertext reference is sent down to the browser, like this one:

```
<a href="/artimus/do/article/view?article=101">Article 101</a>
```

The baseStyle forward is used differently than the others here. It is not meant to generate a hyperlink for the user to follow. Instead, it refers to a style sheet file stored inside our web application. On the pages, we can load the style sheet using a tag like this:

```
<LINK rel="stylesheet" type="text/css"
    href="<html:rewrite forward='baseStyle'/>">
```

Another way to do this would be

```
<LINK rel="stylesheet" type="text/css"
    href="<html:rewrite page='/assets/styles/base.css/'>">
```

but that binds the link to a system path. You couldn't reorganize your file system without changing all your JSPs, which is something Struts tries to avoid.

The Artimus style sheet is rather simple and just defines some base fonts and table sizes. We won't present the style sheet source here, but if you're interested in what it looks like, you now know how to find it—check the global forward in the struts-config.xml!

15.9 /find/Recent

By default, the Artimus welcome Action is mapped to /do/find/Recent. This action displays a list of the last 20 articles posted. This is one of several search operations. Artimus can also find articles by author, title, content, or time span. Listing 15.7 shows the Artimus Find actions described in the Struts configuration (struts-config.xml).

Listing 15.7   /WEB-INF/struts-config.xml (Find actions)

```
<action
        path="/find/Recent"
        forward="/do/find/Last?articles=20"/>

    <action
        path="/find/Last"
        type="org.apache.struts.scaffold.ProcessAction"
        parameter="org.apache.artimus.article.FindByLast"
        name="articleForm"
      validate="false">
        <forward
            name="success"
            path=".article.Result"/>
    </action>

  <action
        path="/find/Author"
        type="org.apache.struts.scaffold.ProcessAction"
        parameter="org.apache.artimus.article.FindByCreator"
        name="articleForm"
      validate="false">
        <forward
            name="success"
            path=".article.Result"/>
    </action>

  <action
        path="/find/Title"
        type="org.apache.struts.scaffold.ProcessAction"
        parameter="org.apache.artimus.article.FindByTitle"
        name="articleForm"
        validate="false">
        <forward
            name="success"
            path=".article.Result"/>
    </action>
```

```
<action
        path="/find/Content"
        type="org.apache.struts.scaffold.ProcessAction"
        parameter="org.apache.artimus.article.FindByContent"
        name="articleForm"
        validate="false">
     <forward
          name="success"
          path=".article.Result"/>
   </action>
<action
        path="/find/Hours"
        type="org.apache.struts.scaffold.ProcessAction"
        parameter="org.apache.artimus.article.FindByHours"
        name="articleForm"
        validate="false">
     <forward
          name="success"
          path=".article.Result"/>
   </action>
```

As you can see in listing 15.7, our /find/Recent action is really an alias. It simply turns around and forwards the request to do/find/Last while making the URI a query string by concatenating ?articles=20. This parameter restricts the /find/ Last action to returning 20 articles. To display more or fewer articles, you would just need to change this setting in the Struts configuration.

You will notice that the Find actions are very similar. The only real difference is that each has a different parameter property. The parameter is the full classname for the business logic object that can execute the search operation. As recommended by the Struts User Guide, Artimus implements business logic objects as plain Java classes that are not tied to Struts or the web tier. This makes the business logic objects easy to write and allows them to be used in other environments.

You might also notice that the paths in our local forwards do not look like system paths to JSPs. They are in fact references to Tiles Definitions. We cover Tiles in chapter 11, and we see how Artimus uses Tiles in section 15.10. As a convention, we've named our definitions using dots where a URI would usually put a slash. This is to distinguish the definitions from actual system paths. The dots have no special meaning to Tiles.

Listing 15.8 shows the source code for our FindByLast class. We'll cover the hotspots in the following sections. All the search classes are implemented in a similar way. After we present this one, you should be able to follow the source for the others without any difficulty.

Take careful note that this is a business class that is being called by a Struts Action object. This is not a Struts class. It executes the business logic and then *returns the result* to a Struts Action.

Listing 15.8   org.apache.artimus.article.FindByLast

```
package org.apache.artimus.article;
import org.apache.commons.scaffold.lang.ParameterException;
import org.apache.commons.scaffold.util.ProcessResultBase;
import org.apache.commons.scaffold.util.ResultList;
import org.apache.commons.scaffold.util.ResultListBase;
import org.apache.artimus.lang.Tokens;
        // [15.9.1] extends bean
public class FindByLast extends Bean {
     public static final String PROPERTY = Tokens.LAST;
     public Object execute(Object parameters) throws Exception {
             // [15.9.2] super.execute
     super.execute(parameters);
             // [15.9.3] getArticles
      Integer articles = getArticles();
       if (null==articles) {
           throw new ParameterException();
       }
             // [15.9.4] findByLast and ResultList
      ResultList list = new ResultListBase(
          Access.findByLast(this,articles)
      );
      list.setLegend(PROPERTY,articles.toString());
             // [15.9.5] ProcessResult
      return new ProcessResultBase(list);

     } // execute
} // end FindByLast
```

15.9.1 *extends bean*

Artimus uses a "coarse-grained" bean approach (see chapter 5) for both its ActionForms and the business logic beans. The Bean super class contains all the properties used by the other business logic beans in the Artimus `article` package. In a larger application, each package might have its own base bean, perhaps managed by different members of the development team.

The Bean super class in turn extends the Scaffold ProcessBeanBase class (`org.apache.commons.scaffold.util.ProcessBeanBase`). This is a very light class that provides a couple of convenience properties and, more important, a standard entry method for invoking the bean.

A standard entry method lets another process, such as a Struts Action, call each object in the same way, regardless of its subclass. Struts uses this same Inversion of Control technique [Johnson] in calling whatever Actions your application defines. Scaffold defines an Executable interface (`org.apache.commons.scaffold.util. Executable`) that provides the entry method for the ProcessBeans, and consequently the Artimus business beans.

Artimus instantiates a new business bean for each request, like the FindByLast class shown in listing 15.8, in much the same way that Struts might instantiate a new ActionForm. Another approach would be to write the business beans as singletons, like the Struts Actions, so that they are instantiated only once for each application. This could provide better performance in some cases, with the trade-off that the business beans would have to be thread-safe.

15.9.2 super.execute

The FindByLast class of our business bean is entered through its `execute` method. As shown in listing 15.8, it starts out by calling the super class `execute` method. The default behavior inherited from ProcessBeanBase is to cast the `parameters` object as a Map and use it to populate itself via reflection. The standard `BeanUtils.populate` utility method handles the data transfer. This is the same utility Struts uses to populate ActionForm beans.

The interface is designed so that any application that can create a Map can call the `FindByLast.execute` method without being bound to Struts or HTTP.

15.9.3 getArticles

The FindByLast class in listing 15.8 needs one parameter: the number of articles to return. This must be passed as one of the Map entries in the `parameters` object. If it was duly passed, the super class `execute` method should have found it and used it to populate our bean's `articles` property. If `getArticles()` returns null, FindByLast throws a ParameterException (`org.apache.commons.scaffold. lang.ParameterException`).

Since missing parameters is a common occurrence in multitier applications, Scaffold defines a standard exception for this, based on a chained exception class (`org.apache.commons.scaffold.lang.ChainedException`). Other tiers can add their own exceptions to the chain if needed.

15.9.4 Access.findByLast and ResultList

The FindByLast class in listing 15.8 is a denizen of the business tier. Its job is to gather parameters for the resource-tier class, obtain the result, and pass the result back to the application layer. Artimus groups the data-access methods needed by a package into an Access class. The methods in this class take plain Java parameters, like Integers and Strings, and return an Object or Collection of Objects.

Scaffold provides a useful set of JDBC utilities to help with this process, but any data-access approach, or combination of approaches, could be used within the Access class. Artimus, for example, uses both JDBC and Lucene [ASF, Lucene] to perform different operations. For more about using Artimus with various data services, see chapter 14.

Artimus implements the Access class using static methods, but it could also be implemented as a singleton to provide more flexibility. An entirely different class could also be implemented and invoked from the business beans.

You could also implement the data-access routines directly in the business bean, in the same way you could implement everything in a Struts Action. But that would not provide for the optimal number of component layers recommended by many application architects. Many modern designs include a discrete set of components for the application, business, data access, and resource layers. Table 15.2 shows some common architectural layers and corresponding Artimus components.

Table 15.2   Common layers and Artimus components

Architectural layer	Artimus components
Presentation	JavaServer Pages, JSP tags
Control	ActionServlet, ActionForms, ActionForwards, ActionMappings, Actions
Business	ProcessBeans, ResultList, ProcessResult, MessageResources, Properties
Data access	Access class, StatementUtils, LuceneUtils, ConnectionAdaptor, JDBC driver
Resource	DBMS, Lucene

ResultList

The Java language provides a very useful Collection interface (java.util. Collection). A Collection is often used to transport the result of a data-access operation to the presentation tier. In practice, the presentation needs to know a little bit more about the result. There is usually a legend describing the Collection and there are often some column headers, both of which may need to be localized. The presentation page may also need to know how many members are in the Collection, if any. Very often, the page will need an Iterator to scroll through the members of the Collection.

The ResultList interface in the Scaffold package (`org.apache.commons.scaffold.util.ResultList`) wraps all of these requirements up into a tidy bundle. A ResultList extends Collection, and so can be used anywhere a Collection can be used. But it also provides additional properties for the convenience of the presentation tier. See chapter 14 for more about the ResultList object (section 14.4).

The FindByLast class in listing 15.8 wraps the Collection returned by the Access class method to create a ResultList object. It also sets the `legend` property on the ResultList. On the presentation page, the legend will be rendered at the top as `last=20` and be part of the standard page description, `20 matches for last=20`. This makes it easy to customize the same presentation page for all the search methods.

15.9.5 *ProcessResult*

There are a variety of outcomes to a business operation. Some operations may return a single object. Other operations will return a collection of objects. Some may just return a message or even suggest a change in the workflow. Often, an operation returns an object that needs to be stored in a context available to other components. This could be a servlet context, a JNDI context, some type of custom context, or just a property on another object.

The Scaffold ProcessResult interface (`org.apache.commons.scaffold.util.ProcessResult`) defines a transfer object that can describe several possible outcomes. ProcessResultBase is a standard bean class that implements the ProcessResult interface. Any operation may return a data object or collection, a list of messages, dispatch advice, or any combination of the three. It may also request that the object be stored under a certain attribute name for use by another component.

Table 15.3 shows the ProcessResult properties (implemented by ProcessResultBase) that are used to relate the outcome of the operation. The business bean sets the properties, and the ProcessAction acts on them.

Table 15.3   ProcessResult properties

Property	Description
name	Contains the attribute name for the result object, or null if a default name should be used.
scope	Specifies the application scope or other context for storing the result object as an attribute.
singleForm	Specifies whether the result is an Object or Collection of Objects.

Table 15.3   ProcessResult properties *(continued)*

Property	Description
exposed	Specifies whether the result should be exposed as an attribute [true].
data	Specifies the object containing the result of the operation.
aggregate	Specifies whether this ProcessResult is a collection of other ProcessResults [false].
messages	Contains a list of messages for the application tier, keyed to the application's message resources.
dispatch	Contains special routing advice for the controller. May be a path or a logical name (for example, the ActionForward name). Rarely used.
dispatchPath	Specifies whether dispatch advice is a logical name (preferred) or a URI.

Our FindByLast operation is simply returning a collection of objects, which it can wrap in a standard ProcessResultBase object. So, it can just call a default constructor on the way out. (The simple things *can* still be simple.) We'll show a more advanced use of the ProcessResult object when we create the items for the Artimus main menu in section 15.15.

15.9.6 *ProcessAction*

All of the Find actions shown in listing 15.7 call the Scaffold ProcessAction (org.apache.struts.scaffold.ProcessAction). This Action object in turn invokes the business bean class given as the parameter property, like the FindByLast class we presented in sections 15.9.1 through 15.9.5.

ProcessAction is a sophisticated object developed and refined over the course of writing several different Struts applications. It extends the Scaffold BaseHelperAction, which is covered in chapter 8. The BaseHelperAction handles the nuts and bolts of instantiating the business bean (or beans) from the parameter property. The ProcessAction then simply has to invoke the bean and cope with the result.

To invoke our business bean, ProcessAction extracts a Map (java.util.Map) from the incoming ActionForm (if there is one) and calls our bean's execute method, passing it the Map. This is the same Inversion of Control technique the ActionServlet uses when it calls an Action. The differences are that:

- Our business beans are not bound to any web-tier classes.
- Our business beans can make API contract demands that cannot be made at the web-tier level.

The latter difference means that we can do things like expect that data be present and of the correct type—or throw a serious exception if it isn't. On the web tier, invalid input is usually a user error that we should politely correct in the normal course. At this level, bad data usually represents a programming flaw that requires the attention of a developer or administrator.

The API contract for a ProcessBean, like our FindByLast bean (sections 15.9.1 through 15.9.5), is to take whatever parameters it needs from a Map and return the outcome in a ProcessResult. The action uses the ProcessResult object to determine the outcome of the operation. This is the same pattern an ActionServlet uses when it looks at the ActionForward to determine its next step.

If the ProcessResult includes messages, the ProcessAction wraps them up as ActionErrors or (since Struts 1.1) ActionMessage objects. If the result includes data, the action saves the object or collection of objects to the appropriate scope. If the result includes special dispatch advice, the action finds or creates the appropriate ActionForward. The action does all this by analyzing the ProcessResult properties shown in table 15.3.

In the case of our FindByLast operation, shown in listing 15.8, the bean simply returned a ResultList collection wrapped in a default ProcessResult object. The ProcessAction will then just save the ResultList collection in request scope, using the default RESULT attribute name, and forward control to success.

If for some reason the articles parameter was missing (section 15.9.3), the ProcessAction would automatically catch and log the Exception, wrap the message in an ActionError, and forward control to failure instead.

In either case, we will be routing control out to the presentation layer, where either our ResultList or our Exception message will be displayed to the user. Which brings us to Tiles.

15.10 *tiles.xml and Article.jsp*

We noted that the path for the local forwards shown in listing 15.6 were references to Tiles Definitions (we discuss Tiles in chapter 11). These are loaded from a tiles.xml configuration file, which is much like the struts-config.xml or the web.xml file. Listing 15.9 shows the Tiles configuration file for Artimus.

Listing 15.9   /WEB-INF/tiles.xml (Artimus 1.0)

```
<tiles-definitions>
    <definition name=".article.Base" path="/article/common/layouts/
  Article.jsp">
      <put name="title"      value ="${title}"/>
```

```
        <put name="header"     value="/article/common/header.jsp"/>
        <put name="message"    value="/article/common/message.jsp"/>
        <put name="content"    value="${content}"/>
        <put name="navbar"     value="/article/common/navbar.jsp"/>
    </definition>
    <definition name=".article.Result" extends=".article.Base">
        <put name="title"      value="article.Result.title"/>
        <put name="content"    value="/article/content/result.jsp"/>
    </definition>
    <definition name=".article.View" extends=".article.Base">
        <put name="title"      value="article.View.title"/>
        <put name="content"    value="/article/content/view.jsp"/>
    </definition>
    <definition name=".article.Form" extends=".article.Base">
        <put name="title"      value="article.Form.title"/>
        <put name="header"     value="/article/common/headerForm.jsp"/>
        <put name="content"    value="/article/content/form.jsp"/>
    </definition>
    <definition name=".article.Menu" extends=".article.Base">
        <put name="title"      value="article.Menu.title"/>
        <put name="content"    value="/article/content/menu.jsp"/>
        <put name="navbar"     value="/article/common/navbarMenu.jsp"/>
    </definition>
</tiles-definitions>
```

Our Tiles configuration file defines a base layout definition and four display pages: Result, View, Form, and Menu. The display pages inherit most of their markup from the base definition. We simply need to provide a title String and content tile. The title Strings are actually given as keys in our application's message resources. This keeps the literal text from being buried in a programmer's configuration file and makes Artimus easier to localize later.

As a convention, we've named our definitions using dots where a URI would usually put a slash. This is to distinguish the definitions from actual system paths. The dots have no special meaning to Tiles.

With Tiles enabled, when the ActionServlet processes an ActionForward, the Tiles Definitions are checked first. If the ActionForward path matches a Tiles Definition name, the ActionServlet creates a Tiles context for the Definition and forwards control to the URI specified by the Definition's path. The path usually leads to a JSP page that renders the response using the Tiles tags and the details from the Definition. Listing 15.10 shows the base tile for our Article page.

Listing 15.10   /pages/tiles/layouts/Article.jsp

```
<%@ taglib uri="/tags/struts-bean" prefix="bean" %>
<%@ taglib uri="/tags/struts-html" prefix="html" %>
<%@ taglib uri="/tags/tiles" prefix="tiles" %>
<!-- [15.10.1] useAttribute-->
<tiles:useAttribute name="title" scope="request"/>
<html:html>
<HEAD>
<html:base/>
<!-- [15.10.2] baseStyle-->
<LINK rel="stylesheet" type="text/css" href="<html:rewrite
  forward='baseStyle'/>">
<!-- [15.10.3] title-->
<TITLE><bean:message key="app.title"/> - <bean:message name="title"/></TITLE>
</HEAD>
<!-- [15.10.4 tiles -->
<tiles:get name="header"/>
<tiles:get name="message"/>
<tiles:get name="content"/>
<tiles:get name="navbar"/>
</BODY>
</html:html>
```

15.10.1   *useAttribute*

Tiles uses its own context, akin to the standard session or request context. When Tiles Definitions, like those in listing 15.9, use put on a value, they are putting it into the Tiles context. The <useAttribute> tag, shown in listing 15.10, makes the value available to one of the standard contexts. The default is the page context. Our <useAttribute> tag specified request scope so that other tiles can have access to the title attribute too. (Each tile has its own page context.)

The title attribute is a key in our application's message resources, which we use later in the page.

15.10.2   *baseStyle*

To help maintain consistency, our tiles all use the same set of styles. To make it easy to swap in another style sheet, in listing 15.10 we maintain the path to the style sheet as an ActionForward. The rewrite tag returns the path to the style sheet from the Struts configuration.

15.10.3 *title*

Since the `title` attribute passed to our page is a key in the application's message resources, in listing 15.10 we use the `<bean:message>` tag to render the actual text. We also look up another message, the app.title. This ends up generating a page title like "Artimus—Article Search Result."

15.10.4 *Tiles*

Most of the page rendered by listing 15.10 comes from the component tiles. The layout page refers to the tile using logical names. The paths to the JSPs are given in the Definition shown in listing 15.9. When the ActionServlet processes an ActionForward that uses a Tiles Definition, the servlet puts the Definition into the Tiles context where the layout page will find it. In the case of our results page, the layout would include the standard header.jsp, message.jsp, and navbar.jsp, along with the result.jsp content tile.

Since the Artimus pages are quite simple, the markup in these tiles does not amount to much. In pages that use more complex markup, the savings can be significant. Listings 15.11, 15.12, and 15.13 show the JSP source for the header, message, and navbar tiles, respectively.

Listing 15.11   /article/common/heading.jsp

```
<%@ taglib uri="/tags/struts-bean" prefix="bean" %>
<%@ taglib uri="/tags/struts-html" prefix="html" %>
<BODY>
<!-- OUTER TABLE -->
<TABLE class="outer">
<TR>
<TD align="center">
<!-- INNER TABLE -->
<TABLE class="inner">
<TR>
<TD class="heading" colspan="3"><bean:message name="title"/></TD>
</TR>
```

Listing 15.12   /article/common/message.jsp (1.0)

```
<%@ taglib uri="/tags/struts-bean" prefix="bean" %>
<%@ taglib uri="/tags/struts-html" prefix="html" %>
<%@ taglib uri="/tags/struts-validator" prefix="validator" %>
<validator:errorsExist>
<TR>
<TD class="error" colspan="3">
   <UL>
   <validator:errors id="error">
```

```
      <LI><bean:write name="error"/></LI>
   </validator:errors>
   </UL>
</TD>
</TR>
</validator:errorsExist>
<validator:messagesExist>
<TR>
<TD class="message" colspan="3">
   <UL>
   <validator:messages id="message">
      <LI><bean:write name="message"/></LI>
   </validator:messages>
   </UL>
</TD>
</TR>
</validator:messagesExist>
```

Listing 15.13   /article/common/navbar.jsp

```
<%@ taglib uri="/tags/struts-html" prefix="html" %>
</TABLE>
</TD>
</TR>
<TR>
<TD class="navbar">
<html:link forward="done">DONE</html:link>
</TD>
</TR>
</TABLE>
```

Listing 15.12 uses the Struts Validator 1.0 tags to display both error and confirmation messages. This tag set was integrated into the Struts 1.1 taglibs. When we migrate Artimus to Struts 1.1 in the next chapter, this tile will be replaced with one that uses the newer tags.

The message tile is used to print whatever errors and/or messages are found in the request. Artimus does not use the <html:error> tag to render the error messages. The design of this tag makes it easy to render messages but encourages you to put HTML markup into the message resource files. Instead, we use the Struts Validator 1.0 tag set. The validator's errors and messages tags work like iterators. In each iterator, the next message is exposed under whatever ID you specify. The <bean:write> tag can then render the message like any other String.

Like Struts 1.1, the validator tags support the idea of two message queues: one for actual errors, and another for other messages. Our message tile prints the errors

first and then the messages. The Scaffold BaseAction (`org.apache.commons.`
`scaffold.BaseAction`) supports the message-only queue for both Struts 1.0 and
Struts 1.1.

Being able to put complicated code, like that shown in listing 15.12, onto a tile
saves us from having to copy and paste this block onto every page that has to display messages.

As mentioned, we will need to change the taglibs used in listing 15.12 when we
migrate to Struts 1.1, but the layout and output strategy will remain the same.
Because it is a tile, we will also need to make the changes in only one place. Without tiles, we would have to update every page that displays messages (which in
Artimus is all of them).

Listings 15.11 and 15.13 are straightforward examples of Tiles/JSP markup.
Specifying these segments as tiles means that we can avoid copying and pasting
the same markup into all of our pages. Our result, view, form, and menu tiles contain only the markup unique to each of those pages.

The content tile for our results page is covered in section 15.11.

15.11 *result.jsp*

Because the result.jsp is a tile rather than a complete JSP, the markup in
listing 15.14 gets right down to business. All the usual HTML chrome is provided by
other tiles, so all the result tile has to do is render the unique content for this page.

When the ProcessAction (section 15.9.6) put our ResultList into the request
context, it used the default attribute name RESULT. This means we can access any
property on the result list using the various Struts tags and specifying
`name="RESULT"`.

The ResultList that we received back from the business tier is not a collection
of ActionForm beans. What we have is a collection of our business beans
(`org.apache.artimus.article.Bean`). But since we designed our ActionForm
so that its property names match the business bean's property names, we can use
whichever bean is most convenient.

The Struts framework needs an ActionForm to automatically capture and validate HTTP parameters. Otherwise, it doesn't matter what sort of JavaBean you use
to transport your data. The tags bind to the property names, not to the bean type.

Of course, technically, passing the business bean straight through to the page
is a kluge. During implementation, we arranged that our business-layer and
presentation-layer property names would match. However, since these layers are
not adjacent, the business layer should be able to change its property names without affecting the presentation page [POSA].

Happily, in practice, the business layer could do just that. Our bean does not come directly from the business layer but is *relayed* to the presentation layer by the controller. In the event that the property names ever change, the controller is there to wrap the business bean into an adaptor object that matches up the property names again. Bothering with that now has no intrinsic value, so we cut to the chase and pass along the business bean, as shown in listing 15.14.

Listing 15.14   /article/common/result.jsp

```
<%@ taglib uri="/tags/struts-bean" prefix="bean" %>
<%@ taglib uri="/tags/struts-html" prefix="html" %>
<%@ taglib uri="/tags/struts-logic" prefix="logic" %>
<!-- [15.11.1] legend -->
<TR class="message">
<TD align="center" colspan="3">
<bean:write name="RESULT" property="size"/>
matches for
<bean:write name="RESULT" property="legend"/>
</TD>
</TR>
   <!-- [15.11.2] isResult? -->
<logic:notEqual name="RESULT" property="size" value="0">
<TR class="subhead">
<TH>id</TH>
<TH>article</TH>
<TH>contributed</TH>
</TR>
<TR>
<!-- [15.11.3] RESULT -->
<logic:iterate id="row" name="RESULT" property="iterator">
<TR>
  <TD nowrap>
    <bean:write name="row" property="article"/>
  </TD>
  <TD width="100%">
    <html:link forward="article" paramName="row"
          paramProperty="article" paramId="article">
      <bean:write name="row" property="title"/>
    </html:link>
  </TD>
  <TD nowrap>
    <bean:write name="row" property="contributedDisplay"/>
  </TD>
 </TR>
</logic:iterate>
</TR>
</logic:notEqual>
```

15.11.1 *The legend*

At the top of the result tile in listing 15.14, we print a description for the page. The description is assembled from some of the properties provided by the ResultList object (section 15.9.4). The `size` property returns the number of entries in the Collection. The `legend` property is created on the business tier. For the /find/Recent action (section 15.9), the legend would usually read `20 matches for last=20`.

The same result tile is used by all the search operations. The legend serves to customize the page and keep users informed as to where they are in a workflow.

15.11.2 *isResult?*

Many search operations return no matches. The result tile shown in listing 15.14 checks the `size` property of the ResultList to see if any matches were returned. If we do have entries, the column headings for the table are printed, and we continue to iterate over the Collection entries.

If there were zero matches, we can skip the rest of the markup. In this case, the only content printed for this tile would be the legend `0 matches for....`

15.11.3 *RESULT*

When there are matches, the Struts `<logic:iterate>` tag is used to scroll through the Collection. During the iteration, each entry will be exposed as a scripting variable named `row`. The ResultList object provides a standard `getIterator()` method that works well with the Struts tag. The block of code in this row (`<TR>` ... `</TR>`) is generated for each entry in this collection. The markup that is sent to the browser looks something like this:

```
<TR>
  <TD nowrap>101</TD>
  <TD width="100%">
    <a href="/artimus/do/view/Article?article=101">
      Welcome to Artimus
    </a>
  </TD>
  <TD nowrap>2002-12-25 18:30:03</TD>
</TR>
```

<html:link>

The `<html:link>` tag starts by retrieving the `path` property of the `article` global forward (section 15.8), which is /do/view/Article. The `paramProperty` and `paramId` properties specify to use `article` as the name (or id) of a query string parameter and the result of `row.getArticle()` for its value. The `<html:link>` tag adds the servlet context (/artimus) and pastes it all together to create a hyperlink like this:

```
<a href="/artimus/do/view/Article?article=101">Welcome to Artimus</a>
```

This link could also have been written as

```
<html:link page="/do/view/Article" paramName="row" paramProperty="article"
    paramId="article">
```

but that embeds more of our API detail into the page. Using an ActionForward documents that we need a hyperlink that goes to the `article` and also makes it easy to change our `article` hyperlinks later.

One example would be an intranet environment where everyone using the application was a Contributor. During a period of heavy editing, the users might prefer to skip the view stage and go directly to the editing page. If you changed the ActionForward for `article` from /do/View/article to /do/Edit/article, the link would be changed wherever it appeared in the application. Later, if they change their minds again (as users are wont to do), a single modification puts it all back.

contributedDisplay

There are many properties in an application that need to be rendered in a particular way. The database may store a telephone number as a simple `String` of numerals, but your business requirements might say that telephone numbers must be formatted with spaces or hyphens to make them easier to read.

A good way to handle these requirements is with a helper method. The helper method starts with the original database value and then modifies it to meet the business requirements. One requirement may be that a person's name be in all uppercase letters. Elsewhere, there may be a requirement that the person's name be displayed last name first. Using the helper pattern, we can store the original value once in our transfer object and modify it as needed. A `personAllCap` method can concatenate the name properties and return the result in all uppercase letters. A `personDirectoryStyle` method can return another concatenation of the name properties, starting with the last name and not changing the case. Both methods can draw on the same base set of properties and just render them differently.

STRUTS TIP   Use Display properties to convert and transform data.

Dates are another place where we can use helpers. Internally, the database stores the contributed date as a binary Timestamp. But when we send the date between the business and application tiers, we would prefer to represent it as a String that the users can view and edit.

Artimus uses a contributedDisplay helper property to render the Timestamp as a String and then convert it back to a Timestamp later. The ActionForm just uses the String property, contributedDisplay. On the business tier, there are two properties: a Timestamp contributed property, to hold the database value, and the String contributedDisplay helper property:

```
private Timestamp contributed = ConvertUtils.getTimestamp();
public Timestamp getContributed() {
      return (this.contributed);
   }

public void setContributed(Timestamp contributed) {
      this.contributed = contributed;
   }

public void setContributedDisplay(String contributedDisplay) {
      if (null==contributedDisplay)
         this.contributed = null;
      else
         this.contributed = Timestamp.valueOf(contributedDisplay);
   }

public String getContributedDisplay() {
      Timestamp contributed = getContributed();
      if (null==contributed)
         return null;
      else
         return contributed.toString();
   }
```

Note that the contributedDisplay property has no field of its own. It gets what it needs from the contributed property, munges the value, and returns the desired result.

Again, these are methods on the article business bean (org.apache.artimus. article.Bean). The ActionForm we use for editing, shown in listing 15.15, just stores contributedDisplay as a simple String property. The business bean handles the conversion issues.

The date handling in the application is rudimentary and could be improved in future releases of the application.

Listing 15.15   org.apache.artimus.struts.Form

```java
public class Form extends BaseForm {
    private String primaryKey = null;
    public String getPrimaryKey() {
        return (this.primaryKey);
    }
    public void setPrimaryKey(String primaryKey) {
        this.primaryKey = primaryKey;
    }

    private String marked = ConvertUtils.STRING_ZERO;
    public String getMarked() {
        return (this.marked);
    }
    public void setMarked(String marked) {
        this.marked = marked;
    }

    private String hours = null;
    public String getHours() {
        return (this.hours);
    }
    public void setHours(String hours) {
        this.hours = hours;
    }

    private String articles = null;
    public String getArticles() {
        return (this.articles);
    }
    public void setArticles(String articles) {
        this.articles = articles;
    }

    private String article = null;
    public String getArticle() {
        return (this.article);
    }
    public void setArticle(String article) {
        this.article = article;
    }

    private String contributor = null;
    public String getContributor() {
        return (this.contributor);
    }
    public void setContributor(String contributor) {
        this.contributor = contributor;
    }

    private String contributedDisplay =
        ConvertUtils.getTimestamp().toString();
```

```
public String getContributedDisplay() {
    return this.contributedDisplay;
}
public void setContributedDisplay(String contributedDisplay) {
    this.contributedDisplay = contributedDisplay;
}

private String creator = null;
public String getCreator() {
    return (this.creator);
}
public void setCreator(String creator) {
    this.creator = creator;
}

private String title = null;
public String getTitle() {
    return (this.title);
}

public void setTitle(String title) {
    this.title = title;
}

private String contentDisplayHtml = null;
public String getContentDisplayHtml() {
    return (this.contentDisplayHtml);
}
public void setContentDisplayHtml(String contentDisplayHtml) {
    this.contentDisplayHtml = contentDisplayHtml;
}

} // end Form
```

15.12 *Article actions*

When a user selects an article link from the results page (section 15.11), the result
is a call to the application's /article/View action. Listing 15.16 shows how /article
/View and the other Article actions are defined in the Struts configuration.

Listing 15.16   /WEB-INF/struts-config.xml (the Article actions)

```
<action
      path="/article/View"
      type="org.apache.struts.scaffold.ProcessAction"
      parameter="org.apache.artimus.article.FindByArticle"
      name="articleForm"
      scope="request"
      validate="false">
```

```
        <forward
            name="success"
            path=".article.View"/>
    </action>

<action
        path="/admin/article/Edit"
        type="org.apache.struts.scaffold.ProcessAction"
        parameter="org.apache.artimus.article.FindByArticle"
        name="articleForm"
        scope="request"
        validate="false">
        <forward
            name="success"
            path=".article.Form"/>
    </action>

<action
        path="/admin/article/Input"
        forward=".article.Form"
        name="articleForm"
        scope="request"
        validate="false"/>

<action
        path="/admin/article/Store"
        type="org.apache.struts.scaffold.ProcessAction"
        parameter="org.apache.artimus.article.Store"
        name="articleForm"
        scope="request"
        validate="true"
        input=".article.Form">
        <forward
            name="success"
            path=".article.View"/>
    </action>

<action
        path="/admin/article/Delete"
        type="org.apache.struts.scaffold.ProcessAction"
        parameter="org.apache.artimus.article.Delete"
        name="articleForm"
        scope="request"
        validate="false">
        <forward
            name="success"
            path=".article.Menu"/>
    </action>

  <action
        path="/admin/article/Restore"
        type="org.apache.struts.scaffold.ProcessAction"
        parameter="org.apache.artimus.article.Restore"
```

```
            name="articleForm"
            scope="request"
            validate="false">
          <forward
                name="success"
                path=".article.Menu"/>
      </action>
```

Like the Find actions presented earlier (listing 15.7), most of the Article actions shown in listing 15.16 use the standard ProcessAction to launch a business bean. The business bean is specified as the `parameter` property. The actions also all share the `articleForm` form bean, which defines the properties needed by all of these actions. Most of these do not require validation, the exception being the Store action.

Our View action uses the FindByArticle business class to locate the article by its ID number. If the operation is successful, the request is forwarded to the article view page:

```
<forward
      name="success"
      path=".article.View"/>
```

The system path to the view page is handled through a Tiles definition (section 15.10):

```
<definition name=".article.View" extends=".article.Base">
      <put name="title"      value="article.View.title"/>
      <put name="content"    value="/pages/article/view.jsp"/>
  </definition>
```

On the other hand, if it does not succeed, our global `failure` ActionForward (section 15.8) comes into play:

```
<forward
      name="failure"
      path="/do/Menu"/>
```

which sends the request to the Menu action and ultimately the menu page. (We cover the Artimus menu in section 15.15.)

The same pattern repeats for the other actions. The ProcessAction creates a Map from the ActionForm properties and passes it to the business bean. The business bean executes the business operation and returns the result. The ProcessAction analyzes the outcome and routes control to `success` or `failure`.

QUERY Success and failure: is that all there is? Of course, the architecture is not restricted to success and failure. It's just that in practice, these are enough to handle the vast majority of tasks. In section 15.15, we make better use of the flexibility afforded by ActionForwards when we use them as routers for our menuing tasks.

While the backroom actions are becoming a bit dull, things are starting to heat up on the presentation layer. Let's take a look at the view.jsp tile and see how it adjusts its presentation according to the user's security role.

15.13 *view.jsp*

Most often, a user reaches the view page from the results page (section 15.11) by clicking on an article's title. It can also be reached directly from the menu page, using the article ID. (We cover the menu actions in section 15.15.)

Listing 15.17 shows our view.jsp tile. Remember this is just the content tile. Other tiles, as specified by the Tiles Definition and layout page (section 15.10), provide the rest of the markup.

This listing introduces a tag we haven't used before: <req:isUserInRole>. This comes out of the Jakarta Taglibs Request tag library. It tests the user's security role, as declared in our deployment descriptor (section 15.4.6). The view page uses it to determine whether to print the Edit and Delete buttons.

As with the results page (section 15.11), the bean behind this form is not an ActionForm but an instance of our business bean.

Listing 15.17   /article/common/view.jsp

```
<%@ taglib uri="/tags/struts-html" prefix="html" %>
<%@ taglib uri="/tags/struts-bean" prefix="bean" %>
<%@ taglib uri="/tags/struts-logic" prefix="logic" %>
<%@ taglib uri="/tags/tiles" prefix="tiles" %>
<%@ taglib uri="/tags/request" prefix="req" %>
<TR>
<!-- [15.13.1] headline-->
<TD class="headline" colspan="3">
<H2><bean:write name="articleForm" property="title"/></H2></TD>
</TR>
<TR>
<TD class="author" colspan="3">by <bean:write name="articleForm"
  property="creator"/>
</TD>
</TR>
```

```
<TR>
<!-- [15.13.2] content -->
<TD class="article" colspan="3">
<bean:write name="articleForm" property="contentDisplayHtml"
            filter="false"/></TD>
</TR>
<!-- [15.13.3] contributor -->
<req:isUserInRole role="contributor">
<TR>
<TD colspan="3"><HR /></TD>
</TR>
<TR>
<%-- DELETE --%>
<logic:equal name="articleForm" property="marked" value="0">
      <html:form action="/admin/article/Delete">
      <TD class="button.left"><html:submit>DELETE</html:submit></TD>
      <html:hidden property="article"/>
      </html:form>
</logic:equal>
<%-- RESTORE --%>
<logic:equal name="articleForm" property="marked" value="1">
      <html:form action="/admin/article/Restore">
      <TD class="button.left">
      <html:submit>RESTORE</html:submit>
      </TD>
      <html:hidden property="article"/>
      </html:form>
</logic:equal>
<html:form action="/admin/article/Edit">
<TD class="button" colspan="2">
<html:hidden property="article"/>
<html:submit>EDIT</html:submit>
<html:cancel>CANCEL</html:cancel>
</TD>
</html:form>
</TR>
</req:isUserInRole>
```

15.13.1 *headline*

Making good use of our style sheet, the page shown in listing 15.17 prints the title and creator (or author) properties at the top of the tile. The style sheet reference is defined by the layout page (section 15.10).

15.13.2 *content*

Our article content is inserted into the page as a single String. Note that in listing 15.17, the <bean:write> tag for the contentDisplayHtml property has the `filter` property set to false. This lets HTML through to the page. The default setting for `<bean:write>` is `filter=true`. The filter escapes the HTML tags to be sure they do not spoil surrounding markup or create any security issues.

The API contract with the `contentDisplayHtml` property is that the method is responsible for handling any markup issues. If the raw `content` property were called instead, then the filter should be left on.

The `contentDisplayHtml` property is another example of the helper pattern. The helper pattern is also used with the `contributedDisplay` property (section 15.11.3).

QUERY   Why do we need a `contentDisplayHtml` helper method? Isn't coping with HTML markup something a JSP should do? It's the job of the presentation layer to take data returned from the other tiers and display it to the user. Sometimes that data will be plain text that needs to be surrounded with markup. Other times, it may be an HTML segment that must be positioned in relation to the other HTML markup on the page. In the case of `contentDisplayHtml`, the content may be stored in some other format and have to be transformed to HTML before display. Since the JSP cannot be expected to cope with any arbitrary format, it becomes the job of the business tier to manage the transformation. The content may also be made available to other components, aside from a JSP, that understand HTML.

15.13.3 *contributor*

As mentioned, the `<req:isUserInRole>` is used to determine whether to print the contributor controls. There would be other ways to handle this, but, in practice, this is the most common approach.

Some MVC mavens might complain that the security role is not a concern of the presentation layer and should not be embedded in the markup. But, in practice, many presentation designs revolve around a user's role in the application. If they are logged on, the storyboard goes, the page looks like this. If they are not, it looks like this instead.

So, we could develop two content tiles, one for contributors and one for noncontributors. We could also use Tiles to arrange it so the contributor tile is included only for contributors. But those are just semantic differences.

The important point is that the security role is being determined through a custom tag *that we control for our application*. The page only knows what the tag tells it. If we want to determine the role in an entirely different way, we can replace the implementation of the tag without changing the markup on the page. The tag itself provides the layering expected by a Model 2/MVC design.

But the critical point is that the tag is not the final arbiter of security. When the operation is requested, the user's credentials will be automatically checked before it is executed. Being able to request an operation is not enough; you must also be able to access the action's URI. The access permissions are outside the presentation layer's control.

delete / restore

Another bit of logic in listing 15.17 is the testing of our `marked` property. The `marked` property indicates whether the article has been selected for deletion. If `marked` is set to 0, it hasn't been marked. So, we display a Delete button and point it at the delete action. The /admin/article/Delete action sets `marked` to 1. All of the standard FindBy operations are designed to ignore `marked` articles, so the record appears to be deleted.

The exception is the FindByArticle operation. If we know the article's ID, we can still bring it up even after it's been deleted. In this case, the Delete button does not display, and the Restore button displays instead (`marked` equals 1). The /admin/article/Restore action sets `marked` back to 0, and the article is effectively undeleted.

So why do we go around Robin Hood's barn just to delete a record? In practice, removing records from a table is often a task best left to the database administrator's discretion. The space consumed by a record is rarely a concern these days, and ad-hoc deletions may degrade a system's performance. Artimus starts by marking the articles for deletion, but defers actually removing them to another operation. Better safe than sorry.

edit

Aside from deleting and restoring, a contributor can also elect to edit an article. The /admin/article/Edit action, shown in listing 15.17, simply forwards to the edit page. Since the URI is under /admin/*, the container will allow access only to a user in the contributor or manager role (section 15.4.8).

15.14 *form.jsp*

As with the view.jsp (section 15.13), the form.jsp is only one tile of a larger page. The full source for our edit page is shown in listing 15.18. Since the tags for client-side validation changed slightly between Struts 1.0 and Struts 1.1, we will present the updated 1.1 version of this page in the next chapter. Listing 15.18 shows the (nearly identical) 1.0 version.

For the record, this is actually the "Add / Edit" page. Our business bean is smart enough to tell an insert from an update, and so we can use the same page for both tasks.

Listing 15.18   **/article/content/form.jsp**

```
<%@ taglib uri="/tags/struts-html" prefix="html" %>
<%@ taglib uri="/tags/struts-bean" prefix="bean" %>
<%@ taglib uri="/tags/struts-logic" prefix="logic" %>
<html:form action="/admin/article/Store"
      onsubmit="return validateArticleForm(this);">
<TR>
<TD class="label" nowrap>Title:</TD>
<TD class="input" colspan="2">
<html:text property="title" size="50" maxlength="255"/></TD>
</TR>
<TR>
<TD class="label" nowrap>Author:</TD>
<TD class="input">
<html:text property="creator" size="30" maxlength="75"/></TD>
<TD class="hint">Full name of person who originated the article.</TD>
</TR>
<!-- [15.14.1] article content -->
<TR>
<TD class="label" nowrap>Article:</TD>
<TD class="input" colspan="2">
<!-- The Struts html:textarea tag does not support wrapping -->
<!-- so we use this trick instead -->
<textarea name="contentDisplayHtml" rows="12" cols="50" tabindex="2"
  wrap="soft">
<bean:write name="articleForm" property="contentDisplayHtml"/>
</textarea>
</TD>
</TR>
<!-- [15.14.2] contributed / contributor -->
<html:hidden property="contributedDisplay"/>
<html:hidden property="contributor"/>
<!-- [15.14.3] article id -->
</TR><TD class="label" nowrap>Article ID:</TD>
<logic:notPresent name="articleForm" property="article">
      <TD class="dimmed"><i><html:hidden property="article"/>not assigned</
   i></TD>
</logic:notPresent>
<logic:present name="articleForm" property="article">
      <TD class="input"><html:hidden property="article"/>
      <bean:write name="articleForm" property="article"/></TD>
```

```
</logic:present>
<TD> </TD>
</TR>
<TR>
<TD class="button" colspan="3">
<html:submit>SAVE</html:submit>
<html:cancel>CANCEL</html:cancel>
</TD>
</TR>
</html:form>
<!-- [15.14.4] client-side validation (1.0)-->
<validator:javascript formName="articleForm"/>
```

So, is the bean behind this page an instance of our business bean or have we finally resorted to an ActionForm?

The answer? The bean behind this form is an instance of our business bean *or* an ActionForm. When we retrieve an article to edit, the page is populated by a business bean that we received from the business tier. If we are creating a new article, or our article fails web-tier validation, then the page would be rendered using an ActionForm.

Changing bean types is transparent to the tags. The tags only look at the property names; the bean type is immaterial. As long as the property names match, any number of beans can share the same page.

15.14.1 *Article content*

Listing 15.18 uses a `<textarea>` element to allow an article's content to be edited. The Struts html taglib does offer an `<html:textarea>` tag to generate this element, but we have chosen not to use it. In our `<textarea>` element, we would like to use the `wrap=soft` attribute. This attribute is not an official HTML 4.01 attribute for the `<textarea>` element, but the popular browsers interpret it to mean that long lines within the text area should be wrapped to fit. You can do the same thing by hand, but users may complain if this feature is not used.

Being standards-conscious, the Struts team will not add a `wrap` attribute to the `<html:textarea>` tag, unless and until it is made part of the official specification. So, caught between a rock and the user base, we resorted to creating our own dynamic `<textarea>` element. This is very simple to do. Just start by coding the HTML element the old-fashioned way, and then use `<bean:write>` to populate it.

In the view page (section 15.13), we added `filter=false` to the `<bean:write>` tag so that it would not escape any HTML tags that might be found in the content text. This lets the contributors use HTML in their articles. On the edit side, we leave the filtering on so the tags are escaped. Otherwise, we wouldn't be able to edit them. This makes it easy to roundtrip the HTML for editing.

Like the handling of our contributed date (section 15.11.3), the way content is rendered is crude but adequate. The feature could be vastly improved in later releases. Ideally, various content types should be supported; HTML, when used, should be validated and/or converted to XHTML before acceptance, and so forth.

But like most applications, Artimus had to meet a ship date, and feature triage put these niceties further down the list.

15.14.2 *Contributed / contributor*

A future version of Artimus is slated to support tracking the contributor and selecting the contribution date. The properties were added, but we are not ready to fully implement the features yet. So, in listing 15.18, for now we are just passing the properties as hidden fields. (Sound familiar?)

15.14.3 *Article ID*

As mentioned, this page is used for both adding and updating articles. The business bean tells the difference by looking for an article ID. If there's no article ID, then it's an insert. Otherwise, it's an update. In listing 15.18, we use the `<logic:present>` and `<logic:notPresent>` tags to print either the article ID or the legend `not assigned`.

15.14.4 *Validation*

The Struts Validator is designed so that it can perform both server-side and client-side validations using the same set of rules. The validators and validation rules are defined in XML files. The standard ActionForm `validate` method can be hooked into the Validator framework. Most applications, like Artimus, can just use the Struts Validator to handle the prima facie validators. You can also extend the standard validators with your own plug-ins, or call the Struts Validator and then apply your own set of handcoded validations. For more about the Validator, see chapter 12.

Server-side validations

The server-side validators are Java classes that are configured through XML for each field that needs to be checked. Listing 15.19 shows our validation.xml file.

Listing 15.19   /WEB-INF/validation.xml

```xml
<form-validation>
  <global>
    <validator name="required"
               classname="com.wintecinc.struts.validation.StrutsValidator"
               method="validateRequired"
               msg="errors.required">
      <javascript><![CDATA[
        function validateRequired(form) {
            var bValid = true;
            var focusField = null;
            var i = 0;
            var fields = new Array();
            oRequired = new required();

            for (x in oRequired) {
                if ((form[oRequired[x][0]].type == 'text' ||
form[oRequired[x][0]].type == 'textarea' || form[oRequired[x][0]].type ==
'select' || form[oRequired[x][0]].type == 'radio' ||
form[oRequired[x][0]].type == 'password') && form[oRequired[x][0]].value
== '') {
                    if (i == 0)
                        focusField = form[oRequired[x][0]];

                    fields[i++] = oRequired[x][1];

                    bValid = false;
                }
            }

            if (fields.length > 0) {
                focusField.focus();
                alert(fields.join('\n'));
            }

            return bValid;
        }]]>
      </javascript>
    </validator>
  </global>
  <formset>
    <form name="articleForm">
      <field
         property="title"
         depends="required">
            <arg0 key="article.title.displayname"/>
      </field>
      <field
         property="creator"
         depends="required">
            <arg0 key="article.creator.displayname"/>
      </field>
```

```
<field
    property="contentDisplayHtml"
    depends="required">
        <arg0 key="article.content.displayname"/>
    </field>
</form>
</formset>
</form-validation>
```

The validations for the article form simply check to see if all the fields have been completed. The Validator is integrated with the message resources, so we can use the same message keys to identify the fields. Any messages generated by a failed client-side validation will display on our message tile.

Client-side validators

The Struts Validator also supports JavaScript validations. Each validator has its own script, which the framework automatically combines into a single, seamless script. The scripts are identified by the name of the ActionForm bean. To call the script:

- Add an `onsubmit` JavaScript event handler to the form tag.
- Insert a `<validator:javascript>` tag anywhere on the page citing the form name.

See listing 15.18 to see how these two elements are used by the edit JSP. Note that the name of the script is the same as the name of the form, but with a *validate* prefix.

15.15 /do/Menu

The final set of actions in Artimus is the menu actions. Links to the menu actions are provided on the default navbar tile. The menu is also the default failure page if another is not specified. In addition to the default action that leads to the menu page, there are several other menu actions in Artimus. The menu page uses these actions to provide access to the various search operations we saw in section 15.9. Listing 15.20 shows the Artimus menu actions.

Listing 15.20　/WEB-INF/struts-confg.xml (the menu actions)

```xml
<!-- [15.15.1] logon -->
<action
    path="/admin/Menu"
    forward="/do/Menu"/>

<!-- [15.15.2] menu -->
 <action
    path="/Menu"
    name="menuForm"
    type="org.apache.struts.scaffold.ExistsAttributeAction"
    parameter="application;HOURS">
    <forward
        name="success"
        path=".article.Menu"/>
    <forward
        name="failure"
        path="/do/MenuCreate"/>
 </action>

<!-- [15.15.2] menu init -->
  <action
      path="/MenuCreate"
      name="menuForm"
      type="org.apache.struts.scaffold.ProcessAction"
      parameter="org.apache.artimus.article.MenuCreate">
    <forward
        name="success"
        path="/do/Menu"/>
    <forward
        name="failure"
        path=".article.Menu"/>
  </action>

<!-- [15.16.2] find -->
<action
      path="/menu/Find"
      type="org.apache.struts.scaffold.ParameterAction"
      name="menuForm"
      validate="false"
      parameter="keyValue">
    <forward
        name="title"
        path="/do/find/Property?keyName=title&amp;keyValue="/>
    <forward
        name="author"
        path="/do/find/Property?keyName=creator&amp;keyValue="/>
    <forward
        name="content"
        path="/do/find/Property?keyName=content&amp;keyValue="/>
    <forward
```

```
            name="article"
            path="/do/article/View?article="/>
</action>

<!-- [15.16.4] contributor -->
<action
    path="/menu/Contributor"
    type="org.apache.struts.scaffold.RelayAction"
    name="menuForm"
    validate="false">
    <forward
        name="input"
        path="/do/admin/article/Input"/>
</action>

<!-- [15.16.5] manager -->
<action
    path="/menu/Manager"
    type="org.apache.struts.scaffold.RelayAction"
    name="menuForm"
    validate="false">
    <forward
        name="reload"
        path="/do/admin/Reload"/>
    <forward
        name="createResources"
        path="/do/admin/CreateResources"/>
</action>
```

The first three listed are used to display the menu page. The others are used by the menu page itself. We'll cover the latter actions in section 15.16, when we present the JSP code for the menu page.

15.15.1 *logon*

The /admin/Menu action in listing 15.20 is just a little trick to get the container to present a logon challenge. By using a URI below /admin/, the container will ensure that a user is logged in before displaying the menu page (again). This then lets the menu page display options based on the user's role, as we did on the view page (15.13).

15.15.2 *menu*

Our menu page provides several option lists. Rather than hardcode these into the JSP, or generate them on every request, Artimus stores them as application attributes. This works well as long as the attributes exist but gets messy if they don't.

To help ensure that the attributes are created before the page displays, the default menu command, /Menu, shown in listing 15.20, uses a standard Scaffold Action to test for the existence of one of the attributes. The ExistsAttribute-Action expects the scope to check (application, session, request) to be given as the first token of the parameter property. The attributes to check for are given as the remaining tokens of the parameter property. In this case, we told Exists-AttributeAction to check if there is an attribute named HOURS in application scope. If there is, the Action branches to success. Otherwise, ExistsAttributeAction branches to failure.

If the HOURS attribute isn't in application scope, the actions fails, and control is forwarded to the /menu/Create action. This action uses (surprise!) ProcessAction to execute a business bean that creates the option lists we need for the menu page. Listing 15.21 shows the source for the MenuCreate bean.

Listing 15.21   org.apache.artimus.article.MenuCreate

```
package org.apache.artimus.article;
import java.util.List;
import java.util.ArrayList;
import org.apache.artimus.lang.Tokens;
import org.apache.commons.scaffold.util.LabelValueBean;
import org.apache.commons.scaffold.util.ProcessBeanBase;
import org.apache.commons.scaffold.util.ProcessResult;
import org.apache.commons.scaffold.util.ProcessResultBase;

public class MenuCreate extends ProcessBeanBase {
    public Object execute(Object parameters) throws Exception {
      <!-- [15.15.3 Our controls] -->
      ArrayList controls = new ArrayList();
      ArrayList hours = new ArrayList();
          hours.add(new LabelValueBean("Day", "24"));
          hours.add(new LabelValueBean("Week", "168"));
          hours.add(new LabelValueBean("Month", "720"));
        saveResult(Tokens.MENU_HOURS,hours,controls);
      ArrayList find = new ArrayList();
          find.add(new LabelValueBean("-- select --", "done"));
          find.add(new LabelValueBean("Title", "title"));
          find.add(new LabelValueBean("Author", "author"));
          find.add(new LabelValueBean("Content", "content"));
          find.add(new LabelValueBean("ID", "article"));
        saveResult(Tokens.MENU_FIND,find,controls);
    ArrayList contributor = new ArrayList();
          contributor.add(new LabelValueBean("Add Article", "input"));
        saveResult(Tokens.MENU_CONTRIBUTOR,contributor,controls);
      ArrayList manager = new ArrayList();
  manager.add(new LabelValueBean("Test channel", "channel""));
  manager.add(new LabelValueBean("Delete marked", "remove""));
```

```
            manager.add(new LabelValueBean("Reload config", "reload"));
            manager.add(new LabelValueBean("Create resources", "create"));
      saveResult(Tokens.MENU_MANAGER,manager,controls);

          <!-- [15.15.5 Our results] -->
           ProcessResult results = new ProcessResultBase(controls);
              results.setAggregate(true); // I'm a list of other results
           return (Object) results;
      }

   <!-- [15.15.4] saveResult -->
    private void saveResult(String name, List items, List controls) {
         ProcessResult result = new ProcessResultBase(items);
         result.setName(name);
        result.setScope(org.apache.commons.scaffold.lang.Tokens.APPLICATION);
         controls.add(result);
      }
   } // end MenuCreate
```

15.15.3 *Our controls*

All told, our menu page hosts four controls with option lists. Each of these can be saved as a separate attribute in the application scope. This makes them easier to use separately, if needed.

The MenuCreate bean in listing 15.21 first creates an ArrayList to hold the collections of options as they are instantiated. Each option is represented as a LabelValueBean (a JavaBean with a label property and a value property).

15.15.4 *saveResult*

Since we are on the business tier, the attribute cannot actually be saved to the application context … at least not yet. The ProcessAction can do this when the result is returned from the business tier to the web tier, but we have to tell it what to do. The result object is used to store the settings we want the action to use when it saves the attribute for us.

The settings we want to store are encapsulated in a utility saveResult method. This creates a new ProcessResult for the list, gives it an attribute name, and sets the scope to application. The ProcessAction can then use these settings to save the attribute in the right place under the right name.

15.15.5 *Our results*

Once all the option lists are created and saved to our control list, we can return the result to the ProcessAction. To do this, we wrap our list in yet another ProcessResult, but set this ProcessResult to be an aggregation. This tells the

ProcessAction to process each entry as a separate ProcessResult. Each of our option lists is then stored as a separate attribute in the application context, just as if each had been a separate business operation.

In fact, we could refactor MenuCreate into separate business beans at any time. The MenuCreate bean could just as easily call an HoursCreate bean, a Find-Create bean, and so forth, and return an aggregation of those results. The rest of the application would be unaffected. It just calls MenuCreate without caring how it is created.

This is the essence of a Model 2/MVC layered architecture. As long as the API between the layers is retained, we should be able to change one layer's implementation without affecting the adjoining layer. The other side of the coin is that we should be able to change the API between two layers without affecting other layers above or below them. While these can be difficult design requirements to meet in practice, the return on investment can be significant over the life of an application.

After saving our objects to application scope, the ProcessAction returns its success forward. For the /menu/Create mapping in listing 15.20, this routes us back to the default /Menu action. But this time, the ExistsAttributeAction succeeds, and control is forwarded to the menu page.

15.16 *menu.jsp*

The menu page renders the option lists we generated in the /menu/Create action (section 15.15.2). The lists are used to populate controls for listing recently posted articles and for finding articles by title, author, or keyword. There are also special menus for users in the contributor or manager role.

Listing 15.22 shows the source for our menu.jsp tile.

Listing 15.22   /article/common/menu.jsp

```
<%@ taglib uri="/tags/struts-html" prefix="html" %>
<%@ taglib uri="/tags/struts-bean" prefix="bean" %>
<%@ taglib uri="/tags/struts-logic" prefix="logic" %>
<%@ taglib uri="/tags/request" prefix="req" %>
<!-- [15.16.1] /find/Hours -->
<html:form action="/find/Hours">
<TR>
<TD class="label">List articles posted in the last:</TD>
<TD class="input">
<logic:iterate id="row" name="HOURS"
   type="org.apache.commons.scaffold.util.LabelValueBean">
<html:radio property="hours" value="<%=row.getValue()%>"/>
   <bean:write name="row" property="label"/>
```

```
</logic:iterate>
</TD>
<TD class="input">
<html:submit property="submit" value="GO"/>
</TD>
</TR>
</html:form>
<!-- [15.16.2] /menu/Find -->
<html:form action="/menu/Find">
<TR>
<TD class="label" nowrap>Find articles by: </TD>
<TD class="input">
<html:select property="dispatch">
<html:options collection="FIND" labelProperty="label" property="value" />
</html:select>
<html:text property="keyValue" size="10" maxlength="30"/>
</TD>
<TD><html:submit>GO</html:submit></TD>
</TR>
</html:form>
<!-- [15.16.3] /find/Last -->
<html:form action="/find/Last">
<TR>
<TD> </TD><html:hidden property="articles" value="20"/>
<TD class="input"><html:submit property="submit"> LATEST NEWS </
  html:submit></TD>
<TD> </TD>
</TR>
</html:form>
<!-- [15.16.4] /menu/Contributor -->
<req:isUserInRole role="contributor">
<html:form action="/menu/Contributor">
<TR >
<TD class="label" nowrap>Contributor options: </TD>
<TD class="input">
<html:select property="dispatch">
<html:options collection="CONTRIBUTOR" property="value"
  labelProperty="label"/>
</html:select>
</TD>
<TD><html:submit>GO</html:submit></TD>
</TR>
</html:form>
</req:isUserInRole>
<!-- [15.16.5] /menu/Manager-->
<req:isUserInRole role="manager">
<html:form action="/menu/Manager">
<TR>
<TD class="label" nowrap>Manager options: </TD>
<TD class="input">
<html:select property="dispatch">
```

```
<html:options collection="MANAGER" property="value" labelProperty="label"/>
</html:select>
</TD>
<TD><html:submit>GO</html:submit></TD>
</TR>
</html:form>
</req:isUserInRole>
```

15.16.1 /find/Hours

The `<html:radio>` tag in Struts 1.0 lacks some of the niceties found in some of the other Struts tags. The /find/Hours form in listing 15.22 has to do a little jury-rigging to get the tag to work with the list of labels and values set up by the /menu/Create action (section 15.15.2).

Since we need to generate several radio buttons, we start by nesting the `<html:radio>` tag inside `<logic:iterate>`. On each iteration, we expose the next LabelValue bean from the list we stored under the attribute HOURS. Within the loop, we start writing a `<html:radio>` but as usual, but switch over to a scriptlet to provide the value. The runtime expression (`<%=row.getValue()%>`) gets the value property from the current bean, and then `<bean:write>` prints the label.

When rendered, our radio tags resolve to

```
<input type="radio" name="hours" value="24"> Day
<input type="radio" name="hours" value="168"> Week
<input type="radio" name="hours" value="720"> Month
```

When one of these is selected and submitted, we end up with the query string equivalent of

```
/artimus/find/Hours?hours=24
```

15.16.2 /menu/Find

The /menu/Find form in listing 15.22 prints a list of options followed by a text input field. The list is taken from the Find list generated by the /menu/Create action (section 15.15.2) and includes the label/value entries shown in table 15.4.

The form lets the user select a search flavor (Title, Author, Content, ID) and then enter a qualifier in the text input field. Listing 15.22 shows the mapping for our /menu/Find action. It submits our form to the Scaffold ParameterAction, populating a Scaffold MenuForm bean on the way. The MenuForm is a convenience class for maintaining menu pages, like this one. It captures the `dispatch` and `keyValue` properties we used in the /menu/Find form. This saves defining utility properties like this on our application's ActionForms.

Table 15.4   The Find menu entries

Label	Value
Title	title
Author	author
Content	content
ID	article
– select –	done

The ParameterAction is used to complete a query string by adding an additional parameter. What request parameter to append is specified as the `parameter` property to the ActionMapping. The query string is selected from one of the local forwards.

In listing 15.20, the mapping for the /menu/Find action includes local forwards like this one:

```
<forward
name="article"
        path="/do/article/View?article="/>
```

When the ID label is selected from the menu, the browser will submit the query string equivalent of

```
/artimus/menu/Find?dispatch=article&keyValue=101
```

The ParameterAction looks for the `dispatch` parameter and uses that as the name of the forward with our base query string. The base query string is retrieved from the forward's `path`, and the runtime parameter value is appended. In our example, this results in the query string equivalent of

```
/artimus/do/article/View?article=101
```

We could have done the same thing by using a standalone form for /article/View with a text input control named `article`. But then we would need to do the same for the Title, Author, and Content searches. The MenuForm and ParameterAction let us add any number of search types to our list and let them share an input box, even if they expect parameters with different names.

15.16.3 /find/Last

The /find/Last form in listing 15.22 replicates the functionality for the default /find/Recent action. It uses a hidden field to set the number of articles to list at 20.

We could have also used a hyperlink to the `welcome` forward here, or even directly to the /do/find/Recent action. The one thing we couldn't do, without making some changes, is use /find/Recent as the target of an `<html:form>`.

Why not? If you check the /find/Recent mapping in listing 15.7, you'll see we neglected to specified a form bean. If you try to use a form bean–less mapping with the `<html:form>` tag, it will complain that it can't find the bean. Since the primary purpose of the `<html:form>` tag is to populate elements from an Action-Form, not specifying an Action generates an error.

Of course, we could have just specified a form bean for /find/Recent. There's even a NullForm class in Scaffold (`org.apache.struts.scaffold.NullForm`) for this very purpose. Another workaround would have been to jury-rig an HTML form like this:

```
<FORM action="<html:rewrite forward='welcome'/>" method="POST">
<TR>
<TD> </TD>
<TD class="input"><INPUT type="submit" value=" LATEST NEWS " name="SUBMIT">
    </TD>
<TD> </TD>
</TR>
</FORM>
```

But it seemed simplest to just use the hidden field.

15.16.4 /menu/Contributor

Some features may be available only to contributors. In listing 15.22, the `<req:isUserInRole>` tag is used to omit or include a list of contributor commands. We also used this tag on the view page (section 15.13) to omit or include the Edit and Delete buttons.

Right now, the only item on the contributor-only command list is adding articles. While a button could have been used instead, we went ahead and set up an options list, just to make it easier to add other commands later. This also makes it consistent with the /menu/Manager menu in the next section.

Since this command doesn't need any qualifiers, we don't need to use the ParameterAction again. We can use a RelayAction instead. Like the ParameterAction, the RelayAction (`org.apache.struts.scaffold.RelayAction`) looks for a `dispatch` parameter and uses it to select an ActionForward.

Our list of contributor commands stored by the /menu/Create action renders as a short, one-item list:

```
<select name="dispatch">
  <option value="input">Add Article</option></select>
```

When the Add Article option is selected and the form submitted, the browser generates a request for

```
/artimus/do/menu/Contributor?dispatch=input
```

The controller passes this to the RelayAction. The `dispatch` parameter tells the RelayAction to search for a forward named `input` (starting with the mapping's local forwards), like this one:

```
<forward
    name="input"
    path="/do/admin/article/Input"/>
```

The /admin/ portion assures that the user will be logged in before the request is honored. If the request is accepted, it is forwarded on to the article Input action. As shown back in listing 15.16, the Input action simply forwards outs to the edit page.

Since we haven't retrieved an article, our ActionForm is blank, and an empty form is presented to the contributor. If this form is submitted, the article Store action will see that the article ID is blank and insert the new article into the database.

15.16.5 /menu/Manager

The /menu/Manager form in listing 15.22 uses the same approach as the contributor menu (section 15.16.4) but with a different list of commands. Like the contributor menu, this list is restricted to users in the manager role. Our default Artimus user is both a contributor and a manager. So, both menus will display if you log in using the Artimus user credentials.

15.17 *Summary*

Whew! We've come a long way on our journey through Artimus. At this point, we've been through all the essential components. There are several business bean classes that we did not present, but these are all straightforward variations on the two that we did present. Of course, the full source code for all the classes is available through the book's website [Husted].

In the next chapter, we retrofit Artimus for Struts 1.1 so that it can take advantage of the many whiz-bang features offered in the new release.

16

Redux: migrating to Struts 1.1

This chapter covers

- Updating an application for 1.0
- Using dynamic ActionForms
- Implementing Action-based security
- Configuring Tiles and Validator 1.1

> *You only ever write one software application, then you spend*
> *the rest of your life going back and rewriting it.*
> —Craig McClanahan's computer science professor

16.1 Next station, Struts 1.1

Since its release in June 2000, Struts 1.0 has quickly become a very successful product. Thousands of applications now in production are based on Struts. With the advent of Struts 1.1, many teams will be updating their applications to take advantage of the new features. In this chapter, we help blaze the upgrade path by retrofitting our Artimus 1.0 application for Struts 1.1.

First, it's important to note that most Struts 1.0 applications will be able to run under Struts 1.1 out of the box. All that really needs to be done is to:

- Swap in the Struts 1.1 and Commons JARs.
- Rebuild everything, including the JSPs.

If you were using some of the Struts classes that were moved to the Commons, you may have to change a few `import` statements before your application will build. But that should be all you need to do to get up and running.

Several Struts classes were found to have uses outside the framework. Between Struts 1.0 and Struts 1.1, these were repackaged and moved to the Jakarta Commons [ASF, Commons]. The new classes you *may* need to import are as follows:

- Commons BeanUtils package (`org.apache.commons.beanutils`) replaces `org.apache.struts.utils.BeanUtils`, `org.apache.struts.utils.ConvertUtils`, and `org.apache.struts.utils.PropertyUtils`.

- Commons Collections package (`org.apache.commons.collections`) replaces `org.apache.struts.util.ArrayStack`, `org.apache.struts.util.FastArrayList`, `org.apache.struts.util.FastHashMap`, and `org.apache.struts.util.FastTreeMap`.

- Commons Digester package (`org.apache.commons.digester`) replaces `org.apache.struts.digester.*`.

If you are using the 1.0 versions of Tiles and the Struts Validator, you will also have to:

- Change any `import` statements that refer to the com.wintec.* packaging of the Validator.

- Change any `import` statements that refer to the components version of Tiles (although this would be rare).

- Remove references to Tiles or the Validator from your web.xml.

- Add new references to the struts-config.xml to load the integrated versions of Tiles and the Validator.

We will go through this process step by step with our Artimus application so you can see how it's done. But before getting on with that, let's take a quick look at the goodies Struts 1.1 has to offer.

NOTE   The Commons BeanUtils offers significantly better conversion capabilities than the original Struts 1.0 utility. It also changes a fundamental assumption. When converting from `Strings` to numeric types, the Struts 1.0 BeanUtil converts null to null for numeric object types (like `Integer`) but null to 0 (zero) for the native types (like `int`). The Commons version converts null numerics to 0 in either case. If your code expects null `Strings` to convert to null numeric objects, you may have to tweak your code. There is a switch in the ActionServlet (`convertNull`) that can tell Struts to observe the 1.0 behavior. But if you are using BeanUtils in your own code, you may have to adjust your own classes as well.

16.1.1 *Struts 1.1 feature roundup*

The new features offered by Struts 1.1 cover the entire range of the framework, from high-level support for modular applications to low-level tweaks to many of the tags. Table 16.1 summarizes the exciting new features in the Struts 1.1 release and indicates where you can find more information.

Table 16.1   New features in Struts 1.1 (beta 1)

Feature	Classes or package and description
Multiple Message-Resources	(`org.apache.struts.config.MessageResourcesConfig`) You can now load multiple message resource bundles from the Struts configuration, making it easier to organize your application's resources.
Modular applications	(`org.apache.struts.config.*`) There is new support for organizing an application into modules, or subapplications. Each module has its own set of configuration files and can be developed as if it were a single application. Most Struts 1.0 applications can be used as application modules with only minor changes to the configuration file. For more about application modules, see chapter 4.

Table 16.1   **New features in Struts 1.1 (beta 1)** *(continued)*

Feature	Classes or package and description
Dynamic ActionForms	`(org.apache.struts.action.DynaActionForm)` A specialized subclass of ActionForm allows you to define whatever JavaBean properties you need from the Struts configuration file. For fully dynamic, configuration-free ActionForms, you can also use mapped-backed ActionForms. See chapter 5 for more about ActionForms and dynamic ActionForms.
Roles attribute for Actions	`(org.apache.struts.action.ActionConfig.roles)` You can now register a list of JAAS security roles with an ActionMapping. If the user is not in a role on the list, then access is denied. This works just like standard container-based security but allows you to apply authorization to a specific ActionMapping rather than to just a URL pattern. This can be used along with or instead of container-based security. By providing your own RequestProcessor, you enable other security schemes to use this property.

Separate queues for messages and errors	`(org.apache.struts.action.ActionMessage)`
	 `(org.apache.struts.action.ActionMessages)`
	 `(org.apache.struts.taglib.logic.MessagesPresentTag)`
	 `(org.apache.struts.taglib.logic.MessagesNotPresentTag)`
	 `(org.apache.struts.taglib.html.MessagesTag)`
	 A new generic message class can be used to separate other messages from error-type messages. The message queue is exposed through the `saveMessages` method of the Action class (chapter 8) and the message tags in the html taglib (chapter 10).

Lookup-DispatchAction	`(org.apache.struts.actions.LookupDispatchAction)` A new version of the standard Struts LookupAction makes it easier to combine several operations into an Action and select the operations from localized controls on the presentation page.
SwitchAction	`(org.apache.struts.actions.SwitchAction)` A new standard Action makes it easy to forward a request from one application module to another.
Declarative exception handling	`(org.apache.struts.action.ExceptionHandler)` Rather than catch Exceptions within your Actions, you can let them pass back up to the controller and be caught by a Struts ExceptionHandler. You can register handlers for as many or as few Exception classes as needed. The default handler wraps the Exception message in an instance of ActionErrors and forwards control to a specified URI. You can also create your own ExceptionHandler subclasses to provide other behaviors.
Request-Processor component	`(org.apache.struts.action.RequestProcessor)` You can easily customize how a module handles each request by providing a RequestProcessor subclass. The RequestProcessor object provides several extension points that make it easy to change only what needs to be changed.
PlugIn Actions to manage resources	`(org.apache.struts.PlugIn)` To load your own resources, you can register a PlugIn Action with the controller. This gives you the opportunity to create a resource at startup and destroy it at shutdown, without creating your own specialized servlet or ActionServlet subclass.

Table 16.1   New features in Struts 1.1 (beta 1) *(continued)*

Feature	Classes or package and description
Commons Logging interface	`(org.apache.commons.logging)` The Struts ActionServlet and related components now implement the Commons Logging interface, making it easier to integrate Struts with advanced logging packages like Log4j and the Java 1.4 logging package.
LabelValueBean	`(org.apache.struts.utils.LabelValueBean)` Many JSP tags need to display controls with both a label and a value. This convenience object works well with tags that expect a bean with a `label` and a `value` method. For more about the Struts taglibs, see chapter 10.
Nested taglibs	`(org.apache.struts.taglib.nested.*)` The nested tags extend the base Struts tags to allow them to relate to each other in a nested nature. For more about the Struts taglibs, see chapter 10.
New `empty`/ `notEmpty` tags	`(org.apache.struts.taglib.logic.EmptyTag)` New logic tags make it easier to test fields that may be null or may contain empty strings.
New `frame` tag	`(org.apache.struts.taglib.html.Frame)` A new HTML `frame` tag makes it easier to create hyperlinks between frames, with all the capabilities of the Struts HTML link tag.
New `options-Collection` tag	`(org.apche.struts.taglib.html.OptionsCollection)` The new HTML `optionsCollection` tag makes it easy to store a collection that you use to populate a control on the ActionForm with the other properties.
New `idName` property on radio tag	`(org.apache.struts.taglib.html.RadioTag)` To make it easier to write a series of dynamic radio buttons, you can indicate a bean with the radio tag's value with the new `idName` attribute.
New `indexed` tag property	`(button, checkbox, file, hidden, image, link, password, radio, select, submit, text, textarea)` Many pages create a series of controls using an iterator. Several of the HTML tags now support the `indexed` property, which gives the control a unique name on each iterator.
New Java-ScriptValidator tags	`(org.apache.struts.taglib.html.JavaScriptValidatorTag)` The Struts Validator lets you create individual JavaScript validators for the fields on your forms and insert them all using a single tag.

Tiles framework	`(org.apache.struts.Tiles)`
	`(org.apache.struts.taglib.Tiles)`
	The Tiles framework is now integrated with the core Struts distribution. This advanced document assembly package for JavaServer Pages makes it easy to create pages by combining reusable fragments.

Struts Validator	`(org.apache.struts.Validator)` The Struts Validator makes it easy to generate client-side and server-side validations from the same configuration.

1.0 vs 1.1   When this book was written, Struts 1.1 beta release 2 was in circulation. Some details may have changed between beta 2 and the final release. Be sure to check the book's website [Husted] for any errata.

Of course, most applications do not use every feature in Struts 1.0, and most will also not use every new feature in Struts 1.1. But there should be something on this list that can benefit most applications.

16.1.2 Features we can use

For our initial Artimus migration, we decided to move to the integrated versions of Tiles and the Validator and to implement two new features: DynaActionForms and action-based security.

In Artimus 1.0, we had to create an ActionForm subclass to handle our simple set of input properties. In Struts 1.1, we can use a *DynaActionForm* (`org.apache.struts.action.DynaActionForm`) instead and avoid creating a new Java subclass. You still need to declare the properties for a DynaActionForm, but since these declarations can be in XML, they are much easier to maintain.

The new *action-based security* feature means that we can apply Declarative Security to individual mappings rather than rely on URL patterns registered with the container.

Struts 1.1 also bundles Tiles and the Validator as part of the standard distribution. These work the same way as they did in Artimus 1.0 but are initialized differently. We will also need to change the tag names on the Artimus 1.0 message tile to use the built-in versions of the Validator 1.0 tags.

We explored the Artimus feature set and implementation in chapter 15. In this chapter we focus only on the parts of the Artimus 1.0 codebase that are being retrofitted for Struts 1.1. We will not discuss the Artimus application design or functionality in any great detail. To get the most out of this chapter, you may need to read chapter 15 first.

DynaActionForms and action-based security are only a taste of the new features in Struts 1.1. But our list for Artimus is probably representative of what the first round of your own enhancement pass would look like.

16.2 Baseline changes

A good portion of our upgrade activity is going to take place just within the Struts configuration file (struts-config.xml). Two baseline changes involve Tiles and the

Validator. In Struts 1.1, these components are integrated into the main distribution and need to be loaded differently. We also need to remove an action mapping to an obsolete standard Action. We'll make these three changes first, and then make a second pass for the features on our discretionary list.

But the very first thing we need to do is pop in the new Struts 1.1 JARs for the other packages. We will need to fuss a bit with Tiles and the Struts Validator (because they were moved into the core codebase), but everything else is plug and play.

The Struts 1.1 distribution comes with a handy library distribution with most of the new files we need. To get started on an upgrade, you just need to download the library distribution and place those files in the WEB-INF/lib folder of your application.

If you want to follow along as we update Artimus, start with the Artimus 1.0 distribution from the book website [Husted]. Also download the Scaffold 1.1 library distribution from the site. Then, copy all the files from the Struts 1.1 library distribution under the Artimus WEB-INF/lib folder, along with the two Scaffold JARs. You can overwrite any files of the same name with the 1.1 versions. If your application, like Artimus, is using a build of Tiles that uses the `org.apache.struts` packaging, you should also remove the tiles.jar and the tiles.tld now. Otherwise, there will be class loader conflicts with the 1.1 versions in the Struts JAR.

NOTE The Java JAR files use the popular ZIP archive format. You can open a JAR with any ZIP file browser to see what's inside. The paths to the files indicate how they are packaged.

If your application imported any of the Struts util packages that were moved to the Commons (see section 16.1), you will have to change the `import` statements to refer to the new versions:

```
// import org.apache.struts.util.BeanUtils; // Struts 1.0.x
import org.apache.commons.beanutils.BeanUtils; // Struts 1.1
```

Artimus doesn't import any of the Struts 1.0 utility classes directly, so we don't have to make any Java source changes to it.

At this point, you should be able to run a clean build of Artimus without any compile-time errors. If the Ant build tool [ASF, Ant] is on your system path, you can run a clean build by changing to WEB-INF/src and entering

```
> ant clean.build
```

However, Artimus itself is not quite ready to go. The configuration files are still set to load the 1.0 versions of Tiles and the Validator. Let's look at what changes we need to make to get the new versions up and running.

16.2.1 *Tiles in Struts 1.1*

Tiles lets you construct a page from component parts using a descriptor called a *Tiles Definition*. Like other framework objects, the Definition object can be created via an XML configuration file. The XML element declares a layout page and passes it the names of the components (or *tiles*) to insert at runtime. Chapter 11 covers Tiles in detail.

Tiles works this magic by watching for ActionForwards that refer to one of its Definitions. When it sees a path that matches one of its Definitions, Tiles assembles the page and passes it along for the JSP service to render.

Although it is one of the fancier Struts components, moving from the optional Tiles 1.0 to the integrated Tiles 1.1 package is a simple operation. In Struts 1.0, Tiles had to subclass the ActionServlet and several methods. In Struts 1.1, Tiles uses the new RequestProcessor object (`org.apache.struts.action.Request-Processor`). The ActionServlet will then delegate the request processing to the new RequestProcessor.

By using a RequestProcessor, we can use the rest of the ActionServlet without creating a formal subclass. When application modules are being used (see chapter 4), each module can have its own RequestProcessor.

Besides the RequestProcessor, Tiles also needs to load its Definitions from an XML document. In Struts 1.0, the ActionServlet subclass handled this task for us. In Struts 1.1, we can use a PlugIn Action to do the same thing. A PlugIn Action has an `init()` method, just like a servlet. We register PlugIns via the Struts configuration file. The ActionServlet will call the `init()` method for each PlugIn at startup and its `destroy()` method at shutdown. This is a great way to create and release application-scope resources, like the Tiles Definitions.

Besides loading the Definitions, the Tiles PlugIn Action (`org.apache.struts.tiles.TilesPlugInAction`) also sets up the Tiles RequestProcessor (`org.apache.struts.tiles.TilesRequestProcessor`). This way, you don't have to bother with configuring both the TilesRequestProcessor and the Tiles PlugIn. However, if you need to load your own RequestProcessor later, be sure to make it a subclass of the TilesRequestProcessor. (For more about RequestProcessors and PlugIns, see chapter 9.)

Listing 16.1 shows the `<plug-in>` element that you can add to the struts-config.xml. The PlugIn section of the struts-config.xml appears at the very end,

just before the closing `</struts-config>` element, after the `<action-map-`
`pings>` element and any of the other new sections.

```
<!--- other elements -->

</action-mappings>

<plug-in className="org.apache.struts.tiles.TilesPlugin">  <set-property
    property="definitions-config"
    value="/WEB-INF/tiles-defs.xml"/>
</plug-in>

</struts-config>
```

NOTE   In the Struts 1.0 configuration, all the elements were enclosed. There
was an `<action-mappings>` element for the `<action>` elements and a
`<form-beans>` element for the `<form-bean>` element. In Struts 1.1,
several elements, such as `<plug-in>`, are not enclosed; there is no
`<plug-ins>` element.

For more about configuring Struts applications generally, including using the
`<set-property>` element, see chapter 4.

   The Tiles package is part of the standard Struts 1.1 JAR. We will need to adjust
the deployment descriptor to load the new tag library descriptor (TLD), but we
will *not* need to change any of the pages or the Tiles configuration file.

   Here's our new Tiles TLD reference in the deployment descriptor (web.xml):

```
<taglib>
  <taglib-uri>/tags/tiles</taglib-uri>
  <!-- <taglib-location>/WEB-INF/lib/tiles.tld</taglib-location> -->
   <taglib-location>/WEB-INF/lib/struts-tiles.tld</taglib-location>
</taglib>
```

For backward-compatibility, we took advantage of the logical nature of the
`<taglib-uri>` and did *not* change the reference from *tiles* to *struts-tiles*. Since this
is still a small application, it would not have been hard to change the tiles, but
since we didn't *have* to make those changes now, we left them for later and just
changed the `taglib-location` to match the new TLD name.

   We can also remove the reference to the TilesComponent servlet from our
web.xml and go back to using the default ActionServlet:

```
<servlet>
    <servlet-name>action</servlet-name>
    <!-- org.apache.struts.tiles.ActionComponentServlet -->
    <servlet-class>org.apache.struts.action.ActionServlet</servlet-class>
    <! -- … -->
```

We can now safely delete the tiles.jar and tiles.tld from our WEB-INF/lib folder (if you haven't already). The Tiles classes are now in the main struts.jar, and a struts-tiles.tld was included in the Struts 1.1 library distribution.

1.0 vs 1.1   To make it easy to compare the Struts 1.0 and Struts 1.1 versions of the configuration files, we left the originals in a conf_1_0 folder in the Artimus 1.1 source distribution. When we deploy the source files (see section 15.3.1), the archival versions are not copied to the public application. The source for the Struts 1.1 versions are in the /WEB-INF/src/conf folder.

Before closing struts-config.xml, we need to do one more thing: at the top of the file, change the DTD reference from

```
<!DOCTYPE struts-config PUBLIC "-//Apache Software Foundation//DTD Struts
    Configuration 1.0//EN" "http://jakarta.apache.org/struts/dtds/struts-
    config_1_0.dtd">
```

to

```
<!DOCTYPE struts-config PUBLIC "-//Apache Software Foundation//DTD Struts
    Configuration 1.1 //EN" "http://jakarta.apache.org/struts/dtds/struts-
    config_1_1.dtd">
```

This tells the Digester to use the correct DTD for Struts 1.1

In the deployment descriptor (WEB-INF/src/conf/web.xml), we can now replace the `<servlet-class>` reference to the *ActionComponentServlet* with a reference to the standard ActionServlet `org.apache.struts.action.ActionServlet`.

This is all we need to do to get Tiles back into action. But we still need to make similar changes for the Validator before we can try running the application.

NOTE   As discussed in section 15.3.1, all the source files for Artimus are kept below WEB-INF/src. This includes all Java, XML, JSP, and Properties files. The Ant build file deploys the source files when the application is compiled.

16.2.2 *Validator in Struts 1.1*

Moving the Validator from 1.0 to 1.1 is another straightforward operation, though packaging changes will force us to adjust some pages at the end.

The Struts Validator vets the properties on an ActionForm to be sure the values at least *look* valid. This is to help keep incorrect input away from the business tier, the way a receptionist might keep unwanted callers from bothering a busy executive.

The Validator comes in two distinct parts. First, there is a registry of the different validators the application can use. One validator might check if a field has any input at all. Another might check if the input is of an expected length. The Validator comes bundled with several basic validators, and you can also plug in your own. The second part of the Validator is the actual validations. The validation section describes your forms and fields so that you can link specific validators with specific fields. Chapter 12 covers the Struts Validator in detail.

Like most components these days, the Validator is configured through XML. The 1.0 version of the Validator used a servlet to initialize its resources. In Struts 1.1, a new PlugIn Action is used instead. The ValidatorPlugInAction replaces the ValidatorServlet we used with Artimus 1.0.

Listing 16.2 shows the <plug-in> element we can add to our struts-config.xml to initialize the Struts Validator.

Listing 16.2   /WEB-INF/src/conf/struts-config.xml (the Validator PlugIn element)

```
<plug-in
className="org.apache.struts.validator.ValidatorPlugIn">
<set-property
    property="pathnames"
    value="/WEB-INF/validator-rules.xml,/WEB-INF/validation.xml"/>
</plug-in>
```

The Struts 1.0 validator used a single file to store both the validator configurations and the form validations. In Struts 1.1, we can use separate configuration files: a validation-rules.xml for the validators and the trusty validation.xml for our form validations. The thinking is that the *validators* (validator-rules.xml) can be copied between applications. But the form *validations* (validation.xml) tend to be different for each application. By using separate files, we make it easier to change the standard validators without upsetting our validations.

For Artimus, we can move the new validator-rules.xml from the WEB-INF/lib directory (it was in the library distribution) into our WEB-INF/src/conf folder. Since this file has all the validators we need, we can edit the old validation.xml file (also in the conf folder) and delete the segment for the `<global><validator>` ... `</validator></global>` elements at the top. The `<formset>` element at the bottom remains, with the one `<form>` element for our `articleForm`.

1.0 vs 1.1   As this book was being finalized, a DTD was being added for the Struts Validator. For Struts 1.1 final, you may need to add a DTD to the validator configuration files. Check the book's website [Husted] for any errata.

In the deployment descriptor (WEB-INF/src/conf/web.xml), we can now remove the *validator* `<servlet>` element completely, since the new PlugIn loads the Validator's resources. We can also remove the struts-validator `<taglib>` element, since the tags we need are now in the main Struts JAR. To avoid any confusion, you should also remove the struts-validator.jar and struts-validator.tld files from the WEB-INF/lib folder. In Struts 1.1, the Validator package is in the main JAR, and the Validator tags are now in the html and logic taglibs.

16.2.3 *ReloadAction in Struts 1.1*

The complexities of modular applications and other considerations led to the removal of the several administrative Actions supplied in the Struts 1.0 distribution. This purge included the very handy ReloadAction (`org.apache.struts.actions.ReloadAction`).

Sadly, we must remove the mapping for the Reload command from the Artimus 1.1 struts-config.xml, since it no longer exists. At the end of the chapter, we will be also making the corresponding change to our menu action.

16.2.4 *Other baseline changes to web.xml and struts-config.xml*

There are none.

That's right. To retrofit Artimus for Struts 1.1, we had to:

- Remove an obsolete `<action>` element.
- Insert two new configuration elements to the struts-config.xml.
- Remove two obsolete elements from the web.xml.
- Amend a taglib reference.

But that's it as far as the struts-config.xml and web.xml go. Most applications would not even need to do this much.

The only bad news is that the packaging for the Validator tags changed when it was integrated into Struts 1.1. Since we were using the optional Validator component in Artimus 1.0, we will need to make some minor changes to our pages to reflect the new tag names.

16.2.5 *message.jsp (1.1)*

When the Struts Validator was integrated with Struts 1.1, its tags were integrated with the existing taglibs. So instead of referring to `<validator:messages-Exist>`, we can now refer to `<logic:messagesExist>`. The implementation of the underlying tags is the same; only the packaging has changed.

Listing 16.3 shows our updated message.jsp. Since this is a tile shared by the other pages, we had to make this change only in a single file, even though every page on the site can display messages.

Listing 16.3   /WEB-INF/src/pages/article/common/message.jsp

```jsp
<%@ taglib uri="/tags/struts-bean" prefix="bean" %>
<%@ taglib uri="/tags/struts-html" prefix="html" %>
<%-- [1.0] Tag is part of html in 1.1
<%@ taglib uri="/tags/struts-validator" prefix="validator" %>
--%>
<%@ taglib uri="/tags/struts-logic" prefix="logic" %>
<logic:messagesPresent>
<TR>
<TD class="error" colspan="3">
   <UL>
   <html:messages id="error">
      <LI><bean:write name="error"/></LI>
   </html:messages>
   </UL>
</TD>
</TR>
</logic:messagesPresent>
<logic:messagesPresent message="true">
<TR>
<TD class="message" colspan="3">
   <UL>
   <html:messages id="message" message="true">
      <LI><bean:write name="message"/></LI>
   </html:messages>
   </UL>
</TD>
</TR>
</logic:messagesPresent>
```

1.0 vs 1.1   To make it easy to compare the Struts 1.0 and Struts 1.1 versions of the JavaServer Pages, we left copies of any source files that were changed by giving them the file extension .1_0—not because we needed to, but because we just wanted to have the old versions on hand for reference. When we deploy the source files (see section 15.3.1), these archival versions are not copied to the public application.

16.2.6   *form.jsp (1.1)*

We also need to tweak the tags in our form tile, as shown in listing 16.4. Again this is just a matter of changing the tag names. The actual JSP code is unchanged.

Listing 16.4   /WEB –INF/src/pages/article/content/form.jsp

```
<%@ taglib uri="/tags/struts-html" prefix="html" %>
<%@ taglib uri="/tags/struts-bean" prefix="bean" %>
<%@ taglib uri="/tags/struts-logic" prefix="logic" %>
<%-- [1.0] Tag is part of html in 1.1
<%@ taglib uri="/tags/struts-validator" prefix="validator" %>
--%>
<html:form action="/admin/article/Store" onsubmit="return
  validateArticleForm(this);">
<TR>
<TD class="label" nowrap>Title:</TD>
<TD class="input" colspan="2">
<html:text property="title" size="50" maxlength="255"/></TD>
</TR>
<TR>
<TD class="label" nowrap>Author:</TD>
<TD class="input">
<html:text property="creator" size="30" maxlength="75"/></TD>
<TD class="hint">Full name of person who originated the article.</TD>
</TR>
<TR>
<TD class="label" nowrap>Article:</TD>
<TD class="input" colspan="2">
<!-- The Struts html:textarea tag does not support wrapping -->
<!-- so we use this trick instead -->
<textarea name="contentDisplayHtml" rows="12" cols="50" tabindex="2"
  wrap="soft">
<bean:write name="articleForm" property="contentDisplayHtml"/>
</textarea>
</TD>
</TR>
<html:hidden property="contributedDisplay"/>
<html:hidden property="contributor"/>
</TR><TD class="label" nowrap>Article ID:</TD>
```

```
<logic:notPresent name="articleForm" property="article">
    <TD class="dimmed"><i><html:hidden property="article"/>not assigned
        </i></TD>
</logic:notPresent>
<logic:present name="articleForm" property="article">
    <TD class="input"><html:hidden property="article"/>
        <bean:write name="articleForm" property="article"/></TD>
</logic:present>
<TD> </TD>
</TR>
<TR>
<TD class="button" colspan="3">
<html:submit accesskey="S">SAVE</html:submit>
<html:cancel accesskey="C">CANCEL</html:cancel>
</TD>
</TR>
</html:form>
<%--
<validator:javascript formName="articleForm"/>
--%
<html:javascript formName="articleForm"/>
```

In section 16.3.3, we will need to make one other change to this page, after we implement a new feature. But for now, all we need to do is adjust the validator tag names.

At this point, our first pass at Artimus 1.1 should be up and running. If you run a clean build and start your container, you should be able to click through the application and use it normally. The only thing to avoid is the Reload action we removed from the Struts configuration. We haven't changed the menu yet, so it will still be listed, even though its mapping is not available. Let's take care of that next.

NOTE Be sure to compile the application before trying it. Also be sure to compile it with the Ant build file after making changes to any of the files. The originals are all kept below the WEB-INF/src folder. You must rebuild the application after any changes, including changes to files like web.xml and struts-config.xml.

16.2.7 *MenuCreate (1.1)*

Struts 1.1 removed the Reload administrative action that we had offered on our manager's menu. In section 16.2.3, we removed the mapping to the Reload-Action. Now we can remove it from the menu by deleting a line from the class that creates our menu object.

In our *MenuCreate* business object bean (org.apache.artimus.article.
MenuCreate), originally presented back in listing 15.21, we revised the block for
the manager's menu from

```
ArrayList manager = new ArrayList();
manager.add(new LabelValueBean("Reload Config", "reload"));
manager.add(new LabelValueBean("Create Resources", "createResources"));
saveResult(Tokens.MENU_MANAGER,manager,controls);
```

to

```
ArrayList manager = new ArrayList();
manager.add(new LabelValueBean("Create Resources", "createResources"));
saveResult(Tokens.MENU_MANAGER,manager,controls);
```

The menu page does not need to be changed, since it just wrote out the menu list
without knowing what options were available.

Of course, an alternative here would have been to create a reload page that
explained the command was not available in this version. But in this case, it was
simplest to revise the business bean.

LabelValueBean

In Struts 1.1, a LabelValueBean object was added to the Struts util package, just
like the one in the Scaffold util package. We could move our dependency on the
LabelValueBean from the Scaffold class to the Struts class, but we decided to stick
with the Scaffold version. The MenuCreate class is a business bean and, ideally,
should not import classes from Struts. So rather than introduce a dependency in
MenuCreate on the Struts JAR, we left the dependency with the framework-
independent Scaffold Commons package instead.

16.2.8 Onward

After confirming our reconfigured application is up and running under Struts 1.1,
we can move on to the discretionary changes.

16.3 Discretionary changes

To get the most out of Struts 1.1, we decided to make four discretionary changes.
As part of this iteration, we will also:

- Configure a DynaActionForm bean.
- Add roles to our protected mappings to implement action-based security.
- Add a new configuration element to load the default message resources.

16.3.1 *Form to DynaActionForm*

Artimus 1.0 declared one custom ActionForm that it defined in the Struts configuration as the `articleForm`:

```
<!-- Article Form Bean -->
    <form-bean
        name="articleForm"
        type="org.apache.artimus.struts.Form"/>
```

Like most ActionForms, our `articleForm` was nothing but a set of simple properties. It just buffered the form input until the properties could be validated and transferred to our business bean. JavaBean properties aren't hard to set up, but it can get to be a pain after a while.

Struts 1.1 offers a new way to define an ActionForm that is nothing but a set of simple properties. The DynaActionForm class lets you define the properties in XML as part of the `<form-bean>` element. To another component, a DynaActionForm looks and feels just like a conventional JavaBean. It can be used anywhere a "regular" ActionForm class can be used. A DynaActionForm can also be used with any development tool designed to use JavaBeans, just as if you had coded all the properties by hand.

If you are using the Struts Validator, a DynaValidatorForm class is available so you can use DynaForms with the Validator. This can eliminate the need for a discrete ActionForm class altogether. Listing 16.5 shows what our `articleForm` from listing 15.15 looks like coded as a DynaActionForm.

> **Listing 16.5**   /WEB-INF/struts-config.xml (<form-bean> element)

```
<form-bean
        name="articleForm"
        type="org.apache.struts.validator.DynaValidatorForm">
    <form-property
            name="keyName"
        type="java.lang.String"/>
    <form-property
            name="keyValue"
        type="java.lang.String"/>
    <form-property
            name="marked"
            type="java.lang.String"
            initialValue="0"/>
    <form-property
            name="hours"
            type="java.lang.String"/>
    <form-property
            name="articles"
```

```
                    type="java.lang.String"/>
            <form-property
                name="article"
                type="java.lang.String"/>
            <form-property
                name="contributor"
                type="java.lang.String"/>
            <form-property
                name="contributedDisplay"
                type="java.lang.String"/>
            <form-property
                name=" "
                type="java.lang.String"/>
            <form-property
                name="creator"
                type="java.lang.String"/>
            <form-property
                name="title"
                type="java.lang.String"/>
            <form-property
                name="contentDisplayHtml"
                type="java.lang.String"/>
    </form-bean>
```

All we need to do is remove the old `articleForm` `<form-bean>` element from our struts-config.xml and add this element in its place. Since we don't have a reload action in Struts 1.1, we need to reload the application before testing our DynaBean.

With our dynamic `articleForm` in place, we can now remove the `org.apache. artimus.struts.Form` class from the Artimus 1.1 codebase, along with the descendant class, `org.apache.artimus.article.struts.ArticleForm`. Our Form class is officially obsolete.

NOTE   If you use DynaForms in your own application, be aware that the default `reset` method sets all the dynamic properties to their initial value (that is, null). With conventional ActionForms, the default `reset` does nothing.

16.3.2 *Action-based security*

Our Artimus 1.0 application relies on container-based security to ensure that only authorized users have access to the Actions that insert, edit, or delete articles. We told the container to reserve access to any URI that started with /admin/* to those users in the manager, editor, or contributor role. In Artimus 1.0, this was handled by the `<auth-constraint>` element in the web.xml.

Struts 1.1 lets you take container-based security a step further. An ActionMapping can specify its own list of security roles that may access it. So to protect our article edit Action, we can just add a `roles` attribute to the mapping, like this:

```
<action
        roles="manager"
        path="/admin/CreateResources"
        type="org.apache.struts.scaffold.ProcessAction"
        parameter="org.apache.artimus.CreateResources">
        <forward
            name="success"
            path="/do/find/Recent"/>
</action>
```

Before invoking the Action associated with this mapping, the controller will now check to see if the user making the request has been assigned any of the listed security roles. The controller uses the same API the container uses when it checks for requests for URI matching the /admin/* pattern. So, action-based security is not a *new* system but a progressive use of the *existing* system.

This progressive use does not conflict with the authorization constraints we set up in Artimus 1.0. In fact, the ActionMapping complements the standards. We could continue to use our original authentication scheme unchanged. After a request passes the container's constraints, Struts will apply the ActionMapping's constraints. This can let you fine-tune the constraints without requiring changes to the application-wide deployment descriptor.

Meanwhile, you can also use it as an alternative to the container constraints. Using the stock `url-pattern` approach, we have to adjust our URI command structure to match the security constraints. This can be made to work, but often interferes with the way Struts developers tend to use action mappings. Right now, we have all of our `article` commands under /article, except for those that are secured (these are under /admin/article). That's not a big deal now, but it can start to get complicated when modular applications, with their own `url-pattern` requirements, are added to the equation.

With action-based security in place, we can specify which mappings must be protected and can use whatever URIs we like. So before where we had a mapping like

```
<action
        path="/admin/article/Edit"
        type="org.apache.struts.scaffold.ProcessAction"
        parameter="org.apache.artimus.article.FindByArticle"
        name="articleForm"
```

```
        scope="request"
        validate="false">
      <forward
          name="success"
          path=".article.Form"/>
    </action>
```

we could now use a mapping like

```
<action
    roles="contributor,manager"
    path="/article/Edit"
    type="org.apache.struts.scaffold.ProcessAction"
    parameter="org.apache.artimus.article.FindByArticle"
    name="articleForm"
    scope="request"
    validate="false">
  <forward
      name="success"
      path=".article.Form"/>
</action>
```

How or when users log on, how we registered them with the system, or what happens when they are authorized or unauthorized does not change one bit. We are just moving from declaring security based on a URL pattern to declaring exactly which operations we want to secure.

For more about action-based security, see chapter 7.

Consequences

Removing /admin from the path means that we will need to update any pages that refer to that URI. If making this change were problematic, we could leave the ActionMapping path as it was. We could also put in a Struts forward from /admin/article/store to /article/store until the pages could be updated. This would allow both paths to work during a transition period. Of course, a redirect can also be made at the container level, but doing this sort of refactoring in the strut-config.xml itself can be simpler.

One reason for making this change now is to simplify using Artimus as an application module later. The conventional url-pattern approach to Declarative Security can become complicated when we are also using url-patterns to identify application modules.

Nearly all of the changes can be made within the struts-config.xml. Just look for /admin throughout the file. If /admin is found in an <action> path, remove /admin and add a roles attribute. If it is any other path, just remove the /admin component from the path.

The exceptions are

```
<forward name="logon" path="/do/admin/Menu"/>
```

and

```
<action path="/admin/Menu" forward="/do/Menu"/>
```

This is a little trick to get the container to ask for the user's credentials. The /admin path forces the challenge. If they pass, we just go back to the menu (but logged in this time). Otherwise, the browser puts up the standard Unauthorized screen.

16.3.3 *Action path changes*

Since the `<html:form>` tag uses an embedded reference to the ActionMapping path, changing any of those paths means updating the tags. While the ActionMappings are *virtual* references, they are not true *logical* references. Other components use the URI paths and have their own expectations about how they should work.

Our change to action-based security is a double-edged sword. It simplified our internal API but forced us to make changes to the external API. We could have mitigated these changes with workarounds, but because Artimus is such a small application, we can just bite the bullet and do the right thing.

The two pages that need to use the new action paths are the form.jsp and view.jsp.

/WEB-INF/src/pages/articles/content/form.jsp

The action path for the `<html:form>` tag in our form tile can be changed from /admin/article/store to /article/store.

/WEB-INF/src/pages/articles/content/view.jsp

Likewise, the action path for the `<html:form>` tag in our view tile can be changed from /admin/article/Store to /article/Store.

16.3.4 *Application resources in Struts 1.1*

The support for application modules in Struts 1.1 brought about a change to the way the name of the default resource bundle is specified. In Struts 1.0, the name of the application resource bundle was an initialization parameter to ActionServlet. And, though deprecated, it still is. But since each application module must be able to specify its own application resources, you can now specify the name of the bundle in the Struts configuration file instead.

A new configuration element, `<message-resources>`, can be used to specify the name of the bundle instead of using the ActionServlet `<init-param>`. This element, shown in listing 16.6, must be placed after the `<controller>` element (if any) and before the `<plug-in>` elements (if any).

Listing 16.6   /WEB-INF/struts-config.xml (`<message-resources>` element)

```
<message-resources
    parameter="resources.application"/>
```

Since each application module has its own Struts configuration, each module can have its own default message resources bundle. If an application (or module) would like to use more than one message bundle, you can specify more than one `<message-resources>` element. Any additional message resources elements must also specify the `key` attribute for the bundle.

Just like our `<init-param>` in Artimus 1.0, here we tell Struts to look for a file named application.properties in the resource package (or folder). Our build file places the resource package under the /WEB-INF/classes folder to ensure that our bundles are on the `CLASSPATH`, where the container can find them.

With the `<message-resources>` element in place, we can now remove the application `<init-param>` from the ActionServlet element in the web.xml.

For the future

Of course, Artimus does not need to use the new `<message-resources>` element. As the application stands, we can pass the resource bundle name to Artimus via the `<init-param>` element, and everything will work just the same. However, since Artimus might make a good module in a larger application, we converted the `<init-param>` element to a `<message-resources>` element, just in case.

16.4 Summary

For now, this is all we need to do to christen Artimus a Struts 1.1 application. We are now using the integrated versions of the Struts Validator and Tiles, the DynaActionForm for our form beans, and role-based security to protect our Actions.

Of course, there are a few more items we could handle in a second iteration:

- Convert the ArtimusServlet to a PlugIn.
- Reconfigure Artimus into a default application and an articles module, to make Artimus easier to plug into a larger, multimodule application.
- Implement a frames interface using the new `frame` tag.

But sufficient unto the day are the features thereof.

17

Velocity: replacing JSPs

Change is the constant, the signal for rebirth, the egg of the phoenix.
—Christina Baldwin

17.1 Moving to Velocity templates

Change is at the core of computer science. Without variables, virtually all computer programs would be useless curiosities—intellectual exercises producing the same, predetermined result over and over again. Being able to say $z=x+y$ and provide our own x and y is what makes programs useful. People expect applications to be easy to modify, both inside and out. Developers expect application frameworks to make these changes easy to implement.

In this chapter, we look at making a seemingly drastic change to our application—ditching JavaServer Pages and using Velocity templates instead. You may be surprised at how easy an overhaul like this can be—at least when using a framework like Struts.

17.2 Change makes the framework

Being able to quickly construct an application is only half the battle. It is well known that more than half of the cost of an application is spent on maintenance [Linday]. The Struts framework streamlines maintenance by encapsulating the details most likely to change. Chief among these details are the pages referenced by an Action.

In this chapter, we change the entire presentation layer for the logon application we built in chapter 3 from JavaServer Pages to another popular presentation technology, Velocity templates.

Like Struts, Velocity [ASF, Velocity] is an open source product hosted at the Apache Jakarta site. It is well suited for use in a Model 2/MVC architecture. Velocity can be especially useful when the page designers are not Java engineers or JavaServer Page enthusiasts.

Changing from JSP to Velocity may sound like a bigger deal than it is. The key to many application-wide changes in Struts is the configuration file. The configuration file is designed so that most implementation details—such as the name of a presentation page or template—can be stored in this central location. If all the hyperlinks used by a web application go through ActionForwards, then just changing the Struts configuration can alter what page each link references. Of course, when we built our logon application in chapter 3, we were careful to use

ActionForwards rather than any type of direct hyperlink. For more about Action-Forwards and the Struts configuration file, see chapter 4.

Let's introduce Velocity templates, find out how they work, and then plug them into our logon application.

17.3 Why we need Velocity

So, if we already have JavaServer Pages, why do we need Velocity templates?

17.3.1 Velocity is light, fast, and versatile

Velocity templates tend to require less code than a corresponding JavaServer Page and render just as quickly. While Velocity templates can be used with several web application frameworks, including Struts, Velocity itself is not tied to web applications. Velocity templates can be used with any Java application that needs to create customized output at runtime. This can be an important consideration when deploying an application in multiple environments. Velocity is a versatile tool and can also be used to generate SQL, PostScript, e-mail, or XML from templates.

17.3.2 Velocity works well with others

The Velocity codes display well in visual HTML editors, so page designers usually find Velocity templates easier to work with than JavaServer Pages. At this writing, support for JSP custom tags in most HTML editors is minimal or nonexistent. In practice, JSP tags actually look too much like HTML tags. Most visual HTML editors hide tags they don't know, making them *harder* to use with JavaServer Pages rather than easier. Sad, but true.

Meanwhile, dynamic web pages based on Velocity templates can be easily edited using off-the-shelf tools like Allaire HomeBase, Macromedia Dreamweaver, or Microsoft FrontPage, to name a few. Ironically, since Velocity markup does *not* look like HTML, standard editing software treats the Velocity codes like text. Page designers can view and edit the codes without difficulty.

17.3.3 Velocity is simple but powerful

It's been noted that the *Velocity Template Language* (VTL) is an API that "you can fit on a matchbook cover." From an HTML page designer's viewpoint, that's a very good thing. Most people can be up and running with Velocity the same day. At the same time, the VTL has proven to be a complete solution; you can do with it whatever you need to do. A summary of the VTL is shown in table 17.1.

Table 17.1   The Velocity Template Language

Element	Description
`#set`	Establishes the value of a reference
`#if` / `#elseif` / `#else`	Provides output that is conditional on the truth of statements
`#foreach`	Loops through a list of objects
`#include`	Renders local file(s) that are not parsed by Velocity
`#parse`	Renders a local template that is parsed by Velocity
`#stop`	Stops the template engine
`#macro`	Defines a Velocimacro (VM), a repeated segment of a VTL template, as required
`##`	Specifies a single-line comment
`#* ... *#`	Specifies a multiline comment
`${variable}`	Provides a variable reference (to an attribute in the context)
`${purchase.Total}`	References a property—for example, returns the value of `purchase.Total` or `purchase.getTotal()`
`${purchase.setTitle("value")}`	References a method —for example, calls `purchase.setTitle("value")`

In this chapter, we present the practical example of using Velocity templates as the presentation layer of our logon application. For more about Velocity, visit the Velocity website at Jakarta [ASF, Velocity]. You may be surprised by how much it can really do.

17.4 *Using Velocity with web applications*

Pages in a conventional website are static and unchanging. They can be read from the disk as HTML files and returned to the browser. The web browser then reads the HTML and displays the formatted page. Pages in a dynamic web application have to be customized for each user. In practice, most of the page is static and unchanging; only a few details ever actually change.

In chapter 10, we describe the strategy of using a server page to combine the static markup with the dynamic data. A template provides the static portion of a server page. This template includes a mixture of HTML markup and the special codes that customize the page.

A JSP uses scriptlets and JSP tags to create the customizations. The JSP template is compiled into a special servlet. The JSP servlet renders the HTML markup and processes the JSP code. When a JSP page is requested, the container actually calls the compiled JSP servlet. It doesn't load and process the template again.

In Velocity (as in most server page systems), the templates are actually used at runtime to create the response. A central engine reads the template, processes the codes, and returns the customized result. In a web environment, the Velocity servlet returns the result as a response to the HTTP request.

When the template is processed, the Velocity Template Engine is also given a runtime context that contains variable information. This is similar to the servlet contexts used by web applications but is not bound to the web tier. Since Velocity provides its own context object, the same Velocity Template Engine can be used with web applications and with conventional Java applications.

In a web application, Velocity can adopt the standard servlet context and use it as the Velocity context. When the Velocity servlet adopts a context, it employs the same scoping strategy as is used with JSP tags. The request scope is checked first, then the session scope, and finally the application scope. But to the Engine, it looks like a single context.

When the Engine renders a template, it looks for Velocity *statements* and *references*. Velocity statements are identified by a pound sign (#) and a keyword appearing at the beginning of a line. The references are to variables in the context. References are identified by a dollar sign ($) followed by a reference name. Any Java object can be placed in the context and used as a reference. The reference can access any public method on a Java class. (Table 17.1 contains the Velocity statements and references.)

17.4.1 *Using Velocity with servlet resources*

Much of the communication between components in a web application involves four standard resources provided by the Servlet API: the application context, the session, the request, and the response. The application context lets components share data and services. The session object provides data and services regarding each user. The request and response objects work together to fulfill the infamous HTTP request-response cycle (see chapter 1).

Since a dynamic page is just another component in a web application, it should have access to the same resources as other components. Velocity provides a standard VelocityViewServlet, which makes it easy to integrate Velocity with any servlet in your application.

Among other things, this servlet automatically creates and populates the Velocity context with the usual suspects from the Servlet API. Table 17.2 lists the Velocity attributes (or tools) and the API objects they represent.

Table 17.2   Velocity servlet tools

Context key	Class	Remarks
`$application`	`javax.servlet.ServletContext`	The servlet context
`$session`	`javax.servlet.http.HttpSession`	The current session, if one exists
`$request`	`javax.servlet.http.HttpServletRequest`	The current servlet request
`$response`	`javax.servlet.http.HttpServletResponse`	The current servlet response

Since this "gang of four" are now just objects in the Velocity context, they can be accessed with the Velocity Template Language (see table 17.1).

Let's compare accessing these tools with doing the same thing with a custom tag. The Jakarta Taglibs project [ASF, Taglibs] offers a Request tag library that exposes the properties of the pending HttpServletRequest, just like the `$request` Velocity tool does. To check a user's security role using the `<request>` tag, we could say this:

```
<request:isUserInRole role="contributor">
      <%-- … -%>
</request:isUserInRole>
```

The same check is done in Velocity:

```
#if $request.isUserInRole("contributor")
      # …
#endif
```

Any other method or property of the request, session, application, or response objects can be accessed in the same way—but without the red tape of creating and importing a tag library. Once the HttpServletRequest object is placed in the Velocity context, you can access it using the *object's native API*, not one being passed through a custom tag implementation.

17.4.2   *Using Velocity with context attributes*

Most web applications, especially Struts applications, make good use of the standard servlet contexts. Objects we can all share are posted in the application context. Objects that pertain to an individual user go into the session context. If the object is just being used to create a HTTP response, we tuck it away in the request context.

These contexts are contained within the standard servlet resources we introduced in section 17.4.1. So, we could always get at them this way:

```
<P>Username: ${session.getAttribute("username")}</P>
```

But that's a bit too verbose for Velocity-land. To avoid so much typing, Velocity supports the same type of automatic scoping found in most JSP tag implementations. When we refer to an attribute, the request context is checked first, then the session, and finally the application. Each of the contexts provided by the request, session, and application resources are chained together, but to the Velocity Template Engine, they all look like the same context.

This means we can get at our username this way instead:

```
<P>Username: $!user.username</P>
```

Internally, Velocity will check the standard request context for the user object. Not finding it, it will try the session context. When it finds the user attribute in the session context, Velocity returns the result of the user.getUserName() method. If the user attribute was not found anywhere, the exclamation point (!) tells Velocity to return a blank string instead.

Out of the box, the Velocity Template Language and VelocityViewServlet provide all the generic functionality provided by the Struts bean and logic taglibs, along with several others, such as the Jakarta request taglib.

But what about the special resources provided by the Struts framework? The attribute keys used by Struts are verbose and not easy for page designers to remember or type. The HTML tags usually handle all that.

Point taken. Happily, Velocity provides a special toolkit for Struts that does for the Struts API what it did for the Servlet API. The Struts framework objects are exposed as Velocity "tools" that can be used with a minimum of fuss.

17.4.3 *How Velocity works with Struts*

The objects defined in the Struts configuration (see chapter 4) create a database of the JavaBeans, hyperlinks, actions, and messages to be used with an application. Many of the JSP tag extensions bundled with Struts—<html:link>, for example—are designed to look up information from this database.

Struts exposes this database of configuration objects through the standard servlet contexts. Any other servlet, in the application can access the Struts configuration objects—if they know where to look. The JSP tags bundled with Struts use a class called RequestUtils (org.apache.struts.util.RequestUtils) to access the configuration objects. But any other component in the application can do the same thing.

In fact, the VelocityStruts toolkit and its view tools do for a Struts Velocity Template application *exactly* what the RequestUtils and bundled taglibs do for a Struts JSP application.

17.4.4 *The VelocityStruts toolkit*

The VelocityStruts toolkit makes it easy to use Velocity templates with Struts. The kit includes the VelocityViewServlet (see section 17.4.1) and the Velocity View tools for Struts.

The VelocityViewServlet is loaded into the application along with the Struts ActionServlet. The Velocity servlet is configured to match some URL pattern, most often *.vm, in the usual way. Once the Velocity servlet is loaded, we can start forwarding to VM files in *exactly* the same way we forward to JSP files. If we create a logon.vm page out of our login.jsp page, we can change the forwards from

```
<forward
    name="continue"
    path="/pages/Logon.jsp"/>
```

to

```
<forward
    name="continue"
    path="/pages/Logon.vm"/>
```

In practice, Struts doesn't render the JSP. That's handled by a service bundled with your container. So, Struts can forward to the VelocityViewServlet just as easily as it forwards to the JSP service. From the controller's perspective, they are all just URIs.

In a Struts JSP, the real magic is handled by the custom tags. They know how to access the Struts configuration and use those objects to customize the page.

In a Struts Velocity template, the View tools know all the same magic words and can access the Struts configuration just like the Struts taglibs do. Where we forwarded to JSPs, we can now forward to VMs. Where we used custom tags, we can now use View tools. It's really that simple.

But no coincidence …

Sun originally designed JSP tags to be a means for a JavaServer Page to access Java-Beans. Most carefully designed taglibs, like the ones bundled with Struts, are based on this fundamental design principle. The application creates JavaBeans to encapsulate data. The JSP tags access the JavaBean, wrap the data in HTML markup, and output the result.

The Velocity Template Language uses the same design pattern. Objects are placed in a shared context by another component. The template language processes the data provided by those objects and outputs the result.

From a distance, pages coded for Velocity tools or JSP tags will look very much alike. They are both trying to do the same things in much the same way for all the same reasons. The implementations differ, but the strategy remains the same.

17.4.5 *The Struts View tools*

As we've mentioned, much of the functionality provided by the Struts taglibs is already built into the Velocity Template Language and VelocityViewServlet. The Struts-specific features are provided through a set of four JavaBeans, or tools, that the servlet makes available to your templates (like the Servlet API resources covered in section 17.4.1). Table 17.3 itemizes the four Struts-specific Velocity View tools.

Table 17.3 Velocity Struts View tools (`org.apache.velocity.tools.struts`)

Context key	Class	Remarks
`$msg`	MessageTool	Provides access to the Struts message resources for internationalized output
`$errors`	ErrorsTool	Provides methods to check for and output Struts error messages
`$link`	LinkTool	Provides methods to work with URIs
`$form`	FormTool	Provides miscellaneous methods to work with forms and form beans in the context of Struts applications

Let's take a look at a Struts JSP and a Struts Velocity template.

17.5 *Our logon templates*

Since they are both designed to do the same thing, the Velocity templates and JSP versions of our pages look very much alike, especially when you compare them closely. (Form follows function.) You may be surprised to discover that you already know enough about Velocity to read through the template source. If you get stuck, look back to table 17.1 as a quick reference (or scribble it down on any handy matchbook). Welcome.vm appears in figure 17.1a, and Welcome.jsp appears in figure 17.1b.

As you can see, the markup is more alike than it is different, and the same commentary we presented back in chapter 3 (section 3.3.2) would apply here,

```
<HTML>
<HEAD>
<TITLE>Welcome!</TITLE>
<BASE href="$link.baseRef">
</HEAD>
<BODY>
#if( $user )
<H3>Welcome $user.username!</H3>
#else
<H3>Welcome World!</H3>
#end
$!errors.msgs()
<UL>
<LI><A
  href="$link.setForward('logon')">
  Sign in</A></LI>
#if( $user )
<LI><A href=
  "$link.setForward('logoff')">
  Sign out</A></LI>
#end
</UL>
<IMG src='struts-power.gif'
  alt='Powered by Struts'>
<IMG src='velocity-power.gif'
  alt='Powered by Velocity'>
</BODY>
</HTML>
```

a.

```
<%@ taglib uri="/tags/struts-bean"
  prefix="bean" %>
<%@ taglib uri="/tags/struts-html"
  prefix="html" %>
<%@ taglib uri="/tags/struts-logic"
  prefix="logic" %>
<HTML>
<HEAD>
<TITLE>Welcome!</TITLE>
<html:base/>
</HEAD>
<BODY>
<logic:present name="user">
<H3>Welcome <bean:write name="user"
  property="username"/>!</H3>
</logic:present>
<logic:notPresent scope="session"
  name="user">
<H3>Welcome World!</H3>
</logic:notPresent>
<html:errors/>
<UL>
<LI><html:link forward="logon">Sign
  in</html:link></LI>
<logic:present name="user">
<LI><html:link forward="logoff">Sign
  out</html:link></LI>
</logic:present>
</UL>
<IMG src='struts-power.gif'
  alt='Powered by Struts'>
</BODY>
</HTML>
```

b.

Figure 17.1   (a.) Welcome.vm and (b.) Welcome.jsp

block by block. The versions of the logon page are just as similar, as shown in figures 17.2a and 17.2b.

While it may appear that the Velocity versions require that more HTML markup be used on a page, it can be much easier to write a Velocity template using today's visual HTML editors. To HTML editing software, the Velocity markup looks like the control's initial value. (And, in a sense, it is.) The Velocity markup can then be input via any editing software's normal dialog boxes and displayed on a test page outside the running application. So, in practice, *less* HTML is actually written by human beings.

```
<HTML>
<HEAD>
<TITLE>Sign in, Please!</TITLE>
</HEAD>
<BODY>
$!errors.msgs()
<FORM method="POST"
  action="$link.setAction('/Logon
  Submit')">
<TABLE border="0" width="100%">
<TR>
<TH align="right">Username:</TH>
<TD align="left"><INPUT type="text"
  name="username"
  value="$!logonForm.username"></TD
  >
</TR>
<TR>
<TH align="right">Password:</TH>
<TD align="left"><INPUT
  type="password" name="password"
  value="$!logonForm.password"></TD
  >
</TR>
<TR>
<TD align="right"><INPUT
  type="submit" value="Submit"
  name="submit"></TD>
<TD align="left"><INPUT type="reset"
  value="Reset"name="reset"></TD>
</TR>
</TABLE>
</FORM>
</BODY>
</HTML>
```

a.

```
<%@ taglib uri="/tags/struts-html"
  prefix="html" %>
<HTML>
<HEAD>
<TITLE>Sign in, Please!</TITLE>
</HEAD>
<BODY>
<html:errors/>
<html:form action="/LogonSubmit"
  focus="username">
<TABLE border="0" width="100%">
<TR>
<TH align="right">Username:</TH>
<TD align="left"><html:text
  property="username"/></TD>
</TR>
<TR>
<TH align="right">Password:</TH>
<TD align="left"><html:password
  property="password"/></TD>
</TR>
<TR>
<TD
  align="right"><html:submit/></TD>
<TD align="left"><html:reset/></TD>
</TR>
</TABLE>
</html:form>
</BODY>
</HTML
```

b.

Figure 17.2   (a.) Logon.vm and (b.) Logon.jsp

Similar functionality is becoming available for JavaServer Pages. There are some add-ins for Dreamweaver 4 [ASF, CTLX], but the marketplace, regrettably, has been slow to provide direct support for JSP custom tags. Meanwhile, Velocity templates can be easily coded using any off-the-shelf HTML editor. In practice, the HTML page designers working with a Velocity template tend to enter less application-specific code than they would with a JSP.

With a framework like Struts, you have your choice of presentation systems and can use whichever one is the best fit for your application and team members.

An updated version of the logon application from chapter 3 is available on the book website [Husted] as logon-velocity.war. You can download this application and install it in your container to see Velocity in action. You can log on using the names of any of the book's authors, as shown in table 17.4. Use the first name as the userId and the last name as the password.

Table 17.4   Default logons

userId	Password
Ted	Husted
Cedric	Dumoulin
George	Franciscus
David	Winterfeldt
Craig	McClanahan

The passwords are case sensitive, so be sure to use an initial capital letter.

Let's take a look at the changes we had to make to the configuration to get the logon Velocity application up and running.

17.6   Setting up VelocityViewServlet

Before we can actually test our Velocity templates, we need access to the Velocity Template Engine. Usually, you need to create your own instance of the engine designed to work with a particular application. But since web applications based on a framework (like Struts) have very similar needs, the Velocity team provides a standard VelocityViewServlet (`org.apache.velocity.tools.view.servlet. VelocityViewServlet`) that takes care of everything for us.

17.6.1   Installing the VelocityViewServlet

The VelocityViewServlet itself is in the velocity-tools-view.jar in the logon application's WEB-INF/lib folder. The web.xml in the logon distribution also includes the Velocity servlet configuration, and is a working example of configuring both the ActionServlet and Velocity servlet in the same file.

Aside from the velocity-tools-view.jar, we also added the velocity-tools-library.jar, the velocity-tools-struts.jar, and the dom4j.jar to our lib folder. For Struts 1.0.2, you will also need to add the jakarta-commons-collection.jar. But, given the usual Struts JARs, that's it!

Of course, the latest version of the Velocity Struts toolkit is available from the Velocity website at Jakarta [ASF, Velocity].

Given the requisite JARs, we just need to configure our deployment descriptor (web.xml) to load the Velocity servlet and add a toolbox.xml configuration file to WEB-INF for our new toys.

17.6.2 *Deploying the Velocity servlet*

Like any servlet, the VelocityViewServlet is deployed through the web application deployment descriptor. Listing 17.1 shows the servlet configuration element we added to the logon application's web.xml.

Listing 17.1   /WEB-INF/web.xml (Velocity servlet element)

```
<!-- Define Velocity template compiler -->
  <servlet>
    <servlet-name>velocity</servlet-name>
    <servlet-class>
      org.apache.velocity.tools.view.servlet.VelocityViewServlet
    </servlet-class>
    <init-param>
      <param-name>toolbox</param-name>
      <param-value>/WEB-INF/toolbox.xml</param-value>
    </init-param>
<load-on-startup>10</load-on-startup>
  </servlet>
  <!-- Map *.vm files to Velocity -->
  <servlet-mapping>
    <servlet-name>velocity</servlet-name>
    <url-pattern>*.vm</url-pattern>
  </servlet-mapping>
```

The toolbox parameter

As we've mentioned, the Struts configuration is exposed to the Velocity template using a handy set of predefined objects that Velocity calls *tools*. The tools are helper objects that give you quick and easy access to framework objects. Other tools can help out with date transformations, math calculations, and whatever else you might need to do within your presentation page. Tools can help extend a Velocity template in much the same way a custom tag can extend a JSP.

The Struts View tools are only one of a number of toolkits planned by the Velocity team. The `toolbox` parameter is used to specify the tool configuration file. This is where we can load the Struts tools and any others we might ever need. Conceptually, this is very much like deploying a custom tag library that a JSP might use. We take a closer look at the Velocity toolbox in section 17.6.3.

The properties parameter

Velocity is a full-featured component and offers a number of configuration options. These can be placed in a Properties file and adjusted for your application. Our application doesn't need to change any of the Velocity defaults, so we've omitted the velocity.properties file. For more about the different ways Velocity can be configured, consult the documentation at the Velocity website [ASF, Velocity].

17.6.3 The toolbox configuration file

Our toolbox configuration file, shown in listing 17.2, simply loads the Struts View tools. Other tools that you or others develop can also be loaded here.

Listing 17.2   /WEB-INF/toolbox.xml

```xml
<?xml version="1.0"?>

<toolbox>
  <tool>
     <key>toolLoader</key>
     <class>org.apache.velocity.tools.tools.ToolLoader</class>
  </tool>
  <tool>
     <key>link</key>
     <class>org.apache.velocity.tools.struts.LinkTool</class>
  </tool>
  <tool>
     <key>msg</key>
     <class>org.apache.velocity.tools.struts.MessageTool</class>
  </tool>
  <tool>
     <key>errors</key>
     <class>org.apache.velocity.tools.struts.ErrorsTool</class>
  </tool>
  <tool>
     <key>form</key>
     <class>org.apache.velocity.tools.struts.FormTool</class>
  </tool>
</toolbox>
```

If for any reason you need to change the name of a tool, you can change the name parameter here, and it will be exposed under the new attribute name.

17.7 *Setting up struts-config*

At this point, changing over to Velocity templates is simply a matter of replacing *.jsp* with *.vm* in the struts-config. You could even do this with a search and replace. The converted struts-config is shown in listing 17.3.

Listing 17.3   /WEB-INF/conf/struts-config.xml

```xml
<?xml version="1.0" encoding="ISO-8859-1" ?>
<!DOCTYPE struts-config PUBLIC "-//Apache Software Foundation//DTD Struts
   Configuration 1.0//EN" "http://jakarta.apache.org/struts/dtds/struts-
   config_1_0.dtd">
<struts-config>
<form-beans>
      <form-bean
      name="logonForm"
      type="app.LogonForm"/>
   </form-beans>
<global-forwards>
    <forward
      name="logoff"
      path="/Logoff.do"/>
    <forward
      name="logon"
      path="/Logon.do"/>
    <forward
      name="welcome"
      path="/Welcome.do"/>
</global-forwards>
<action-mappings>
    <action
      path="/Welcome"
      type="org.apache.struts.actions.ForwardAction"
      parameter="/pages/Welcome.vm"/>
    <action
      path="/Logon"
      type="org.apache.struts.actions.ForwardAction"
      parameter="/pages/Logon.vm"/>

    <action
      path="/LogonSubmit"
      type="app.LogonAction"
      name="logonForm"
      scope="request"
      validate="true"
      input="/pages/Logon.vm">
      <forward
          name="success"
          path="/pages/Welcome.vm"/>
   </action>
```

```
<action
    path="/Logoff"
    type="app.LogoffAction">
    <forward
        name="success"
        path="/pages/Welcome.vm"/>
</action>
</action-mappings>
</struts-config>
```

If you make this change in the logon application's configuration, or the one you are building yourself, then you should be ready to take the application for a test drive. It should look just like the other, except for the additional "Powered by Velocity" image on the welcome page, as shown in figure 17.3.

Figure 17.3
The welcome screen of the logon application using Velocity templates

Of course, you can also mix and match JavaServer Pages and Velocity templates in the same application. A very good way to start out with Velocity is to replace a single JavaServer Page at a time. It's not an either/or proposition. The choice is yours.

17.8 *Summary*

Velocity is an excellent way to handle the presentation layer of any MVC application, including web applications based on the Struts framework. The Velocity View tools for Struts make it easy to access the framework's resources. The VelocityViewServlet make it just as easy to access the Servlet API resources, along with any other helpers you might be tucking away in one of the contexts.

Since Velocity and JSP custom tags share a common design philosophy, moving from one to the other is a straightforward process. A custom tag and a Velocity declaration or tool can be exchanged on a one-to-one basis.

In an MVC web environment like Struts, Velocity templates and custom tags are playing on a level field. Which technology is best for your application is more about *who* will be creating the presentation layer than *what* they should be creating it with. If Java engineers already comfortable with JavaServer Pages are creating the presentation pages, then JSPs remain a solid choice. On the other hand, if your engineers will be working with page designers using tools designed for static HTML pages, then Velocity templates may be the better choice.

If for any reason you need to mix and match JSPs and Velocity templates, you can do that too. The technologies are not mutually exclusive. In fact, they play well together.

The important thing is that by using a layered architecture and a versatile framework like Struts, you reserve the option of making your own choices. You *can* make the decision.

Design patterns

*A pattern is an idea that has been useful in one practical context
and will probably be useful in others.*

—Martin Fowler

Design patterns are often mentioned in development discussions today. Struts itself implements a number of classic designs, starting with Model-View-Controller (MVC). Understanding which patterns Struts uses, and why, makes it much easier to "program with the grain," so you can create applications that make the best use of the Struts components.

As we show in this appendix, although no one person or group of people wrote the patterns, using them together has a synergistic effect. Relying on patterns, and being able to discuss how they are used, leads to better and better designs over the life of an application.

But where did the design patterns come from? How did they become such an important element in application architecture?

A.1   *A brief history of design patterns*

It can be said that Struts "stands on the shoulders of giants." Let's introduce the little giants we call *design patterns*, and provide pointers for further research.

The software community has known the value of design patterns for some time. In the 1970s, a number of books were published documenting patterns in civil engineering and architecture. The software community took note and began to refer to *patterns* found in their own work. Interest in software design patterns has peaked in recent years, especially in the Java community. The patterns themselves are often deceptively simple. Here's an excerpt from a well-known pattern catalog defining a very simple, yet very useful pattern:

Adapter Pattern.   Convert the interface of a class into another interface clients expect. Adapter lets classes work together that couldn't otherwise because of incompatible interfaces. [Go4]

Developers approach these patterns like Zen sayings. This sentence is the complete definition of the Adapter pattern. But entire chapters can be written to discuss what a pattern like this means.

The use of these seemingly simple patterns, such as Adapter, has a synergistic effect on an application's architecture, making programs easier to write, and more important, easier to maintain. A prime mover in the current wave of interest in design patterns has been the *Design Patterns* book [Go4], published in 1994. This was joined by other pattern classics, including *Working with Objects: The Ooram Software Engineering Method* [Ooram] in 1995 and *Pattern-Oriented Software Architecture* [POSA] in 1996. Sun then drove the point home with its J2EE Blueprints website [Sun, Blueprints] and its subsequent publication of *Core J2EE Patterns* [Go3] in 2001.

The many ideas in each of these works have built on each other and have created a coherent patterns literature. Struts builds soundly on the classic patterns described in these references. Next, we discuss the history and importance of design patterns and how they are used in the Struts framework.

A.1.1 The Gang of Four

... consider the excellent but difficult book Design Patterns.
—Alistair Cockburn

Once upon a time, Erich Gamma, Richard Helm, Ralph Johnson, and John Vlissides put their collective heads together and developed a catalog of design patterns, the venerable *Design Patterns: Elements of Reusable Object-Oriented Software* [Go4]. This so-called Gang of Four did not invent the patterns; they carefully selected and documented a core set of patterns known to be useful. This has been an immensely popular work, and has led to software patterns being a common topic of discussion in development teams around the world.

The underlying theme of the patterns is that most problems are not unique; often, we need to solve the same class of problems over and over again. By describing these solutions on their own terms, we find it easier to see the pattern behind the solution, and reapply the idea the next time a similar situation comes along.

Design Patterns catalogs 23 truly useful patterns—including Adapter, Decorator, Facade, Factory Method, Singleton, and many others—that developers now consider their stock in trade.

Design patterns and frameworks make for a very good match. Both are really trying to do the same thing: save developers the work of reinventing the wheel. In chapter 2, we show how these and other patterns are implemented in Struts.

One thing expert designers know not to do is solve every problem from first principles. Rather, they reuse solutions that have worked for them in the past. When they find a good solution they use it again and again [Go4].

A.1.2 J2EE Blueprints

To position Java as the platform of choice for robust, scalable applications, Sun offers up the Java 2 Enterprise Edition (J2EE). This is a feature-rich platform that draws on a number of technologies, including Enterprise JavaBeans (EJBs). These advanced technologies are very easy to misuse. More than one team has found that poor design choices can quickly rob a J2EE application of its performance and scalability advantages.

To help developers design better applications, Sun developed the J2EE Blueprints [Sun, Blueprints]. The Blueprints are a set of guidelines, design patterns, and sample code, all meant to embody the J2EE best practices. The Blueprints are primarily available online, but a companion book, *Designing Enterprise Applications with the J2EE Platform* [Sun, J2EE], is available.

The Blueprints clearly define the terms most often used in web architecture circles, including tiers, business logic, clients, CGI, and component-based design. Regardless of whether you are writing a J2EE application or a Java 2 Standard Edition (J2SE) application, the Blueprints give you an excellent background on designing Java web applications.

A.1.3 *Core J2EE Patterns*

Sun's *Core J2EE Patterns*, by Deepak Alur, John Crupi, and Dan Malks [Go3], has much in common with *Design Patterns* (including a foreword by Grady Booch). There is no overlap between the books; *Core J2EE Patterns* intentionally builds on the foundation laid down by the Gang of Four. But this "Gang of Three" extends the focus to patterns for building robust, scalable applications, like those designed for the J2EE platform.

While the book is ostensibly about J2EE patterns, since they are *patterns* the book's advice can be applied to any compatible technology. The Core patterns work well with any Java web application, regardless of whether EJBs are used on the backend.

The key point about the J2EE patterns is that they stress building applications in tiers, with strong abstractions, layering, and clean separation between the presentation, business, and integration tiers. Struts is designed to provide that same separation, and is a good fit with the overall focus of the book. In fact, *Core J2EE Patterns* uses Struts as the example implementation for the Synchronizer Token pattern in the book's refactoring section.

A.2 *Why patterns are important*

The most important thing about patterns is that they are *proven solutions*. Each catalog mentioned here includes only patterns that have been found useful by multiple developers in multiple projects. The cataloged patterns are also *well defined*; the authors describe each pattern with great care and in its own context, so that it will be easy for you to apply the pattern to your own circumstances. The cataloged patterns also form a *common vocabulary* among developers. We can use terms like *adapter* and *facade* during design discussions and communicate exactly what we have in mind. Each pattern carries documented consequences, both good and bad, and developers can choose a pattern, forewarned and forearmed. Since great care is put into cataloging the patterns, they also represent a set of *best practices* for teams to follow.

A.3 What patterns won't do

Patterns are a roadmap, not a strategy. The catalogs will often present some source code as an example strategy, but that would just be one possible implementation. Selecting a pattern is not the same as importing a class; you still have to implement the pattern in the context of your application. Patterns will not help you determine what application you should be writing—only how to best implement the application once the feature set and other requirements are determined. Patterns help with the *what* and the *how*, but not with the *why* or *when*.

A.4 Struts—a Who's Who of design patterns

Patterns and frameworks are a good combination. But patterns can be used again and again throughout an application. Struts provides a concrete example of how many of the cataloged patterns can be implemented. In looking through the catalogs, selecting patterns for use in your own applications, you may find it helpful to see how Struts has made good use of the same patterns.

After all, if Struts is your application framework, it is now part and parcel of your own application. Using the same pattern in the same way will help you get the most out of both Struts and your own hard work.

Working from the descriptions in the *Core J2EE Patterns* catalog, the Struts architecture implements several key patterns, including Service to Worker, Front Controller, Singleton, Dispatcher, View Helper, Value Object, Composite View, and Synchronizer Token, among others. Table A.1 shows the many patterns implemented by Struts components.

Table A.1 Patterns implemented by Struts classes

Pattern(s)	Struts component(s)
Service to Worker	ActionServlet, Action
Command [Go4], Command and Controller, Front Controller, Singleton, Service Locator	ActionServlet, Action
Dispatcher, Navigator	ActionMapping, ActionServlet, Action, ActionForward
View Helper, Session Facade, Singleton	Action
Transfer Objects (fka Value Objects), Value Object Assembler	ActionForm, ActionErrors, ActionMessages
View Helper	ActionForm, ContextHelper, tag extensions
Composite View, Value Object Assembler	Template taglib, Tiles taglib

Since Struts 1.1

Since Struts 1.1

Table A.1 Patterns implemented by Struts classes *(continued)*

Pattern(s)	Struts component(s)
Synchronizer Token	Action
Decorator [Go4]	ActionMapping

Let's take a closer look at the key patterns.

A.4.1 *The Service to Worker pattern*

At the highest level, Struts implements a *Service to Worker* pattern. This is a "macro" pattern that incorporates two others, *Front Controller* and *View Helper*.

The Front Controller pattern

In chapter 2, we see that the ActionServlet receives user gestures and state changes. Another way to say it is that the ActionServlet provides a centralized access point for request handling. This called the *Front Controller* pattern, and it is a key feature of the Model 2 approach. This pattern allows the centralization of code relating to system services, security services, content retrieval, view management, and navigation, so that application code is not endlessly duplicated or commingled with view content.

The Command / Command and Controller patterns

Like many Front Controllers, Struts implements a dispatcher component (or Action class) to handle such details as content retrieval and view management. The ActionServlet invokes a known method on the Action and passes it details of the request to delegate responsibility for the response. This is known as the *Command and Controller* strategy [Go3] and is based on the *Command* pattern [Go4]. The Struts Action classes play a strong role in view management.

The Service Locator pattern

Many data persistence components rely on standard DataSource objects (`javax.sql.DataSource`) to provide access to the underlying storage system. Most often the store is a JDBC database, but a DataSource can be used to connect to any type of system. The ActionServlet can maintain a list of DataSource objects keyed to a logical name that you specify in the Struts configuration. Other objects can retrieve the DataSource object ("locate the service") by name without knowing any other implementation detail. Struts developers can switch JDBC drivers, connection pools, and so forth, just by changing which DataSource is registered under a logical name.

The View Helper pattern

Also in chapter 2, we see that the ActionForm contains the data for a state change. The framework expects the data being entered into the system to be encapsulated in a JavaBean. One of the things that Struts does for you is to take an HTTP request and transfer its parameters into an ActionForm bean. Using JavaBeans to transfer business data to a view component is known as the *View Helper* pattern [Go3]. The Struts framework exposes several shared resources in the servlet contexts so that they can be used by other components, especially those on the presentation layer. While not always simple JavaBeans, the Struts resources are another type of view helper.

A.4.2   The Singleton pattern

In a multithreaded environment such as Java, there is often no advantage to having several copies of the same object floating around. Servlets, for example, are multithreaded and can handle any number of requests without spawning a new object. Struts applies this same principle to its Actions, and instantiates only one Action per application. This enhances performance but puts the responsibility of writing thread-safe Actions on the developer.

A.4.3   The Session Facade pattern

The interaction between the model and the rest of your application can be quite complex. Encapsulating these details into a single object with a simple interface can make an application much easier to write and maintain. Struts encourages encapsulating such details with its Action classes. An Action has a well-defined interface and some general responsibilities, but is mainly a white box where an application can do whatever needs to be done.

This is known as the *Session Facade* pattern: the Action class "abstracts the underlying business object interaction and provides a service layer that exposes only the required interfaces" [Go3].

Struts also uses a Session Facade pattern in the design of the message resources component. The complexity of selecting the user's locale is hidden. The components simply ask for a message by key, and the message resources provide the correct message for the user's locale.

A.4.4   Value Object / Value Object Assembler patterns

One thing leads to another. Often, a process will require several pieces of information in order to complete. In the olden days of Teletype programs, we had to ask for everything one piece at a time. Now, with form-based dialog boxes, we can ask for everything we need at once.

This functionality can be especially important when our application is using a remote server and there is some lag between requests. We need to get as much information as we can up front, because sending the information to the server and back takes longer than we would like.

In J2EE circles, the information we want to collect into a single packet is called a *value object*. A value object encapsulates business data, so that a single call can be made to send and receive our data [Go3]. The Struts ActionForm is one example of a value object. It collects the fields we need from an HTML form all at once, so that the information can be validated all at once and either returned together for correction or sent along for processing by the Action.

The Struts ActionErrors is another example of a value object. Here we can collect several related error messages together so they can be displayed at once, corrected together, and resubmitted.

The Struts ActionForms can also use nested JavaBeans. This lets you divide the properties you need to collect into different JavaBeans, which may be obtained from different parts of your model. Various beans can be made members of your ActionForm class and referred to using a dotted syntax. (See chapter 5 for details.)

This is known as the *Value Object Assembler* pattern: you build a composite value object using other value objects so that the data set can be treated as a single entity.

A.4.5 *The Composite View pattern*

Often, a screen presentation is made up of several individual displays, or a *Composite View* [Go4]. The Struts 1.0 Template tags use this pattern to build a JavaServer Page from several standard pages. Typically, this is used to provide a common set of navigational elements to a page, which can be changed throughout the site by editing a single page.

A.4.6 *The Synchronizer Token pattern*

An ongoing problem in a web application is the lag between a request and its response. In some applications, this can be a serious problem when a request should be submitted only once—for example, when a user is checking out a shopping cart and placing an order. Since placing the order can take some time, there may be a few minutes before the response is generated. It is easy for the user to become impatient and click the Submit button again. This can generate another request—and a duplicate order.

One strategy to prevent this is to set a *synchronizer token* in the user's session and include the token's value in the form we need to protect. When the form is submitted, the Action clears the token. If a later submission finds that its token is missing, the Action can forgo the duplicate submission.

The Struts Action class implements a synchronizer token strategy, which is also exposed in the tag extensions.

A.4.7 *The Decorator pattern*

The Action object is a multithreaded singleton. This is generally a good thing, but it can make the Action harder to reuse for similar operations. The Action-Mapping class is used to extend the Action *object* rather than the Action *class*. An ActionMapping gives a specific Action object additional responsibilities and new functionality, which embodies the *Decorator pattern* [Go4].

The struts-config API

The format used by the Struts configuration file (struts-config.xml) is described by the struts-config Document Type Definition (DTD), as given by the DOCTYPE element at the head of the file:

```
<!DOCTYPE struts-config PUBLIC
"-//Apache Software Foundation//DTD Struts Configuration 1.1//EN"
"http://jakarta.apache.org/struts/dtds/struts-config_1_1.dtd"
```

The DTD should be considered the official reference document for the struts-config format, in the same way that the JavaDocs are the official reference document for the frameworks Java objects. For your convenience, we have formatted the comments from the struts-config DTD as a standard API reference. Several supporting elements used by the DTD are not documented here, because they are not an essential part of the public API. For complete details, see the reference copy of the DTD at http://jakarta.apache.org/struts/dtds/struts-config_1_1.dtd.

> **1.0 vs 1.1**   When this book went to press, Struts 1.1 beta release 2 was in circulation. Some details may have changed between beta 2 and the final release. Be sure to check the book's website [Husted] for any errata.

B.1   *<struts-config>*

The `<struts-config>` element is the root of the configuration file hierarchy. It contains nested elements for all of the other configuration settings. Table B.1 shows the Struts configuration elements.

Table B.1   `<struts-config>` elements

Element	Description
set-property	Specifies the method name and initial value of an additional JavaBean configuration property
data-sources	Specifies a set of DataSource objects (JDBC 2.0 Standard Extension)
data-source	Specifies a DataSource object to be instantiated, configured, and made available as a servlet context attribute (or application-scope bean)
global-exceptions	Describes a set of exceptions that might be thrown by an Action object
exception	Registers an ExceptionHandler for an exception type
form-beans	Describes the set of form bean descriptors for this application module
form-bean	Describes an ActionForm subclass that can be referenced by an `<action>` element
form-property	Describes a JavaBean property that can be used to configure an instance of a DynaActionForm or a subclass thereof
global-forwards	Describes a set of ActionForward objects that are available to all Action objects as a return value
forward	Describes an ActionForward that is to be made available to an Action as a return value
action-mappings	Describes a set of ActionMappings that are available to process requests matching the URL pattern our ActionServlet registered with the container
action	Describes an ActionMapping object that is to be used to process a request for a specific module-relative URI
controller	Describes the ControllerConfig bean that encapsulates an application module's runtime configuration

Since Struts 1.1

Since Struts 1.1

Since Struts 1.1

Table B.1 `<struts-config>` **elements** *(continued)*

Element	Description
message-resources	Describes a MessageResources object with message templates for this module
plug-in	Specifies the fully qualified classname of a general-purpose application plug-in module that receives notification of application startup and shutdown events

B.1.1 *<set-property>*

The `<set-property>` element specifies the method name and initial value of an additional JavaBean configuration property. When the object representing the surrounding element is instantiated, the accessor for the indicated property is called and passed the indicated value. The `<set-property>` element is especially useful when a custom subclass is used with `<forward>`, `<action>`, or `<plug-in>` elements. The subclass can be passed whatever other properties may be required to configure the object without changing how the struts-config is parsed. The attributes shown in table B.2 are defined.

Table B.2 `<set-property>` **attributes**

Attribute	Description
property	The name of the JavaBeans property whose setter method will be called
value	The string representation of the value to which this property will be set, after suitable type conversion

B.1.2 *<data-sources>*

The `<data-sources>` element describes a set of DataSource objects (JDBC 2.0 Standard Extension).

The individual DataSource objects are configured through nested `<data-source>` elements.

B.1.3 *<data-source>*

The `<data-source>` element describes a DataSource object (JDBC 2.0 Standard Extension) that will be instantiated, configured, and made available as a servlet context attribute (or application-scope bean). Any object can be specified as long as it implements `javax.sql.DataSource` and can be configured entirely from Java-Bean properties. Table B.3 shows the attributes for the `<data-source>` element.

Table B.3 `<data-source>` **attributes**

Attribute	Default/Description
className	(org.apache.struts.config.DataSourceConfig) The configuration bean for this DataSource object. If specified, the object must be a subclass of the default configuration bean.
key	(org.apache.struts.action.DATA_SOURCE) The servlet context attribute key under which this data source will be stored. The default is the value specified by the string constant defined by Action. DATA_SOURCE_KEY. The application module prefix (if any) is appended to the key (${key}$prefix). Note that the application module prefix includes the leading slash, so the default data source for a module named foo is stored under org.apache.struts.action.DATA_SOURCE/foo.
type	(org.apache.struts.util.GenericDataSource) The fully qualified Java classname for this data source object. The class must implement javax.sql.DataSource, and the object must be configurable entirely from JavaBean properties.
Nested element	
set-property	See table B.2.

B.1.4 *<global-exceptions>*

The `<global-exceptions>` element describes a set of exceptions that might be thrown by an Action object. The handling of individual exception types is configured through nested exception elements. An `<action>` element may override a global exception handler by registering a local exception handler for the same exception type.

B.1.5 *<exception>*

The `<exception>` element registers an ExceptionHandler for an exception type. Table B.4 shows the attributes for the `<exception>` element.

Table B.4 `<exception>` **attributes**

Attribute	Default/Description
bundle	(org.apache.struts.action.MESSAGE) The servlet context attribute for the message resources bundle associated with this handler. The default attribute is the value specified by the string constant declared at org.apache.struts.Action.MESSAGES_KEY.
className	(org.apache.struts.config.ExceptionConfig) The configuration bean for this ExceptionHandler object. If specified, className must be a subclass of the default configuration bean.

Table B.4 `<exception>` **attributes** *(continued)*

Attribute	Default/Description
`handler`	`(org.apache.struts.action.ExceptionHandler)` The fully qualified Java classname for this exception handler.
`key`	No default The key to use with this handler's message resource bundle that will retrieve the error message template for this exception.
`path`	No default The module-relative URI to the resource that will complete the request/response if this exception occurs.
`scope`	`(request)` The context (request or session) that is used to access the ActionError object for this exception.
`type`	No default The fully qualified Java classname of the exception type to register with this handler.
`description`	Descriptive (paragraph-length) text about the surrounding element, suitable for use in GUI tools.
`display-name`	A short (one-line) description of the surrounding element, suitable for use in GUI tools.
`icon`	A small-icon and large-icon element that specifies the location, relative to the Struts configuration file, for small and large images used to represent the surrounding element in GUI tools.
Nested element	
`set-property`	See table B.2.

B.1.6 *<form-beans>*

The `<form-beans>` element describes the set of form bean descriptors for this application module. An optional `type` attribute may be specified, as shown in table B.5.

Table B.5 `<form-beans>` attribute

Attribute	Default/Description
type	`(org.apache.struts.config.FormBeanConfig)` The fully qualified Java classname to use when instantiating ActionFormBean objects. If specified, the object must be a subclass of the default class type. (Deprecated)
Nested element	
form-bean	See table B.6.

In Struts 1.0, you must set the default implementation class name with the `form-Bean` initialization parameter to the Struts controller servlet.

B.1.7 *<form-bean>*

The `<form-bean>` element describes an ActionForm subclass (`org.apache.struts.action.ActionForm`) that can be referenced by an `<action>` element. Table B.7 shows the attributes for the `<form-bean>` element.

Table B.6 `<form-bean>` attributes

Attribute	Default/Description
className	`(org.apacheapache.struts.config.FormBeanConfig)` The configuration bean for this form bean object. If specified, the object must be a subclass of the default configuration bean.
dynamic	(true) if `type` equals `org.apache.struts.action.DynaActionForm` (false) otherwise If the form bean `type` is a DynaActionForm subclass (that you created), then (and only then) set this attribute to true. If the type is set to the default DynaActionForm or any conventional ActionForm subclass, then this attribute can be omitted.
name	No default The unique identifier for this form bean. Referenced by the `<action>` element to specify which form bean to use with its request.
type	No default The fully qualified Java classname of the ActionForm subclass to use with this form bean.
description	Descriptive (paragraph-length) text about the surrounding element, suitable for use in GUI tools.
display-name	A short (one-line) description of the surrounding element, suitable for use in GUI tools.

Table B.6 `<form-bean>` **attributes** *(continued)*

Attribute	Default/Description
icon	A small-icon and large-icon element that specifies the location, relative to the Struts configuration file, for small and large images used to represent the surrounding element in GUI tools.
Nested elements	
set-property	See table B.2.
form-property	See table B.6.

B.1.8 *<form-property>*

Since Struts 1.1 The `<form-property>` element describes a JavaBean property that can be used to configure an instance of a DynaActionForm or a subclass thereof. This element is used only when the `type` attribute of the enclosing `<form-bean>` element is `org.apache.struts.action.DynaActionForm` or a subclass of DynaActionForm. If a custom DynaActionForm subclass is used, then the `dynamic` attribute of the enclosing `<form-bean>` element must be set to true. The attributes shown in table B.6 are defined.

Table B.7 `<form-property>` **attributes**

Attribute	Default/Description
className	(org.apache.struts.config.FormPropertyConfig) The configuration bean for this form property object. If specified, the object must be a subclass of the default configuration bean.
initial	(null) or (0) The string representation of the initial value for this property. If not specified, primitives will be initialized to zero and objects initialized to null.
name	No default The name of the JavaBean property described by this element.
type	No default The fully qualified Java classname of the field underlying this property, optionally followed by [] to indicate that the field is indexed.
Nested element	
set-property	See table B.2.

B.1.9 *<global-forwards>*

The `<global-forwards>` element describes a set of ActionForward objects (`org.apache.struts.action.ActionForward`) that are available to all Action objects as a return value. The individual ActionForwards are configured through nested `<forward>` elements. An `<action>` element may override a global forward by defining a local `<forward>` element of the same name.

An optional `type` attribute may be specified to the `<global-forwards>` element, as shown in table B.8.

Table B.8 `<global-forwards>` attribute

Attribute	Default/Description
type	`(org.apache.struts.action.ActionForward)` The fully qualified Java classname to use when instantiating ActionForward objects. If specified, the object must be a subclass of the default class type. (Deprecated)
Nested element	
forward	See table B.9.

In Struts 1.0, you must set the default implementation classname with the `actionForward` initialization parameter to the Struts controller servlet.

B.1.10 *<forward>*

The `<forward>` element describes an ActionForward that is to be made available to an Action as a return value. An ActionForward is referenced by a logical name and encapsulates a URI. A `<forward>` element may be used to describe both global and local ActionForwards. Global forwards are available to all the Action objects in the application module. Local forwards can be nested within an `<action>` element and are only available to an Action object when it is invoked through that ActionMapping.

The attributes shown in table B.9 can be used with the `<forward>` element.

Table B.9 `<forward>` **attributes**

Attribute	Default/Description
className	`(org.apache.struts.action.ActionForward)` The fully qualified Java classname of the ActionForward subclass to use for this object. If specified, `className` must be a subclass of the default object.
contextRelative	(false) Set this to true if, in a modular application, the `path` attribute starts with a slash (/) and should be considered relative to the entire web application rather than the module.
name	No default The unique identifier for this forward. Referenced by the Action object at run-time to select (by its logical name) the resource that should complete the request/response.
path	No default The module-relative or context-relative path to the resource that is encapsulated by the logical name of this ActionForward. If the path is to be considered context-relative when used in a modular application, then the `contextRela-tive` attribute should be set to true. This value should begin with a slash (/) character.
redirect	(false) Set to true if a redirect instruction should be issued to the user agent so that a new request is issued for this forward's resource. If true, `RequestDis-patcher.Redirect` is called. If false, `RequestDispatcher.forward` is called instead.
description	Descriptive (paragraph-length) text about the surrounding element, suitable for use in GUI tools.
display-name	A short (one-line) description of the surrounding element, suitable for use in GUI tools.
icon	A small-icon and large-icon element that specifies the location, relative to the Struts configuration file, for small and large images used to represent the surrounding element in GUI tools.
Nested element	
set-property	See table B.2.

Since Struts 1.1

B.1.11 *<action-mappings>*

The `<action-mappings>` element describes a set of ActionMapping objects (`org.apache.struts.action.ActionMapping`) that are available to process requests matching the URL pattern our ActionServlet registered with the container. The individual ActionMappings are configured through nested `<action>` elements. Table B.10 shows the attribute for the `<action-mappings>` element.

Table B.10 `<action-mappings>` **attribute**

Attribute	Default/Description
type	`(org.apache.struts.action.ActionMapping)` The fully qualified Java classname to use when instantiating ActionMapping objects. If specified, the object must be a subclass of the default class type.
Nested element	
action	See table B.11.

In Struts 1.0, you must set the default implementation classname with the `actionMapping` initialization parameter to the Struts controller servlet.

B.1.12 *<action>*

The `<action>` element describes an ActionMapping object that is to be used to process a request for a specific module-relative URI. Table B.11 shows the attributes for the `<action>` element.

Table B.11 `<action>` **attributes**

Attribute	Default/Description
attribute	*(Set to* name *property)* The name of the request-scope or session-scope attribute that is used to access our ActionForm bean, if it is other than the bean's specified name. Optional if name is specified, otherwise not valid.
className	`(org.apache.struts.action.ActionMapping)` The fully qualified Java classname of the ActionMapping subclass to use for this action mapping object. Defaults to the type specified by the enclosing `<action-mappings>` element or `org.apache.struts.action.ActionMapping` if not specified.
forward	No default The module-relative path of the servlet or other resource that will process this request, instead of the Action class specified by type. Exactly one of forward, include, or type must be specified.
include	No default The module-relative path of the servlet or other resource that will process this request, instead of the Action class specified by type. Exactly one of forward, include, or type must be specified.

Table B.11 `<action>` **attributes** *(continued)*

Attribute	Default/Description
input	No default The module-relative path of the action or other resource to which control should be returned if a validation error is encountered. Valid only when name is specified. Required if name is specified and the input bean returns validation errors. Optional if name is specified and the input bean does not return validation errors.
name	No default The name of the form bean, if any, that is associated with this action mapping.
path	No default The module-relative path of the submitted request, starting with a / character, and without the filename extension if extension mapping is used. Note: Do not include a period in your pathname, because it will look like a filename extension and cause your Action to not be located.
parameter	No default A general-purpose configuration parameter that can be used to pass extra information to the Action object selected by this action mapping.
prefix	No default A prefix used to match request parameter names to ActionForm property names, if any. Optional if name is specified, otherwise not allowed.
roles	No default A comma-delimited list of security role names that are allowed access to this ActionMapping object.
scope	No default The context (request or session) that is used to access our ActionForm bean, if any. Optional if name is specified, otherwise not valid.
suffix	No default A suffix used to match request parameter names to ActionForm bean property names, if any. Optional if name is specified, otherwise not valid.
type	No default The fully qualified Java classname of the Action subclass (org.apache.struts.action.Action) that will process requests for this action mapping. Not valid if either the forward or include attribute is specified. Exactly one of forward, include, or type must be specified.
unknown	(false) Set to true if this object should be configured as the default action mapping for this module. If a request does not match another object, it will be passed to the Action-Mapping object with unknown set to true. Only one ActionMapping can be marked as unknown within a module.

Since Struts 1.1

Table B.11   `<action>` **attributes**   *(continued)*

Attribute	Default/Description
validate	(true) Set to true if the `validate` method of the ActionForm bean should be called prior to calling this action mapping, or set to false if you do not want the `validate` method called.
description	Descriptive (paragraph-length) text about the surrounding element, suitable for use in GUI tools.
display-name	A short (one-line) description of the surrounding element, suitable for use in GUI tools.
icon	A small-icon and large-icon element that specifies the location, relative to the Struts configuration file, for small and large images used to represent the surrounding element in GUI tools.
Nested elements	
set-property	See table B.2.
exception	See table B.4.
forward	See table B.9.

Any `<action>` may contain `icon`, `display-name`, `description`, `set-property`, `exception`, or `forward` elements.

B.1.13   *<controller>*

The `<controller>` element describes the ControllerConfig bean (`org.apache.struts.config.ControllerConfig`) that encapsulates an application module's runtime configuration. The attributes shown in table B.12 are defined.

Table B.12   `<controller>` **attributes**

Attribute	Default/Description
bufferSize	(4096) The size of the input buffer to use when processing file uploads.
className	(org.apache.struts.config.ControllerConfig) The fully qualified Java classname of the ControllerConfig subclass for this controller object. If specified, the object must be a subclass of the default class.

Table B.12 `<controller>` **attributes** *(continued)*

Attribute	Default/Description
`contentType`	(text/html) The default content type (and optional character encoding) to be set on each response. May be overridden by the Action, JSP, or other resource to which the request is forwarded.
`debug`	(0) The debugging detail level for this module.
`forwardPattern`	(AP) A replacement pattern defining how the `path` attribute of a `<forward>` element is mapped to a context-relative URL when it starts with a slash (and when the `contextRelative` property is false). This value may consist of any combination of the following: $A—Replaced by the `app` prefix of this module $P—Replaced by the `path` attribute of the selected `<forward>` element $$—Causes a literal dollar sign to be rendered $x (where x is any character not defined above)—Silently swallowed, reserved for future use If not specified, the default `forwardPattern` is AP, which is consistent with the previous behavior of forwards.
`inputForward`	(false) Set to true if you want the `input` attribute of `<action>` elements to be the name of a local or global ActionForward, which will then be used to calculate the ultimate URL. Set to false (the default) to treat the `input` parameter of `<action>` elements as a module-relative path to the resource to be used as the input form.
`locale`	(true) Set to true if you want a Locale object stored in the user agent's session if not already present.
`maxFileSize`	(250M) The maximum size (in bytes) of a file to be accepted as a file upload. Can be expressed as a number followed by a K, M, or G, which are interpreted to mean kilobytes, megabytes, or gigabytes, respectively.
`multipartClass`	(org.apache.struts.upload.DiskMultipartRequestHandler) The fully qualified Java classname of the multipart request handler class to be used with this module.
`nocache`	(false) Set to true if you want Struts to add HTTP headers for defeating caching to every response from this module.

Since Struts 1.1

Since Struts 1.1

Table B.12 `<controller>` **attributes** *(continued)*

Attribute	Default/Description
`pagePattern`	(AP) A replacement pattern defining how the `page` attribute of custom tags using it is mapped to a context-relative URL of the corresponding resource. This value may consist of any combination of the following: $A—Replaced by the `app` prefix of this module $P—Replaced by the value of the `page` attribute $$—Causes a literal dollar sign to be rendered $x (where x is any character not defined above)—Silently swallowed, reserved for future use If not specified, the default `forwardPattern` is AP, which is consistent with the previous behavior of URL evaluation for `page` attributes.
`processorClass`	(`org.apache.struts.action.RequestProcessor`) The fully qualified Java classname of the RequestProcessor class to be used with this module.
`TempDir`	(Directory provided by servlet container) The temporary working directory to use when processing file uploads.
Nested element	
`set-property`	See table B.2.

Since Struts 1.1

B.1.14 *<message-resources>*

The `<message-resources>` element describes a MessageResources object with message templates for this module. The attributes shown in table B.13 are defined.

Table B.13 `<message-resources>` **attributes**

Attribute	Description
`className`	(`org.apache.struts.config.MessageResourcesConfig`) The configuration bean for this message resources object. If specified, the object must be a subclass of the default configuration bean.
`factory`	(`org.apache.struts.util.PropertyMessageResourcesFactory`) The fully qualified Java classname of the MessageResourcesFactory subclass to use for this message resources object.
`key`	(`org.apache.struts.action.MESSAGE`) The servlet context attribute under which this message resources bundle will be stored. The default attribute is the value specified by the string constant at (`org.apache.struts.Action.MESSAGES_KEY`). The application module prefix (if any) is appended to the key (`${key}${prefix}`). Note that the application module prefix includes the leading slash, so the default message resource bundle for a module named `foo` is stored under `org.apache.struts.action.MESSAGE/foo`.

Table B.13 `<message-resources>` **attributes** *(continued)*

Attribute	Description
null	(true) Set to true if you want your message resources to return a null string for unknown message keys, or false to return a message with the bad key value.
parameter	A configuration parameter to be passed to the `createResources` method of our factory object.
Nested element	
set-property	See table B.2.

B.1.15 *<plug-in>*

The `<plug-in>` element specifies the fully qualified classname of a general-purpose application plug-in module that receives notification of application startup and shutdown events. An instance of the specified class is created for each element, and can be configured with nested `<set-property>` elements. The attribute shown in table B.14 is supported.

Table B.14 `<plug-in>` **attribute**

Attribute	Default/Description
className	(org.apache.struts.PlugIn) The fully qualified Java classname of the plug-in class; must implement.
Nested element	
set-property	See table B.2.

Taglib quick reference

Each of the Struts taglibs is very well documented, and the distribution provides both a Developer's Guide and complete technical documentation. However, it does not provide an overview of the tag names, properties, and descriptions all in one place. This appendix fills that gap, and can be useful when you are looking for a particular tag or just want to check for the name of a known property. For more about the Struts taglibs, see chapter 10.

Table C.1 shows the bean taglib, table C.2 the html taglib, table C.3 the logic taglib, table C.4 the template taglib, and table C.5 the tiles taglib quick reference.

Table C.1 Bean taglib quick reference

Tag name	Properties	Description
cookie	id, name, multiple, value	Defines a scripting variable based on the value(s) of the specified request cookie
define	id, name, property, scope, toScope, type, value	Defines a scripting variable based on the value(s) of the specified bean property
header	id, name, multiple, value	Defines a scripting variable based on the value(s) of the specified request header
include	anchor, forward, href, id, name, page, transaction	Loads the response from a dynamic application request and makes it available as a bean
message	arg0, arg1, arg2, arg3, arg4, bundle, key, locale, name, property, scope	Renders an internationalized message string to the response
page	id, property	Exposes a specified item from the page context as a bean
parameter	id, name, value, multiple	Defines a scripting variable based on the value(s) of the specified request parameter
resource	id, input, name	Loads a web application resource and makes it available as a bean
size	collection, id, name, property, scope	Defines a bean containing the number of elements in a Collection or Map
struts	id, form, forward, mapping	Exposes a named Struts internal configuration object as a bean
write	bundle, filter, format, formatKey, ignore, locale, name, property, scope	Renders the value of the specified bean property to the current JspWriter

Table C.2 Html taglib quick reference

Tag name	Properties	Description
Img	access, align, alt, altKey, border, bundle, height, hspace, imageName, ismap, locale, lowsrc, name, on*, paramId, page, pageKey, paramName, paramProperty, paramScope, property, scope, src, srcKey, style, styleClass, styleId, usemap, vspace, width	Renders an HTML img tag

Table C.2 Html taglib quick reference *(continued)*

Tag name	Properties	Description
link	accesskey, anchor, forward, href, indexed, indexId, linkName, name, on*, page, paramId, paramName, paramProperty, paramScope, property, scope, style, scope, style, styleClass, styleId, tabindex, target, title, transaction	Renders an HTML anchor or hyperlink
Javascript-Validator	DynamicJavascript, formName, method, page, src, staticJavascript	Renders JavaScript validation based on the validation rules loaded by the ValidatorPlugIn
messages	id, bundle, locale, name, property, header, footer, message	Conditionally displays a set of accumulated messages
multibox	accesskey, disabled, name, on*[a], property, style, styleClass, styleId, tabIndex, value	Renders a checkbox input field
option	bundle, disabled, key, locale, style, styleClass, value	Renders a select option
options	collection, labelName, labelProperty, name, property, style, styleClass	Renders a collection of select options
password	accessKey, disabled, indexed, maxlength, name, on*, property, readonly, redisplay, style, styleClass, styleId, size, tabindex, value	Renders a password input field
radio	accesskey, disabled, name, on*, property, style, styleClass, styleId, tabIndex, value	Renders a radio button input field
reset	accesskey, disabled, name, on*, property, style, styleClass, styleId, tabIndex, value	Renders a reset button input field
rewrite	anchor, forward, href, name, page, paramId, paramName, paramProperty, paramScope, property, scope, transaction	Renders a URI
select	accesskey, disabled, name, on*, property, style, styleClass, styleId, tabIndex, value	Renders a select element
submit	accesskey, disabled, name, on*, property, style, styleClass, styleId, tabIndex, value	Renders a Submit button
text	accesskey, disabled, name, on*, property, readonly, style, styleClass, styleId, tabIndex, value	Renders an input field of type text
textarea	accesskey, disabled, name, on*, property, readonly, style, styleClass, styleId, tabIndex, value	Renders a text area

a. on*—Indicates that the tag includes the JavaScript event properties: onblur, onchange, onclick, ondblclick, onfocus, onkeydown, onkeypress, onkeyup, onmousedown, onmousemove, onmouseout, onmouseover, onmouseup

Table C.3   Logic taglib quick reference

Tag name	Properties	Description
empty	name, property, scope	Evaluates the nested body content of this tag if the requested variable is either null or an empty string
equal	cookie, header, name, parameter, property, scope, value	Evaluates the nested body content of this tag if the requested variable is equal to the specified value
forward	Name	Forwards control to the page specified by the specified ActionForward entry
greaterEqual	cookie, header, name, parameter, property, scope, value	Evaluates the nested body content of this tag if the requested variable is greater than or equal to the specified value
greaterThan	cookie, header, name, parameter, property, scope, value	Evaluates the nested body content of this tag if the requested variable is greater than the specified value
iterate	collection, id, indexId, length, name, offset, property, scope, type	Repeats the nested body content of this tag over a specified collection
lessEqual	cookie, header, name, parameter, property, scope, value	Evaluates the nested body content of this tag if the requested variable is greater than or equal to the specified value
lessThan	cookie, header, name, parameter, property, scope, value	Evaluates the nested body content of this tag if the requested variable is less than the specified value
match	cookie, header, location, name, parameter, property, scope, value	Evaluates the nested body content of this tag if the specified value is an appropriate substring of the requested variable
messagesNotPresent	name, property, message	Generates the nested body content of this tag if the specified message is not present in this request
messagesPresent	name, property, message	Generates the nested body content of this tag if the specified message is present in this request
notEmpty	name, property, scope	Evaluates the nested body content of this tag if the requested variable is neither null nor an empty string
notEqual	cookie, header, name, parameter, property, scope, value	Evaluates the nested body content of this tag if the requested variable is not equal to the specified value

Table C.3   Logic taglib quick reference *(continued)*

Tag name	Properties	Description
notMatch	cookie, header, location, name, parameter, property, scope, value	Evaluates the nested body content of this tag if the specified value is not an appropriate substring of the requested variable
notPresent	cookie, header, name, parameter, property, role, scope, value	Generates the nested body content of this tag if the specified value is not present in this request
present	cookie, header, name, parameter, property, role, scope, value	Generates the nested body content of this tag if the specified value is present in this request
redirect	anchor, forward, href, name, page, paramId, paramName, paramProperty, paramScope, property, scope, transaction	Renders an HTTP Redirect

Table C.4   Template taglib quick reference

Tag name	Properties	Description
insert	name	Inserts (includes, actually) a template. Templates are JSPs that include parameterized content. That content comes from put tags that are children of insert tags.
put	template, role, name, content, direct	Puts content into request scope.
get	flush, name, role	Gets the content from request scope that was put there by a put tag.

Table C.5   Tiles taglib quick reference

Tag name	Properties	Description
Add	beanName, beanProperty, beanScope, content, direct, role, type, value	Adds an element to the surrounding list. Equivalent to put, but for a list element.
Definition	extends, id, page, role, scope, template	Creates a tile/component/template definition bean.
Get	flush, ignore, name, role	Gets the content from request scope that was put there by a put tag.
GetAsString	ignore, name, role	Renders the value of the specified tile/component/template attribute to the current JspWriter.

Table C.5   Tiles taglib quick reference *(continued)*

Tag name	Properties	Description
Import-Attribute	ignore, name, role	Imports the tile's attribute in the specified context.
InitComponent-Definitions	classname, file	Initializes the tile/component definitions factory.
Insert	attribute, beanName, beanProperty, beanScope, component, controllerclass, controllerUrl, definition, flush, ignore, name, page, role, template	Inserts a tile/component/template.
Put	beanName, beanProperty, beanScope, content, direct, name, role, type, value	Puts an attribute into tile/component/template context.
PutList	name	Declares a list that will be passed as an attribute to a tile.
UseAttribute	classname, id, ignore, name, scope	Uses the attribute value inside the page.

glossary

abstract.　A Java class, or method, that has not been implemented. Concrete classes are said to implement abstract classes.

accessor.　A JavaBean method used to expose a JavaBean property. See *JavaBean.*

adaptor.　A Java class used as a proxy between two classes.

Apache Software Foundation.　A membership-based, nonprofit corporation existing to provide organizational, legal, and financial support for the Apache open source software projects.

API contract.　A popular way to view a method's signature: as a contract between the method and its caller.

application context.　An area of memory used to store objects. The application context is visible to all servlets contained within a web application.

application framework.　A specialized framework used to provide an application infrastructure to build applications. See *framework.*

application programming interface (API).　A set of methods, or functions, used to interface between software components.

Artimus.　A news poster application that serves as an example to demonstrate the deployment of an enterprise-grade, best practices application using Struts, Tiles, and the Validator.

blackbox framework.   See *frameworks, blackbox.*

business layer.   See *business tier.*

business logic.   Programming logic used to achieve business functionality. See *business object.*

business object.   An object that encapsulates business logic. See *business logic.*

business tier.   An architecture layer representing business logic.

Cascading Style Sheets (CSS).   Programming logic used by the browser to build presentation features, such as color and fonts.

ChainedException.   A Java class extending `java.lang.Exception`. A chained exception maintains a list of all thrown exceptions.

chrome.   Visually appealing application features.

client tier.   An architecture layer representing clients interacting with the application.

Cocoon.   An XML publishing framework from Apache that is based on pipelined SAX processing.

cohesion.   A term used to describe a strong relationship between the responsibilities and functionality of an object.

Common Gateway Interface (CGI).   The first widely used standard for producing dynamic content. CGI uses standard operating system features to create a bridge between the web server and other applications on the host machine.

connection pool.   A set of cached resource connections.

container.   See *servlet container.*

context.   See *application context, session context,* and *request context.*

Controller.   A software component, such as a servlet, that acts as an initial point of contact for requests. The Controller provides common services such as authorization, error management, and invocation of business logic navigational flow.

convert.   See *data conversion.*

cookies.   Files written by the web browser on the client machine to maintain persistence information between requests.

coupling.   A dependency between objects, components, systems, or devices.

CRUD.   An acronym used to describe *Create Read Update Delete* operations.

data conversion.   The process of moving data from one type to another, such as from a `String` to an `Integer`.

data transformation.   The process of changing the internal format of a data, such as removing unwanted punctuation from a `String`.

decorator pattern.   A pattern that attaches additional responsibilities to an object dynamically. Decorators provide a flexible alternative to subclassing for extending functionality [Go4].

decoupling.   A lack of dependency between objects, components, systems, or devices.

deployment descriptor.   A file containing configuration information.

descriptor objects.   Objects containing configuration information.

design pattern.   A description of solutions, strategies, and consequences, intended to be used repeatedly to solve problems. Design patterns are used as a communication tool among architects, designers, and developers.

Digester.   A set of Java classes designed to trigger actions when specified XML node patterns are recognized during XML document parsing. The Digester is commonly used to create Java object representations of configuration information based on XML input. See *deployment descriptor* and *descriptor objects.*

DynaBean.   Specialized subclass of ActionForm that allows the creation of form beans with dynamic sets of properties, without requiring the developer to create a Java class for each type of form bean.

EAR.   A platform-independent file format used to combine a set of WAR files into a single file. EAR files are used to deploy combined servlet and EJB applications.

encapsulation.   A term used to describe the conccalment of details between objects.

Enterprise JavaBeans (EJB).   J2EE components used to provide remote access to reusable logic.

entries.   Key-value pairs contained within Properties files.

Extensible Markup Language (XML).   A set of markup tags used to provide meaning to content. XML is a subset of the Standard Generalized Markup Language (SGML).

Extensible Stylesheet Language (XSL).   A language for expressing style sheets. It consists of XSTL, XPath, and XSL formatting objects. See *XSLT, XML Path Language,* and *XSL formatting objects.*

extension point.   Specific locations in a framework used to customize or override behavior. See also *framework.*

factory.   A pattern used to create objects. See *design pattern.*

five-tier model.   A depiction of architectural layering. Under the five-tier model, an architecture is separated according to areas of responsibility: client, presentation, business, integration, and resource. See *client tier, presentation tier, business tier, integration tier,* and *resource tier.*

framework.   A reusable, semi-complete application that can be specialized to produce custom applications [Johnson]. Frameworks have well-defined interfaces that trigger event-handling logic.

frameworks, blackbox.   Frameworks that tend to define interfaces for pluggable components and then provide base starter components based on those interfaces. The interface and base components will often provide hotspot methods that can be used as is or overridden to provide special behavior. [Johnson] See also *extension point.*

frameworks, whitebox.   Frameworks that rely heavily on object-oriented language features such as inheritance and dynamic binding. [Johnson]

handshaking.   The agreed-upon interaction between two objects, components, systems, or devices.

hotspot.   See *extension point.*

i18n.   An acronym for internationalization. The acronym is derived from the observation that there are 18 characters between the first and last characters in the word *internationalization.* See *internationalization.*

immutable.   A term used to indication that an object or property cannot be changed. Contrast *mutable.*

integration layer.   See *integration tier.*

integration tier.   An architecture layer representing logic responsible for interaction with the resource tier. See *resource tier.*

internationalization.   The application design activity that permits an application to respond to the needs of multiple languages and regions.

introspection.   The process of identifying which JavaBean properties are available on an object. Introspection is a specialized form of reflection. Java makes this service available through a set of classes in the `java.bean` package.

Inversion of Control.   A design pattern where objects register with a framework as a handler for an event.

J2EE (Java 2 Enterprise Edition).   A suite of tools, runtime environments, and APIs designed to provide a foundation for enterprise computer systems.

J2EE blueprints.   A set of guidelines, patterns, and code provided by Sun Microsystems Inc. to illustrate best practices on the Java platform.

JAR (Java Archive).   A platform-independent file format used to combine multiple files into a single file.

Jasper.   The component within the Tomcat application server responsible for generating servlets from JavaServer Pages.

Java 2 Platform, Standard Edition (J2SE).   A suite of tools, runtime environments, and APIs used to create applications in Java.

Java Database Connectivity (JDBC).   A Java API used to access ODBC-compliant databases.

Java Internationalization Toolkit.   A toolkit for rapid Java applications internationalization and localization development.

Java Naming Directory Interface (JNDI).   A standard extension to the Java platform, providing Java-enabled applications with a unified interface to multiple naming and directory services in the enterprise.

Java Virtual Machine (JVM).   Software used to execute the byte code created by the Java compiler.

JavaBean.   A Java class conforming to well-known conventions permitting other Java classes to use the Java Reflection API as a facility for discovery and interaction.

JavaServer Pages Standard Tag Library (JSTL).   A library of JSP tags that provide functionality common to many JSP applications.

Jetspeed.   An open source Java and XML implementation of an enterprise information portal. Jetspeed makes network resources, such as applications and databases, available to end users via a web browser, Wireless Access Protocol (WAP) phone, pager, or any other device.

jsessionid. An HTTP parameter containing a unique number used to identify the user's session.

Lightweight Directory Access Protocol (LDAP). A protocol used to access directory services.

Locale. A standard Java object representing a specific geographical, political, or cultural region.

locale-sensitive. A term used to describe components with the ability to alter their behavior by locality. See *Locale.*

localization. An application design activity that permits an application to respond to the needs of multiple locales. See *Locale.*

markup. The collection of commands placed in a file to provide formatting instructions rather than visible text or content. HTML uses a tag-based markup system.

message protocol. A technique based on reflection that allows objects to share information by observing a common naming convention in lieu of sharing a common hierarchy.

modal. A user-interface element that claims all the user input for an application. Other elements of the application cannot be accessed until the element is dismissed.

Model. An architectural concept representing the data container. The Model is the gateway between the data repository and the Controller and View. JavaBeans are commonly, but not exclusively, used to represent the Model in Struts.

Model-View-Controller (MVC). A term used to describe an architecture that separates the Model, View, and Controller. See *Model, View,* and *Controller.*

multithreaded. A term used to describe Java objects designed to be used as threads. See *thread.*

mutable. A term used to indicate that an object, or property, can be changed. Contrast *immutable.*

nonmodal. The opposite of modal. See *modal.*

nonmutable. See *immutable.*

Observer pattern. A design pattern in which one object is notified when another object's state changes.

overload. A term used to describe methods or constructors with the same name but a different set of parameters.

performant. A French word meaning *efficient*. Software engineers often use the word *performant* to describe a process or device that performs well.

pluggable. An object-oriented design strategy that allows objects to be developed independently of an application and then incorporated without changing the base code. Pluggable components are often created by a third party.

Poolman. An open source tool providing a means of pooling and caching Java objects, SQL queries, and results across multiple databases.

presentation layer. See *presentation tier.*

presentation tier. An architecture layer representing presentation logic. Struts resides in the presentation tier.

Properties file. A simple text file used to record key-values pairs. See *entries.*

Protected Variation. A design principle that encourages the encapsulation of the predicted points of change.

redirect. A term used to describe a message sent to a browser to initiate a request to another URL.

refactoring. The process of modifying software so that it does not change its interface. See *encapsulation.*

reflection. The process of determining what member fields and methods are available on an object. Java makes this service available through a set of classes in the `java.lang.reflect` package.

regular expression. Syntax used to discover string patterns.

request context. An area of memory used to store objects. The request context is visible to all objects having access to an execution thread of the servlet request.

Resin. An application server that is an alternative to Tomcat.

resource bundle. A locale-sensitive Properties file. See *locale-sensitive* and *Properties file.*

resource layer. See *resource tier.*

resource tier. An architecture layer representing resource assets, such as databases and legacy systems. See *five-tier model.*

Rich Site Summary (RSS). An XML format designed for sharing headlines and other web content.

servlet.   Java programs executing within a servlet container.

servlet container.   An environment within an application server responsible for managing the servlet life cycle. See *servlet.*

session context.   An area of memory used to store objects. The session context is visible to all objects having visibility to a user's session.

static content.   Content on the web that comes directly from text or data files, such as HTML or JPEG files. These files might be changed from time to time, but they are not altered automatically when requested by a web browser. Dynamic content, on the other hand, is generated on the fly, typically in response to an individualized request from a browser.

synchronizer token.   A pattern used to protect the application against duplicate requests.

Tag Library Descriptor (TLD).   An XML file used to associate JSP tag extensions with the Java classes that implement them.

thread.   A programming feature that allows multiple blocks of code to be executed concurrently within the same instance of an object.

thread-safe.   A programming technique employing programming language features to control access to resources available to threads. See *thread.*

Tiles.   A Java-based template engine designed to work with or without Struts.

Tomcat.   An open source Apache application server used as the official Reference Implementation for Java Servlet and JavaServer Pages technologies.

transaction.   An atomic unit of work.

transfer object.   An object that efficiently commutes fine-grained data by sending a coarse-grained view of the data. Often treated as synonymous to value object. See *value object.*

Turbine.   A servlet-based application framework. An alternative to Struts. See *application framework.*

Unicode.   A universal character-encoding scheme defining a numerical mapping for every character irrespective of platform or programming language.

Uniform Resource Identifier (URI).   A string identifying a resource on the Internet or other computer network. A resource could be a document, image, downloadable file, electronic mailbox, and so forth.

URL rewriting. A strategy for achieving session tracking by appending session information to the URL.

value object. An object that efficiently commutes fine-grained data by sending a coarse-grained view of the data. Value objects and transfer objects are sometimes considered to be synonymous, but purists make a distinction between the two terms. A purist definition of value object limits the definition to granular objects such as dates or money. Transfer objects are an aggregation of value objects. See *transfer object.*

Velocity. A Java-based template engine.

View. Represents the application from the user perspective. JSPs and HTML pages are considered components of the View.

virtual resource. A resource that does not map to a file but is processed by a programming component.

Web Archive (WAR). A platform-independent file format used to combine a set of servlet application files into a single file. WAR files are used to deploy servlet applications. See *servlet.*

XML. See *Extensible Markup Language (XML).*

XML Path Language (XPath). An expression language used by XSLT to access, or refer to, parts of an XML document.

XPath. See *XML Path Language (XPath).*

XSL. See *Extensible Stylesheet Language (XSL).*

XSL formatting objects. An XML vocabulary for specifying formatting semantics.

XSLT. A language for transforming XML documents into other XML documents.

references

[Adalon] Synthis Corporation, Synthis Adalon, http://www.synthis.com/products/adalon/overview.jsp.

[Ambler] Ambler, Scott W., "Mapping Objects to Relational Databases," http://www.ambysoft.com/mappingObjects.pdf, and "The Design of a Robust Persistence Layer for Relational Databases," http://www.ambysoft.com/persistenceLayer.pdf.

[ASF, Ant] Apache Software Foundation, Apache Ant, Java-based build tool, http://jakarta.apache.org/ant/index.html.

[ASF, AppDev] Apache Software Foundation, "Developing Applications with Tomcat," http://jakarta.apache.org/tomcat/tomcat-3.2-doc/appdev.

[ASF, Artimus] Apache Software Foundation, Artimus example application, http://sourceforge.net/projects/struts.

[ASF, Cocoon] Apache Software Foundation, Apache Cocoon XML publishing framework, http://xml.apache.org/cocoon/.

[ASF, Commons] Apache Software Foundation, Jakarta Commons Repository, http://jakarta.apache.org/commons.

[ASF, CTLX] Apache Software Foundation, Custom Tag Library Extension for Dreamweaver UltraDev, http://jakarta.apache.org/taglibs/doc/ultradev4-doc/.

[ASF, ECS] Apache Software Foundation, Jakarta Element Construction Set, http://jakarta.apache.org/ecs.

[ASF, Jetspeed] Apache Software Foundation, Jetspeed Enterprise Information Portal, http://jakarta.apache.org/jetspeed/site/.

[ASF, License] Apache Software Foundation, Apache Software License, http://apache.org/LICENSE.

[ASF, Lucene] Apache Software Foundation, Jakarta Lucene Text Search Engine, http://jakarta.apache.org/lucene.

[ASF, OBJ] Apache Software Foundation, ObjectRelationalBridge, http://jakarta.apache.org/ojb/.

[ASF, Regexp] Apache Software Foundation, Jakarta Regexp, http://jakarta.apache.org/regexp/.

[ASF, Scaffold] Apache Software Foundation, Scaffold package, http://jakarta.apache.org/commons.

[ASF, Struts] Apache Software Foundation, Jakarta Struts Framework 1.0, http://jakarta.apache.org/struts.

[ASF, Taglibs] Apache Software Foundation, Jakarta Taglibs Repository, http://jakarta.apache.org/taglibs.

[ASF, Tiles] The Tiles Document Assembly Framework, http://jakarta.apache.org/struts/userGuide/dev_tiles.html.

[ASF, Tomcat] Apache Software Foundation, Tomcat, http://jakarta.apache.org/tomcat.

[ASF, Torque] Apache Software Foundation, Torque, http://jakarta.apache.org/turbine/torque.

[ASF, Turbine] Apache Software Foundation, Turbine, http://jakarta.apache.org/turbine.

[ASF, Validator] Apache Software Foundation, Jakarta Commons Validator, http://jakarta.apache.org/commons/.

[ASF, Velocity] Apache Software Foundation, Velocity Template Engine, http://jakarta.apache.org/velocity/.

[Bayern] Bayern, Shawn, *JSTL in Action* (Greenwich, CT: Manning Publications, 2002; ISBN: 193011052), http://www.manning.com/bayern/index.html.

[Braga, et al] Braga, Christiano de O. , Marcus Felipe M.C. da Fontoura, Edward H. Hoeusler, and Carlos Jose P. de Lucena, "Formalized OO Frameworks and Framework Instantiation," (1998), http://www.almaden.ibm.com/cs/people/fontoura/papers/wmf98.pdf.

[Camino] Scioworks Pte Ltd, Scioworks Camino, Visual Modeling Tool for Struts Applications, http://www.scioworks.com/scioworks_camino.html.

[Castor] Castor, Castor open source data binding framework for Java, http://castor.exolab.org/.

[CKNOW] Computer Knowledge, http://www.cknow.com/ckinfo/acro_a/api_1.shtml.

[Cockburn] Cockburn, Alistair, "Characterizing People as Non-Linear, First-Order Components in Software Development," http://alistair.cockburn.us/.

[Console] Holmes, James, "Struts Console," http://www.jamesholmes.com/struts/.

[Date] Date, Chris J., and Hugh Darwen (contributor), *A Guide to the SQL Standard* (Boston: Addison-Wesley, 1997; ISBN: 0201964260).

[dbForms] dbForms, http://dbforms.org/.

[Dragan] Dragan, Richard V., "Enterprise JavaBeans (EJB) Best Practices," http://www.extremetech.com/print_article/0,3428,a=11791,00.asp.

[Earles] Earles, John, "Frameworks! Make Room for Another Silver Bullet," http://www.cbd-hq.com/PDFs/cbdhq_000301je_frameworks.pdf.

[EJS] Vermeulen, Allan, Scott W. Ambler, Greg Bumgardner, Eldon Metz, Trevor Misfeldt, Jim Shur, and Patrick Thompson, *The Elements of Java Style* (Cambridge: Cambridge University Press, 2000; ISBN: 0521777682).

[Expresso] JCorporate, Expresso Web Application Development Framework, http://jcorporate.com/.

[Fayad] Mohamed Fayad and Douglas C. Schmidt, "Object-Oriented Application Frameworks." *Communications of the ACM*, Special Issue on Object-Oriented Application Frameworks, Vol. 40, No. 10, October 1997, http://www.cs.wustl.edu/~schmidt/CACM-frameworks.html.

[Fields] Fields, Duane K., Mark A. Kolb, Shawn Bayern, *Web Development with Java-Server Pages, 2nd Edition* (Greenwich, CT: Manning Publications, 2001; ISBN: 193011012X), http://www.manning.com/fields2.

[Foote] Foote, Brian and Joseph Yoder, "Big Ball of Mud Programming," http://devcentre.org/mud/mudmain.htm.

[Fowler] Fowler, Martin, *Refactoring: Improving the Design of Existing Code* (Boston: Addison-Wesley, 1999; ISBN: 0201485672).

[Gabrick] Gabrick, Kurt A. and David B. Weiss, *J2EE and XML Development* (Greenwich, CT: Manning Publications, 2002; ISBN: 1930110308), http://www.manning.com/gabrick.

[Go3] Alur, Deepak, John Crupi, Dan Malks, *Core J2EE Patterns* (Upper Saddle River, NJ: Prentice Hall PTR, 2001; ISBN: 0130648841).

[Go4] Gamma, Erich , Richard Helm, John Vlissides, Ralph Johnson, *Design Patterns: Elements of Reusable Object-Oriented Software* (Boston: Addison-Wesley, 1995; ISBN: 0201633612).

[Goetz] Goetz, Brian "Exceptional Practices," http://www.javaworld.com/javaworld/jw-08-2001/jw-0803-exceptions.html.

[Gosling, JLE] Gosling, James and Henry McGilton, "The Java Language Environment—A White Paper," http://java.sun.com/docs/white/langenv/index.html.

[Hatcher] Hatcher, Erik, and Steve Loughran, *Java Development with Ant* (Greenwich, CT: Manning Publications, 2002; ISBN 1930110588), http://www.manning.com/hatcher/.

[Husted] Husted, Ted, Cedric Dumoulin, George Franciscus, and David Winterfeldt, *Struts in Action* (Greenwich, CT: Manning Publications, 2002; ISBN 1930110502), http://www.manning.com/husted/.

[Improve] Improve, Struts Layout Taglib, http://struts.application-servers.com/.

[IS0-3166, ISO-639] ISO 3166 Codes (Countries) http://www.chemie.fu-berlin.de/diverse/doc/ISO_3166.html and code for the representation of names of languages, http://www.ics.uci.edu/pub/ietf/http/related/iso639.txt.

[ISO 8859-1] ISO, ISO 8859-1 character set overview, http://www.htmlhelp.com/reference/charset/.

[Jack] Anonymous, "The House That Jack Built," http://www.enchantedlearning.com/Jackshouse.html.

[jEdit] Pestov, Slava, et al., jEdit open source programmer's text editor, http://jedit.sourceforge.net/.

[Jikes] IBM, Jikes Java bytecode compiler, http://oss.software.ibm.com/developerworks/opensource/jikes/.

[Johnson] Johnson, Ralph, and Brian Foote, "Designing Reusable Classes," *Journal of Object-Oriented Programming.* SIGS, 1, 5 (June/July 1988), 22–35, http://www.laputan.org/drc/drc.html.

[JRF] is.com, JRelationalFramework, http://jrf.sourceforge.net/.

[JUnit] JUnit, http://junit.org/.

[Kovitz] Kovitz, Benjamin L., *Practical Software Requirements* (Greenwich, CT: Manning Publications, 1998; ISBN 1884777597), http://www.manning.com/Kovitz/.

[Larman] Larman, Craig, *Applying UML and Patterns, An Introduction to Object-Oriented Analysis and Design and the Unified Process* (Upper Saddle River, NJ: Prentice Hall PTR, 2001; ISBN 0130925691).

[Linday] Linday, James, "The Software Process," http://bmrc.berkeley.edu/courseware/ba293/spring01/lectures/process/.

[Macromedia] Macromedia, Inc., http://www.macromedia.com/.

[Martin] Martin, Robert C., *Designing Object-Oriented C++ Applications Using the Booch Method* (Englewood Cliffs, NJ: Prentice Hall, 1995; ISBN 0132038374).

[McConnell] McConnell, Steve, *Code Complete* (Redmond, WA: Microsoft Press, 1993; ISBN: 1556154844).

[Netscape] Netscape Communications Corporation, JavaScript Reference, http://developer.netscape.com/tech/javascript/.

[ObjectAssembler] ObjectVenture Corporation, ObjectAssembler, http://www.objectventure.com/products/objectassembler.html.

[Objectwave] Objectwave Corporation, X2J: Code Generator for Struts, http://www.objectwave.com/html/tools/tool1_3.htm.

[Ooram] Reenskaug, Trygve, P. Wold, and O. A. Lehne, *Working with Objects: The Ooram Software Engineering Method* (Englewood Cliffs, NJ: Prentice Hall, 1995; ISBN: 0134529308).

[Osage] Osage Persistence Plus XML, http://osage.sourceforge.net/.

[POSA] Buschmann, Frank, Regine Meunier, Hans Rohnert, Peter Sommerlad, and Michael Stal, *A System of Patterns: Pattern-Oriented Software Architecture* (New York: John Wiley & Sons, 1996; ISBN: 0471958697).

[Ramaiah] Ramaiah, Ravindran, Struts Code Generator, http://husted.com/struts/resources/codemaker.htm.

[Ramsay] Ramsay, Stephen, "Using Regular Expressions," http://etext.lib.virginia.edu/helpsheets/regex.html.

[Resin] Caucho Technology, Resin Java Web Server, http://www.caucho.com/.

[Rodrigues] Rodrigues, Lawrence H., *The Awesome Power of JavaBeans* (Greenwich, CT: Manning Publications, 1998; ISBN: 1884777562), http://www.manning.com/Rodrigues/.

[Roman] Roman, Ed, Scott W. Ambler, Tyler Jewell, and Floyd Marinescu, *Mastering Enterprise JavaBeans* (New York: John Wiley & Sons, 2001; ISBN: 0471417114).

[Schmidt] Schmidt, Douglas C., "Applying Design Patterns and Frameworks to Develop Object-Oriented Communication Software," *Handbook of Programming Languages*, Volume I, edited by Peter Salus (Indianapolis: Macmillan Computer Publishing, 1997).

[Shachor] Shachor, Gal, Adam Chace, and Magnus Rydin, *JSP Tag Libraries* (Greenwich, CT: Manning Publications, 2001; ISBN: 193011009X), http://www.manning.com/shachor/.

[Simper] Field-Elliot, Bryan, "Simple Persistence in Java," http://sourceforge.net/projects/simper/.

[Sun, Blueprints] J2EE Blueprints, http://java.sun.com/j2ee/blueprints/.

[Sun, Business Logic] Sun Microsystems, J2EE Blueprints, Section 5.2, http://java.sun.com/blueprints/guidelines/designing_enterprise_applications/ejb_tier/business_logic/index.html.

[Sun, Data Access Objects] Sun Microsystems, J2EE Blueprints, http://java.sun.com/blueprints/patterns/DAO.html.

[Sun, DAO Factories] Sun Microsystems, J2EE Blueprints, http://java.sun.com/blueprints/corej2eepatterns/Patterns/DataAccessObject.html.

[Sun, i18n] Sun Microsystems, Sun Java Tutorial, Internationalization Trail, http://java.sun.com/docs/books/tutorial/i18n/.

[Sun, J2EE] Sun Microsystems, "Designing Enterprise Applications with the J2EE Platform," http://java.sun.com/blueprints/guidelines/designing_enterprise_applications.

[Sun, JAAS] Java Authentification and Authorization Service, http://java.sun.com/products/jaas/.

[Sun, Java] Sun Microsystems, Java Technology, http://java.sun.com/.

[Sun, JavaBeans] Sun Microsystems, JavaBean Trail, http://java.sun.com/docs/books/tutorial/javabeans.

[Sun, JBS] Sun Microsystems, JavaBean Specification, http://java.sun.com/products/javabeans/docs/spec.html.

[Sun, JDBC] Sun Microsystems, The Java Tutorial—Trail: JDBC, http://java.sun.com/docs/books/tutorial/jdbc.

[Sun, JDK] Sun Microsystems, the Java Developers Kit, http://java.sun.com/j2se/.

[Sun, JILKIT] Sun Microsystems, Java Internationalization and Localization Toolkit 2.0, http://java.sun.com/products/jilkit/.

[Sun, JSF] Sun Microsystems, JavaServer Faces, http://jcp.org/jsr/detail/127.jsp.

[Sun, JSP] Sun Microsystems, JavaServer Pages Technology, http://java.sun.com/products/jsp.

[Sun, JST] Sun Microsystems, Java Servlet Technology, http://java.sun.com/products/servlet/.

[Sun, JSTL] Sun Microsystems, JSP Standard Tag Library, http://jakarta.apache.org/taglibs/doc/standard-doc/intro.html.

[Sun, JTL] Sun Microsystems, JSP Tag Library Technology page, http://java.sun.com/products/jsp/taglibraries.html.

[Sun, N2AC] Sun Microsystems, Native-to-ASCII Converter, http://java.sun.com/j2se/1.4/docs/tooldocs/win32/native2ascii.html.

[Sun, MVC] Sun Microsystems, J2EE Patterns, http://swjscmail1.java.sun.com/cgi-bin/wa?A2=ind0106&L=j2eepatterns-interest&D=0&P=2671.

[Sun, Properties] Sun Microsystems, the Java Tutorial, http://java.sun.com/docs/books/tutorial/essential/attributes/properties.html.

[Sun, Servlets] Sun Microsystems, the Java Tutorial—Trail: Servlets, http://java.sun.com/docs/books/tutorial/servlets.

[Sun, TagExt] Sun Microsystems, "Classes and Interfaces for the Definition of JavaServer Pages Tag Libraries," http://java.sun.com/j2ee/sdk_1.3/techdocs/api/javax/servlet/jsp/tagext/package-summary.html.

[Sun, Trails] Sun Microsystems, Java Tutorial, http://java.sun.com/docs/books/tutorial/.

[W3C, CSS] W3C, Cascading Style Sheets, http://www.w3.org/Style/CSS/.

[W3C, HTML] W3C, Hypertext Markup Language, http://www.w3.org/MarkUp/.

[W3C, HTML4] W3C, Hypertext Markup Language, http://www.w3.org/TR/html401/.

[W3C, URI] W3C, Uniform Resource Identifiers (URI): Generic Syntax, http://www.ietf.org/rfc/rfc2396.txt.

[W3C, URL] W3C, Uniform Resource Locator (URL): Generic Syntax, http://www.ietf.org/rfc/rfc2396.txt.

[W3C, XML] W3C, Extensible Markup Language, http://www.w3.org/XML/.

[Williamson] Williamson, Alan R., *Java Servlets by Example* (Greenwich, CT: Manning Publications, 1999; ISBN: 188477766X), http://www.manning.com/Williamson/.

[XDoclet] Schaefer, Andreas, Ara Abrahamian, Aslak Hellesoy, Dmitri Colebatch, Rickard Oberg, Vincent Harcq, et al, Extended Javadoc Doclet Engine, http://xdoclet.sourceforge.net/.

Regarding material attributed to the W3C

Copyright FAQ) are satisfied, the right to create modifications or derivatives is sometimes granted by the W3C to individuals complying with those requirements.

THIS DOCUMENT IS PROVIDED "AS IS," AND COPYRIGHT HOLDERS MAKE NO REPRESENTATIONS OR WARRANTIES, EXPRESS OR IMPLIED, INCLUDING, BUT NOT LIMITED TO, WARRANTIES OF MERCHANTABILITY, FITNESS FOR A PARTICULAR PURPOSE, NON-INFRINGEMENT, OR TITLE; THAT THE CONTENTS OF THE DOCUMENT ARE SUITABLE FOR ANY PURPOSE; NOR THAT THE IMPLEMENTATION OF SUCH CONTENTS WILL NOT INFRINGE ANY THIRD PARTY PATENTS, COPYRIGHTS, TRADEMARKS OR OTHER RIGHTS. COPYRIGHT HOLDERS WILL NOT BE LIABLE FOR ANY DIRECT, INDIRECT, SPECIAL OR CONSEQUENTIAL DAMAGES ARISING OUT OF ANY USE OF THE DOCUMENT OR THE PERFORMANCE OR IMPLEMENTATION OF THE CONTENTS THEREOF.

The name and trademarks of copyright holders may NOT be used in advertising or publicity pertaining to this document or its contents without specific, written prior permission. Title to copyright in this document will at all times remain with copyright holders.

Regarding the original source code provided with this book and its example applications

The Apache Software License, Version 1.1

Copyright (c) 2000 The Apache Software Foundation. All rights reserved.

Redistribution and use in source and binary forms, with or without modification, are permitted provided that the following conditions are met:

1. Redistributions of source code must retain the above copyright notice, this list of conditions and the following disclaimer.

2. Redistributions in binary form must reproduce the above copyright notice, this list of conditions and the following disclaimer in the documentation and/or other materials provided with the distribution.

3. The end-user documentation included with the redistribution, if any, must include the following acknowledgment: "This product includes software developed by the Apache Software Foundation (http://www.apache.org/)." Alternately, this acknowledgment may appear in the software itself, if and wherever such third-party acknowledgments normally appear.

4. The names "Apache" and "Apache Software Foundation" must not be used to endorse or promote products derived from this software without

prior written permission. For written permission, please contact apache@apache.org.

5 Products derived from this software may not be called "Apache", nor may "Apache" appear in their name, without prior written permission of the Apache Software Foundation.

THIS SOFTWARE IS PROVIDED "AS IS" AND ANY EXPRESSED OR IMPLIED WARRANTIES, INCLUDING, BUT NOT LIMITED TO, THE IMPLIED WARRANTIES OF MERCHANTABILITY AND FITNESS FOR A PARTICULAR PURPOSE ARE DISCLAIMED. IN NO EVENT SHALL THE APACHE SOFTWARE FOUNDATION OR ITS CONTRIBUTORS BE LIABLE FOR ANY DIRECT, INDIRECT, INCIDENTAL, SPECIAL, EXEMPLARY, OR CONSEQUENTIAL DAMAGES (INCLUDING, BUT NOT LIMITED TO, PROCUREMENT OF SUBSTITUTE GOODS OR SERVICES; LOSS OF USE, DATA, OR PROFITS; OR BUSINESS INTERRUPTION) HOWEVER CAUSED AND ON ANY THEORY OF LIABILITY, WHETHER IN CONTRACT, STRICT LIABILITY, OR TORT (INCLUDING NEGLIGENCE OR OTHERWISE) ARISING IN ANY WAY OUT OF THE USE OF THIS SOFTWARE, EVEN IF ADVISED OF THE POSSIBILITY OF SUCH DAMAGE.

==

This software consists of voluntary contributions made by many individuals on behalf of the Apache Software Foundation. For more information on the Apache Software Foundation, please see <http://www.apache.org/>. Portions of this software are based upon public domain software originally written at the National Center for Supercomputing Applications, University of Illinois, Urbana-Champaign.

index

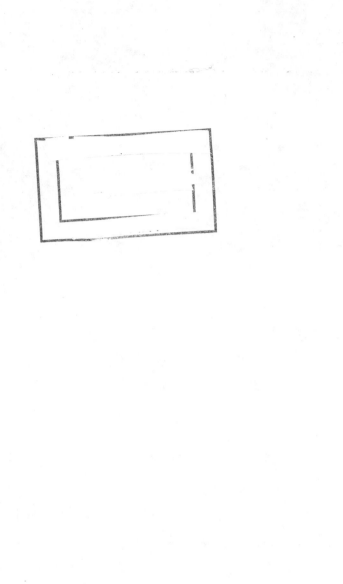